A-Z GLASGOW

Key to Map Pages	
Large Scale City Centre	6-254
Map Pages	6-256

REFERENCE

Motorway	**M8**	Map Continuation ▲ **86**	Large Scale City Centre ▲ **4**	
A Road	A77	Car Park Selected	**P**	
Under Construction		Church or Chapel	†	
Proposed		Cycle Route	☞	
B Road	B812	Fire Station	■	
Dual Carriageway		Hospital	**H**	
One Way Street	➡	House Numbers (A and B Roads only)	13 8	
Traffic flow on A Roads is also indicated by a heavy line on the driver's left.	➡	Information Centre	**i**	
Junction Name	TOWNHEAD INTERCHANGE	National Grid Reference	⁶60	
Restricted Access		Police Station (Open 24 Hours)	▲	
Pedestrianized Road		Post Office	★	
Track/Footpath	-------	Toilet	▽	
Residential Walkway	....	with facilities for the Disabled	♿	
Railway Level Crossing / Station / Tunnel		Viewpoint	☀ ☀	
Underground Station	Ⓤ	Educational Establishment	◰	
Local Authority Boundary	— · — ·	Hospital or Hospice	◰	
Posttown Boundary		Industrial Building	◰	
Postcode Boundary within Posttowns	— — —	Leisure or Recreational Facility	◰	
Built-up Area	MILL ST.	Place of Interest	◰	
		Public Building	◰	
		Shopping Centre or Market	◰	
		Other Selected Buildings	◰	

SCALE

Map Pages 6-165 1:18,103

0   ¼   ½ Mile

0   250   500   750 Metres

3½ inches (8.89 cm) to 1 mile   5.52 cm to 1 km

Map Pages 4-5 1:9051

0   ⅛   ¼ Mile

0   100   200   300   400 Metres

7 inches (17.78 cm) to 1 mile   11.05 cm to 1 km

Copyright of Geographers' A-Z Map Company Limited

Head Office:
Fairfield Road, Borough Green, Sevenoaks, Kent TN15 8PP
Telephone 01732 781000 (Enquiries & Trade Sales)
01732 783422 (Retail Sales)
www.a-zmaps.co.uk
Copyright © Geographers' A-Z Map Co. Ltd.

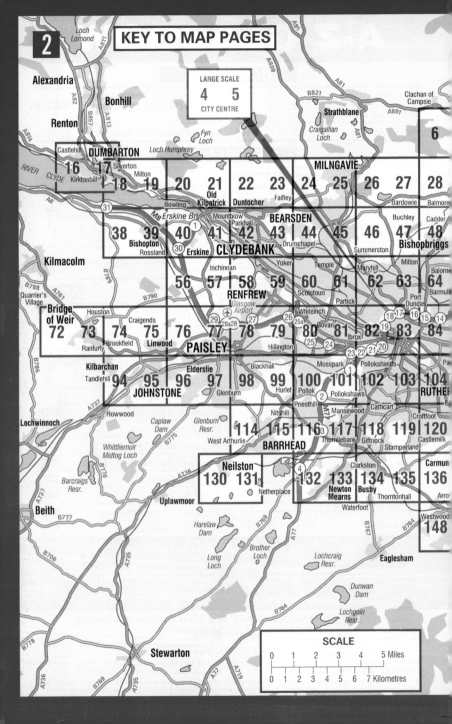

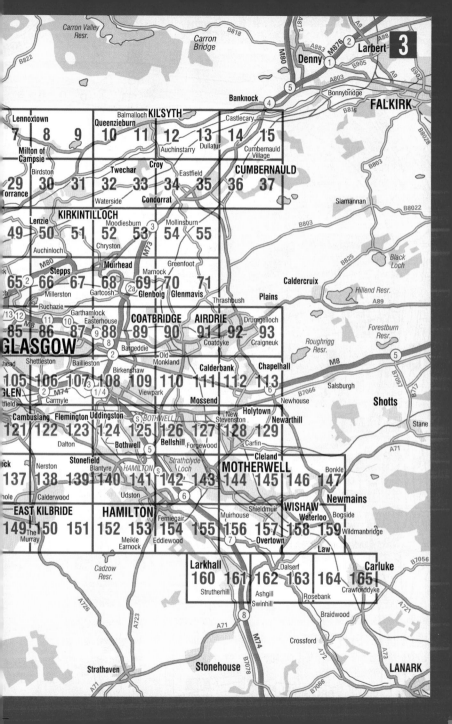

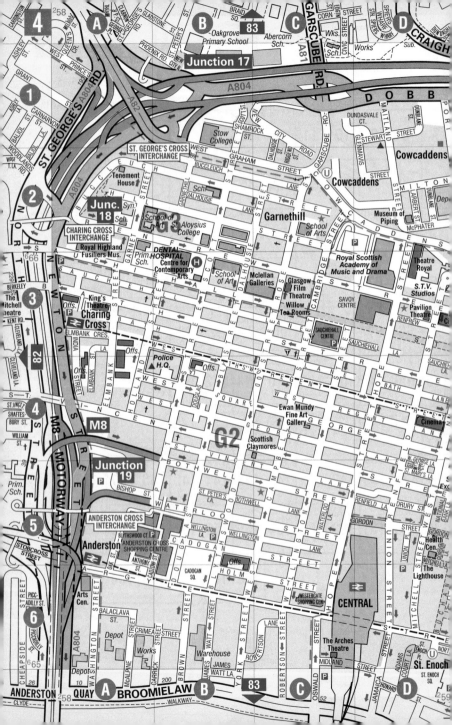

6

²60

Baillie
Hill

Crosshouse

Kier
Hill

Rosedene

Wellbank **A891**

Kilwinnet

Hall

Cricket
Grd. Weir
Hall

Balcorrach

1

79

East
Lodge

STRATHBLANE

Hole

Capieston
House

P o w

West
Lodge

Glazert Wood

A891

2

Lovers'
Leap

Bank
Wood

Tennis
Ct.

Nurses
Home

Ten.
Cts.

**LENNOX CASTLE
HOSPITAL** **H**

BOULEVARD

CASTLE
VIEW

Pavilion

Sew
Wo

678

Craigend
Wood

Filter
House

The White
House

Campsie
House

Bowl
Grns.

South
Lodge

Baldow

3

Clochcore
Wood

Reservoir

Baldow
Plantation

Drum
Plantation

4

Mounthuillie

Baldow

Glasgow

77

G66

W

5

Cattle
Grid

Muirh

6

Peathill
Wood

Newlands

Glenwynd
Wood

G64

Glenwhap

76

²60

A

Wa

B

Waterfall

28

61

C

D

Upp
Carles

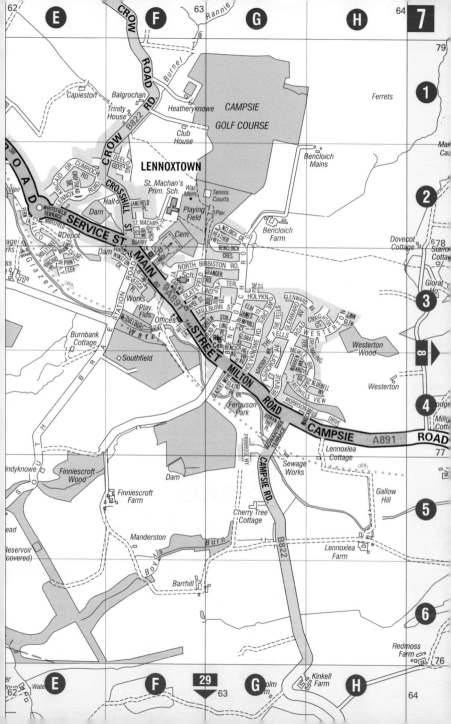

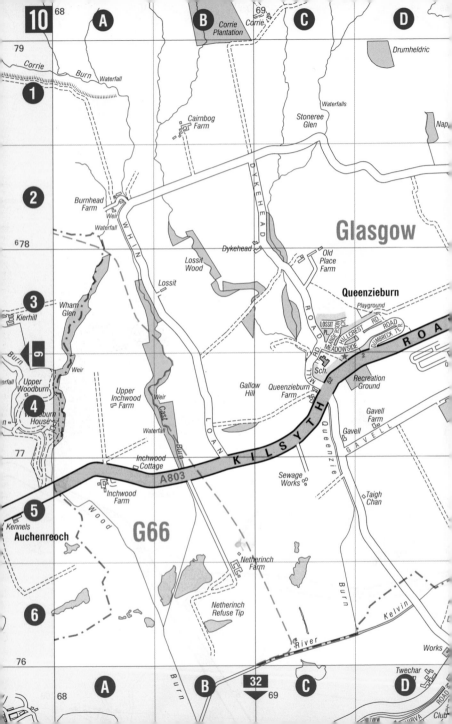

79

A

B

Corrie Plantation

69 Corrie

C

D

Drumheldric

Corrie Burn Waterfall

1

Cairnbog Farm

Stoneree Glen

Waterfalls

Nap

2

Burnhead Farm

Weir

Waterfall

WHIN

DYKEHEAD

Dykehead

Lossit Wood

Lossit

Old Place Farm

Glasgow

Queenzieburn

Playground

678

3

Wham Glen

Kierhill

9

Upper Woodburn

Weir

Cast

LOSSIT PL

HANDERSON CR

HILLCREST RD

MEADOWSIDE

DUMBRECK TCR

ROAD

ROAD

Sch.

Recreation Ground

ROAD

4

Woodburn House

Waterfall

Upper Inchwood Farm

Weir

Burn

Gallow Hill

Queenzieburn Farm

KILSYTH

Queenzie

Gavell Farm

Gavell

GAVELL

77

Inchwood Cottage

A803

LOAN

Sewage Works

Taigh Chan

5

Kennels

Auchenreoch

Inchwood Farm

Wood

G66

Netherinch Farm

Burn

Kelvin

6

Netherinch Refuse Tip

River

Works

76

A

68

Burn

B

69

C

Twechar

D

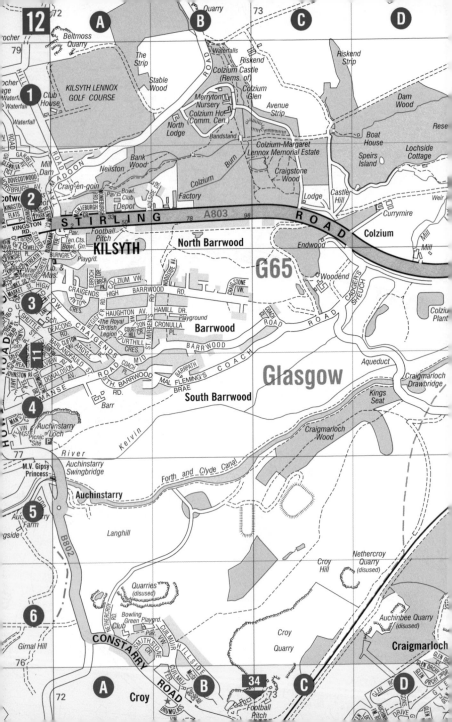

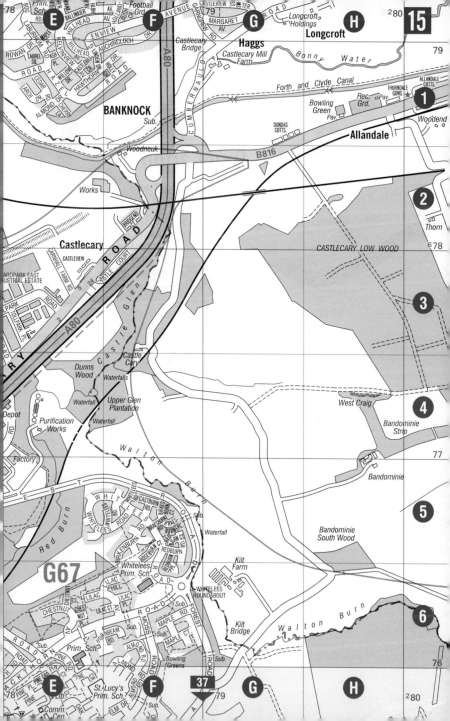

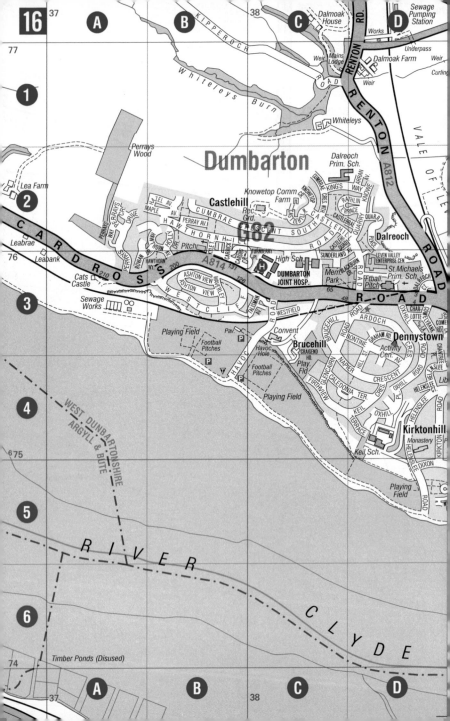

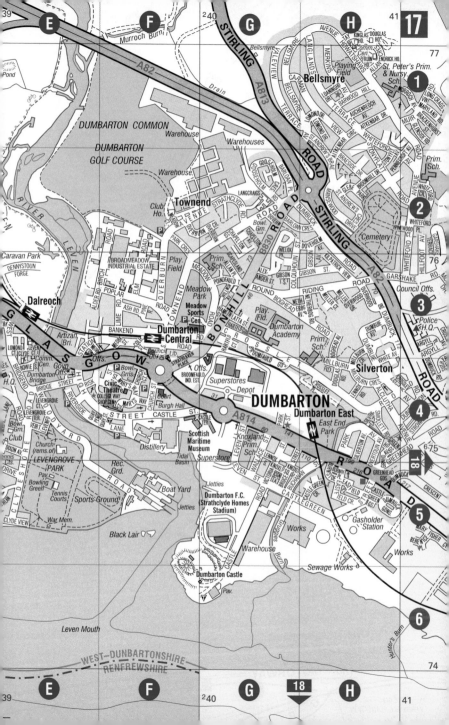

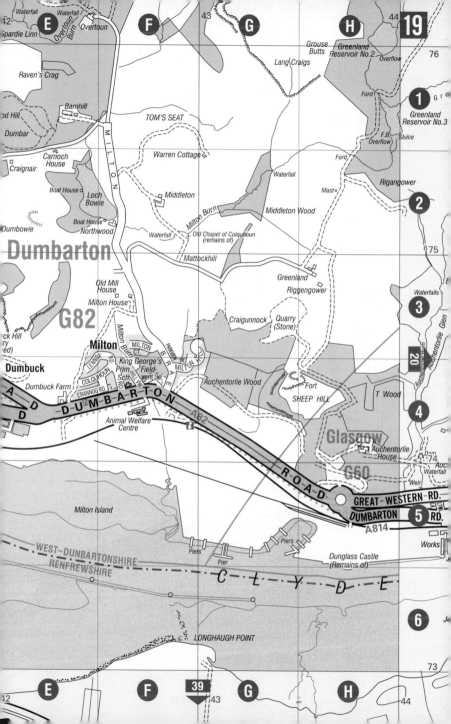

44 245

A   B   C   D

1

LOCH HUMPHREY
(Reservoir)
Boat Shed

Grouse Butts

Greenland
Reservoir No.3

C R A I G A R E S T I E

Dam

K I L P A

2 Rigangower

675

Bow Linn

Waterfalls

Reservoir

Waterfall

3

Waterfall

McKellar's
Wood

Quarry (Disused)

19

Lonendale
Wood

Hill of Dun

Glenarbuck

Haw Craig

4 T Wood

Auchentorlie
Cottage

K I L P A

Auchentorlie
House 74

Dam

High
Auchentorlie

East Wood

Bowling

Torwood Villa

Lodge

Gavinburn Co

Waterfall

Waterfalls

Glenarbuck House

G R E A T   W E S T E R N   R O A D   D U M B A R

MANSE

Dunarbuck
Cottage

Weir

Lodge

Weir

5 D U M B A R T O N

SCOTT AVENUE

A82

A814

Gavinbur

Bowling

Works

Jetty

Frisky
Wharf

Bowling Harbour

Pier

Lock

Basin

Library G

ROMAN CRESCENT

ess Castle
(ns of)

R I V E R

Jetty

WEST DUNBARTONSHIRE
RENFREWSHIRE

Lock

C L Y D E

ROMAN

Chapel Hill

CRESCENT

Depot
GAV

PORTPATRICK

6 Jetty

73

Donald's Quay
Light

44 A   B   40 C   D on Beacon

245

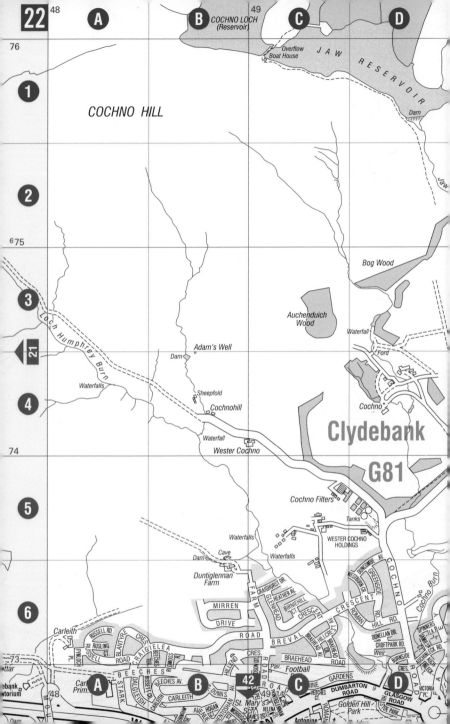

22 48   A   B   49   C   D

COCHNO LOCH
(Reservoir)

JAW RESERVOIR

76

Overflow
Boat House

1

COCHNO HILL

Dam

Jaw

2

675

Bog Wood

3

Loch Humphrey Burn

Adam's Well

Auchenduich
Wood

Waterfall

Ford

21

Dam

Sheepfold

Waterfalls

Cochno

4

Cochnohill

Waterfall

Wester Cochno

Clydebank

74

G81

Cochno Filters

5

Tanks

Waterfalls

WESTER COCHNO
HOLDINGS

Waterfalls

Cave

Dam

Duntiglennan
Farm

DUNCOMBE AV.

GREENSIDE

COCHNO

Cochno Burn

6

MIRREN

DRIVE

FARM ROAD

CRAIGHURST DR.

GLENEAD

HEATHER AV.

BIRNIEHILL

CRES.

CRESCENT

WESTBURN.

HILL RD.

ROMAN

DUNELLAN DR.

CROFTPARK RD.

Weir

SPINNERS

BURNSIDE

Carleith

RUSSELL RD.

RUSLING
CT.

BLANTYRE

CRES.

CRAIGIELEA

BEECHES

REMUS CT.

HILLEND

BREVAL

BRAEHEAD AV.

BRAEHEAD

CRESCENT

ROMAN

RD.

AUCHNACRAIG RD.

VICTORIA
PL.

73

PENILEE
PL.

RUSSELL
RD.

ROAD

STARK

CRAIGTON

DALGLEISH

BEECHES

CARLEITH

AV.

BEECHES AV.

DUNN ST.

CRES.

BRAEHEAD
ROAD

Pav. Football

VEITCHES CT.

GARDENS

DUMBARTON

ROAD

GLASGOW
ROAD

CRES.

48

A

Carl
Prim.

ebank
atorium

Dam

B

42 49

St. Mary's
Sch.

HOGAN

MORRISON

JAMES

HELENA

C

D

Golden Hill
Park

Antonine

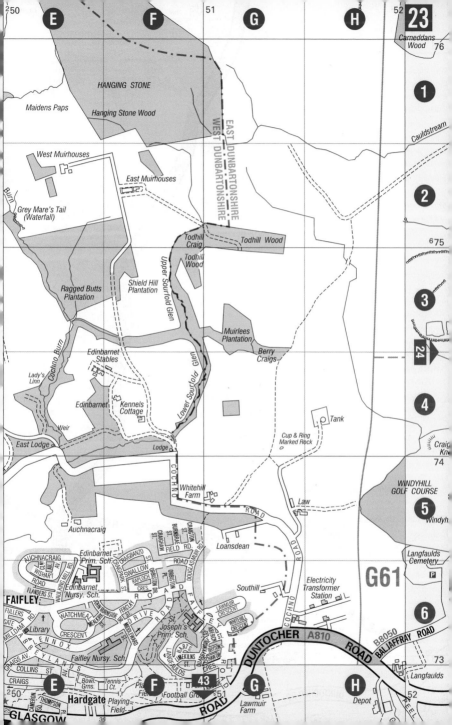

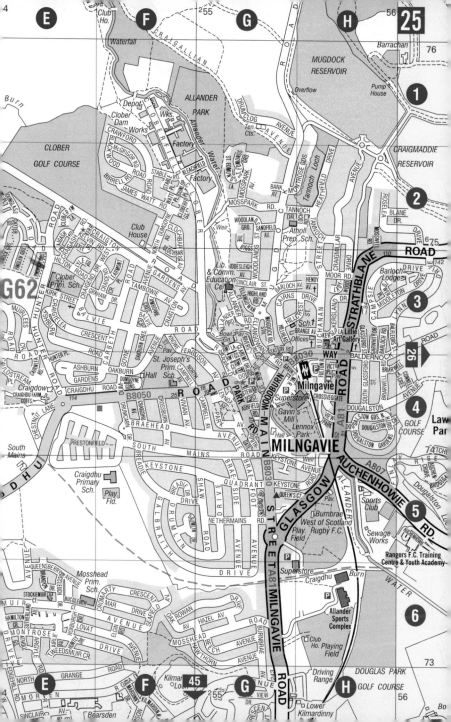

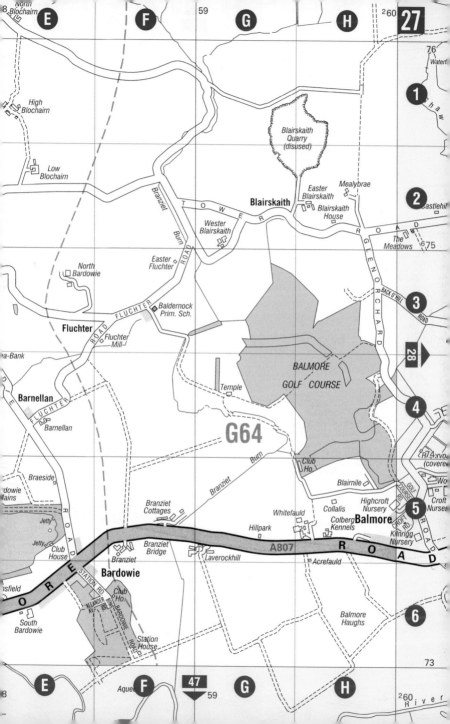

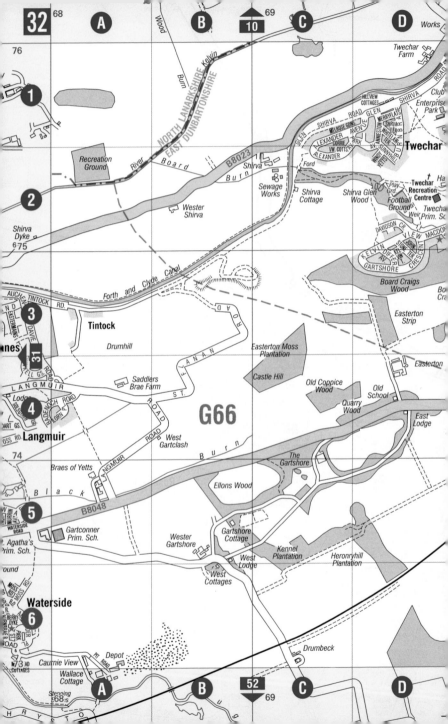

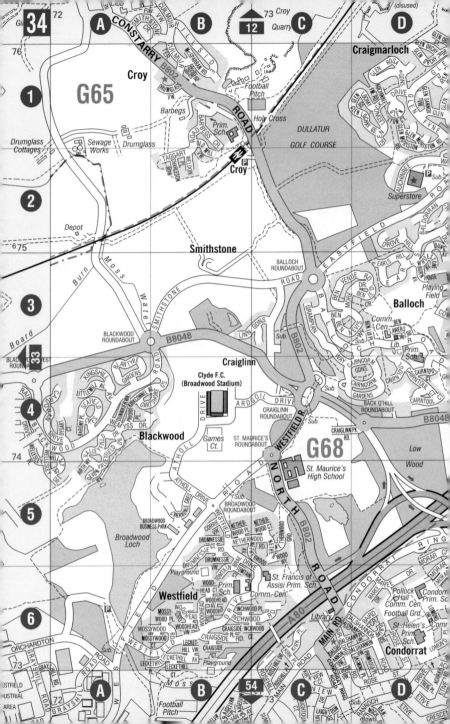

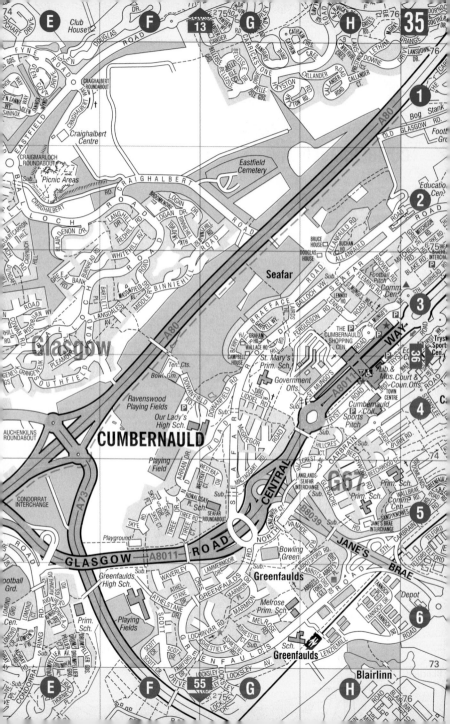

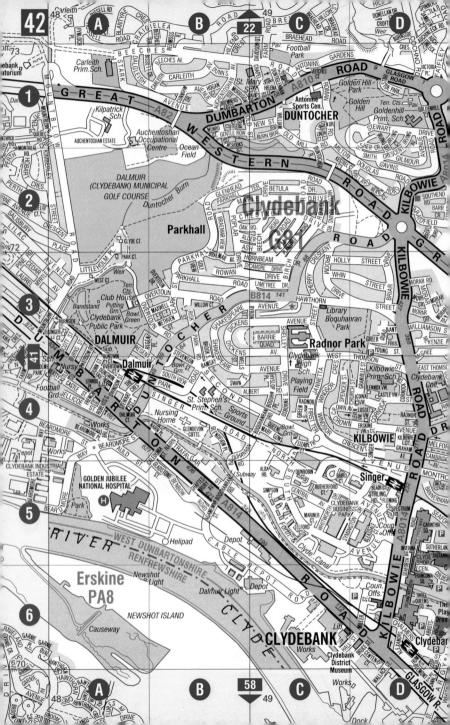

Blairlinn

1

BLAIRLINN IND. EST.

2

Wester
Blairlinn

Garngribboch

Auchenkilns
Holdings

Cumbernauld
Rugby Football
Club
Playing Field

Playing
Field

North
Myvot

Burn

Millcroft
Corn Mill

Milncroft
Farm

Madgiscroft
Quarry

Cragside

Lochside
Cottage

3

Milncroft Wood

South
Myvot

Hallbrae

North Bellstane
Plantation

Mill Lade

Loanhead

Bellstane
Lodge

4

Summerhill

Shank Burn

Clay
Pit

**Airdrie
ML6**

Broomlee Strip

Summerhill Strips

Shank
Bridge

Bellstane

Summerfield
Strip

Mossywood

South
Bellstane
Plantation

5

GAIN AND SHANKBURN

The Gains

B802

Douglas
Glen

Mossywood
Clumps

Cullochrig
Plantation

6

Blackcraig
Wood

Cleddans

Black Craig

New West
Lodge

East
Lodge

Heatherfield
Wood

Douglas
Plantation

Mosshouse

West Lodge

Hairstanes

East Lodge
Wood

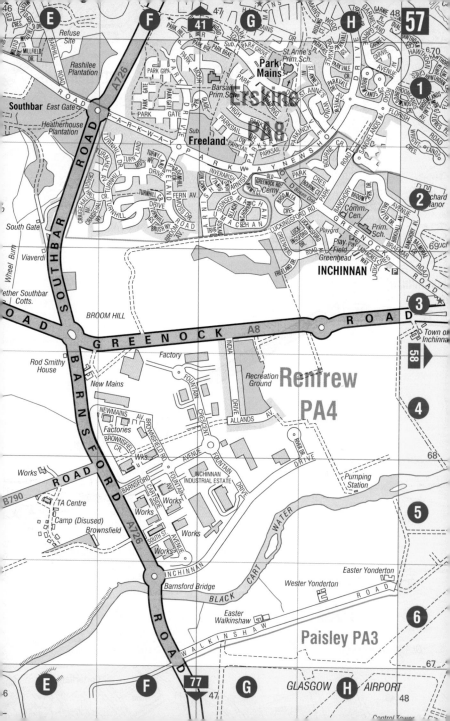

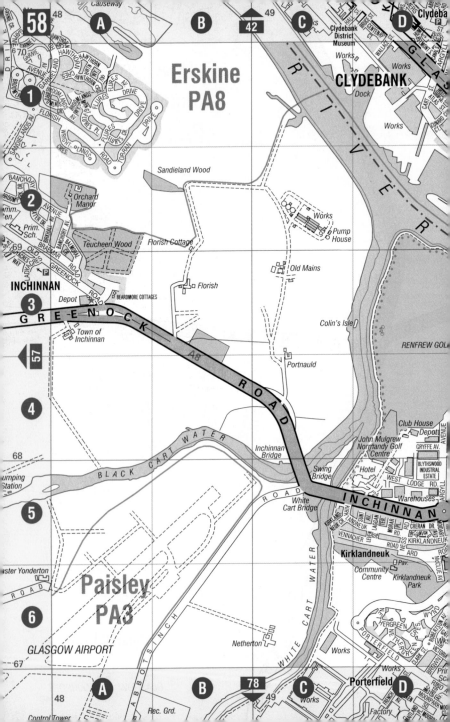

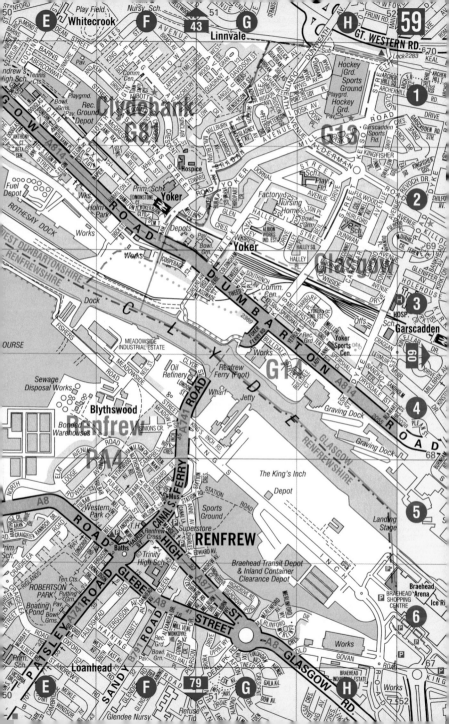

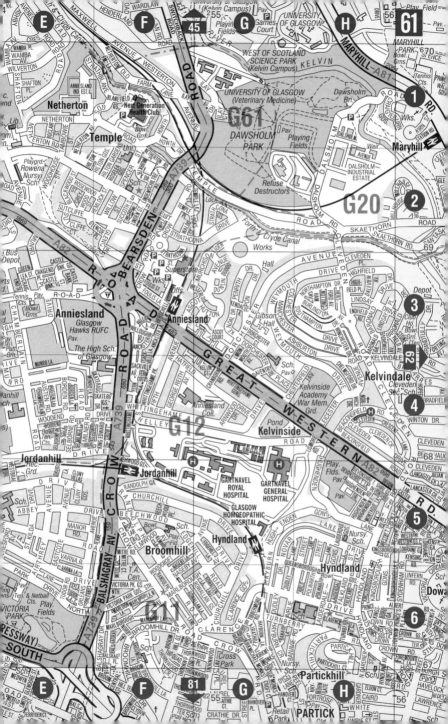

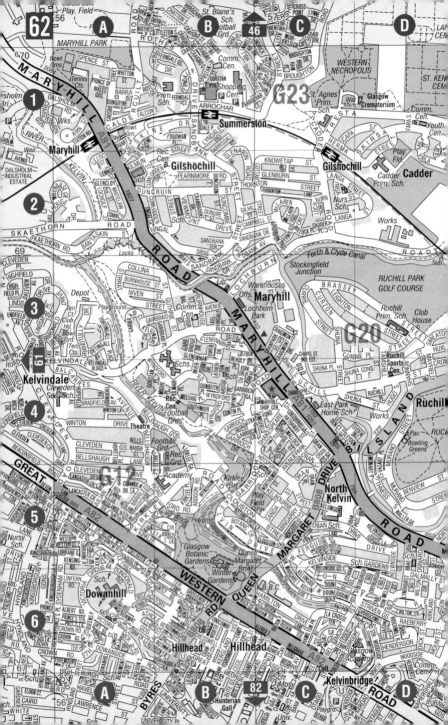

E
F
G
H
47
59
260
670
POSSIL LOCH
(Bird Sanctuary)
Forth & Clyde Canal
BALMORE
BALMORE INDUSTRIAL ESTATE
Milton
Colston
Lambhill
Lambhill Bridge
Glasgow
G22
Possilpark & Parkhouse
Ashfield
Possil Park
Milton Park
Bowl.-Grns.
Tennis Cts.
Library
Comm. Cen.
St. Augustine's Prim. & Sec. Schs.
Hockey Grds.
Playing Fields
Chirnsyde Sports Cen.
Playing Field
Chirnsyde Prim. Sch.
Milton Sch.
Depot
POSSIL PARK TRADING CEN.
DENMARK STREET INDUS. CENTRE
HAWTHORN
STREET
B808
DRIVE
ROAD
Keppoch Park
Saracen Park
Hawthorn Prim. Sch.
Cowlairs Nth. Junc.
Cowlairs West Junc.
COWLAIRS INDUSTRIAL ESTATE
Cowlairs
Partick Thistle F.C. (Firhill Park)
Football Ground
Wester Common Prim. Sch.
Firhill
Millennium Cen.
Hamiltonhill
Works
St. Teresa's Prim. Sch.
Keppoch Prim. Sch.
COWLAIRS PARK (Rec. Grd.)
G21
SARACEN ST.
CRAIGHALL RD.
A879
GARSCUBE ROAD
A81
OAKBANK INDUS. EST.
Warehouse
G4
PORT DUNDAS INDUS. EST.
Distillery
Sighthill Prim. Sch.
SIGHTHILL CEMETERY
EAGLE HEIGHTS
64
83
68
69
67
1
2
3
4
5
6

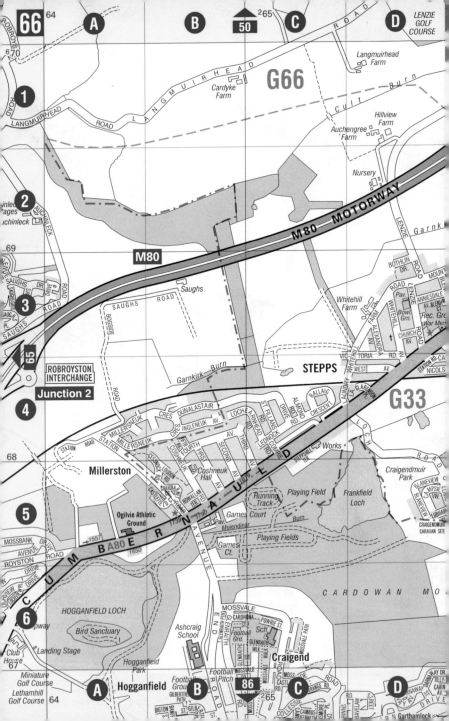

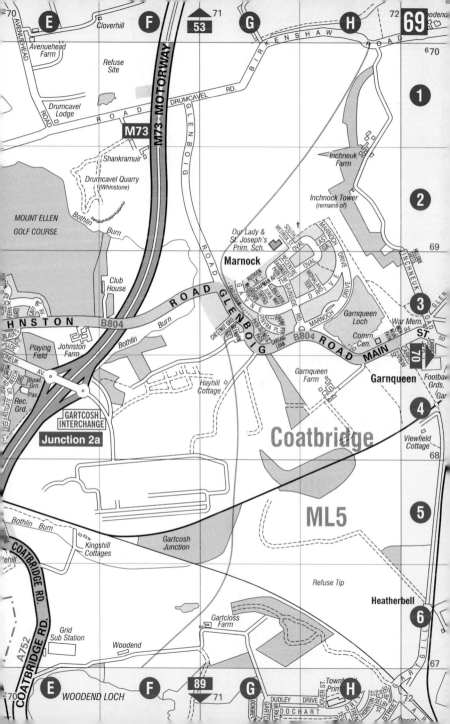

New West J
Lodge
74 YETTS HOLE RD
West Lodge
Hairstanes
Cottage
East Lodge
Wood
Foot o' Loan
Wood
East
Gartmillan
West
Gartmillan
Arderyth
Wellhouse
Greenfield
LINSBURN
ROAD
Firknowe

Black Craig
East
Lodge
rfield
od
CONDORRAT
B802
Glenmill
Shank Burn

Glenmill
Wood

Drumbowie
Farm
BRACKENHIRST
ROAD

Cullochrig
CULLOCHRIG
ROAD
BRACKENHIRST
Brackenhirst
Plantation
670

1
2
69
3

BRACKENHIRST GDNS
Ryding
Brackenhirst
Farm
B802
Gas Storage
Depot

Airdrie
ML6

Ryden
Mains

Cemetery

Reservoir
(covered)

New
Monkland

Cemetery
New Monkland
Prim. Sch.

Laverock
Knowe

4

ARRAN DR
STRATHCARRON DR
BANCHORY
AV
MORAL HILL
CRATHIE
BRIMCLIFF
NORWOOD DRIVE
ARRAN DR
GS. DR.
B803
ROAD
68

5

ROAD
RAEBOG

Norwood
Rochsoles

Crowhill
Plantation

AIRDRIE
GOLF
COURSE

MAINS
RYDEN
Comm.
Cen.
WADDELL
QUARRY ST.
ST.
KIRKSTYLE
MACARTHUR
AV.
WADDELL
PL
Playground

Football
Ground
Bowl.
Grn.

CLEDDANS VW.
45
LOCHVIEW CT.
GLEN VIEW ST.
27
190
LOCHBURN LA.
LOCHBURN
MAINS
MELDRUM
GLENWELL
ST.

GLENMAVIS

Blackwalk
Plantation

Roughcraig
Glen
STRATHSPEY CR
STRATHBLANE CR.
STRIVEN CR.
STRATHCONA

6

67

Braidenhill
Farm
Dryflat
B803
GLENMAVIS
BRIDGE
B802
COATBRIDGE

South
Lodge
GLENMAVIS
ROAD

Club
Ho. Golfhill

DRIVE
STRATHMORE
STRATHTAY
BLUEBELL
WAY
TUMMEL DR.
LOCHEARN CR
PRINGHAM
CRAIGMOCHAN
STAINEY
BRAE
STRATHPEFFER
PL
76
STRATHBRAAN
DRYFEN
MUIRHOUSE
DRIVE

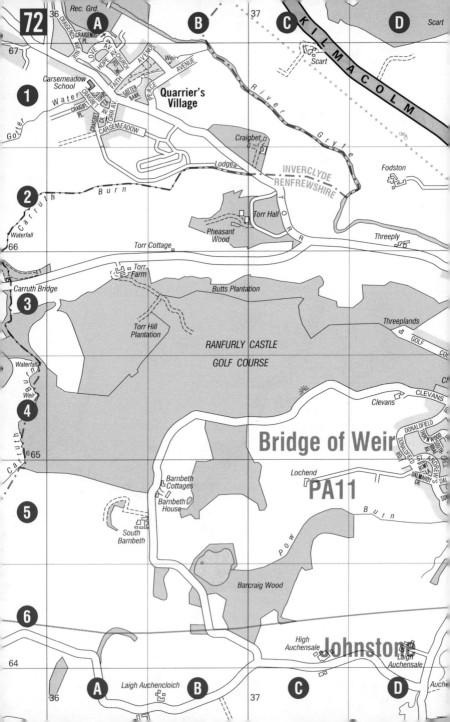

72

36   Rec. Grd.

67

A   **B**   **C**   **D**

Scart

KILMACOLM

CRAIGENDS PL

OVE AV
HOPE AV
FAITH
CHURCH
AVENUE
Weir
AVENUE

Scart

1

Carsemeadow
School

Water
CRAIGBET
PL
CRAIGBET CR
CRAIGBET AV
TORR AV
GUTTER
BANK
PEACE

**Quarrier's
Village**

River
Gryfe

Craigbet

Goter

CARSEMEADOW

Lodges

INVERCLYDE
RENFREWSHIRE

Fodston

2

Carruth   Burn

TORR

Torr Hall

Threeply

Waterfall

66

Torr Cottage

Pheasant
Wood

3

Torr
Farm

Butts Plantation

Carruth Bridge

Torr Hill
Plantation

Threeplands

GOLF   CO

RANFURLY CASTLE

GOLF COURSE

4

Waterfall

Weir

Carruth

Clevans

CLEVANS

Cl

Bridge of Weir

DONALDFIELD
THORN
WOOD
SOUTH CRES.
DONALDFIELD
ROW
ST. ANDREW'S

665

Lochend

PA11

BGMT
DALMAHOY'S
CR
ST. ANDREW'S DAL
DALMAHOY'S
SUN

5

Barnbeth
Cottages

Barnbeth
House

Pow   Burn

South
Barnbeth

6

Barcraig Wood

64

High
Auchensale

Johnstone

Laigh
Auchensale

Auche

A   Laigh Auchencloich   **B**   **C**   **D**

36   37

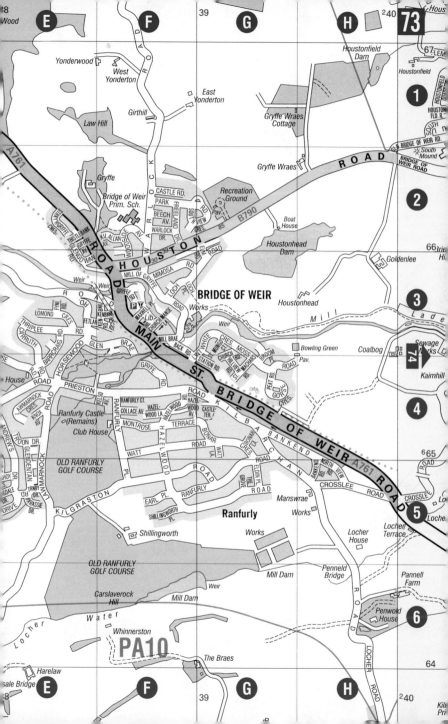

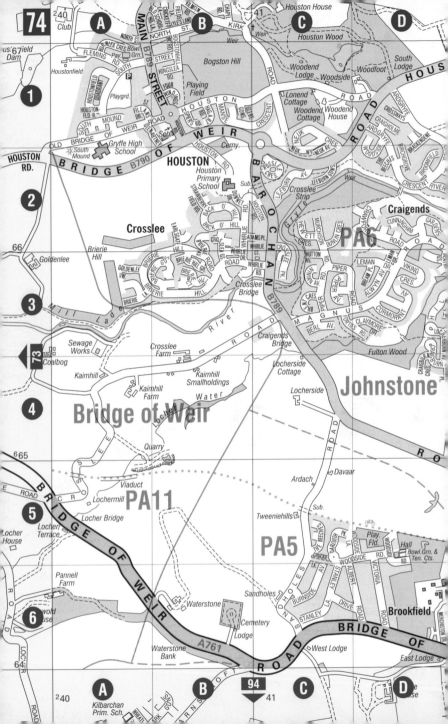

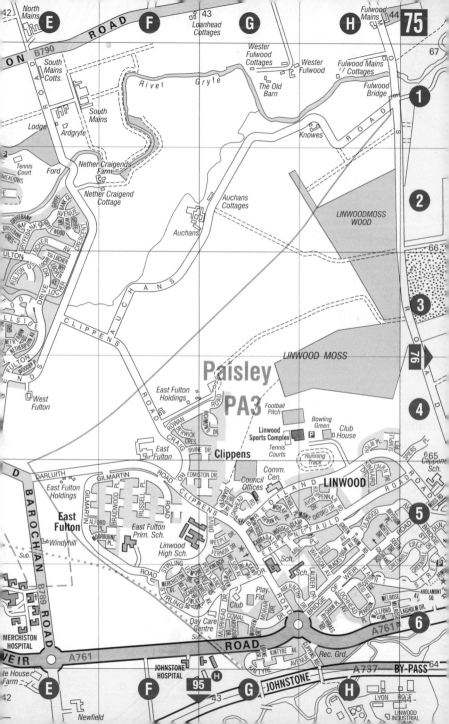

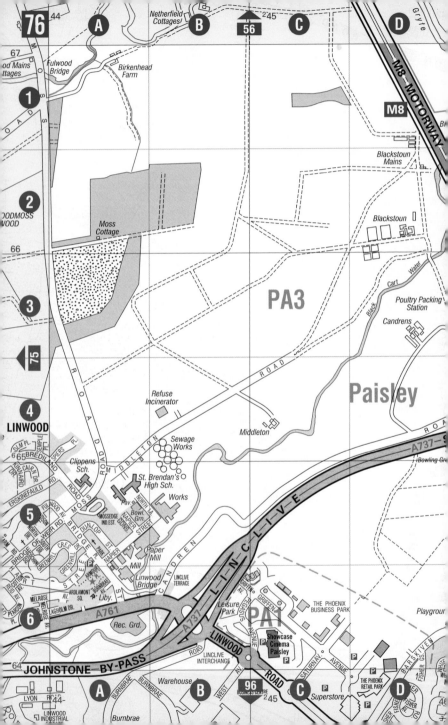

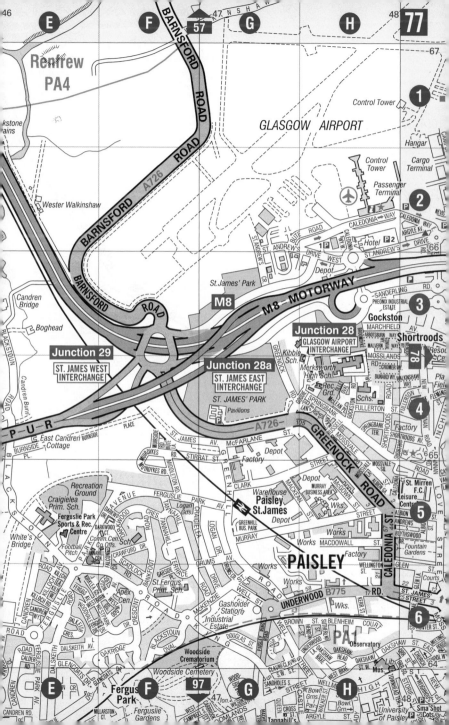

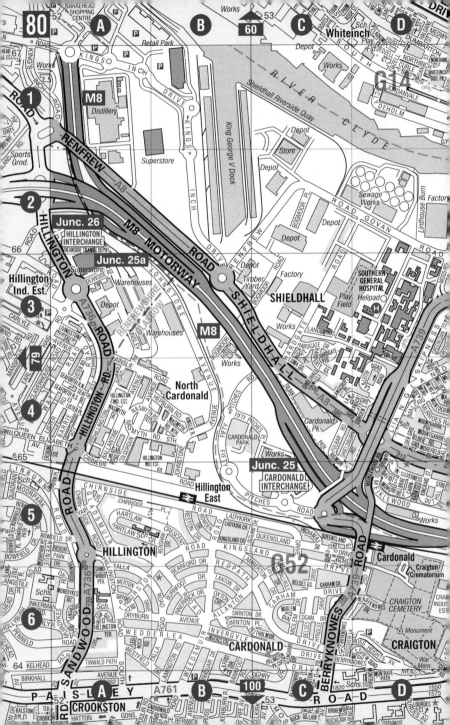

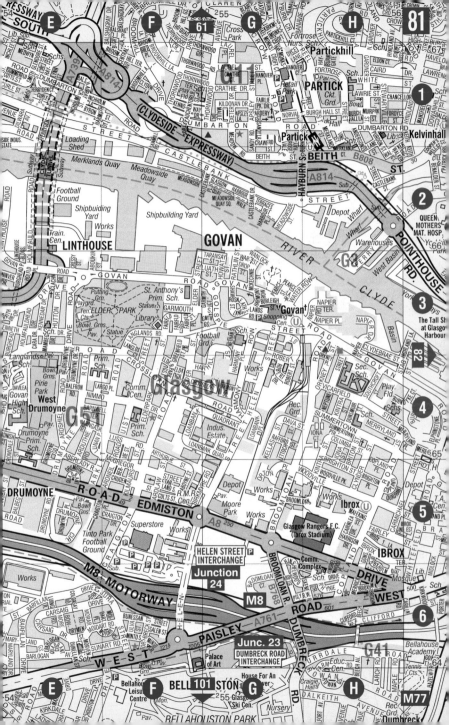

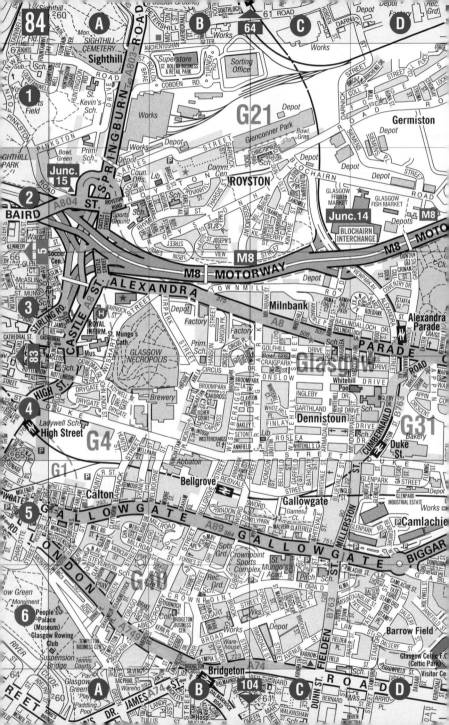

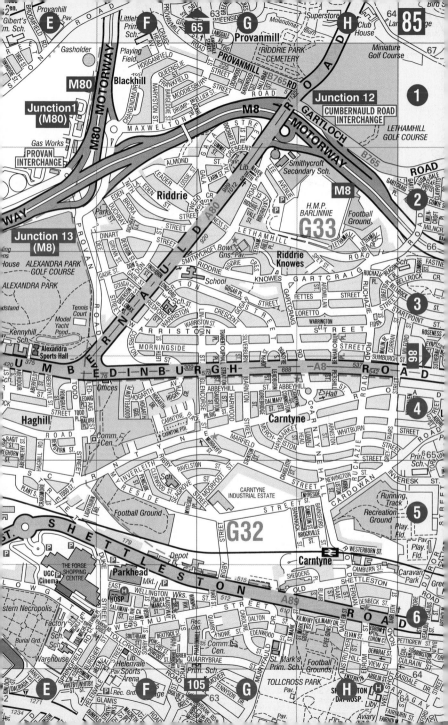

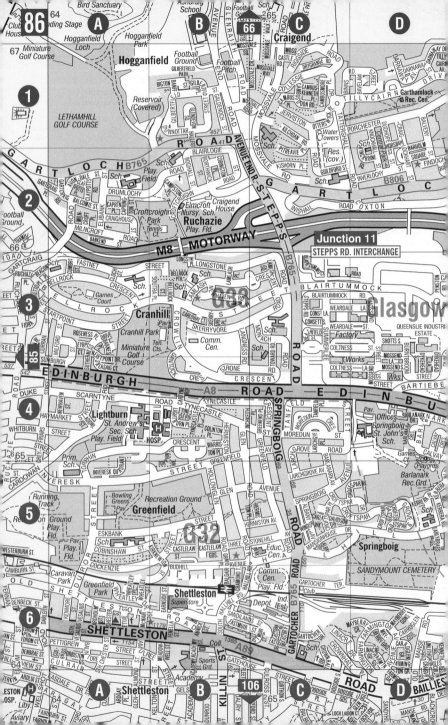

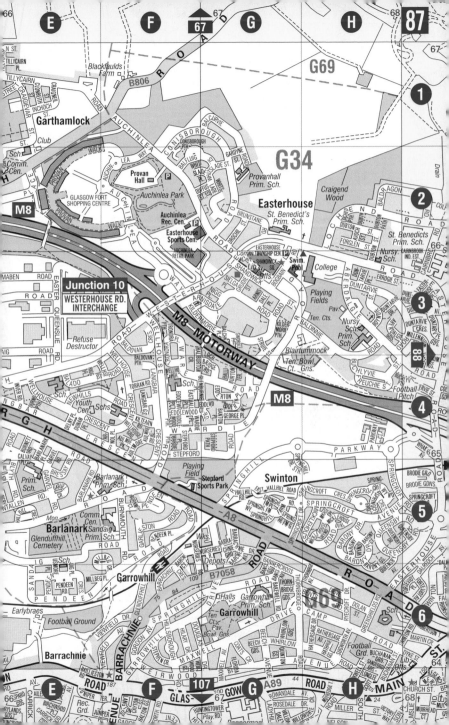

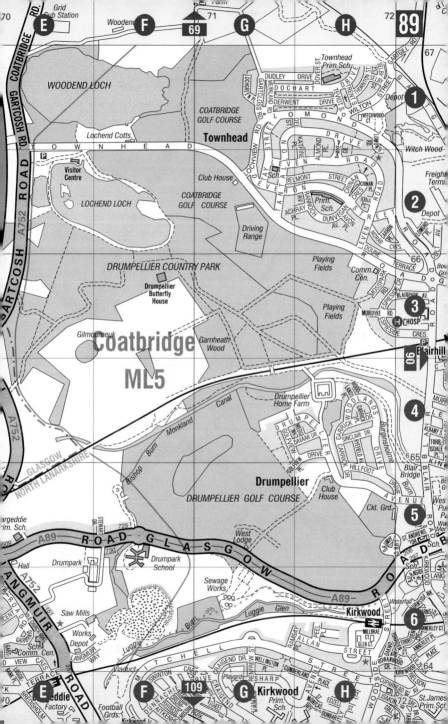

Airdrie
ML6

PLAINS

Meadowhall
House

BALLOCHNEY RD.

Meadowhall

Playing Fields

Playing Flds.

St. David's
Primary
School

Depots

AIRDRIE

St. Phillip's
School

ROAD MAIN STREET

A89

BURNTESIDE

Weir

Waterfall

Sewage
Farm

Hillhead

EASTER MOFFAT
GOLF COURSE

Club Ho.

Greystones

CHURCH CR.

Depot

CONNOR ST.

Katherine
Cottage

Play.
Fld.

Katherine
Park

WESTER
MOFFAT
HOSPITAL

Wester Moffat
Farm

TOWERS ROAD

ROAD

A89

Dunrobin

North Calder Water

Ponds

Caldervale
Forge

Caldervale
High Sch.

Weir

Warehouses

Dunrobin
Prim. Sch.

Warehouses

Petersburn

Moffat
Mills

Bowl.
Grn.

Burn
Wood

Warehouses

STEPENDS ROAD

Rec.
Grd.

Comm.
Cen.

ROUGHRIGG

ROAD

Gimmerscroft

Weir

Kameyknowe
Cottage

Knowehead

CRAIGENS

Glenview

ROAD

Mill Farm

GARTNESS DRIVE

Gartness

Bowhouse

BOWHOUSE

Damhead
Farm

Clattering Burn

DUNISTON ROAD

Easter
Dunsyston

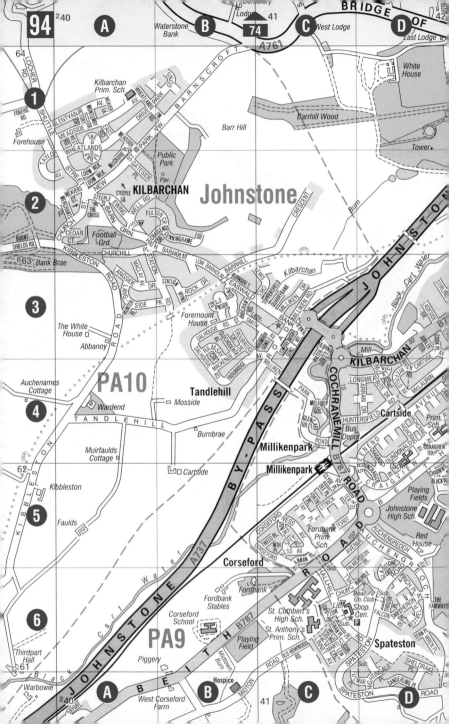

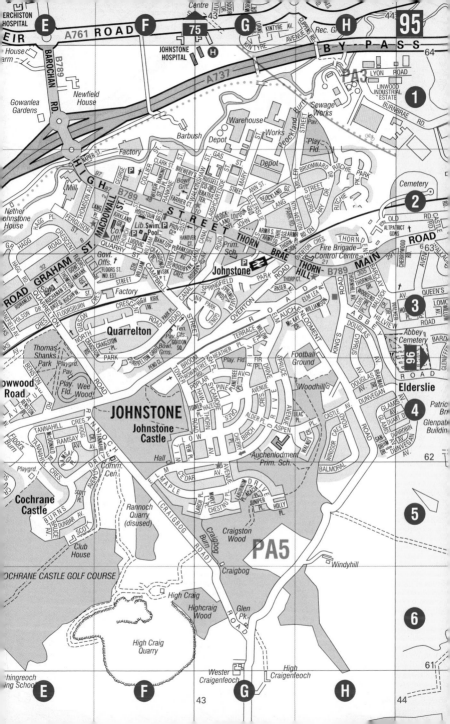

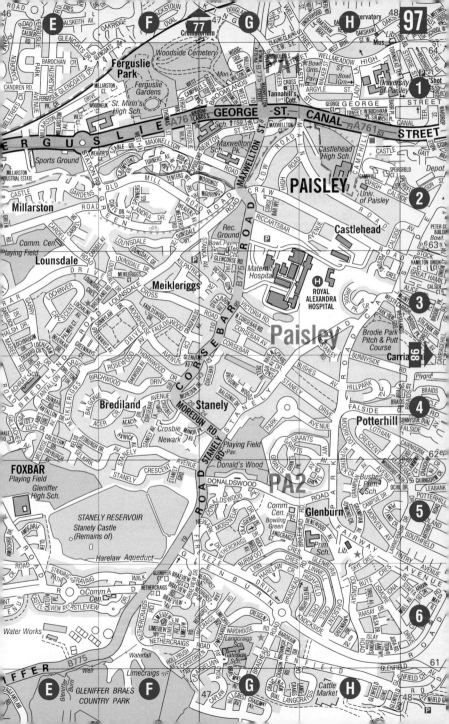

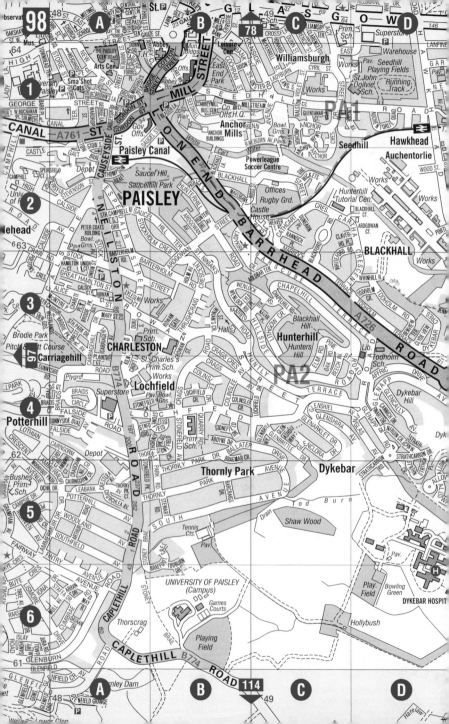

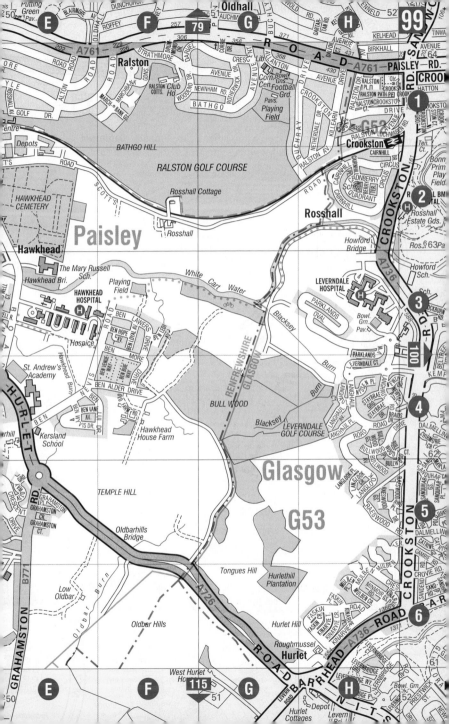

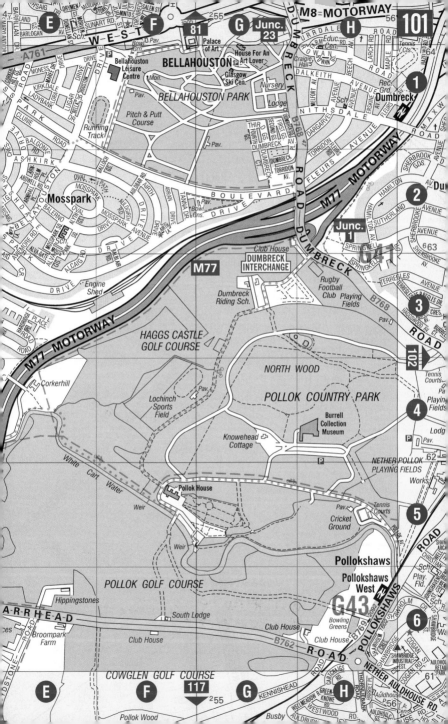

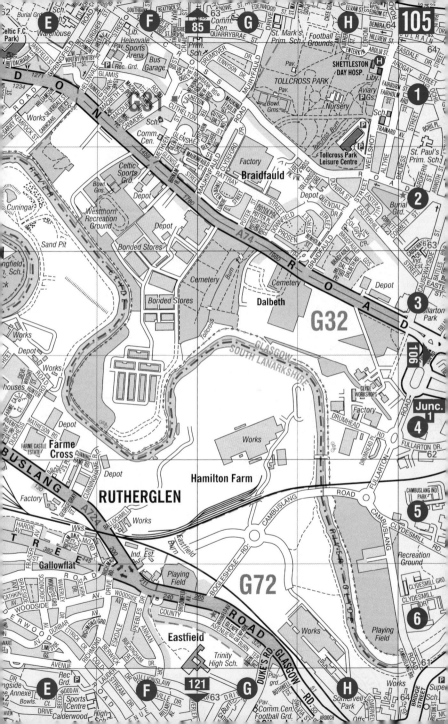

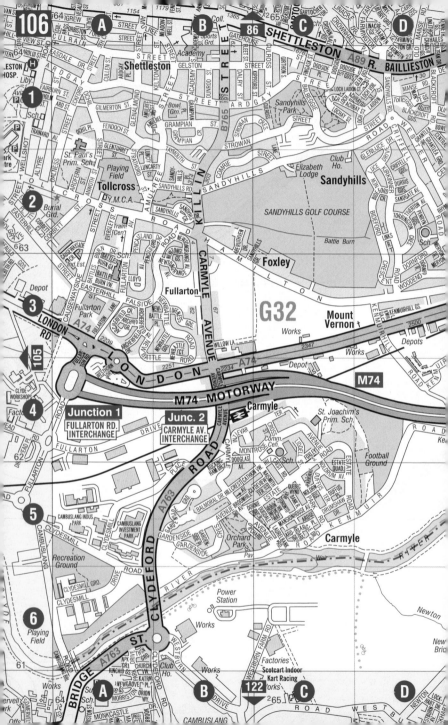

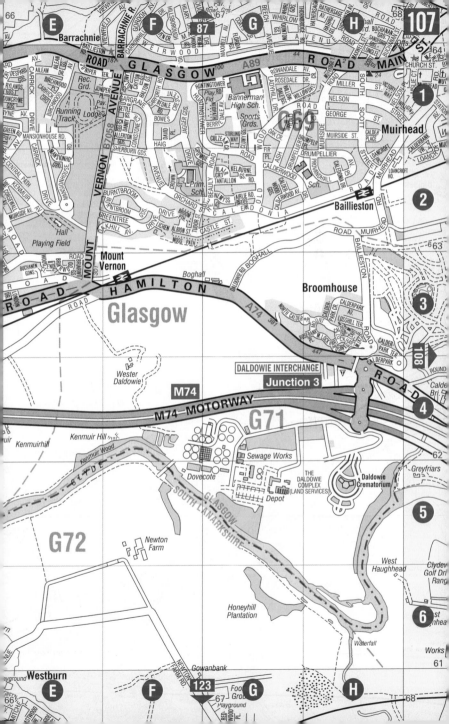

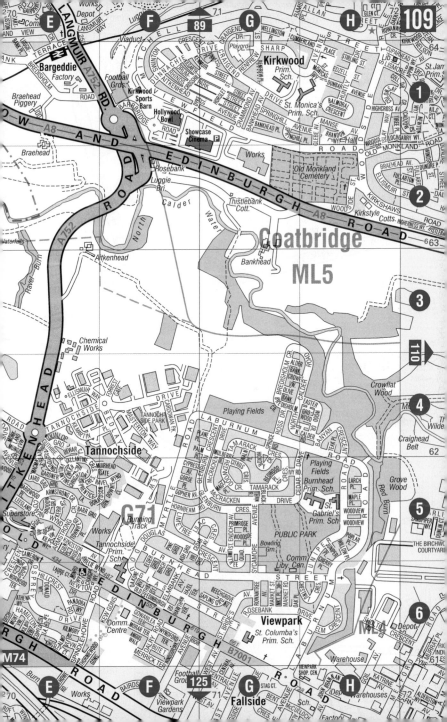

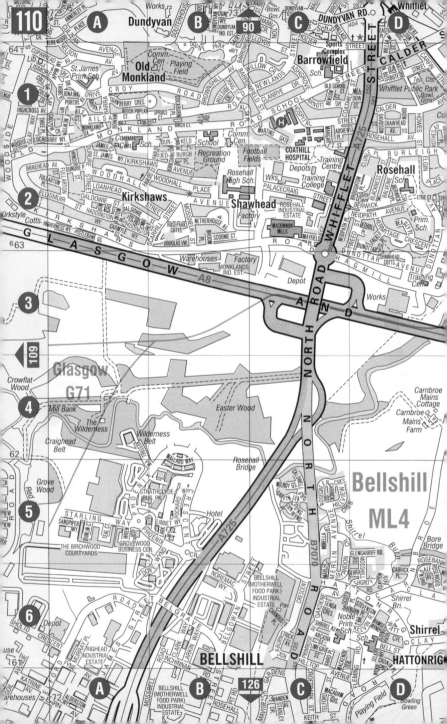

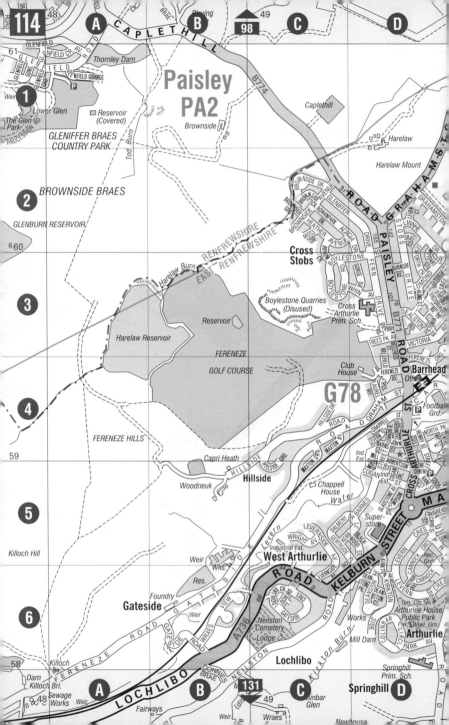

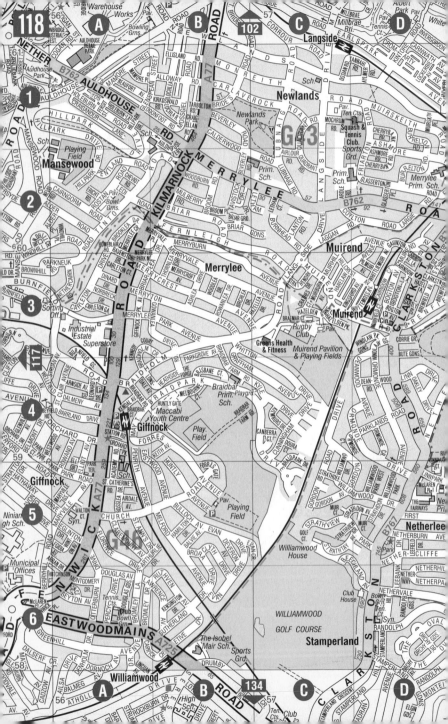

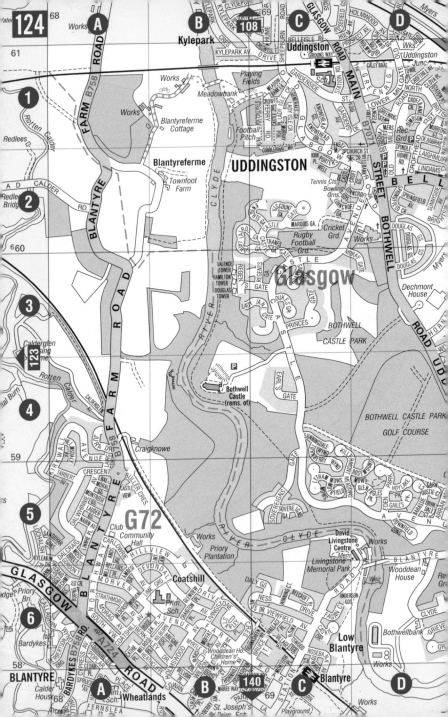

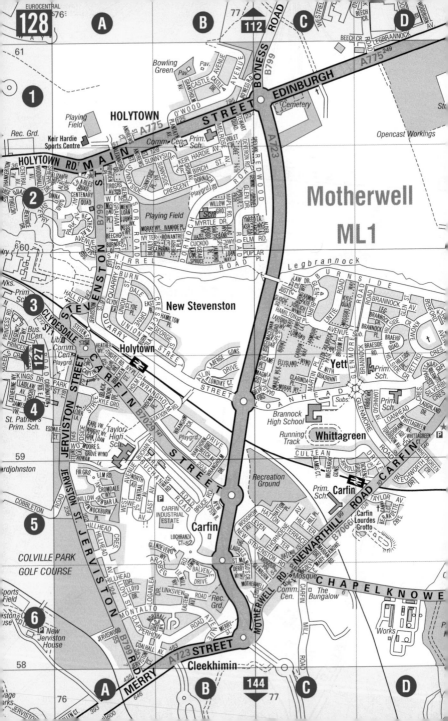

128

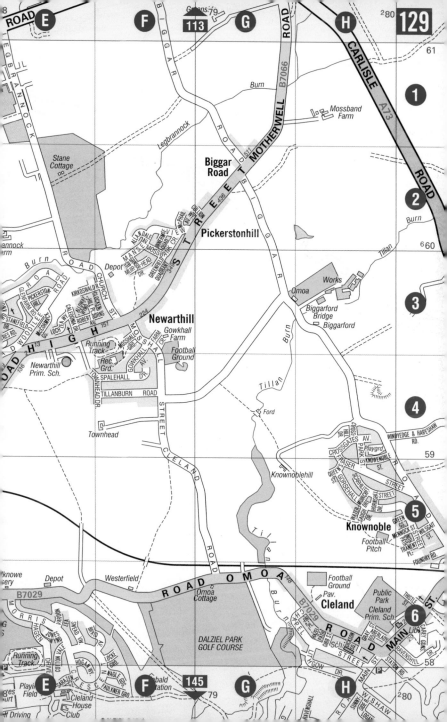

130 46

A   Killoch   B   Water   47   C   Waterfall   D
58   Waterfalls   Killoch   Killoch Bri.
                                                       Glen   Waterfall
Witch   Dam
Burn   ROAD   Auchentiber
1   FERENEZE   FERENEZE
        Foreside   Works

2   FERENEZE   SEA BRAE   BROADLIE   ROAD   BROADLIE
                            LOCHLIBO   HOLEHOUSE   G78   Prim.
                            Mill   Res.   (Dis.)   Sch.

        A736   Lodge   Weir   CROFTHEAD   MILLVIEW   Neilston
57   High   COTTAGES   Playing
        LOCHLIBO   Holehouse   Holehouse   Field
3   Crofthead   Dam   Farm   Bowl
        Cowdon Burn   House   Sidney   Grn.
                            Cottage   Football   COMMORE
        Smiddyhill   Brimstone   Bridge   ICE CREAM CR.   GLEN ORRIN WY.
                    Lodge   GLEN MARK RD.   KINGSTON AV.   CRAIG
        Crumyards   UPLAWMOOR   Water   Glen   GLEN FINLET CR.   KINGSTON AV.
        Cottage   ROAD   GLEN MUIR RD.
4   MUIRHEAD   Crumyards   GLEN ISLA AV.   GLEN FALLOCH CR.
                            Levern   Glen   Kilburn   Water
                    Midgehole   Works   Water
56   Glen   Neilstonside   Works   Craig
        Jaapston   Cottage   Neilst.
        Farm   ROAD   Neilstonside   Craig   Craig
                        Bridge   Neilstonside   of   Cottage
5   MUIRHEAD   Hill   Neilston   Craig
                            Levern   Wood
        Braeface   NEILSTON
        Farm   MUIRHEAD   Links   Craighall   PAD
6   Neilstonside   or   Boat   Overflow
        Waterside   Levern   Water   House
        Aboon   ROAD   CRAIGHALL
6 55   the Brae   A   B   DAM   C   D
        46   A   47   B   C   D

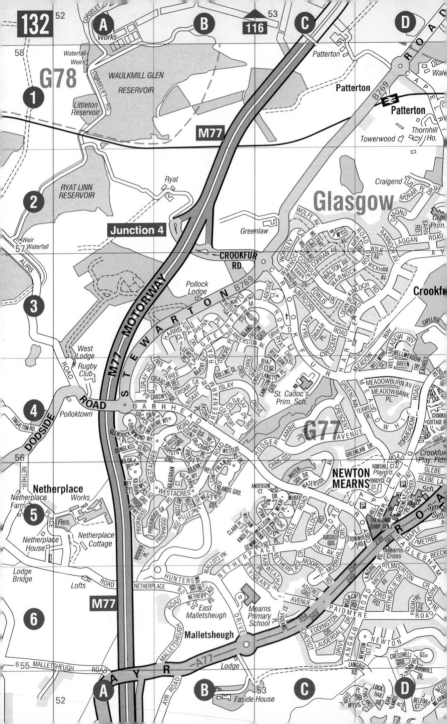

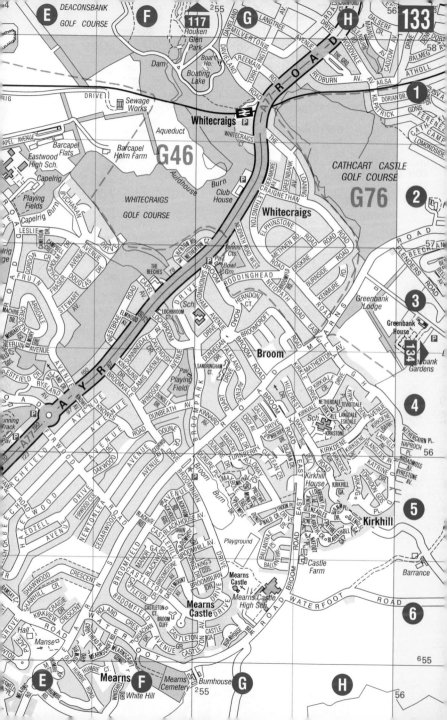

DEACONSBANK GOLF COURSE

Rouken Glen Park **117**

CATHCART CASTLE GOLF COURSE

G46

G76

WHITECRAIGS GOLF COURSE

Whitecraigs

Whitecraigs

Greenbank Lodge

Greenbank House

134

Broom

Kirkhill

Mearns Castle

Mearns Castle High Sch.

Castle Farm

Barrance

Mearns

Mearns Cemetery

White Hill

Burnhouse

WATERFOOT ROAD

(1) (2) (3) (4) (5) (6)

E F G H

260

58

A

B

120

61

C

CATHKIN BRAES
GOLF COURSE

D

G45

ROAD

Curling
Pond

1

BUSBY R.

GALLOWHILL
THE WILLOWS
CREST
PLATFIELD RD.
MANSE
MAR OAKS
GREEN
BEECHES
SYCAMORE
WAYSIDE

B759

Muir
Farm

CARMUNNOCK

C
A
T
H
K
I
N

ROAD

KIRK
PATHE
ROAD
GLEBE AV.
CRAIGHALL
PARK
CRAGNELL PARK

GLASGOW
SOUTH LANARKSHIRE

2

Ren
(GR

KITTOCHSIDE
PARK LEE DR.

Prim.
Sch.

57
GDNS.

Parklea

Bellcraig

Highflat
Farm

WATERSIDE

ROAD

3

135

ROAD

KITTOCHSIDE

Braefoot

Rockcrest

G76

Waters

4

Waterbank

Wester
Kittochside

Kittochside

CAIRNMUIR

Stepends
Bridge

Philipshill Sewage
Works

STERFIELD

56

ROAD

Kittochside
Farm

Eastend

Dykehead
Farm

KITTOCHSIDE
RD.

Kittochside

CARMUNNOCK

GLEN RD.

Cemetery

Museum of
Scottish
Country Life

Mill
Cottage

Philipshill

5

EAST

KILBRIDE

A725

ROAD

STERFIELD RD.

PHILIPSHILL

PHILIPSHILL
GATE

Hotel

EWARTFIELD

ROAD

WINTER'S
CASTLEGLEN
PARK
CASTLEHILL
CASTLE
GATES

Castleglen

CASTLEGLEN

MACKENZIE
GDNS.

MANOR

MACKENZIE
PL.
CALCOL

EWAN
PK.

CAIRN
MACDONALD

AVENUE

McCALLUM

MAYOR
McKAY PL. McCALL

MACKAY

MACFI

CRESC.

MACNEILL GS.
MAC-NEILL DR.

MACNINE
MACINDR.
GRO.

MACFIE

Supermark
Comm
Cen

PLACE

Castle Hill

Kittoch

Rough
Hill

WATER

ROAD

HA

WBANK

Industrial Estate

James

WATT

PLACE

DIXON

PLACE

College
Milton

6

head
ourt
AD

Kingsknowe

park

Q
U
E
E
N
S
W
A
Y

A726

ROAD

A726

Government
Offices

ROAD

ROAD

GLENBURN

GLENBURN WY.

GLENBURN

WESTGARTH
PLACE
SPRINGBURN PL.

RONNIE
PLACE

ROAD
ARROTSHOLE

West
Mains

655

A

BARBANA
ROAD

GLASGOW
SOUTHERN ORBITAL

REDWOOD

Ind. Est.

PEEL PARK
(IND. EST.)

REDWOOD
CRESCENT

REDWOOD PLACE

PEEL PARK

B

GLENBURN
PLACE

148

6.1 MILTON

C

ROAD

EAST

D

B761

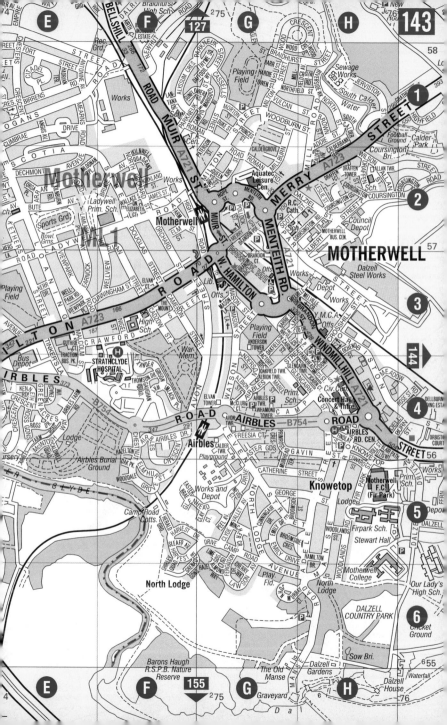

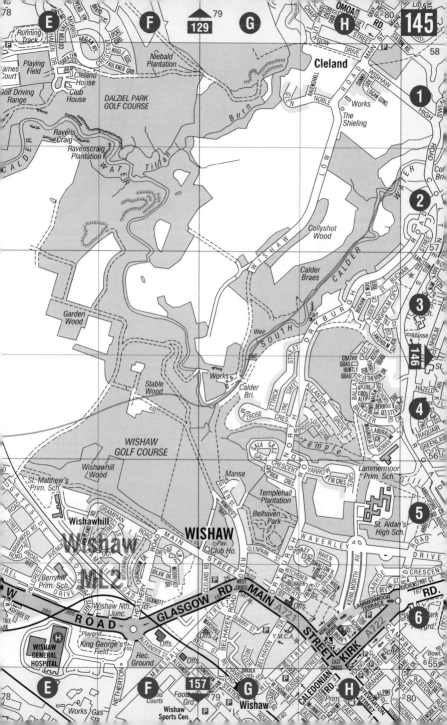

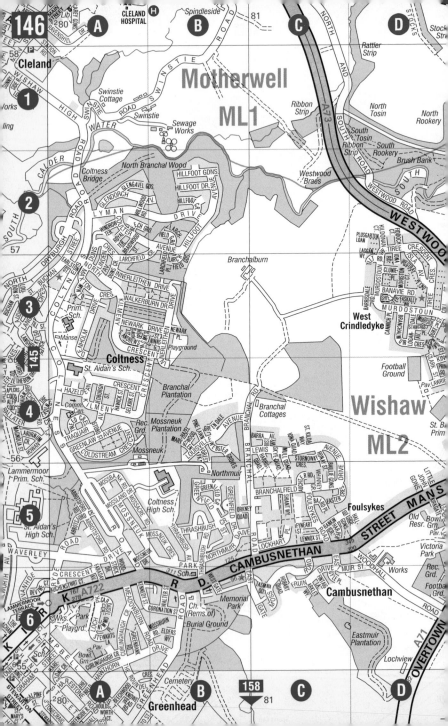

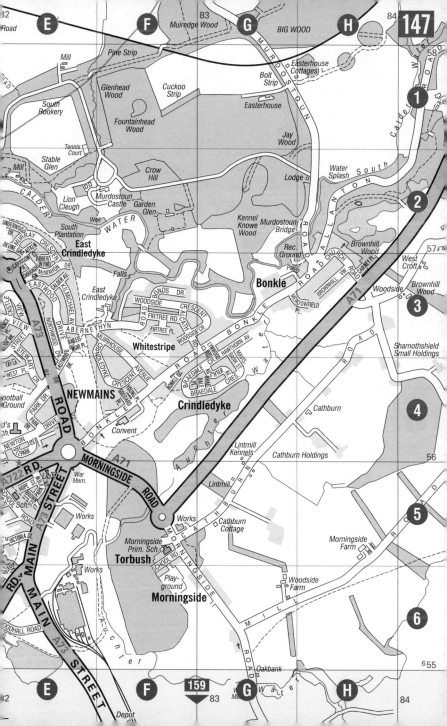

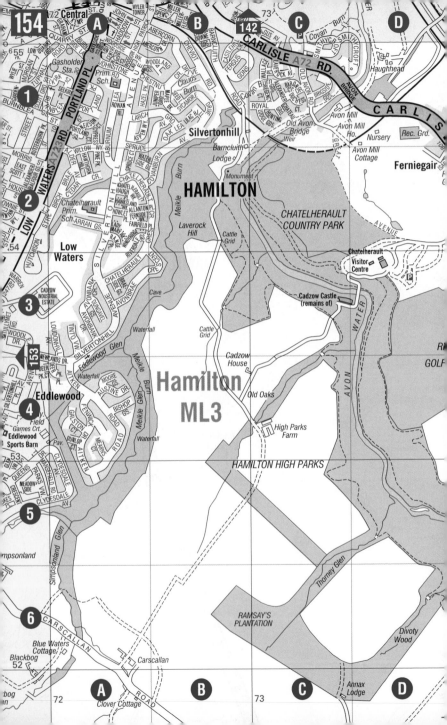

Grid references (top): E · F · G · H
Grid references (right, top to bottom): 1 · 2 · 3 · 4 · 5 · 6
Grid references (bottom): E · F · G · H

M74

275
143

76
Low Bri.

The Old Manse
Barons Haugh
R.S.P.B. Nature
Reserve

Dalzell
Gardens

Wate 655

Dalzell
House

Graveyard

Dalzell
Burn

Motherwell

ML1

NORTH LANARKSHIRE
SOUTH LANARKSHIRE

RIVER

CLYDE

Ea
P

Hall

162

Depot

M74 MOTORWAY

54

PARK DR.
ROSS TERR.
CLYDE
HAMILTON
PARK
CASTLE HILL CR.
AVENUE

Allanton

Allanton Ter.

Sewage
Works

Saw Mill

b House

A72

M74

156

ARTON

COURSE

Low
Merryton

BELVIDERE

PLANTATION

CARLISLE

ROAD

Merryton
Farm Cotts.

LANARK RD. END LANARK

A72

ROAD

53

Garden Centre

Larkhall

ML9

West of Scotland
Go-Kart Circuit

MERRYTON ROAD

Dykehead
Cottage

von
aes

B7078

High Merryton

MERRYTON ROAD

CRESCENT
SHIEL DR.
FYNE

MORR.
VINHE

Lodge

CRESCENT
SIDLAW
WY.
PENTLAND
LAMM.
CAMP.
PENTLAND
FINVR
WIND
CRESCENT
WESTHORN
DAVE BARRIE AV.
HAMILTON RD.
SUMMERLEE

DEER
BEE.
MOORF.
BIRCH
CRO.

ROAD

Lodge
Fairholm
Bridge

160

275

LARKHALL

BEATON
FAIR.
SUNNY.
MERRYTON
STREET
WESTHORN
HAMILTON RD.
War
Mem.
GREEN
QUEEN
LONDON

52

HAMILTON

ST.

BRIGE HILL
CHEST.
NUT
MAP.
PRIM.
BRONE
ASH
CHEST.

Sewage
Works

Playground

99

760

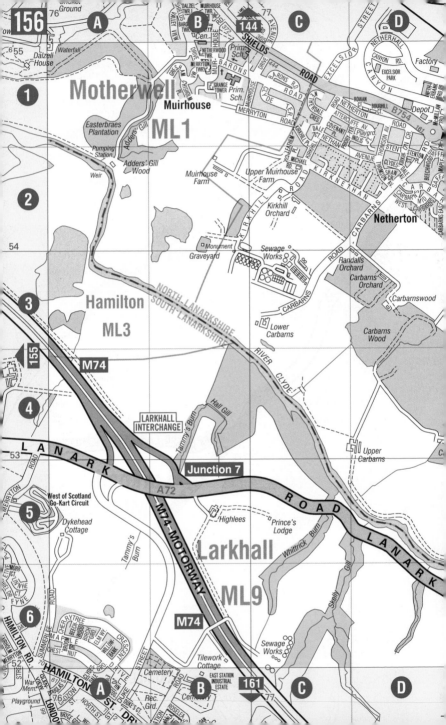

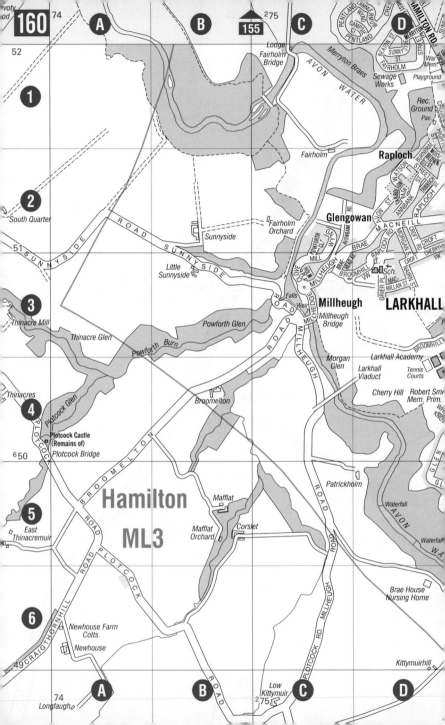

160 74

52

A **B** 275 **C** **D**

155

1

2

South Quarter

51

SUNNYSIDE

ROAD

SUNNYSIDE

Sunnyside

Little
Sunnyside

3

Thinacre Mill

Thinacre Glen

Powforth Glen

Powforth Burn

Falls

Weir

Thinacres

4

Plotcock Glen

Plotcock Castle
(Remains of)
Plotcock Bridge

6 50

5

East
Thinacremuir

Hamilton

ML3

Broomelton

Mafflat

Mafflat
Orchard

Corset

6

CRAIGTHORNHILL

PLOTCOCK

ROAD

BROOMELTON

ROAD

Newhouse Farm
Cotts.

Newhouse

49

74
Longfaugh

A **B** **C** 275 **D**

Low
Kittymuir

Lodge
Fairholm
Bridge

AVON WATER

Merryton Braes

Sewage
Works

Fairholm

Fairholm
Orchard

PENTLAND
PENTLAND
CT
CAMPSIE
CREST
FAIR
MUIR
WOOD
HAMILTON RD.
MERRYTON
STREET
BEATON ST.
FAIRHOLM
SUNNY
ST.
War
Mem.
Playground

Rec.
Ground
Pav.

Raploch

BURNBRAE
MOSS
ST.
BLOWN
ARBULLION
PL.
W-ATSON
ST.
BURNBRAE
ST.
THROBCH
ST.

ARBULLION
PARK
AVONBANK
RAPLOCH
ST.
VICK
ST.
MORGAN
ST.
CROFT
ST.
CHERRYH

Glengowan

LARKHALL

MILLHEUGH

RAPLOCH RD.
BRAE

PONFORTH
PL.
MILL

BROOMHILL
VW.

GRIER PL.
MAC-
MILLAN ST.
Sch.

Millheugh

Millheugh
Bridge

Morgan
Glen

MILLHEDGE

ROAD

MILLHEUGH

Larkhall Academy

Larkhall
Viaduct

Tennis
Courts

Cherry Hill

Robert Sm
Mem. Prim.

GLEN

BROOMHILL

WHI
KNO

AVON

Patrickholm

Waterfall

MILLHEUGH
ROAD

PLOTCOCK RD.

Brae House
Nursing Home

Waterfall

W

GLEN

Kittymuirhill

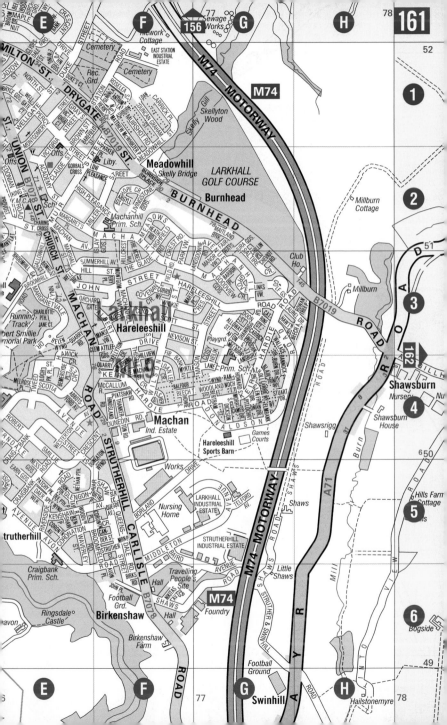

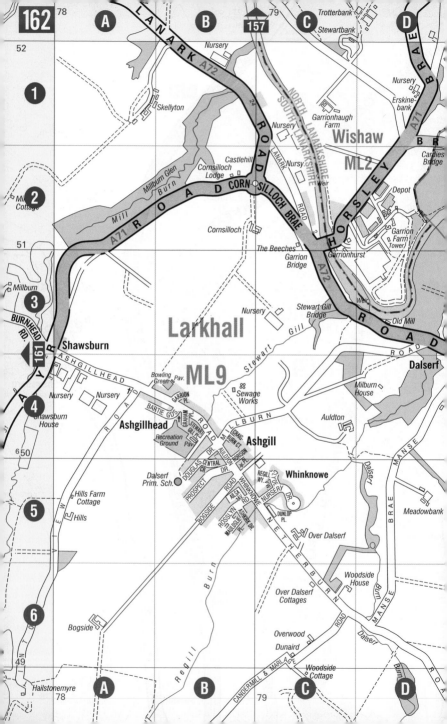

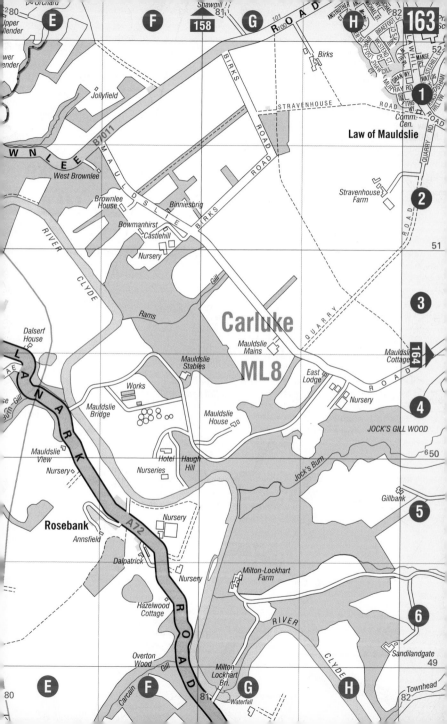

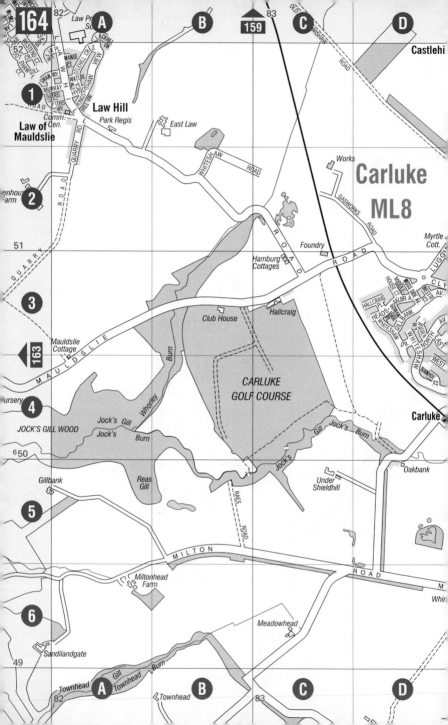

164

Law Prim Sc

Law Hill

Law of Mauldslie

Park Regis

East Law

WHITESHAW ROAD

Works

Carluke ML8

Greenhouse Farm

QUARRY ROAD

Myrtle Cott.

Foundry

Hamburg Cottages

GASWORKS ROAD

ROAD

LUGGI

CLY

HALLCRAIG PL

Mauldslie Cottage

163

MAULDSLIE

Club House

Hallcraig

HEADS

WHITESHAW

GILLBANK

WEST

MANROE CT

WHITESHAW

CARLUKE GOLF COURSE

Carluke

Nursery

Whorley Burn

JOCK'S GILL WOOD

Jock's Gill

Jock's Burn

Jock's Gill

Jock's Burn

Jock's Gill

Oakbank

Gillbank

Reas Gill

Under Shieldhill

RAES ROAD

MILTON ROAD

Miltonhead Farm

M

Whir

Meadowhead

Sandilandgate

Townhead Gill

Townhead Burn

Townhead

Castlehi

Comm. Cen.

82 **83** **OLD WISHAW ROAD** **C** **D**

51

650

49

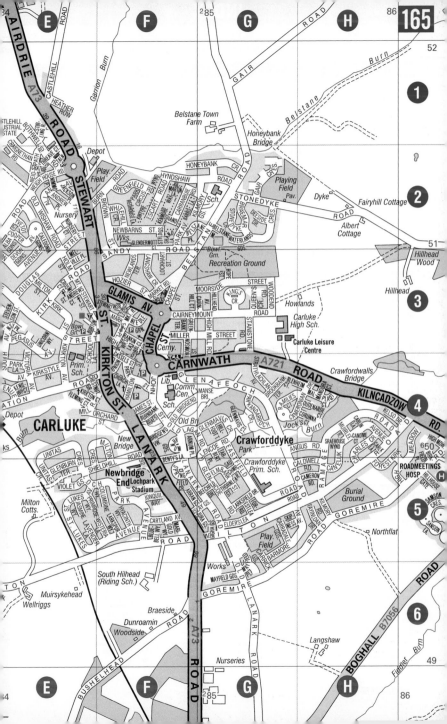

INDEX

Including Streets, Places & Areas, Industrial Estates, Selected Flats & Walkways,
Junction Names, Stations and Selected Places of Interest.

HOW TO USE THIS INDEX

1. Each street name is followed by its Postal District and then by its Locality abbreviation(s) and then by its map reference;
   e.g. **Abbeycraig Rd.** G34: Glas . . . .2B **88** is in the Glasgow 34 Postal District and the Glasgow Locality and is to be found in square 2B on page **88**. The page number is shown in bold type.

2. A strict alphabetical order is followed in which Av., Rd., St., etc. (though abbreviated) are read in full and as part of the street name;
   e.g. **Adams Pl.** appears after **Adamson St.** but before **Adamswell St.**

3. Streets and a selection of flats and walkways too small to be shown on the maps, appear in the index with the thoroughfare to which it is connected shown in brackets; e.g. **Abbey Wlk.** G69: Barg . . . .6D **88** (off Abercrombie Cres.)

4. Addresses that are in more than one part are referred to as not continuous.

5. Places and areas are shown in the index in **BLUE TYPE** and the map reference is to the actual map square in which the town centre or area is located and not to the place name shown on the map; e.g. **AIRDRIE** 3H **91**

6. An example of a selected place of interest is **Auchinvole Castle** 5G **11**

7. Junction names are shown in the index in **CAPITAL LETTERS**; e.g. **ANDERSTON CROSS INTERCHANGE** 5A **4**

8. An example of a station is **Airbles Station (Rail)** . . . .4G **143**. Included are Rail **(Rail)** and Underground **(Und.)** Stations.

9. Map references shown in brackets; e.g. **Adams Ct. La.** G1: Glas . . . .5F **83** (6D **4**) refer to entries that also appear on the large scale pages **4** & **5**.

GENERAL ABBREVIATIONS

Arc. : Arcade	**Ent.** : Enterprise	**Pde.** : Parade
Av. : Avenue	**Est.** : Estate	**Pk.** : Park
Bk. : Back	**Fld.** : Field	**Pas.** : Passage
Blvd. : Boulevard	**Gdn.** : Garden	**Pl.** : Place
Bri. : Bridge	**Gdns.** : Gardens	**Quad.** : Quadrant
Bldg. : Building	**Ga.** : Gate	**Ri.** : Rise
Bldgs. : Buildings	**Gt.** : Great	**Rd.** : Road
Bus. : Business	**Grn.** : Green	**Rdbt.** : Roundabout
Cvn. : Caravan	**Gro.** : Grove	**Shop.** : Shopping
Cen. : Centre	**Hgts.** : Heights	**Sth.** : South
Chu. : Church	**Ho.** : House	**Sq.** : Square
Circ. : Circle	**Ind.** : Industrial	**Sta.** : Station
Cir. : Circus	**Intl.** : International	**St.** : Street
Cl. : Close	**Junc.** : Junction	**Ter.** : Terrace
Coll. : College	**La.** : Lane	**Twr.** : Tower
Comn. : Common	**Lit.** : Little	**Trad.** : Trading
Cnr. : Corner	**Lwr.** : Lower	**Up.** : Upper
Cott. : Cottage	**Mans.** : Mansions	**Va.** : Vale
Cotts. : Cottages	**Mkt.** : Market	**Vw.** : View
Ct. : Court	**Mdw.** : Meadow	**Vs.** : Villas
Cres. : Crescent	**Mdws.** : Meadows	**Vis.** : Visitors
Cft. : Croft	**M.** : Mews	**Wlk.** : Walk
Dpt. : Depot	**Mt.** : Mount	**W.** : West
Dr. : Drive	**Mus.** : Museum	**Yd.** : Yard
E. : East	**Nth.** : North	

LOCALITY ABBREVIATIONS

Air : **Airdrie**	Bri W : **Bridge of Weir**	Dals : **Dalserf**
Alla : **Allandale**	Brkfld : **Brookfield**	Denn : **Dennyloanhead**
Anna : **Annathill**	Busby : **Busby**	Dull : **Dullatur**
Ashg : **Ashgill**	C'bnk : **Calderbank**	Dumb : **Dumbarton**
Auch : **Auchinloch**	Camb : **Cambuslang**	Dun : **Duntocher**
Bail : **Baillieston**	Cam G : **Campsie Glen**	E Kil : **East Kilbride**
Balder : **Baldernock**	Card : **Cardross**	Eld : **Elderslie**
Balm : **Balmore**	Carf : **Carfin**	Ersk : **Erskine**
Bank : **Banknock**	Carl : **Carluke**	Faif : **Faifley**
Bant : **Banton**	Crmck : **Carmunnock**	Fern : **Ferniegair**
Bard : **Bardowie**	Carm : **Carmyle**	Flem : **Flemington**
Barg : **Bargeddie**	C'cry : **Castlecary**	G'csh : **Gartcosh**
Barr : **Barrhead**	Chap : **Chapelhall**	Gart : **Gartness**
Bear : **Bearsden**	Chry : **Chryston**	Giff : **Giffnock**
Bell : **Bellshill**	Clar : **Clarkston**	Glas : **Glasgow**
Birk : **Birkenshaw**	Cle : **Cleland**	Glas A : **Glasgow Airport**
B'rig : **Bishopbriggs**	Clyd : **Clydebank**	Glass : **Glassford**
B'ton : **Bishopton**	Coat : **Coatbridge**	Glenb : **Glenboig**
Blan : **Blantyre**	Crsfd : **Crossford**	Glenm : **Glenmavis**
B'bri : **Bonnybridge**	C'lee : **Crosslee**	Grng : **Greengairs**
Both : **Bothwell**	Croy : **Croy**	Hag : **Haggs**
Bowl : **Bowling**	Cumb : **Cumbernauld**	Ham : **Hamilton**

Hard : **Hardgate**
Hill : **Hillington Ind. Est.**
Holy : **Holytown**
Hous : **Houston**
How : **Howwood**
Inch : **Inchinnan**
John : **Johnstone**
Kilb : **Kilbarchan**
Kils : **Kilsyth**
Kirk : **Kirkintilloch**
Lang : **Langbank**
Lark : **Larkhall**
Law : **Law**
Len : **Lennoxtown**
Lenz : **Lenzie**
Lin : **Linwood**
Loch : **Lochwinnoch**
Longc : **Longcroft**
Mille : **Millerston**
Miln : **Milngavie**

Milt : **Milton**
Milt C : **Milton of Campsie**
Mollin : **Mollinsburn**
Mood : **Moodiesburn**
Moss : **Mossend**
Moth : **Motherwell**
Muirh : **Muirhead**
Neil : **Neilston**
Ners : **Nerston**
Neth : **Netherlee**
N'hill : **Newarthill**
N'hse : **Newhouse**
Newm : **Newmains**
New S : **New Stevenston**
Newt : **Newton**
Newt M : **Newton Mearns**
Old K : **Old Kilpatrick**
Over : **Overtown**
Pais : **Paisley**
Plain : **Plains**

Q'riers : **Quarriers Village**
Quar : **Quarter**
Queen : **Queenzieburn**
Renf : **Renfrew**
Rent : **Renton**
Rigg : **Riggend**
Roger : **Rogerton**
Rose : **Rosebank**
Ruth : **Rutherglen**
Shaw : **Shawsburn**
Step : **Stepps**
Tann : **Tannochside**
T'bnk : **Thornliebank**
T'hall : **Thorntonhall**
Torr : **Torrance**
Twe : **Twechar**
Udd : **Uddingston**
View : **Viewpark**
Water : **Waterfoot**
Wis : **Wishaw**

A

Abbey Cl. PA1: Pais 1A **98**
Abbeycraig Rd. G34: Glas 2B **88**
Abbeydale Way G73: Ruth 4E **121**
Abbey Dr. G14: Glas 5E **61**
Abbeyfield Ho. G46: Giff 4H **117**
   ML5: Coat 5A **90**
Abbeygreen St. G34: Glas 2C **88**
Abbeyhill St. G32: Glas 4G **85**
Abbeylands Rd. G81: Faif. 6E **23**
Abbeymill Bus. Cen. PA1: Pais 1B **98**
Abbey Pl. ML6: Air 1C **112**
Abbey Rd. PA5: Eld 3H **95**
Abbey Wlk. *G69: Barg* *6D 88*
   (off Abercrombie Cres.)
   ML9: Lark *1F 161*
   (off Duncan Graham St.)
Abbotsburn Way PA3: Pais 3H **77**
Abbotsford G64: B'rig 5E **49**
Abbotsford Av. G73: Ruth 6D **104**
   ML3: Ham 3F **141**
   ML9: Lark 4E **161**
Abbotsford Brae G74: E Kil 6G **137**
Abbotsford Ct. G67: Cumb 6H **35**
Abbotsford Cres. ML2: Wis 5A **146**
   ML3: Ham 3F **141**
   PA2: Pais 6B **96**
Abbotsford Dr. G66: Kirk 5E **31**
Abbotsford La. ML4: Bell 1B **126**
Abbotsford Pl. G5: Glas 1F **103**
   (not continuous)
   G67: Cumb 6H **35**
   ML1: Holy. *2A 128*
   (off Ivy Ter.)
Abbotsford Rd. G61: Bear 1C **44**
   G67: Cumb 6H **35**
   G81: Clyd 6D **42**
   ML2: Wis 5A **146**
   ML3: Ham 3E **141**
   ML6: Chap 4E **113**
Abbotshall Av. G15: Glas 4G **43**
Abbotsinch Rd. PA4: Renf 6A **58**
Abbotsinch Rd. PA3: Glas A 2A **78**
Abbots Ter. ML6: Air 1C **112**
Abbot St. G41: Glas 4C **102**
   PA3: Pais 5B **78**
Abbott Cres. G81: Clyd 1F **59**
ABC Cinema 3D **118**
Aberconway St. G81: Clyd 1E **59**
Abercorn Av. G52: Hill 3G **79**
Abercorn Cres. ML3: Ham 1B **154**
Abercorn Dr. ML3: Ham 6B **142**
Abercorn Ind. Est. PA3: Pais 5B **78**
Abercorn Pl. G23: Glas 6C **46**
Abercorn Rd. G77: Newt M 3C **132**
Abercorn St. G81: Faif 6G **23**
   PA3: Pais 6A **78**
Abercrombie Cres. G69: Barg 6D **88**
Abercrombie Dr. G61: Bear 5B **24**
Abercrombie Ho. G75: E Kil. 2A **148**

Abercrombie Pl. G65: Kils 2F **11**
Abercromby Cres. G74: E Kil 6B **138**
Abercromby Dr. G40: Glas 5B **84**
Abercromby Pl. G74: E Kil 6B **138**
Abercromby St. G40: Glas 6A **84**
   (not continuous)
Aberdalgie Path *G34: Glas* *3H 87*
   (off Aberdalgie Rd.)
Aberdalgie Rd. G34: Glas 3H **87**
Aberdeen Rd. ML6: Chap 1D **112**
Aberdour Dr. G31: Glas 4E **85**
Aberfeldy Av. ML6: Plain 1F **93**
Aberfeldy St. G31: Glas 4E **85**
Aberfoyle St. G31: Glas 4E **85**
Aberlady Pl. G51: Glas 4E **81**
Aberlady St. ML1: Cle 6H **129**
Abernethy Dr. PA3: Lin 6G **75**
Abernethyn Rd. ML2: Newm 3E **147**
Abernethy Pk. G74: E Kil 1F **149**
Abernethy St. G31: Glas 5E **85**
Aberuthven Dr. G32: Glas 2B **106**
Abiegail Pl. G72: Blan 6B **124**
Aboukir St. G51: Glas 3E **81**
Aboyne Dr. PA2: Pais 4B **98**
Aboyne St. G51: Glas 5F **81**
ABRONHILL 1E **37**
Acacia Dr. G78: Barr 2C **114**
   PA2: Pais 4F **97**
Acacia Pl. PA5: John 5G **95**
Acacia Way G72: Flem 2E **123**
Academy Ct. ML5: Coat 4C **90**
Academy Pk. G51: Glas 1A **102**
   ML6: Air 4A **92**
Academy Pl. ML5: Coat 4C **90**
Academy Rd. G46: Giff 5A **118**
Academy St. G32: Glas 1B **106**
   ML5: Coat. 4C **90**
   ML6: Air 4A **92**
   ML9: Lark 2E **161**
Academy Ter. ML4: Bell 2D **126**
Acer Cres. PA2: Pais 4E **97**
Acer Gro. ML6: Chap 2E **113**
Achamore Cres. G15: Glas 3G **43**
Achamore Dr. G15: Glas 3G **43**
Achamore Gdns. G15: Glas 3G **43**
Achamore Rd. G15: Glas 3G **43**
Achnasheen Rd. ML6: Air 5G **93**
Achray Dr. PA2: Pais 4E **97**
Achray Pl. G62: Miln 2D **24**
   ML5: Coat 2H **89**
Achray Rd. G67: Cumb 6D **34**
Acorn Ct. G40: Glas 1B **104**
Acorn St. G40: Glas 1B **104**
Acredyke Cres. G21: Glas 2E **65**
Acredyke Pl. G21: Glas 3E **65**
Acredyke Rd. G21: Glas 2D **64**
   G73: Ruth 5B **104**
Acre Rd. G20: Glas 6H **45**
Acres, The ML9: Lark 3F **161**
Acre Valley Rd. G64: Torr 3D **28**
Adam Av. ML6: Air 4B **92**

Adams Ct. La. G1: Glas 5F **83** (6D **4**)
Adamslie Cres. G66: Kirk 5A **30**
Adamslie Dr. G66: Kirk 5A **30**
Adamson St. ML4: Moss 2F **127**
Adamswell St. G21: Glas 6A **64**
Adamswell Ter. G69: Mood 5E **53**
Addie St. ML1: Moth 1H **143**
Addiewell Pl. ML5: Coat 1C **110**
Addiewell St. G32: Glas 4A **86**
Addison Gro. G46: T'bnk 3F **117**
Addison Pl. G46: T'bnk. 3F **117**
Addison Rd. G12: Glas 5B **62**
   G46: T'bnk 3E **117**
Adelaide Ct. G81: Clyd 2H **41**
Adelaide Rd. G75: E Kil 4D **148**
Adele St. ML1: Moth 5H **143**
Adelphi Cen. G5: Glas 6H **83**
Adelphi St. G5: Glas 6H **83**
   (Commercial Rd., not continuous)
   G5: Glas 6H **83**
   (Gorbals St.)
Admiral St. G41: Glas 6C **82**
Admiralty Gdns. G60: Old K 2F **41**
Admiralty Gro. G60: Old K 2F **41**
Admiralty Pl. G60: Old K 2F **41**
Advance Pl. *PA11: Bri W* *3F 73*
   (off Main St.)
Advie Pl. G42: Glas 5F **103**
Affric Av. ML6: Plain 1G **93**
Affric Dr. PA2: Pais 4D **98**
Afton Cres. G61: Bear 4H **45**
Afton Dr. PA4: Renf 6G **59**
Afton Gdns. G72: Blan 3H **139**
   ML5: Coat. 6F **91**
Afton Rd. G67: Cumb 2B **36**
   ML9: Lark 3G **161**
Afton St. G41: Glas 5C **102**
   ML9: Lark 3G **161**
Afton Vw. G66: Kirk 4F **31**
Afton Way PA2: Pais 4D **96**
Agamemnon St. G81: Clyd 5B **42**
Agate Ter. *ML4: Bell.* *3C 126*
   (off Diamond St.)
Agnew Av. ML5: Coat 4E **91**
Agnew Gro. ML4: Bell 2H **125**
Agnew La. G42: Glas 4E **103**
Aigas Cotts. *G13: Glas* *4F 61*
   (off Fern La.)
Aikenhead Rd. G42: Glas 2F **103**
   G44: Glas 1G **119**
Aikman Pl. G74: E Kil. 5B **138**
Aikman Rd. ML1: Moth 4D **142**
Ailort Loan *ML2: Newm.* *3D 146*
   (off Tiree Cres.)
Ailean Dr. G32: Glas. 1E **107**
Ailean Gdns. G32: Glas 1E **107**
Aillort Pl. G74: E Kil. 6G **137**
Ailort Av. G44: Glas 2E **119**
Ailsa Av. ML1: Moth 2D **142**
   ML9: Ashg 5B **162**
Ailsa Ct. ML3: Ham 2B **152**
   ML5: Coat. 1A **110**

Ailsa Cres. ML1: Moth. 2D **142**
Ailsa Dr. G42: Glas 6D **102**
  G46: Giff. 1H **133**
  G66: Kirk. 3F **31**
  G71: Both 3E **125**
  G73: Ruth. 2B **120**
  G81: Hard 1E **43**
  PA2: Pais 6H **97**
Ailsa Pl. ML5: Coat 1B **110**
Ailsa Rd. G64: B'rig 5D **48**
  ML5: Coat. 1A **110**
  PA4: Renf 1E **79**
Ailsa Twr. G72: Camb 4G **121**
Ainslie Av. G52: Hill 3A **80**
Ainslie Rd. G52: Hill 4A **80**
                              (not continuous)
  G67: Cumb 2C **36**
Airbles Cres. ML1: Moth 4F **143**
Airbles Dr. ML1: Moth 4F **143**
Airbles Farm Rd. ML1: Moth. 5E **143**
Airbles Rd. ML1: Moth. 4G **143**
Airbles Station (Rail) 4G **143**
Airbles St. ML1: Moth 4G **143**
Airbles Twr. ML1: Moth 4G **143**
Airdale Av. G46: Giff 5A **118**
AIRDRIE 3H **91**
Airdriehill Rd. ML6: Air 1C **92**
Airdriehill St. ML6: Air 1C **92**
Airdrie Leisure Cen. 2C **92**
Airdrie Rd ML6: Air, Plain. 2F **93**
Airdrie Rd. G65: Kils 2H **11**
  G67: Cumb 1D **54**
                          (Condorrat Ring Rd.)
  G67: Cumb. 6C **34**
                                   (Main Rd.)
  G67: Mollin 3H **53**
  ML8: Carl 6H **159**
Airdrie Station (Rail) 4A **92**
Airdrie United F.C. 5C **92**
Aird's La. *G1: Glas*. *5G **83***
                               (off Bridgegate)
Airgold Dr. G15: Glas. 3H **43**
Airgold Pl. G15: Glas 3H **43**
Airlie Av. G61: Bear 6E **25**
Airlie Dr. ML4: Bell 1C **126**
Airlie Gdns. G73: Ruth. 3F **121**
Airlie La. G12: Glas 6H **61**
Airlie Rd. G69: Bail 2G **107**
Airlie St. G12: Glas 6G **61**
Airlink Ind. Est. PA3: Glas A 3A **78**
Airlour Rd. G43: Glas 2C **118**
Airth Ct. ML1: Moth 6F **127**
Airth Dr. G52: Glas 2F **101**
Airth La. G52: Glas 2F **101**
Airth Pl. *G52: Glas* *2F **101***
                                    (off Airth La.)
Airthrey Av. G14: Glas 6E **61**
Airthrey La. *G14: Glas* *5E **61***
                                  (off Airthrey Av.)
Airth Way G68: Cumb 5A **34**
Aitchison Ct. ML6: Air 3H **91**
Aitchison St. ML6: Air 4G **91**
Aitkenbar Circ. G82: Dumb 2H **17**
Aitkenbar Dr. G82: Dumb 1H **17**
Aitken Cl. ML2: Newm 2E **147**
Aitkenhead Av. ML5: Coat 1F **109**
Aitkenhead Rd. G69: Barg, Tann . . .5E **109**
  G71: Barg, Tann 5E **109**
  ML6: Chap 3D **112**
Aitken Rd. ML3: Ham. 4A **154**
Aitken St. G31: Glas. 4D **84**
  ML6: Air 2A **92**
Alasdair Ct. G78: Barr 5E **115**
Alba Gdns. ML8: Carl 2E **165**
Alba Ho. G81: Clyd. 5C **42**
Albans Cres. ML1: Moth 1D **142**
Albany G74: E Kil 5C **138**
Albany Av. G32: Glas 5C **86**
Albany Cotts. *G13: Glas* *4F **61***
                                     (off Fern La.)
Albany Dr. G73: Ruth. 1D **120**
Albany Pl. G71: Both 5F **125**
Albany Quad. G32: Glas 5C **86**
Albany Rd. ML3: Ham 4G **153**

Albany St. G40: Glas 1C **104**
  ML5: Coat 4A **90**
Albany Ter. G72: Camb 4G **121**
Albany Way PA3: Pais 3A **78**
Albany Wynd *ML9: Lark* *1F **161***
                            (off Duncan Graham St.)
Alba Way ML3: Ham 5G **153**
  ML9: Lark. *4G **161***
                               (off Keir Hardie Rd.)
Alberta Av. G75: E Kil 3D **148**
  . . . . .3B **90**
Alberta Cres. G75: E Kil 3E **149**
Alberta Pk. G75: E Kil. 3F **149**
Alberta Pl. G75: E Kil 3F **149**
Albert Av. G42: Glas. 4D **102**
Albert Bri. G5: Glas 6G **83**
Albert Cres. ML6: Air. 4B **92**
Albert Cross G41: Glas 2D **102**
Albert Dr. G41: Glas 3A **102**
  G61: Bear 4H **45**
  G73: Ruth 2D **120**
  ML9: Lark 3F **161**
Albert Pl. ML6: Air. 3B **92**
Albert Quad. ML1: Holy 2A **128**
Albert Rd. G12: Glas 6H **61**
  G42: Glas 4E **103**
  G66: Lenz 4C **50**
  G81: Clyd 4B **42**
  PA4: Renf 6E **59**
  PA5: Brkfld 6C **74**
Albert St. ML1: Moth. 2H **143**
  ML3: Ham 3F **141**
  ML5: Coat. 4C **90**
                                   (not continuous)
Albert Ter. ML3: Ham 3E **141**
Albion Ct. *ML5: Coat* *5E **91***
                                   (off Clifton Pl.)
Albion Ga. G1: Glas 4H **83** (6G **5**)
  PA3: Pais 5H **77**
Albion Rovers F.C. 5E **91**
Albion St. G1: Glas 5H **83** (6G **5**)
  G69: Bail 2F **107**
  ML1: Moth 4G **143**
  ML5: Coat 4D **90**
  PA3: Pais 5A **78**
Albion Twr. ML1: Moth 4G **143**
Albion Way G75: E Kil 6H **149**
Albion Works Ind. Est. G13: Glas . . .2G **59**
Alcaig Rd. G52: Glas 3E **101**
Alcath Rd. ML2: Newm 3F **147**
Alclutha Av. G82: Dumb 4H **17**
Alder Av. G66: Lenz 2B **50**
  ML3: Ham 2A **154**
Alder Bank G71: View 4G **109**
Alder Ct. G75: E Kil 6E **149**
  G78: Barr 6E **115**
Alder Cres. G75: E Kil 6E **149**
Alder Ga. G72: Flem 2E **123**
Alder Gro. ML5: Coat. 5D **90**
Alder La. ML1: Holy. 2C **128**
  ML1: New S 4A **128**
Alderman Pl. G13: Glas 3C **60**
Alderman Rd. ML3: Glas 2H **59**
Alder Pl. G43: Glas 2A **118**
  G75: E Kil 6E **149**
  PA5: John. 4G **95**
Alder Rd. G43: Glas 2H **117**
  G66: Milt C. 6B **8**
  G67: Cumb 3D **36**
  G81: Clyd 2B **42**
  G82: Dumb 3E **17**
Alderside Gdns. G71: Udd 6C **108**
Alderside Pl. G71: Both 4F **125**
Alderstocks G75: E Kil 6G **149**
Alderston Pl. ML4: Bell 3A **126**
Alderston Way ML4: Bell 1A **126**
Aldersyde Av. ML2: Wis 5D **144**
Aldersyde Pl. G72: Blan. 6A **124**
Alexander Av. G65: Twe 2C **32**
  G71: View. 1G **125**
Alexander Balfour Gdns.
  ML3: Ham2H **153**
Alexander Cres. G5: Glas 1G **103**
Alexander Gdns. ML3: Ham. 1C **154**

Alexander Gibson Way
  ML1: Moth 4F **143**
Alexander Pl. G66: Kirk. 6H **31**
Alexander St. G81: Clyd 6D **42**
  G82: Dumb. 3G **17**
  ML2: Wis 6F **145**
  ML5: Coat 3D **90**
  ML6: Air 4G **91**
Alexander Ter. G78: Neil 3C **130**
Alexandra Av. G33: Step 3D **66**
  G66: Lenz 3C **50**
Alexandra Ct. G31: Glas 3D **84**
Alexandra Dr. PA2: Pais 2F **97**
  PA4: Renf 6F **59**
Alexandra Gdns. G66: Lenz 3C **50**
Alexandra Pde. G31: Glas 3A **84**
Alexandra Parade Station (Rail) . . .3D **84**
Alexandra Pk. G66: Lenz 3C **50**
Alexandra Pk. St. G31: Glas 3D **84**
Alexandra Rd. G66: Lenz. 3C **50**
Alexandra Sports Hall 3E **85**
Alexandra St. G66: Kirk 5C **30**
Alford Av. G66: Kirk 5B **30**
Alford Pl. PA3: Lin 5E **75**
Alford Quad. ML2: Wis 4H **145**
Alford St. G21: Glas 6H **63**
Alfred La. *G12: Glas*. *6C **62***
                                    (off Cecil St.)
Alfred Ter. G12: Glas 6C **62**
Algie St. G41: Glas 5D **102**
Algoma Pl. G75: E Kil 3D **148**
Alice Av. ML4: Bell. 3C **126**
Alice St. PA2: Pais 3A **98**
Aline Ct. G78: Barr. 3D **114**
Alison Lea G74: E Kil 6B **138**
Allan Av. ML8: Carl 2E **165**
  PA4: Renf 2G **79**
Allan Ct. G75: E Kil 4A **148**
Allan Cres. G82: Dumb 1H **17**
ALLANDALE 1H **15**
Allandale Av. ML1: N'hill 2F **129**
Allandale Cotts. FK4: Alla 1H **15**
Allandale Path *G72: Blan*. *2B **140***
                               (off Winton Cres.)
Allander Av. G62: Bard 6F **27**
Allander Dr. G64: Torr 5C **28**
Allander Gdns. G64: B'rig 3B **48**
Allander Ho. *G67: Cumb* *4H **35***
                         (in Cumbernauld Shop. Cen.)
Allander Rd. G62: Miln 3G **25**
  G82: Glas. 5G **63**
Allander St. G22: Glas 5G **63**
Allander Wlk. *G67: Cumb* *4H **35***
                         (in Cumbernauld Shop. Cen.)
Allands Av. PA4: Inch 4G **57**
Allanfauld Rd. G65: Kils 1H **11**
  G67: Cumb 3H **35**
Allan Glen Gdns. G64: B'rig. 3C **48**
Allan Pl. G40: Glas 3D **104**
  G75: E Kil 4A **148**
  G82: Dumb 3G **17**
Allanshaw Gdns. ML3: Ham. 6F **141**
Allanshaw Gro. ML3: Ham 1F **153**
Allanshaw Ind. Est. ML3: Ham 6G **141**
Allanshaw St. ML3: Ham. 6G **141**
Allan St. G40: Glas 3D **104**
  ML1: Moth 2H **143**
  ML5: Coat 6H **89**
ALLANTON 2E **155**
Allanton Av. PA1: Pais 1G **99**
Allanton Dr. G52: Glas 6B **80**
Allanton Gro. ML2: Wis. 4H **145**
Allanton Lea ML3: Ham. 3G **153**
Allanton Pl. ML3: Ham 2A **154**
Allanton Rd. ML2: Newm 2H **147**
Allanton St. ML3: Fern 3F **155**
Allan Twr. ML1: Moth 2H **143**
Allbany Cres. ML1: Holy 2H **127**
Allendale G74: E Kil 6E **137**
Allender Rd. G61: Bear 4D **44**
Allen Way PA4: Renf 2F **79**
Allerdyce Ct. G15: Glas 6G **43**
Allerdyce Dr. G15: Glas. 6H **43**
Allerdyce Pl. G15: Glas 6H **43**

Allerdyce Rd. G15: Glas 6G 43
Allershaw Pl. ML2: Wis 3F 157
Allershaw Rd. ML2: Wis 3F 157
Allershaw Ter. ML2: Wis 3F 157
Allerton Gdns. G69: Bail. 1F 107
Alleysbank Rd. G73: Ruth 4D 104
Allison Av. PA8: Ersk 5D 40
Allison Dr. G72: Camb 1A 122
Allison Pl. G42: Glas 3E 103
  G69: G'csh 5C 68
  G77: Newt M 5C 132
Allison St. G42: Glas 3E 103
Allnach Pl. G34: Glas. 3C 88
Alloway Av. PA2: Pais 5D 98
Alloway Ct. G66: Kirk. 3G 31
Alloway Cres. G73: Ruth 2B 120
  PA2: Pais 5D 98
Alloway Dr. G66: Kirk. 3F 31
  G73: Ruth. 2B 120
  G77: Newt M 5G 133
  G81: Clyd 4E 43
  PA2: Pais 5D 98
Alloway Gdns. G66: Kirk 3G 31
  ML3: Ham 2B 152
Alloway Gro. G66: Kirk. 3F 31
  G66: Pais 5E 99
Alloway Quad. G66: Kirk 4G 31
Alloway Rd. G43: Glas 1B 118
  G74: E Kil. 5D 138
  ML6: Air 3F 93
Alloway St. ML9: Lark 3G 161
Alloway Ter. G66: Kirk 3F 31
Alloway Wynd ML1: N'hill 3E 129
Almada Gro. ML3: Ham. 5H 141
Almada La. ML3: Ham. 5H 141
Almada St. ML3: Ham 5G 141
Alma St. G40: Glas. 6C 84
Almond Av. PA4: Renf 1G 79
Almond Bank G61: Bear. 5C 44
Almond Cres. PA2: Pais. 3D 96
Almond Dr. FK4: Bank 1E 15
  G66: Lenz 2B 50
  G74: E Kil 2B 150
  PA7: B'ton 5H 39
Almond Pl. ML1: Holy 3B 128
  ML5: Coat 2H 89
Almond Rd. G33: Step 4C 66
  G61: Bear. 5D 44
  G67: Cumb 6F 15
Almond St. G33: Glas. 2F 85
Almond Va. G71: Tann 6E 109
Almond Vw. G15: Glas 5B 44
Almond Way ML1: Moth 6G 143
Alness Cres. G52: Glas 2E 101
Alness St. ML3: Ham. 2H 153
Alness Ter. ML3: Ham 1H 153
Alpine Gro. G71: Tann 6D 108
Alsatian Av. G81: Clyd 5F 43
Alsh Ter. ML3: Ham 2E 153
Alston Av. ML5: Coat 3D 90
Alston Gdns. G61: Bear 5B 24
Altnacreag Gdns. G69: Mood. . . . 4E 53
Alton Ct. G66: Kirk 5E 31
      (off Highfield Rd.)
Alton Rd. PA1: Pais 1E 99
Altpatrick Gdns. PA5: Eld 2H 95
Altyre St. G32: Glas 2H 105
Alva Gdns. G52: Glas 3E 101
  G61: Bear. 6D 24
Alva Ga. G52: Glas 2E 101
Alva Pl. G66: Lenz 3E 51
Alwyn Av. PA6: C'lee 3D 74
Alwyn Ct. G74: E Kil. 6G 137
Alyssum Cres. ML1: Moth 1F 143
Alyth Cres. G76: Clar 1E 135
Alyth Gdns. G52: Glas 2E 101
  G76: Clar 1E 135
Ambassador Way PA4: Renf. 2F 79
Amber Ter. ML4: Bell 3C 126
Ambleside G75: E Kil 5B 148
Ambleside Ri. ML3: Ham 6G 153
Ambrose Ct. ML3: Ham 5F 141
      (off Burnbank Rd.)
Amethyst Av. ML4: Bell 3C 126

AMF Bowling 4D 82
Amisfield St. G20: Glas 4C 62
Amochrie Dr. PA2: Pais 5E 97
Amochrie Glen PA2: Pais 5E 97
Amochrie Rd. PA2: Pais 4D 96
Amochrie Way PA2: Pais 4D 96
      (off Amochrie Rd.)
Amulree Pl. G32: Glas 1A 106
Amulree St. G32: Glas 2A 106
Ancaster Dr. G13: Glas 3F 61
Ancaster La. G13: Glas. 3F 61
Anchor Av. PA1: Pais 1C 98
Anchor Bldgs. PA1: Pais 1B 98
Anchor Cres. PA1: Pais 2C 98
Anchor Dr. PA1: Pais 1C 98
Anchor La. G2: Glas 4G 83 (5E 5)
ANCHOR MILLS. 1C 98
Anchor Wynd PA1: Pais 2C 98
Ancroft St. G20: Glas. 6E 63
Andersen Ct. G75: E Kil 5G 149
Anderside G75: E Kil 6G 149
Anderson Av. G65: Kils. 2F 11
Anderson Ct. G77: Newt M 5C 132
  ML4: Bell 2D 126
Anderson Cres. G65: Queen. 3C 10
Anderson Dr. G77: Newt M 5C 132
  PA4: Renf 5F 59
Anderson Gdns. G72: Blan. 6C 124
Anderson La. ML6: Air. 3A 92
Anderson Rd. PA7: B'ton 3G 39
Anderson St. G11: Glas. 1H 81
  ML1: Moth 4G 143
  ML3: Ham 4D 140
  ML6: Air 3A 92
Anderson Twr. ML1: Moth 3G 143
ANDERSTON. 4D 82
ANDERSTON CROSS INTERCHANGE
      . . . . 5A 4
Anderston Cross Shop. Cen.
      . . . . 4E 83 (5A 4)
  G2: Glas. 4E 83 (5A 4)
Anderston Quay G3: Glas . . 5D 82 (6A 4)
Anderston Station (Rail) 4E 83 (5A 4)
Andrew Av. G66: Lenz 4D 50
  PA4: Renf. 6G 59
Andrew Dr. G81: Clyd. 1E 59
Andrew Pl. ML8: Carl 2E 165
Andrew Sillars Av. G72: Camb . . 2B 122
Andrews St. PA3: Pais 5A 78
Andrew St. G74: E Kil 2H 149
Anford Pl. G72: Blan 2C 140
Angela Way G71: Udd 1D 124
Angle Ga. G14: Glas 5D 60
Angus Av. G52: Glas 2C 100
  G64: B'rig 1E 65
  G74: E Kil 1B 150
  ML1: Moth 1E 143
  ML3: Ham 6C 142
  ML6: Air 6A 92
Angus Gdns. G71: Tann 5D 108
Angus Oval G52: Glas 1B 100
Angus Pl. G52: Glas. 1B 100
  G74: E Kil 1B 150
Angus Rd. ML8: Carl 4G 165
Angus St. G21: Glas 5A 64
  G81: Clyd 1G 59
Angus Wlk. G71: View 6F 109
Anish Pl. G15: Glas 3G 43
Annan Av. G75: E Kil 4A 148
Annan Ct. ML5: Coat 5B 90
Annan Cres. ML6: Chap. 4D 112
Annandale St. G42: Glas 2F 103
Annan Dr. G61: Bear 4C 44
  G73: Ruth 6F 105
Annan Glade ML1: Moth 6A 144
Annan Gro. ML1: Moth 6A 144
Annan Ho. G67: Cumb. 4H 35
      (in Cumbernauld Shop. Cen.)
Annan Pl. PA5: John 5C 94
Annan St. G42: Glas 5E 103
  ML1: Moth 6A 144
Annan Way G67: Cumb 4H 35
      (in Cumbernauld Shop. Cen.)
ANNATHILL. 5B 54
Annathill Gdns. ML5: Anna 5B 54

Annbank St. G31: Glas 5B 84
  ML9: Lark. 2D 160
Ann Ct. ML3: Ham 4E 141
Anne Av. PA4: Renf 5F 59
Anne Cres. G66: Lenz 4D 50
Annerley Ct. ML5: Coat 6A 90
Annerley Pl. ML5: Coat 6A 90
Anne's M. ML3: Ham 6B 142
Annette St. G42: Glas 3E 103
Annfield Gdns. G72: Blan. 6A 124
Annfield Pl. G31: Glas 4B 84
Annick Dr. G61: Bear 4C 44
Annick St. G32: Glas 6B 86
  G72: Camb 2D 122
Anniesdale Av. G33: Step 3D 66
Annieshill Vw. ML6: Plain 1G 93
ANNIESLAND 3F 61
Anniesland Cres. G14: Glas. 4A 60
Anniesland Ind. Est. G13: Glas . . 1E 61
Anniesland Rd. G13: Glas 3C 60
  G14: Glas 4A 60
Anniesland Station (Rail) 3F 61
Anniston G65: Twe 1D 32
Anniversary Av. G75: E Kil 4E 149
Annsfield Rd. ML3: Ham. 4G 153
Ann St. ML3: Ham 4E 141
  PA5: John. 2G 95
Ansdell Av. G72: Blan 2A 140
Anson Av. G40: Glas. 1B 104
Anson Way PA4: Renf. 2E 79
Anstruther Ct. ML8: Law 6D 158
Anstruther St. G32: Glas 6H 85
  ML8: Law. 6D 158
Antermony Rd. G66: Milt C 5C 8
Anthony Ct. G81: Clyd 1E 59
Anthony St. G2: Glas 4E 83 (5A 4)
Antigua Way G75: E Kil 2C 148
Anton Cres. G65: Kils. 3A 12
Antonine G66: Kirk. 3H 31
Antonine Av. ML1: Moth 1E 143
Antonine Gdns. G81: Dun 1C 42
Antonine Rd. G61: Bear 1B 44
  G68: Dull 5E 13
Antonine Sports Cen. 1C 42
Antrim La. ML9: Lark 1F 161
Anwoth St. G32: Glas 2A 106
Apartments, The G46: Giff. 6H 117
      (off Milverton Rd.)
Apollo Path ML1: Holy. 2B 128
Appin Ct. G66: Kirk 4H 31
Appin Cres. G31: Glas. 4D 84
Appin Rd. G31: Glas 4D 84
Appin Ter. G73: Ruth 3F 121
  ML3: Ham 5C 140
Appin Way G71: Both 4E 125
  ML5: Coat. 1A 110
  ML6: Glenm 5H 71
Appleby Cl. G75: E Kil 5B 148
Appleby St. G22: Glas 6F 63
Applecross Gdns. G69: Mood 4D 52
Applecross Quad. ML2: Wis 4H 145
Applecross Rd. G66: Kirk 4H 31
Applecross St. G4: Glas 6F 63
Appledore Cres. G71: Both 4E 125
Appleyard Ct. ML4: Bell 4B 126
Apsley La. G11: Glas 1G 81
Apsley St. G11: Glas 1G 81
Aqua Av. ML3: Ham 1C 152
Aqua Ct. ML3: Ham 1C 152
Aquatec Leisure Cen. 2G 143
Aquila Way ML8: Carl 3D 164
Araburn Dr. G75: E Kil 6G 149
Aranthrue Cres. PA4: Renf. 5E 59
Aranthrue Dr. PA4: Renf. 5E 59
Aray St. G20: Glas 3B 62
Arbroath Av. G52: Glas 1B 100
Arbroath Gro. ML3: Ham 1F 153
Arbuckle Pl. ML6: Plain 1G 93
Arbuckle Rd. ML6: Plain 1H 93
Arcadia St. G40: Glas. 6A 84
  ML4: Bell 6C 110
Arcan Cres. G15: Glas 5B 44
Archerfield Av. G32: Glas. 3A 106
Archerfield Cres. G32: Glas. 3A 106

Archerfield Dr.—Arthur St.

Archerfield Dr. G32: Glas 3A **106**
Archerfield Gro. G32: Glas. 3A **106**
Archerhill Av. G13: Glas. 1A **60**
Archerhill Cotts. G13: Glas 1A **60**
Archerhill Cres. G13: Glas 1B **60**
Archerhill Gdns. G13: Glas 1A **60**
Archerhill Rd. G13: Glas 1H **59**
Archerhill Sq. G13: Glas 1H **59**
Archerhill Ter. G13: Glas 1A **60**
(not continuous)
Arches Theatre 4F 83 (6C 4)
Archibald Ter. G66: Milt C 5B **8**
Archiebald Pl. ML4: Bell 3F **127**
Arch Way G65: Kils 2H **11**
Ardargie Dr. G32: Carm 5C **106**
Ardargie Gro. G32: Carm. 5C **106**
Ardargie Pl. G32: Carm 5C **106**
Ardbeg Av. G64: B'rig 6E **49**
G73: Ruth. 4G **121**
Ardbeg Rd. ML1: Carf 5B **128**
Ardbeg St. G42: Glas 3E **103**
Ardconnel St. G46: T'bnk 3F **117**
ARDEN 3D **116**
Arden Av. G46: T'bnk 5E **117**
Ardenclutha Av. ML3: Ham 5F **141**
Arden Ct. ML3: Ham 2H **153**
ML6: Air 3F ***91***
(off Monkscourt Av.)
Ardencraig Dr. G45: Glas 5B **120**
Ardencraig Gdns. G45: Glas 5C **120**
Ardencraig Pl. G45: Glas 4A **120**
Ardencraig Quad. G45: Glas 5B **120**
Ardencraig Rd. G45: Glas 6G **119**
Ardencraig St. G45: Glas 4C **120**
Ardencraig Ter. G45: Glas 5B **120**
Ardencraig Workspace G45: Glas . . . 5C **120**
Arden Dr. G46: Giff 5H **117**
Arden Gro. G65: Kils 1G **11**
Ardenlea G71: Tann 6D **108**
Ardenlea St. G40: Glas 2D **104**
Arden Pl. G46: T'bnk 5E **117**
Arden Rd. ML3: Ham 1G **153**
Arden St. ML6: Plain 1G **93**
Arden Ter. ML3: Ham. 1G **153**
Ardery St. G11: Glas 1G **81**
Ardessie St. G23: Glas. 6B **46**
Ardfern Rd. ML6: Air 5F **93**
Ardfern St. G32: Glas. 2A **106**
Ardgay Pl. G32: Glas 1A **106**
Ardgay St. G32: Glas 1A **106**
Ardgay Way G73: Ruth 4D **120**
Ardgoil Dr. G68: Cumb. 4B **34**
Ardgour Ct. G72: Blan 3D **140**
Ardgour Dr. PA3: Lin 6G **75**
Ardgour Pde. ML1: Carf. 6C **128**
Ardgowan Av. PA2: Pais. 2B **98**
Ardgowan Ct. PA2: Pais. 2D **98**
Ardgowan Dr. G71: Tann 6D **108**
Ardgowan St. PA2: Pais 3B **98**
Ardgowan Ter. La. *G3: Glas 2B* ***82***
(off Radnor St.)
Ardgryfe Cres. PA6: Hous 1D **74**
Ardholm St. G32: Glas. 6A **86**
Ardhu Pl. G15: Glas 3A **44**
Ardlamont Sq. PA3: Lin 6A **76**
Ard La. *ML2: Newm. 3D* ***146***
(off Clunie Pl.)
Ardlaw St. G51: Glas 5F **81**
Ardle Rd. G43: Glas 2C **118**
Ard Loan *ML1: Holy 2A* ***128***
(off Howden Pl.)
Ardlui Gdns. G62: Miln 2D **24**
Ardlui St. G32: Glas. 1H **105**
Ardmaleish Cres. G45: Glas 5A **120**
Ardmaleish Dr. G45: Glas 5H **119**
Ardmaleish Rd. G45: Glas. 5H **119**
Ardmay Cres. G44: Glas 6G **103**
Ardmillan St. G33: Glas. 3H **85**
Ardmory Av. G42: Glas. 6H **103**
Ardmory La. G42: Glas 6A **104**
Ardmory Pl. G42: Glas 6A **104**
Ardnahoe Av. G42: Glas. 5H **103**
Ardnahoe Pl. G42: Glas. 5H **103**
Ardneil Rd. G51: Glas. 5F **81**
Ardnish St. G51: Glas. 4E **81**
Ardoch Cres. G82: Dumb. 3D **16**
Ardoch Gdns. G72: Camb 1H **121**
Ardoch Gro. G72: Camb. 1H **121**
Ardoch Path *ML2: Newm. 3D* ***146***
(off Tiree Cres.)
Ardochrig G75: E Kil. 6H **149**
Ardoch Rd. G61: Bear 2H **45**
Ardoch St. G22: Glas 5F **63**
Ardoch Way G69: Mood. 5D **52**
Ardo Gdns. G51: Glas 6G **81**
Ardressie Pl. G20: Glas 4B **62**
Ard Rd. PA4: Renf 5D **58**
Ardshiel Rd. G51: Glas. 4E **81**
Ardsloy La. G14: Glas 5A **60**
Ardsloy Pl. G14: Glas. 5A **60**
Ard St. G32: Glas 1A **106**
Ardtoe Cres. G33: Step 4E **67**
Ardtoe Pl. G33: Step 4E **67**
Arduthie Rd. G51: Glas 4E **81**
Ardwell Rd. G52: Glas 2E **101**
Argosy Way PA4: Renf 2E **79**
Argus Av. ML6: Chap 3C **112**
Argyle Av. PA3: Glas A 2A **78**
Argyle Cres. ML3: Ham 6D **140**
ML6: Air 1H **111**
Argyle Dr. ML3: Ham 5E **141**
Argyle Gdns. G66: Len. 4G **7**
Argyle Rd. G61: Bear 6E **25**
Argyle St. G1: Glas 4G **83** (6E **5**)
G2: Glas. 4E **83** (6A **4**)
G3: Glas 2B **82**
PA1: Pais 1H **97**
Argyle Street Station (Rail)
. . . . 5G **83** (6E **5**)
Argyll Arc. G1: Glas 4G **83** (6D **4**)
Argyll Av. G82: Dumb 1C **18**
PA4: Renf. 5D **58**
Argyll Gdns. ML9: Lark 2F **161**
Argyll Pl. G65: Kils. 3A **12**
G74: E Kil 6C **138**
G82: Dumb. 1C **18**
ML4: Bell 5B **126**
Argyll Rd. G81: Clyd 1D **58**
Arisaig Dr. G52: Glas. 2D **100**
G61: Bear. 4H **45**
Arisaig Pl. G52: Glas 2E **101**
Arisdale Cres. G77: Newt M 3E **133**
Arkaig Av. ML6: Plain. 1F **93**
Arkaig Pl. G77: Newt M. 5H **133**
Arkaig St. ML2: Wis. 2H **157**
Ark La. G31: Glas. 4B **84**
ARKLESTON 3E **79**
Arkleston Ct. PA3: Pais 3D **78**
Arkleston Cres. PA3: Pais 4D **78**
ARKLESTON INTERCHANGE 3C **78**
Arkleston Rd. PA1: Pais. 5D **78**
PA4: Renf. 3C **78**
Arkle Ter. G72: Camb. 4G **121**
Arklet Rd. G51: Glas. 5E **81**
Arklet Way ML2: Wis 6C **146**
Arkwrights Way PA1: Pais 2F **97**
Arlington Baths Club 1D **82**
Arlington Pl. *G3: Glas 2D* ***82***
(off Arlington St.)
Arlington St. G3: Glas 2D **82**
Armadale Ct. G31: Glas 3C **84**
Armadale Path G31: Glas. 3C **84**
Armadale Pl. G31: Glas 3C **84**
Armadale St. G31: Glas 4C **84**
Armine Path ML1: N'hill. 3C **128**
Armour Av. ML6: Air 4G **91**
Armour Ct. G66: Kirk 4G **31**
G72: Blan 3H **139**
Armour Dr. G66: Kirk 4G **31**
Armour Gdns. G66: Kirk. 4G **31**
Armour Gro. ML1: Moth. 5A **144**
Armour Pl. G66: Kirk 4G **31**
ML1: N'hill 3C **128**
PA3: Lin 6A **76**
PA5: John. 2G **95**
Armour Sq. PA5: John 2G **95**
Armour St. G4: Glas. 5A **84**
PA5: John. 2G **95**
Armstrong Cres. G71: Tann 5E **109**
Armstrong Gro. G75: E Kil 4F **149**
Arnbrae Rd. G65: Kils. 2F **11**
Arngask Rd. G51: Glas. 4E **81**
Arnhall Pl. G52: Glas 2E **101**
Arnhem St. G72: Camb 2D **122**
Arnholm Pl. G52: Glas 2E **101**
Arnisdale Pl. G34: Glas 3G **87**
Arnisdale Rd. G34: Glas 3G **87**
Arnisdale Way G73: Ruth 3D **120**
Arnish PA8: Ersk 2G **57**
Arniston St. G32: Glas 4H **85**
Arniston Way PA3: Pais 4C **78**
Arnold Av. G64: B'rig 6C **48**
Arnol Pl. G33: Glas. 4F **87**
Arnott Dr. ML5: Coat 1C **110**
Arnott Quad. ML1: Moth 6E **127**
Arnott Way G72: Camb. 1A **122**
Arnprior Cres. G45: Glas 4H **119**
Arnprior Gdns. G69: Mood 5D **52**
Arnprior Quad. G45: Glas 3H **119**
Arnprior Rd. G45: Glas 3H **119**
Arnprior St. G45: Glas 3H **119**
Arnside Av. G46: Giff 4A **118**
Arnum Gdns. ML8: Carl 4F **165**
Arnum Pl. ML8: Carl. 4F **165**
Arnwood Dr. G12: Glas 4G **61**
Aron Ter. G72: Camb 4H **121**
Aros Dr. G52: Glas 2D **100**
Aros La. G52: Glas. 3D **100**
Arran G74: E Kil 2C **150**
Arran Av. G82: Dumb. 2D **16**
ML5: Coat. 1F **111**
PA3: Glas A 1A **78**
(not continuous)
Arran Dr. G46: Giff 5A **118**
G52: Glas 2F **101**
G66: Kirk 3E **31**
G67: Cumb 5F **35**
ML6: Air. 2H **91**
ML6: Glenm 4H **71**
PA2: Pais 6A **98**
PA5: John. 4D **94**
Arran Gdns. ML3: Ham 2A **154**
ML8: Carl 5F **165**
Arran La. G69: Mood 5E **53**
Arran Path *ML9: Lark. 4G* ***161***
(off Stuart Dr.)
Arran Pl. G81: Clyd 5E **43**
ML5: Coat. 1F **111**
PA3: Lin 5G **75**
Arran Rd. ML1: Moth 2E **143**
PA4: Renf 1F **79**
Arran Twr. G72: Camb 4G **121**
Arran Vw. G65: Kils 3H **11**
Arranview St. ML6: Chap. 4E **113**
Arran Way G71: Both 5D **124**
G73: Ruth. 2B **120**
Arrochar Ct. G23: Glas. 1B **62**
Arrochar Dr. G23: Glas. 6B **46**
Arrochar Path *G23: Glas 6B* ***46***
(off Arrochar Rd.)
Arrochar St. G23: Glas. 6B **46**
Arrol Pl. G40: Glas. 1D **104**
Arrol St. G52: Hill. 4G **79**
(not continuous)
Arrotshole Ct. G74: E Kil 6D **136**
Arrotshole Rd. G74: E Kil. 1D **148**
Arrowsmith Av. G13: Glas 1D **60**
Arthur Av. G78: Barr. 6D **114**
ML6: Air. 5H **91**
ARTHURLIE 6D **114**
Arthurlie Av. G78: Barr. 5E **115**
Arthurlie Dr. G46: Giff 5A **118**
G77: Newt M 6D **132**
Arthurlie Gdns. G78: Barr 5E **115**
Arthurlie St. G51: Glas 4F **81**
G78: Barr 5E **115**
Arthur Pl. G76: Busby 3C **134**
Arthur Rd. PA2: Pais 5A **98**
Arthur St. G3: Glas 2B **82**
G76: Busby. 3C **134**
ML3: Ham 4H **141**
PA1: Pais 6G **77**

Arundel Dr. G42: Glas 6E 103
    G64: B'rig 3D 48
Ascaig Cres. G52: Glas 3E 101
Ascog Rd. G61: Bear 5F 45
Ascog St. G42: Glas 3E 103
Ascot Av. G12: Glas 3F 61
Ascot Ct. G12: Glas 3G 61
Ash Av. G75: E Kil 5E 149
Ashbank Cres. ML6: Chap 2E 113
Ashburn Gdns. G62: Miln 4E 25
Ashburn Loan ML9: Lark 1F 161
Ashburn Rd. G62: Miln 3E 25
Ashburton La. G12: Glas 3H 61
                                    (off Ashburton Rd.)
Ashburton Pk. G75: E Kil 4C 148
Ashburton Rd. G12: Glas 3H 61
Ashbury Ct. PA3: Lin 6H 75
                                    (off Melrose Av.)
Ashby Cres. G13: Glas 6E 45
Ash Ct. G75: E Kil 5E 149
Ashcroft G74: E Kil 4D 138
Ashcroft Av. G66: Len 4G 7
Ashcroft Dr. G44: Glas 1A 120
Ashcroft Wlk. G66: Len 4G 7
Ashdale Dr. G52: Glas 2E 101
Ashdene St. G22: Glas 2F 63
Asher Rd. ML6: Chap 3E 113
Ashfield G64: B'rig 4C 48
Ashfield Rd. G62: Miln 4G 25
    G76: Clar 3C 134
    ML8: Law 5D 158
Ashfield Station (Rail) 4G 63
Ashfield St. G22: Glas 5G 63
                                    (not continuous)
ASHGILL 4B 162
ASHGILLHEAD 4A 162
Ashgillhead Rd. ML9: Shaw 4A 162
Ashgill Pl. G22: Glas 3G 63
Ashgill Rd. G22: Glas 2F 63
Ash Gro. G64: B'rig 1D 64
    G66: Lenz 2B 50
Ashgrove G69: Mood 6D 52
Ash Gro. G71: View 5F 109
Ashgrove ML5: Coat 1C 110
    ML6: Air 4D 92
Ash Gro. ML8: Law 5D 158
Ashgrove Rd. ML4: Bell 6D 110
Ashgrove St. G40: Glas 3C 104
Ashiestiel Ct. G67: Cumb 6G 35
Ashiestiel Pl. G67: Cumb 6G 35
Ashiestiel Rd. G67: Cumb 6G 35
Ashkirk Dr. G52: Glas 2E 101
    ML9: Ashg 5B 162
Ashland Av. ML3: Ham 5H 153
Ashlea Dr. G46: Giff 3B 118
Ashlea Gdns. ML6: Plain 1F 93
Ashley Dr. G71: Both 2F 125
Ashley La. G3: Glas 1A 4
Ashley Pk. G71: View 1G 125
Ashley Pl. G72: Blan 1A 140
Ashley St. G3: Glas 2D 82 (1A 4)
Ashmore Rd. G43: Glas 2D 118
    G44: Glas 2D 118
    G75: E Kil 5E 149
    PA5: John 4G 95
Ash Pl. FK4: Bank 1E 15
    G75: E Kil 5E 149
Ash Rd. G67: Cumb 6D 14
                                    (not continuous)
    G69: Bail 2G 107
    G81: Clyd 2B 42
    G82: Dumb 3F 17
Ashton Gdns. G69: G'csh 3E 69
Ashton Grn. G74: E Kil 1G 149
Ashton La. G12: Glas 6B 62
                                    (not continuous)
Ashton La. Nth. G12: Glas 1B 82
Ashton Rd. G12: Glas 1B 82
    G73: Ruth 4C 104
Ashton St. ML1: Moth 5F 127
Ashton Vw. G82: Dumb 3B 16
Ashton Way PA2: Pais 5C 96
Ashtree Ct. G60: Old K 1F 41
Ashtree Gro. G77: Newt M 6C 132
Ashtree Pk. ML2: Wis 6E 145

Ashtree Rd. G43: Glas 5A 102
Ashvale Cres. G21: Glas 5A 64
Ash Wlk. G73: Ruth 4E 121
    ML1: Holy 2B 128
Ashwood ML2: Wis 2E 157
Ashworth Ter. ML3: Ham 5E 141
Ash Wynd G72: Flem 3E 123
Aspen Dr. G21: Glas 6C 64
Aspen Pl. G72: Flem 2E 123
    PA5: John 4G 95
Aspen Way ML3: Ham 1A 154
Asquith Pl. ML4: Bell 2F 127
Aster Dr. G45: Glas 4C 120
Aster Gdns. G53: Glas 4C 116
    ML1: Moth 4G 143
Athelstane Dr. G67: Cumb 6F 35
Athelstane Rd. G13: Glas 2C 60
Athena Way G71: Tann 6E 109
Athole Gdns. G12: Glas 6A 62
Athole La. G12: Glas 6A 62
Atholl Av. G52: Hill. 3G 79
                                    (not continuous)
    G64: Torr 4D 28
Atholl Ct. G66: Kirk 4H 31
    G72: Blan 3D 140
Atholl Cres. PA1: Pais 5G 79
Atholl Dr. G46: Giff 1A 134
    G68: Cumb 5B 34
Atholl Gdns. G46: Glas 5F 117
    G61: Bear 6E 25
    G64: B'rig 4B 48
    G73: Ruth 3G 121
Atholl La. G69: Mood 5E 53
Atholl Pl. G46: Glas 4F 117
    ML5: Coat 2D 110
    PA3: Lin 5G 75
Atholl St. ML3: Ham 3F 141
Atholl Ter. G46: Glas 5F 117
                                    (off Woodlands Pk.)
    G71: Tann 4D 108
Atlas Ind. Est. G21: Glas 5B 64
Atlas Pl. G21: Glas 5B 64
Atlas Rd. G21: Glas 5A 64
Atlas Sq. G21: Glas 5B 64
Atlas St. G81: Clyd 1D 58
Atlin Dr. ML1: New S 4B 128
Attercliffe Av. ML2: Wis 1C 156
Attlee Av. G81: Clyd 6F 43
Attlee Pl. G81: Clyd 6F 43
                                    (off Attlee Av.)
Attow Rd. G43: Glas. 2H 117
Auburn Dr. G78: Barr 6F 115
Auchans Rd. PA6: Hous 3F 75
AUCHENBACK 6F 115
Auchenbothie Cres. G33: Glas. . . . 3G 65
Auchenbothie Pl. G33: Glas 4F 65
Auchencrow St. G34: Glas 3B 88
Auchencruive G62: Miln. 5A 26
Auchendavie Rd. G66: Kirk 3H 31
Auchendavie Steading
    G66: Kirk 3H 31
Auchengeich Rd. G69: Mood 3B 52
Auchengilloch G75: E Kil 6G 149
Auchengleich Gdns. G69: Mood . . . 5D 52
Auchenglen Dr. G69: Mood 5D 52
Auchengreoch Av. PA5: John. 5D 94
Auchengreoch Rd. PA5: John 5D 94
Auchenhowie G62: Miln. 5A 26
Auchenhowie Rd.
    G62: Bard, Miln 5H 25
Auchenkilns Rd. G67: Cumb 1F 55
Auchenkilns Rdbt. G68: Cumb . . . 4E 35
Auchenlodment Rd. PA5: John . . . 3G 95
AUCHENREOCH 5H 9
Auchenreoch Av. G82: Dumb 1H 17
Auchenstewart Ct. ML2: Wis 6A 146
AUCHENTIBBER 6F 139
Auchentibber Rd. G72: Blan 6F 139
AUCHENTORLIE 2D 98
Auchentorlie Quad. PA1: Pais 1D 98
Auchentorlie St. G11: Glas 1F 81
Auchinairn Av. G81: Dun 1B 42
Auchinairn Est. G81: Clyd. 1A 42
Auchinairn Ter. G21: Glas. 1B 84

AUCHINAIRN 1D 64
Auchinairn Gdns. G64: B'rig. 1F 65
Auchinairn Rd. G64: B'rig 1F 65
Auchinbee Farm Rd. G68: Cumb. . . 1D 34
Auchinbee Way G68: Cumb. 2D 34
Auchincampbell Rd. ML3: Ham . . . 6H 141
Auchincloch Dr. FK4: Bank. 1F 15
Auchineden Ct. G61: Bear 6C 24
Auchingill Path G34: Glas 2B 88
                                    (off Auchingill Pl.)
Auchingill Pl. G34: Glas. 2B 88
Auchingill Rd. G34: Glas. 2A 88
                                    (not continuous)
Auchingramont Ct. ML3: Ham. . . . 6H 141
Auchingramont Rd. ML3: Ham . . . 5H 141
Auchinlea Retail Pk. G34: Glas . . . 3F 87
Auchinlea Rd. G34: Glas 1F 87
Auchinlea Way G34: Glas. 2F 87
Auchinleck Av. G33: Glas. 3G 65
Auchinleck Cres. G33: Glas 3G 65
Auchinleck Dr. G33: Glas. 3G 65
Auchinleck Gdns. G33: Glas 3G 65
Auchinleck Rd. G33: Glas 2H 65
Auchinleck Ter. G81: Hard. 6D 22
    G81: Hard. 6D 22
AUCHINLOCH
    Banknock 1C 14
    Lenzie 5D 50
Auchinloch Rd. G66: Lenz 3D 50
Auchinloch St. G21: Glas. 6B 64
AUCHINRAITH 3C 140
Auchinraith Av. ML3: Ham 3F 141
Auchinraith Rd. G72: Blan 3B 140
Auchinraith Ter. G72: Blan 3C 140
                                    (not continuous)
AUCHINSTARRY 5A 12
Auchintibber Ct. G72: Blan 4C 140
Auchinvole Castle 5G 11
Auchinvole Cres. G65: Kils. 3F 11
Auchmannoch Av. PA1: Pais 6G 79
Auchnacraig Rd. G81: Faif, Hard . . 5E 23
Auchter Av. ML2: Newm 4G 147
Auchter Rd. ML2: Wis 5C 146
Auckland Pk. G75: E Kil 3C 148
Auckland Pl. G81: Clyd 3H 41
Auckland St. G22: Glas. 6F 63
Auldbar Rd. G52: Glas 2F 101
Auldbar Ter. PA2: Pais 3C 98
Auldburn Pl. G43: Glas. 1H 117
Auldburn Rd. G43: Glas. 1H 117
Auldearn Rd. G21: Glas 2E 65
Auldgirth Rd. G52: Glas 2F 101
Auldhame St. ML5: Coat 3A 90
Auldhouse Av. G43: Glas 1H 117
Auldhouse Ct. G43: Glas 1H 117
Auldhouse Gdns. G43: Glas. 1H 117
Auldhouse Retail Pk.
    G43: Glas 6A 102
Auldhouse Rd. G43: Glas. 1H 117
    G75: E Kil 6F 149
Auldhouse Ter. G43: Glas 1B 118
Auld Kirk Mus. 4C 30
Auld Kirk Rd. G72: Camb. 4C 122
Auldkirk, The G76: Busby 4E 135
Auldmurroch Dr. G62: Miln 3D 24
Auld Rd., The G67: Cumb 1A 36
Auld's Brae ML6: Air 3A 92
Auldton Ter. ML9: Ashg 4B 162
Aultbea St. G22: Glas 1F 63
Aultmore Gdns. G33: Glas 4F 87
Aultmore Pk. G33: Glas 4F 87
Aultmore Rd. G33: Glas 4F 87
Aursbridge Cres. G78: Barr 5F 115
Aursbridge Dr. G78: Barr 5F 115
Aurs Cres. G78: Barr 5F 115
Aurs Dr. G78: Barr 6F 115
Aurs Glen G78: Barr 6E 115
Aurs Pl. G78: Barr 5G 115
Aurs Rd. G78: Barr. 4F 115
Austen La. G13: Glas. 4E 61
Austen Rd. G13: Glas. 4E 61
Austine Dr. ML3: Ham 4A 154
Avenel Rd. G13: Glas. 6E 45

Avenue End Rd. G33: Glas 5B 66
Avenuehead Rd. G69: Mood 6D 52
Avenuepark St. G20: Glas 5C 62
Avenue St. G40: Glas 6C 84
G73: Ruth 4D 104
Avenue, The (Shop. Cen.)
  G77: Newt M 5D 132
Aviemore Gdns. G61: Bear 2H 45
Aviemore Rd. G52: Glas 3E 101
Avoch St. G34: Glas 2H 87
Avon Av. G61: Bear 4H 45
  ML8: Carl 3E 165
Avonbank Cres. ML3: Ham 3A 154
Avonbank Rd. G73: Ruth 6B 104
  ML9: Lark 2C 160
Avonbrae Cres. ML3: Ham 3A 154
Avon Bri. ML3: Ham 1C 154
Avonbridge Dr. ML3: Ham 6B 142
Avondale Av. G74: E Kil 2H 149
Avondale Dr. PA1: Pais 5D 78
Avondale Pl. G74: E Kil 3A 150
Avondale St. G33: Glas 2A 86
Avon Dr. ML4: Bell 3E 127
  PA3: Lin 5H 75
Avonhead G75: E Kil 6G 149
Avonhead Av. G67: Cumb 6E 35
Avonhead Gdns. G67: Cumb 6E 35
Avonhead Pl. G67: Cumb 6E 35
Avonhead Rd. G67: Cumb 6E 35
Avon Ho. ML3: Ham 4A 142
Avon Pl. ML5: Coat 2H 89
  ML9: Lark 6F 161
Avon Rd. G46: Giff 5H 117
  G64: B'rig 1C 64
  ML9: Lark 5E 161
Avonside Gro. ML3: Ham 6B 142
Avonspark St. G21: Glas 6C 64
Avon St. ML1: Moth 4F 143
  ML3: Ham 6A 142
  ML9: Lark 2D 160
Avon Twr. ML1: Moth 4G 143
Avon Wlk. G67: Cumb 3H 35
  (in Cumbernauld Shop. Cen.)
Avon Wynd ML2: Newm 3D 146
Aylmer Rd. G43: Glas 1D 118
Ayr Dr. ML6: Air 6A 92
Ayr Rd. G46: Giff 2G 133
  G77: Newt M 6A 132
  ML9: Lark, Shaw 6H 161
Ayr St. G21: Glas 5B 64
Ayton Pk. Nth. G74: E Kil 6B 138
Ayton Pk. Sth. G74: E Kil 6B 138
Aytoun Dr. PA8: Ersk 4D 40
Aytoun Rd. G41: Glas 1B 102
Azalea Gdns. G72: Flem 2E 123

B

Babylon Av. ML4: Bell 4C 126
Babylon Dr. ML4: Bell 4C 126
Babylon Pl. ML4: Bell 5C 126
Babylon Rd. ML4: Bell 4C 126
Backbrae St. G65: Kils 3H 11
  (not continuous)
Back Causeway G31: Glas 6F 85
Backmuir Cres. ML3: Ham 3F 141
Backmuir Pl. ML3: Ham 3F 141
Backmuir Rd. G15: Glas 3B 44
  ML3: Ham 3F 141
Bk. o'Barns ML3: Ham 5A 142
Bk. o'Dykes Rd. G66: Kirk 6H 31
Back o' Hill PA6: C'lee 2B 74
Back o' Hill Rd. G64: Balm, Torr . . . 3H 27
BACK O'HILL RDBT. 4D 34
Back Row ML3: Ham 5A 142
Bk. Sneddon St. PA3: Pais 6A 78
Badenheath Pl. G68: Cumb 2H 53
Badenheath Ter. G67: Mollin 3H 53
Badenoch Rd. G66: Kirk 4H 31
Bagnell St. G21: Glas 4B 64
Bahamas Way G75: E Kil 2C 148
Bailie Dr. G61: Bear 6D 24
Bailie Fyfeway ML2: Over 4H 157

Baillie Dr. G71: Both 4E 125
  G74: E Kil 5B 138
Baillie Gdns. ML2: Wis 5C 146
Baillie Pl. G74: E Kil 5C 138
Baillies La. ML6: Air 4A 92
Bailliesmuir Pl. ML2: Newm 3E 147
BAILLIESTON 6A 88
Baillieston Rd. G32: Glas 1D 106
  G71: Udd 2H 107
Baillieston Station (Rail) 2H 107
Baillie Wynd G71: Tann 5E 109
Bainsford St. G32: Glas 5H 85
Bain St. G40: Glas 5A 84
  ML6: Air 1B 92
  ML9: Lark 5F 161
Baird Av. G52: Hill 3G 79
Baird Brae G4: Glas 6F 63
Baird Ct. G81: Clyd 5C 42
Baird Cres. G67: Cumb 6D 34
  (not continuous)
Baird Dr. G61: Bear 2D 44
  PA8: Ersk 4D 40
Baird Hill G75: E Kil 3F 149
Baird Pl. ML2: Wis 5C 146
  ML4: Bell 6C 110
Bairds Av. G71: View 1F 125
Bairds Cres. ML3: Ham 6G 141
Bairdsland Vw. ML4: Bell 2D 126
Baird St. G4: Glas 2H 83 (2G 5)
  ML5: Coat 4C 90
Baker St. G41: Glas 4C 102
Bakewell Rd. G69: Bail 6G 87
Balaclava St. G3: Glas 4E 83 (6A 4)
Balado Rd. G33: Glas 4E 87
Balbeggie St. G32: Glas 1C 106
Balbeg St. G51: Glas 5E 81
Balblair Rd. G52: Glas 3F 101
Balcary Pl. ML6: Chap 4E 113
Balcarres Av. G12: Glas 4A 62
Balcastle Gdns. G65: Kils 1F 11
Balcomie St. G65: Kils 2E 11
Balcomie St. G33: Glas 2A 86
Balcomie Ter. ML3: Ham 3F 153
Balcurvie Rd. G34: Glas 1G 87
BALDERNOCK 3D 26
Baldernock Rd.
  G62: Balder, Miln 4H 25
Baldinnie Rd. G34: Glas 3H 87
Baldoran Dr. G66: Milt C 5B 8
Baldorran Cres. G68: Cumb 2D 34
Baldovan Cres. G33: Glas 3F 87
Baldovan Path G33: Glas 4F 87
Baldovie Rd. G52: Glas 1C 100
Baldragon Rd. G34: Glas 2H 87
Baldric Rd. G13: Glas 3C 60
Balerno Dr. G52: Glas 2E 101
Balfleurs St. G62: Miln 3H 25
Balfluig St. G34: Glas 2F 87
Balfour St. G20: Glas 3B 62
Balfour Ter. G75: E Kil 4H 149
Balfour Wynd ML9: Lark 4F 161
Balfron Cres. ML3: Ham 6D 140
Balfron Dr. ML5: Coat 2E 111
Balfron Rd. G51: Glas 4E 81
  PA1: Pais 6F 79
Balgair Dr. PA1: Pais 6D 78
Balgair Pl. G22: Glas 5F 63
Balgair St. G22: Glas 4F 63
Balgair Ter. G32: Glas 6B 86
Balglass Gdns. G22: Glas 5F 63
Balglass St. G22: Glas 5F 63
Balgonie Av. PA2: Pais 4E 97
Balgonie Dr. PA2: Pais 4G 97
Balgonie Rd. G52: Glas 1E 101
Balgonie Woods PA2: Pais 4G 97
Balgownie Cres. G46: T'bnk 5G 117
Balgray Cres. G78: Barr 5F 115
Balgrayhill Rd. G21: B'rig, Glas . . . 3B 64
Balgray Rd. G77: Newt M 4A 132
Balintore St. G32: Glas 6A 86
Baliol La. G3: Glas 2A 4
Baliol St. G3: Glas 2D 82 (1A 4)

Baljaffray Rd. G61: Bear 6H 23
Baljaffray Shop. Cen. G61: Bear . . . 5C 24
Ballagan Pl. G62: Miln 3D 24
Ballaig Av. G61: Bear 2D 44
Ballaig Cres. G33: Step 4C 66
Ballantay Quad. G45: Glas 4C 120
Ballantay Rd. G45: Glas 4C 120
Ballantay Ter. G45: Glas 4C 120
Ballantine Av. G52: Hill 4A 80
Ballantrae G74: E Kil 1F 149
Ballantrae Cres. G77: Newt M 6G 133
Ballantrae Dr. G77: Newt M 5G 133
Ballantrae Rd. G72: Blan 4C 140
Ballantrae Wynd ML1: Holy 2A 128
  (off Beauly Pl.)
Ballater Cres. ML2: Wis 4H 145
Ballater Dr. G61: Bear 5F 45
  PA2: Pais 4B 98
  PA4: Inch 2H 57
Ballater Pl. G5: Glas 1H 103
Ballater St. G5: Glas 6G 83
Ballater Way ML5: Glenb 3G 69
Ballayne Dr. G69: Mood 4E 53
Ballerup Ter. G75: E Kil 5G 149
BALLIESTON 1A 108
Ballindalloch Dr. G31: Glas 3C 84
Ballindalloch La. G31: Glas 3C 84
Ballinkier Av. FK4: Bank 1E 15
BALLOCH 3D 34
Balloch Gdns. G52: Glas 2F 101
Ballochmill Rd. G73: Ruth 5F 105
Ballochmyle G74: E Kil 5D 138
Ballochmyle Cres. G53: Glas 5A 100
Ballochmyle Dr. G53: Glas 5A 100
Ballochmyle Gdns. G53: Glas 5A 100
Ballochmyle Pl. G53: Glas 5A 100
Ballochney La. ML6: Air 1G 91
Ballochney Rd. ML6: Air 1E 93
Ballochney St. ML6: Air 1G 91
Ballochnie Dr. ML6: Plain 1F 93
Balloch Rd. G68: Cumb 3C 34
  ML6: Air 5G 93
BALLOCH RDBT. 3C 34
Balloch Vw. G67: Cumb 3H 35
Ballogie Rd. G44: Glas 6F 103
BALMALLOCH 2G 11
Balmalloch Rd. G65: Kils 2F 11
Balmartin Rd. G23: Glas 6B 46
Balmedie PA8: Ersk 5E 41
Balmeg Av. G46: Giff 1A 134
Balmerino Pl. G64: B'rig 1F 65
Balmoral Av. ML6: Glenm 4H 71
Balmoral Cres. ML5: Coat 1H 109
  PA4: Inch 2A 58
Balmoral Dr. G32: Carm 5B 106
  G61: Bear 5G 45
  G72: Camb 2G 121
  PA7: B'ton 6A 40
Balmoral Gdns. G71: Tann 4D 108
  G72: Blan 3A 124
Balmoral Path ML9: Lark 3G 161
  (off Alloway St.)
Balmoral Pl. G74: E Kil 2E 149
Balmoral Rd. PA5: Eld 5H 95
Balmoral St. G14: Glas 6B 60
BALMORE 5A 28
Balmore Dr. ML3: Ham 3E 153
Balmore Ind. Est. G22: Glas 1F 63
Balmore Pl. G22: Glas 3F 63
Balmore Rd. G23: Glas 1D 46
  G62: Balm, Bard 6D 26
  G64: Balm, Torr 5H 27
Balmore Sq. G22: Glas 4F 63
Balmuildy Rd. G23: Glas 3E 47
  G64: B'rig 3G 47
BALORNOCK 3D 64
Balornock Rd. G21: Glas 4C 64
Balruddery Pl. G64: B'rig 1F 65
Balshagray Av. G11: Glas 6F 61
Balshagray Cres. G14: Glas 1E 81
Balshagray Dr. G11: Glas 6F 61
Balshagray La. G11: Glas 1F 81
Balshagray Pl. G11: Glas 6F 61
Baltic Ct. G40: Glas 2C 104

Baltic La. G40: Glas 2C **104**
Baltic Pl. G40: Glas 1C **104**
Baltic St. G40: Glas 1C **104**
(not continuous)
Balure Pl. G31: Glas. 4E **85**
Balvaird Cres. G73: Ruth. 6C **104**
Balvaird Dr. G73: Ruth. 6C **104**
Balvenie Dr. ML6: Air 6B **128**
Balvenie St. ML5: Coat 2D **110**
Balveny St. G33: Glas 1D **86**
Balvicar Dr. G42: Glas. 4D **102**
Balvicar St. G42: Glas. 3D **102**
Balvie Av. G15: Glas 6A **44**
G46: Giff 5B **118**
Balvie Cres. G62: Miln 3F **25**
Balvie Rd. G62: Miln 3E **25**
Banavie La. G11: Glas. 6G **61**
Banavie Rd. G11: Glas. 6G **61**
ML2: Newm 3D **146**
Banchory Av. G43: Glas 2H **117**
ML6: Glenm 4H **71**
PA4: Inch 2H **57**
Banchory Cres. G61: Bear 5G **45**
Banchory Rd. ML2: Wis. 4H **145**
Banff Av. ML6: Air 1A **112**
Banff Pl. G75: E Kil. 3E **149**
Banff Quad. ML2: Wis 4H **145**
Banff St. G33: Glas. 1B **86**
Bangorshill St. G46: T'bnk 3F **117**
Bank Av. G62: Miln 2G **25**
Bankbrae Av. G53: Glas 1A **116**
Bankend PA11: Bri W. 4G **73**
Bankend Rd. G82: Dumb 3F **17**
PA11: Bri W 5H **73**
Bankend St. G33: Glas. 2A **86**
Bankfield Dr. ML3: Ham 4H **153**
Bankfoot Dr. G52: Glas. 6B **80**
Bankfoot Pl. G77: Newt M 5H **133**
Bankfoot Rd. G52: Glas 1B **100**
PA3: Pais 6F **77**
Bankglen Rd. G15: Glas 3B **44**
Bankhall St. G42: Glas 3F **103**
BANKHEAD 1B **120**
Bankhead Av. G13: Glas. 3A **60**
ML4: Bell 4D **126**
ML5: Coat 1G **109**
ML6: Air 4D **92**
Bankhead Dr. G73: Ruth 6C **104**
Bankhead Pl. ML5: Coat 1G **109**
ML6: Air 4D **92**
Bankhead Rd. G66: Kirk 6G **31**
G73: Ruth. 1B **120**
G76: Crmck 2H **135**
Bankholm Pl. G76: Busby 4D **134**
Bankier Rd. FK4: Bank 1E **15**
Bank La. PA1: Pais. 6B **78**
BANKNOCK 1E **15**
Banknock St. G32: Glas 5G **85**
Bank Pk. G75: E Kil. 3F **149**
Bank Rd. G32: Carm 5C **106**
Bankside Av. PA5: John 2F **95**
Banks Rd. G66: Kirk. 4D **30**
Bank St. G12: Glas 1C **82**
G72: Camb 1A **122**
G78: Barr 5E **115**
G78: Neil 2D **130**
ML5: Coat. 5A **90**
ML6: Air 3A **92**
PA1: Pais 1B **98**
(not continuous)
Banktop Pl. PA5: John 2F **95**
Bank Vw. ML6: Chap 3D **112**
Bankview Cres. G66: Kirk 5A **30**
Bankview Dr. G66: Kirk 5A **30**
Bank Way ML9: Lark 1F **161**
(off Carrick Pl.)
Bannatyne Av. G31: Glas. 4D **84**
Bannercross Av. G69: Bail 6G **87**
Bannercross Dr. G69: Bail 5G **87**
Bannercross Gdns. G69: Bail. 6G **87**
Banner Dr. G13: Glas 6C **44**
Bannerman Dr. ML4: Bell 2F **127**
Bannerman Pl. G81: Clyd 5D **42**

Banner Rd. G13: Glas 6C **44**
Bannockburn Dr. ML9: Lark 4G **161**
Bannockburn Pl. ML1: New S 5A **128**
Bantaskin St. G20: Glas 2A **62**
BANTON 1G **13**
Banton Pl. G33: Glas 4G **87**
Banton Rd. G65: Kils 2E **13**
Banyan Cres. G71: View 4H **109**
Barassie G74: E Kil 6F **137**
Barassie Ct. G71: Both 5D **124**
Barassie Cres. G68: Cumb 5H **13**
Barassie Dr. PA11: Bri W 5E **73**
Baraston Rd. G64: Torr 2B **28**
Barbados Grn. G75: E Kil 2C **148**
Barbana Rd. G74: E Kil 1A **148**
Barbegs Cres. G65: Croy 1B **34**
Barberry Av. G53: Glas. 5B **116**
Barberry Gdns. G53: Glas 5B **116**
Barberry Pl. G53: Glas. 5C **116**
Barbeth Gdns. G67: Cumb. 1D **54**
Barbeth Pl. G67: Cumb. 1C **54**
Barbeth Rd. G67: Cumb. 1C **54**
Barbeth Way G67: Cumb 1C **54**
Barbrae Pl. G71: Both 4E **125**
Barbreck Rd. G41: Glas. 3D **102**
Barcaldine Av. G69: Chry 1H **67**
Barcapel Av. G77: Newt M 2E **133**
Barchan's Rd. PA10: Kilb. 3B **94**
Barclay Av. PA5: Eld 3H **95**
Barclay Ct. G60: Old K 1F **41**
Barclay Rd. ML1: Moth 3D **142**
Barclay Sq. PA4: Renf 2D **78**
Barclay St. G21: Glas. 4B **64**
G60: Old K 2F **41**
Barcloy Pl. ML6: Chap 4E **113**
Barcraigs Dr. PA2: Pais 5B **98**
Bard Av. G13: Glas. 1B **60**
BARDOWIE 6F **27**
Bardowie Ind. Est. *G22: Glas* *5G 63*
(off Bardowie St.)
Bardowie Rd. G62: Bard. 6F **27**
Bardowie St. G22: Glas 5F **63**
(not continuous)
Bardrain Av. PA5: Eld. 3A **96**
Bardrain Rd. PA2: Pais. 6G **97**
Bardrill Dr. G64: B'rig 6A **48**
Bardykes Rd. G72: Blan. 1H **139**
Barefield St. ML9: Lark 1E **161**
Bargany Rd. G53: Glas. 4A **100**
Bargaran Rd. G53: Glas 2B **100**
BARGARRAN 5D **40**
Bargarran Rd. PA8: Ersk 5D **40**
Bargarran Sq. PA8: Ersk 4D **40**
Bargarron Dr. PA3: Pais 4C **78**
BARGEDDIE 6D **88**
Bargeddie Station (Rail) 1E **109**
Bargeddie St. G33: Glas 1F **85**
Barhill Cotts. *G65: Twe* *1D 32*
(off Main St.)
Barhill La. G65: Twe 1D **32**
Bar Hill Pl. G65: Kils 3F **11**
Barhill Ter. G65: Twe 1E **33**
Barholm Sq. G33: Glas 1D **86**
Barke Rd. G67: Cumb 2A **36**
Barkly Ter. G75: E Kil 3E **149**
BARLANARK 5E **87**
Barlanark Av. G32: Glas 4C **86**
Barlanark Cres. G33: Glas 4D **86**
Barlanark Dr. G33: Glas 4D **86**
Barlanark Pl. G32: Glas 5C **86**
G33: Glas 4E **87**
Barlanark Rd. G33: Glas 4D **86**
Barlandfauld St. G65: Kils 3A **12**
Barleybank G66: Kirk 5C **30**
Barlia Dr. G45: Glas 4A **120**
Barlia Gdns. G45: Glas 4A **120**
Barlia Gro. G45: Glas 4A **120**
Barlia Sports Complex 4A **120**
Barlia St. G45: Glas 4A **120**
Barlia Ter. G45: Glas 4A **120**
Barloan Cres. G82: Dumb 2G **17**
Barloan Pl. G82: Dumb 2G **17**
Barloch Av. G62: Miln 3G **25**

Barloch Rd. G62: Miln 3H **25**
Barloch St. G22: Glas 5G **63**
Barlogan Av. G52: Glas 6E **81**
Barlogan Quad. G52: Glas 6E **81**
Barmore Av. ML8: Carl 5G **165**
BARMULLOCH. 5E **65**
Barmulloch Rd. G21: Glas 5C **64**
Barnard Gdns. G64: B'rig. 3C **48**
Barnbeth Rd. G53: Glas. 3B **100**
Barncluith Ct. ML3: Ham 6B **142**
Barncluith Rd. ML3: Ham 6B **142**
BARNELLAN 4E **27**
Barnes Pl. G33: Glas 3A **86**
Barnes St. G78: Barr 5D **114**
Barnett Path *G72: Blan.* *2B 140*
(off Winton Cres.)
Barnflat St. G73: Ruth 4D **104**
Barn Grn. PA10: Kilb 2A **94**
BARNHILL 1A **140**
Barnhill Dr. G21: Glas 6C **64**
G77: Newt M 6D **132**
ML3: Ham 1B **152**
Barnhill Rd. G82: Dumb 2C **18**
Barnhill Station (Rail) 6B **64**
Barnkirk Av. G15: Glas 4A **44**
Barns Ct. G78: Barr 4D **114**
Barnscroft PA10: Kilb. 1B **94**
Barnsford Av. PA4: Inch 5F **57**
Barnsford Rd. PA3: Glas A 3E **77**
PA4: Inch 4E **57**
Barns St. G81: Clyd 6E **43**
Barnswood Pl. G71: Both 4F **125**
Barnton St. G32: Glas 4G **85**
Barnwell Ter. G51: Glas 4E **81**
Barnwood Rd. PA8: Ersk 3E **41**
Barochan Cres. PA3: Pais 1E **97**
Barochan Pl. G53: Glas 2B **100**
Barochan Rd. G53: Glas. 2B **100**
PA5: Brkfld 2C **74**
PA6: Hous 2C **74**
(Bridge of Weir Rd.)
PA6: Hous 6B **38**
(Reilly Rd.)
Baronald Dr. G12: Glas 3H **61**
Baronald Ga. G12: Glas 3H **61**
Baronald St. G73: Ruth 4D **104**
Baron Ct. ML3: Ham 1C **154**
Barone Dr. G76: Clar 1A **134**
Baronhall Dr. G72: Blan. 1A **140**
Baronhill G67: Cumb 6A **14**
Baron Path G69: Barg 6D **88**
Baron Rd. PA3: Pais. 5C **78**
Baronscourt Dr. PA1: Pais 1D **96**
Baronscourt Gdns. PA1: Pais. 1D **96**
Baronscourt Rd. PA1: Pais 1D **96**
Barons Ga. G71: Both 3C **124**
Barons Haugh R.S.P.B. Nature Reserve
. . . . 1F **155**
Barons Rd. ML1: Moth 1B **156**
Barons Twr. ML1: Moth 6B **144**
Baron St. PA4: Renf 1E **79**
Barony Ct. G69: Bail. 5H **87**
Barony Dr. G69: Bail. 5H **87**
Barony Gdns. G69: Bail 6H **87**
Barony Pl. G68: Cumb 4A **34**
Barony Wynd G69: Bail 5H **87**
Barra Av. ML2: Wis 4C **146**
ML5: Coat. 1A **110**
PA4: Renf 2E **79**
BARRACHNIE 6E **87**
Barrachnie Av. G69: Bail 5G **87**
Barrachnie Ct. G69: Bail. 5F **87**
Barrachnie Cres. G69: Bail 6F **87**
Barrachnie Dr. G69: Bail. 5G **87**
Barrachnie Gro. G69: Bail 5G **87**
Barrachnie Rd. G69: Bail. 6F **87**
Barrack St. G4: Glas. 5H **83**
ML3: Ham 5H **141**
Barra Cres. G60: Old K 2G **41**
Barra Dr. ML6: Air 5E **93**
Barra Gdns. G60: Old K 2G **41**
Barra Pl. ML5: Coat 1A **110**
Barra Rd. G60: Old K 2G **41**

Barras, The 5A 84
(off Moncur St.)
Barra St. G20: Glas 1A 62
Barr Av. G78: Neil. 1E 131
Barrbridge Rd. G69: Barg, Coat . . 1F 109
ML5: Barg, Coat 1F 109
Barrcraig Rd. PA11: Bri W 4E 73
Barr Cres. G81: Hard 2D 42
Barr Gro. G71: Tann 5E 109
BARRHEAD 5E 115
Barrhead Community Mus. 5E 115
Barrhead Rd. G43: Glas 6E 101
G53: Glas 1H 115
G77: Newt M 4A 132
PA2: Pais 2B 98
Barrhead Sports Cen. 4E 115
Barrhead Station (Rail) 4D 114
Barrhill Ct. G66: Kirk 5G 31
Barrhill Cres. PA10: Kilb 3B 94
Barrhill Rd. G66: Kirk 5G 31
Barriedale Av. ML3: Ham. 6F 141
Barrie Quad. G81: Clyd 3C 42
Barrie Rd. G52: Hill 4A 80
G74: E Kil 4D 138
Barrie St. ML1: Moth. 3G 143
Barrington Dr. G4: Glas 1D 82
Barrisdale Rd. G20: Glas 1B 62
ML2: Newm 3D 146
Barrisdale Way G73: Ruth. 3D 120
Barrland Dr. G46: Giff 4A 118
Barrland St. G41: Glas 2E 103
Barrmill Rd. G43: Glas 2G 117
BARROWFIELD
Coatbridge. 1C 110
BARROW FIELD
Glasgow 6C 84
Barrowfield St. G40: Glas 6C 84
(not continuous)
ML5: Coat. 1B 110
Barrpath G65: Kils 4B 12
Barr Pl. G77: Newt M. 4C 132
PA1: Pais 1H 97
Barrs La. ML8: Carl 2F 165
Barr St. G20: Glas 6E 63
ML1: Moth 1G 143
Barr Ter. G74: E Kil 1G 149
BARRWOOD 3B 12
Barrwood Pl. G71: Tann 5E 109
Barrwood St. G33: Glas 1G 85
Barry Gdns. G72: Blan 3A 140
Barscube Ter. PA2: Pais. 3C 98
Barshaw Dr. PA1: Pais 5C 78
Barshaw Pl. PA1: Pais 6F 79
Barshaw Rd. G52: Glas 5G 79
Barskiven Rd. PA1: Pais 1D 96
Barterholm Rd. PA2: Pais 3A 98
Bartholomew St. G40: Glas 2C 104
Bartiebeith Rd. G33: Glas 4D 86
Bartie Gdns. ML9: Ashg. 4A 162
Bartonhall Av. ML2: Wis 2B 158
Barty's Rd. ML4: Bell 2E 127
Barwood Hill G82: Dumb 1H 17
Bassett Av. G13: Glas. 1B 60
Bassett Cres. G13: Glas. 1B 60
Bathgate St. G31: Glas 5C 84
Bathgo Av. PA1: Pais 1G 99
Bath La. G2: Glas 3E 83 (3A 4)
(not continuous)
Bath St. G2: Glas. 3E 83 (3A 4)
Batson St. G42: Glas 3F 103
BATTLEFIELD 5E 103
Battlefield Av. G42: Glas 6E 103
Battlefield Cres. G42: Glas 5E 103
Battlefield Gdns. G42: Glas 5E 103
Battlefield Rd. G42: Glas 5D 102
Battle Pl. G41: Glas 5D 102
Battles Burn Dr. G32: Glas 3A 106
Battles Burn Ga. G32: Glas 3A 106
Battles Burn Vw. G32: Glas 3A 106
Bavelaw St. G33: Glas 1D 86
Bayfield Av. G15: Glas 4A 44
Bayfield Ter. G15: Glas 4A 44
Beacon Pl. G33: Glas. 3H 85
Beaconsfield Rd. G12: Glas. 4H 61

Beard Cres. G69: G'csh 4E 69
Beardmore G31: Glas. 5D 84
Beardmore Cotts. PA4: Inch 3A 58
Beardmore Pl. G81: Clyd. 4A 42
Beardmore St. G81: Clyd. 4H 41
Beardmore Way G81: Clyd 5H 41
Bearford Dr. G52: Glas 6B 80
BEARSDEN 2C 44
Bearsden Rd. G13: Glas 3F 61
G61: Bear 3F 61
Bearsden Shop. Cen. G61: Bear . . 3G 45
Bearsden Ski & Board Club 1D 44
Bearsden Station (Rail) 3E 45
Beaton Rd. G41: Glas 3C 102
Beaton St. ML9: Lark. 1D 160
Beatrice Dr. ML1: Holy 2H 127
Beatrice Gdns. PA6: C'lee 3D 74
Beatson Wynd G71: Tann 4E 109
Beattock St. G31: Glas 6F 85
Beattock Wynd ML3: Ham 6E 141
Beatty St. G81: Clyd. 4A 42
Beaufort Av. G43: Glas. 1A 118
Beaufort Dr. G66: Kirk 5B 30
Beaufort Gdns. G64: B'rig 6A 48
Beauly Cres. ML2: Wis 2H 157
Beauly Dr. PA2: Pais 4C 96
Beauly Pl. G20: Glas 4B 62
G64: B'rig 5F 49
G69: Chry. 6B 52
G74: E Kil 1F 149
ML1: Holy. 2A 128
ML5: Coat 2D 110
Beauly Rd. G69: Bail 2G 107
Beaumont Ga. G12: Glas 1A 82
Beckfield Cres. G33: Glas. 2F 65
Beckfield Dr. G33: Glas 2F 65
Beckfield Ga. G33: Glas 2F 65
Beckfield Gro. G33: Glas. 2F 65
Beckfield Pl. G33: Glas 2F 65
Beckfield Wlk. G33: Glas 2F 65
Beckford St. ML3: Ham 4G 141
Beckford St. Bus. Cen. ML3: Ham
. . . . 4H 141
Bedale Rd. G69: Bail 1F 107
Bedcow Vw. G66: Kirk 6F 31
Bedford Av. G81: Clyd 5F 43
Bedford La. G5: Glas 6F 83
Bedford St. G5: Glas. 6F 83
Bedlay Castle 6C 52
Bedlay Ct. G69: Mood 4E 53
Bedlay Pl. ML5: Anna 5B 54
Bedlay Vw. G71: Tann 4F 109
Bedlay Wlk. G69: Mood 4E 53
Beech Av. G41: Glas 1H 101
(not continuous)
G61: Bear. 6G 25
G69: Bail 6G 87
G72: Camb 1H 121
G73: Ruth 3E 121
G77: Newt M 5D 132
ML1: New S 4B 128
ML9: Lark. 3H 161
PA11: Bri W 2F 73
PA2: Pais 4C 98
PA5: Eld 3A 96
Beechbank Av. ML6: Air 2H 91
Beech Ct. ML5: Coat 1A 110
Beech Cres. G72: Flem. 3E 123
G77: Newt M 6E 133
ML1: N'hse. 6D 112
(not continuous)
Beech Dr. G81: Clyd. 2C 42
Beeches Av. G81: Dun 1B 42
Beeches Rd. G81: Dun. 1A 42
Beeches Ter. G81: Dun 6B 22
Beeches, The G72: Blan. 2A 140
(off Burnbrae Rd.)
G77: Newt M. 3F 133
PA5: Brkfld 5C 74
PA6: Hous 2D 74
Beechfield Dr. ML8: Carl 5G 165
Beech Gdns. G69: Bail. 6G 87
Beech Gro. G69: G'csh. 4E 69
Beechgrove G69: Mood 5D 52

Beech Gro. G75: E Kil 5D 148
ML2: Wis 2A 146
ML8: Law 5D 158
Beechgrove Av. G71: View. 6G 109
Beechgrove Quad. ML1: Holy 2A 128
Beechgrove St. G40: Glas 3D 104
Beechland Av. G44: Neth 5C 118
Beechlands Dr. G76: Clar. 3A 134
Beechmount Rd. G66: Lenz 3C 50
Beech Pl. G64: B'rig 1D 64
G72: Blan 2C 140
Beech Rd. G64: B'rig 1D 64
G66: Lenz. 1C 50
ML1: N'hse. 6C 112
PA5: John. 4D 94
Beech Ter. ML9: Lark 4F 161
Beechtree Ter. G66: Milt C. 6C 8
Beechwood ML2: Wis 2D 156
ML9: Lark. 6A 156
Beechwood Av. G73: Ruth 1E 121
G76: Clar 3A 134
ML3: Ham. 3F 153
Beechwood Ct. G61: Bear 4F 45
G67: Cumb. 5H 35
Beechwood Cres. ML2: Wis. 1A 158
Beechwood Dr. G11: Glas. 5F 61
ML5: Coat. 6E 91
PA4: Renf 2D 78
Beechwood Gdns. G69: Mood. . . . 6D 52
ML4: Bell 3E 127
BEECHWOOD GATE 6C 64
Beechwood Gro. G78: Barr 6E 115
Beechwood La. G61: Bear 4F 45
Beechwood Pl. G11: Glas. 5F 61
ML4: Bell 3E 127
Beechwood Rd. G67: Cumb. 4H 35
Beechworth Dr. ML1: N'hill 5D 128
Beecroft Pl. G72: Blan. 6C 124
Beil Dr. G13: Glas 2H 59
Beith Dr. ML6: Air 1A 112
Beith Rd. PA9: How 6A 94
Beith St. G11: Glas 2G 81
Belford Ct. G77: Newt M 6D 132
Belford Gro. G77: Newt M 6D 132
Belfron Pl. ML5: Coat. 1E 111
Belgowan St. ML4: Bell 6B 110
Belgrave St. ML4: Bell. 6B 110
Belgrave Ter. G12: Glas. 6C 62
Belhaven Ho. ML2: Wis. 6G 145
Belhaven Pk. G69: Muirh. 2A 68
Belhaven Rd. ML2: Wis. 6G 145
ML3: Ham 6C 140
Belhaven Ter. G12: Glas 5A 62
G73: Ruth 1E 121
ML2: Wis 6G 145
Belhaven Ter. W. G12: Glas 5A 62
Belhaven Ter. W. La. G12: Glas. . . . 5A 62
BELLAHOUSTON 1F 101
Bellahouston Dr. G52: Glas 2E 101
Bellahouston La. G52: Glas 1E 101
Bellahouston Leisure Cen. 1F 101
Bellahouston Pk. 1G 101
Bellairs Pl. G72: Blan 6A 124
Bellas Pl. ML6: Plain. 1G 93
Bellcraig Ct. G76: Busby 4F 135
Bell Dr. G72: Blan 5A 140
Belleisle Av. G71: Udd. 6C 108
Belleisle Ct. G68: Cumb 1G 35
Belleisle Cres. PA11: Bri W 5E 73
Belleisle Dr. G68: Cumb 1G 35
Belleisle Gdns. G68: Cumb. 1G 35
Belleisle Gro. G68: Cumb 1G 35
Belleisle St. G42: Glas 4F 103
Bellevue Av. G66: Kirk 5B 30
Bellevue Rd. G66: Kirk 5B 30
Bellfield Ct. G78: Barr 3D 114
Bellfield Cres. G78: Barr. 3D 114
Bellfield Dr. ML2: Wis 1A 158
Bellfield Rd. G66: Kirk. 5B 30
Bellfield St. G31: Glas 5C 84
Bellflower Av. G53: Glas 4C 116
Bellflower Ct. G74: E Kil 6E 137
Bellflower Gdns. G53: Glas 4C 116
Bellflower Gro. G74: E Kil 5E 137

Bellflower Pl. G53: Glas 4C 116
Bell Grn. E. G75: E Kil 3H 149
Bell Grn. W. G75: E Kil 3G 149
Bellgrove Station (Rail) 5B 84
Bellgrove St. G40: Glas 5B 84
Bellhaven Ter. La. G12: Glas 5A 62
        (off Horslethill Rd.)
Bellisle Ter. ML3: Ham 4F 153
Bellrock Ct. G33: Glas 3B 86
Bellrock Cres. G33: Glas 3A 86
Bellrock Path G33: Glas 3B 86
Bellrock St. G33: Glas 3A 86
Bellscroft Av. G73: Ruth 6B 104
Bellsdyke Rd. ML6: Air 5H 91
Bellsfield Dr. G72: Blan 3B 140
Bellshaugh Ct. G12: Glas 4A 62
Bellshaugh Gdns. G12: Glas 4A 62
Bellshaugh La. G12: Glas 4A 62
Bellshaugh Pl. G12: Glas 4A 62
Bellshaugh Rd. G12: Glas 4A 62
BELLSHILL 2C 126
Bellshill Cultural Cen. 2C 126
Bellshill (Motherwell Food Pk.) Ind. Est.
  ML4: Bell 6C 110
        (Belgowan St.)
  ML4: Bell 1B 126
        (Belgrave St.)
Bellshill Rd. G71: Both 1G 141
  G71: Udd 2D 124
  ML1: Moth 4E 127
Bellshill Station (Rail) 2C 126
Bellside Rd. ML1: N'hse 5G 113
  ML6: Chap 3E 113
BELLSMYRE 1H 17
Bellsmyre Av. G82: Dumb 1G 17
Bell St. G1: Glas 4H 83 (6G 5)
  G81: Clyd 2F 59
  ML2: Wis 6F 145
  ML4: Bell 6D 110
  ML6: Air 3H 91
  PA4: Renf 5F 59
Belltrees Cres. PA3: Pais 1E 97
Bell Vw. Ct. PA4: Renf 5F 59
Bellvue Cres. ML4: Bell 3A 126
Bellvue Way ML5: Coat 1E 111
Bellwood St. G41: Glas 6C 102
Bellziehill Rd. ML4: Bell 2A 126
Belmar Ct. PA3: Lin 6A 76
        (off Langholm Dr.)
Belmont Av. G71: Udd 6C 108
Belmont Ct. G66: Kirk 5D 30
      (off Willowbank Gdns.)
Belmont Cres. G12: Glas 6C 62
Belmont Dr. G46: Giff 4H 117
  G73: Ruth 6D 104
  G75: E Kil 3D 148
  G78: Barr 6F 115
Belmont Ho. G75: E Kil 3D 148
        (off Riverton Dr.)
Belmont La. G12: Glas 6C 62
      (off Gt. Western Rd.)
Belmont Rd. G21: Glas 3B 64
  G72: Camb 4G 121
  PA3: Pais 5C 78
Belmont St. G12: Glas 6C 62
  G65: Kils 2G 11
  G81: Clyd 1D 58
  ML2: Over 5H 157
  ML5: Coat 2G 89
Belses Dr. G52: Glas 6C 80
Belses Gdns. G52: Glas 6C 80
Belstane M. ML8: Carl 2G 165
Belstane Pk. ML8: Carl 2F 165
Belstane Pl. G71: Both 4E 125
Belstane Rd. G67: Cumb 2H 55
  ML8: Carl 3F 165
Belsyde Av. G15: Glas 5A 44
Beltane St. G3: Glas 3D 82
  ML2: Wis 1G 157
Beltrees Av. G53: Glas 4A 100
Beltrees Cres. G53: Glas 4A 100
Beltrees Rd. G53: Glas 4A 100
Belvidere Cres. G64: B'rig 5D 48
  ML4: Bell 3D 126

Belvidere Rd. ML4: Bell. 3C 126
Belvoir Pl. G72: Blan. 1B 140
Bemersyde G64: B'rig 5E 49
Bemersyde Av. G43: Glas 2H 117
Bemersyde Pl. ML9: Lark 4E 161
Bemersyde Rd. PA2: Pais 5B 96
Ben Aigan Pl. G53: Glas 3C 116
Ben Alder Dr. PA2: Pais 4F 99
Benalder St. G11: Glas 2A 82
Benarty Gdns. G64: B'rig. 5D 48
Benbecula G74: E Kil 2C 150
Benbow Rd. G81: Clyd. 5B 42
Ben Buie Way PA2: Pais. 4F 99
Bencloich Av. G66: Len 3G 7
Bencloich Cres. G66: Len 2G 7
Bencloich Rd. G66: Len. 3G 7
Bencroft Dr. G44: Glas 2A 120
Ben Donich Pl. G53: Glas 3D 116
Ben Edra Pl. G53: Glas 3D 116
Benford Av. ML1: N'hill 3D 128
Benford Knowe ML1: N'hill. 3E 129
Bengairn St. G31: Glas. 4E 85
Bengal Pl. G43: Glas 6A 102
Bengal St. G43: Glas 6A 102
Ben Garrisdale Pl. G53: Glas 3D 116
Ben Glas Pl. G53: Glas 3D 116
Benhar Pl. G33: Glas. 4H 85
Benholm St. G32: Glas. 2H 105
Ben Hope Av. PA2: Pais 3F 99
Ben Laga Pl. G53: Glas 3D 116
Ben Lawers Dr. G68: Cumb 3D 34
  PA2: Pais 3F 99
Ben Ledi Av. PA2: Pais 3F 99
Ben Ledi Cres. G68: Cumb 3D 34
Ben Loyal Av. PA2: Pais 3F 99
Ben Lui Dr. PA2: Pais 4E 99
Ben Lui Pl. G53: Glas 3D 116
  G68: Cumb. 3D 34
Ben Macdui Gdns.
  G53: Glas 3D 116
Ben More Dr. G68: Cumb. 3C 34
  PA2: Pais 3F 99
Benmore Twr. G72: Camb 4G 121
Bennan Sq. G42: Glas. 3G 103
Benn Av. PA1: Pais. 1B 98
Ben Nevis Pl. PA2: Pais 4E 99
Ben Nevis Way G68: Cumb 3C 34
Benny Lynch Ct. G5: Glas 6G 83
Benson St. ML5: Coat 1C 110
Benston Pl. PA5: John 4E 95
Benston Rd. PA5: John 4E 95
Bent Cres. G71: View. 1G 125
Bentfoot Rd. ML2: Over 5A 158
Benthall St. G5: Glas. 1H 103
Bentinck St. G3: Glas 2C 82
Bent Rd. ML3: Ham 1G 153
  ML6: Chap 2D 112
Bents Rd. G69: Bail 6H 87
Benty's La. ML8: Carl 5F 165
Ben Uird Pl. G53: Glas. 3D 116
Ben Vane Av. PA2: Pais. 4E 99
Ben Venue Rd. G68: Cumb 3C 34
Ben Venue Way PA2: Pais 4F 99
Benvie Gdns. G64: B'rig 5D 48
Benview Rd. G76: Clar. 2C 134
Benview St. G20: Glas 5D 62
Benview Ter. PA2: Pais 3C 98
Ben Vorlich Dr. G53: Glas 2D 116
Ben Vorlich Pl. G53: Glas 3D 116
Benvue Rd. G66: Len. 4G 7
Ben Wyvis Dr. PA2: Pais 4E 99
Berelands Cres. G73: Ruth 6A 104
Berelands Pl. G73: Ruth 6A 104
Berenice Pl. G82: Dumb 3C 18
Beresford Av. G14: Glas. 5E 61
Berkeley St. G3: Glas 3C 82 (3A 4)
Berkley Dr. G72: Blan. 6A 124
Berkley Ter. La. G3: Glas. 3B 82
        (off Granville St.)
Berl Av. PA6: C'lee 3C 74
Bernadette Cres. ML1: Carf. 5D 128
Bernadette St. ML1: N'hill 4D 128
Bernard Path G40: Glas 1C 104
        (off Bernard Ter.)

Bernard St. G40: Glas 1C 104
Bernard Ter. G40: Glas. 1C 104
Berneray St. G22: Glas 2G 63
Bernisdale Dr. G15: Clyd 4F 43
Bernisdale Gdns. G15: Clyd. 4F 43
Bernisdale Pl. G15: Clyd 4F 43
Berridale Av. G44: Glas 2E 119
Berriedale G75: E Kil 3A 148
Berriedale Av. G69: Bail. 1G 107
Berriedale Quad. ML2: Wis. 4H 145
Berryburn Rd. G21: Glas 5E 65
Berry Dyke G66: Kirk 6H 31
Berryhill Dr. G46: Giff 5H 117
Berryhill Rd. G46: Giff. 6H 117
Berry Hill Rd. G67: Cumb 3G 35
Berryknowe G66: Kirk 6H 31
       (off Bk. o'Dykes Rd.)
Berryknowe Av. G69: Chry 2A 68
Berryknowes Av. G52: Glas 6C 80
Berryknowes Dr. G52: Glas 6D 80
Berryknowes La. G52: Glas 6C 80
Berryknowes Rd. G52: Glas 1C 100
Bertram St. G41: Glas 4C 102
  ML3: Ham. 3E 141
  ML9: Lark. 4G 161
Bervie St. G51: Glas 5F 81
Berwick Cres. ML6: Air 6H 91
  PA3: Lin 4F 75
Berwick Dr. G52: Glas 1B 100
  G73: Ruth 6F 105
Berwick Pl. G74: E Kil 6C 138
  ML5: Coat 2D 110
Berwick St. ML3: Ham 4F 141
  ML5: Coat 2D 110
Bessemer Dr. G75: E Kil 6A 150
Beta Cen. G81: Clyd. 2E 59
Betula Dr. G81: Clyd 2C 42
Bevan Gro. PA5: John 3E 95
Beveridge Ter. ML4: Bell 3F 127
Beverley Rd. G43: Glas 1B 118
Bevin Av. G81: Clyd 6F 43
Bideford Cres. G32: Glas. 2D 106
Bield, The ML2: Wis 1A 158
BIGGAR ROAD 2G 129
Biggar Rd. ML1: N'hse. 5F 113
  ML6: Chap 4E 113
Biggar St. G31: Glas 5D 84
Bigton St. G33: Glas 1B 86
Billings Rd. ML1: Moth 4D 142
Bilsland Ct. G20: Glas 4F 63
Bilsland Dr. G20: Glas 4D 62
Binend Rd. G53: Glas. 5C 100
Binniehill Rd. G68: Cumb 2F 35
Binnie Pl. G40: Glas. 6A 84
Binns Rd. G33: Glas. 1C 86
Birch Av. G76: Busby 3D 134
Birch Brae ML3: Ham. 2A 154
Birch Ct. ML5: Coat 1B 110
Birch Cres. G76: Busby 3D 134
  PA5: John. 4G 95
Birch Dr. G66: Lenz 2D 50
  G72: Camb 1C 122
Birchend Dr. G21: Glas 1D 84
Birchend Pl. G21: Glas. 1D 84
Birchfield Dr. G14: Glas 5B 60
Birchfield Rd. ML3: Ham 6F 141
Birch Gro. G71: View 6F 109
  ML9: Lark. 6A 156
Birchgrove PA6: Hous 2D 74
Birch Knowe G64: B'rig 1D 64
Birchlea Dr. G46: Giff. 3B 118
Birchmount Ct. ML6: Air 3D 92
Birch Pl. G72: Blan. 1B 140
  G72: Flem 3F 123
  PA4: Renf. 1D 78
Birch Quad. ML6: Air. 4D 92
Birch Rd. G67: Cumb 2E 37
  G81: Clyd 3C 42
  G82: Dumb 3F 17
Birch St. G5: Glas 2H 103
  ML1: Holy. 2B 128
Birch Vw. G61: Bear. 2G 45
Birchview Dr. G76: Busby 5D 134
Birch Way PA4: Renf 1D 78

Birchwood Av.—Blythswood St.

Birchwood Av. G32: Glas 1E 107
Birchwood Courtyards, The
ML4: Bell 5A 110
Birchwood Dr. PA2: Pais 4E 97
Birchwood Pl. G32: Glas 1E 107
Birdsfield Ct. ML3: Ham 3D 140
Birdsfield Dr. G72: Blan 3B 140
Birdsfield St. ML3: Ham 3D 140
BIRDSTON 2C 30
Birdstone Rd. G66: Kirk 3C 30
Birdston Rd. G21: Glas 3E 65
G66: Milt C 5C 8
Birgidale Rd. G45: Glas 5H 119
Birgidale Ter. G45: Glas 5H 119
Birkdale G74: E Kil 6E 137
Birkdale Ct. G71: Both 5D 124
Birkdale Cres. G68: Cumb 5H 13
Birkdale Wood G68: Cumb 5A 14
Birkenburn Rd. G67: Cumb 5F 15
Birken Rd. G66: Lenz 3E 51
BIRKENSHAW
Glasgow 5D 108
Larkhall 6F 161
Birkenshaw Ind. Est. G71: Tann 4C 108
Birkenshaw Rd. G69: G'csh 1G 69
ML5: Glenb 6A 54
Birkenshaw Sports Hall 4D 108
Birkenshaw St. G31: Glas 4D 84
Birkenshaw Way *PA3: Pais 3A 78*
(off Mosslands Rd.)
Birkfield Pl. ML8: Carl 4H 165
Birkhall Av. G52: Glas 1H 99
PA4: Inch 2H 57
Birkhall Dr. G61: Bear 5F 45
Birkhill Av. G64: B'rig 5D 48
Birkhill Gdns. G64: B'rig 5D 48
Birkhill Rd. ML3: Ham 4H 153
Birkmyre Rd. G51: Glas 5F 81
Birks Ct. ML8: Law 1H 163
Birkshaw Brae ML2: Wis 3G 157
Birkshaw Pl. ML2: Wis 3G 157
Birkshaw Twr. ML2: Wis 3F 157
Birks Rd. ML8: Carl 1G 163
ML9: Lark 6F 161
Birkwood St. G40: Glas 3D 104
Birmingham Rd. PA4: Renf 2D 78
Birnam Av. G64: B'rig 5D 48
Birnam Cres. G61: Bear 2H 45
Birnam Pl. G77: Newt M 5H 133
ML3: Ham 6C 140
Birnam Rd. G32: Glas 2F 105
Birness Dr. G43: Glas 5B 102
Birnie Ct. G21: Glas 5E 65
BIRNIEHILL 3H 149
Birniehill Ct. G81: Hard 6C 22
BIRNIEHILL RDBT. 3A 150
Birnie Rd. G21: Glas 5E 65
Birnock Av. PA4: Renf 2G 79
Birrell Rd. G62: Miln 2F 25
Birrens Rd. ML1: Moth 1E 143
Birsay Rd. G22: Glas 2F 63
BISHOPBRIGGS 6C 48
Bishopbriggs Ind. Est. G64: B'rig 2C 64
Bishopbriggs Station (Rail) 6C 48
Bishopdale G74: E Kil 6E 137
Bishop Gdns. G64: B'rig 5A 48
ML3: Ham 4A 154
Bishopmill Pl. G21: Glas 5E 65
Bishopmill Rd. G21: Glas 4E 65
Bishops Ga. G64: B'rig 6B 48
G74: T'hall 6G 135
(not continuous)
Bishopsgate Dr. G21: Glas 2A 64
Bishopsgate Gdns. G21: Glas 2A 64
Bishopsgate Pl. G21: Glas 2A 64
Bishopsgate Rd. G21: Glas 2A 64
Bishops Pk. G74: T'hall 6F 135
Bishop St. G2: Glas 4E 83 (5A 4)
BISHOPTON 4G 39
Bishopton Station (Rail) 6H 39
Bisset Ct. *PA5: John 4E 95*
(off Tannahill Cres.)
Bissett Cres. G81: Dun 1A 42
Blackadder Pl. G75: E Kil 4A 148
Blackbog Rd. ML6: Rigg 5G 55
Blackbraes Rd. G74: E Kil 5B 138
Blackbull Cl. ML8: Carl 3F 165
Blackburn Cres. G66: Kirk 5G 31
G82: Dumb 3D 16
Blackburn Sq. G78: Barr 6F 115
Blackburn St. G51: Glas 5B 82
Blackbyres Ct. G78: Barr 3F 115
Blackbyres Rd. G78: Barr 1E 115
Blackcraig Av. G15: Glas 4A 44
Blackcroft Av. ML6: Gart 6E 93
Blackcroft Gdns. G32: Glas 1D 106
Blackcroft Rd. G32: Glas 1D 106
Blackdyke Rd. G66: Kirk 5E 31
Blackfarm Rd. G77: Newt M 5F 133
Blackfaulds Rd. G73: Ruth 5A 104
Blackford Rd. PA2: Pais 3C 98
Blackfriars St. G1: Glas 4H 83 (6G 5)
BLACKHALL 2C 98
Blackhall Ct. PA2: Pais 2D 98
Blackhall La. PA1: Pais 2B 98
Blackhall St. PA1: Pais 2B 98
BLACKHILL 1F 85
Blackhill Pl. G33: Glas 1F 85
Blackhill Rd. G23: Glas 5B 46
Blackhill Vw. ML8: Law 6E 159
Blackhouse Av. G77: Newt M 5F 133
Blackhouse Gdns. G77: Newt M 5F 133
Blackhouse Rd. G77: Newt M 5F 133
Blackie St. G3: Glas 2B 82
Blacklands Pl. G66: Lenz 3E 51
Blacklands Rd. G74: E Kil 2F 149
Blacklaw Dr. G74: E Kil 2B 150
Blacklaw La. PA3: Pais 6A 78
Blackmoor Pl. ML1: New S 4A 128
Blackmoss Dr. ML4: Bell 3B 126
Blackness St. ML5: Coat 2D 110
Blackstone Av. G53: Glas 5C 100
Blackstone Cres. G53: Glas 4C 100
Blackstoun Av. PA3: Lin 5H 75
Blackstoun Oval PA3: Pais 6F 77
Blackstoun Rd. PA3: Pais 3E 77
Black St. G4: Glas 2H 83 (2H 5)
ML6: Air 2B 92
Blackswell La. ML3: Ham 6B 142
Blackthorn Av. G66: Lenz 2A 50
Blackthorn Gro. G66: Lenz 2B 50
Blackthorn Rd. G67: Cumb 1D 36
G71: View 5G 109
BLACKTHORN RDBT. 2E 37
Blackthorn St. G22: Glas 4A 64
BLACKWOOD 4A 34
Blackwood G75: E Kil 6F 149
Blackwood Av. G77: Newt M 6F 133
PA3: Lin 6G 75
Blackwood Gdns. ML1: Moth 6E 127
Blackwood Rd. G62: Miln 1F 25
G68: Cumb 4H 33
BLACKWOOD RDBT. 3A 34
Blackwoods Cres. G69: Mood 5D 52
ML4: Bell 3E 127
Blackwood St. G13: Glas 2E 61
G78: Barr 5D 114
Blackwood Ter. PA5: John 5D 94
BLACKWOOD W. RDBT. 4H 33
Bladda La. PA1: Pais 1B 98
Blades Ct. G69: G'csh 3E 69
Bladnoch Dr. G15: Glas 5C 44
Blaeloch Av. G45: Glas 6G 119
Blaeloch Dr. G45: Glas 6F 119
Blaeloch Ter. G45: Glas 6F 119
Blaeshill Rd. G75: E Kil 3A 148
Blairardie Dr. G13: Glas 6B 44
G15: Glas 6B 44
Blairathol Av. G11: Glas 6G 61
Blairathol Gdns. G11: Glas 6G 61
Blairatholl Cres. G77: Newt M 5H 133
Blair Atholl Dr. ML9: Lark 4G 161
Blairatholl Ga. G77: Newt M 5H 133
Blairbeth Dr. G44: Glas 6F 103
Blairbeth Pl. *G73: Ruth 2D 120*
(off Blairbeth Rd.)
Blairbeth Rd. G73: Ruth 2C 120
Blairbeth Ter. G73: Ruth 2E 121
Blair Ct. G81: Clyd 5D 42
Blair Cres. G69: Bail 2G 107
Blairdardie Rd. G15: Glas 6B 44
Blairdenan Av. G69: Mood 4E 53
Blairdenon Dr. G68: Cumb 2E 35
Blair Dr. G66: Milt C 6B 8
Blair Gdns. G64: Torr 4D 28
G77: Newt M 4B 132
Blairgowrie Rd. G52: Glas 1C 100
Blairgrove Ct. ML5: Coat 5A 90
Blairhall Av. G41: Glas 5D 102
BLAIRHILL 4B 90
Blairhill Av. G66: Kirk 1G 51
Blairhill Pl. ML5: Coat 4A 90
Blairhill Station (Rail) 3A 90
Blairhill St. ML5: Coat 4A 90
Blairholm Dr. ML4: Bell 4D 126
Blair Ho. G67: Cumb 2A 36
BLAIRLINN 1H 55
Blairlinn Ind. Est. G67: Cumb 1H 55
Blairlinn Rd. G67: Cumb 1H 55
Blairlogie St. G33: Glas 2B 86
Blairmore Av. PA1: Pais 6E 79
Blairpark Av. ML5: Coat 3A 90
Blair Path ML1: Moth 4H 143
Blair Rd. ML5: Coat 4A 90
PA1: Pais 6G 79
BLAIRSKAITH 2H 27
Blairston Av. G71: Both 6E 125
Blairston Gdns. G71: Both 6F 125
Blair St. G32: Glas 6H 85
Blairtum Dr. G73: Ruth 2D 120
Blairtummock Rd. G33: Glas 3C 86
(not continuous)
Blake Rd. G67: Cumb 3A 36
Blane Dr. G62: Miln 2H 25
Blanefield Gdns. G13: Glas 1F 61
Blane St. ML5: Coat 3C 90
Blaneview G33: Step 5D 66
BLANTYRE 3A 140
Blantyre Ct. PA8: Ersk 4E 41
Blantyre Cres. G81: Dun 6A 22
Blantyre Dr. PA7: B'ton 3G 39
Blantyre Farm Rd. G71: Udd 2A 124
G72: Blan 6A 124
BLANTYREFERME 1B 124
Blantyre Gdns. G68: Cumb 4A 34
Blantyre Ind. Est. G72: Blan 4C 140
Blantyre Mill Rd. G71: Both 5D 124
Blantyre Rd. G71: Both 5E 125
Blantyre Sports Cen. 1C 140
Blantyre Station (Rail) 1C 140
Blantyre St. G3: Glas 2B 82
Blaven Ct. G69: Bail 1A 108
Blawart Hill St. G14: Glas 4H 59
Bleachfield G62: Miln 2F 25
Bleasdale Ct. G81: Clyd 5D 42
Blenheim Av. G33: Step 3D 66
G75: E Kil 4E 149
Blenheim Ct. G33: Step 3D 66
G65: Kils 2H 11
ML8: Carl 4G 165
PA1: Pais 6H 77
BLOCHAIRN INTERCHANGE 3C 84
Blochairn Rd. G21: Glas 2C 84
Bluebell Gdns. G45: Glas 5C 120
ML1: Moth 5E 127
Bluebell Wlk. ML1: New S 4A 128
Bluebell Way G66: Len 4H 7
ML6: Air 1H 91
ML8: Carl 5F 165
Blueknowes Rd. ML8: Law 6D 158
(not continuous)
Bluevale St. G31: Glas 5C 84
Blyth Pl. G33: Glas 5D 86
Blyth Rd. G33: Glas 5E 87
BLYTHSWOOD 4F 59
Blythswood Av. PA4: Renf 5F 59
Blythswood Ct. G2: Glas 4E 83 (5A 4)
Blythswood Dr. PA3: Pais 5H 77
Blythswood Ind. Est. PA4: Renf 5D 58
Blythswood Rd. PA4: Renf 5F 59
Blythswood Sq. G2: Glas 3E 83 (4B 4)
Blythswood St. G2: Glas 4E 83 (6B 4)

176 A-Z Glasgow

Boardwalk, The G75: E Kil	4A **150**	
Bobbins Ga. PA1: Pais	2F **97**
Boclair Av. G61: Bear	3F **45**
Boclair Cres. G61: Bear	3G **45**
G64: B'rig	5C **48**
Boclair Rd. G61: Bear	3G **45**
G62: Miln	1B **46**
G64: B'rig	6C **48**
Boclair St. G13: Glas	1E **61**
Bodden Sq. ML1: N'hse	6E **113**
Boden Ind. Est. G40: Glas	1D **104**
Boden St. G40: Glas	1C **104**
Bodmin Gdns. G69: Mood	4D **52**
Bogany Ter. G45: Glas	5A **120**
Bogbain Rd. G34: Glas	3G **87**
Boggknowe G71: Tann	5B **108**
Boghall Rd. G71: Udd	3G **107**
ML8: Carl	6H **165**
Boghall St. G33: Glas	2B **86**
BOGHEAD	3H **49**
Boghead Av. G82: Dumb	3H **17**
Boghead Rd. G21: Glas	4C **64**
G66: Lenz	3A **50**
G82: Dumb	3G **17**
Bogleshole Rd. G72: Camb	6G **105**
Bogmoor Pl. G51: Glas	2C **80**
Bogmoor Rd. G51: Glas	3B **80**
Bog Rd. FK4: Bank	1E **15**
BOGSIDE	3G **159**
Bogside Rd. G33: Mille	3A **66**
G65: Kils	4H **11**
ML9: Ashg	5B **162**
Bogside St. G40: Glas	1D **104**
Bogstonhill Rd. PA6: Hous	1B **74**
Bogs Vw. ML4: Bell	4B **126**
Bogton Av. G44: Glas	3D **118**
Bogton Av. La. G44: Glas	3D **118**
Boleyn Rd. G41: Glas	3C **102**
Bolingbroke G74: E Kil	5C **138**
Bolivar Ter. G42: Glas	5G **103**
Bolton Dr. G42: Glas	5F **103**
Bolton Ter. G66: Len	3G **7**
Bon Accord Rd. G76: Busby	3D **134**
Bon Accord Sq. G81: Clyd	1D **58**
Bonar Cres. PA11: Bri W	4G **73**
Bonar La. PA11: Bri W	4G **73**
Bonawe St. G20: Glas	5D **62**
Bonds Dr. ML2: Newm	3F **147**
Bo'ness Rd. ML1: Holy	1C **128**
Boness St. G40: Glas	1D **104**
Bonhill Rd. G82: Dumb	3G **17**
Bonhill St. G22: Glas	6F **63**
BONKLE	3G **147**
Bonkle Gdns. ML2: Newm	4F **147**
Bonkle Rd. ML2: Newm	4F **147**
Bonnar St. G40: Glas	2C **104**
Bonnaughton Rd. G61: Bear	1B **44**
Bonnyholm Av. G53: Glas	2A **100**
Bonnyrigg Dr. G43: Glas	2G **117**
Bonnyton La. ML3: Ham	4F **153**
Bontine Av. G82: Dumb	3D **16**
Bonyton Av. G13: Glas	3H **59**
Boon Dr. G15: Glas	5B **44**
Boquhanran Pl. G81: Clyd	4C **42**
Boquhanran Rd. G81: Clyd	5B **42**
	(not continuous)
Borden La. G13: Glas	4E **61**
Borden Rd. G13: Glas	4E **61**
Border Way G66: Kirk	5E **31**
Boreland Dr. G13: Glas	2A **60**
ML3: Ham	1C **152**
Boreland Pl. G13: Glas	3B **60**
Bore Rd. ML6: Air	2B **92**
Borgie Cres. G72: Camb	2A **122**
Borland Dr. ML9: Lark	5F **161**
Borland Rd. G61: Bear	4G **45**
Borron St. G4: Glas	6G **63**
Borrowdale G75: E Kil	6B **148**
Borthwick Dr. G75: E Kil	4A **148**
Borthwick St. G33: Glas	2B **86**
Bosfield Cnr. G74: E Kil	6H **137**
Bosfield Pl. G74: E Kil	6H **137**
Bosfield Rd. G74: E Kil	6G **137**

Boswell Ct. G42: Glas	6D **102**
Boswell Dr. G72: Blan	2B **140**
Boswell Pk. G74: E Kil	5C **138**
Boswell Sq. G52: Hill	4H **79**
Bosworth Rd. G74: E Kil	5B **138**
Botanic Cres. G20: Glas	5B **62**
Botanic Cres. La. G20: Glas	5B **62**
Bothlin Dr. G33: Step	3D **66**
Bothlyn Av. G66: Kirk	6E **31**
Bothlyn Cres. G69: G'csh	2D **68**
Bothlyn Rd. G69: Chry	1B **68**
BOTHWELL	5E **125**
Bothwell Bri. G71: Both	1G **141**
Bothwell Castle	4B **124**
Bothwellhaugh Quad.
ML4: Bell	4B **126**
Bothwellhaugh Rd. ML1: Moth	6B **126**
Bothwell Ho. ML3: Ham	4A **142**
Bothwell La. G12: Glas	1C **82**
	(off Glasgow St.)
G2: Glas	4E **83** (5B **4**)
Bothwell Pk. Ind. Est.
G71: Udd	2E **125**
Bothwellpark Pl. ML4: Bell	1H **125**
Bothwellpark Rd. G71: Both	5F **125**
Bothwell Pl. ML5: Coat	4B **90**
PA2: Pais	5C **96**
Bothwell Rd. G71: Udd	2D **124**
ML3: Ham	2G **141**
ML8: Carl	1E **165**
Bothwell St. G2: Glas	4E **83** (5B **4**)
G72: Camb	1G **121**
ML3: Ham	4G **141**
Bothwick Way PA2: Pais	5C **96**
Boulevard, The G66: Len	2C **6**
Bourhill Ct. ML2: Wis	1D **156**
Bourne Ct. PA4: Inch	2H **57**
Bourne Cres. PA4: Inch	2H **57**
Bourne St. ML3: Ham	6B **142**
Bourock Sq. G78: Barr	6F **115**
Bourtree Rd. ML3: Ham	1C **152**
Bouverie St. G14: Glas	3G **59**
G73: Ruth	6B **104**
Bowden Dr. G52: Glas	5B **80**
Bowden Pk. G75: E Kil	3E **149**
Bower St. G12: Glas	6C **62**
Bowerwalls St. G78: Barr	3F **115**
Bowes Cres. G69: Bail	1F **107**
Bowfield Av. G52: Glas	5H **79**
Bowfield Cres. G52: Glas	5H **79**
Bowfield Dr. G52: Glas	5H **79**
Bowfield Path G52: Glas	5H **79**
Bowfield Pl. G52: Glas	5H **79**
Bowhousebrae Rd. ML6: Gart	1E **113**
Bowhouse Dr. G45: Ruth	2C **120**
Bowhouse Gdns. G45: Ruth	2C **120**
Bowhouse Gro. G45: Glas	3C **120**
Bowhouse Pl. G45: Glas	3C **120**
Bowhouse Rd. ML6: Gart	6E **93**
Bowie St. G82: Dumb	4E **17**
BOWLING	5B **20**
Bowling Grn. La. G14: Glas	6D **60**
	(off Westland Dr.)
Bowling Grn. Rd. G14: Glas	6D **60**
G32: Glas	1D **106**
G44: Glas	2E **119**
G69: Chry	1B **68**
Bowling Grn. St. ML4: Bell	2D **126**
Bowling Grn. Vw. G72: Flem	3F **123**
Bowling Station (Rail)	5A **20**
Bowling St. ML5: Coat	4B **90**
Bowmanflat ML9: Lark	2E **161**
Bowmont Gdns. G12: Glas	6A **62**
Bowmont Hill G64: B'rig	3C **48**
Bowmont Pl. G72: Camb	2C **122**
G75: E Kil	4A **148**
Bowmont Ter. G12: Glas	6A **62**
Bowmore Gdns. G71: Tann	5C **108**
G73: Ruth	4G **121**
Bowyer Vennel ML4: Bell	1B **126**
Boyd Dr. ML1: Moth	2D **142**
Boydstone Pl. G46: T'bnk	2G **117**

Boydstone Rd. G43: Glas, T'bnk	1E **117**
G53: Glas	1E **117**
Boyd St. G42: Glas	4F **103**
Boylestone Rd. G78: Barr	3C **114**
Boyle St. G81: Clyd	1F **59**
Boyndie Path G34: Glas	3H **87**
Boyndie St. G34: Glas	3H **87**
Brabloch Cres. PA3: Pais	5B **78**
Bracadale Dr. G69: Bail	1B **108**
Bracadale Gdns. G69: Bail	1B **108**
Bracadale Gro. G69: Bail	1A **108**
Bracadale Rd. G69: Bail	1A **108**
Brackenbrae Av. G64: B'rig	5A **48**
Brackenbrae Rd. G64: B'rig	6B **48**
Brackendene PA6: Hous	2D **74**
Brackenhill Dr. ML3: Ham	4F **153**
Brackenhill Rd. ML8: Law	5E **159**
Brackenhirst Gdns. ML6: Glenm	3F **71**
Brackenhirst Rd. ML6: Glenm	3F **71**
Brackenhurst St. G82: Dumb	1H **17**
Brackenrig Rd. G46: T'bnk	5E **117**
Bracken St. G22: Glas	3F **63**
ML1: New S	4A **128**
Bracken Ter. G71: Both	4E **125**
Bracken Way ML9: Lark	4G **161**
	(off Donaldson Rd.)
Brackla Av. G81: Clyd	1G **59**
Bradda Av. G73: Ruth	3E **121**
Bradfield Av. G12: Glas	4A **62**
Bradshaw Cres. ML3: Ham	6C **140**
Brady Cres. G69: Mood	4E **53**
BRAEDALE	3D **142**
Braedale ML3: Ham	6E **141**
Braedale Av. ML1: Moth	3D **142**
ML6: Air	4B **92**
Braedale Cres. ML2: Newm	4F **147**
Braedale Pl. ML2: Newm	4G **147**
Braeface Rd. G67: Cumb	3G **35**
Braefield Dr. G46: T'bnk	4G **117**
Braefoot Av. G62: Miln	5G **25**
Braefoot Ct. ML8: Law	6D **158**
Braefoot Cres. ML8: Law	1H **163**
PA2: Pais	6B **98**
BRAEHEAD	6H **135**
Braehead G72: Blan	3B **140**
Braehead Arena	6A **60**
Braehead Av. G62: Miln	4F **25**
G78: Neil	2D **130**
G81: Dun	6C **22**
ML5: Coat	2H **109**
ML9: Lark	3C **160**
Braehead Cres. G81: Dun	6C **22**
Braehead Curling & Ice Rinks	6A **60**
Braehead Dr. ML4: Bell	3B **126**
Braehead Ind. Est. PA4: Renf	1H **79**
Braehead Loan ML8: Carl	5H **165**
	(off Charles Cres.)
Braehead Pl. ML4: Bell	3B **126**
Braehead Quad. G78: Neil	2D **130**
ML1: N'hill	3D **128**
Braehead Rd. G67: Cumb	2B **36**
G74: T'hall	6G **135**
G81: Dun	6C **22**
PA2: Pais	6G **97**
Braehead Shop. Cen. G51: Glas	6A **60**
Braehead St. G5: Glas	2H **103**
G66: Kirk	4C **30**
Braemar Av. G81: Clyd	3B **42**
Braemar Ct. G44: Glas	3C **118**
Braemar Cres. G61: Bear	5F **45**
ML8: Carl	2G **165**
PA2: Pais	4B **98**
Braemar Dr. PA5: Eld	4H **95**
Braemar Rd. G73: Ruth	4G **121**
PA4: Inch	2H **57**
Braemar St. G42: Glas	6D **102**
ML3: Ham	3F **141**
Braemar Vw. G81: Clyd	2B **42**
Braemore Gdns. G22: Glas	5H **63**
Braemount Av. PA2: Pais	6G **97**
Braes Av. G81: Clyd	6F **43**
Braesburn Ct. G67: Cumb	5F **15**
Braesburn Pl. G67: Cumb	5F **15**
Braesburn Rd. G67: Cumb	5F **15**

Braeside Av. G62: Miln 5G **25**
 G69: Mood 5D **52**
 G73: Ruth 6E **105**
Braeside Cres. G69: Barg 6D **88**
 G78: Barr 6G **115**
Braeside Dr. G78: Barr 6F **115**
 G82: Dumb 2H **17**
Braeside Gdns. ML3: Ham 3A **154**
Braeside La. ML9: Lark 1F **161**
 (off Carrick Pl.)
Braeside Pl. G72: Camb 3B **122**
Braeside Rd. ML1: N'hill 3D **128**
Braeside St. G20: Glas 5D **62**
Braeside Way ML9: Lark 4F **161**
 (off Keir Hardie Rd.)
Braes o'Yetts G66: Kirk 5G **31**
Braeview Av. PA2: Pais 6F **97**
Braeview Dr. PA2: Pais 6F **97**
Braeview Gdns. PA2: Pais 6F **97**
Brae Vw. Pl. G74: E Kil 5B **138**
Braeview Rd. PA2: Pais 6F **97**
Braid Av. ML1: Cle 6E **129**
Braidbar Ct. G46: Giff 4A **118**
Braidbar Farm Rd. G46: Giff 3B **118**
 (not continuous)
Braidbar Rd. G46: Giff 4A **118**
Braidcraft Pl. G53: Glas 5C **100**
Braidcraft Rd. G53: Glas 4C **100**
Braidcraft Ter. G53: Glas 4D **100**
BRAIDFAULD 2G **105**
Braidfauld Gdns. G32: Glas 2H **105**
Braidfauld Pl. G32: Glas 3H **105**
Braidfauld St. G32: Glas 3H **105**
Braidfield Gro. G81: Hard 2D **42**
Braidfield Rd. G81: Hard 2D **42**
Braidholm Cres. G46: Giff 4A **118**
Braidholm Rd. G46: Giff 4A **118**
Braidhurst Ind. Est. ML1: Moth . . 6F **127**
Braidhurst Sports Barn 6F **127**
Braidhurst St. ML1: Moth 1G **143**
Braidley Cres. G75: E Kil 6G **149**
Braidpark Dr. G46: Giff 4B **118**
Braids Circle PA2: Pais 4A **98**
Braids Dr. G53: Glas 4H **99**
Braids Ga. PA2: Pais 4H **97**
Braid Sq. G4: Glas 1E **83** (1B **4**)
Braids Rd. PA2: Pais 4A **98**
Braid St. G4: Glas 1E **83**
Braidwood Pl. PA3: Lin 5F **75**
Braidwood St. ML2: Wis 2A **146**
Bramah Av. G75: E Kil 4H **149**
Bramble Ct. G66: Len 3E **7**
Brambling Ct. ML2: Wis 2F **157**
Bramley Pl. G66: Lenz 3E **51**
 ML6: Air 5E **93**
Brampton G75: E Kil 5B **148**
Branchalfield Dr. ML2: Wis 5C **146**
Branchalmuir Cres.
 ML2: Newm 3D **147**
Branchal Rd. ML2: Wis 4B **146**
Branchock Av. G72: Camb 3D **122**
Brancumhall Rd. G74: E Kil 6D **138**
Brandon Arc. ML1: Moth 3G **143**
Brandon Ct. ML3: Ham 5G **141**
Brandon Dr. G61: Bear 6E **25**
Brandon Gdns. G72: Camb 2G **121**
Brandon Ho. ML3: Ham 4A **142**
Brandon Pde. E. ML1: Moth 2G **143**
Brandon Pde. Sth. ML1: Moth. . . . 3G **143**
Brandon Pl. ML4: Bell 4A **126**
Brandon St. G31: Glas 5B **84**
 ML1: Moth 3H **143**
 ML3: Ham 6A **142**
Brandon Way ML5: Coat 1H **109**
Brand Pl. G51: Glas 5A **82**
Brand St. G51: Glas 5A **82**
Brankholm Brae ML3: Ham 5B **140**
Branklyn Cl. G13: Glas 3D **60**
Branklyn Ct. G13: Glas. 3D **60**
Branklyn Cres. G13: Glas. 3D **60**
Branklyn Gro. G13: Glas. 3D **60**
Branklyn Pl. G13: Glas. 3D **60**
BRANKUMHALL. 6C **138**

Brannock Av. ML1: N'hill 3D **128**
Brannock Pl. ML1: N'hill 3D **128**
Brannock Rd. ML1: N'hill. 4D **128**
Brassey St. G20: Glas 3C **62**
Breadalbane Cres. ML1: Moth. . . . 6F **127**
Breadalbane Gdns. G73: Ruth . . . 3F **121**
Breadalbane St. G3: Glas 3D **82**
Breadie Dr. G62: Miln. 5F **25**
Breamish Pl. G75: E Kil 5B **148**
Bream Pl. PA6: C'lee 3D **74**
Brechin Pl. G64: B'rig 6E **49**
Brechin St. G3: Glas. 3C **82**
Breck Av. PA2: Pais 6B **96**
BREDILAND 4E **97**
Brediland Rd. PA2: Pais 6C **96**
 PA3: Lin 5G **75**
Bredin Way ML1: Moth 1D **142**
Bredisholm Cres. G71: View 4G **109**
Bredisholm Dr. G69: Bail 1A **108**
Bredisholm Rd. G69: Bail 1A **108**
 (not continuous)
 G69: Barg 1D **108**
 (not continuous)
Bredisholm Ter. G69: Bail 1A **108**
Bredland Rd. PA2: Pais 3E **97**
Bremners Cotts. G81: Dun. 1B **42**
Brenfield Av. G44: Glas 3D **118**
Brenfield Dr. G44: Glas 3D **118**
Brenfield Rd. G44: Glas 3D **118**
 G44: Neth 3D **118**
Brent Av. G46: T'bnk 2F **117**
Brent Ct. G74: E Kil 6G **137**
Brent Cres. PA6: C'lee 3C **74**
Brent Dr. G46: T'bnk 2F **117**
Brent Gdns. G46: T'bnk 2F **117**
Brent Rd. G46: T'bnk 2F **117**
 G74: E Kil 6G **137**
Brent Way G46: T'bnk. 2F **117**
Brentwood Av. G53: Glas 3A **116**
Brentwood Dr. G53: Glas 3B **116**
Brentwood Sq. G53: Glas 3B **116**
Brereton St. G42: Glas 4G **103**
Bressay G74: E Kil 6G **137**
Bressay Rd. G33: Glas 5E **87**
Bressay Wynd ML2: Newm 3D **146**
 (off Tiree Cres.)
Breval Cres. G81: Dun, Hard 6C **22**
Brewery St. PA3: John 2F **95**
Brewster Av. PA3: Pais. 4C **78**
Briar Bank G66: Milt C. 6B **8**
Briarbush Way G72: Blan 1A **140**
Briarcroft Dr. G33: Glas 2F **65**
Briarcroft Pl. G33: Glas 3G **65**
Briarcroft Rd. G33: Glas 3F **65**
Briar Dr. G81: Clyd. 3D **42**
Briar Gdns. G43: Glas 2B **118**
Briar Gro. G43: Glas. 2B **118**
Briarlea Dr. G46: Giff 3A **118**
Briar Neuk G64: B'rig 1D **64**
Briar Rd. G43: Glas 2B **118**
 G66: Kirk. 5F **31**
Briar Wlk. G66: Kirk. 5G **31**
Briarwell La. G62: Miln 4H **25**
Briarwell Rd. G62: Miln. 4H **25**
Briarwood Ct. G32: Glas 3E **107**
Briarwood Gdns. G32: Glas 3E **107**
Briarwood Rd. ML2: Wis 5E **145**
Brick La. PA3: Pais 6B **78**
Bridgebar St. G78: Barr 3G **115**
Bridgeburn Dr. G69: Mood. 5C **52**
Bridgeford Av. ML4: Bell 6E **111**
Bridgegait G62: Miln 5A **26**
Bridgegate G1: Glas 5G **83**
Bridgegate Path G1: Glas 5H **83**
 (off Saltmarket)
BRIDGEND 4C **52**
Bridgend PA7: B'ton. 4G **39**
Bridgend Cotts. G66: Kirk 6G **31**
Bridgend Ct. G68: C'cry 2F **15**
Bridgend Cres. G69: Mood 5C **52**
Bridgend Pl. G69: Mood 5C **52**
Bridgend Rd. PA5: Eld 2A **96**
Bridgend Vw. ML8: Carl 4F **165**
BRIDGE OF WEIR 3F **73**

Bridge of Weir Rd. PA11: Bri W 4G **73**
 PA3: Lin 6H **75**
 PA5: Brkfld 6C **74**
 PA6: Hous 2A **74**
Bridge Pl. G62: Miln 4G **25**
Bridge St. G5: Glas. 5F **83**
 G72: Camb 1A **122**
 G81: Clyd 4A **42**
 G82: Dumb 4E **17**
 ML2: Wis 6E **145**
 ML3: Ham 1G **153**
 PA1: Pais 1A **98**
 PA3: Pais 5A **76**
Bridge Street Station (Und.) 6F **83**
BRIDGETON 1B **104**
Bridgeton Bus. Cen. G40: Glas . . . 6B **84**
Bridgeton Cross G40: Glas. 6B **84**
Bridgeton Station (Rail) 1B **104**
Bridgewater Ind. Pk. PA8: Ersk . . . 5F **41**
Bridgewater Shop. Cen.
 PA8: Ersk 5F **41**
Bridgeway Ct. G66: Kirk. 6F **31**
Bridgeway Pl. G66: Kirk. 6F **31**
Bridgeway Rd. G66: Kirk 6F **31**
Bridgeway Ter. G66: Kirk 6F **31**
Bridie Ter. G74: E Kil 5C **138**
Brierie Av. PA6: C'lee 2B **74**
Brierie Gdns. PA6: C'lee 3B **74**
Brierie Hill Ct. PA6: C'lee 3B **74**
Brierie Hill Gro. PA6: C'lee 3B **74**
Brierie Hill Rd. PA6: C'lee 3A **74**
Brierie La. PA6: C'lee. 3A **74**
Brigbrae Av. ML4: Bell 4E **127**
Brigham Pl. G23: Glas 1C **62**
Brighton Pl. G51: Glas. 5H **81**
Brighton St. G51: Glas 5H **81**
Brightside Av. G71: Udd 2D **124**
Bright St. G21: Glas 2B **84**
Brig o'Lea Ter. G78: Neil 3D **130**
Brigside Gdns. ML3: Ham 1C **154**
Brisbane Ct. G46: Giff 4B **118**
Brisbane Rd. PA7: B'ton 4H **39**
Brisbane St. G42: Glas 6E **103**
 G81: Clyd 3H **41**
Brisbane Ter. G75: E Kil 4E **149**
Britannia Way G81: Clyd 5D **42**
 PA4: Renf 2E **79**
Briton St. G51: Glas 4H **81**
Brittain Way ML1: Holy 6H **111**
Broadcroft G66: Kirk. 4C **30**
 (not continuous)
Broadcroft Rd. G66: Kirk 4C **30**
Broadford St. G4: Glas. 1G **83**
Broadholm St. G22: Glas 3F **63**
Broadleys Av. G64: B'rig 4B **48**
Broadlie Ct. G78: Neil 2D **130**
Broadlie Dr. G13: Glas. 3A **60**
Broadlie Rd. G78: Neil. 2C **130**
Broadloan PA4: Renf 1E **79**
Broadmeadow Ind. Est.
 G82: Dumb 3F **17**
Broadmoss Av. G77: Newt M 5A **134**
Broad Sq. G72: Blan. 1A **140**
Broad St. G40: Glas 6B **84**
Broadway, The ML2: Wis 5E **145**
Broadwood Bus. Pk. G68: Cumb . . 5B **34**
Broadwood Dr. G44: Glas 1F **119**
BROADWOOD RDBT. 5B **34**
Broadwood Stadium 4B **34**
Brockburn Cres. G53: Glas. 5B **100**
Brockburn Rd. G53: Glas 3A **100**
Brockburn Ter. G53: Glas 5C **100**
Brocklin Pk. G75: E Kil. 4A **148**
Brock Oval G53: Glas 1C **116**
Brock Pl. G53: Glas 6C **100**
Brock Rd. G53: Glas. 1B **116**
Brock Ter. G53: Glas 1C **116**
Brockville St. G32: Glas. 5H **85**
Brodick Av. ML1: Moth 2D **142**
Brodick Dr. G74: E Kil 6F **137**
Brodick Pl. G77: Newt M 5A **132**
Brodick Sq. G64: B'rig 1E **65**
Brodick St. G21: Glas. 2C **84**
Brodie Pk. Av. PA2: Pais 3A **98**

Brodie Pk. Cres. PA2: Pais 3H 97
Brodie Pk. Gdns. PA2: Pais 3A 98
Brodie Pl. G74: E Kil. 6F 137
Brodie Rd. G21: Glas 2F 65
Brogan Cres. ML1: Moth 2D 142
Bromley Dr. G46: Giff. 6A 118
Bromley La. G46: Giff 6A 118
Bron Way G67: Cumb. 4A 36
Brookbank Ter. ML8: Carl 4G 165
BROOKFIELD 6D 74
Brookfield Av. G33: Glas 2F 65
Brookfield Cnr. G33: Glas. 2F 65
Brookfield Dr. G33: Glas. 2F 65
Brookfield Gdns. G33: Glas 2F 65
Brookfield Ga. G33: Glas. 2F 65
Brookfield Pl. G33: Glas 2G 65
Brooklands E Kil 2C 148
Brooklands Av. G71: Udd 6C 108
Brooklea Dr. G46: Giff 2A 118
Brooklime Dr. G74: E Kil 5E 137
Brooklime Gdns. G74: E Kil 5E 137
Brooklyn Pl. ML2: Over 5H 157
Brookside St. G40: Glas. 6C 84
Brook St. G40: Glas 6B 84
    G81: Clyd 3B 42
BROOM 4H 133
Broom Av. PA8: Ersk. 2F 57
Broomburn Dr. G77: Newt M 5F 133
Broom Cliff G77: Newt M 6F 133
Broom Cres. G75: E Kil. 6F 149
    G78: Barr 2C 114
Broomcroft Rd. G77: Newt M 3G 133
Broom Dr. G81: Clyd 3C 42
    ML9: Lark. 6A 156
Broomdyke Way PA3: Pais. 3H 77
Broomelton Rd. ML3: Ham 5A 160
Broomfauld Gdns. G82: Dumb 3G 17
                                (not continuous)
Broomfauld Ind. Est. G82: Dumb . . . 4F 17
Broomfield PA6: Hous 2D 74
Broomfield Av. G72: Camb. 6F 105
    G77: Newt M. 6F 133
Broomfield Ct. G21: Glas 6E 65
Broomfield La. G21: Glas. 4B 64
Broomfield Pl. G21: Glas 4B 64
Broomfield Rd. G21: Glas 4B 64
    G46: Giff. 3G 133
    ML9: Lark 5F 161
Broomfield St. ML6: Air. 4B 92
Broomfield Ter. G71: Tann 4D 108
Broomfield Wlk. G66: Kirk. 5D 30
Broom Gdns. G66: Lenz 1B 50
BROOMHILL
    Glasgow 6F 61
    Kirkintilloch 3E 31
Broomhill Av. G11: Glas 1F 81
    G32: Carm 5B 106
    G77: Newt M. 5F 133
Broomhill Ct. G66: Kirk 4D 30
                                    (off Eastside)
    ML9: Lark 3E 161
Broomhill Cres. ML4: Bell 4B 126
    PA8: Ersk 2F 57
Broomhill Dr. G11: Glas 6F 61
    G73: Ruth. 2D 120
    G82: Dumb. 2H 17
Broomhill Farm M. G66: Kirk. 4E 31
Broomhill Gdns. G11: Glas. 6F 61
    G77: Newt M. 5F 133
Broomhill Ga. ML9: Lark 3E 161
Broomhill Ind. Est. G66: Kirk. 3E 31
Broomhill La. G11: Glas. 6F 61
Broomhill Path G11: Glas. 1F 81
                                (off Broomhill Dr.)
Broomhill Pl. G11: Glas 1F 81
Broomhill Rd. ML9: Lark. 3D 160
Broomhill Ter. G11: Glas. 1F 81
Broomhill Vw. ML9: Lark. 3C 160
BROOMHOUSE 3H 107
Broomieknowe Dr. G73: Ruth 1D 120
Broomieknowe Gdns. G73: Ruth. . . 1C 120
Broomieknowe Rd. G73: Ruth. . . . 1D 120
Broomielaw G1: Glas 5E 83 (6A 4)
Broomknoll St. ML6: Air 4A 92

Broomknowe G68: Cumb 2F 35
Broomknowes Av. G66: Lenz 3E 51
Broomknowes Rd. G21: Glas. 5C 64
Broomlands Av. PA8: Ersk. 1H 57
Broomlands Cres. PA8: Ersk 1H 57
Broomlands Gdns. PA8: Ersk 1H 57
Broomlands Rd. G67: Cumb 5A 36
Broomlands St. PA1: Pais 1F 97
Broomlands Way PA8: Ersk. 1A 58
Broomlea Cres. PA4: Inch 2G 57
Broomlee Rd. G67: Cumb 1H 55
Broomloan Ct. G51: Glas. 6G 81
Broomloan Pl. G51: Glas. 5G 81
Broomloan Rd. G51: Glas 5G 81
Broompark Av. G72: Blan 3A 140
Broompark Cir. G31: Glas 4B 84
Broompark Cres. ML6: Air 1A 92
Broompark Dr. G31: Glas 4B 84
    G77: Newt M 4G 133
    PA4: Inch 2H 57
Broompark La. G31: Glas. 4B 84
Broompark Rd. G72: Blan 2A 140
    ML2: Wis 5D 144
Broompark St. G31: Glas. 4B 84
Broom Path G69: Bail. 2F 107
Broom Pl. G43: Glas 2B 118
    ML1: N'hill 3C 128
    ML5: Coat. 2B 110
    PA11: Bri W 4G 73
Broom Rd. G43: Glas 2B 118
    G67: Cumb. 6D 14
    G77: Newt M 3G 133
Broom Rd. E. G77: Newt M 6G 133
Broomside Cres. ML1: Moth 5G 143
Broomside St. ML1: Moth 5G 143
Broomstone Av. G77: Newt M 6F 133
Broom Ter. PA5: John 4F 95
Broomton Rd. G21: Glas 2E 65
Broomvale Dr. G77: Newt M 4F 133
Broomward Dr. PA5: John 2H 95
Brora Cres. ML3: Ham 3D 152
Brora Dr. G46: Giff 5B 118
    G61: Bear. 3H 45
    PA4: Renf 6G 59
Brora Gdns. G64: B'rig. 6D 48
Brora Rd. G64: B'rig 6D 48
Brora St. G33: Glas 2F 85
Broughton G75: E Kil 6G 149
Broughton Dr. G23: Glas 1C 62
Broughton Gdns. G23: Glas. 6D 46
Broughton Pl. ML3: Ham 6E 141
    ML5: Coat 2D 110
Broughton Rd. G23: Glas. 1C 62
Brouster Ga. G74: E Kil 2G 149
Brouster Hill G74: E Kil 2G 149
Brouster Pl. G74: E Kil 2G 149
Brown Av. G81: Clyd 1F 59
    G82: Dumb. 1C 18
Brownhill Rd. G43: Glas 3H 117
Brownhill Vw. ML2: Newm 3H 147
Brownieside Pl. ML6: Plain 1G 93
Brownieside Rd. ML6: Plain 1H 93
Brownlee Rd. ML8: Carl, Law 1D 162
Brownlie St. G42: Glas 5F 103
Brown Pl. G72: Camb. 1A 122
Brown Rd. G67: Cumb 3H 35
BROWNSBURN 1C 112
Brownsburn Ind. Est. ML6: Air 6B 92
Brownsburn Rd. ML6: Air 1B 112
Brownsdale Rd. G73: Ruth 6B 104
Brownsfield Cres. PA4: Inch 4F 57
Brownsfield Rd. PA4: Inch 4F 57
Brownshill Av. ML5: Coat 1B 110
Brownside Av. G72: Camb. 2G 121
    G78: Barr 2C 114
    PA2: Pais 6G 97
Brownside Cres. G78: Barr 2C 114
    G78: Barr 2C 114
Brownside Dr. G13: Glas 3A 59
    G78: Barr 2C 114
Brownside Gro. G78: Barr 2C 114
Brownside M. G72: Camb 2G 121
Brownside Rd. G73: Ruth. 2F 121
Brownsland Ct. G69: G'csh 3D 68
Brown's La. PA1: Pais 1A 98

Brown St. G2: Glas 4E 83 (6B 4)
    ML1: Moth 1H 143
    ML2: Newm 5E 147
    ML3: Ham 1A 154
    ML5: Coat. 6C 90
    ML8: Carl 2F 165
    ML9: Lark 1E 161
    PA1: Pais 6G 77
    PA4: Renf 1D 78
Bruar Way ML2: Newm 3D 146
                                (off Tiree Cres.)
Bruce Av. ML1: Moth 2F 143
    PA3: Pais 4C 78
    PA5: John 5E 95
Bruce Ct. ML6: Air 3E 93
Brucefield Pl. G34: Glas 3B 88
BRUCEHILL 3C 16
Bruce Ho. G67: Cumb 2H 35
Bruce Loan ML2: Over 5A 158
Bruce Pl. G75: E Kil 4H 149
Bruce Rd. G41: Glas. 1C 102
    ML1: New S 5B 128
    PA3: Pais 5C 78
    PA4: Renf 2C 78
    PA7: B'ton 3G 39
Bruce's Loan ML9: Lark. 3G 161
                                (off Keir Hardie Rd.)
Bruce St. G81: Clyd 6D 42
    G82: Dumb. 5G 17
    ML4: Bell 2D 126
    ML5: Coat 3D 90
    ML6: Plain 1G 93
Bruce Ter. G72: Blan 6C 124
    G75: E Kil 4H 149
Brunel Way G75: E Kil 3H 149
Brunstane Rd. G34: Glas. 2G 87
Brunswick Cen. G21: Glas 4D 64
Brunswick Ho. G81: Clyd 1H 41
Brunswick La. G1: Glas. 4G 83 (6F 5)
Brunswick St. G1: Glas 4G 83 (6F 5)
Brunton St. G44: Glas 2D 118
Bruntsfield Av. G53: Glas. 4B 116
Bruntsfield Gdns. G53: Glas 4B 116
Bryan St. ML3: Ham. 4F 141
Bryce Gdns. ML9: Lark 1E 161
Bryce Pl. G75: E Kil 5E 149
Brydson Pl. PA3: Lin 5H 75
Bryson Ct. ML3: Ham 4H 153
Bryson St. G81: Faif. 6G 23
Buccleuch Av. G52: Hill 3G 79
    G76: Clar 2B 134
Buccleuch Ct. G61: Bear 6E 25
Buccleuch La. G3: Glas. 2E 83 (2B 4)
Buccleuch St. G3: Glas 2E 83 (2A 4)
Buchanan Av. PA7: B'ton 3H 39
Buchanan Bus. Pk. G33: Step 3F 67
Buchanan Ct. G33: Step. 3E 67
                                (not continuous)
Buchanan Cres. G64: B'rig. 1E 65
    ML3: Ham. 1F 153
Buchanan Dr. G61: Bear 3G 45
    G64: B'rig 1E 65
    G66: Lenz 4D 50
    G72: Camb 1G 121
    G73: Ruth. 1D 120
    G77: Newt M 2E 133
    ML8: Law 5E 159
Buchanan Galleries (Shop. Cen.)
    G1: Glas. 3G 83 (4E 5)
Buchanan Gro. G69: Bail 6H 87
Buchanan Pl. G64: Torr 4D 28
Buchanan St. G1: Glas 4E 83 (6D 4)
    G62: Miln 3H 25
    G69: Bail 1H 107
    G82: Dumb. 5G 17
    ML5: Coat. 5A 90
    ML6: Air 4A 92
    PA5: John 3E 95
Buchanan Street Station (Und.)
    . . . . 3G 83 (4E 5)
Buchanan Way PA5: John 3E 95

Buchandyke Rd. G74: E Kil	5B **138**	
Buchanen Gdns. G32: Glas	3E **107**	
Buchan Ga. G74: E Kil	6B **138**	
Buchan Ho. G67: Cumb	2H **35**	
Buchan Rd. ML1: New S	4A **128**	
Buchan St. ML2: Wis	3H **145**	
ML3: Ham	3G **153**	
Buchan Ter. G72: Camb	4G **121**	
Buchlyvie Gdns. G64: B'rig	2B **64**	
Buchlyvie Path G34: Glas	4H **87**	
Buchlyvie Rd. PA1: Pais	6G **79**	
Buchlyvie St. G34: Glas	4H **87**	
Buckie PA8: Ersk	4E **41**	
Buckie Wlk. ML4: Bell	1C **126**	
Buckingham Ct. ML3: Ham	5C **140**	
Buckingham Dr. G32: Carm	5B **106**	
G73: Ruth	6F **105**	
Buckingham St. G12: Glas	6B **62**	
Buckingham Ter. G12: Glas	6B **62**	
Bucklaw Gdns. G52: Glas	1C **100**	
Bucklaw Pl. G52: Glas	1C **100**	
Bucklaw Ter. G52: Glas	1C **100**	
Buckley St. G22: Glas	3H **63**	
Bucksburn Rd. G21: Glas	5E **65**	
Buckthorne Pl. G53: Glas	4B **116**	
Buddon St. G40: Glas	1E **105**	
Budhill Av. G32: Glas	6B **86**	
Budshaw Av. ML6: Chap	3C **112**	
Bulldale Ct. G14: Glas	4H **59**	
Bulldale St. G14: Glas	3G **59**	
Buller Cres. G72: Blan	5A **124**	
Bullionslaw Dr. G73: Ruth	1F **121**	
Bulloch Av. G46: Giff	5B **118**	
Bull Rd. G76: Busby	3D **134**	
Bullwood Av. G53: Glas	5H **99**	
Bullwood Ct. G53: Glas	5H **99**	
Bullwood Dr. G53: Glas	4H **99**	
Bullwood Gdns. G53: Glas	4H **99**	
Bullwood Pl. G53: Glas	4H **99**	
Bunbury Ter. G75: E Kil	3E **149**	
Bunessan St. G52: Glas	6F **81**	
Bunhouse Rd. G3: Glas	2A **82**	
Burch Hall La. G11: Glas	1H **81**	
Burghead Dr. G51: Glas	3E **81**	
Burghead Pl. G51: Glas	3E **81**	
Burgher St. G31: Glas	6E **85**	
Burgh Hall St. G11: Glas	1H **81**	
Burgh La. *G12: Glas*	*6B 62*	
(off Cresswell St.)		
Burleigh Rd. G71: Both	4F **125**	
Burleigh St. G51: Glas	3G **81**	
ML5: Coat	2D **110**	
Burley Pl. G74: E Kil	1B **148**	
Burlington Av. G12: Glas	3H **61**	
Burmola St. G22: Glas	5F **63**	
Burnacre Gdns. G71: Udd	6C **108**	
Burnawn Ga. G33: Glas	2F **65**	
Burnawn Gro. G33: Glas	2F **65**	
Burnawn Pl. G33: Glas	2F **65**	
BURNBANK	4E **141**	
Burnbank Braes ML8: Carl	4F **165**	
Burnbank Cen. ML3: Ham	4E **141**	
Burnbank Dr. G78: Barr	6E **115**	
Burnbank Gdns. G20: Glas	1D **82**	
ML3: Ham	*4E 141*	
(off Burnbank Rd.)		
Burnbank La. G20: Glas	1D **82**	
Burnbank M. G66: Lenz	3D **50**	
Burnbank Pl. G20: Glas	1E **83**	
Burnbank Quad. ML6: Air	3H **91**	
Burnbank Rd. ML3: Ham	4E **141**	
Burnbank St. ML5: Coat	3D **90**	
ML6: Air	3H **91**	
Burnbank Ter. G20: Glas	1D **82**	
G65: Kils	2H **11**	
Burnblea Gdns. ML3: Ham	1A **154**	
Burnblea St. ML3: Ham	1H **153**	
Burnbrae G65: Twe	2D **32**	
Burn Brae G81: Dun	1C **42**	
Burnbrae Av. G61: Bear	6G **25**	
G69: Mood	5D **52**	
PA3: Lin	6A **76**	
Burnbrae Dr. G73: Ruth	2F **121**	
PA3: Lin	2B **96**	

Burnbrae Gdns. G53: Glas	1D **116**	
Burnbrae Pl. G74: E Kil	1E **149**	
Burnbrae Rd. G66: Auch	5E **51**	
G66: Kirk	6H **31**	
G69: Chry, Lenz	3H **51**	
G72: Blan	2A **140**	
PA3: Lin	1H **95**	
Burnbrae St. G21: Glas	5C **64**	
G81: Faif	5F **23**	
ML9: Lark	2D **160**	
Burncleugh Av. G72: Camb	3A **122**	
Burn Cres. ML1: New S	3A **128**	
ML6: Chap	3D **112**	
Burncrooks Av. G61: Bear	6C **24**	
G74: E Kil	1E **149**	
Burncrooks Ct. G81: Dun	1B **42**	
Burndyke Ct. G51: Glas	4H **81**	
Burndyke Sq. G51: Glas	4A **82**	
Burnet Rose Ct. G74: E Kil	5E **137**	
Burnet Rose Gdns.		
G74: E Kil	5E **137**	
Burnet Rose Pl. G74: E Kil	5E **137**	
Burnett Rd. G33: Glas	4E **87**	
Burnfield Av. G46: Giff	3H **117**	
Burnfield Cotts. G46: Giff	3H **117**	
Burnfield Dr. G43: Glas	3H **117**	
Burnfield Gdns. G46: Giff	3A **118**	
Burnfield Rd. G43: Glas	2G **117**	
G46: Giff	3A **118**	
BURNFOOT.	2G **91**	
Burnfoot Cres. G73: Ruth	2F **121**	
PA2: Pais	5G **97**	
Burnfoot Dr. G52: Glas	6B **80**	
Burnfoot Rd. ML6: Air	3G **91**	
Burngill Pl. *PA11: Bri W*	*3F 73*	
(off Kilmalcom Rd.)		
Burngreen G65: Kils	3H **11**	
Burngreen Ter. G67: Cumb	6B **14**	
Burnhall Pl. ML2: Wis	2B **158**	
Burnhall Rd. ML2: Wis	1A **158**	
Burnhall St. ML2: Wis	2B **158**	
Burnham Rd. G14: Glas	5A **60**	
Burnhaven PA8: Ersk	5E **41**	
BURNHEAD.	2G **161**	
Burnhead Rd. G43: Glas	2C **118**	
G68: Cumb	3E **35**	
ML6: Air	1C **92**	
ML9: Lark	2F **161**	
Burnhead St. G71: View	5F **109**	
Burnhill Quad. G73: Ruth	5B **104**	
Burnhill Sports Cen.	5B **104**	
Burnhill St. G73: Ruth	5B **104**	
Burnhouse Brae G77: Newt M	6G **133**	
Burnhouse Cres. ML3: Ham	2F **153**	
Burnhouse Rd. ML3: Ham	2F **153**	
Burnhouse St. G20: Glas	3A **62**	
(not continuous)		
Burniebrae ML6: Air	3G **91**	
Burniebrae Rd. ML6: Chap	2E **113**	
Burn La. ML1: New S	3A **128**	
Burnlea Cres. PA6: Hous	1A **74**	
Burnlip Rd. ML5: Glenb	5C **70**	
ML6: Glenm	5C **70**	
Burnmouth Ct. G33: Glas	5F **87**	
Burnmouth Pl. G61: Bear	2G **45**	
Burnmouth Rd. G33: Glas	5F **87**	
Burnock Pl. G75: E Kil	4A **148**	
Burnpark Av. G71: Udd	6B **108**	
Burn Pl. G72: Camb	6G **105**	
Burn Rd. ML8: Carl	2F **165**	
Burns Av. PA7: B'ton	4H **39**	
Burns Ct. G66: Kirk	4G **31**	
Burn's Cres. ML6: Air	5B **92**	
PA5: John	5E **95**	
Burns Gdns. G72: Blan	6A **124**	
Burns Gro. G46: T'bnk	5G **117**	
BURNSIDE	2E **121**	
Burnside G61: Bear	6C **24**	
Burnside Av. G66: Kirk	6B **30**	
G78: Barr	3D **114**	
ML4: Bell	3E **127**	
ML6: C'bnk	3B **112**	
PA5: Brkfld	6C **74**	

Burnside Ct. G61: Bear	1C **44**	
G73: Ruth	2E **121**	
G81: Clyd	3A **42**	
ML1: Moth	5B **144**	
ML5: Coat	*6B 90*	
(off Kirk St.)		
Burnside Cres. G72: Blan	3C **140**	
G81: Hard	6D **22**	
Burnside Gdns. G76: Clar	2B **134**	
PA10: Kilb	3B **94**	
Burnside Ga. G73: Ruth	2E **121**	
Burnside Gro. PA5: John	3E **95**	
Burnside Ind. Est.		
G65: Kils	3G **11**	
Burnside La. ML3: Ham	1A **154**	
Burnside Pl. G82: Dumb	5H **17**	
ML9: Lark	2F **161**	
PA3: Pais	4E **77**	
(not continuous)		
Burnside Quad. ML1: Holy.	2A **128**	
Burnside Rd. G46: Giff	3H **133**	
G73: Ruth	2E **121**	
ML1: N'hill	3C **128**	
ML5: Coat	2E **91**	
PA5: Eld	4A **96**	
Burnside Station (Rail)	2E **121**	
Burnside St. G82: Dumb	5H **17**	
ML1: Moth	5B **144**	
Burnside Ter. *G82: Dumb*	*5H 17*	
(off Burnside Pl.)		
PA10: Kilb	3B **94**	
Burnside Twr. *ML1: Moth*	*5A 144*	
(off Burnside Ct.)		
Burnside Vw. ML5: Coat	6A **90**	
Burnside Wlk. ML5: Coat	6A **90**	
Burns La. ML6: Chap	2D **112**	
Burns Loan *ML9: Lark*	*1F 161*	
(off Carrick Pl.)		
Burns Pk. G74: E Kil	1A **150**	
Burns Path ML4: Bell	6D **110**	
Burns Rd. G66: Kirk	4F **31**	
G67: Cumb	3B **36**	
ML6: Chap	1D **112**	
Burns St. G4: Glas	1F **83**	
G81: Clyd	3A **42**	
ML3: Ham	1H **153**	
Burns Way ML1: N'hill	3C **128**	
Burntbroom Dr. G69: Bail	2F **107**	
Burntbroom Gdns. G69: Bail	2F **107**	
Burntbroom St. G33: Glas	3D **86**	
Burn Ter. G72: Camb	6G **105**	
Burnthills Ind. Est. *PA5: John*	*2F 95*	
(off High St.)		
Burntshields Rd. PA10: Kilb	2A **94**	
Burn Vw. G67: Cumb	2C **36**	
Burnwood Dr. ML6: Air	5G **93**	
Burra Gdns. G64: B'rig	5F **49**	
Burrell Collection Mus.	4H **101**	
Burrell Ct. G41: Glas	3A **102**	
Burrell's La. G4: Glas	4A **84** (5H **5**)	
Burrelton Rd. G43: Glas	1D **118**	
Burton La. G42: Glas	4E **103**	
ML8: Carl	3E **165**	
BUSBY.	3D **134**	
Busby Equitation Cen.	5E **135**	
Busby Rd. G76: Clar	1C **134**	
G76: Crmck	3G **135**	
ML4: Bell	4B **126**	
Busby Station (Rail)	4E **135**	
Bush Cres. ML2: Wis	1A **158**	
Bushelhead Rd. ML8: Carl	6E **165**	
Bushes Av. PA2: Pais	4H **97**	
Busheyhill St. G72: Camb	2A **122**	
Bute G74: E Kil	2C **150**	
Bute Av. ML1: Moth	2E **143**	
PA4: Renf	2F **79**	
Bute Cres. G60: Old K	2G **41**	
G61: Bear	5F **45**	
PA2: Pais	6H **97**	
Bute Dr. G60: Old K	2G **41**	
PA5: John	4D **94**	
Bute Gdns. G12: Glas	1B **82**	
G44: Neth	3D **118**	
G60: Old K	1G **41**	

Bute La. G12: Glas 1B **82**
  PA3: Pais 4F **77**
Bute Pl. G60: Old K 1G **41**
Bute Rd. G66: Kirk. 5H **31**
  PA3: Glas A 2G **77**
Bute St. ML3: Ham 3F **141**
  ML5: Coat 1D **110**
Bute Ter. G71: View 6F **109**
  G73: Ruth. 2C **120**
Bute Twr. G12: Camb 4G **121**
Butler Wynd ML4: Bell 2B **126**
Butterbiggins Rd. G42: Glas . . 2E **103**
Butterburn Pk. St.
  ML3: Ham 1H **153**
Butterfield Pl. G41: Glas 2E **103**
Buttermere G75: E Kil 6B **148**
Byars Rd. G66: Kirk. 5B **30**
Byrebush Rd. G53: Glas. 4C **100**
Byres Av. PA3: Pais 5C **78**
Byres Cres. PA3: Pais 5C **78**
Byres Rd. G11: Glas. 1A **82**
  ML1: N'hill 3E **129**
  PA5: Eld 3B **96**
Byrestone Av. G77:
  Newt M. 5A **134**
Byron Ct. G71: Both 5F **125**
Byron St. G11: Glas 1E **81**
  G81: Clyd 3C **42**
Byshot Path G22: Glas 5H **63**
Byshot St. G22: Glas 5H **63**

C

Cable Dpt. Rd. G81: Clyd. 5B **42**
CADDER
  Bishopbriggs 2D **48**
  Gilshochill 2D **62**
Cadder Ct. G64: B'rig 2D **48**
Cadder Gro. G20: Glas. 2C **62**
                  (off Cadder Rd.)
Cadder Pl. G20: Glas 2C **62**
Cadder Rd. G20: Glas 1C **62**
  G23: Glas 1C **62**
  G64: B'rig. 2D **48**
Cadder Way G64: B'rig 2D **48**
Cadell Gdns. G74: E Kil 4D **138**
Cadger's Sheuch G65: Kils. 3C **12**
Cadoc St. G72: Camb. 2B **122**
Cadogan Sq. G2: Glas 4E **83** (6B **4**)
Cadogan St. G2: Glas 4E **83** (5B **4**)
Cadzow Av. G46: Giff 1H **133**
Cadzow Bri. ML3: Ham 5A **142**
Cadzow Castle 3C **154**
Cadzow Cres. ML5: Coat 1A **110**
Cadzow Dr. G72: Camb 2H **121**
  ML4: Bell 3F **127**
Cadzow Grn. G74: E Kil 1F **149**
Cadzow Ho. ML3: Ham 4A **142**
Cadzow Ind. Est. ML3: Ham 3H **153**
Cadzow La. ML3: Ham. 5A **142**
Cadzow Pk. ML3: Ham. 5A **142**
Cadzow St. G2: Glas 4E **83** (6A **4**)
  ML1: Moth 3F **143**
  ML3: Ham 5A **142**
  ML9: Lark 1E **161**
Caerlaverock Pl. G72: Blan 3A **140**
Caird Dr. G11: Glas 1H **81**
Caird Gdns. ML3: Ham 4G **141**
Caird Pk. ML3: Ham 4H **141**
Caird St. ML3: Ham 4G **141**
Caird Ter. G61: Bear 6D **24**
             (off Grampian Way)
Cairhill Trad. Est. ML6: Air 5A **92**
Cairn Av. PA4: Renf 2G **79**
Cairnbairn Ct. ML8: Carl 2F **165**
          (off Carranbuie Rd.)
Cairnban St. G51: Glas 5D **80**
Cairnbrook Ind. Est. G34: Glas . . 2A **88**
Cairnbrook Rd. G34: Glas 3A **88**
Cairn Ct. G74: E Kil 5G **137**
  ML1: Moth 4H **143**
Cairncraig St. G40: Glas 1E **105**
Cairndow Av. G44: Glas 3D **118**

Cairndow Av. La. G44: Glas. 3D **118**
Cairndow Ct. G44: Glas 3D **118**
Cairndow Pl. ML2: Wis 2H **157**
Cairn Dr. PA3: Lin 5H **75**
Cairndyke Cres. ML6: Air. 5A **92**
Cairneymount Rd. ML8: Carl 3F **165**
Cairney Pl. ML2: Newm. 3H **147**
Cairngorm Cres. G61: Bear 1B **44**
  G78: Barr 6E **115**
  ML2: Wis 6F **145**
  PA2: Pais 4A **98**
Cairngorm Gdns.
  G68: Cumb. 4D **34**
Cairngorm Rd. G43: Glas. 2A **118**
CAIRNHILL 6H **91**
Cairnhill Av. ML6: Air 6A **92**
Cairnhill Cir. G52: Glas 2H **99**
Cairnhill Ct. ML8: Carl 3F **165**
Cairnhill Cres. ML5: Coat. 2F **111**
Cairnhill Dr. G52: Glas 2H **99**
Cairnhill Pl. G52: Glas. 2H **99**
Cairnhill Rd. G61: Bear 6F **45**
  ML6: Air. 6H **91**
Cairnhope Av. ML6: Air 6H **91**
Cairnlea Dr. G51: Glas. 5H **81**
Cairnlea Gdns. ML4: Bell. 4D **126**
Cairnlea Rd. G62: Miln 4E **25**
Cairnmuir Rd. G73: Ruth. 2H **137**
  G74: Roger 3F **137**
  G76: Crmck, Roger. 4C **136**
Cairnoch Hill G68: Cumb 3E **35**
Cairn Pl. G74: E Kil 5G **137**
Cairnryan G74: E Kil 6F **137**
CAIRNS 3C **122**
Cairns Av. G72: Camb 2B **122**
Cairns Dr. G62: Miln 3G **25**
Cairnsmore Dr. G61: Bear 6B **24**
Cairnsmore Rd. G15: Glas. 5G **43**
Cairns Rd. G72: Camb 3B **122**
  PA7: B'ton 3G **39**
Cairns St. ML1: Moth 3G **143**
Cairn St. G21: Glas 3B **64**
Cairnswell Av. G72: Camb 3C **122**
Cairnswell Pl. G72: Camb 3C **122**
Cairntoul Ct. G68: Cumb 4D **34**
Cairntoul Dr. G14: Glas 3A **60**
Cairntoul Pl. G14: Glas 4A **60**
Cairn Vw. G66: Kirk 6H **31**
  ML6: Air. 5H **91**
Cairnview Rd. G66: Milt C 6B **8**
Cairnwood Dr. ML6: Air 6H **91**
Caithness Rd. G74: E Kil 6C **138**
Caithness St. G20: Glas. 5D **62**
  G4: Glas 1F **83**
  G72: Blan 3A **140**
Cala Sona Ct. ML2: Wis. 3E **157**
Calcots Path G34: Glas 2A **88**
Calcots Pl. G34: Glas. 2A **88**
Caldarvan St. G22: Glas. 6F **63**
Caldeen Rd. ML5: Coat 6D **90**
Calder Av. G78: Barr 6E **115**
  ML2: Newm 3E **147**
  ML5: Coat 1D **110**
CALDERBANK 3B **112**
Calderbank Rd. ML6: Air 1A **112**
Calderbank Ter. ML1: Moth. 2H **143**
Calderbank Vw. G69: Bail 1A **108**
Calderbankview Cotts.
  ML6: C'bnk. 1A **112**
CALDERBRAES 5C **108**
Calderbraes Av. G71: Tann 4C **108**
Calder Ct. ML5: Coat. 1D **110**
              (off Whifflet St.)
Caldercuilt Rd. G20: Glas 1A **62**
  G23: Glas 1A **62**
Calder Dr. G72: Camb 2A **122**
  ML4: Bell 3E **127**
Calder Ga. G64: B'rig. 3B **48**
Calderglen Av. G72: Blan. 4A **124**
Calderglen Country Pk. 6E **139**
Calderglen Country Pk. Vis. Cen.
  . . . . 5D **150**
Calderglen Rd. G74: E Kil 2C **150**
Caldergrove ML1: Moth. 2G **143**

Calderpark G71: Udd 4H **107**
Calderpark Av. G71: Udd. 3H **107**
Calderpark Cres. G71: Udd 3H **107**
Calderpark Ter. G71: Udd 3H **107**
Calder Pl. G69: Bail 1H **107**
Calderrigg Pl. ML6: Air 4E **93**
Calder Rd. G71: View 4H **109**
  G72: Blan 2H **123**
  ML4: Moss 2E **127**
  PA3: Pais 6E **77**
Calderside Gro. G74: E Kil 5E **139**
Calderside Rd. G72: Blan 3D **150**
Calder St. G42: Glas. 3E **103**
  G72: Blan 1B **140**
  ML5: Coat 1D **110**
  ML6: C'bnk 3C **112**
Calder Twr. G74: E Kil 4B **150**
  ML1: Moth 4G **143**
Caldervale St. ML6: Gart 1E **113**
Calder Vw. ML1: Moth. 2H **143**
  ML3: Ham 3F **153**
Calderview Av. ML5: Coat 1F **111**
CALDERWOOD 6B **138**
Calderwood Av. G69: Bail 2G **107**
Calderwood Dr. G69: Bail 2G **107**
  G72: Blan 3B **140**
Calderwood Gdns. G69: Bail . . . 2G **107**
  G74: E Kil 5E **139**
Calderwood Rd. G43: Glas 1B **118**
  G73: Ruth 6E **105**
  G74: E Kil 2A **150**
Calderwood Sq. G74: E Kil 6B **138**
              (off Pollock Pl.)
Caldwell Av. G13: Glas 3A **60**
  PA3: Lin 6F **75**
Caldwell Gro. ML4: Bell. 5C **110**
Caldwell Quad. ML1: Moth 4E **143**
Caldwell Rd. ML8: Carl 5H **165**
Caledonia Av. G5: Glas 2G **103**
  G73: Ruth. 5D **104**
Caledonia Ct. PA3: Pais. 5H **77**
Caledonia Dr. G69: Bail 2H **107**
  ML1: N'hill 3E **129**
Caledonia Gdns. ML8: Carl 2E **165**
Caledonian Av. ML4: Bell 3B **126**
Caledonian Ct. G74: E Kil 3G **149**
Caledonian Cres. G12: Glas. . . . 1C **82**
              (off Otago St.)
Caledonian Pk. ML2: Wis 6D **144**
Caledonian Rd. ML2: Wis 2G **157**
  ML9: Lark 2E **161**
Caledonia Rd. G5: Glas 1F **103**
  G69: Bail 2G **107**
  G81: Clyd 4B **42**
  PA3: Pais 6H **77**
Caledonia Ter. G82: Dumb 4C **16**
Caledonia Wlk. ML3: Ham 2A **154**
         (off Chatelherault Cres.)
Caledonia Way G52: Glas A. 2H **77**
Caledonia Way E. PA3: Glas A . . . 2A **78**
Caledonia Way W. PA3: Glas A . . . 2H **77**
Caledon La. G12: Glas. 1A **82**
           (off Highburgh Rd.)
Caledon St. G12: Glas 1A **82**
Caley Brae G71: Udd 1D **124**
Calfhill Rd. G53: Glas 2B **100**
Calfmuir Rd. G66: Kirk, Lenz. . . . 6G **31**
Calgary Pk. G75: E Kil 3F **149**
Calgary Pl. G75: E Kil. 3F **149**
Calgary St. G4: Glas 2G **83** (2F **5**)
Calico Way G66: Len 2E **7**
Callaghan Wynd G72: Blan 6H **123**
Callander Ct. G68: Cumb. 1H **35**
Callander Rd. G68: Cumb 1H **35**
  ML6: Chap 4D **112**
Callander St. G20: Glas 6E **63**
Callieburn Ct. G64: B'rig 1C **64**
Callieburn Rd. G64: B'rig. 1C **64**
Callon St. ML6: Air 4A **92**
Cally Av. G15: Glas 4A **44**
Calside PA2: Pais. 3H **97**
Calside Av. PA2: Pais 2H **97**
Calside Ct. PA2: Pais 3A **98**

CALTON 5A 84
Calton Entry G40: Glas. 5A 84
    (off Stevenson St.)
Calvay Cres. G33: Glas 4D 86
Calvay Pl. G33: Glas 4E 87
Calvay Rd. G33: Glas 4D 86
Cambourne Rd. G69: Mood. 4D 52
Cambridge Av. G81: Clyd. 4D 42
Cambridge Rd. PA4: Renf 1E 79
Cambridge St. G2: Glas. 3F 83 (3C 4)
    G3: Glas 3F 83 (3C 4)
Camburn St. G32: Glas. 6H 85
Cambusdoon Rd. G33: Glas. . . . 1C 86
Cambuskenneth Gdns. G32: Glas. . 6D 86
Cambuskenneth Pl. G33: Glas. . 1C 86
CAMBUSLANG 1A 122
Cambuslang Bri. G32: Glas. 6A 106
Cambuslang Ind. Pk. G32: Glas. . 5A 106
Cambuslang Investment Pk.
    G32: Glas 5A 106
Cambuslang Rd. G32: Glas. . . . 5H 105
    G72: Camb 5G 105
    (Bogleshole Rd.)
    G72: Camb 6F 105
    (Farmeloan Rd.)
    G73: Ruth. 4D 104
Cambuslang Station (Rail) 1H 121
Cambusmore Pl. G33: Glas 1C 86
CAMBUSNETHAN 6C 146
Cambusnethan St. ML2: Wis. . . . 5C 146
Cambus Pl. G33: Glas 1C 86
Camden St. G5: Glas 1G 103
Camden Ter. G5: Glas 1G 103
Camellia Dr. ML2: Wis. 2E 157
Camelon Cres. G72: Blan. 2B 140
Camelon St. G32: Glas 5H 85
Cameron Av. PA7: B'ton. 3H 39
Cameron Ct. G52: Hill 4H 79
    G73: Ruth. 6C 104
    G81: Clyd 1E 59
    ML6: Air 3E 93
Cameron Cres. G76: Crmck. . . . 2A 136
    ML3: Ham 6F 141
Cameron Dr. G61: Bear 4G 45
    G71: Tann 5E 109
    G77: Newt M 2E 133
Cameronian Dr. ML8: Carl. 4G 165
Cameronian Pl. ML4: Bell 4A 126
Cameronian Way ML9: Lark 4G 161
Cameron Path ML9: Lark. 4G 161
    (off Donaldson Rd.)
Cameron Rd. ML8: Carl. 5H 165
Cameron Sq. G81: Hard. 1E 43
Cameron St. G52: Hill 4G 79
    G81: Clyd 1E 59
    ML1: Moth 3F 143
    ML5: Coat 3D 90
Cameron Way G72: Blan 1B 140
Camie Ct. G66: Kirk 5C 30
CAMLACHIE 6D 84
Camlachie St. G31: Glas 6D 84
    (not continuous)
Campbell Av. G62: Miln. 4G 25
    G82: Dumb 1C 18
    PA7: B'ton 3H 39
Campbell Cres. G71: Both 3E 125
    G77: Newt M 3E 133
Campbell Dr. G61: Bear. 2D 44
    G78: Barr 5E 115
    G82: Dumb 1C 18
Campbell Ho. G67: Cumb 4G 35
Campbell La. ML3: Ham 6A 142
Campbell Pl. G64: Torr 4D 28
    G75: E Kil 4G 149
Campbell St. G20: Glas 2B 62
    ML2: Wis 6H 145
    ML3: Ham 6A 142
    ML4: Bell 2C 126
    PA4: Renf 5F 59
    PA5: John 3F 95
Campbell Ter. G82: Dumb 1C 18
Camphill PA1: Pais 2H 97
Camphill Av. G41: Glas 5C 102
    G66: Kirk 5C 30

Camphill Ct. PA2: Pais 2H 97
Camphill Gdns. PA7: B'ton 4A 40
Camphill Ho. G41: Glas. 4D 102
Campion Rd. ML1: Moth 1G 143
Camp Rd. G69: Bail 6H 87
    G73: Ruth. 3B 104
    ML1: Moth 5G 143
Camps Cres. PA4: Renf 1G 79
Campsie Av. G78: Barr 6E 115
Campsie Ct. G66: Kirk 1C 50
    ML5: Coat 2E 111
    ML9: Lark. 6H 155
Campsie Cres. ML6: Air 3H 91
Campsie Dr. G61: Bear 6D 24
    G62: Miln 3H 25
    G66: Len 5G 7
    PA2: Pais 5H 97
    PA3: Glas A 1A 78
    PA4: Renf 3C 78
Campsie Pl. G69: Chry 1A 68
Campsie Recreation Cen. 3G 7
Campsie Rd. G64: Torr 4E 29
    G66: Kirk 4B 30
    G66: Len 5G 7
    (Rowantree Ter.)
    G66: Len, Milt C 4H 7
    (MacCabe Gdns.)
    ML2: Wis 5E 145
Campsie St. G21: Glas. 4B 64
Campsie Vw. G33: Step. 5D 66
    G66: Kirk 5A 30
    G67: Cumb 2B 36
    G69: Barg 6D 88
    G69: Chry 1A 68
    G71: Tann 5E 109
    G72: Flem 4E 123
    ML3: Ham 1D 152
Campton Pl. G33: Glas. 2B 86
Camp St. ML1: Moth 4G 143
Camstradden Dr. E. G61: Bear. . 3C 44
Camstradden Dr. W. G61: Bear . . 3C 44
Camus Pl. G15: Glas 3H 43
Canal Av. PA5: John 3G 95
Canal Bank G23: Glas. 2E 63
    (off Balmore Rd.)
Canal Gdns. PA5: Eld. 2B 96
Canal La. G66: Kirk 4D 30
    PA4: Renf 5F 59
Canal Rd. PA5: John 3F 95
Canal St. G4: Glas. 2G 83 (1F 5)
    G66: Kirk 4D 30
    G81: Clyd 1D 58
    PA1: Pais 1H 97
    PA4: Renf 5F 59
    PA5: Eld 2B 96
    PA5: John. 2G 95
Canal Ter. PA1: Pais. 1A 98
Canberra Av. G81: Clyd 3H 41
Canberra Ct. G46: Giff 4C 118
Canberra Dr. G75: E Kil 3E 149
Candermill & Marlage Rd.
    ML9: Ashg 6B 162
Cander Rigg G64: B'rig 3C 48
Cander St. ML9: Lark 5F 161
Candimilne Ct. ML8: Carl 4H 165
Candleriggs G1: Glas 4H 83 (6G 5)
Candren Rd. PA3: Lin 6B 76
    PA3: Pais 1E 97
    (not continuous)
Candren Way PA3: Pais 6E 77
Caneluk Av. ML8: Carl 5H 165
Canmore Pl. G31: Glas. 1F 105
Canmore St. G31: Glas 1F 105
Cannerton Cres. G66: Milt C 6B 8
Cannerton Pk. G66: Milt C 6B 8
Cannich Dr. PA2: Pais 4D 98
Cannich Pl. ML2: Newm 3D 146
Canniesburn Dr. G61: Bear 5C 44
Canniesburn Sq. G61: Bear 5F 45
CANNIESBURN TOLL 5F 45
Canniesburn Rd. G61: Bear 4D 44
Canobie Av. G74: E Kil 5H 137
Canobie St. G34: Glas 2B 88

Canon Ct. ML1: Carf 5D 128
Canongate G74: E Kil 5D 138
Canterbury G75: E Kil 5D 148
Cantieslaw Dr. G74: E Kil. 6A 138
Canting Way G51: Glas 4A 82
Canyon Rd. ML2: Wis 1D 156
Capel Av. G77: Newt M 3F 133
Capel Gro. G74: E Kil 6B 138
Capelridge Dr. G74: E Kil. 1B 150
Capelrig Dr. G77: Newt M 1D 132
Capelrig La. G77: Newt M 3D 132
Capelrig Rd. G77: Newt M. 1D 132
Capelrig St. G46: T'bnk 3F 117
Caper House Play Barn 5D 136
Caplaw Pl. ML2: Wis 3F 157
Caplaw Rd. PA2: Pais 6G 97
Caplaw Twr. ML2: Wis 3F 157
Caplethill Rd. PA2: Pais. 6A 98
Caprington Pl. G33: Glas 2A 86
Caprington St. G33: Glas 2A 86
Cara Dr. G51: Glas 3E 81
Caravelle Way PA4: Renf 2F 79
Carbarns ML2: Wis 2D 156
Carbarns E. ML2: Wis 2D 156
Carbarns Rd. ML2: Wis 3C 156
Carbarns W. ML2: Wis 2D 156
Carberry Rd. G41: Glas 3B 102
Carbeth Rd. G62: Miln 4F 25
Carbeth St. G22: Glas. 5F 63
Carbisdale St. G22: Glas. 4A 64
Carbost St. G23: Glas. 6B 46
Carbrach Loan ML2: Newm 3D 146
    (off Tiree Cres.)
CARBRAIN 4A 36
Carbrain Ind. Est.
    G67: Cumb 4B 36
Carbrook St. G21: Glas 2C 84
    PA1: Pais 1G 97
Cardarrach St. G21: Glas 5C 64
Cardean Rd. ML4: Moss 1G 127
Cardell Av. PA2: Pais 2E 97
Cardell Cres. ML6: Chap 3D 112
Cardell Dr. PA2: Pais 2E 97
Cardell Rd. PA2: Pais 2E 97
CARDONALD 6B 80
Cardonald Dr. G52: Glas 1A 100
Cardonald Gdns. G52: Glas 1B 100
Cardonald Pk. G51: Glas 4B 80
Cardonald Pl. Rd.
    G52: Glas 1B 100
Cardonald Station (Rail) 5D 80
Cardowan Dr. G33: Step 4D 66
    G68: Cumb 4A 34
Cardowan Pk. G71: Tann 4F 109
Cardowan Rd. G32: Glas. 5H 85
    G33: Step 3E 67
Cardow Rd. G21: Glas 5E 65
Cardrona St. G33: Glas 6B 66
Cardross Ct. G31: Glas. 4B 84
Cardross Rd. G82: Card, Dumb . . 2A 16
    G82: Dumb 3B 16
Cardross St. G31: Glas. 4B 84
Cardwell St. G41: Glas. 1E 103
Careston Pl. G64: B'rig. 6F 49
Carey Gdns. ML1: Cle 6H 129
CARFIN 5B 128
Carfin Ind. Est. ML1: Carf 5B 128
Carfin Lourdes Grotto. 5D 128
Carfin Mill Rd. ML1: Carf 6C 128
Carfin Rd. ML1: N'hill 5D 128
    ML2: Wis 5C 144
Carfin Station (Rail). 5D 128
Carfin St. G42: Glas 3F 103
    ML1: New S 4A 128
    ML5: Coat 1D 110
Carfrae St. G3: Glas. 3A 82
Cargill Sq. G64: B'rig. 1E 65
Carham Cres. G52: Glas 6C 80
Carham Dr. G52: Glas 6C 80
Caribou Grn. G75: E Kil 3D 148
Carillon Rd. G51: Glas 6A 82
Carinthia Sq. G81: Clyd 5D 42
Carisbrooke Cres. G64: B'rig. . . . 3D 48

Carlaverock Rd. G43: Glas. 1B 118
Carleith Av. G81: Dun 1B 42
Carleith Quad. G51: Glas. 4D 80
Carleith Ter. G81: Dun 1B 42
Carleston St. G21: Glas 5B 64
Carleton Ct. G46: Giff 3A 118
Carleton Dr. G46: Giff 3A 118
Carleton Ga. G46: Giff 3A 118
Carlibar Av. G13: Glas 3H 59
Carlibar Dr. G78: Barr 4E 115
Carlibar Gdns. G78: Barr 4E 115
Carlibar Rd. G78: Barr. 4D 114
Carlile PI. PA3: Pais 5A 78
Carlin La. ML8: Carl 4H 165
Carlin's PI. G66: Len 3F 7
Carlisle La. ML6: Air 4C 92
Carlisle Rd. ML1: N'hse 6G 113
    ML3: Fern, Ham 6B 142
    ML6: Air 5C 92
    ML9: Lark 5G 155
                            (Lanark Rd. End)
    ML9: Lark 5F 161
                                (Strutherhill)
Carlisle St. G21: Glas 6H 63
Carlock Wlk. G32: Glas 5C 86
Carlouk La. ML8: Carl 4H 165
Carloway Ct. G33: Glas 3B 86
Carlowrie Av. G72: Blan. 5A 124
CARLSTON 3G 29
Carlton Ct. G5: Glas. 5F 83
Carlton PI. G5: Glas 5F 83
CARLUKE 3F 165
Carluke Leisure Cen. 3G 165
Carluke Station (Rail) 4D 164
Carlyle Av. G52: Hill. 3H 79
Carlyle Dr. G74: E Kil 1A 150
Carlyle Ter. G73: Ruth 4D 104
    G74: E Kil 1B 150
Carmaben Rd. G33: Glas. 3D 86
Carman Vw. G82: Dumb 1G 17
Carment Dr. G41: Glas 5B 102
Carmichael Path ML5: Glenb. . . . 3G 69
                                (off Oval, The)
Carmichael PI. G42: Glas 6D 102
Carmichael St. G51: Glas 5H 81
    ML8: Law. 6D 158
Carmichael Way ML8: Law 6D 158
CARMUNNOCK 2H 135
Carmunnock By-Pass
    G76: Crmck 6G 119
Carmunnock La. G44: Glas 2F 119
Carmunnock Rd. G44: Glas 6F 103
    G45: Glas 6G 119
    G74: E Kil 1F 149
    G76: Busby 4E 135
    G76: Crmck 6G 119
                        (Carmunnock By-Pass)
    G76: Crmck 4C 136
                            (Kittochside Rd.)
CARMYLE 5C 106
Carmyle Av. G32: Carm, Glas. . . . 3B 106
CARMYLE AV. INTERCHANGE 4B 106
Carmyle Gdns. ML5: Coat 2A 110
Carmyle Station (Rail) 4B 106
Carna Dr. G44: Glas. 2G 119
Carnarvon St. G3: Glas 2D 82 (1A 4)
Carnbooth Ct. G45: Glas 5B 120
CARNBROE 1E 111
Carnbroe Rd. ML4: Bell 6D 110
    ML5: Coat 1F 111
Carneddans Rd. G62: Miln. 1C 24
Carnegie Hill G75: E Kil 3F 149
Carnegie PI. G75: E Kil. 3F 149
Carnegie Rd. G52: Hill. 4A 80
                            (not continuous)
Carnoch St. G23: Glas 6B 46
Carnock Cres. G78: Barr 6D 114
Carnock Gdns. G62: Miln 3E 25
Carnock Rd. G53: Glas 5C 100
Carnoustie Cres. G64: B'rig 6E 49
    G75: E Kil 5C 148
Carnoustie PI. G5: Glas 6D 82
    ML4: Bell 6C 110

Carnoustie St. G5: Glas 6D 82
Carnoustie Way G68: Cumb 5H 13
CARNTYNE 4G 85
Carntyne Gdns. G32: Glas 4G 85
Carntynehall Rd. G32: Glas 4H 85
Carntyne Ind. Est. G32: Glas 5G 85
Carntyne Path G32: Glas 4F 85
Carntyne PI. G32: Glas 4F 85
Carntyne Rd. G31: Glas 5E 85
    G32: Glas 4F 85
Carntyne Station (Rail) 5H 85
CARNWADRIC 3E 117
Carnwadric Rd. G46: T'bnk 3E 117
Carnwath Av. G43: Glas 1D 118
Carnwath Rd. ML8: Carl 4F 165
Caroline St. G31: Glas 6G 85
Carolside Av. G76: Clar 2C 134
Carolside Dr. G15: Glas 4B 44
Carolside Gdns. G76: Clar 2C 134
Carousel Cres. ML2: Wis. 6A 146
Carradale Cres. G68: Cumb. 5B 34
Carradale Gdns. G64: B'rig 6E 49
    ML8: Carl 5G 165
Carradale PI. PA3: Lin. 5G 75
Carradale St. ML5: Coat 4B 90
                            (not continuous)
Carranbuie Rd. ML8: Carl 2F 165
Carrbridge Dr. G20: Glas. 3B 62
Carresbrook Av. G66: Kirk 1G 51
CARRIAGEHILL 4A 98
Carriagehill Av. PA2: Pais 3A 98
Carriagehill Dr. PA2: Pais 4A 98
Carrickarden Rd. G61: Bear 4F 45
Carrick Ct. G66: Kirk 3G 31
Carrick Cres. G46: Giff 6A 118
    ML2: Wis 5G 145
Carrick Dr. G32: Glas 1E 107
    G73: Ruth. 2C 120
    ML5: Coat 4H 89
Carrick Gdns. G72: Blan. 3B 140
    ML3: Ham 1C 152
    ML4: Bell 5C 110
    ML8: Carl 5G 165
Carrick Gro. G32: Glas. 1E 107
Carrick PI. ML4: Bell 4H 89
    ML5: Coat 4H 89
    ML5: Glenb. 3A 70
    ML9: Lark 1F 161
Carrick Rd. G64: B'rig 6E 49
    G67: Cumb 1A 36
    G73: Ruth 2B 120
    G74: E Kil 6H 137
    PA7: B'ton 5A 40
CARRICKSTONE 6G 13
Carrickstone Rd. G68: Cumb. 6G 13
CARRICKSTONE RDBT. 6G 13
Carrickstone Vw. G68: Cumb 6H 13
Carrick St. G2: Glas. 4E 83 (6B 4)
    ML9: Lark 3G 161
Carrick Ter. G82: Dumb 3B 16
Carrick Vw. ML5: Glenb 3A 70
Carrick Way G71: Both. 4E 125
Carriden PI. G33: Glas 4E 87
Carrington St. G4: Glas. 1D 82 (1A 4)
Carroglen Gdns. G32: Glas 6D 86
Carroglen Gro. G32: Glas. 6D 86
Carroll Cres. ML1: Carf 5C 128
Carron Ct. G72: Camb 2E 123
                                (off Mill Rd.)
    G72: Camb 2D 122
                                (Arnhem St.)
    ML3: Ham 2F 153
Carron Cres. G22: Glas 4H 63
    G61: Bear. 4C 44
    G64: B'rig. 6D 48
    G66: Lenz 3E 51
Carron Dr. PA7: B'ton 5A 40
Carron Ho. G67: Cumb 4H 35
                (in Cumbernauld Shop. Cen.)
    G67: Cumb. 4H 35
                            (off Town Cen.)
Carron PI. G22: Glas 4A 64
    G75: E Kil 6H 149
    ML5: Coat 2H 89

Carron St. G22: Glas 4A 64
    ML2: Wis 2H 157
Carron Way G67: Cumb. 3H 35
                (in Cumbernauld Shop. Cen.)
    ML1: N'hill 3C 128
    PA3: Pais 4C 78
Carrour Gdns. G64: B'rig 5B 48
Carr Quad ML4: Moss 2F 127
Carruth Rd. PA11: Bri W 3E 73
Carsaig Dr. G52: Glas. 6E 81
Carsaig Loan ML5: Glenb 3G 69
Carscallan Rd. ML3: Ham, Quar . . 5H 153
Carsegreen Av. PA2: Pais. 6F 97
Carse Vw. Dr. G61: Bear 1G 45
Carstairs Ct. G40: Glas 3B 104
Carswell Gdns. G41: Glas 3C 102
Carswell Rd. G77: Newt M 4B 132
Cartbank Gdns. G44: Glas 3E 119
Cartbank Rd. G44: Neth 3D 118
Cartbank Rd. G44: Glas 3D 118
Cartcraigs Rd. G43: Glas 1H 117
Cartha Cres. PA2: Pais. 2C 98
Cartha St. G41: Glas 6C 102
Cartland Av. ML8: Carl 5F 165
Cart La. PA3: Pais 5A 78
Cartsbridge Rd. G76: Busby 3C 134
CARTSIDE 4D 94
Cartside Av. PA4: Inch 5F 57
    PA5: John. 4D 94
Cartside Dr. G76: Busby. 3E 135
Cartside PI. G76: Busby 4D 134
Cartside Quad. G42: Glas 6E 103
Cartside Rd. G76: Busby 4D 134
Cartside St. G42: Glas 6D 102
Cart St. G81: Clyd 1D 58
Cartvale La. PA3: Pais 5A 78
Cartvale Rd. G42: Glas 6D 102
Cartview Ct. G76: Busby 3D 134
Cart Wlk. PA1: Pais 1B 98
Cartyne Rd. G32: Glas 4B 86
Caskie Dr. G72: Blan 6C 124
Cassells St. ML1: Moth 1G 143
Cassels Gro. ML1: Moth 6E 127
Cassels St. ML1: Moth 1G 143
    ML8: Carl 4F 165
Cassiltoun Gdns. G45: Glas. 5H 119
Cassley Av. PA4: Renf 1H 79
Castburn Rd. G67: Cumb 5F 15
Castle Av. G71: Both, Udd 3C 124
    ML1: Holy. 1B 128
    PA5: Eld 4H 95
Castle Bank Ct. G13: Glas 3E 61
Castlebank Dr. G11: Glas. 2G 81
Castle Bank Gdns. G13: Glas 3E 61
Castlebank PI. G11: Glas 2G 81
Castlebank St. G11: Glas 2F 81
                            (not continuous)
Castle Bank Vs. G13: Glas 3E 61
Castlebay Dr. G22: Glas. 6G 47
Castlebay PI. G22: Glas 1G 63
Castlebay St. G22: Glas. 1G 63
Castlebrae G82: Dumb. 2C 16
Castlebrae Gdns. G44: Glas 1F 119
CASTLECARY 3E 15
Castle Cary 4F 15
Castlecary Rd.
    G68: C'cry, Cumb. 5C 14
Castle Chimmins Av.
    G72: Camb 3D 122
Castle Chimmins Gdns.
    G72: Camb 4D 122
Castle Chimmins Rd.
    G72: Camb 4D 122
Castle Ct. G66: Kirk 5D 30
    G68: C'cry. 3F 15
Castle Cres. PA7: B'ton 5H 39
Castlecroft Gdns. G71: Udd. 2D 124
Castle Dr. ML1: Holy 1B 128
Castlefern Rd. G73: Ruth 4D 120
Castlefield Ct. G33: Mille. 5B 66
Castlefield Gdns. G75: E Kil 6D 148
Castle Gait G53: Glas. 5A 100
    PA1: Pais 2H 97

Castle Gdns.—Chapelknowe Rd.

Castle Gdns. G69: Mood 5D **52**
  PA2: Pais 2E **97**
Castle Ga. G71: Both 2C **124**
  G77: Newt M 6G **133**
Castleglen Rd. G74: E Kil 5B **136**
Castlegreen Cres. G82: Dumb. . . 5H **17**
Castlegreen Gdns.
  G82: Dumb. 5H **17**
Castlegreen La. G82: Dumb 5G **17**
Castlegreen St. G82: Dumb. 5G **17**
Castle Gro. G65: Kils 1G **11**
CASTLEHEAD 2H **97**
CASTLEHILL
  Carluke 1E **165**
  Dumbarton 2C **16**
Castlehill Cres. FK4: Bank 1E **15**
Castle Hill Cres. ML3: Fern 2E **155**
Castlehill Cres. ML3: Ham 1B **154**
  ML6: Chap 4F **113**
  ML8: Law 1A **164**
  PA4: Renf 5F **59**
Castlehill Dr. G77: Newt M 5F **133**
Castlehill Grn. G74: E Kil 5B **136**
Castlehill Ind. Est. ML8: Carl. . . 1E **165**
Castlehill Quad. G82: Dumb. . . . 2C **16**
Castlehill Rd. G61: Bear 1B **44**
  G82: Dumb. 2C **16**
  ML2: Wis 3F **157**
  ML8: Carl 1E **165**
Castlehill Vw. G65: Kils 1G **11**
Castlelaw Gdns. G32: Glas 5B **86**
Castlelaw St. G32: Glas 5B **86**
Castle Mains Rd. G62: Miln 3D **24**
CASTLEMILK 4A **120**
Castlemilk Arc. G45: Glas 4A **120**
Castlemilk Cres. G44: Glas 2A **120**
Castlemilk Dr. G45: Glas 4A **120**
Castlemilk Rd. G44: Glas. 1A **120**
                (Croftend Av.)
  G44: Glas 6A **104**
                 (Curtis Av.)
Castlemilk Sports Cen. 4A **120**
Castlemilk Swimming Pool 4A **120**
Castlemount Av. G77: Newt M . . 6F **133**
Castle Pl. G71: Udd 1C **124**
Castle Quad. ML6: Air 4D **92**
Castle Rd. G77: Newt M 5C **132**
  G82: Dumb. 5G **17**
  ML6: Air 4D **92**
  PA11: Bri W 2F **73**
  PA5: Eld 2A **96**
Castle Sq. G81: Clyd 4A **42**
Castle St. G11: Glas 2A **82**
  G4: Glas 3A **84** (5H **5**)
  G69: Bail 2G **107**
  G73: Ruth 5C **104**
  G81: Clyd 4A **42**
  G82: Dumb 4F **17**
  ML3: Ham 5B **142**
  ML6: Chap 3D **112**
  PA1: Pais 1H **97**
Castle Ter. G82: Dumb 4G **17**
  PA11: Bri W 4G **73**
           (off Kilbarchan Rd.)
Castleton Av. G64: B'rig 2A **64**
  G77: Newt M. 6F **133**
Castleton Ct. G45: Glas 5B **120**
  G77: Newt M. 6F **133**
Castleton Cres. G77: Newt M. . . 6F **133**
Castleton Dr. G77: Newt M 6F **133**
Castleton Gro. G77: Newt M . . . 6F **133**
Castleview G66: Cam G 1B **6**
Castle Vw. G66: Len 2C **6**
Castleview G68: Cumb 3E **15**
Castle Vw. G72: Blan 5A **124**
  G81: Clyd 4D **42**
  ML2: Newm 3E **147**
Castleview Av. PA2: Pais 6E **97**
Castleview Dr. PA2: Pais 6E **97**
Castleview Pl. PA2: Pais 6E **97**
Castleview Ter. FK4: Hag. 1G **15**
Castle Way G67: Cumb 1C **36**
  G69: Barg. 6D **88**
Castle Wynd G71: Both 5F **125**

Cathay St. G22: Glas 1G **63**
Cathburn Rd. ML2: Newm 5F **147**
CATHCART 1E **119**
Cathcart Castle 2F **119**
Cathcart Cres. PA2: Pais 2C **98**
Cathcart Pl. G73: Ruth. 6B **104**
Cathcart Rd. G42: Glas. 3F **103**
  G73: Ruth. 6B **104**
Cathcart Station (Rail) 1E **119**
Cathedral Sq. G4: Glas 4A **84**
           (not continuous)
Cathedral St. G1: Glas . . . 3G **83** (4E **5**)
Catherine St. G66: Kirk 5C **30**
  ML1: Moth 5G **143**
Catherines Wlk. G72: Blan. 3B **140**
Catherine Way ML1: New S. . . . 4H **127**
CATHKIN. 5F **121**
Cathkin Av. G72: Camb 1G **121**
  G73: Ruth. 6E **105**
Cathkin Braes Country Pk. 5D **120**
Cathkin By-Pass G73: Ruth 4F **121**
Cathkin Ct. G45: Glas. 5B **120**
Cathkin Cres. G68: Cumb 6G **13**
Cathkin Gdns. G71: Tann 4C **108**
Cathkin Pl. G72: Camb 1G **121**
Cathkin Recreation Cen. 5F **103**
Cathkin Rd. G42: Glas 6D **102**
  G71: Tann. 4C **108**
  G73: Ruth. 1B **136**
  G76: Crmck 1A **136**
Cathkin Vw. G32: Carm 5B **106**
Cathkinview Pl. G42: Glas 6E **103**
Cathkinview Rd. G42: Glas 6E **103**
Catrine G74: E Kil 1F **149**
Catrine Av. G81: Clyd 4F **43**
         (off Kirkoswald Dr.)
Catrine Ct. G53: Glas 5A **100**
Catrine Cres. ML1: Moth 6A **144**
Catrine Gdns. G53: Glas 5A **100**
Catrine Pl. G53: Glas 5A **100**
Catrine Rd. G53: Glas 5A **100**
Catrine St. ML9: Lark 3G **161**
Catriona Way ML1: Holy 2B **128**
Catter Gdns. G62: Miln. 2E **25**
Cauldstream Pl. G62: Miln. 4E **25**
Causewayside Cres. G32: Glas . . 2A **106**
Causewayside St. G32: Glas . . . 3A **106**
Causeyside St. PA1: Pais. 1A **98**
             (Forbes Pl.)
  PA1: Pais 2A **98**
          (Thompson Brae)
Causeystanes G72: Blan 2B **140**
         (off Winton Cres.)
Cavendish Ct. G5: Glas. 1F **103**
Cavendish Dr. G77: Newt M . . . 3F **133**
Cavendish Pl. G5: Glas. 1F **103**
Cavendish St. G5: Glas. 1F **103**
Cavin Dr. G45: Glas. 3A **120**
Cavin Rd. G45: Glas. 3A **120**
Cawder Ct. G68: Cumb 6F **13**
Cawder Pl. G68: Cumb 6G **13**
Cawder Rd. G68: Cumb. 6G **13**
Cawder Vw. G68: Cumb. 6G **13**
Cawder Way G68: Cumb 6G **13**
Cawdor Cres. PA7: B'ton 5H **39**
Cawdor Way G74: E Kil. 6F **137**
Cayton Gdns. G69: Bail. 1F **107**
Cecil St. G12: Glas 6B **62**
  G76: Clar 2C **134**
  ML5: Coat. 6C **90**
Cedar Av. G71: View. 5F **109**
  G81: Clyd 3H **41**
  PA5: John 5F **95**
Cedar Ct. G20: Glas 1E **83**
  G72: Flem 3E **123**
  G75: E Kil 6E **149**
  PA10: Kilb. 2A **94**
Cedar Dr. G66: Lenz. 2C **50**
  G71: View. 5G **109**
  G75: E Kil 6E **149**
Cedar Gdns. G73: Ruth 3E **121**
  ML1: N'hill 3C **128**
  ML8: Law 5D **158**

Cedar La. ML1: Holy 3B **128**
  ML6: Air 4C **92**
Cedar Pl. G72: Blan 6A **124**
  G75: E Kil 6E **149**
  G78: Barr 6F **115**
Cedar Rd. FK4: Bank 1E **15**
  G64: B'rig. 1D **64**
  G66: Milt C 6C **8**
  G67: Cumb. 2D **36**
Cedar St. G20: Glas 1E **83**
Cedar Wlk. G64: B'rig 1D **64**
Cedarwood Av.
  G77: Newt M. 5F **133**
Cedric Pl. G13: Glas 2D **60**
Cedric Rd. G13: Glas 2D **60**
Celtic F.C. 6D **84**
Celtic F.C. Vis. Cen. 1D **104**
Celtic Pk. 6D **84**
Celtic St. G20: Glas 2A **62**
Cemetery Rd. G52: Glas 1D **100**
  G72: Blan 3A **140**
Centenary Av. ML6: Air 4F **91**
Centenary Ct. G78: Barr 5D **114**
          (off Cochrane St.)
  G81: Clyd 6D **42**
Centenary Gdns. ML3: Ham . . . 1A **154**
  ML5: Coat. 6B **90**
Centenary Quad. ML1: Holy . . . 2A **128**
Central Av. G11: Glas 1F **81**
  G32: Glas 2D **106**
  G71: View. 1G **125**
  G72: Blan 4C **140**
  G72: Camb 1H **121**
  G81: Clyd 5C **42**
  ML1: Holy 2H **127**
  ML1: New S 5A **128**
Central Cres. ML9: Ashg 5B **162**
Central Gro. G32: Glas. 1D **106**
  G72: Camb 1H **121**
Central Path G32: Glas. 2E **107**
Central Rd. PA1: Pais 6A **78**
Central Station (Rail) 4F **83** (6D **4**)
Central Way G67: Cumb 5G **35**
  PA1: Pais 6A **78**
Cen. for Contemporary Arts 3B **4**
Centre Pk. Ct. ML5: Coat. 6C **90**
CENTRE RDBT., THE 2H **149**
Centre St. G5: Glas. 6E **83**
  ML5: Glenb 3G **69**
  ML6: Chap 3D **112**
Centre, The G78: Barr 5D **114**
Centre Way St. G78: Barr 4D **114**
Ceres Gdns. G64: B'rig. 6F **49**
Cessnock Pl. G72: Camb 2D **122**
Cessnock Rd. G33: Mille 4B **66**
Cessnock Station (Und.) 5A **82**
Cessnock St. G51: Glas 5A **82**
Chalmers Ct. G40: Glas 5B **84**
          (off Millroad Dr.)
  G71: Udd 1D **124**
Chalmers Cres. G75: E Kil 4H **149**
Chalmers Dr. G75: E Kil. 4H **149**
Chalmers Ga. G40: Glas 5A **84**
         (off Claythorn St.)
Chalmers Pl. G40: Glas 5A **84**
         (off Claythorn St.)
Chalmers St. G40: Glas 5A **84**
  G81: Clyd 6D **42**
Chamberlain La. G13: Glas 4E **61**
Chamberlain Rd. G13: Glas 3E **61**
Chancellor St. G11: Glas 1H **81**
CHANTINGHALL 6F **141**
Chantinghall Rd. ML3: Ham. . . . 6F **141**
Chantinghall Ter. ML3: Ham . . . 6F **141**
Chantree Ct. ML1: N'hill. 4C **128**
CHAPEL 1G **159**
Chapel Ct. G73: Ruth. 5B **104**
Chapelcross Av. ML6: Air 2A **92**
CHAPELHALL 3E **113**
Chapelhall Ind. Est.
  ML6: Chap 1D **112**
CHAPEL HILL 6D **20**
Chapelhill Rd. PA2: Pais 3C **98**
Chapelknowe Rd. ML1: Carf 6C **128**

Chapel Pl. G78: Neil 2D **130**
Chapel Rd. G81: Dun 1C **42**
 ML2: Newm 2F **159**
 PA6: Hous 1B **74**
Chapelside Av. ML6: Air 3A **92**
Chapelside Rd. G74: Ners 3A **138**
Chapel St. G20: Glas 4C **62**
 G66: Len 3F **7**
 G73: Ruth. 5B **104**
 ML1: Cle. 6H **129**
 ML3: Ham *6A 142*
 (off Leechlee Rd.)
 ML6: Air 3A **92**
 ML8: Carl 3F **165**
Chapel St. Ind. Est. G20: Glas. 3C **62**
Chapelton Av. G61: Bear 3F **45**
 G82: Dumb. 2G **17**
Chapelton Gdns. G61: Bear 3F **45**
 G82: Dumb. 2G **17**
Chapelton Rd. G67: Cumb 1E **55**
Chapelton St. G22: Glas 3F **63**
Chaplet Av. G13: Glas 1C **60**
Chapman Av. ML5: Coat. 3G **69**
Chapman St. G42: Glas 3E **103**
Chappell St. G78: Barr. 4D **114**
Charing Cross ML9: Lark 2E **161**
Charing Cross La. *G3: Glas* *3D 82*
 (off Granville St.)
Charing Cross Station (Rail)
 . . . . 3E **83 (3A 4)**
Charles Av. PA4: Renf 5F **59**
Charles Cres. G66: Lenz 4D **50**
 ML8: Carl 4H **165**
Charleson Row G65: Croy 2B **34**
Charles Path ML6: Chap 4D **112**
Charles Quad. ML1: Holy. 2A **128**
Charles Rennie Mckintosh Society
 . . . . 5E **63**
Charles St. G21: Glas. 2A **84**
 G65: Kils 2H **11**
 ML2: Wis 5C **144**
CHARLESTON 3A **98**
Charleston Ga. *PA2: Pais*. *2A 98*
 (off Sth. Campbell St.)
Charlotte Av. G71: Torr 5D **28**
Charlotte Path ML9: Lark 3E **161**
Charlotte Pl. PA2: Pais 3A **98**
Charlotte St. G1: Glas 5H **83**
 G82: Dumb 3D **16**
Charnwood Av. PA5: John 5D **94**
Chartwell Rd. PA7: B'ton. 4H **39**
Chassels St. ML5: Coat 3C **90**
Chateau Gro. ML3: Ham 1C **154**
Chatelherault 3D **154**
Chatelherault Av. G72: Camb 2G **121**
Chatelherault Country Pk. 2C **154**
Chatelherault Country Pk. Vis. Cen.
 . . . . 3D **154**
Chatelherault Cres. ML3: Ham . . . 2A **154**
Chatelherault Wlk. ML3: Ham. . . . 2A **154**
Chatham G75: E Kil 4E **149**
Chatton St. G23: Glas. 6B **46**
Cheapside St. G3: Glas. . . . . . 4D **82 (6A 4)**
Chelmsford Dr. G12: Glas 4H **61**
Cherry Bank G66: Lenz 2B **50**
Cherrybank Rd. G43: Glas 1D **118**
Cherrybank Wlk. ML6: Air 3F **91**
Cherry Cres. G81: Clyd 3C **42**
Cherryhill Vw. ML9: Lark. 2D **160**
Cherry La. FK4: Bank 1E **15**
Cherry Pl. G64: B'rig 1D **64**
 G66: Milt C 1B **30**
 G71: View. 6H **109**
 ML1: Holy 2B **128**
 PA5: John. 4G **95**
Cherrytree Cres. ML9: Lark 6A **156**
Cherrytree Dr. G72: Flem 3E **123**
Cherry Wlk. ML1: Moth. 6G **143**
Cherrywood Rd. PA5: Eld. 3A **96**
Chesterfield Av. G12: Glas. 4G **61**
Chesters Cres. ML1: Moth. 1E **143**
Chesters Pl. G73: Ruth 6B **104**
Chesters Rd. G61: Bear 3C **44**
Chester St. G32: Glas. 6A **86**

Chestnut Av. G67: Cumb 6E **15**
 PA7: B'ton 2F **39**
 (not continuous)
Chestnut Ct. G66: Milt C 6B **8**
 G67: Cumb 6E **15**
Chestnut Cres. G71: View 6H **109**
 G75: E Kil 5E **149**
 ML3: Ham 1A **154**
Chestnut Dr. G66: Lenz 1B **50**
 G81: Clyd 2B **42**
Chestnut Gro. G69: G'csh 3G **69**
 G72: Blan 1A **140**
 ML1: Moth 4F **143**
 ML8: Carl 4E **165**
 ML9: Lark 6A **156**
Chestnut La. G62: Miln 4E **25**
Chestnut Pl. G67: Cumb. 6E **15**
 PA5: John. 5G **95**
Chestnut St. G22: Glas. 4H **63**
Chestnut Way G72: Flem 3E **123**
Cheviot Av. G78: Barr. 5E **115**
Cheviot Cl. G13: Glas. 3B **60**
Cheviot Ct. ML5: Coat 2E **111**
 ML6: Air 1B **92**
Cheviot Cres. ML2: Wis 5F **145**
Cheviot Dr. G77: Newt M 6C **132**
Cheviot Gdns. G61: Bear 6D **24**
Cheviot Rd. G43: Glas 2A **118**
 ML3: Ham 1B **154**
 ML9: Lark. 3G **161**
 PA2: Pais 4A **98**
Cheviot St. G72: Blan. 2A **140**
Chillin Pl. ML9: Lark 2G **161**
Chirmorie Cres. G53: Glas. 4A **100**
Chirmorie Pl. G53: Glas. 4A **100**
Chirnside Ct. G72: Blan 4D **140**
Chirnside Pl. G52: Glas 5A **80**
Chirnside Rd. G52: Glas 5A **80**
Chirnsyde Sports Cen. 2H **63**
Chisholm Av. PA7: B'ton 4A **40**
Chisholm Dr. G77: Newt M 3E **133**
Chisholm Pl. ML1: Moth 1B **156**
Chisholm St. G1: Glas 5H **83**
 ML5: Coat 3D **90**
Chrighton Grn. G71: Tann 5E **109**
Chriss Av. ML3: Ham 4H **153**
Christchurch Pl. G75: E Kil 4D **148**
Christian St. G43: Glas 5A **102**
Christie La. PA3: Pais 6A **78**
Christie Pl. G72: Camb 2A **122**
Christie St. ML4: Bell 2F **127**
 PA1: Pais 6B **78**
Christopher St. G21: Glas 2C **84**
CHRYSTON 6B **52**
Chryston Rd. G66: Kirk 1H **51**
 G69: Chry 1B **68**
Chryston Valley Bus. Cen.
 G69: Chry 1A **68**
Chuckie La. PA5: Brkfld 5C **74**
Church Av. G33: Step. 3D **66**
 G73: Ruth 2E **121**
 ML2: Newm 5D **146**
Church Ct. G82: Dumb 4F **17**
Church Cres. ML3: Ham 5H **153**
 ML6: Air 2E **93**
Church Dr. G66: Lenz 1C **50**
Church Hill PA1: Pais 6A **78**
Churchill Av. G74: E Kil 2H **149**
 PA5: John. 6C **94**
Churchill Cres. G71: Both 4F **125**
Churchill Dr. G11: Glas. 5F **61**
 PA7: B'ton 4H **39**
Churchill Pl. PA10: Kilb 2A **94**
Church La. G65: Kils 3H **11**
 (not continuous)
 ML2: Newm 5D **146**
 ML5: Coat. 4C **90**
 ML8: Carl 4F **165**
Church Manse La.
 PA11: Bri W 3F **73**
Church Pl. G60: Old K 1E **41**
 G73: Ruth. 5D **104**
Church Rd. G69: Muirh 2A **68**
 G76: Busby 3D **134**

Church Rd. ML2: Newm. 2H **147**
 PA11: Bri W 4G **73**
 PA11: Q'riers 1A **72**
Church St. G11: Glas 1A **82**
 G65: Kils 3H **11**
 G69: Bail. 1A **108**
 G71: Udd 2D **124**
 G72: Blan 2C **140**
 G81: Clyd 4D **42**
 G82: Dumb 4F **17**
 ML1: N'hill 3F **129**
 ML3: Ham 5A **142**
 ML5: Coat. 4C **90**
 ML9: Lark. 2E **161**
 PA10: Kilb. 2A **94**
 PA5: John. 2F **95**
Church Vw. G72: Camb 6A **106**
 ML5: Coat. 4C **90**
Church Vw. Ct. G66: Len 2F **7**
Church Vw. Gdns. ML4: Bell 2C **126**
Circus Dr. G31: Glas. 4B **84**
Circus Pl. G31: Glas. 4B **84**
Circus Pl. La. G31: Glas. 3B **84**
Citadel Pl. ML1: Moth 1E **143**
Citizen La. G2: Glas . . . . . . 4G **83 (5E 5)**
Citizens' Theatre 6G **83**
Citrus Cres. G71: View. 5G **109**
Cityford Cres. G73: Ruth 6B **104**
Cityford Dr. G73: Ruth 1B **120**
City Hall . . . . 4H **83 (6G 5)**
Civic Sq. *ML1: Moth* *4H 143*
 (off Camp St.)
Civic St. G4: Glas . . . . 1F **83 (1C 4)**
Civic Theatre 4F **17**
Civic Way G66: Kirk 6C **30**
Clachan Dr. G51: Glas 3E **81**
Clachan, The ML2: Wis 6H **145**
CLADDENS 3E **51**
Claddens Pl. G66: Lenz 3E **51**
Claddens Quad. G22: Glas. 3G **63**
Claddens St. G22: Glas 3F **63**
Claddens Wynd G66: Lenz 3E **51**
Cladence Gro. G75: E Kil. 6H **149**
Claire St. ML2: Newm 4E **147**
Clairinish Gdns. PA4: Renf 2E **79**
Clairmont Gdns. G3: Glas 2D **82**
Clair Rd. G64: B'rig 6F **49**
Clamp Rd. ML2: Wis 5C **144**
Clamps Gro. G74: E Kil 3A **150**
Clamps Ter. G74: E Kil. 3B **150**
Clamps Wood G74: E Kil 3A **150**
Clanrye Dr. ML5: Coat 1C **110**
Clapperhow Rd. ML1: Carf 6A **128**
Claremont Av. G66: Kirk 5B **30**
Claremont Dr. G62: Miln 4G **25**
Claremont Gdns. G62: Miln 4G **25**
Claremont Ho. G74: E Kil 2C **150**
Claremont Pl. *G3: Glas* *2D 82*
 (off Lynedoch Ter.)
Claremont St. G3: Glas 3C **82**
 (not continuous)
Claremont Ter. G3: Glas 2D **82**
Claremont Ter. La. *G3: Glas* *2D 82*
 (off Clifton St.)
Claremount Av. G46: Giff 5A **118**
Clarence Dr. G11: Glas 6G **61**
 G12: Glas 6G **61**
 PA1: Pais 6C **78**
Clarence Gdns. G11: Glas 6G **61**
Clarence La. *G12: Glas*. *6H 61*
 (off Hyndland Rd.)
Clarence St. G81: Clyd 4D **42**
 PA1: Pais 6C **78**
Clarendon Pl. G33: Step 4D **66**
 G4: Glas. . . . . 1E **83 (1A 4)**
Clarendon Rd. ML2: Wis 2E **157**
Clarendon St. G20: Glas. 1E **83**
Clare St. G21: Glas 2C **84**
Clarinda Ct. G66: Kirk 3G **31**
Clarinda Pl. ML1: N'hill 4C **128**
Clarion Cres. G13: Glas 1A **60**
Clarion Rd. G13: Glas. 2A **60**
Clark Pl. G64: Torr 5E **29**
 G77: Newt M 5B **132**

CLARKSTON
Airdrie 3D 92
Glasgow 2C 134
Clarkston Av. G44: Glas 3D 118
Clarkston Dr. ML6: Air 4D 92
Clarkston Rd. G44: Glas 3D 118
  G44: Neth 1C 134
  G76: Clar 1C 134
Clarkston Station (Rail) 2C 134
Clark St. G81: Clyd 3B 42
  ML2: Newm 4D 146
  ML6: Air .4B 92
  PA3: Pais 5G 77
  PA4: Renf 6D 58
  PA5: John 2F 95
Clark Way ML4: Bell 6B 110
Clarkwell Rd. ML3: Ham 1C 152
Clarkwell Ter. ML3: Ham 6D 140
Clathic Av. G61: Bear 3G 45
Claude Av. G72: Camb 3E 123
Claude St. ML9: Lark 2E 161
Claud Rd. PA3: Pais 5C 78
Clavens Rd. G52: Glas. 5G 79
Claverhouse Pl. PA2: Pais 2C 98
Claverhouse Rd. G52: Hill 4H 79
Clavering St. E. PA1: Pais 6G 77
Clavering St. W. PA1: Pais 6G 77
Clay Ct. ML1: Moth 5G 143
Clay Cres. ML4: Bell 6D 110
Clayhouse Rd. G33: Step 5E 67
Claymore Dr. PA6: C'lee. 3D 74
Claypotts Pl. G33: Glas 2A 86
Claypotts Rd. G33: Glas 2A 86
Clay Rd. ML4: Bell 6D 110
Clayslaps Rd. G3: Glas 2B 82
Claythorn Av. G40: Glas 5A 84
Claythorn Ct. G40: Glas 5A 84
  (off Claythorn St.)
Claythorn Pk. G40: Glas 6A 84
Claythorn St. G40: Glas 5A 84
Claythorn Ter. G40: Glas 5A 84
Clayton Cir. G40: Glas 5A 84
Clayton Path G67: Bell 6D 110
Clayton Ter. G31: Glas 4B 84
Clearfield Av. ML3: Ham 5F 141
CLEDDANS 4F 31
Cleddans Cres. G81: Hard 1E 43
Cleddans Rd. G66: Kirk 4E 31
  G81: Hard 2E 43
Cleddans Vw. G81: Clyd. 4E 43
  (off Kirkoswald Dr.)
  ML6: Glenm 5G 71
Cleddens Ct. G64: B'rig 6C 48
  ML6: Air 3F 91
  (off Monkscourt Av.)
CLEEKHIMIN 6B 128
Cleeves Quad. G53: Glas 2A 116
Cleeves Rd. G53: Glas. 2A 116
Cleghorn St. G22: Glas. 6F 63
Cleish Av. G61: Bear 6C 24
CLELAND 6H 129
Cleland La. G5: Glas 6G 83
Cleland Pl. G74: E Kil 1A 150
Cleland Rd. ML1: Carf 6C 128
  ML1: Cle .4F 129
  ML2: Wis 6G 145
Cleland St. G5: Glas 6G 83
Clelland Av. G64: B'rig 1C 64
Clem Attlee Gdns. ML9: Lark 3F 161
Clerwood St. G32: Glas 5F 85
Cleuch Gdns. G76: Clar 1B 134
Clevans Rd. PA11: Bri W 4D 72
Cleveden Cres. G12: Glas 4H 61
Cleveden Cres. La. G12: Glas 4H 61
Cleveden Dr. G12: Glas 4H 61
  G73: Ruth 1E 121
Cleveden Dr. La. G12: Glas 5A 62
Cleveden Gdns. G12: Glas 4A 62
Cleveden La. G12: Glas 3H 61
  (off Northampton Dr.)
Cleveden Pl. G12: Glas 3H 61
Cleveden Rd. G12: Glas 2H 61
Cleveland La. G3: Glas 3A 4
Cleveland St. G3: Glas. 3D 82

Clifford Gdns. G51: Glas 6H 81
Clifford La. G51: Glas 6A 82
Clifford Pl. G51: Glas. 6B 82
  (off Clifford La.)
Clifford St. G51: Glas 6H 81
Clifford Rd. G3: Glas 1D 82
Cliftonhill Stadium 5E 91
Clifton Pl. G3: Glas 2C 82
  (off Clifton St.)
  ML5: Coat. 5E 91
Clifton Rd. G46: Giff 4H 117
Clifton St. G3: Glas 2C 82
Clifton Ter. G72: Camb 4G 121
  PA5: John. 3G 95
  (off Auchenlodment Rd.)
CLIFTONVILLE 4E 91
Cliftonville Ct. ML5: Coat. 5E 91
  (off Clifton Pl.)
CLINCARTHILL 6C 104
Clincarthill Rd. G73: Ruth 6C 104
Clincart Rd. G42: Glas 5F 103
CLIPPENS .5G 75
Clippens Rd. PA3: Lin 6H 75
  PA6: Hous. 3E 75
Cloan Av. G15: Glas 5B 44
Cloan Cres. G64: B'rig. 3D 48
Clober Farm La. G62: Miln 2E 25
Cloberfield G62: Miln 1F 25
Cloberfield Gdns. G62: Miln. 2F 25
Cloberhill Rd. G13: Glas 6C 44
Clober Rd. G62: Miln 2F 25
Clochbar Av. G62: Miln. 2F 25
Clochbar Gdns. G62: Miln 3F 25
Clochoderick Av. PA10: Kilb. 3B 94
Cloch St. G33: Glas 3A 86
Clockerhill Pl. ML1: N'hill 3E 129
Clock Sq. G67: Cumb. 4H 35
  (in Cumbernauld Shop. Cen.)
Cloister Av. ML6: Air 1C 112
Clonbeith St. G33: Glas 1E 87
Closeburn St. G22: Glas 4G 63
Cloth St. G78: Barr 5E 115
Clouden Rd. G67: Cumb 3B 36
Cloudhowe Ter. G72: Blan 6A 124
Clouston Ct. G20: Glas 5C 62
Clouston La. G20: Glas 5C 62
Clouston St. G20: Glas. 5B 62
Clova Pl. G71: Udd 1D 124
Clova St. G46: T'bnk. 3F 117
Clove Mill Wynd ML9: Lark 3C 160
Clovend Dr. G73: Ruth. 4D 120
Clovenstone Rd. G21: Glas. 2C 84
Clovergate G64: B'rig. 6A 48
Cloverhill Pl. G69: Chry. 1A 68
Cloverhill Ter. G74: E Kil 2G 149
Cloverhill Vw. G74: E Kil 2F 149
Clunie Pl. ML2: Newm. 3D 146
  ML5: Coat 2D 110
Clunie Rd. G52: Glas 1E 101
Cluny Av. G61: Bear 5G 45
  PA4: Renf .6E 23
Cluny Dr. G61: Bear 5G 45
  G77: Newt M 4B 132
  PA3: Pais .5C 78
Cluny Gdns. G14: Glas 5E 61
  G69: Bail .1G 107
Cluny Vs. G14: Glas 5E 61
Clutha Pl. G75: E Kil 4C 148
Clutha St. G51: Glas 5B 82
Clyde Av. G64: Torr 5D 28
  G71: Both 6D 124
  G78: Barr .6F 115
  ML3: Fern 2E 155
CLYDEBANK 4D 42
Clydebank Bus. Pk. G81: Clyd 5C 42
Clydebank Crematorium
  G81: Dun .1H 41
Clydebank District Mus. 6C 42
Clydebank Ind. Est. G81: Clyd. 5H 41
Clydebank Megabowl 6E 43
Clydebank Station (Rail) 6D 42
Clydebrae Dr. G71: Both 1F 141
Clydebrae St. G51: Glas 3H 81
Clyde Bri. ML3: Ham 4D 142

Clydebuilt. 6A 60
Clyde Ct. G81: Clyd 2A 42
  G82: Dumb 3E 17
  ML5: Coat. 5E 91
  (off Clifton Pl.)
Clyde Dr. ML4: Bell 3E 127
Clyde F.C. 4B 34
Clydeford Dr. G32: Glas 2G 105
  G71: Udd .6B 108
Clydeford Rd. G32: Glas 6A 106
  G72: Camb 1B 122
Clydeholm Rd. G14: Glas 1D 80
Clydeholm Ter. G81: Clyd. 2F 59
Clyde Ho. ML3: Ham 4A 142
Clyde La. ML1: New S 3A 128
Clydeneuk Dr. G71: Udd 6B 108
Clyde Pl. G5: Glas 5E 83
  G72: Camb 3D 122
  ML1: New S 3A 128
  PA5: John. 5C 94
Clyde Rd. PA3: Pais. 4D 78
CLYDESDALE 4H 127
Clydesdale Av. ML2: Wis. 2D 156
  ML3: Ham 5H 153
  PA3: Pais .2C 78
Clydesdale Pl. ML3: Ham 5H 153
Clydesdale St. ML3: Ham 5G 141
  ML4: Bell .3F 127
  ML9: Lark 1E 161
Clyde Shop. Cen. G81: Clyd 5D 42
Clydeshore Rd. G82: Dumb 5E 17
Clydeside Expressway G11: Glas. . . .1F 81
  G14: Glas 6D 60
  G3: Glas 3B 82
Clydeside Ind. Est. G31: Glas 1D 80
Clydeside Rd. G73: Ruth 3B 104
Clydesmill Dr. G32: Glas 6A 106
Clydesmill Gro. G32: Glas 6A 106
Clydesmill Pl. G32: Glas 5H 105
Clydesmill Rd. G32: Glas 5H 105
Clyde Sq. G67: Cumb 4H 35
  (in Cumbernauld Shop. Cen.)
Clyde St. G1: Glas 5G 83
  G81: Clyd .1E 59
  ML5: Coat. 4E 91
  ML8: Carl 3D 164
  PA4: Renf .4F 59
Clyde Ter. G71: Both 6E 125
  ML1: Moth 1C 156
Clyde Twr. G74: E Kil 4B 150
  ML1: Moth 4G 143
  (off Airbles Rd.)
Clyde Tunnel G51: Glas 2E 81
Clydevale G71: Both 6F 125
Clyde Valley Av. ML1: Moth 5G 143
Clydeview G71: Both 6G 125
Clyde Vw. G82: Dumb 5E 17
  ML3: Ham 2F 153
  ML9: Ashg 5C 162
  PA2: Pais .3D 98
Clyde Vw. Ct. G60: Bowl 5A 20
Clydeview La. G11: Glas 1F 81
Clydeview Shop. Cen. G72: Blan
  . . . . .2C 140
Clydeview Ter. G32: Carm 5C 106
Clyde Wlk. G67: Cumb 4H 35
  (in Cumbernauld Shop. Cen.)
Clyde Walkway G3: Glas 6A 4
Clyde Way G67: Cumb 4H 35
  (in Cumbernauld Shop. Cen.)
  PA3: Pais .4D 78
Clydeway Ind. Est. G3: Glas 3C 82
  (off Finnieston Sq.)
Clyde Workshops G32: Glas 4H 105
Clynder St. G51: Glas 5H 81
Clyth Dr. G46: Giff 5B 118
Coach Cl. G65: Kils 3C 12
Coach Pl. G65: Kils 4A 12
Coach Rd. G65: Kils. 4B 12
Coalburn Rd. G71: Both 2F 125
Coalhall Av. ML1: Carf. 6A 128
Coalhill St. G31: Glas 6D 84
Coatbank St. ML5: Coat 6D 90

Coatbank Way ML5: Coat 5D 90
COATBRIDGE 4C 90
Coatbridge Central Station (Rail)
. . . . .4B 90
Coatbridge College Sports Cen. . . .4D 90
Coatbridge Indoor Bowling Club
. . . . .4F 91
Coatbridge Ind. Est. ML5: Coat . . .2C 90
Coatbridge Outdoor Sports Complex
. . . . .6B 90
Coatbridge Rd. G69: Bail. 6B 88
G69: Barg. 5D 88
G69: G'csh 5E 69
ML5: Coat 2D 90
ML5: Glenb. 4B 70
ML6: Glenm 2D 90
Coatbridge Sunnyside Station (Rail)
. . . . .3C 90
COATDYKE 5F 91
Coatdyke Station (Rail) 4F 91
Coathill St. ML5: Coat 1C 110
Coats Cres. G69: Bail. 6G 87
Coats Dr. PA2: Pais. 2F 97
COATSHILL 6A 124
Coatshill Av. G72: Blan 6A 124
Coats Observatory 6H 77
Coats St. ML5: Coat. 5D 90
Cobbett Rd. ML1: Moth 4D 142
Cobblerigg Way G71: Udd 2C 124
Cobbleton Rd. ML1: New S 5H 127
Cobden Rd. G21: Glas 1B 84
Cobington Pl. G33: Glas. 2B 86
Cobinshaw St. G32: Glas. 5A 86
Coburg St. G5: Glas 6F 83
(Kilbarchan St.)
G5: Glas 5F 83
(Norfolk St.)
Cochno Rd. G81: Faif 5F 23
G81: Hard. 6D 22
Cochno St. G81: Clyd. 1E 59
COCHRANE CASTLE 5E 95
Cochrane Ct. G62: Miln 5A 26
Cochranemill Rd. PA5: John 4C 94
Cochrane Sq. PA3: Lin. 5H 75
Cochrane St. G1: Glas. 4G 83 (5F 5)
G78: Barr. 5D 114
Cochrane St. ML4: Bell. 2B 126
Cochran St. PA1: Pais 1B 98
Cockburn Pl. ML5: Coat 1B 110
Cockels Loan PA4: Renf 2D 78
Cockenzie St. G32: Glas. 6A 86
Cockerhill Rd. G52: Glas. 4D 100
Cockhill Way ML4: Bell 1H 125
Cockmuir St. G21: Glas 5C 64
Coddington Cres. ML1: Holy 6H 111
Cogan Pl. G78: Barr. 5D 114
Cogan Rd. G43: Glas 1A 118
Cogan St. G43: Glas. 6A 102
G78: Barr 5D 114
Colbert St. G40: Glas 1B 104
Colbreggan Ct. G81: Hard. 1E 43
Colbreggan Gdns. G81: Hard. 1E 43
Colbreggan Pl. G81: Hard 1E 43
Colchester Dr. G12: Glas 3G 61
Coldingham Av. G14: Glas. 3G 59
Coldstream Cres. ML2: Wis. 4A 146
Coldstream Dr. G73: Ruth 6F 105
PA2: Pais 4E 97
Coldstream Pl. G21: Glas. 6G 63
Coldstream Rd. G81: Clyd 6D 42
Coldstream St. G72: Blan 2B 140
Cole G74: E Kil 3C 150
Colebrooke Pl. G12: Glas. 6C 62
Colebrooke St. G12: Glas. 6C 62
Colebrooke Ter. G12: Glas. 6C 62
Colebrook St. G72: Camb 1A 122
Coleridge G75: E Kil. 4C 148
Coleridge Av. G71: Both. 4F 125
Colfin St. G34: Glas 2A 88
Colgrain St. G20: Glas 3E 63
Colgrave Cres. G32: Glas 2H 105
Colinbar Circ. G78: Barr 6D 114
Colinslee Av. PA2: Pais 4B 98
Colinslee Cres. PA2: Pais 4B 98

Colinslee Dr. PA2: Pais 4B 98
Colinslie Rd. G53: Glas 5D 100
Colinton Pl. G32: Glas 4B 86
Colintraive Av. G33: Glas. 6G 65
Colintraive Cres. G33: Glas. 6G 65
Collace Av. PA11: Bri W 4F 73
Colla Gdns. G64: B'rig 5F 49
College Ga. G65: Bear 1C 44
College La. G1: Glas 4H 83 (6H 5)
COLLEGE MILTON 6D 136
College St. G1: Glas 4H 83 (6G 5)
G82: Dumb 3F 17
Coll. Way Shop. Cen. G82: Dumb . .4F 17
Collessie Dr. G33: Glas 1C 86
Collier St. PA5: John 2F 95
Colliertree Rd. ML6: Air 3D 92
Collina St. G20: Glas. 4B 62
Collins Gallery 4H 83 (5G 5)
Collins St. G4: Glas 4A 84 (5H 5)
G81: Faif 1E 43
Coll Lea ML3: Ham 2D 152
Coll Pl. G21: Glas 1D 84
ML6: Air 6C 92
Collree Gdns. G34: Glas 4A 88
Coll St. G21: Glas 1D 84
ML2: Newm 3D 146
Collylinn Rd. G61: Bear 3E 45
Colmonell Av. G13: Glas 2H 59
Colonsay G74: E Kil 4B 150
Colonsay Av. PA4: Renf 2E 79
Colonsay Cres. ML5: Coat. 1H 109
Colonsay Dr. G77: Newt M. 4B 132
Colonsay Rd. G52: Glas. 6E 81
PA2: Pais 6H 97
Colquhoun Av. G52: Hill. 4A 80
Colquhoun Ct. G41: Glas 1A 102
Colquhoun Dr. G61: Bear. 2D 44
Colquhoun Pk. G52: Hill. 4B 80
(off Hepburn Rd.)
Colquhoun Rd. G82: Milt 4E 19
Colquhoun St. G82: Dumb. 3G 17
Colson Pl. ML4: Bell. 4E 127
COLSTON 2A 64
Colston Av. G64: B'rig 2B 64
Colston Dr. G64: B'rig 2B 64
Colston Gdns. G64: B'rig 2A 64
ML6: Air 4C 92
Colston Gro. G64: B'rig 2B 64
Colston Path G64: B'rig 2A 64
Colston Pl. G64: B'rig 2A 64
ML6: Air 4C 92
Colston Rd. G64: B'rig 2A 64
ML6: Air 4C 92
Colston Ter. ML6: Air. 4C 92
Colt Av. ML5: Coat 3A 90
Coltmuir Cres. G64: B'rig. 1A 64
Coltmuir Dr. G64: B'rig 1A 64
Coltmuir Gdns. G64: B'rig 1A 64
Coltmuir St. G22: Glas 3F 63
COLTNESS 3A 146
Coltness Dr. ML4: Bell 3D 126
Coltness La. G33: Glas. 4C 86
Coltness Rd. ML2: Wis 3A 146
Coltness St. G33: Glas. 3C 86
Coltpark Av. G64: B'rig 1A 64
Coltpark La. G64: B'rig 1B 64
Colt Pl. ML5: Coat 3C 90
Coltsfoot Dr. G53: Glas 4B 116
Coltswood Ct. ML5: Coat. 3C 90
Coltswood Rd. ML5: Coat 2C 90
Colt Ter. ML5: Coat 3C 90
Columba G81: Clyd. 5F 43
Columba Cres. ML1: Moth. 5F 127
Columba Path G72: Blan 1A 140
Columba Sports Complex
. . . . .1C 110
Columba St. G51: Glas 4H 81
Columbia Pl. G75: E Kil. 3D 148
Columbia Way G75: E Kil. 3D 148
Columbine Way ML8: Carl 5F 165
Colvend La. G40: Glas 2B 104
Colvend St. G40: Glas 2B 104

Colville Dr. G73: Ruth 1F 121
Colvilles Pl. G75: E Kil. 5B 150
Colvilles Rd. G75: E Kil 6A 150
Colwood Av. G53: Glas 3A 116
Colwood Gdns. G53: Glas 4A 116
Colwood Path G53: Glas 3A 116
Colwood Pl. G53: Glas 4A 116
Colwood Sq. G53: Glas 4A 116
Colwyn Ct. ML6: Air 2A 92
COLZIUM .1C 12
Colzium Vw. G65: Kils 3A 12
Combe Quad. ML4: Bell 4A 126
Comedie Rd. G33: Step 5E 67
Comely Bank ML3: Ham 6D 140
Comelybank La. G82: Dumb 3D 16
Comelybank Rd. G82: Dumb 3D 16
Comelypark Pl. G31: Glas 5C 84
(off Comelypark St.)
Comelypark St. G31: Glas 5B 84
Commerce St. G5: Glas 6F 83
Commercial Ct. G5: Glas 6H 83
Commercial Rd. G78: Barr. 4E 115
Common Grn. ML3: Ham 5A 142
Commonhead Av. ML6: Air 2H 91
Commonhead La. ML6: Air 2H 91
Commonhead Rd. G34: Glas 3B 88
Commonhead St. ML6: Air 2H 91
Commonside St. ML6: Air 2H 91
Commore Av. G78: Barr 6F 115
Commore Dr. G13: Glas. 2A 60
Commore Pl. G78: Neil 3C 130
Community Av. ML4: Bell. 5C 126
Community Pl. ML4: Bell. 4D 126
Community Rd. ML4: Bell 4B 126
Comrie Cres. ML3: Ham 6B 140
Comrie Rd. G33: Step 4C 66
Comrie St. G32: Glas. 2B 106
Conan Ct. G72: Camb 2D 122
Conan St. G46: T'bnk 3E 117
Condor Glen ML1: Holy 6G 111
CONDORRAT 6C 34
CONDORRAT INTERCHANGE 5D 34
Condorrat Ring Rd.
G67: Cumb. 6D 34
Condorrat Rd. G67: Cumb 4D 54
ML6: Glenm 1F 71
Coneypark Cres. FK4: Bank 1C 14
Coneypark Pl. FK4: Bank 1C 14
Congress Rd. G3: Glas. 4B 82
Congress Way G3: Glas. 4C 82
Conifer Pl. G66: Lenz. 1B 50
Conisborough Path G34: Glas 1F 87
Conisborough Rd. G34: Glas 1F 87
Coniston G75: E Kil 6B 148
Coniston Cres. ML3: Ham 5G 153
Coniston Dr. ML4: Bell. 4D 126
Conistone Cres. G69: Bail 1F 107
Connal St. G40: Glas 2D 104
Connell Cres. G62: Miln. 4A 26
Conniston St. G32: Glas. 4G 85
Connor Rd. G78: Barr 4D 114
Connor St. ML6: Air 2E 93
Conolly's Land G81: Hard 1C 42
(off Dumbarton Rd.)
Conon Av. G61: Bear 4C 44
Conservation Pl. ML2: Wis 1H 157
Consett La. G33: Glas. 3C 86
Consett St. G33: Glas. 3C 86
Constarry Rd. G65: Croy 6A 12
Contin Pl. G20: Glas. 4B 62
Convair Way PA4: Renf 2F 79
Conval Way PA3: Pais 3H 77
Cook St. G5: Glas 6E 83
Coolgardie Grn. G75: E Kil. 4E 149
Coolgardie Pl. G75: E Kil 4E 149
Cooperage Pl. G3: Glas 3A 82
Co-operative Ter. PA5: John 2G 95
Cooper Av. ML8: Carl 2E 165
Cooper's Well St. G11: Glas 2A 82
Copenhagen Av. G75: E Kil 5G 149
Copland Pl. G51: Glas 5H 81
Copland Quad. G51: Glas 5H 81
Copland Rd. G51: Glas 6H 81
Coplaw Ct. G42: Glas. 2E 103

Coplaw St. G42: Glas 2E **103**
Copperfield La. G71: Tann 6E **109**
Coral Mt. Gdns. G66: Kirk 6E **31**
Corbett Ct. G32: Glas 2H **105**
Corbett St. G32: Glas 2H **105**
Corbie Pl. G62: Miln 3D **24**
Corbiston Way G67: Cumb 3B **36**
Cordiner St. G44: Glas 6F **103**
CORKERHILL 3D **100**
Corkerhill Gdns. G52: Glas 1E **101**
Corkerhill Pl. G52: Glas 3D **100**
Corkerhill Rd. G52: Glas 2D **100**
Corkerhill Station (Rail) 3D **100**
Corlaich Av. G42: Glas 6A **104**
Corlaich Dr. G42: Glas 6A **104**
Cormack Av. G64: Torr 4E **29**
Cormorant Av. PA6: C'lee 3D **74**
Cornaig Rd. G53: Glas 5B **100**
Cornalee Gdns. G53: Glas 5A **100**
Cornalee Pl. G53: Glas 5A **100**
(not continuous)
Cornalee Rd. G53: Glas 5B **100**
Cornelian Ter. ML4: Bell 3C **126**
Cornelia St. ML1: Moth 6D **126**
Cornhill Dr. ML5: Coat 3A **90**
Cornhill St. G21: Glas 4C **64**
Cornish Ct. ML5: Coat 3B **90**
Cornock Cres. G81: Clyd 4D **42**
Cornock St. G81: Clyd 4D **42**
Cornsilloch Brae ML9: Lark 2B **162**
Corn St. G4: Glas 1F **83** (1C **4**)
Cornwall Av. G73: Ruth 2F **121**
Cornwall Ct. G74: E Kil 2H **149**
Cornwall St. G41: Glas. 6B **82**
G74: E Kil 2F **149**
Cornwall St. Sth. G41: Glas. 6B **82**
Cornwall Way G74: E Kil 2H **149**
Coronation Av. ML9: Lark 5E **161**
Coronation Cres. ML9: Lark 5E **161**
Coronation Pl. G69: G'csh 2C **68**
ML9: Lark 5F **161**
Coronation Rd. ML1: New S 3H **127**
Coronation Rd. E. ML1: New S . . 4H **127**
Coronation St. ML2: Wis 6B **146**
Coronation Way G61: Bear. 5F **45**
Corpach Pl. G34: Glas 2B **88**
Corporation Yd. G15: Glas. 4H **43**
Corra Linn ML3: Ham 6E **141**
Corran Av. G77: Newt M 3C **132**
Corran St. G33: Glas 3H **85**
Correen Gdns. G61: Bear 6B **24**
Corrie Brae G65: Kils 2G **11**
Corrie Ct. ML3: Ham 1D **152**
Corrie Dr. ML1: Moth. 2D **142**
PA1: Pais 1G **99**
Corrie Gro. G44: Neth 3D **118**
Corrie Pl. G66: Lenz 3E **51**
Corrie Rd. G65: Kils 2G **11**
Corrie Vw. G68: Cumb 5B **34**
Corrie Way ML9: Lark 3F **161**
Corrour Rd. G43: Glas 6B **102**
G77: Newt M 3C **132**
Corsebar Av. PA2: Pais 3G **97**
Corsebar Cres. PA2: Pais 4G **97**
Corsebar Dr. PA2: Pais 3G **97**
Corsebar La. PA2: Pais 4F **97**
Corsebar Rd. PA2: Pais 4F **97**
Corsebar Way PA2: Pais 2G **97**
CORSEFORD 6B **94**
Corseford Av. PA5: John 5C **94**
Corsehill Path G34: Glas 3A **88**
Corsehill Pl. G34: Glas 3A **88**
Corsehill St. G34: Glas 3A **88**
Corselet Rd. G53: Glas 4A **116**
G78: Barr 1A **132**
Corse Rd. G52: Glas 5G **79**
Corsewall St. G32: Glas. 2E **107**
Corsewall St. ML5: Coat 4A **90**
Corsford Dr. G53: Glas 1C **116**
Corsock Av. ML3: Ham. 1C **152**
Corsock St. G31: Glas 4D **84**
Corston St. G33: Glas 3F **85**
Cortachy Pl. G64: B'rig 6F **49**

Coruisk Dr. G76: Clar 1B **134**
Coruisk Way PA2: Pais. 5C **96**
Corunna Ct. ML8: Carl 4H **165**
Corunna St. G3: Glas 3C **82**
Coshneuk Rd. G33: Mille 4B **66**
Cosy Neuk ML9: Lark 4G **161**
Cottar St. G20: Glas 2C **62**
Cotton Av. PA3: Lin 6H **75**
Cotton St. G40: Glas. 3C **104**
PA1: Pais 1B **98**
Cotton St. Ent. Pk. G40: Glas. . . . 3B **104**
Cotton Va. ML1: Cle 1E **145**
Coulin Gdns. G22: Glas 5H **63**
Coulter Av. ML2: Wis 2A **146**
ML5: Coat 3A **90**
Countess Way G69: Barg 6E **89**
(off Princess Dr.)
County Av. G72: Camb 6F **105**
County Pl. PA1: Pais 6A **78**
County Sq. PA1: Pais 6A **78**
Couper Pl. G4: Glas 2H **83** (2G **5**)
Couper St. G4: Glas 2H **83** (2G **5**)
Coursington Cres. ML1: Moth 2A **144**
Coursington Gdns.
ML1: Moth 2H **143**
Coursington Rd. ML1: Moth 2H **143**
(not continuous)
Coursington Twr. ML1: Moth. . . . 2H **143**
(off Coursington Rd.)
Courthill G61: Bear 1D **44**
Court Hill G65: Kils 3A **12**
Courthill Av. G44: Glas. 2F **119**
Courthill Cres. G65: Kils 3A **12**
Coustonholm Rd. G43: Glas. 6B **102**
Couther Quad. ML6: Air. 1A **92**
Covanerton Rd. ML3: Ham 2B **154**
Covenant Cres. ML9: Lark 3F **161**
Covenanters Way
ML2: Over 5A **158**
Covenany Pl. ML2: Wis 1C **156**
Coventry Dr. G31: Glas 3D **84**
Cowal Cres. G66: Kirk 4H **31**
Cowal Dr. PA3: Lin 6G **75**
Cowal St. G20: Glas 2A **62**
Cowal Vw. G81: Clyd 4D **42**
Cowan Cres. G78: Barr 4F **115**
Cowan La. G12: Glas 1C **82**
(off Glasgow St.)
Cowan Rd. G68: Cumb 3D **34**
Cowan St. G12: Glas 1C **82**
Cowan Wilson Av. G72: Blan 1B **140**
Cowan Wynd G71: Tann 5E **109**
ML2: Over 4A **158**
COWCADDENS 2F **83** (1E **5**)
Cowcaddens Rd.
G4: Glas 2F **83** (2C **4**)
Cowcaddens Station (Und.)
. . . . 2F **83** (2C **4**)
Cowden Dr. G64: B'rig 4C **48**
Cowdenhill Cir. G13: Glas 1D **60**
Cowdenhill Pl. G13: Glas 1D **60**
Cowdenhill Rd. G13: Glas 1D **60**
Cowden St. G51: Glas 4D **80**
Cowdray Cres. PA4: Renf 6F **59**
Cowgate G66: Kirk 4C **30**
Cowglen Rd. G53: Glas 6C **100**
COWLAIRS 5A **64**
Cowlairs Ind. Est. G21: Glas 5H **63**
Cowlairs Rd. G21: Glas 5A **64**
(off Kemp St.)
G21: Glas 5A **64**
(Millarbank St.)
Coxdale Av. G66: Kirk 5B **30**
Coxhill St. G21: Glas 6H **63**
Coxton Pl. G33: Glas 2D **86**
Coylton Cres. ML3: Ham 2C **152**
Coylton Rd. G43: Glas 2C **118**
Crabb Quad. ML1: Moth 6E **127**
Cragdale G74: E Kil 6E **137**
Craggan Dr. G14: Glas 3H **59**
Crags Av. PA2: Pais 4B **98**
Crags Cres. PA2: Pais 3B **98**
Crags Rd. PA2: Pais 4B **98**

Cragwell Pk. G76: Crmck. 2A **136**
Craigallan Av. G72: Camb 3D **122**
Craigallian Av. G62: Miln 1F **25**
Craiganour La. G43: Glas 1A **118**
Craiganour Pl. G43: Glas 1A **118**
Craigard Pl. G73: Ruth. 4F **121**
Craigash Quad. G62: Miln 2E **25**
Craigash Rd. G62: Miln 3E **25**
Craigbank Dr. G53: Glas 1A **116**
Craigbank Rd. ML9: Lark 5E **161**
Craigbank St. ML9: Lark 4E **161**
Craigbanzo St. G81: Faif. 5F **23**
Craigbarnet Av. G64: Torr 5C **28**
Craigbarnet Cres. G33: Mille 5B **66**
Craigbarnet Rd. G62: Miln. 3D **24**
Craigbet Av. PA11: Q'riers 1A **72**
Craigbet Cres. PA11: Q'riers 1A **72**
Craigbet Pl. PA11: Q'riers 1A **72**
Craigbo Av. G23: Glas 6B **46**
Craigbo Ct. G23: Glas 1B **62**
Craigbo Dr. G23: Glas 6B **46**
Craigbog Av. PA5: John 4D **94**
Craigbog Rd. PA5: John. 5F **95**
Craigbo Pl. G23: Glas 1B **62**
Craigbo Rd. G23: Glas 1B **62**
Craigbo St. G23: Glas 6B **46**
Craigburn Av. PA6: C'lee 3D **74**
Craigburn Ct. ML9: Ashg 4B **162**
Craigburn Cres. PA6: C'lee 4D **74**
Craigburn Pl. PA6: C'lee 4D **74**
Craigburn St. ML3: Ham 3H **153**
Craig Cres. G66: Kirk. 6H **31**
(off Bk. o'Dykes Rd.)
Craigdhu Av. G62: Miln 4F **25**
ML6: Air 4E **93**
Craigdhu Farm Cotts. G62: Miln . . . 4E **25**
Craigdhu Rd. G61: Bear. 5D **24**
(not continuous)
Craigdonald Pl. PA5: John 2F **95**
Craigellan Rd. G43: Glas 1B **118**
Craigelvan Av. G67: Cumb 1B **54**
Craigelvan Ct. G67: Cumb 1B **54**
Craigelvan Dr. G67: Cumb 1B **54**
Craigelvan Gdns. G67: Cumb 1B **54**
Craigelvan Gro. G67: Cumb 1B **54**
Craigelvan Pl. G67: Cumb 1B **54**
Craigelvan Vw. G67: Cumb 1B **54**
Craigenbay Cres. G66: Lenz 2E **51**
Craigenbay Rd. G66: Lenz 3D **50**
Craigenbay St. G21: Glas 5D **64**
Craigencart Ct. G81: Dun. 1B **42**
CRAIGEND 6C **66**
Craigend Cres. G62: Miln. 3F **25**
Craigend Dr. ML5: Coat 1G **109**
Craigend Dr. W. G62: Miln 3E **25**
Craigend Ho. G82: Dumb 3C **16**
CRAIGENDMUIR 5E **67**
Craigendmuir Cvn. Site G33: Step. . . 5E **67**
Craigendmuir Rd. G33: Step 5E **67**
Craigendmuir St. G33: Glas 1F **85**
Craigendon Oval PA2: Pais 6G **97**
Craigendon Rd. PA2: Pais 6G **97**
Craigend Pl. G13: Glas. 3E **61**
Craigend Rd. G67: Cumb 2B **54**
CRAIGENDS 3D **74**
Craigends Av. PA11: Q'riers. 1A **72**
Craigends Dr. PA10: Kilb 2A **94**
Craigends Pl. PA11: Q'riers 1A **72**
Craigends Rd. PA6: C'lee, Hous . . . 4D **74**
Craigend St. G13: Glas. 3E **61**
Craigend Vw. G67: Cumb 2B **54**
Craigenfeoch Av. PA5: John 4D **94**
Craigens Rd. ML6: Gart 6F **93**
Craigfaulds Av. PA2: Pais. 3F **97**
Craigfell Ct. ML3: Ham 1C **152**
Craigflower Av. G53: Glas 3A **116**
Craigflower Gdns. G53: Glas 3A **116**
Craigflower Rd. G53: Glas 4A **116**
Craig Gdns. G77: Newt M 5C **132**
Craighalbert Rd. G68: Cumb 2E **35**
(not continuous)
CRAIGHALBERT RDBT. 1E **35**
Craighalbert Way G68: Cumb 1E **35**
Craighall Quad. G78: Neil 3D **130**

Craighall Rd. G4: Glas 1F **83** (1D **4**)
Craighaw St. G81: Faif 5F **23**
CRAIGHEAD 1E **141**
Craighead Av. G33: Glas 6F **65**
   G66: Milt C 5C **8**
Craighead Dr. G62: Miln 3D **24**
Craighead Rd. G66: Milt C 5C **8**
   PA7: B'ton 5H **39**
Craighead St. G78: Barr 5D **114**
   ML6: Air 3E **93**
Craighead Way G78: Barr 5D **114**
   (not continuous)
Craig Hill G75: E Kil 4E **149**
Craighill Dr. G76: Clar 3B **134**
Craighill Gro. G76: Clar 3B **134**
Craigholme PA6: Hous 1D **74**
Craighouse St. G33: Glas 2A **86**
Craighton Gdns. G66: Len 3H **7**
Craighurst Dr. G81: Dun, Hard .. 6C **22**
Craighurst Rd. G62: Miln 3D **24**
Craigiebar Dr. PA2: Pais 5G **97**
Craigieburn Gdns. G20: Glas 1H **61**
Craigieburn Rd. G67: Cumb 4H **35**
Craigie Dr. G77: Newt M 6E **133**
Craigiehall Av. PA8: Ersk 2E **57**
Craigiehall Cres. PA8: Ersk 2E **57**
Craigiehall Pl. G51: Glas 5B **82**
Craigiehall St. G51: Glas 5C **82**
Craigiehall Way PA8: Ersk 2E **57**
Craigie La. *ML9: Lark* *1F 161*
   (off Duncan Graham St.)
Craigielea Ct. PA4: Renf 5E **59**
Craigielea Cres. G62: Miln 3E **25**
Craigielea Dr. PA3: Pais 5F **77**
Craigielea Pk. PA4: Renf 6E **59**
Craigielea Rd. G81: Dun 6A **22**
   PA4: Renf 6E **59**
Craigielea St. G31: Glas 3C **84**
Craigielinn Av. PA2: Pais 6F **97**
Craigie Pk. G66: Lenz 2E **51**
Craigie St. G42: Glas 3E **103**
Craigievar Pl. G77: Newt M ... 4B **132**
Craigievar St. G33: Glas 1E **87**
Craiglea Pl. ML6: Air 3C **92**
Craiglea Ter. ML6: Plain 1E **95**
Craiglee G75: E Kil 6G **149**
Craigleith St. G32: Glas 5G **85**
CRAIGLINN 4B **34**
Craiglinn Pk. Rd. G68: Cumb ... 4C **34**
CRAIGLINN RDBT. 4C **34**
Craiglockhart St. G33: Glas 1D **86**
Craigmaddie Gdns. G64: Torr ... 5C **28**
Craigmaddie Rd.
   G62: Balder, Bard 3D **26**
Craigmaddie Ter. La. *G3: Glas* ... *2C 82*
   (off Derby St.)
CRAIGMARLOCH 1E **35**
Craigmarloch Av. G64: Torr 5D **28**
CRAIGMARLOCH RDBT. 2E **35**
Craigmillar Av. G62: Miln 3H **25**
Craigmillar Rd. G42: Glas 6E **103**
Craigmochan Av. ML6: Air 1H **91**
Craigmont Dr. G20: Glas 3C **62**
Craigmont St. G20: Glas 3C **62**
Craigmore Pl. ML5: Coat 2A **110**
Craigmore Rd. G61: Bear 6B **24**
Craigmore St. G31: Glas 5E **85**
Craigmore Wynd *ML9: Lark* *1F 161*
   (off Carrick Pl.)
Craigmount Av. PA2: Pais 6G **97**
Craigmount St. G66: Kirk 6D **30**
Craigmuir Cres. G52: Glas 5H **79**
Craigmuir Gdns. G72: Blan 3H **139**
Craigmuir Pl. G52: Glas 5G **79**
Craigmuir Rd. G52: Glas 5G **79**
   G72: Blan 3H **139**
Craigneil St. G33: Glas 1E **87**
Craigneith Castle (Ruins) *6E 139*
Craigneith Ct. G74: E Kil 5E **139**
Craignethan Rd. G46: Giff 2G **133**
   ML8: Carl 2E **165**
CRAIGNEUK
   Airdrie 4D **92**
   Wishaw 5D **144**

Craigneuk Av. ML6: Air 5C **92**
Craigneuk St. ML1: Moth. 4B **144**
   ML2: Wis 4B **144**
Craignure Cres. ML6: Air 4E **93**
Craignure Rd. G73: Ruth. 4D **120**
Craigpark G31: Glas 4C **84**
Craigpark Dr. G31: Glas 4C **84**
Craigpark St. G81: Faif 6F **23**
Craigpark Ter. *G31: Glas* *4C 84*
   (off Craigpark)
Craigpark Way G71: Tann 6E **109**
Craig Pl. G77: Newt M 4B **132**
Craig Rd. G44: Glas 2E **119**
   G78: Neil 3D **130**
   PA3: Lin 4F **75**
Craigs Av. G81: Faif, Hard 1E **43**
Craigsheen Av. G76: Crmck 2H **135**
Craigside Ct. G68: Cumb 6B **34**
Craigside Pl. G68: Cumb 6B **34**
Craigside Rd. G68: Cumb 6B **34**
Craigson Pl. ML6: Air 4F **93**
Craigstone Vw. G65: Kils 3B **12**
Craigston Pl. PA5: John 3F **95**
Craigston Rd. PA5: John 3E **95**
Craig St. G72: Blan 3C **140**
   ML5: Coat. 1B **110**
   ML6: Air 4H **91**
Craigthornhill Rd. ML3: Ham ... 6A **160**
CRAIGTON 6D **80**
Craigton Av. G62: Miln 3F **25**
   G78: Barr 6G **115**
Craigton Cl. G77: Newt M 4B **132**
Craigton Cotts. G62: Miln 1C **24**
Craigton Crematorium G52: Glas .. 6D **80**
Craigton Dr. G51: Glas 5F **81**
   G77: Newt M 4C **132**
   G78: Barr 6G **115**
Craigton Gdns. G62: Miln. 2E **25**
Craigton Ind. Est. G52: Glas 6D **80**
Craigton Pl. G51: Glas 5E **81**
   G72: Blan 6B **124**
Craigton Rd. G51: Glas. 5F **81**
   G62: Miln 2C **24**
   G77: Newt M 6H **131**
Craigton St. G81: Faif 5F **23**
CRAIGTON VILLAGE 2B **24**
Craigvale Cres. ML6: Air 4E **93**
Craigvicar Gdns. G32: Glas ... 1D **106**
Craigview PA5: John 5D **94**
Craigview Pl. ML1: Moth 1H **143**
Craigview Ter. PA5: John 4D **94**
Craigwell Av. G73: Ruth. 1F **121**
Crail St. G31: Glas 1F **105**
Craithie Ct. G11: Glas 1G **81**
Crammond Av. ML5: Coat 1G **109**
Cramond Av. PA4: Renf 1G **79**
Cramond St. G5: Glas 3H **103**
Cramond Ter. G32: Glas 6B **86**
Cranborne Rd. G12: Glas 4G **61**
Cranbrooke Dr. G20: Glas 2B **62**
CRANHILL 3B **86**
Crannog Rd. G82: Milt 4E **19**
CRANSTON HILL 3D **82**
Cranston St. G3: Glas 4D **82**
Cranworth La. *G12: Glas* *6B 62*
   (off Gt. George St.)
Cranworth St. G12: Glas 6B **62**
Crarae Av. G61: Bear 5E **45**
Crarae Pl. G77: Newt M 4A **132**
Crathes Ct. G44: Glas 3C **118**
Crathie Ct. ML8: Carl 2E **165**
Crathie Dr. G11: Glas 1G **81**
   ML6: Glenm 5H **71**
Crathie Pl. G77: Newt M 5H **133**
Crathie Quad. ML2: Wis 4H **145**
Crauchlan Av. PA2: Pais. 5A **98**
Crawford Av. G66: Lenz 4D **50**
Crawford Ct. G46: Giff 6H **117**
Crawford Cres. G71: Udd. 6C **108**
   G72: Blan 6B **124**
Crawford Dr. G15: Glas 6H **43**
   G74: E Kil 1B **150**
CRAWFORDDYKE 4G **165**

Crawford Gdns. G72: Blan 2H **139**
Crawford Hill G74: E Kil 1B **150**
Crawford La. *G11: Glas* *1G 81*
   (off Crawford St.)
Crawford Path *G11: Glas* *1G 81*
   (off Crawford St.)
Crawford Rd. G62: Miln 1F **25**
   G73: Ruth. 3D **120**
   PA6: C'lee. 2D **74**
Crawford St. G11: Glas 1G **81**
   ML1: Moth 3E **143**
   ML3: Ham. 4E **141**
Crawfurd Dr. PA3: Pais. 5F **77**
Crawfurd Gdns. G73: Ruth. 3E **121**
Crawriggs Av. G66: Kirk. 1D **50**
Craw Rd. PA2: Pais 2G **97**
Creamery Rd. ML2: Wis 2B **158**
Crebar Dr. G78: Barr 5E **115**
Crebar St. G46: T'bnk. 3E **117**
Credon Dr. ML6: Air 6A **92**
Credon Gdns. G73: Ruth. 3E **121**
Cree Av. G64: B'rig 6F **49**
Cree Gdns. G32: Glas 6H **85**
Cree Pl. G75: E Kil 2D **148**
Creighton Gro. G74: E Kil 2G **149**
Creran Ct. ML3: Ham 2E **153**
Creran Dr. PA4: Renf 5D **58**
Creran Path *ML2: Newm* *3D 146*
   (off Tiree Cres.)
Crescent Ct. *G81: Clyd.* *4A 42*
   (off Crescent, The)
Crescent Rd. G13: Glas 4B **60**
   G14: Glas 4B **60**
Crescent, The G62: Miln 5G **25**
   G76: Busby. 4E **135**
   G81: Clyd 4A **42**
Cressdale Av. G45: Glas 5H **119**
Cressdale Ct. G45: Glas 5H **119**
Cressdale Dr. G45: Glas 5H **119**
Cressland Dr. G45: Glas 6H **119**
Cressland Pl. G45: Glas. 6H **119**
Cresswell Gro. G77: Newt M. ... 6D **132**
Cresswell La. *G12: Glas* *6B 62*
   (off Cresswell St.)
Cresswell Pl. G77: Newt M 6E **133**
Cresswell St. G12: Glas 6B **62**
Cressy St. G51: Glas 3E **81**
Crest Av. G13: Glas 1B **60**
Crestlea Av. PA2: Pais 5A **98**
Creswell Ter. G71: Udd 1C **124**
Crichton Ct. G45: Glas 5B **120**
Crichton Pl. G21: Glas 5A **64**
Crichton St. G21: Glas 5A **64**
   ML5: Coat. 3C **90**
Cricketfield La. PA6: Hous 1B **74**
Crieff Av. ML6: Chap 4D **112**
Criffell Gdns. G32: Glas 2D **106**
Criffell Rd. G32: Glas. 1D **106**
Criffel Pl. *ML1: N'hill* *4C 128*
   (off Clarinda Pl.)
Crighton Wynd ML4: Bell 2H **125**
Crimea St. G2: Glas 4E **83** (6A **4**)
Crimond Pl. G65: Kils 2F **11**
Crinan Cres. ML5: Coat 2H **89**
Crinan Gdns. G64: B'rig 6E **49**
Crinan Pl. ML4: Bell. 3D **126**
   ML5: Coat 2H **89**
Crinan Rd. G64: B'rig 6E **49**
Crinan St. G31: Glas 3D **84**
CRINDLEDYKE 4G **147**
Crindledyke Cres. ML2: Newm ... 3F **147**
Cripps Av. G81: Clyd. 6F **43**
Croft ML9: Lark 3D **160**
Croftbank Av. G71: Both. 6F **125**
Croftbank Cres. G71: Both 6F **125**
   G71: Udd 1D **124**
Croftbank Ga. G71: Both. 6F **125**
Croftbank St. G21: Glas 5B **64**
Croftburn Dr. G44: Glas 3H **119**
Croftcot Av. ML4: Bell 4B **126**
Croftcroighn Rd. G33: Glas 2B **86**
Croftend Av. G44: Glas. 1A **120**
Croftend La. G44: Glas. 2B **120**
CROFTFOOT 2A **120**

Croftfoot Cres. G45: Glas 3C 120
Croftfoot Dr. G45: Glas 3B 120
Croftfoot Pl. G69: G'csh 3E 69
Croftfoot Quad. G45: Glas 3A 120
Croftfoot Rd. G44: Glas 3H 119
   G45: Glas 3B 120
Croftfoot Station (Rail) 1A 120
Croftfoot St. G45: Glas 3C 120
Croftfoot Ter. G45: Glas 3B 120
Crofthead Cotts. G78: Neil 2C 130
Crofthead Cres. ML4: Bell 4B 126
Crofthead Dr. G66: Len 2E 7
Crofthead La. G66: Kirk 4C 30
                (off W. High St.)
Crofthead Pl. G77: Newt M 6E 133
   ML4: Bell 4B 126
Crofthead St. G71: Udd 2D 124
Crofthill Av. G71: Udd 1D 124
Crofthill Rd. G44: Glas 1H 119
Crofthouse Dr. G44: Glas 3A 120
Croftmont Av. G44: Glas 3A 120
Croftmoraig Av. G69: Mood 3E 53
Crofton Av. G44: Glas 3H 119
Croftpark Av. G44: Glas 3G 119
Croftpark Cres. G72: Blan 3C 140
Croftpark Rd. G81: Hard 6D 22
Croftpark St. ML4: Bell. 1C 126
Croft Pl. ML9: Lark 2D 160
Croft Rd. G64: Balm 5A 28
   G72: Camb 2B 122
   G75: E Kil 4G 149
Croftside Av. G44: Glas 3A 120
Croftspar Av. G32: Glas 5C 86
Croftspar Ct. G32: Glas 5D 86
Croftspar Dr. G32: Glas 5C 86
Croftspar Ga. G32: Glas 5D 86
Croftspar Gro. G32: Glas 5C 86
Croftspar Pl. G32: Glas 5C 86
Croft Way PA4: Renf 2F 79
Croftwood G64: B'rig 3C 48
Croftwood Av. G44: Glas 3H 119
Croftwood Rd. ML3: Ham 2H 153
Croft Wynd G71: Udd 1E 125
Crogal Cres. ML6: Chap 3D 112
Cromalt Cres. G61: Bear 5C 24
Cromarty Av. G43: Glas 1D 118
   G64: B'rig 5F 49
Cromarty Cres. G61: Bear 6F 25
Cromarty Gdns. G76: Clar 6E 119
Cromarty Pl. G69: Chry 6B 52
   G74: E Kil 6C 138
Cromarty Rd. ML6: Air 6H 91
Crombie Gdns. G69: Bail 2F 107
Cromdale St. G51: Glas 4E 81
Cromdale Way ML1: New S 5A 128
Cromer St. G20: Glas 4D 62
Cromer Way PA3: Pais. 4H 77
Crompton Av. G44: Glas 2F 119
Crompton Gro. PA1: Pais 2F 97
Cromwell La. G20: Glas 1E 83
Cromwell St. G20: Glas 1E 83
Crona Dr. ML3: Ham 5C 140
Cronberry Quad. G52: Glas 2H 99
Cronberry Ter. G52: Glas 2H 99
Cronin Pl. ML4: Bell. 6D 110
Cronulla Pl. G65: Kils 3B 12
Crookedshields Rd.
   G72: Camb 2B 138
   G74: Ners 2A 138
CROOKFUR 3C 132
Crookfur Cott. Homes
   G77: Newt M 4D 132
Crookfur Rd. G77: Newt M 3B 132
CROOKSTON 1A 100
Crookston Av. G52: Glas 1A 100
Crookston Castle (Remains of) . . 3B 100
Crookston Ct. G52: Glas 1A 100
Crookston Dr. PA1: Pais. 1H 99
Crookston Gdns. G52: Glas 1H 99
Crookston Gro. G52: Glas 1A 100
Crookstonhill Path G52: Glas 1H 99
            (off Crookston Quad.)
Crookston Path G52: Glas 1H 99
            (off Crookston Quad.)

Crookston Pl. G52: Glas. 1H 99
Crookston Quad. G52: Glas 1H 99
Crookston Rd. G52: Glas 2H 99
   G53: Glas 6A 100
Crookston Station (Rail) 1H 99
Crookston Ter. G52: Glas 1A 100
Crosbie Dr. PA2: Pais. 6C 96
Crosbie La. G20: Glas 1A 62
             (off Crossbie St.)
Crosbie St. G20: Glas 1A 62
Crosbie Wood PA2: Pais. 4F 97
Crossan Dr. G66: Len. 2C 6
Cross Arthurlie St. G78: Barr. 5D 114
Crossbank Av. G42: Glas 4A 104
Crossbank Dr. G42: Glas 4H 103
Crossbank Rd. G42: Glas 4H 103
Crossbank Ter. G42: Glas 4H 103
CROSSBASKET 3F 139
Crossburn Av. G62: Miln. 4F 25
Cross Ct. G64: B'rig 6B 48
Crossdykes G66: Kirk. 6G 31
Crossen La. ML8: Carl. 4H 165
             (off Ramage Rd.)
Crossflat Cres. PA1: Pais. 6C 78
Crossford Dr. G23: Glas 6C 46
Crossgate G66: Kirk. 4D 30
Cross Gates ML4: Bell 3C 126
Crossgates PA7: B'ton 3F 39
Crossgates Av. ML1: Cle 4H 129
Crossgates St. ML9: Lark 1D 160
CROSSHILL
   Baillieston. 6B 88
   Glasgow 4F 103
   G66: Kirk 1D 50
Crosshill Av. G42: Glas 4F 103
Crosshill Dr. G73: Ruth 1D 120
   ML1: Cle. 4H 129
Crosshill Station (Rail) 4F 103
Crosshill Rd. G64: B'rig, Lenz 2E 49
   G66: Lenz. 3H 49
Crosshill St. G66: Len 2F 7
   ML1: Moth 3H 143
   ML5: Coat 2H 93
   ML6: Air 4H 91
Crosshouse Rd. G75: E Kil. 6B 148
Crosslea Gdns. PA6: C'lee 2B 74
CROSSLEE 3B 74
Crosslee Cres. PA6: Hous 2C 74
Crosslee Pk. PA6: C'lee 2C 74
Crosslee Rd. PA11: Bri W 5H 73
Crosslees Dr. G46: T'bnk 4F 117
Crosslees Pk. G46: T'bnk. 4F 117
Crosslees Rd. G46: T'bnk. 5F 117
Crosslee St. G52: Glas 6D 80
CROSSLET 2C 18
Crosslet Av. G82: Dumb 1C 18
Crosslet Ct. G82: Dumb 2C 18
Crosslet Ho. G82: Dumb 2C 18
Crosslet Pl. G82: Dumb 4H 17
Crosslet Rd. G82: Dumb 3G 17
Crossloan Rd. G51: Glas 4F 81
Crossloan Ter. G51: Glas 4F 81
CROSSMILL 3F 115
Crossmill Av. G78: Barr 3F 115
Crossmount Ct. ML8: Carl 3E 165
CROSSMYLOOF. 4B 102
Crossmyloof Gdns. G41: Glas 4B 102
Crossmyloof Station (Rail) 4B 102
Cross Orchard Way ML4: Bell 2C 126
Crosspoint Dr. G23: Glas 6C 46
Cross Rd. PA2: Pais 3F 97
CROSS STOBS. 2C 114
Cross Stone Pl. ML1: Moth 3G 143
Cross St. G32: Carm 4C 106
   PA1: Pais 1G 97
Cross, The PA1: Pais 6A 78
   PA10: Kilb. 2A 94
Crosstobs Rd. G53: Glas 4A 100
Crossveggate G62: Miln. 4H 25
Crossveggate Bus. Pk. G62: Miln . . 4H 25
             (off Crossveggate)
Crossview Av. G69: Bail 6B 88
Crossview Pl. G69: Bail 6B 88
Crossway Gardens 3E 39

Crossways PA6: Hous 1D 74
Cross Wynd G74: E Kil. 1H 149
              (off Hunter St.)
Crovie Rd. G53: Glas 6A 100
Crow Av. ML1: Holy 2B 128
Crowflats Rd. G71: Udd 1C 124
Crowfoot Vw. G71: View 4G 109
Crowford La. G11: Glas 1G 81
             (off Rosevale St.)
Crowhill Cres. ML6: Air 1H 91
Crowhill Rd. G64: B'rig 2B 64
Crowhill St. G22: Glas 3G 63
Crow La. G13: Glas 4F 61
Crowlin Cres. G33: Glas. 3B 86
Crown Av. G81: Clyd 4C 42
Crown Cir. G12: Glas 6A 62
Crown Gdns. G12: Glas 6A 62
Crownhall Pl. G32: Glas 6C 86
Crownhall Rd. G32: Glas 6C 86
Crownpoint Rd. G40: Glas 6B 84
Crownpoint Sports Complex 5B 84
Crown Rd. Nth. G12: Glas 6H 61
Crown Rd. Sth. G12: Glas 6H 61
Crown St. G5: Glas. 1G 103
             (Alexander Cres.)
   G5: Glas 6G 83
              (Ballater St.)
   G5: Glas 1F 103
            (Caledonia Rd.)
   G69: Bail 2F 107
   ML5: Coat 4E 91
   ML6: C'bnk 2B 112
Crown Ter. G12: Glas 6H 61
Crow Rd. G11: Glas 5F 61
   G13: Glas 3F 61
   G66: Len 1F 7
Crow-Wood Cres. ML6: C'bnk 3B 112
Crow-Wood Dr. ML6: Air 4D 92
Crow Wood Rd. G69: Chry 2H 67
Crow-Wood Rd. ML6: C'bnk 3B 112
Crow Wood Ter. G69: Chry 2H 67
CROY. 1A 34
Croy G74: E Kil 6F 137
Croy Pl. G21: Glas 4E 65
Croy Rd. G21: Glas. 4E 65
   ML5: Coat. 1A 110
Croy Station (Rail). 2B 34
Cruachan Av. PA4: Renf 2E 79
Cruachan Dr. G77: Newt M. 6F 133
   G78: Barr 6E 115
Cruachan Rd. G61: Bear 6B 24
   G73: Ruth 4F 121
Cruachan St. G46: T'bnk 3F 117
Cruachan Way G78: Barr 6E 115
Cruden St. G51: Glas 5F 81
Crum Av. G46: T'bnk 4G 117
Crusader Av. G13: Glas 6D 44
Cubie St. G40: Glas 6B 84
Cuckoo Way ML1: Holy 2B 128
Cuilhill Rd. G69: Barg 3D 88
Cuillins, The G69: Mood 3E 53
Cuillin Way G78: Barr 5E 115
Cuilmuir Ter. G65: Croy 1B 34
Cuilmuir Vw. G65: Croy 6B 12
Culbin Dr. G13: Glas 1H 59
Cullen PA8: Ersk. 4E 41
Cullen La. G75: E Kil 4G 149
Cullen Pl. G71: Tann 5E 109
Cullen Rd. G75: E Kil 4F 149
   ML1: Moth 4E 143
Cullen St. G32: Glas 1A 106
Cullins Rd. G73: Ruth 4F 121
Cullins, The G71: Tann 4C 108
Cullion Way ML1: N'hill 2G 129
Cullochrig Rd. ML6: Rigg 5G 55
             (not continuous)
Culloch Rd. G61: Bear 5C 24
Culloden Av. ML4: Bell 3F 127
Culloden St. G31: Glas 3D 84
Culrain Gdns. G32: Glas 6A 86
Culrain St. G32: Glas 6A 86
Culross Hill G74: E Kil 2F 149
Culross La. G32: Glas 1C 106

Culross Pl.—Dalwhinnie Av.

Culross Pl. G74: E Kil 2F 149
ML5: Coat 4B 90
Culross St. G32: Glas 1C 106
Culross Way G69: Mood 4E 53
Culterfell Path ML1: Cle 5H 129
Cult Rd. G66: Lenz 3E 51
Cults St. G51: Glas 5F 81
Culvain Av. G61: Bear 6B 24
Culzean ML6: Glenm 4H 71
Culzean Av. ML5: Coat 6A 90
Culzean Ct. *ML5: Coat 6A 90*
(off Torriden St.)
Culzean Cres. G69: Bail 1G 107
G77: Newt M 4G 133
Culzean Dr. G32: Glas 1D 106
G74: E Kil 6F 137
ML1: Carf 4C 128
Culzean Pl. G74: E Kil 6F 137
Cumberland Pl. G5: Glas 1G 103
ML5: Coat 6G 89
Cumberland St. G5: Glas 6F 83
(not continuous)
CUMBERNAULD 4H 35
Cumbernauld Mus. 4H 35
Cumbernauld Rd.
FK4: C'cry, Longc 1F 15
G31: Glas 4D 84
G33: Glas 4D 84
G33: Mille, Step 5A 66
G33: Step 2G 67
G67: Mollin 3H 53
G68: Mollin 1C 68
G69: Chry 2G 67
G69: Mood 1C 68
G69: Muirh 2A 68
CUMBERNAULD RD. INTERCHANGE 1G 85
Cumbernauld Shop. Cen., The
G67: Cumb 3H 35
Cumbernauld Station (Rail) 5A 36
Cumbernauld Theatre 1B 36
CUMBERNAULD VILLAGE 6B 14
Cumbrae G74: E Kil 2C 150
Cumbrae Ct. G81: Clyd 5D 42
Cumbrae Cres. ML5: Coat 6G 91
Cumbrae Cres. Nth. G82: Dumb 2C 16
Cumbrae Cres. Sth. G82: Dumb 2B 16
Cumbrae Dr. ML1: Moth 1E 143
Cumbrae Pl. ML5: Coat 1G 111
Cumbrae Rd. PA2: Pais 6A 98
PA4: Renf 2F 79
Cumbrae St. G33: Glas 3A 86
Cumlodden Dr. G20: Glas 2A 62
Cumming Dr. G42: Glas 5F 103
Cummock Dr. G78: Barr 6F 115
Cumnock Dr. ML3: Ham 2B 152
ML6: Air 1A 112
Cumnock Rd. G33: Glas 3G 65
Cumroch Rd. G66: Len 2E 7
Cunard Ct. G81: Clyd 1D 58
Cunard St. G81: Clyd 1D 58
Cunningair Dr. ML1: Moth 5G 143
Cunningham Dr. G46: Giff 4C 118
G81: Dun 1B 42
Cunninghame Rd. G73: Ruth 5E 105
G74: E Kil 2G 149
PA10: Kilb 2B 94
Cunningham Gdns. PA6: C'lee 2D 74
Cunningham Rd. G52: Hill 3H 79
Cunningham St. ML1: Moth 3F 143
Cuparhead Av. ML5: Coat 1H 109
Curfew Rd. G13: Glas 6D 44
Curle St. G14: Glas 1D 80
(not continuous)
Curlew Pl. PA5: John 6C 94
Curling Cres. G44: Glas 6G 103
Curlinghaugh Cres. ML2: Wis 6A 146
Curlingmire G75: E Kil 5G 149
Curran Av. ML2: Wis 2E 157
Currie Ct. *PA5: John 4E 95*
(off Tannahill Cres.)
Currie Pl. G20: Glas 3C 62
Currie St. G20: Glas 3C 62
Curtis Av. G44: Glas 5G 103
Curzon St. G20: Glas 3C 62
Cuthbertson St. G42: Glas 2E 103
Cuthbert St. G71: View 6F 109
Cuthelton Dr. G31: Glas 1G 105
Cuthelton St. G31: Glas 1F 105
Cuthelton Ter. G31: Glas 1F 105
Cut, The G71: Udd 2D 124
Cypress Av. G71: View 5F 109
G72: Blan 6A 124
Cypress Ct. G66: Lenz 1B 50
G75: E Kil 6E 149
ML3: Ham 1A 154
Cypress Cres. G75: E Kil 6E 149
Cypress Pl. G75: E Kil 6E 149
Cypress St. G22: Glas 4H 63
Cypress Way G72: Flem 3F 123
Cyprus Av. PA5: Eld 3H 95
Cyril St. PA1: Pais 1C 98

D

Daer Av. PA4: Renf 2G 79
Daer Wlk. ML9: Lark 5E 161
Daer Way ML3: Ham 6E 141
Daffodil Way ML1: Moth 1G 143
Dairsie Ct. G44: Glas 3D 118
Dairsie Gdns. G64: B'rig 1F 65
Dairsie St. G44: Glas 3D 118
Daisy St. G42: Glas 4F 103
Dakala Ct. ML2: Wis 1G 157
Dakota Way PA4: Renf 2F 79
Dalbeattie Braes ML6: Chap 4E 113
DALBETH 3G 105
Dalbeth Pl. G32: Glas 3H 105
Dalbeth Rd. G32: Glas 3H 105
Dalcharn Path *G34: Glas 3G 87*
(off Kildermorie Rd.)
Dalcharn Pl. G34: Glas 3G 87
Dalcraig Cres. G72: Blan 5A 124
Dalcross Pass *G11: Glas 1A 82*
(off Dalcross St.)
Dalcross St. G11: Glas 1A 82
Dalcruin Gdns. G69: Mood 3E 53
Daldowie Av. G32: Glas 2D 106
Daldowie Complex, The (Land Services)
G71: Udd 5G 107
Daldowie Crematorium
G71: Udd 5H 107
DALDOWIE INTERCHANGE 4H 107
Daldowie Rd. G71: Udd 3G 107
Daldowie St. ML5: Coat 2A 110
(not continuous)
Dale Av. G75: E Kil 4E 149
Dale Ct. ML2: Wis 1C 156
Dale Dr. ML1: New S 3A 128
Dale Path *G40: Glas 1B 104*
(off Main St.)
Dale St. G40: Glas 1B 104
(not continuous)
Daleview Av. G12: Glas 3H 61
Daleview Dr. G76: Clar 3B 134
Daleview Gro. G76: Clar 3B 134
Dale Way G73: Ruth 3D 120
Dalfoil Ct. PA1: Pais 1H 99
Dalgarroch Av. G81: Clyd 1G 59
Dalgleish Av. G81: Dun 1A 42
Dalhousie Gdns. G64: B'rig 5B 48
Dalhousie La. G3: Glas 2E 83 (2B 4)
Dalhousie Rd. PA10: Kilb 3B 94
Dalhousie St. G3: Glas 3E 83 (3B 4)
(not continuous)
Dalilea Dr. G34: Glas 2B 88
Dalilea Path *G34: Glas 2B 88*
(off Dalilea Dr.)
Dalilea Pl. G34: Glas 2B 88
Dalintober St. G5: Glas 5E 83
Dalkeith Av. G41: Glas 1H 101
G64: B'rig 4D 48
Dalkeith Rd. G64: B'rig 3D 48
Dalmacoulter Rd. ML6: Air 1B 92
Dalmahoy Cres. PA11: Bri W 5D 72
Dalmahoy St. G32: Glas 4G 85
Dalmally St. G20: Glas 6D 62
DALMARNOCK 2D 104
Dalmarnock Bri. G73: Ruth 3D 104
Dalmarnock Ct. G40: Glas 2D 104
Dalmarnock Dr. G40: Glas 1B 104
Dalmarnock Rd. G40: Glas 1B 104
G73: Ruth 3D 104
Dalmarnock Rd. Ind. Est.
G73: Ruth 4D 104
Dalmarnock Station (Rail) 2C 104
Dalmary Dr. PA1: Pais 5D 78
Dalmellington Ct. *G74: E Kil 1F 149*
(off Dalmellington Dr.)
ML3: Ham 2B 152
Dalmellington Dr. G53: Glas 5A 100
G74: E Kil 1F 149
Dalmellington Rd. G53: Glas 4A 100
Dalmeny Av. G46: Giff 4A 118
Dalmeny Dr. G78: Barr 5C 114
Dalmeny Rd. ML3: Ham 1H 153
Dalmeny St. G5: Glas 3A 104
Dalmoor Dr. ML6: Air 5A 92
DALMUIR 4A 42
Dalmuir Ct. G81: Clyd 4A 42
Dalmuir Station (Rail) 4A 42
Dalnair Pl. G62: Miln 3D 24
Dalnair St. G3: Glas 2A 82
Dalness Pas. *G32: Glas 1A 106*
(off Ochil St.)
Dalness St. G32: Glas 2A 106
Dalnottar Av. G60: Old K 1F 41
Dalnottar Dr. G60: Old K 2F 41
Dalnottar Gdns. G60: Old K 2F 41
Dalnottar Hill Rd. G60: Old K 1F 41
Dalnottar Ter. G60: Old K 1F 41
DALREOCH 3D 16
Dalreoch Av. G69: Bail 6A 88
Dalreoch Ct. G82: Dumb 3D 16
Dalreoch Ho. *G82: Dumb 3D 16*
(off School La.)
Dalreoch Path G69: Bail 6A 88
Dalreoch Station (Rail) 3E 17
Dalriada Cres. ML1: Moth 5F 127
Dalriada Dr. G64: Torr 5E 29
Dalriada St. G40: Glas 1E 105
Dalry Gdns. ML3: Ham 1B 152
Dalrymple Ct. G66: Kirk 6D 30
Dalrymple Dr. G74: E Kil 6G 137
G77: Newt M 5G 133
ML5: Coat 6B 90
Dalry Pl. ML6: Chap 5D 112
Dalry Rd. G71: View 6F 109
Dalry St. G32: Glas 1B 106
DALSERF 3D 162
Dalserf Ct. G31: Glas 6D 84
Dalserf Cres. G46: Giff 6H 117
Dalserf Gdns. G31: Glas 6D 84
Dalserf Path *ML9: Lark 4G 161*
(off Bannockburn Dr.)
Dalserf St. G31: Glas 6D 84
Dalsetter Av. G15: Glas 5H 43
Dalsetter Pl. G15: Glas 5A 44
DALSHANNON 1B 54
Dalshannon Pl. G67: Cumb 6C 34
Dalshannon Rd. G67: Cumb 6D 34
Dalshannon Vw. G67: Cumb 6C 34
Dalshannon Way G67: Cumb 6C 34
Dalsholm Av. G20: Glas 1H 61
Dalsholm Ind. Est. G20: Glas 2H 61
Dalsholm Rd. G20: Glas 2H 61
Dalskeith Av. PA3: Pais 6E 77
Dalskeith Cres. PA3: Pais 6E 77
Dalskeith Rd. PA3: Pais 1E 97
Dalswinton Path G34: Glas 3B 88
Dalswinton St. G34: Glas 3A 88
Dalton Av. G81: Clyd 6G 43
Dalton Cotts. G72: Flem 5F 123
Dalton Hill ML3: Ham 1C 152
Dalton St. G31: Glas 6G 85
Dalveen Ct. G78: Barr 6E 115
Dalveen Dr. G71: Tann 5C 108
Dalveen Quad. ML5: Coat 6F 91
Dalveen St. G32: Glas 6H 85
Dalveen Way G73: Ruth 4E 121
Dalwhinnie Av. G72: Blan 5A 124

Daly Gdns. G72: Blan. 6C **124**
Dalzell Av. ML1: Moth 5A **144**
Dalzell Country Pk. 6H **143**
Dalzell Dr. ML1: Moth 5A **144**
Dalziel Dr. G41: Glas 2A **102**
Dalziel Quad. G41: Glas. 2A **102**
Dalziel Rd. G52: Hill 3H **79**
Dalziel St. ML1: Moth 2H **143**
  ML3: Ham 4F **141**
Dalziel Twr. ML1: Moth 6B **144**
Damshot Cres. G53: Glas 5D **100**
Damshot Rd. G53: Glas 6D **100**
Danby Rd. G69: Bail 1F **107**
Danes Av. G14: Glas 5C **60**
Danes Cres. G14: Glas. 4B **60**
Danes Dr. G14: Glas. 4B **60**
Danes La. Nth. G14: Glas 5C **60**
Danes La. Sth. G14: Glas 5C **60**
Daniel McLaughlin Pl. G66: Kirk . . . 4E **31**
Dargarvel Av. G41: Glas 1H **101**
Dargavel Av. PA7: B'ton. 4H **39**
Dargavel Path G41: Glas 2G **101**
  (off Dumbreck Pl.)
Dargavel Rd. PA7: B'ton 6A **40**
  (not continuous)
Darkwood Ct. PA3: Pais 5F **77**
Darkwood Cres. PA3: Pais 5F **77**
Darkwood Dr. PA3: Pais 5F **77**
Darleith St. G32: Glas 6H **85**
Darley Pl. ML3: Ham 3F **153**
Darley Rd. G68: Cumb. 6G **13**
Darluith Pk. La. PA5: Brkfld 5C **74**
Darluith Rd. PA6: C'lee 5E **75**
Darnaway Av. G33: Glas 1D **86**
Darnaway Dr. G33: Glas 1D **86**
Darnaway St. G33: Glas 1D **86**
Darngavel Ct. ML6: Air. 3F **91**
  (off Monkscourt Av.)
Darnick St. G21: Glas. 6C **64**
Darnley Cres. G64: B'rig 4B **48**
Darnley Gdns. G41: Glas 3C **102**
Darnley Ind. Est. G53: Glas 3B **116**
Darnley Mains Rd. G53: Glas 4C **116**
Darnley Path G46: T'bnk 2E **117**
Darnley Pl. G41: Glas 3C **102**
Darnley Rd. G41: Glas 3C **102**
  G78: Barr 4F **115**
Darnley St. G41: Glas 3D **102**
Darragh Grn. ML2: Newm 3E **147**
Darroch Dr. PA8: Ersk 4D **40**
Darroch Way G67: Cumb 2A **36**
Dartford St. G22: Glas 6F **63**
Darvel Cres. PA1: Pais 1F **99**
Darvel Dr. G77: Newt M 4G **133**
Darwin Pl. G81: Clyd 3H **41**
Darwin Rd. G75: E Kil 3E **149**
Davaar G74: E Kil 2C **150**
Davaar Dr. ML1: Moth 5E **127**
  ML5: Coat 4H **89**
  PA2: Pais 6A **98**
Davaar Pl. G77: Newt M 3C **132**
Davaar Rd. PA4: Renf 2F **79**
Davaar St. G40: Glas 1D **104**
Davan Loan ML2: Newm 3D **146**
  (off Isla Av.)
Dava St. G51: Glas. 4G **81**
Dave Barrie Av. ML9: Lark 6H **155**
Daventry Dr. G12: Glas 4G **61**
David Donnely Pl. G66: Kirk 4C **30**
David Gray Dr. G66: Kirk 4G **31**
David Livingstone Cen. 5C **124**
David Lloyd Leisure 2D **78**
David Pl. G69: Bail 1F **107**
  PA3: Pais 4D **78**
Davidson Cres. G65: Twe 2D **32**
Davidson Gdns. G14: Glas 5E **61**
  (off Westland Dr.)
Davidson La. G14: Glas 5E **61**
  ML8: Carl. 4H **165**
  (off Ramage Rd.)
Davidson Pl. G32: Glas. 5C **86**
Davidson Quad. G81: Dun 1C **42**
Davidson St. G40: Glas 3C **104**
  G81: Clyd 1G **59**

Davidson St. ML5: Coat. 1D **110**
  ML6: Air 3H **91**
Davidson Pl. G66: Lenz. 3F **51**
David St. G40: Glas 6C **84**
  ML5: Coat. 4E **91**
David Way PA3: Pais 4D **78**
Davieland Rd. G46: Giff. 6G **117**
Davie's Acre G74: E Kil 5B **136**
Davies Quad. ML1: Moth 5F **127**
Davie's Sq. G81: Dun. 1C **42**
Davington Dr. ML3: Ham 1B **152**
Daviot St. G51: Glas. 5D **80**
Davlea G51: Glas 4E **81**
Dawson Av. G75: E Kil 2D **148**
Dawson Pl. G4: Glas. 6F **63**
Dawson Rd. G4: Glas 6F **63**
Deaconsbank Av. G46: T'bnk. 6D **116**
Deaconsbank Cres. G46: T'bnk 6D **116**
Deaconsbank Gdns. G46: T'bnk 6E **117**
Deaconsbank Gro. G46: T'bnk. 6D **116**
Deaconsbank Pl. G46: T'bnk 6E **117**
Deacons Rd. G65: Kils 3A **12**
Dealston Rd. G78: Barr 3D **114**
Deanbrae St. G71: Udd 1D **124**
Dean Cres. G69: Chry 6B **52**
  ML3: Ham 2G **153**
DEAN PARK 1G **79**
Dean Pk. Av. G71: Both 5E **125**
Dean Pk. Dr. G72: Camb 3D **122**
Dean Pk. Rd. PA4: Renf 1G **79**
Deans Av. G72: Camb 3D **122**
Deanside Rd. G52: Hill 3A **80**
Deanside Transit Dpt.
  G52: Hill 2A **80**
Deanston Dr. G78: Barr 6D **114**
Deanston Gdns G78: Barr 6D **114**
Deanston Gro. ML5: Coat 2A **110**
Deanston Pk. G78: Barr 6D **114**
Dean St. G81: Clyd. 6E **43**
  ML4: Bell 2D **126**
Deanwood Av. G44: Neth. 4D **118**
Deanwood Rd. G44: Neth 4D **118**
Dechmont G75: E Kil. 6F **149**
Dechmont Av. G72: Camb 4D **122**
  ML1: Moth 2E **143**
Dechmont Cotts. G72: Flem 4F **123**
Dechmont Gdns. G71: Tann. 4C **108**
  G72: Blan 6A **124**
Dechmont Pl. G72: Camb 4D **122**
Dechmont Rd. G71: Tann. 4C **108**
Dechmont St. G31: Glas 1E **105**
  ML3: Ham 1G **153**
Dechmont Vw. G71: Tann. 6E **109**
  ML4: Bell 4B **126**
Dee Av. PA2: Pais 3D **96**
  PA4: Renf 6G **59**
Deedes St. ML6: Air 5F **91**
Dee Dr. PA2: Pais. 4D **96**
Dee Path ML1: Holy 2B **128**
  ML9: Lark 5E **161**
Deep Dale G74: E Kil 6E **137**
Deepdene Rd. G61: Bear 4D **44**
  G69: Mood 5D **52**
Dee Pl. G75: E Kil 4A **148**
  PA5: John 5C **94**
Deerdykes Ct. Nth. G68: Cumb 1A **54**
Deerdykes Ct. Sth. G68: Cumb 2A **54**
Deerdykes Pl. G68: Cumb 1A **54**
Deerdykes Rd. G68: Cumb 1A **54**
DEERDYKES RDBT. 2H **53**
Deerdykes Vw. G68: Cumb 2H **53**
Deer Pk. Ct. ML3: Ham 4H **153**
  ML3: Ham 4A **154**
Deeside Dr. ML8: Carl 2G **165**
Deeside Pl. ML5: Coat. 1F **111**
Dee St. G33: Glas 2F **85**
  ML5: Coat 1H **89**
Dee Ter. ML3: Ham 3F **153**
Delhi Av. G81: Clyd 3G **41**
Dellburn St. ML1: Moth 4A **144**
Dellburn Trad. Est. ML1: Moth 4A **144**

Dell, The G77: Newt M 4H **133**
  ML4: Bell 4F **127**
Delny Pl. G33: Glas 4E **87**
Delvin Rd. G44: Glas 1E **119**
Dempsey Rd. ML4: Bell. 4B **126**
Denbak Av. ML3: Ham 1E **153**
Denbeck St. G32: Glas. 6H **85**
Denbrae St. G32: Glas. 6H **85**
Dene Wlk. G64: B'rig 1E **65**
Denewood Av. PA2: Pais 5H **97**
Denham St. G22: Glas 6F **63**
Denholm Cres. G75: E Kil 3G **149**
Denholm Dr. G46: Giff 6A **118**
  ML2: Wis 3A **146**
Denholm Grn. G75: E Kil 3H **149**
Denholm Ter. ML3: Ham 6C **140**
Denmark St. G22: Glas 5G **63**
Denmark St. Ind. Cen. G22: Glas . . 4G **63**
Denmilne Gdns. G34: Glas 4A **88**
Denmilne Path G34: Glas. 4A **88**
Denmilne Rd. G69: Barg 4B **88**
Denmilne St. G34: Glas. 4A **88**
DENNISTOUN 4C **84**
Dennistoun St. ML4: Bell. 2C **126**
Dennystoun Forge G82: Dumb. 3E **17**
DENNYSTOWN 3D **16**
Dentdale G74: E Kil 6E **137**
Deramore Av. G46: Giff 2G **133**
Derby St. G3: Glas. 3C **82**
Derby Ter. La. G3: Glas 3C **82**
  (off Derby St.)
Derby Wynd ML1: Carf. 6B **128**
Derrywood Rd. G66: Milt C 5C **8**
Derwent Dr. ML5: Coat 1G **89**
Derwent St. G22: Glas 5F **63**
Derwentwater G75: E Kil 5B **148**
Despard Av. G32: Glas. 1D **106**
Despard Gdns. G32: Glas. 1E **107**
Deveron Av. G46: Giff 5B **118**
Deveron Cres. ML3: Ham 5B **140**
Deveron Rd. G61: Bear 5C **44**
  G74: E Kil 2A **150**
  ML1: Holy. 1B **128**
Deveron St. G33: Glas 2F **85**
  ML5: Coat 2G **89**
Deveron Way G67: Cumb 4H **35**
  (in Cumbernauld Shop. Cen.)
  PA2: Pais 4D **96**
Devine Ct. ML2: Wis 6H **145**
Devine Gro. ML2: Newm 2E **147**
Devlin Gro. G72: Blan 2C **140**
Devol Cres. G53: Glas 5B **100**
Devondale Av. G72: Blan 6A **124**
Devon Dr. PA7: B'ton 4A **40**
Devon Gdns. G64: B'rig 4B **48**
  ML8: Carl 3E **165**
Devonhill Av. ML3: Ham 4H **153**
Devon Pl. G41: Glas 1F **103**
Devonport Pk. G75: E Kil 4C **148**
Devonshire Gdns. G12: Glas 5H **61**
Devonshire Gdns. La. G12: Glas . . 5H **61**
Devonshire Ter. G12: Glas 5H **61**
Devonshire Ter. La. G12: Glas 5H **61**
Devon St. G5: Glas. 1F **103**
Devonview Pl. ML6: Air. 5H **91**
Devonview St. ML6: Air. 4H **91**
Devon Wlk. G68: Cumb 5A **34**
Devon Way ML1: Moth 3D **142**
Dewar Cl. G71: Tann 4E **109**
Dewar Dr. G15: Glas 4A **44**
Dewar Ga. G15: Glas 4A **44**
Diamond St. ML4: Bell. 3C **126**
Diana Av. G13: Glas. 1B **60**
Diana Quad. ML1: Holy 2A **128**
Dickens Av. G81: Clyd 3B **42**
Dickens Gro. ML1: Carf 5D **128**
Dickson Sq. ML1: Cle 6H **129**
Dickson St. ML9: Lark 4G **161**
Dicks Pk. G75: E Kil 3F **149**
Dick St. G20: Glas 6D **62**
Differ Av. G65: Twe 3D **32**
Dilwara Av. G14: Glas 1E **81**
Dimity St. PA5: John 3F **95**
DIMSDALE 2A **158**

Dimsdale Cres. ML2: Wis 2A **158**
Dimsdale Rd. ML2: Wis. 2A **158**
Dinard Dr. G46: Giff 3A **118**
Dinart St. G33: Glas 2F **85**
Dinduff St. G34: Glas 2A **88**
Dinmont Av. PA2: Pais 4D **96**
Dinmont Cres. ML1: Moth 5E **127**
Dinmont Pl. *G41: Glas* *4C 102*
           (off Dinmont Rd.)
Dinmont Rd. G41: Glas 4B **102**
Dinmont Way PA2: Pais 4C **96**
Dinnet Way *ML2: Newm* *3D 146*
           (off Isla Av.)
Dinwiddie St. G21: Glas. 1E **85**
Dinyra Pl. ML5: Glenb 3G **69**
Dipple Pl. G15: Glas 5B **44**
Dirleton Dr. G41: Glas 5C **102**
  PA2: Pais 4E **97**
Dirleton Ga. G61: Bear 4D **44**
Dirleton Pl. G41: Glas 5C **102**
Divernia Way G78: Barr 6E **115**
Dixon Av. G42: Glas 3E **103**
  G82: Dumb 4E **17**
Dixon Dr. G82: Dumb. 5D **16**
Dixon Pl. G74: E Kil 6D **136**
Dixon Rd. G42: Glas 4F **103**
Dixons Blazes Ind. Est. G5: Glas. . 2G **103**
Dixon St. G1: Glas 5F **83**
  ML3: Ham 6H **141**
  ML5: Coat 1D **110**
  PA1: Pais 1B **98**
Dobbies Ct. ML8: Law 5E **159**
Dobbie's Loan G4: Glas. 2F **83** (1D **4**)
DOBBIES LOAN INTERCHANGE
  . . . . 2G **83** (1E **5**)
Dobbie's Loan Pl.
  G4: 3H **83** (3G **5**)
Dochart Av. PA4: Renf 2G **79**
Dochart Dr. G68: Cumb 6E **13**
  ML5: Coat 1G **89**
Dochart St. G33: Glas 1G **85**
Dock St. G81: Clyd 2F **59**
Dodhill Pl. G13: Glas 3B **60**
Dodside Gdns. G32: Glas. 1C **106**
Dodside Pl. G32: Glas 1C **106**
Dodside St. G32: Glas 1C **106**
Dolan St. G69: Bail 6H **87**
Dollan Aqua Cen. *2G 149*
Dollar Pk. ML1: Moth 6B **144**
Dollar Ter. *G20: Glas* *1A 62*
           (off Crosbie St.)
Dolley Rd. ML2: Wis 6G **145**
Dolphin Rd. G41: Glas 3B **102**
Dominica Grn. G75: E Kil 2C **148**
Donald Dewar Leisure Cen.
  . . . . *4A 44*
Donaldfield Rd.
  PA11: Bri W 4D **72**
Donaldson Av. G65: Kils 4H **11**
Donaldson Cres. G66: Kirk 6C **30**
Donaldson Dr. PA4: Renf 6E **59**
Donaldson Grn. G71: Tann 5E **109**
Donaldson Pl. G66: Kirk 5D **30**
Donaldson Rd. ML9: Lark 4G **161**
Donaldson St. G66: Kirk 6C **30**
  ML3: Ham. 4E **141**
Donaldswood Pk. PA2: Pais 5G **97**
Donaldswood Rd. PA2: Pais 5G **97**
Donald Ter. ML3: Ham. 2G **153**
Donald Way G71: Tann 6E **109**
Don Av. PA4: Renf 1G **79**
Doncaster St. G20: Glas. 6E **63**
Don Ct. ML3: Ham 3E **153**
Don Dr. PA2: Pais. 4D **96**
Donnelly Way ML2: Wis 5C **144**
Donnies Brae G78: Barr 1F **131**
Donohoe Ct. G64: B'rig 6C **48**
Don Path ML9: Lark 5E **161**
Don Pl. PA5: John 5C **94**
Don St. G33: Glas 3F **85**
Doon Cres. G61: Bear 4D **44**
Doonfoot Ct. G74: E Kil. 1F **149**
Doonfoot Gdns. G74: E Kil 1F **149**
Doonfoot Rd. G43: Glas 1B **118**

Doon Pl. G66: Kirk 3F **31**
Doon Rd. G66: Kirk. 4F **31**
Doonside G67: Cumb 3B **36**
Doonside Twr. ML1: Moth 5B **144**
Doon St. G81: Clyd 4F **43**
  ML1: Moth 5A **144**
  ML9: Lark 3G **161**
Doon Way G66: Kirk. 4G **31**
Dorain Rd. ML1: N'hill 4D **128**
Dora St. G40: Glas 2C **104**
Dorchester Av. G12: Glas 3G **61**
Dorchester Ct. G12: Glas 3G **61**
Dorchester Pl. G12: Glas 3G **61**
Dorian Dr. G76: Clar 1H **133**
Dorlin Rd. G33: Step 4E **67**
Dormanside Ct. G53: Glas 2B **100**
Dormanside Ga. G53: Glas 2B **100**
Dormanside Gro. G53: Glas. 2B **100**
Dormanside Pl. G53: Glas 4C **100**
Dormanside Rd. G53: Glas 2B **100**
           (not continuous)
Dornal Av. G13: Glas 2G **59**
Dornford Av. G32: Glas 3D **106**
Dornford Rd. G32: Glas 3D **106**
Dornie Dr. G32: Carm 5B **106**
Dornie Path *ML2: Newm* *3D 146*
           (off Isla Av.)
Dornoch Av. G46: Giff 6A **118**
Dornoch Ct. ML4: Bell 1C **126**
Dornoch Pl. G64: B'rig 5F **49**
  G69: Chry 6B **52**
  G74: E Kil 1E **149**
Dornoch Rd. G61: Bear 5D **44**
  ML1: Holy. 3B **128**
Dornoch St. G40: Glas 6B **84**
Dornoch Way G68: Cumb. 6A **14**
  ML6: Air 6H **91**
Dorset Sq. *G3: Glas* *3D 82*
           (off Dorset St.)
Dorset St. G3: Glas 3D **82**
Dosk Av. G13: Glas 1H **59**
Dosk Pl. G13: Glas 1H **59**
Double Hedges Rd. G78: Neil . . . 3D **130**
Dougalston Av. G62: Miln 4H **25**
Dougalston Cres. G62: Miln 4H **25**
Dougalston Gdns. Nth. G62: Miln . . 4H **25**
Dougalston Gdns. Sth.
  G62: Miln. 4H **25**
Dougalston Rd. G23: Glas 1C **62**
Douglas Av. G32: Carm 4B **106**
  G46: Giff 6A **118**
  G66: Lenz 2D **50**
  G73: Ruth 2E **121**
  PA5: Eld 3H **95**
Douglas Ct. G66: Lenz. 2D **50**
Douglas Cres. G71: Tann 5F **109**
  ML3: Ham 5H **153**
  ML6: Air 5A **92**
  PA8: Ersk 4D **40**
Douglasdale G74: E Kil 1F **149**
Douglas Dr. G15: Glas. 6H **43**
  G69: Bail 6F **87**
  G71: Both 6E **125**
  G72: Camb 2H **121**
  G75: E Kil 4A **148**
  G77: Newt M 3E **133**
  ML4: Bell 3E **127**
  ML9: Ashg 5B **162**
Douglas Dr. La. G45: Glas 4H **119**
Douglas Gdns. G46: Giff 6A **118**
  G61: Bear 3F **45**
  G66: Lenz 2D **50**
  G71: Udd 2D **124**
Douglas Ga. G72: Camb 2H **121**
Douglas Ho. G67: Cumb 3H **35**
  G82: Dumb. 1H **17**
Douglas La. G2: Glas. 4B **4**
Douglas Muir Dr. G62: Miln 2C **24**
Douglas Muir Gdns. G62: Miln . . . 2C **24**
Douglas Muir Pl. G62: Miln 2C **24**
Douglas Muir Rd. G62: Miln 3D **24**
  G81: Faif 6F **23**
Douglas Pk. Cres. G61: Bear. 1G **45**
Douglas Pk. La. ML3: Ham 5G **141**

Douglas Pl. G61: Bear 2E **45**
  G66: Lenz. 2D **50**
  ML3: Ham 5H **153**
  ML5: Coat. 5B **90**
Douglas Rd. G82: Dumb 4H **17**
  PA4: Renf 3C **78**
Douglas St. G2: Glas. 4E **83** (6B **4**)
  G62: Miln 4G **25**
  G66: Miln 4G **25**
  G71: Tann 5F **109**
  G72: Blan 3A **140**
  ML1: Moth 2F **143**
  ML2: Over 4B **158**
  ML3: Ham 4G **141**
           (not continuous)
  ML6: Air 5A **92**
  ML8: Carl 3E **165**
  ML9: Lark 1E **161**
  PA1: Pais 6G **77**
Douglas Ter. G41: Glas 3D **102**
Douglas Twr. G71: Both 3B **124**
Douglas Vw. ML5: Coat 2B **110**
Dougray Pl. G78: Barr 5E **115**
Dougrie Dr. G45: Glas 4H **119**
Dougrie Gdns. G45: Glas. 5H **119**
Dougrie Pl. G45: Glas 4A **120**
Dougrie Rd. G45: Glas 5G **119**
Dougrie St. G45: Glas 4A **120**
Dougrie Ter. G45: Glas 4H **119**
Doune Cres. G64: B'rig 3D **48**
  G77: Newt M 4F **133**
  ML6: Chap 4D **112**
Doune Gdns. G20: Glas 6C **62**
Doune Gdns. La. G20: Glas 6C **62**
Doune Pk. Way ML5: Coat. 1B **110**
Doune Quad. G20: Glas 6C **62**
Doune Ter. ML5: Coat 2H **89**
Dovecot G43: Glas 5A **102**
Dovecotehall St. G78: Barr 4F **115**
Dovecote Vw. G66: Kirk 6F **31**
DOVECOTHALL 3G **115**
DOVECOTWOOD 2H **11**
Dovecotwood G65: Kils 2H **11**
Doveholm G82: Dumb 2G **17**
Doveholm Av. G82: Dumb 2H **17**
Dove Pl. G75: E Kil. 5B **148**
Dover St. G3: Glas 3C **82**
  ML5: Coat 1H **89**
  G53: Glas 2A **116**
Dove Wynd ML4: Bell. 6A **110**
Dowanfield Rd. G67: Cumb 4F **35**
DOWANHILL 6A **62**
Dowanhill St. G11: Glas. 1A **82**
Dowan Rd.
  G62: Balder, Bard, Miln 6C **26**
Dowanside La. G12: Glas 6B **62**
Dowanside Rd. G12: Glas 6A **62**
Downcraig Dr. G45: Glas. 5H **119**
Downcraig Gro. G45: Glas 5G **119**
Downcraig Rd. G45: Glas. 6G **119**
Downcraig Ter. G45: Glas 5H **119**
Downfield Dr. ML3: Ham 4F **153**
Downfield Gdns. G71: Both 5D **124**
Downfield St. G32: Glas 2G **105**
Downiebrae Rd. G73: Ruth 3D **104**
Downie Cl. G71: Tann. 5F **109**
Downie St. ML3: Ham 2H **153**
Downs St. G21: Glas 4B **64**
Dowrie Cres. G53: Glas 4B **100**
Draffen St. ML1: Moth. 2H **143**
Draffen St. ML1: Moth 2H **143**
Draffen Twr. ML1: Moth. 2H **143**
Drakemire Av. G45: Glas 3G **119**
Drakemire Dr. G45: Glas 5F **119**
Drake St. G40: Glas 6A **84**
Dreghorn St. G31: Glas 4E **85**
Drimmin Rd. G33: Step 4F **67**
Drive Rd. G51: Glas 3E **81**
Drochil St. G34: Glas 2G **87**
Dromore St. G66: Kirk 6D **30**
Drove Hill G68: Cumb 2D **34**
Drumaling Ter. G66: Len 3H **7**
Drumbathie Rd. ML6: Air 3B **92**
Drumbathie Ter. ML6: Air 3C **92**

Drumbeg Dr. G53: Glas 1A **116**
Drumbeg Pl. G53: Glas 1A **116**
Drumbeg Ter. G62: Miln 3D **24**
Drumbottie Rd. G21: Glas 4C **64**
Drumby Cres. G76: Clar 6B **118**
Drumby Dr. G76: Clar 1B **134**
Drumcarn Dr. G62: Miln 4F **25**
Drumcavel Rd. G69: Muirh 2B **68**
Drumchapel Gdns. G15: Glas 5A **44**
Drumchapel Pl. G15: Glas 5B **44**
Drumchapel Rd. G15: Glas 5A **44**
Drumchapel Shop. Cen. G15: Glas . . 4H **43**
Drumchapel Sports Cen. 5H **43**
Drumchapel Station (Rail) 6A **44**
Drumchapel Swimming Pool 5H **43**
Drumclair Pl. ML6: Air 4D **92**
Drumclog Av. G62: Miln 1G **25**
Drumclog Gdns. G33: Glas 3H **65**
Drumcross Rd. G53: Glas 4C **100**
PA7: B'ton 4B **40**
Drumduff G75: E Kil 6F **149**
DRUMGELLOCH 3D **92**
Drumgelloch Station (Rail) 4D **92**
Drumgelloch St. ML6: Air 2D **92**
Drumglass Vw. G65: Croy 1B **34**
DRUMGREW 4F **33**
DRUMGREW RDBT. 4F **33**
Drumhead Pl. G32: Glas 4H **105**
Drumhead Rd. G32: Glas 4H **105**
Drumhill G66: Kirk 3H **31**
Drumilaw Cres. G73: Ruth 2C **120**
Drumilaw Rd. G73: Ruth 2C **120**
Drumilaw Way G73: Ruth 2C **120**
Drumlaken Av. G23: Glas 6A **46**
(off Drumlaken St.)
Drumlaken Ct. G23: Glas 6B **46**
Drumlaken Path G23: Glas 6B **46**
(off Littleton St.)
Drumlaken Pl. G23: Glas 6B **46**
(off Drumlaken Ct.)
Drumlaken St. G23: Glas 6A **46**
Drumlanrig Av. G34: Glas 2A **88**
Drumlanrig Pl. G34: Glas 3B **88**
Drumlin Dr. G62: Miln 5F **25**
Drumloch Gdns. G75: E Kil 6G **149**
Drumlochy Rd. G33: Glas 2A **86**
Drum Mains Pk. G68: Cumb 6G **33**
Drummond Av. G73: Ruth 5B **104**
Drummond Dr. ML2: Wis 1H **157**
PA1: Pais 1F **99**
Drummond Hill G74: E Kil 6B **138**
Drummond Ho. G67: Cumb 2A **36**
Drummond Pl. G74: E Kil 6B **138**
Drummond Way G77: Newt M 4A **132**
Drummore Av. ML5: Coat 2F **111**
Drummore Rd. G15: Glas 2A **44**
Drumnessie Ct. G68: Cumb 5B **34**
Drumnessie Rd. G68: Cumb 5B **34**
Drumnessie Vw. G68: Cumb 5B **34**
Drumore Av. ML6: Chap 4D **112**
Drumover Dr. G31: Glas 1G **105**
DRUMOYNE 5E **81**
Drumoyne Av. G51: Glas 4E **81**
Drumoyne Cir. G51: Glas 5E **81**
Drumoyne Dr. G51: Glas 4E **81**
Drumoyne Pl. G51: Glas 5E **81**
Drumoyne Quad. G51: Glas 5E **81**
Drumoyne Rd. G51: Glas 5E **81**
Drumoyne Sq. G51: Glas 4E **81**
Drumpark St. G46: T'bnk 3F **117**
ML5: Coat 1F **109**
DRUMPELLIER 4H **89**
Drumpellier Av. G67: Cumb 1E **55**
G69: Bail 2H **107**
ML5: Coat 4G **89**
Drumpellier Butterfly House 3F **89**
Drumpellier Country Pk. 3F **89**
Drumpellier Country Pk. Vis. Cen.
. . . . 2E **89**
Drumpellier Ct. G67: Cumb 6E **35**
Drumpellier Cres. ML5: Coat 5H **89**
Drumpellier Gdns.
G67: Cumb 6E **35**
Drumpellier Gro. G67: Cumb 6E **35**

Drumpellier Pl. G67: Cumb 6E **35**
G69: Bail 1H **107**
Drumpellier Rd. G69: Bail 2G **107**
Drumpellier St. G33: Glas 1F **85**
Drumreoch Dr. G42: Glas 5A **104**
Drumreoch Pl. G42: Glas 5A **104**
DRUMRY 4E **43**
Drumry Pl. G15: Glas 5G **43**
Drumry Rd. G81: Clyd 4E **43**
Drumry Rd. E. G15: Glas 5G **43**
Drumry Station (Rail) 5F **43**
Drumsack Av. G69: Chry 1A **68**
Drumsargard Rd. G73: Ruth 2F **121**
Drums Av. PA3: Pais 5G **77**
Drums Cres. PA3: Pais 6G **77**
Drumshangie Pl. ML6: Air 1A **92**
Drumshangie St. ML6: Air 1A **92**
Drumshaw Dr. G32: Carm 5C **106**
Drums Rd. G53: Glas 2A **100**
Drumtrocher St. G65: Kils 3H **11**
Drumvale Dr. G69: Mood 5C **52**
Drury La. Ct. G74: E Kil 5C **138**
(off Bosworth Rd.)
Drury St. G2: Glas 4F **83** (5D **4**)
Dryad St. G46: T'bnk 2E **117**
Dryburgh Av. G73: Ruth 6D **104**
PA2: Pais 4E **97**
Dryburgh Gdns. G20: Glas 6D **62**
Dryburgh Hill G74: E Kil 2F **149**
Dryburgh La. G74: E Kil 2F **149**
Dryburgh Pl. G66: Kirk 5F **31**
ML5: Coat 4B **90**
Dryburgh Rd. G61: Bear 1C **44**
ML2: Wis 6G **145**
Dryburgh St. ML3: Ham 3F **141**
Dryburgh Wlk. G69: Mood 4E **53**
Dryburgh Way G72: Blan 2B **140**
(off Winton Cres.)
Dryburn Av. G52: Glas 6A **80**
Dryden St. ML3: Ham 3F **141**
Drygait PA9: How 6A **94**
Drygate G4: Glas 4A **84**
Drygate St. ML9: Lark 1E **161**
Drygrange Rd. G33: Glas 1C **86**
Drymen Pl. G66: Lenz 4D **50**
Drymen Rd. G61: Bear 1D **44**
Drymen St. G52: Glas 6E **81**
Drymen Wynd G61: Bear 4F **45**
Drynoch Pl. G22: Glas 2F **63**
Drysdale St. G14: Glas 4H **59**
(not continuous)
Duart Dr. G74: E Kil 6F **137**
G77: Newt M 4G **133**
PA5: Eld 4H **95**
Duart St. G20: Glas 1A **62**
Dubs Rd. G78: Barr 4G **115**
Dubton Path G34: Glas 2H **87**
Dubton St. G34: Glas 2H **87**
Duchall Pl. G14: Glas 5B **60**
Duchess Ct. ML3: Ham 1C **154**
Duchess Pl. G73: Ruth 5E **105**
Duchess Rd. G73: Ruth 4E **105**
Duchess Way G69: Barg 6D **88**
(off Park Rd.)
Duchray Dr. PA1: Pais 2G **99**
Duchray La. G33: Glas 2F **85**
Duchray St. G33: Glas 2F **85**
Dudhope St. G33: Glas 1D **86**
Dudley Dr. G12: Glas 6G **61**
ML5: Coat 1G **89**
Dudley La. G12: Glas 6G **61**
Duffus Pl. G32: Carm 5C **106**
Duffus St. G34: Glas 2G **87**
Duffus Ter. G32: Carm 5C **106**
Duich Gdns. G23: Glas 5C **46**
Duisdale Rd. G32: Carm 5C **106**
Duke's Ct. ML9: Lark 1E **161**
Dukes Ga. G71: Both 3C **124**
Dukes Pl. ML3: Ham 5H **153**
Dukes Rd. G69: Barg 6D **88**
Duke's Rd. G72: Camb 1G **121**
G73: Ruth 2E **121**
Duke St. G31: Glas 5D **84**
G4: Glas 4A **84** (5H **5**)

Duke St. ML1: Moth 1G **143**
ML2: Newm 3D **146**
ML3: Ham 6A **142**
ML9: Lark 1E **161**
PA2: Pais 3A **98**
Duke Street Station (Rail) 4D **84**
DULLATUR 5F **13**
Dullatur Rd. G68: Dull 5F **13**
DULLATUR RDBT. 6H **13**
Dulnain St. G72: Camb 2D **122**
Dulsie Rd. G21: Glas 3E **65**
DUMBARTON 4F **17**
Dumbarton Castle 6G **17**
Dumbarton Central Station (Rail)
. . . . 3F **17**
Dumbarton East Station (Rail) 4H **17**
Dumbarton Rd. G11: Glas 1F **81**
G14: Glas 3G **59**
G60: Bowl, Old K 5G **19**
G81: Clyd 3G **41**
G81: Dun, Hard 1B **42**
G82: Milt. 4E **19**
DUMBRECK. 2A **102**
Dumbreck Av. G41: Glas 1G **101**
Dumbreck Ct. G41: Glas 2G **101**
Dumbreck Path G41: Glas 2G **101**
(off Dumbreck Pl.)
Dumbreck Pl. G41: Glas 2G **101**
G66: Lenz 3E **51**
Dumbreck Rd. G41: Glas 6G **81**
DUMBRECK RD. INTERCHANGE . . 6H **81**
Dumbreck Sq. G41: Glas 1G **101**
Dumbreck Station (Rail) 1A **102**
Dumbreck Ter. G65: Queen 3D **10**
Dumbrock Rd. G62: Miln 3D **24**
DUMBUCK 4E **19**
Dumbuck Cres. G82: Dumb 5H **17**
Dumbuck Gdns. G82: Dumb 5H **17**
Dumbuck Rd. G82: Dumb 3H **17**
(Overwood Dr., not continuous)
G82: Dumb. 2H **17**
(Stirling Rd.)
Dumbuie Av. G82: Dumb 3H **17**
Dumfries Cres. ML6: Air 6H **91**
Dumgoyne Av. G62: Miln 4F **25**
Dumgoyne Ct. ML6: Air 1B **92**
(off Thrushbush Rd.)
Dumgoyne Dr. G61: Bear 6D **24**
Dumgoyne Gdns. G62: Miln 4F **25**
Dumgoyne Pl. G76: Clar 2A **134**
Dunagoil Gdns. G45: Glas 5A **120**
Dunagoil Pl. G45: Glas 6A **120**
Dunagoil Rd. G45: Glas 5H **119**
Dunagoil St. G45: Glas 5A **120**
Dunalastair Dr. G33: Mille 4B **66**
Dunan Pl. G33: Glas. 4E **87**
Dunard Ct. ML8: Carl 2F **165**
(off Carranbute Rd.)
Dunard Rd. G73: Ruth 6D **104**
Dunard St. G20: Glas 5D **62**
Dunard Way PA3: Pais 4H **77**
Dunaskin St. G11: Glas 2A **82**
Dunavon Pl. ML5: Coat 1F **111**
Dunbar Av. G73: Ruth 6E **105**
ML5: Coat 1H **109**
PA5: John 5E **95**
Dunbar Dr. ML1: Moth 5A **144**
Dunbar Hill G74: E Kil 2E **149**
Dunbar La. ML1: New S. 5A **128**
Dunbar Pl. G74: E Kil 2E **149**
Dunbar Rd. PA2: Pais 4E **97**
Dunbar St. ML3: Ham 4F **141**
Dunbeath Av. G77: Newt M 4F **133**
Dunbeith Pl. G20: Glas 4B **62**
DUNBETH 4D **90**
Dunbeth Av. ML5: Coat 4D **90**
Dunbeth Ct. ML5: Coat 4D **90**
Dunbeth Rd. ML5: Coat 3D **90**
Dunblane Dr. G74: E Kil 6H **137**
Dunblane Pl. G74: E Kil 1H **149**
ML5: Coat. 1B **110**
Dunblane St. G4: Glas. 2F **83** (1D **4**)
(not continuous)
Dunbrach Rd. G68: Cumb 2D **34**

Dunbritton Rd. G82: Dumb 2C **18**
Duncan Av. G14: Glas 6C **60**
Duncan Ct. ML1: Moth 6F **127**
Duncan Graham St. ML9: Lark. . . .1F **161**
Duncan La. *G14: Glas 6C 60*
(off Gleneagles La. Nth.)
Duncan La. Nth. *G14: Glas 5C 60*
(off Norse La. Nth.)
Duncan McIntosh Rd. G68: Cumb . . .4B **14**
Dun Cann PA8: Ersk. 2G **57**
Duncannon La. Nth. *G14: Glas 5C 60*
(off Earlbank Av.)
Duncanrig Sports Cen. 3D **148**
Duncansby Rd. G33: Glas 5D **86**
Duncarnock Av. G78: Neil. 2E **131**
Duncarnock Cres. G78: Neil 2E **131**
Dunchattan Pl. G31: Glas. 4B **84**
Dunchattan St. G31: Glas. 4B **84**
Dunchurch Rd. PA1: Pais 6F **79**
Dunclutha Dr. G71: Both 6E **125**
Dunclutha St. G40: Glas 3D **104**
Duncolm Pl. G62: Miln 3D **24**
Duncombe Av. G81: Hard 6D **22**
Duncombe St. G20: Glas 2B **62**
Duncombe Vw. G81: Clyd. 4F **43**
Duncraig Cres. PA5: John 5D **94**
Duncrub Dr. G64: B'rig. 6A **48**
Duncruin St. G20: Glas 2A **62**
Duncruin Ter. G20: Glas 2B **62**
Duncryne Av. G32: Glas. 1D **106**
Duncryne Gdns. G32: Glas. 1E **107**
Duncryne Pl. G64: B'rig. 1A **64**
Dundaff Hill G68: Cumb. 3E **35**
Dundas Av. G64: Torr. 5D **28**
Dundas Cotts. FK4: Alla 1G **15**
Dundas Ct. G74: E Kil 1G **149**
Dundashill G4: Glas 1F **83** (1D **4**)
Dundas La. G1: Glas 3G **83** (4E **5**)
Dundas Pl. G74: E Kil 1G **149**
Dundas St. G1: Glas 3G **83** (4E **5**)
(not continuous)
Dundasvale Ct. G4: Glas 2F **83** (1D **4**)
Dundee Dr. G52: Glas 1B **100**
Dundee Path G52: Glas 2C **100**
Dundonald Av. PA5: John 4D **94**
Dundonald Cres. G77: Newt M 5G **133**
Dundonald Dr. ML3: Ham 4H **153**
Dundonald Pl. G78: Neil 2D **130**
Dundonald Rd. G12: Glas 6A **62**
PA3: Pais 4C **78**
Dundonald St. G72: Blan 1A **140**
Dundrennan Rd. G42: Glas 6D **102**
DUNDYVAN. 6B **90**
Dundyvan Gdns. ML5: Coat 6C **90**
Dundyvan Ga. ML5: Coat 6C **90**
Dundyvan Ind. Est. ML5: Coat 6B **90**
Dundyvan La. ML2: Wis 1G **157**
Dundyvan Rd. ML5: Coat 5B **90**
Dundyvan St. ML2: Wis. 1G **157**
Dundyvan Way ML5: Coat 6B **90**
Dunearn Pl. PA2: Pais 2C **98**
Dunearn St. G4: Glas. 1D **82**
Duneaton Wynd ML9: Lark. 5F **161**
Dunedin Dr. G75: E Kil 3C **148**
Dunedin Dr. G75: E Kil 2C **148**
Dunedin Rd. ML9: Lark 4F **161**
Dunedin Ter. G81: Clyd 1E **59**
Dunellan Av. G69: Mood 5E **53**
Dunellan Ct. G69: Mood 5E **53**
Dunellan Cres. G69: Mood 5E **53**
Dunellan Dr. G81: Hard 6D **22**
Dunellan Gdns. G69: Mood 5E **53**
Dunellan Rd. G62: Miln 3C **24**
Dunellan St. G52: Glas. 6E **81**
Dungavel Gdns. ML3: Ham 3A **154**
Dungavel La. *ML8: Carl. 4H 165*
(off Kelso Dr.)
Dungeonhill Rd. G34: Glas 3B **88**
Dunglass Av. G14: Glas 5C **60**
G74: E Kil 6H **137**
Dunglass La. *G14: Glas 5C 60*
(off Norse La. Sth.)
Dunglass La. Nth. *G14: Glas 5C 60*
(off Danes La. Sth.)

Dunglass Pl. G62: Miln 2E **25**
G77: Newt M 4A **132**
Dunglass Rd. PA7: B'ton 5A **40**
Dunglass Sq. G74: E Kil. 1H **149**
Dungoil Av. G68: Cumb 2D **34**
Dungoil Rd. G66: Lenz. 3E **51**
Dungoyne St. G20: Glas. 1A **62**
Dunholme Pk. G81: Clyd 4H **41**
Dunira St. G32: Glas 2H **105**
Duniston Rd. ML6: Air. 1H **113**
Dunivaig Rd. G33: Glas 4D **86**
Dunkeld Av. G73: Ruth 6D **104**
Dunkeld Dr. G61: Bear. 3H **45**
Dunkeld Gdns. G64: B'rig 5D **48**
Dunkeld La. G69: Mood. 5E **53**
Dunkeld Pl. G77: Newt M 5H **133**
ML3: Ham 6C **140**
ML5: Coat. 1B **110**
Dunkeld St. G31: Glas 1E **105**
Dunkenny Pl. G15: Glas. 3H **43**
Dunkenny Rd. G15: Glas 4H **43**
Dunkenny Sq. G15: Glas 4H **43**
Dunlin G12: Glas 3G **61**
G74: E Kil 5G **137**
Dunlin Ct. ML4: Bell. 5A **110**
Dunlin Cres. PA6: C'lee 2C **74**
Dunlop Ct. ML3: Ham 4A **154**
Dunlop Cres. G71: Both 6F **125**
PA4: Renf 5F **59**
Dunlop Gro. G71: Tann. 4E **109**
Dunlop Pl. G62: Miln 2F **25**
ML9: Ashg 5C **162**
Dunlop St. G1: Glas 5G **83**
(not continuous)
G72: Camb 1E **123**
PA3: Lin 5A **76**
PA4: Renf *5F 59*
(off Dunlop Cres.)
Dunlop Twr. *G75: E Kil. 3G 149*
(off Denholm Cres.)
Dunmore Dr. G62: Miln 5A **26**
Dunmore St. G81: Clyd 1E **59**
Dunnachie Dr. ML5: Coat. 1F **109**
Dunnachie Pl. ML5: Coat. 1G **109**
Dunnet Av. ML6: Glenm. 4H **71**
Dunnet Dr. PA6: C'lee. 2B **74**
Dunnichen Gdns. G64: B'rig. 6F **49**
Dunnikier Wlk. G68: Cumb 4A **34**
Dunnottar Wlk. *ML2: Newm 3D 146*
(off Tiree Cres.)
Dunnottar Ct. G74: E Kil. 6E **137**
Dunnottar Cres. G74: E Kil 6E **137**
Dunnottar St. G33: Glas. 1B **86**
G64: B'rig 5F **49**
Dunn Sq. PA1: Pais 1A **98**
Dunn St. G40: Glas 2B **104**
G81: Clyd 4A **42**
G81: Dun 1B **42**
PA1: Pais 6C **78**
Dunns Wood Rd. G67: Cumb. 5D **14**
Dunolly Dr. G77: Newt M 4F **133**
Dunottar Av. ML5: Coat 3D **110**
Dunottar Pl. ML5: Coat 2D **110**
Dun Pk. G66: Kirk 5D **30**
Dunphail Dr. G34: Glas 3B **88**
Dunphail Rd. G34: Glas 3B **88**
Dunragit St. G31: Glas. 4E **85**
DUNROBIN 4E **93**
Dunrobin Av. PA5: Eld 4A **96**
Dunrobin Ct. G74: E Kil 6F **137**
G81: Clyd 5C **42**
Dunrobin Cres. G74: E Kil 6F **137**
Dunrobin Dr. G74: E Kil 6F **137**
Dunrobin Gdns. ML6: Air 5E **93**
Dunrobin Pl. ML5: Coat 4B **90**
Dunrobin Rd. ML6: Air. 4E **93**
Dunrobin St. G31: Glas 5D **84**
Dunrod Hill G74: E Kil 6H **137**
Dunrod St. G32: Glas 1B **106**
Dunscore Brae ML3: Ham 1C **152**
Duns Cres. ML2: Wis 3A **146**
Dunside Dr. G53: Glas 1A **116**
Dunskaith Pl. G34: Glas. 4B **88**

Dunskaith St. G34: Glas. 4B **88**
Dunsmore Rd. PA7: B'ton 3G **39**
Dunsmuir St. G51: Glas. 4H **81**
Duns Path ML5: Coat 2F **111**
Dunster Gdns. G64: B'rig. 3D **48**
Dunswin Av. G81: Clyd 4A **42**
Dunswin Ct. G81: Clyd. 4A **42**
Dunsyre Pl. G23: Glas 6C **46**
Dunsyre St. G33: Glas 3G **85**
Duntarvie Av. G34: Glas. 3A **88**
Duntarvie Cl. G34: Glas. 3A **88**
Duntarvie Cres. G34: Glas. 3A **88**
Duntarvie Dr. G34: Glas. 3H **87**
Duntarvie Gdns. G34: Glas 3A **88**
Duntarvie Pl. G34: Glas 3H **87**
Duntarvie Rd. G34: Glas 3H **87**
Dunterlie Av. G13: Glas 3A **60**
Dunterlie Ct. G78: Barr 4E **115**
DUNTIBLAE 6G **31**
Duntiblae Rd. G66: Kirk. 6G **31**
Duntiglennan Rd. G81: Dun. 1C **42**
DUNTOCHER 1C **42**
Duntocher Rd. G61: Bear 1A **44**
G81: Clyd 4A **42**
G81: Dun 2C **42**
G81: Faif. 6G **23**
Duntreath Av. G13: Glas 1G **59**
G15: Glas 6H **43**
Duntreath Dr. G15: Glas. 6H **43**
Duntreath Gdns. G15: Glas 5H **43**
Duntreath Gro. G15: Glas 6H **43**
Duntreath Ter. G65: Kils 3H **11**
Duntroon Pl. *ML4: Bell 4D 126*
(off Glencalder Cres.)
Duntroon St. G31: Glas 3D **84**
Dunure Dr. G73: Ruth 2B **120**
G77: Newt M 4G **133**
ML3: Ham 1B **152**
Dunure Pl. G77: Newt M 5G **133**
ML5: Coat. 2A **110**
Dunure St. G20: Glas 2B **62**
ML5: Coat. 2A **110**
Dunvegan Av. ML6: Glenm 5G **71**
Dunvegan Av. ML5: Coat 2H **89**
PA5: Eld 4H **95**
Dunvegan Ct. G13: Glas 3B **60**
Dunvegan Dr. G64: B'rig 3C **48**
G77: Newt M 4G **133**
Dunvegan Pl. G71: Tann 5B **108**
G74: E Kil 6F **137**
Dunvegan Quad. PA4: Renf 5D **58**
Dunwan Av. G13: Glas 2H **59**
Dunwan Pl. G13: Glas 2H **59**
Durban Av. G81: Clyd. 3G **41**
Durham St. G41: Glas 6B **82**
Durisdeer Dr. ML3: Ham 2C **152**
Durness Av. G61: Bear. 2H **45**
Durno Path G33: Glas. 4E **87**
Duror St. G32: Glas. 6A **86**
Durris Gdns. G32: Glas 2D **106**
Durrockstock Cres. PA2: Pais 6D **96**
Durrockstock Rd. PA2: Pais 6D **96**
Durrockstock Way PA2: Pais 6D **96**
Durward G74: E Kil. 5E **139**
Durward Av. G41: Glas 4B **102**
Durward Ct. G41: Glas 4B **102**
ML1: Moth 5F **127**
Durward Cres. PA2: Pais 4D **96**
Durward Way PA2: Pais 4D **96**
Duthie Pk. Gdns. G13: Glas. 3D **60**
Duthie Pk. Pl. G13: Glas 3D **60**
Duthil St. G51: Glas 5D **80**
Dyce Av. ML6: Air 1G **111**
Dyce La. G11: Glas 1G **81**
Dyer's La. G1: Glas 5H **83**
Dyer's Wynd PA1: Pais. 6A **78**
Dyfrig St. G72: Blan 1A **140**
DYKEBAR. 4D **98**
Dykebar Av. G13: Glas 3B **60**
Dykebar Cres. PA2: Pais 3D **98**
Dykehead La. G33: Glas 4D **86**
Dykehead Rd. G65: Queen. 2C **10**
G68: Dull 5E **13**

Dykehead Rd. G69: Barg 6D **88**
 ML6: Air 1H **91**
Dykehead Sq. ML3: Ham 6D **140**
Dykehead St. G33: Glas 4D **86**
Dykemuir Pl. G21: Glas 5D **64**
Dykemuir Quad. G21: Glas 5C **64**
Dykemuir St. G21: Glas 5C **64**
Dyke Rd. G13: Glas 2A **60**
 G14: Glas 4H **59**
Dyke St. G69: Bail 6A **88**
 ML5: Coat 1F **109**
Dysart Ct. G68: Cumb 4A **34**
Dysart Way ML6: Air 5G **93**

E

Eagle Cres. G61: Bear 1B **44**
Eagle Hgts. G21: Glas 1H **83**
Eaglesham Ct. G51: Glas 5C **82**
Eaglesham Path ML5: Glenb 3G **69**
Eaglesham Pl. G51: Glas 5C **82**
Eaglesham Rd. G75: E Kil 3A **148**
 G76: Clar 6B **134**
 G77: Newt M 5D **132**
Eagle St. G4: Glas 1G **83**
Earlbank Av. G14: Glas 5C **60**
Earlbank La. Nth. *G14: Glas* *5C 60*
 (off Verona Av.)
 G14: Glas *5C 60*
 (off Earlbank Av.)
Earlbank La. Sth. G14: Glas 5C **60**
Earl Haig Rd. G52: Hill 4H **79**
Earl La. G14: Glas 6C **60**
 (not continuous)
Earl Pl. G14: Glas. 5C **60**
 PA11: Bri W 5F **73**
Earlsburn Rd. G66: Lenz 3E **51**
Earlscourt G69: Mood 6D **52**
Earl's Ga. G71: Both 4C **124**
Earlsgate PA6: C'lee. 2B **74**
Earl's Hill G68: Cumb 3D **34**
Earlspark Av. G43: Glas 1D **118**
Earlston Av. G21: Glas 2B **84**
Earlston Cres. ML5: Coat 2F **111**
Earlston Pl. G21: Glas 2B **84**
Earlston St. ML2: Wis 3A **146**
Earl St. G14: Glas. 5A **60**
Earl Vw. ML1: New S 4A **128**
Earlybraes Gdns. G33: Glas 5D **86**
Earn Av. G61: Bear. 3H **45**
 ML4: Bell 1A **126**
 PA4: Renf 1G **79**
Earn Cres. ML2: Wis 2H **157**
Earn Gdns. ML9: Lark 5E **161**
Earn La. *ML1: Holy* *2A 128*
 (off Howden Pl.)
EARNOCK 1C **152**
Earnock Av. ML1: Moth 3E **143**
Earnock Gdns. ML3: Ham 2D **152**
Earnock Rd. ML3: Ham 1B **152**
Earnock St. G33: Glas. 5F **65**
 ML3: Ham. 5E **141**
Earn Rd. G77: Newt M 2D **132**
Earnside St. G32: Glas. 6B **86**
Earn St. G33: Glas 2G **85**
Easdale G74: E Kil 4B **150**
Easdale Dr. G32: Glas 1A **106**
Easdale Path ML5: Coat 1F **111**
 ML5: Glenb 3G **69**
Easdale Pl. G77: Newt M 4B **132**
Easdale Ri. ML3: Ham 6C **140**
E. Academy St. ML2: Wis 1H **157**
East Av. G71: View. 1G **125**
 G72: Blan 4B **140**
 ML1: New S 5A **128**
 ML6: Plain 1G **93**
 ML8: Carl 3D **164**
 PA4: Renf 6F **59**
EAST BALGROCHAN 3E **29**
Eastbank Dr. G32: Glas 6C **86**
Eastbank Pl. G32: Glas 6C **86**
Eastbank Ri G32: Glas 6C **86**
E. Barns St. G81: Clyd 1F **59**

E. Bath La. G2: Glas 3G **83** (4E **5**)
E. Buchanan M. *PA1: Pais*. *6B 78*
 (off E. Buchanan St.)
E. Buchanan St. PA1: Pais 6B **78**
Eastburn Cres. G21: Glas 3D **64**
Eastburn Pl. G21: Glas 3D **64**
Eastburn Rd. G21: Glas 4D **64**
E. Burnside St. G65: Kils 3H **11**
E. Campbell St. G40: Glas 5A **84**
Eastcote Av. G14: Glas 5E **61**
EAST CRAIGEND 6D **40**
EAST CRINDLEDYKE 3E **147**
Eastcroft G73: Ruth 5D **104**
Eastcroft Ter. G21: Glas 5C **64**
E. Dean St. ML4: Bell 2D **126**
Eastend Av. ML1: Carf 6B **128**
Easterbrae ML1: Moth 5F **143**
Easter Cadder Cotts. G66: Kirk 6H **29**
Easter Craigs G31: Glas. 3D **84**
Easter Cres. ML2: Wis 5C **146**
Easter Garngaber Rd. G66: Lenz . . . 2E **51**
Eastergreens Av. G66: Kirk 6C **30**
Easterhill Pl. G32: Glas 2H **105**
Easterhill St. G32: Glas 2H **105**
EASTERHOUSE 3G **87**
Easterhouse Pl. G34: Glas 3A **88**
Easterhouse Rd. G34: Glas 3A **88**
 G69: Bail 6H **87**
EASTERHOUSE ROAD INTERCHANGE
 . . . . **4A 88**
Easterhouse Sports Cen. 2F **87**
Easterhouse Station (Rail) . . . . [●] **88**
Easterhouse Swimming Pool 3G **87**
Easterhouse Township Cen.
 G34: Glas 2G **87**
Eastermains G66: Kirk 3H **31**
Easter M. G71: Udd 2C **124**
Easter Queenslie Rd. G33: Glas 3E **87**
Easter Rd. G76: Busby 3E **135**
Easterton Av. G76: Busby. 4E **135**
Easterton Cotts. G64: Torr 3E **29**
Easter Wood Cres. G71: View 4H **109**
EASTFIELD 6F **105**
Eastfield Av. G72: Camb 1G **121**
Eastfield Cres. G82: Dumb 5H **17**
Eastfield Pl. G82: Dumb 5H **17**
Eastfield Rd. G21: Glas 5A **64**
 G68: Cumb 3C **34**
 ML8: Carl 4G **165**
Eastfield Ter. ML4: Bell 3F **127**
EAST FULTON 5F **75**
Eastgate G69: G'csh 4E **69**
East Ga. ML2: Wis 6B **146**
 ML5: Glenb 2H **69**
E. George St. ML5: Coat 3D **90**
E. Glebe Ter. ML3: Ham 1H **153**
E. Greenlees Av. G72: Camb 4C **122**
E. Greenlees Cres. G72: Camb 4B **122**
E. Greenlees Dr. G72: Camb 4C **122**
East Greenlees Gro. G72: Camb 4H **121**
E. Greenlees Rd. G72: Camb. 4A **122**
E. Hallhill Road G69: Bail 5G **87**
Easthall Pl. G33: Glas 4F **87**
E. Hamilton St. ML2: Wis 1H **157**
E. High St. ML6: Air 3A **92**
EAST KILBRIDE 2H **149**
East Kilbride Arts Cen. 6H **137**
East Kilbride Ice Rink 3H **149**
East Kilbride Station (Rail)
 . . . . 1G **149**
E. Kilbride Rd. G73: Ruth 2E **121**
 G76: Busby. 2E **121**
East Kilbride Rd. G76: Crmck 5G **135**
East Kilbride Sports Cen. 5C **150**
East Kilbride Village Theatre
 . . . . 1H **149**
East La. PA1: Pais 1C **98**
Eastlea Pl. ML6: Air. 5B **92**
E. Machan St. ML9: Lark 4F **161**
EAST MAINS 1A **150**
E. Mains Rd. G74: E Kil 1G **149**
E. Milton Gro. G75: E Kil 2D **148**
Eastmuir St. G32: Glas. 6B **86**
 ML2: Wis 5C **146**

Easton Pl. ML5: Coat 6D **90**
East Rd. ML1: New S 3A **128**
 PA10: Kilb. 1A **94**
E. Scott Ter. ML3: Ham 2H **153**
EAST SHAWHEAD 3E **111**
Eastside G66: Kirk 4D **30**
Eastside Ind. Est. *G66: Kirk* *4D 30*
 (off Kilsyth Rd.)
E. Springfield Ter. G64: B'rig 1D **64**
E. Station Ind. Est. ML9: Lark 1F **161**
E. Stewart Pl. ML5: Coat 4E **91**
E. Stewart St. ML5: Coat 5E **91**
E. Thomson St. G81: Clyd 4D **42**
E. Thornlie St. ML2: Wis 1H **157**
Eastvale Pl. G3: Glas 3A **82**
E. Wellbrae Cres. ML3: Ham 2F **153**
E. Wellington St. G31: Glas 6F **85**
E. Whitby St. G31: Glas 1E **105**
Eastwood Av. G41: Glas 5B **102**
 G46: Giff 4A **118**
Eastwood Butterfly Kingdom 5F **117**
Eastwood Cres. G46: T'bnk 3F **117**
Eastwood Dr. ML2: Newm 3E **147**
Eastwoodmains Rd. G46: Giff 6H **117**
 G76: Clar 6H **117**
Eastwood Recreation Cen. 5H **117**
Eastwood Rd. G69: Mood 5D **52**
Eastwood Toll G46: Giff 6H **117**
Eastwood Vw. G72: Camb 1E **123**
Eastwood Way *ML9: Lark*. *1F 161*
 (off Antrim La.)
Easwald Bank PA10: Kilb. 3B **94**
Ebroch Dr. G65: Kils. 3A **12**
Ebroch Pk. G65: Kils 3A **12**
Eccles St. G22: Glas. 4A **64**
Eckford St. G32: Glas 1A **106**
Eck Path *ML1: Holy* *2A 128*
 (off Howden Pl.)
Eday St. G22: Glas 3H **63**
Edderton Pl. G34: Glas 4G **87**
Edderton Way G34: Glas 4G **87**
Eddington Dr. G77: Newt M 6C **132**
Eddlewood Pl. G72: Camb. 2D **122**
EDDLEWOOD 4H **153**
Eddlewood Ct. G33: Glas. 4G **87**
Eddlewood Path G33: Glas 4F **87**
Eddlewood Pl. G33: Glas 4F **87**
Eddlewood Rd. G33: Glas. 4F **87**
Eddlewood Sports Barn 4H **153**
Eden Dr. G75: E Kil. 5B **148**
Eden Gdns. G75: E Kil 4B **148**
Eden Gro. G75: E Kil 4B **148**
Eden La. G33: Glas 2F **85**
Eden Pk. G71: Both 5D **124**
Eden Pl. G72: Camb 2D **122**
 PA4: Renf 1G **79**
Edenside G68: Cumb 4B **14**
Eden St. G33: Glas 2F **85**
Edenwood St. G31: Glas 6G **85**
Edgam Dr. G52: Glas 6C **80**
Edgefauld Av. G21: Glas 6B **64**
Edgefauld Dr. G21: Glas. 5B **64**
Edgefauld Pl. G21: Glas 4B **64**
Edgefauld Rd. G21: Glas 5B **64**
Edgehill La. G11: Glas. 5G **61**
Edgehill Rd. G11: Glas 5F **61**
 G61: Bear 1E **45**
Edgemont Pk. ML3: Ham. 3G **153**
Edgemont St. G41: Glas 5C **102**
Edinbeg Av. G42: Glas 5A **104**
Edinbeg Pl. G42: Glas 5A **104**
Edinburgh Rd. G33: Glas 4F **85**
 G69: Bail 5G **87**
 ML1: N'hse 1C **128**
Edington Gdns. G69: Mood 4D **52**
Edington St. G4: Glas 1F **83** (1C **4**)
Edison St. G52: Hill 3G **79**
 (not continuous)
Edmiston Dr. G51: Glas 5F **81**
 PA3: Lin 5F **75**
Edmonstone Ct. G81: Clyd 2F **59**
Edmonstone Dr. G65: Kils 4H **11**
Edmonton Ter. G75: E Kil 3E **149**
Edmund Kean G74: E Kil 4C **138**

Edrick Ct. *ML5: Coat* *5B* **90**
(off Kirk St.)
Edrom Ct. G32: Glas 6H 85
Edrom Path G32: Glas 6H 85
Edrom St. G32: Glas 6H 85
(not continuous)
Edward Av. PA4: Renf 5G 59
Edward St. G65: Kils 2H 11
G69: Barg 6D 88
G81: Clyd 2F 59
ML1: Moth 4H 143
ML3: Ham 1H 153
Edwin St. G51: Glas 6B 82
Edzell Ct. G14: Glas 1D 80
Edzell Dr. G77: Newt M 5E 133
PA5: Eld 3B 96
Edzell Gdns. G64: B'rig 1E 65
ML2: Wis 1G 157
Edzell Pl. G14: Glas 6D 60
Edzell St. G14: Glas 1D 80
ML5: Coat 1H 109
Egidia Av. G46: Giff 5A 118
Egilsay Cres. G22: Glas 1G 63
Egilsay Pl. G22: Glas 1G 63
Egilsay St. G22: Glas 1G 63
Egilsay Ter. G22: Glas 1G 63
Eglinton Ct. G5: Glas 6F 83
Eglinton Dr. G46: Giff 5A 118
Eglinton St. G41: Glas 1E 103
ML5: Coat 3D 90
Egmont Pk. G75: E Kil 4C 148
Eider G12: Glas 2G 61
Eider Av. G75: E Kil 6C 148
Eider Gro. G75: E Kil 6C 148
Eider Pl. G75: E Kil 6C 148
Eighth St. G71: Tann 4C 108
Eildon Cres. ML6: Chap 4F 113
Eildon Dr. G78: Barr 6E 115
Eildon Rd. G66: Kirk 5F 31
Eileen Gdns. G64: B'rig 5D 48
Eilt Wlk. *ML2: Newm* *3D 146*
(off Islay Av.)
Elcho St. G40: Glas 5B 84
Elderbank G61: Bear 4E 45
Elder Cres. G72: Flem 3E 123
Elder Gro. G51: Glas 4D 80
G71: View 5F 109
Elder Gro. Ct. G51: Glas 4D 80
Elderpark Gdns. G51: Glas 4F 81
Elderpark Gro. G51: Glas 4F 81
Elderpark St. G51: Glas 4F 81
Elderslea Rd. ML8: Carl 5G 165
ELDERSLIE 2A 96
Elderslie Leisure Cen. 2B 96
Elderslie St. G3: Glas 2D 82
Elder St. G51: Glas 4F 81
(not continuous)
Elders Way ML2: Wis 6B 146
Eldin Pl. PA11: Bri W 5G 73
PA5: Eld 3H 95
Eldon Ct. G11: Glas 1H 81
Eldon Gdns. G64: B'rig 6A 48
Eldon St. G3: Glas 1C 82
Elgin Av. G74: E Kil 6H 137
Elgin Gdns. G76: Clar 1D 134
Elgin Pl. G65: Kils 2H 11
G74: E Kil 6H 137
ML5: Coat 2D 110
ML6: Air 6G 91
Elgin Rd. G61: Bear 6F 25
Elgin Ter. ML3: Ham 5C 140
Elgin Way ML4: Bell 1C 126
Elibank St. G33: Glas 2A 86
Elie Ct. G68: Cumb 6H 13
Elie St. G11: Glas 1A 82
Eliot Cres. ML3: Ham 2H 153
Eliot Ter. ML3: Ham 1H 153
Elison Ct. ML1: Moth 5B 144
Elizabethan Way PA4: Renf 2E 79
Elizabeth Av. G46: Milt C 5B 8
Elizabeth Ct. G74: E Kil 1H 149
Elizabeth Cres. G46: T'bnk 4G 117
Elizabeth Quad. ML1: Holy 2A 128
Elizabeth St. G51: Glas 6A 82

Elizabeth Wynd ML3: Ham 4H 153
Ella Gdns. ML4: Bell. 3E 127
Ellangowan Ct. G62: Miln 3G 25
Ellangowan Rd. G41: Glas 5A 102
G62: Miln 3G 25
Ellergreen Rd. G61: Bear 3E 45
Ellerslie St. PA5: John 2G 95
Ellesmere St. G22: Glas 6E 63
Ellinger Ct. G81: Clyd 3H 41
Elliot Av. G46: Giff 5A 118
PA2: Pais 6C 96
Elliot Ct. ML1: Moth 6F 127
Elliot Cres. G74: E Kil 1B 150
Elliot Dr. G46: Giff 4A 118
Elliot Pl. G3: Glas 4C 82
Elliot St. G3: Glas 4C 82
(not continuous)
Ellisland G66: Kirk 3H 31
G74: E Kil 6D 138
Ellisland Av. G81: Clyd 4E 43
Ellisland Cres. G73: Ruth 2B 120
Ellisland Dr. G66: Kirk 3G 31
G72: Blan 3H 139
Ellisland Rd. G43: Glas 1B 118
G67: Cumb 3B 36
G76: Busby 4C 134
Ellismuir Farm Rd. G69: Bail. 1B 108
Ellismuir Pl. G69: Bail 1A 108
Ellismuir Rd. G69: Bail 1A 108
Ellismuir St. ML5: Coat 2H 109
(not continuous)
Ellismuir Way G71: Tann 4E 109
Ellis St. ML5: Coat 4C 90
Elliston Av. G53: Glas 2C 116
Elliston Cres. G53: Glas. 2C 116
Elliston Dr. G53: Glas. 2C 116
Ellis Way ML1: Moth 4H 143
Ellon Dr. PA3: Lin. 6G 75
Ellon Gro. PA3: Pais. 4B 78
Ellon Way PA3: Pais. 4B 78
Ellrig G75: E Kil 6F 149
Elm Av. G66: Lenz 1C 50
PA4: Renf 5E 59
Elm Bank G64: B'rig. 6D 48
G66: Kirk 4D 30
Elmbank Av. G71: View 6F 109
Elmbank Cres. G2: Glas . . . 3E 83 (3A 4)
ML3: Ham. 5E 141
Elmbank Dr. ML9: Lark 4G 161
Elmbank St. G2: Glas . . . 3E 83 (4A 4)
ML4: Bell 2C 126
ML8: Carl 5G 165
Elmbank St. La. G2: Glas. 4A 4
Elm Cres. G71: View 6H 109
Elm Dr. G67: Cumb. 1F 37
G72: Camb 2C 122
PA5: John 5F 95
Elmfoot St. G5: Glas 3H 103
Elm Gdns. G61: Bear 1E 45
Elmhurst ML1: Moth. 5F 143
Elmira Rd. G69: Muirh. 2B 68
Elm La. W. *G14: Glas* *6D 60*
(off Lime St.)
Elm Lea PA5: John 3H 95
Elmore Av. G44: Glas 2F 119
Elmore La. G44: Glas 2F 119
Elm Pl. G75: E Kil 5E 149
Elm Quad. ML6: Air 4D 92
Elm Rd. G73: Ruth 3D 120
G81: Clyd 2C 42
G82: Dumb 3F 17
ML1: Holy 2B 128
ML1: New S 5A 128
PA11: Bri W 2G 73
PA2: Pais 4C 98
Elmslie Ct. G69: Bail 1A 108
Elms, The G44: Glas. 3E 119
Elm St. G14: Glas. 6D 60
G66: Len 3G 7
G72: Blan 2C 140
G76: Busby 3D 134
ML1: Moth 2F 143
ML5: Coat 6E 91

Elm St. E. *G14: Glas* *6D 60*
(off Elm St.)
Elmtree Gdns. G45: Glas 3B 120
Elmvale Row G21: Glas 4A 64
Elmvale St. G21: Glas 4A 64
Elm Vw. Ct. ML4: Bell 3F 127
Elm Wlk. G61: Bear 1E 45
Elm Way G72: Flem 3E 123
ML9: Lark 6A 156
Elmwood ML2: Wis 2E 157
Elmwood Av. G11: Glas 5F 61
G77: Newt M 3F 133
Elmwood Ct. G71: Both 5E 125
Elmwood Gdns. G66: Lenz 2A 50
Elmwood La. G11: Glas 5F 61
Elphinstone Cres. G75: E Kil 4H 149
Elphinstone Pl. G51: Glas 4A 82
Elphinstone Rd. G46: Giff 2G 133
Elphin St. G23: Glas 6B 46
Elrig Rd. G44: Glas 2D 118
Elsinore Path G75: E Kil. 6G 149
Elspeth Gdns. G64: B'rig 5E 49
Eltham St. G22: Glas 6F 63
Elvan Ct. ML1: Moth. 3F 143
Elvan Pl. G75: E Kil 4A 148
Elvan St. G32: Glas 6H 85
ML1: Moth 2F 143
Elvan Twr. ML1: Moth 4G 143
Embo Dr. G13: Glas 3B 60
Emerald Ter. ML4: Bell 3C 126
Emerson Rd. G64: B'rig. 6C 48
Emerson Rd. W. G64: B'rig 6C 48
Emily Dr. ML1: Moth 5G 143
Emma Jay Rd. ML4: Bell 2D 126
Empire Way ML1: Moth 6E 127
Endfield Av. G12: Glas. 3H 61
Endrick Bank G64: B'rig 3C 48
Endrick Dr. G61: Bear 4F 45
PA1: Pais 5D 78
Endrick Gdns. G62: Miln 3E 25
Endrick Ho. G82: Dumb 1H 17
Endrick St. G21: Glas. 6H 63
English Row ML6: C'bnk 3C 112
English St. ML2: Wis 6D 144
Ennerdale G75: E Kil 5B 148
Ennisfree Rd. G72: Blan. 1B 140
Ensay St. G22: Glas 2H 63
Enterkin St. G32: Glas. 1H 105
Eriboll Pl. G22: Glas. 2F 63
Eriboll St. G22: Glas. 2F 63
Eribol Wlk. ML1: N'hill. 4D 128
Ericht Rd. G43: Glas. 2A 118
Eriska Av. G14: Glas. 4A 60
Eriskay Av. G77: Newt M 4B 132
ML3: Ham 1D 152
Eriskay Cres. G77: Newt M 4B 132
Eriskay Dr. G60: Old K 1G 41
Eriskay Pl. G60: Old K 1G 41
Erradale St. G22: Glas 2E 63
Errogie St. G34: Glas 3H 87
Errol Gdns. G5: Glas 1G 103
ERSKINE 6F 41
Erskine Av. G41: Glas 1H 101
Erskine Bri. G60: Old K 2E 41
PA7: B'ton 3D 40
Erskine Ct. *ML6: Air* *3E 93*
(off Katherine St.)
Erskine Cres. ML6: Air. 6H 91
Erskinefauld Rd. PA3: Lin 5G 75
Erskine Ferry Rd. G60: Old K 2F 41
Erskine Rd. G46: Giff 3H 133
Erskine Sq. G52: Hill 4H 79
Erskine Swimming Pool 5F 41
Erskine Vw. G60: Old K 1E 41
G81: Clyd 4D 42
Ervie St. G34: Glas. 4A 88
Escart Rd. ML8: Carl 2F 165
Esdaile Ct. ML1: New S 4A 128
Esk Av. PA4: Renf. 1G 79
Eskbank St. G32: Glas 5A 86
Eskdale G74: E Kil 6E 137
G77: Newt M 4H 133
Eskdale Dr. G73: Ruth 6F 105
Eskdale Rd. G61: Bear. 5D 44

Eskdale St. G42: Glas 4F 103
Esk Dr. PA2: Pais 4C 96
Esk St. G14: Glas 4H 59
Esk Wlk. G67: Cumb 4H 35
   (in Cumbernauld Shop. Cen.)
Esk Way PA2: Pais 4C 96
Esmond St. G3: Glas 2A 82
Espedair St. PA2: Pais 2A 98
Espieside Cres. ML5: Coat 3H 89
Esporta Health & Fitness Club
   Finnieston 3C 82
   Hamilton 4B 142
Esporta Health & Racquets 2B 26
Essenside Av. G15: Glas 5B 44
Essex Dr. G14: Glas 5D 60
Essex La. G14: Glas 5D 60
   (not continuous)
Esslemont Av. G14: Glas 4B 60
Esslemont La. G14: Glas 4C 60
Estate Quad. G32: Carm 5C 106
Estate Rd. G32: Carm 5C 106
Etive Av. G61: Bear 3H 45
   ML3: Ham 2E 153
Etive Ct. G67: Cumb 1D 54
   G81: Hard 2E 43
   ML5: Coat 2D 110
Etive Cres. G64: B'rig 6D 48
   G67: Cumb 1D 54
   ML2: Wis 3H 157
Etive Dr. G46: Giff 6B 118
   G67: Cumb 1D 54
   ML6: Air 6C 92
   PA7: B'ton 5A 40
Etive Pl. G67: Cumb 1E 55
Etive St. G32: Glas 6A 86
   ML2: Wis 2H 157
Etna Ind. Est. ML2: Wis 5C 144
Etna St. ML2: Wis 5C 144
Eton La. G12: Glas 1C 82
   (off Gt. George St.)
Etrick Pl. ML4: Bell 6C 110
Etterick Wynd G72: Blan 2A 140
   (off Cheviot St.)
Ettrick Av. PA4: Renf 1H 79
Ettrick Ct. G72: Camb 2D 122
   ML5: Coat 2E 111
Ettrick Cres. G73: Ruth 6E 105
Ettrick Dr. G61: Bear 6C 24
   PA7: B'ton 5A 40
Ettrick Hill G74: E Kil 6A 138
Ettrick Oval PA2: Pais 5C 96
Ettrick Pl. G43: Glas 6B 102
Ettrick Sq. G67: Cumb 4H 35
   (in Cumbernauld Shop. Cen.)
Ettrick St. ML2: Wis 4G 145
Ettrick Ter. PA5: John 5C 94
Ettrick Wlk. G67: Cumb 4H 35
   (in Cumbernauld Shop. Cen.)
Ettrick Way G67: Cumb 4H 35
   (in Cumbernauld Shop. Cen.)
   PA4: Renf 1H 79
Eurocentral ML1: Holy 5H 111
Eurocentral Ind. Est. ML1: Holy . . . 6H 111
EUROCENTRAL JUNC. 4H 111
Evan Cres. G46: Giff 5B 118
Evan Dr. G46: Giff 5B 118
Evanton Dr. G46: T'bnk 4E 117
Evanton Pl. G46: T'bnk 4E 117
Everall Dr. ML2: Newm 4E 147
Everard Ct. G21: Glas 2A 64
Everard Dr. G21: Glas 3A 64
Everard Pl. G21: Glas 2A 64
Everard Quad. G21: Glas 2A 64
Everglades, The G69: Chry 1H 67
Eversley St. G32: Glas 2A 106
Everton Rd. G53: Glas 3C 100
Ewan Mundy Fine Art Gallery
    . . . . 4C 4
Ewart Cres. ML3: Ham 1E 153
Ewart Ter. ML3: Ham 1F 153
Ewing Ct. ML3: Ham 4G 153
Ewing Pl. G31: Glas 6E 85
Ewing St. G73: Ruth. 6C 104
   PA10: Kilb. 2A 94

Ewing Wlk. G62: Miln 4A 26
Excelsior Pk. ML2: Wis 1D 156
Excelsior St. ML2: Wis 1C 156
Exchange Pl. G1: Glas 5E 5
   ML5: Coat. 5C 90
Exeter Dr. G11: Glas 1G 81
Exeter La. G11: Glas 1G 81
   (off Dumbarton Rd.)
Exeter St. ML5: Coat 6C 90
Exhibition Centre Station (Rail) . . . 3C 82
Eynort St. G22: Glas 2E 63
Eyrepoint Ct. G33: Glas 3A 86

F

Factory Rd. ML1: Moth 4G 143
Fagan Ct. G72: Blan 6C 124
FAIFLEY 6E 23
Faifley Rd. G81: Faif, Hard. 6F 23
Fairbairn Cres. G46: T'bnk 5G 117
Fairbairn Path G40: Glas 1C 104
   (off Ruby St.)
Fairbairn St. G40: Glas 1C 104
Fairburn St. G32: Glas 1H 105
Fairfax Av. G44: Glas 2G 119
Fairfield Ct. G76: Busby 4C 134
Fairfield Dr. G76: Busby 4C 134
   PA4: Renf 2F 79
Fairfield Gdns. G51: Glas. 3F 81
Fairfield Pl. G51: Glas 3F 81
   G71: Both 5F 125
   G74: E Kil 1D 148
   ML3: Ham 2A 154
Fairfield St. G51: Glas 3F 81
Fairford Dr. G67: Cumb 6F 35
Fairhaven Av. ML6: Air 5E 93
Fairhaven Rd. G23: Glas 1C 62
FAIRHILL 3G 153
Fairhill Av. G53: Glas. 6C 100
   ML3: Ham 2G 153
Fairhill Cres. ML3: Ham 2G 153
Fairhill Pl. ML3: Ham. 4F 153
Fairholm Av. ML3: Fern 2E 155
Fairholm St. G32: Glas 1H 105
   ML9: Lark. 1D 160
Fairley St. G51: Glas. 5H 81
Fairlie G74: E Kil 6F 137
Fairlie Pk. Dr. G11: Glas 1G 81
Fair Oaks G76: Crmck 1A 136
Fairview Ct. G62: Miln. 4G 25
   (off Main St.)
Fairway G61: Bear 2B 44
Fairway Av. PA2: Pais 5H 97
Fairways ML9: Lark. 2G 161
Fairways, The G44: Neth. 5D 118
   PA5: John. 6D 94
Fairways Vw. G81: Hard. 1F 43
Fairweather Pl.
   G77: Newt M 5C 132
Fairyknowe Gdns. G71: Both 5F 125
Faith Av. PA11: Q'riers 1A 72
Falconbridge Rd. G74: E Kil 5C 138
Falcon Cres. PA3: Pais 5F 77
Falconer Ter. ML3: Ham 2G 153
Falcon Ho. PA3: Pais 4A 78
Falcon Rd. PA5: John 6D 94
Falcon Ter. G20: Glas 1A 62
Falcon Ter. La. G20: Glas 1A 62
   (off Caldercuilt Rd.)
Falfield St. G5: Glas 1E 103
Falkland Av. G77: Newt M 4G 133
Falkland Cres. G64: B'rig 1F 65
Falkland Dr. G74: E Kil. 2E 149
Falkland La. G12: Glas 6H 61
Falkland Pl. G74: E Kil. 2F 149
   ML5: Coat 2D 110
Falkland St. G12: Glas 6H 61
Falloch Rd. G42: Glas 6E 103
   G61: Bear. 5C 44
   G62: Miln 3D 24
FALLSIDE 1G 125
Fallside Av. G71: View. 1G 125

Fallside Rd. G71: Both. 5E 125
Falside Av. PA2: Pais 4A 98
Falside Rd. G32: Glas 3A 106
   PA2: Pais 4H 97
Falstaff G74: E Kil 4C 138
Faraday Av. ML2: Wis 6A 146
Faraday Retail Pk. ML5: Coat 5C 90
Fara St. G23: Glas 1D 62
Farie St. G73: Ruth 5B 104
Farm Ct. G71: Both. 3F 125
Farm Cres. ML1: N'hill 3F 129
Farme Castle Ct. G73: Ruth. 4E 105
Farme Castle Est. G73: Ruth 4E 105
FARME CROSS 4E 105
Farme Cross G73: Ruth 4D 104
Farmeloan Rd. G73: Ruth 5D 104
Farmgate Sq. ML4: Bell. 3B 126
Farmington Av. G32: Glas 6D 86
Farmington Gdns. G32: Glas 6D 86
Farmington Ga. G32: Glas 1D 106
Farmington Gro. G32: Glas 6D 86
Farm La. G71: Udd. 2E 125
   ML4: Bell 4B 126
Farm Pk. G66: Lenz 3D 50
Farm Rd. G41: Glas 6H 81
   G72: Blan 6B 124
   G81: Clyd 4H 41
   G81: Dun, Hard 6C 22
   ML3: Ham 5D 140
Farm St. ML1: Moth. 2F 143
Farm Ter. ML3: Ham 5D 140
Farndale G74: E Kil 6E 137
Farne Dr. G44: Glas 3F 119
Farnell St. G4: Glas 1F 83
Farrier Ct. PA5: John 2F 95
Faskally Av. G64: B'rig. 4A 48
Faskally Wlk. ML2: Newm. 3D 146
Faskin Cres. G53: Glas 6H 99
Faskine Av. ML6: Air 5H 91
   ML6: C'bnk. 3B 112
Faskine Cres. ML6: Air 5H 91
Faskin Pl. G53: Glas 6H 99
Faskin Rd. G53: Glas 6H 99
Fasque Pl. G15: Glas 3G 43
Fastnet St. G33: Glas 3A 86
FAULDHEAD 1H 51
Fauldhouse St. G5: Glas 2H 103
Faulds G69: Bail 6A 88
Faulds Gdns. G69: Bail 6A 88
Fauldshead Rd. PA4: Renf. 6E 59
Faulds La. ML5: Coat. 2B 110
Fauldspark Cres. G69: Bail 5A 88
Faulds St. ML5: Coat 2A 110
Fauldswood Cres. PA2: Pais 3F 97
Fauldswood Dr. PA2: Pais 3F 97
Faulkner Gro. ML1: Cle 1F 145
Fearnmore Rd. G20: Glas 2B 62
Fells, The G66: Len 3G 7
Fellsview Av. G66: Kirk 4F 31
Felton Pl. G13: Glas. 2H 59
Fendoch St. G32: Glas 1A 106
Fenella St. G32: Glas. 6B 86
Fennsbank Av. G73: Ruth. 4F 121
Fenwick Dr. G78: Barr 6E 115
   ML3: Ham 4A 154
Fenwick Pl. G46: Giff. 6H 117
Fenwick Rd. G46: Giff 6H 117
Ferclay St. G81: Faif. 6F 23
Fereneze Av. G76: Clar 1A 134
   G78: Barr 4D 114
   PA4: Renf 3C 78
Fereneze Cres. G13: Glas 3A 60
   ML3: Ham 6D 140
Fereneze Dr. PA2: Pais 5F 97
Fereneze Gro. G78: Barr 4D 114
Fereneze Rd. G78: Neil 2A 130
Fergus Av. PA3: Pais 6E 77
Fergus Ct. G20: Glas 5C 62
Fergus Dr. G20: Glas 5C 62
   PA3: Pais 6E 77
Fergus Gdns. ML3: Ham 1B 154
Fergus La. G20: Glas. 5D 62
Fergus La. G20: Glas 5D 62
Ferguslie PA1: Pais 2D 96
FERGUSLIE PARK 5E 77

Ferguslie Pk. Av. PA3: Pais 6E 77
Ferguslie Pk. Cres. PA3: Pais 1E 97
Ferguslie Park Sports & Recreation Cen.
. . . . 5E 77
(not continuous)
Ferguslie Wlk. PA1: Pais 1F 97
Ferguson Av. G62: Miln 3F 25
PA4: Renf 6F 59
Ferguson Dr. ML1: Moth 6G 143
Ferguson St. PA4: Renf 5F 59
PA5: John 2E 95
Ferguson Way ML6: Air 1B 92
Fergusson Pl. G74: E Kil 4D 138
Fergusson Rd. G67: Cumb 3H 35
Fergusson Ter. G66: Milt C 5C 8
Ferguston Rd. G61: Bear 3F 45
Fernan St. G32: Glas 6H 85
Fern Av. G64: B'rig 1D 64
G66: Lenz 3C 50
PA8: Ersk 2F 57
Fernbank Av. G72: Camb 3C 122
Fernbank St. G21: Glas 4A 64
G22: Glas 4A 64
Fernbrae Av. G73: Ruth 4D 120
Fernbrae Way G73: Ruth 4D 120
Fern Cotts. G13: Glas 4F 61
Ferncroft Dr. G44: Glas 2H 119
Ferndale ML9: Lark 4E 161
Ferndale Ct. G23: Glas 1B 62
Ferndale Dr. G23: Glas 1B 62
Ferndale Gdns. G23: Glas 1B 62
Ferndale Pl. G23: Glas 1B 62
Fern Dr. G78: Barr 3D 114
Ferness Oval G21: Glas 2E 65
Ferness Pl. G21: Glas 2E 65
Ferness Rd. G21: Glas 3E 65
Fern Gro. G69: G'csh 3E 69
Ferngrove Av. G12: Glas 3H 61
FERNHILL. 4D 120
Fernhill Grange G71: Both 6E 125
Fernhill Rd. G73: Ruth 2C 120
FERNIEGAIR 2D 154
Fernie Gdns. G20: Glas 2C 62
Fern La. G12: Glas 4F 61
G13: Glas 4F 61
G66: Len 2E 7
Fernlea G61: Bear 4E 45
Fernleigh Pl. G69: Mood 5D 52
Fernleigh Rd. G43: Glas 2B 118
Fernside Wlk. ML3: Ham 2A 154
Fernslea Av. G72: Blan 1A 140
Fern St. ML1: Moth 5A 144
Ferryden Ct. G14: Glas. 1E 81
Ferryden St. G11: Glas. 1E 81
G14: Glas 1E 81
Ferry Rd. G3: Glas 3H 81
G71: Both 5E 125
G71: Udd 1C 124
Ferry Rd. PA4: Renf 5F 59
PA7: B'ton 4G 39
Fersit Ct. G43: Glas 1A 118
Fersit St. G43: Glas 1A 118
Fetlar Dr. G44: Glas 2G 119
Fetlar Rd. PA11: Bri W 3E 73
Fettercairn Av. G15: Glas. 4G 43
Fettercairn Gdns.
G64: B'rig 6E 49
Fettes St. G33: Glas 3H 85
Fiddoch Ct. ML2: Newm 2D 146
Fidra St. G33: Glas 3H 85
Fielden Pl. G40: Glas 6C 84
Fielden St. G40: Glas 6C 84
Field Gro. G76: Busby 4D 134
Fieldhead Dr. G43: Glas 2G 117
Fieldhead Sq. G43: Glas 2G 117
Field Rd. G76: Busby 4D 134
G81: Faif 5F 23
ML9: Lark 3F 161
Fields La. PA6: Hous 1B 74
Field St. ML3: Ham 2H 153
Fife Av. G52: Glas 1B 100
ML6: Air 6A 92
Fife Ct. G71: Both. 6E 125
Fife Cres. G71: Both. 6E 125

Fife Dr. ML1: Moth 5F 127
Fife Way G64: B'rig 1F 65
Fifth Av. G12: Glas 4F 61
G33: Mille. 4B 66
G72: Blan 4C 140
ML6: Air 3C 92
PA4: Renf 1E 79
Fifty Pitches Pl. G51: Glas. 4B 80
Fifty Pitches Rd. G51: Glas 4B 80
Finart Dr. PA2: Pais 4D 98
Finaven Gdns. G61: Bear. 5B 24
Finch Dr. G13: Glas 1H 59
Finch Pl. PA5: John 6D 94
Findhorn PA8: Ersk. 4E 41
Findhorn Av. PA2: Pais 4D 96
PA4: Renf 6G 59
Findhorn Ct. G75: E Kil 3A 148
Findhorn Pl. G75: E Kil 3A 148
Findhorn St. G33: Glas 3F 85
Findlay Ct. ML1: Moth 1F 143
(from Roman Rd.)
Findlay St. G65: Kils 3H 11
ML1: Moth 4H 143
Findochty PA8: Ersk 4E 41
Findochty St. G33: Glas 2D 86
Fingal La. G20: Glas 2A 62
Fingal St. G20: Glas 2B 62
Fingalton Rd. G77: Newt M 4A 132
Fingask St. G32: Glas 1C 106
Finglas Av. PA2: Pais 4D 98
Finglen Gdns. G62: Miln 3E 25
Finglen Pl. G53: Glas. 3B 116
Fingleton Av. G78: Barr 6F 115
Finhaven St. G32: Glas 2G 105
Finlarig St. G34: Glas 4A 88
Finlas Pl. G21: Glas 4H 63
Finlas St. G22: Glas 5H 63
Finlay Dr. G31: Glas 4C 84
PA3: Lin 6F 75
Finlay Rd. G62: Miln. 5H 25
Finlayson Dr. ML6: Air 4E 93
Finlayson Quad. ML6: Air 4E 93
Finlaystone St. ML5: Coat 4A 90
Finnart Sq. G40: Glas 2B 104
Finnart St. G40: Glas 2B 104
FINNIESTON 3C 82
Finnieston Crane. 4C 82
Finnieston Sq. G3: Glas. 3C 82
Finnieston St. G3: Glas 4C 82
Fintaig La. ML2: Wis 6C 146
Fintrie Ter. ML3: Ham 5C 140
Fintry Av. PA2: Pais 5A 98
Fintry Ct. ML5: Coat 2E 111
Fintry Cres. G64: B'rig 6E 49
G78: Barr 6E 115
Fintry Dr. G44: Glas 6G 103
Fintry Gdns. G61: Bear 5C 24
Firbank Av. G64: Torr. 5D 28
Fir Bank Av. ML9: Lark 3F 161
Firbank Quad. ML6: Chap 2E 113
Firbank Ter. G78: Barr 6G 115
Fir Ct. G72: Flem 3E 123
ML5: Coat 1A 110
Firdon Cres. G15: Glas. 6A 44
Fir Dr. G75: E Kil 6D 148
Fir Gro. G71: View 5F 109
ML1: New S 5A 128
FIRHILL. 5E 63
Firhill Av. ML6: Air 5H 91
Firhill Pk. 5E 63
Firhill Rd. G20: Glas 5D 62
Firhill St. G20: Glas 5E 63
Firlee G75: E Kil. 3B 148
Fir Pk. 5H 143
Firpark Rd. G64: B'rig 1D 64
Firpark St. G31: Glas 3B 84
Fir Pk. St. ML1: Moth 5H 143
Firpark Ter. G31: Glas 4B 84
Fir Pl. G69: Bail 2G 107
G72: Camb 1C 122
ML1: Cle. 6H 129
PA5: John. 4G 95

First Av. G33: Mille. 4B 66
G44: Neth 5D 118
G61: Bear 4G 45
G66: Auch 6D 50
G71: Tann. 5C 108
G82: Dumb 3C 18
PA4: Renf 1E 79
First Gdns. G41: Glas. 1G 101
Firs, The G44: Glas. 2F 119
First Rd. G72: Blan. 4C 140
First St. G71: Tann. 5D 108
First Ter. G81: Clyd 4C 42
Firthview Ter. G82: Dumb 4C 16
Firtree Pl. ML2: Newm 3F 147
Firtree Rd. ML2: Newm 3F 147
Fir Vw. ML6: C'bnk 3B 112
Firwood Courts G77: Newt M 5E 133
Firwood Dr. G44: Glas. 1G 119
Firwood Rd. G77: Newt M 4E 133
Fischer Gdns. PA1: Pais 1D 96
Fisher Av. G65: Kils 3H 11
PA1: Pais 1D 96
Fisher Ct. G31: Glas. 4B 84
Fisher Cres. G81: Hard 1D 42
Fisher Dr. PA1: Pais. 1D 96
Fishers Rd. PA4: Renf 3E 59
Fisher St. ML9: Lark. 4F 161
Fisher Way PA1: Pais. 1D 96
Fishescoates Av. G73: Ruth. 3E 121
(not continuous)
Fishescoates Gdns. G73: Ruth. . . . 2F 121
Fitness First Health Club 3F 103
Fitzalan Dr. PA3: Pais 5C 78
Fitzalan Rd. PA4: Renf. 2C 78
Fitzroy La. G3: Glas 3C 82
Fitzroy Pl. G3: Glas 3C 82
(off Royal Cres.)
Flakefield G74: E Kil 1D 148
Flanders St. G81: Hard 6E 23
Flaxford Gro. ML1: Moth 5F 127
Flaxmill Av. ML2: Wis 5D 144
Flax Rd. G71: Udd 2E 125
Fleet Av. PA4: Renf 2G 79
Fleet St. G32: Glas 1B 106
Fleming Av. G69: Chry. 1A 68
G81: Clyd 1F 59
Fleming Ct. G81: Clyd 5D 42
ML1: Moth 5A 144
ML3: Ham 5C 140
ML8: Carl 4E 165
Fleming Pl. G75: E Kil 3G 149
Fleming Rd. G67: Cumb 3H 35
ML4: Bell 1D 126
PA6: Hous 1A 74
PA7: B'ton 4H 39
Fleming St. G31: Glas 5D 84
PA3: Pais 4A 78
FLEMINGTON
Cambuslang 3E 123
Motherwell 5B 144
Flemington Ind. Est.
G72: Flem 3E 123
Flemington Ind. Pk.
ML1: Moth 4C 144
Flemington Rd. G72: Camb 2E 139
Flemington St. G21: Glas. 6A 64
ML1: Moth 4A 144
Fleming Way ML3: Ham 5B 140
Flenders Av. G76: Clar 3A 134
Flenders Rd. G76: Clar 3A 134
Fleurs Av. G41: Glas 1H 101
Fleurs Rd. G41: Glas 1H 101
Flinders Pl. G75: E Kil 3D 148
Flloyd St. ML5: Coat 4B 90
Floorsburn Cres. PA5: John. 3E 95
Floors St. PA5: John 3E 95
Floors St. Ind. Est. PA5: John 3F 95
Flora Gdns. G64: B'rig 5E 49
Florence Dr. G46: Giff 5A 118
Florence Gdns. G73: Ruth 3E 121
Florence St. G5: Glas. 1G 103
(off Caledonia Rd.)
G5: Glas 6G 83
(Ballater St.)

Florida Av. G42: Glas 5F **103**
Florida Cres. G42: Glas 5F **103**
Florida Dr. G42: Glas 5E **103**
Florida Gdns. G69: Bail 6G **87**
Florida Sq. G42: Glas 5F **103**
Florida St. G42: Glas 5F **103**
Florish Rd. PA8: Ersk 1H **57**
Flowerdale Pl. G53: Glas 4B **116**
Flowerhill Ind. Est.
  ML6: Air 3B **92**
Flowerhill St. ML6: Air 3B **92**
FLUCHTER 3E **27**
Fluchter Rd. G62: Balm, Bard . . . 4E **27**
  G64: Balm 3F **27**
Flures Av. PA8: Ersk. 1A **58**
Flures Cres. PA8: Ersk. 1A **58**
Flures Dr. PA8: Ersk. 1A **58**
Flures Pl. PA8: Ersk. 1A **58**
Fochabers Dr. G52: Glas 5C **80**
Fogo Pl. G20: Glas 3B **62**
Foinhaven Dr. G46: T'bnk 2F **117**
Foinhaven Gdns. G46: T'bnk 1F **117**
Foinhaven Way G46: T'bnk 1G **117**
Footfield Rd. ML4: Bell 3B **126**
Forbes Dr. G40: Glas 6B **84**
  ML1: Moth 5D **126**
Forbes Pl. PA1: Pais 1A **98**
Forbes St. G40: Glas 5B **84**
Fordneuk St. G40: Glas 6C **84**
Fordoun St. G34: Glas 3B **88**
Ford Rd. G12: Glas. 5B **62**
  G77: Newt M 6D **132**
Fordyce Ct. G77: Newt M. 5D **132**
Fordyce St. G11: Glas. 1H **81**
Foremount Ter. La. *G12: Glas* *6A* **62**
  (off Hyndland Rd.)
Fore Row ML3: Ham 5A **142**
Forest Av. ML3: Ham 5H **153**
Forestburn Ct. *ML6: Air* *4F* **91**
  (off Monkscourt Av.)
Forest Dr. G71: Both 4E **125**
  ML4: Bell 4E **127**
Forest Gdns. G66: Lenz 3A **50**
Foresthall Cres. G21: Glas. 6C **64**
Foresthall Dr. G21: Glas 6C **64**
  (not continuous)
Forest Kirk ML8: Carl. 5H **165**
Forest La. ML3: Ham 5H **153**
Forestlea Rd. ML8: Carl 5G **165**
Forest Pk. ML2: Wis 4B **146**
Forest Pl. G66: Lenz 3A **50**
  PA2: Pais 3A **98**
Fore St. G14: Glas 6C **60**
Forest Rd. G67: Cumb 5D **14**
  ML9: Lark 3F **161**
Forest Vw. G67: Cumb 2C **36**
Forfar Av. G52: Glas. 1B **100**
Forfar Cres. G64: B'rig 1E **65**
Forgan Gdns. G64: B'rig. 1F **65**
Forge Dr. ML5: Coat. 4B **90**
Forge Pl. G21: Glas 1D **84**
Forge Rd. ML6: Air. 5F **93**
Forge Row ML3: C'bnk 2C **112**
Forge, The G46: Giff 4B **118**
FORGEWOOD 6F **127**
Forgewood Path ML6: Air. 5F **93**
Forgewood Rd. ML1: Moth 5E **127**
Forglen St. G34: Glas 2H **87**
Formby Dr. G23: Glas. 6B **46**
Forres Av. G46: Giff. 4A **118**
Forres Cres. ML4: Bell. 1C **126**
Forres Ga. G46: Giff 5B **118**
Forres Quad. ML2: Wis 4H **145**
Forres St. G23: Glas. 6C **46**
  G72: Blan 3A **140**
Forrest Dr. G61: Bear. 4B **24**
Forrester Ct. G64: B'rig 1B **64**
Forrestfield Cres. G77: Newt M. . . 4E **133**
Forrestfield Gdns. G77: Newt M . . 4D **132**
Forrestfield St. G21: Glas 2C **84**

Forrest Ga. G71: Tann 4F **109**
  ML3: Ham. 2F **153**
Forrest St. G40: Glas 6C **84**
  G72: Blan 2D **140**
  ML6: Air 3C **92**
  (not continuous)
Forsyth St. ML6: Air. 3B **92**
Fort Antonine Theatre 6B **48**
Forteviot Av. G69: Bail 6A **88**
Forteviot Pl. G69: Bail 6A **88**
Forth Av. PA2: Pais 4D **96**
Forth Ct. G75: E Kil 4A **148**
Forth Cres. G75: E Kil 3A **148**
Forth Gro. G75: E Kil 4A **148**
Forth Pl. ML9: Lark 5F **161**
  PA5: John. 5C **94**
Forth Rd. G61: Bear. 5D **44**
  G64: Torr 5D **28**
Forth St. G41: Glas 2D **102**
  G81: Clyd 1E **59**
Forth Ter. ML3: Ham 3F **153**
Forth Wlk. *G67: Cumb* *4H* **35**
  (in Cumbernauld Shop. Cen.)
Forth Way *G67: Cumb* *4H* **35**
  (in Cumbernauld Shop. Cen.)
Forties Ct. G46: T'bnk 2F **117**
Forties Cres. G46: T'bnk 2G **117**
Forties Gdns. G46: T'bnk. 2G **117**
Forties Rd. PA6: C'lee 3C **74**
Forties Way G46: T'bnk 2G **117**
Fortieth Av. G75: E Kil 6H **149**
Fortingale Av. G12: Glas 3A **62**
Fortingall Pl. G12: Glas 3A **62**
Fortingall Rd. G72: Blan 4D **140**
Fortrose St. G11: Glas. 1H **81**
Forum Pl. ML1: Moth 1D **142**
Fossil Gro. G66: Kirk. 4G **31**
Fossil Rd. 6D **60**
Foswell Pl. G15: Glas 2H **43**
Fotheringay La. G41: Glas. 3B **102**
Fotheringay Rd. G41: Glas. 3B **102**
Foulis La. G13: Glas. 3F **61**
Foulis St. G13: Glas 3F **61**
FOULSYKES 5C **146**
Foulsykes Rd. ML2: Wis 5C **146**
Foundry La. G78: Barr 5E **115**
Foundry Rd. ML1: Cle 5H **129**
Fountain Av. PA4: Inch. 5F **57**
Fountain Cres. PA4: Inch 4F **57**
Fountain Dr. PA4: Inch. 5G **57**
Fountainwell Av. G21: Glas 1H **83**
Fountainwell Dr. G21: Glas 1H **83**
Fountainwell Path G21: Glas 6H **63**
Fountainwell Pl. G21: Glas 1H **83**
Fountainwell Rd. G21: Glas. 1H **83**
Fountainwell Sq. G21: Glas 1A **84**
Fountainwell Ter. G21: Glas 1A **84**
Fourth Av. G33: Mille 4B **66**
  G66: Auch 6D **50**
  G82: Dumb 3C **18**
  PA4: Renf 1E **79**
Fourth Gdns. G41: Glas 1G **101**
Fourth Rd. G72: Blan 4C **140**
Fourth St. G71: Tann 4D **108**
Four Windings PA6: Hous 1B **74**
Fowlis Dr. G77: Newt M 3C **132**
FOXBAR 4D **96**
Foxbar Cres. PA2: Pais 6C **96**
Foxbar Dr. G13: Glas 3B **60**
  PA2: Pais 6C **96**
Foxbar Rd. PA2: Pais 6B **96**
  PA5: Eld 6B **96**
Foxes Gro. G66: Lenz. 2E **51**
Foxglove Pl. G53: Glas 4B **116**
Fox Gro. ML1: Moth. 2D **142**
Foxhills Pl. G23: Glas 6C **46**
FOXLEY 3C **106**
Foxley St. G32: Carm. 4C **106**
Fox St. G1: Glas 5F **83**
Foyers Ter. G21: Glas 5C **64**
Foyes Ct. G13: Glas 3B **60**
Francis St. G5: Glas 1E **103**
Franconia Sq. G81: Clyd. 6D **42**

Frankfield Rd. G33: Step 4E **67**
Frankfield St. G33: Glas. 1F **85**
Frankfort St. G41: Glas 4C **102**
Franklin Pl. G75: E Kil 2D **148**
Franklin St. G40: Glas 2B **104**
Fraser Av. G73: Ruth 5E **105**
  G77: Newt M 3E **133**
  G82: Dumb 1C **18**
  PA5: John. 3G **95**
  PA7: B'ton 3H **39**
Fraser Ct. ML3: Ham 1F **153**
  ML6: Air *3E* **93**
  (off Katherine St.)
Fraser Cres. ML3: Ham 1F **153**
Fraser Gdns. G66: Kirk 5B **30**
Fraser St. G72: Camb 1G **121**
  ML1: Cle. 5H **129**
Frazer River Twr. G75: E Kil 3F **149**
Frazer St. G40: Glas. 6C **84**
Frederick St. ML5: Coat. 3A **90**
FREELAND 2F **57**
Freeland Brae *G75: E Kil* *3H* **149**
  (off Telford Rd.)
Freeland Ct. G53: Glas. 1C **116**
Freeland Cres. G53: Glas. 1B **116**
Freeland Dr. G53: Glas 1B **116**
  PA11: Bri W 2F **73**
  PA4: Inch 3G **57**
Freeland La. *G75: E Kil* *3H* **149**
  (off Telford Rd.)
Freeland Pl. G66: Kirk. 5D **30**
Freeland Rd. PA8: Ersk 2F **57**
Freelands Ct. G60: Old K 3G **41**
Freelands Cres. G60: Old K. 2G **41**
Freelands Pl. G60: Old K 3G **41**
Freelands Rd. G60: Old K 2G **41**
Freesia Ct. ML1: Moth 4G **143**
French St. G40: Glas 2B **104**
  G81: Clyd 4A **42**
  ML2: Wis 6H **145**
  PA4: Renf 1D **78**
Freuchie St. G34: Glas. 4H **87**
Frew St. ML6: Air. 3A **92**
Friar Av. G64: B'rig 4D **48**
Friarscourt Av. G13: Glas. 6D **44**
Friarscourt La. *G13: Glas* *1D* **60**
  (off Knightscliffe Av.)
Friarscourt Rd. G69: Chry 6H **51**
Friars Cft. G66: Kirk 5E **31**
Friars Pl. G13: Glas. 1D **60**
Friars Way ML6: Air. 1C **112**
Friarton Rd. G43: Glas. 2D **118**
Friendship Way PA4: Renf 2F **79**
Frood St. ML1: Moth 6E **127**
Fruin Av. G77: Newt M 3E **133**
Fruin Dr. ML2: Wis. 6C **146**
Fruin Ho. G82: Dumb. 1H **17**
Fruin Pl. G22: Glas 5G **63**
Fruin Ri. ML3: Ham 1C **152**
Fruin Rd. G15: Glas 6H **43**
Fruin St. G22: Glas 5G **63**
Fulbar Av. PA4: Renf 5E **59**
Fulbar Ct. PA4: Renf. 5F **59**
Fulbar Cres. PA2: Pais 3D **96**
Fulbar Gdns. PA2: Pais 3D **96**
Fulbar La. PA4: Renf 5F **59**
Fulbar Path G51: Glas 4C **80**
Fulbar Rd. G51: Glas 4C **80**
  PA2: Pais 3D **96**
Fulbar St. PA4: Renf. 5F **59**
FULLARTON 3A **106**
Fullarton Av. G32: Glas 3A **106**
Fullarton Dr. G32: Glas 4A **106**
Fullarton La. G32: Glas 3A **106**
Fullarton Pl. ML5: Coat 2H **109**
Fullarton Rd. G32: Glas. 5H **105**
  G68: Cumb. 6G **13**
FULLARTON ROAD INTERCHANGE
  . . . . 4A **106**
Fullarton St. ML5: Coat 2A **110**
Fullers Ga. G81: Faif 6E **23**
Fullerton St. PA3: Pais 4H **77**
Fullerton Ter. PA3: Pais 4A **78**
Fullwood Ind. Est. ML3: Ham 5F **141**

Fulmar Ct. G64: B'rig 1B 64
Fulmar Pk. G74: E Kil 6F 137
Fulmar Pl. PA5: John 6C 94
Fulton Cres. PA10: Kilb 2A 94
Fulton Dr. PA6: C'lee 3E 75
Fulton Gdns. PA6: C'lee 3E 75
Fulton Rd. G62: Miln 4H 25
Fulton St. G13: Glas 2D 60
Fulwood Av. G13: Glas 2H 59
  PA3: Lin 5H 75
Fulwood Pl. G13: Glas 2H 59
Furlongs, The ML3: Ham 4A 142
Fyneart St. ML2: Wis 5C 146
Fyne Av. ML4: Bell 6A 110
Fyne Ct. ML3: Ham 2E 153
Fyne Cres. ML9: Lark 6H 155
Fyne Way ML1: Holy 2A 128
  (off Howden Pl.)
Fynloch Pl. G81: Dun 6A 22
Fyvie Av. G43: Glas 2G 117
Fyvie Cres. ML6: Air 4F 93

G

Gadie Av. PA4: Renf 1G 79
Gadie St. G33: Glas 3F 85
Gadloch Av. G66: Auch 5D 50
Gadloch Gdns. G66: Lenz 4D 50
Gadloch St. G22: Glas 3G 63
Gadloch Vw. G66: Auch 5D 50
Gadsburn Ct. G21: Glas 3E 65
Gadshill St. G21: Glas 2B 84
Gailes Pl. G71: Both 5D 124
Gailes Rd. G68: Cumb 6H 13
Gailes St. G40: Glas 1D 104
Gain & Shankburn Rd.
  G67: Cumb 6D 54
Gainburn Ct. G67: Cumb 1B 54
Gainburn Cres. G67: Cumb 2B 54
Gainburn Gdns. G67: Cumb 2B 54
Gainburn Pl. G67: Cumb 1B 54
Gainburn Vw. G67: Cumb 1C 54
Gain Rd. G67: Cumb 6B 54
  ML5: Glenb 6B 54
Gainside Rd. ML5: Glenb 3G 69
Gairbraid Av. G20: Glas 3A 62
Gairbraid Ct. G20: Glas 3A 62
Gairbraid Pl. G20: Glas 3B 62
Gairbraid Ter. G69: Barg 6E 89
Gair Cres. ML2: Wis 2H 157
  ML8: Carl 2G 165
Gairloch Gdns. G66: Kirk 4H 31
Gair Rd. ML8: Carl 1G 165
Gala Av. PA4: Renf 1G 79
Gala Cres. ML2: Wis 4G 145
Gala St. G33: Glas 1G 85
Galbraith Cres. ML8: Law 5E 159
Galbraith Dr. G51: Glas 3D 80
  G62: Miln 5F 25
Galdenoch St. G33: Glas 1B 86
Gallacher Av. PA2: Pais 4E 97
Gallacher Ct. ML1: Moth 6B 144
  PA1: Pais 6G 77
Gallan Av. G23: Glas 6C 46
Gallery of Modern Art 5E 5
Galloway Av. ML3: Ham 4G 153
Galloway Dr. G73: Ruth 4D 120
Galloway Rd. G74: E Kil 6C 138
  ML6: Air 6H 91
Galloway St. G21: Glas 3B 64
GALLOWFLAT 6E 105
Gallowflat St. G73: Ruth 5D 104
GALLOWGATE 6C 84
Gallowgate G1: Glas 5H 83
GALLOWHILL 4D 78
Gallowhill ML9: Lark 3E 161
Gallowhill Av. G66: Lenz 1C 50
Gallowhill Ct. PA3: Pais 3C 78
Gallowhill Gro. G66: Kirk 6C 30
Gallowhill Rd. G66: Kirk, Lenz 1C 50
  G76: Crmck 1H 135
  PA3: Pais 5B 78
Galston Av. G77: Newt M 4G 133

Galston Ct. ML3: Ham 4A 154
Galston St. G53: Glas 1H 115
Galt Pl. G75: E Kil 4F 149
Gamrie Dr. G53: Glas 6A 100
Gamrie Gdns. G53: Glas 6A 100
Gamrie Rd. G53: Glas 5A 100
Gannochy Dr. G64: B'rig 6E 49
Gantock Cres. G33: Glas 4B 86
GARDENHALL 4A 148
Gardenhall G75: E Kil 3A 148
Gardenhall Ct. G75: E Kil 3A 148
Gardenside ML4: Bell 3C 126
Gardenside Av. G32: Carm 5B 106
  G71: Udd 1C 124
Gardenside Cres. G32: Carm 5B 106
Gardenside Gro. G32: Carm 5B 106
Gardenside Pl. G32: Carm 5B 106
Gardenside Rd. ML3: Ham 1H 153
Gardenside St. G71: Udd 1C 124
Garden Sq. Wlk. ML6: Air 3F 91
Garden Veteran's Cotts.
  PA7: B'ton 2D 40
Gardner Gro. G71: Tann 5E 109
Gardner St. G11: Glas 1H 81
Gardyne St. G34: Glas 2G 87
Garelochn Av. ML6: Air 1H 91
  PA2: Pais 3E 97
Garfield Av. ML4: Bell 2E 127
Garfield Dr. ML4: Bell 3E 127
Garfield St. G31: Glas 5C 84
Garforth Rd. G69: Bail 1F 107
Gargrave Av. G69: Bail 1F 107
Garion Dr. G13: Glas 4B 60
Garlieston Rd. G33: Glas 5H 87
Garmouth Ct. G51: Glas 3G 81
Garmouth Gdns. G51: Glas 3G 81
Garmouth St. G51: Glas 3F 81
GARNETHILL 2E 83 (2C 4)
Garnethill St. G3: Glas 2E 83 (2B 4)
Garnet St. G3: Glas 2E 83 (3A 4)
Garngaber Av. G66: Lenz 2D 50
Garngaber Ct. G66: Lenz 2E 51
Garngrew Rd. FK4: Hag 1F 15
Garnhall Farm Rd. G68: Cumb 3E 15
Garnie Av. PA8: Ersk 6H 41
Garnie Cres. PA8: Ersk 6H 41
Garnieland Rd. PA8: Ersk 6H 41
Garnie La. PA8: Ersk 1H 57
Garnie Oval PA8: Ersk 6H 41
Garnie Pl. PA8: Ersk 6H 41
GARNKIRK 3G 67
Garnkirk La. G33: Step 4E 67
Garnock Pl. G74: E Kil 2B 150
Garnock St. G21: Glas 2B 84
GARNQUEEN 4H 69
Garrell Av. G65: Kils 2H 11
Garrell Gro. G65: Kils 1H 11
Garrell Pl. G65: Kils 3G 11
Garrell Rd. G65: Kils 3G 11
Garrell Way G65: Kils 3G 11
Garrioch Cres. G20: Glas 4B 62
Garrioch Dr. G20: Glas 4B 62
Garrioch Ga. G20: Glas 4B 62
Garriochmill Rd. G20: Glas 5B 62
  (not continuous)
Garrioch Quad. G20: Glas 4B 62
Garrioch Rd. G20: Glas 5B 62
Garrion Bus. Pk. ML2: Wis 3H 157
Garrion Pl. ML9: Ashg 4B 162
Garrion St. ML2: Over 5A 158
Garrochmill Way G20: Glas 6D 62
  (off Henderson St.)
GARROWHILL 6G 87
Garrowhill Dr. G69: Bail 6F 87
Garrowhill Station (Rail) 6F 87
Garry Av. G61: Bear 5H 45
Garry Dr. PA2: Pais 3E 97
Garry St. G44: Glas 6E 103
Garscadden Rd. Sth. G13: Glas 1A 60
  G15: Glas 1H 59
  (off Gt. Western Rd.)
Garscadden Station (Rail) 3A 60
Garscadden Vw. G81: Clyd 4F 43

Garscube Rd. G20: Glas 6E 63
  G4: Glas 2F 83 (1C 4)
Garshake Av. G82: Dumb 1C 18
Garshake Rd. G82: Dumb 3H 17
Garshake Ter. G82: Dumb 1C 18
Gartartan Rd. PA1: Pais 6H 79
Gartcarron Hill G68: Cumb 2E 35
Gartcloss Rd. ML5: Coat 1G 89
Gartconnell Dr. G61: Bear 1E 45
Gartconnell Gdns. G61: Bear 1E 45
Gartconnell Rd. G61: Bear 1E 45
Gartconner Av. G66: Kirk 5H 31
GARTCOSH 4D 68
Gartcosh Rd. G69: Barg 5D 88
  (Coatbridge Rd.)
  G69: Barg 3E 89
  (Cuilhill Rd.)
  G69: G'csh 1E 89
Gartcosh Wlk. ML4: Bell 2B 126
Gartcraig Path G33: Glas 2H 85
  (off Gartcraig Rd.)
Gartcraig Pl. G33: Glas 2H 85
Gartferry Av. G69: Mood 5D 52
Gartferry Rd. G68: Mollin 5C 52
  G69: Chry 5B 52
  G69: Mood 5C 52
Gartferry St. G21: Glas 5C 64
Gartfield St. ML6: Air 5B 92
Gartgill Rd. ML5: Coat 1A 90
GARTHAMLOCK 1E 87
Garthland Dr. G31: Glas 4C 84
Garthland La. PA1: Pais 6B 78
Garth St. G1: Glas 4G 83 (6F 5)
GARTLEA 5B 92
Gartlea Av. ML6: Air 4A 92
Gartlea Gdns. ML6: Air 4B 92
Gartleahill ML6: Air 5A 92
Gartlea Rd. ML6: Air 4A 92
Gartliston Rd. ML5: Coat 6B 70
Gartliston Ter. G69: Barg 6E 89
Gartloch Rd. G33: G'csh, Glas 2C 86
  G33: Glas 1H 85
  G69: G'csh 6H 67
Gartly St. G44: Glas 3D 118
Gartmore Gdns. G71: Tann 5C 108
Gartmore La. G69: Mood 5E 53
Gartmore Rd. PA1: Pais 1D 98
Gartmore Ter. G72: Camb 4G 121
GARTNESS 6E 93
Gartness Dr. ML6: Gart 6E 93
Gartness Rd. ML6: Air 2G 113
Gartocher Dr. G32: Glas 6C 86
Gartocher Rd. G32: Glas 6C 86
Gartocher Ter. G32: Glas 6C 86
Gartons Rd. G21: Glas 4E 65
GARTSHERRIE 2B 90
Gartsherrie Av. ML5: Glenb 4B 70
Gartsherrie Ind. Est. ML5: Coat 2B 90
Gartsherrie Rd. ML5: Coat 3A 90
Gartshore Cres. G65: Twe 3D 32
Gartshore Gdns. G68: Cumb 4A 34
Garturk St. G42: Glas 3F 103
  ML5: Coat 1D 110
Garvald Ct. G40: Glas 2D 104
Garvald St. G40: Glas 2D 104
Garve Av. G44: Glas 3E 119
Garvel Cres. G33: Glas 5E 87
Garvel Pl. G62: Miln 3D 24
Garvel Rd. G33: Glas 5E 87
  G62: Miln 3D 24
Garvin Lea ML4: Bell 5C 110
Garvock Dr. G43: Glas 2H 117
Garwhitter Dr. G62: Miln 3H 25
Gascoyne G75: E Kil 4E 149
Gaskin Path G33: Step 4E 67
Gask Pl. G13: Glas 1H 59
Gas St. PA5: John 2G 95
Gasworks Rd. ML8: Carl 2C 164
Gatehouse St. G32: Glas 6B 86
GATESIDE 6B 114
Gateside Av. G65: Kils 3F 11
  G72: Camb 2D 122
Gateside Cres. G78: Barr 6C 114
  ML6: Air 3A 92

Gateside Pk.—Glebe St.

Gateside Pk. G65: Kils 2F **11**
Gateside Pl. PA10: Kilb 2A **94**
Gateside Rd. G78: Barr 6B **114**
   ML2: Wis 5E **145**
Gateside St. G31: Glas 5D **84**
   ML3: Ham 1A **154**
Gateway, The G74: E Kil 5A **138**
Gaughan Quad. ML1: Moth 4F **143**
Gauldry Av. G52: Glas 2C **100**
Gauze St. PA1: Pais 6A **78**
Gavell Rd. G65: Queen 4D **10**
Gavinburn Gdns. G60: Old K 6D **20**
Gavinburn Pl. G60: Old K 6E **21**
Gavinburn St. G60: Old K 6E **21**
Gavin's Mill Rd. G62: Miln 4G **25**
Gavins Rd. G81: Hard 2D **42**
Gavin St. ML1: Moth 4G **143**
Gavinton St. G44: Glas 2D **118**
Gayne Dr. ML5: Glenb 3G **69**
Gean Ct. G67: Cumb 1F **37**
Gear Ter. G40: Glas 3D **104**
Geary St. G23: Glas 6B **46**
Geddes Hill G74: E Kil 5B **138**
Geddes Rd. G21: Glas 2E **65**
Geelong Gdns. G66: Len 2F **7**
Geils Av. G82: Dumb 2C **18**
Geils Quad. G82: Dumb 2C **18**
Gelston St. G32: Glas 1B **106**
Gemini Gro. ML1: Holy 2B **128**
Gemmel Pl. G77: Newt M 5B **132**
Generals Ga. G71: Udd 1C **124**
Gentle Row G81: Dun 1B **42**
George Av. G81: Clyd 4E **43**
George V Bri. G5: Glas 5F **83**
George Ct. ML2: Wis 1E **157**
George Ct. ML3: Ham 4E **141**
   PA1: Pais 1H **97**
George Cres. G81: Clyd 4E **43**
George Gray St. G73: Ruth 5E **105**
George La. PA1: Pais 1A **98**
George Mann Ter. G73: Ruth 3C **120**
George Pl. PA1: Pais 1A **98**
George Reith Av. G12: Glas 4F **61**
George Sq. G2: Glas 4G **83** (5E **5**)
George St. G1: Glas 4G **83** (5F **5**)
   G69: Bail 1H **107**
   G78: Barr 4D **114**
   ML1: Moth 5G **143**
   ML1: New S 3B **128**
   ML3: Ham 4E **141**
   ML4: Bell 2B **126**
   ML6: Air 4G **91**
   ML6: Chap 2D **112**
   PA1: Pais 1G **97**
      (Broomlands St.)
   PA1: Pais 1H **97**
      (George Ct.)
George St. PA5: John 2F **95**
George Way ML9: Lark 1F **161**
      (off Duncan Graham St.)
Gerard Pl. ML4: Bell 6D **110**
GERMISTON 1D **84**
Gertrude Pl. G78: Barr 5C **114**
Ghillies La. ML1: Moth 6E **127**
Gibbon Cres. G74: E Kil 6C **138**
Gibb St. ML1: Cle 6H **129**
   ML6: Chap 2D **112**
Gibson Av. G82: Dumb 3H **17**
Gibson Cres. PA5: John 3E **95**
Gibson Hgts. G4: Glas 4A **84**
      (off Drygate)
Gibson Quad. ML1: Moth 6E **127**
Gibson Rd. PA4: Renf 3D **78**
Gibson St. G12: Glas 1B **82**
   G40: Glas 5A **84**
   G82: Dumb 3G **17**
GIFFNOCK 4A **118**
Giffnock Pk. Av. G46: Giff 3A **118**
Giffnock Station (Rail) 4A **118**
Giffnock Tennis Squash & Hockey Club
   . . . . 6A **118**
Gifford Dr. G52: Glas 6A **80**
Gifford Wynd PA2: Pais 3D **96**
Gigha Gdns. ML8: Carl 5G **165**

Gigha Quad. ML2: Wis 2E **157**
Gilbank La. ML9: Lark 3G **161**
      (off Shawrigg Rd.)
Gilbertfield Path G33: Glas 1B **86**
Gilbertfield Pl. G33: Glas 1B **86**
Gilbertfield Rd.
   G72: Camb, Flem 4C **122**
Gilbertfield St. G33: Glas 1B **86**
Gilbert St. G3: Glas 3A **82**
Gilchrist Ct. PA5: John 4E **95**
      (off Tannahill Cres.)
Gilchrist Gdns. G71: Both 6F **125**
Gilchrist St. ML5: Coat 3D **90**
Gilchrist Way ML2: Wis 2A **158**
Gilderdale G74: E Kil 1E **149**
Gilfillan Pl. ML2: Over 4A **158**
Gilfillan Way PA2: Pais 5C **96**
Gilhill St. G20: Glas 2B **62**
Gillbank Av. ML8: Carl 3D **164**
Gillburn St. ML2: Over 5A **158**
Gillies Cres. G74: E Kil 4D **138**
Gillies La. G69: Bail 1A **108**
Gill Rd. ML2: Over 4A **158**
      (not continuous)
Gilmartin Rd. PA3: Lin 5E **75**
Gilmerton St. G32: Glas 1A **106**
Gilmour Av. G74: T'hall 6F **135**
   G81: Hard 2D **42**
Gilmour Cres. G73: Ruth 5B **104**
Gilmour Dr. ML3: Ham 1D **152**
Gilmour Pl. G5: Glas 1G **103**
   ML4: Bell 2A **126**
   ML5: Coat 3B **90**
Gilmour St. G81: Clyd 3E **43**
   PA1: Pais 6A **78**
Gilmourton Cres. G77: Newt M . . . 6D **132**
GILSHOCHILL 2B **62**
Gilshochill Station (Rail) 2C **62**
Gimmerscroft Cres. ML6: Air 5F **92**
Girthon St. G32: Glas 1C **106**
Girvan Cres. ML6: Chap 4D **112**
Girvan St. G33: Glas 2F **85**
Glade, The ML9: Lark 3F **161**
Gladney Av. G13: Glas 1G **59**
Gladsmuir Rd. G52: Glas 5A **80**
GLADSTONE 6H **39**
Gladstone Av. G78: Barr 5D **114**
   PA5: John 6D **94**
Gladstone Ct. ML3: Ham 4E **141**
Gladstone St. G4: Glas 1E **83** (1A **4**)
   G81: Clyd 5B **42**
   ML4: Bell 2D **126**
Glaive Rd. G13: Glas 6D **44**
Glamis Av. G77: Newt M 4F **133**
   ML8: Carl 3F **165**
   PA5: Eld 4H **95**
Glamis Ct. ML1: Carf 5C **128**
Glamis Dr. G74: E Kil 6H **137**
Glamis Gdns. G64: B'rig 3D **48**
Glamis Rd. G31: Glas 1F **105**
Glanderston Av. G77: Newt M . . . 3B **132**
Glanderston Ct. G13: Glas 1A **60**
Glanderston Dr. G13: Glas 3A **60**
Glanderston Ga. G77: Newt M . . . 3B **132**
Glanderston Rd.
   G78: Neil, Newt M 3H **131**
Glandston Av. G78: Barr 5G **115**
GLASGOW 4G **83** (5F **5**)
Glasgow Academical Athletic Ground
   . . . . 3D **60**
Glasgow Airport PA3: Glas A 1H **77**
GLASGOW AIRPORT INTERCHANGE
   . . . . 3H **77**
Glasgow & Edinburgh Rd.
   G69: Bail 6B **88**
   G69: Barg 1D **108**
   ML1: Holy 4A **112**
   ML1: N'hse 5E **113**
   ML4: Bell 4G **111**
   ML5: Coat 1D **108**
Glasgow Botanic Gardens 5B **62**
Glasgow Bri. G5: Glas 5F **83**
Glasgow Bri. Cotts. G66: Kirk . . . 6G **29**
      (off Kirkintilloch Rd.)

Glasgow Crematorium G23: Glas . . . 1D **62**
Glasgow Film Theatre 3F **83** (3C **4**)
Glasgow Fish Mkt. G21: Glas 2D **84**
Glasgow Fort Shop. Cen.
   G34: Glas 2E **87**
Glasgow Fruit Mkt. G21: Glas 2C **84**
Glasgow Golf Course 4A **46**
Glasgow Green Football Cen. . . . 1A **104**
Glasgow Harbour Terraces
   G11: Glas 2G **81**
Glasgow Hawks R.U.F.C. 3E **61**
Glasgow Necropolis G31: Glas . . . 4A **84**
Glasgow Rd. G62: Miln 5G **25**
   G65: Kils 3E **11**
   G66: Kirk 6H **29**
   G67: Cumb 5E **35**
      (Condorrat Ring Rd.)
   G67: Cumb 1B **36**
      (Old Glasgow Rd.)
   G69: Bail 1F **107**
   G69: Barg, Coat 5F **89**
   G71: Tann, Udd 4A **108**
   G72: Blan 6H **123**
   G72: Camb 6G **105**
      (Duke's Rd.)
   G72: Camb 6H **121**
      (E. Kilbride Rd.)
   G73: Ruth 5H **121**
      (E. Kilbride Rd.)
   G73: Ruth 3B **104**
      (Shawfield Rd.)
   G74: Ners 2A **138**
   G76: Water 6B **134**
   G78: Barr 3F **115**
   G81: Clyd 1D **58**
   G81: Hard 1D **42**
   G82: Dumb, Milt 3E **17**
   ML2: Wis 6D **144**
   ML3: Ham 4E **141**
   ML5: Barg, Coat 5F **89**
   PA1: Pais 6B **78**
   PA4: Renf 6G **59**
Glasgow Rowing Club 6A **84**
Glasgow Royal Concert Hall
   . . . . 3G **83** (3E **5**)
Glasgow School of Art 3E **83** (3B **4**)
Glasgow Science Cen. 4B **82**
Glasgow's Grand Ole Opry 5C **82**
Glasgow Ski Cen. 1G **101**
Glasgow Southern Orbital
   G74: E Kil 2A **148**
   G74: E Kil 6A **136**
Glasgow St. G12: Glas 6C **62**
Glassel Rd. G34: Glas 2B **88**
Glasserton Pl. G43: Glas 2D **118**
Glasserton Rd. G43: Glas 2D **118**
Glassford St. G1: Glas 4G **83** (6F **5**)
   G62: Miln 3H **25**
   ML1: Moth 5A **144**
Glassford Twr. ML1: Moth 5A **144**
      (off Burnside Ct.)
Glaudhall Av. G69: G'csh 2C **68**
Glazert Dr. G66: Len 1C **6**
Glazert Mdw. G66: Len 4G **7**
Glazert Pk. Dr. G66: Len 4G **7**
Glazert Pl. G66: Milt C 6B **8**
Glebe Av. G71: Both 5F **125**
   G76: Crmck 2H **135**
   ML5: Coat 1H **109**
Glebe Ct. G4: Glas 3H **83** (3H **5**)
Glebe Cres. G74: E Kil 2H **149**
   ML3: Ham 1G **153**
   ML6: Air 3D **92**
Glebe Gdns. PA6: Hous 1B **74**
Glebe La. G77: Newt M 5D **132**
Glebe Pk. G82: Dumb 2H **17**
Glebe Pl. G72: Camb 2B **122**
   G73: Ruth 5B **104**
Glebe Rd. G77: Newt M 5D **132**
Glebe St. G4: Glas 2H **83** (2H **5**)
      (Kennedy St.)
   G4: Glas 3A **84** (3H **5**)
      (McAslin St., not continuous)

Glebe St.—Gleniffer Braes Country Pk.

Glebe St. G74: E Kil 1H **149**
ML3: Ham 1G **153**
ML4: Bell 2B **126**
PA4: Renf 6F **59**
Glebe, The G71: Both 5F **125**
Glebe Wynd G71: Both 5F **125**
Gleddoch Rd. G52: Glas 5G **79**
Gledstane Rd. PA7: B'ton 5H **39**
Glenacre Cres. G71: Tann 5C **108**
Glenacre Dr. G45: Glas 4H **119**
ML6: Air 5D **92**
Glenacre Gro. G45: Glas 3A **120**
Glenacre Quad. G45: Glas 4H **119**
Glenacre Rd. G67: Cumb 5H **35**
Glenacre St. G45: Glas 4H **119**
Glenacre Ter. G45: Glas 4H **119**
Glenafeoch Rd. ML8: Carl 4F **165**
Glen Affric G74: E Kil 2B **150**
Glen Affric Av. G53: Glas 3D **116**
Glen Affric Way *ML6: Chap 4D* ***112***
(off Glen Avon Dr.)
Glenafton Vw. ML3: Ham 3F **153**
Glen Alby Pl. G53: Glas 3C **116**
Glenallan Ter. ML1: Moth 6F **127**
Glenallan Way PA2: Pais 6B **96**
Glen Almond G74: E Kil 1D **150**
Glenalmond Rd. G73: Ruth 4F **121**
Glenalmond St. G32: Glas 1A **106**
Glenalva Ct. G65: Kils 2H **11**
Glenapp Av. PA2: Pais 4D **98**
Glenapp Pl. G69: Mood 4D **52**
Glenapp Rd. PA2: Pais 4D **98**
Glenapp St. G41: Glas 2D **102**
Glenarklet Dr. PA2: Pais 4C **98**
Glen Arroch G74: E Kil 2B **150**
Glenartney PA6: Hous 1A **74**
Glenartney Rd. G69: Chry 6A **52**
Glenashdale Way PA2: Pais 4C **98**
Glen Av. G32: Glas 5B **86**
G69: Mood 5D **52**
G78: Neil 2E **131**
ML9: Lark 5D **160**
Glenavon Ct. ML3: Ham 2F **153**
Glen Avon Dr. ML6: Chap 4D **112**
Glenavon Rd. G20: Glas 2B **62**
Glenbank Av. G66: Lenz 3D **50**
Glenbank Dr. G46: T'bnk 5F **117**
Glenbank Rd. G66: Lenz 3D **50**
Glenbarr St. G21: Glas 2B **84**
Glen Bervie G74: E Kil 1B **150**
Glenbervie Cres. G68: Cumb 1H **35**
Glenbervie Pl. G23: Glas 6B **46**
G77: Newt M 4A **132**
GLENBOIG 3A **70**
Glenboig Farm Rd.
ML5: Glenb 3A **70**
Glenboig New Rd. ML5: Glenb 3B **70**
Glenboig Rd. G69: G'csh 1F **69**
Glen Brae PA11: Bri W 3E **73**
Glenbrittle Dr. PA2: Pais 4C **98**
Glenbrittle Way PA2: Pais 4C **98**
Glenbuck Av. G33: Glas 3H **65**
Glenbuck Dr. G33: Glas 3H **65**
GLENBURN 5H **97**
Glenburn Av. G69: Bail 6A **88**
G69: Mood 5D **52**
G72: Camb 2F **121**
ML1: N'hill 3C **128**
Glenburn Ct. *G66: Kirk 5D* ***30***
(off Willowbank Gdns.)
G74: E Kil 6C **136**
Glenburn Cres. G66: Milt C 6C **8**
G71: View 5G **109**
PA2: Pais 5H **97**
Glenburn Gdns. G64: B'rig 5B **48**
ML5: Glenb 3G **69**
Glenburnie Pl. G34: Glas 4F **87**
Glenburn La. G20: Glas 2C **62**
Glenburn Rd. G46: Giff 6H **117**
G61: Bear 2D **44**
G74: E Kil 6C **136**
ML3: Ham 6F **141**
PA2: Pais 5F **97**
Glenburn St. G20: Glas 2C **62**
Glenburn Ter. ML1: Carf 6C **128**
ML8: Carl 5E **165**
Glenburn Wlk. G69: Bail 6A **88**
Glenburn Way G74: E Kil 6B **136**
Glenburn Wynd *ML9: Lark 1F* ***161***
(off Muirshot Rd.)
Glencairn Av. ML2: Wis 5D **144**
Glencairn Ct. *PA3: Pais 3D* ***78***
(off Montgomery Rd.)
Glencairn Dr. G41: Glas 3B **102**
G69: Mood 5C **52**
G73: Ruth 5B **104**
Glencairn Gdns. G41: Glas 3C **102**
G72: Camb 2D **122**
Glencairn La. G41: Glas 3C **102**
Glencairn Path *G32: Glas 5C* ***86***
(off Mansionhouse Dr.)
Glencairn Rd. G67: Cumb 3C **36**
G82: Dumb 4C **16**
PA3: Pais 4C **78**
Glencairn St. G66: Kirk 6D **30**
ML1: Moth 4G **143**
Glencairn Twr. ML1: Moth 4G **143**
Glen Calder Ct. ML6: Air 6D **92**
Glencalder Cres. ML4: Bell 4D **126**
Glen Cally G74: E Kil 1B **150**
Glencally Av. PA2: Pais 4D **98**
Glen Cannich G74: E Kil 2B **150**
Glen Carron G74: E Kil 2B **150**
Glencart Gro. PA10: John 4C **94**
Glencleland Rd. ML2: Wis 5D **144**
Glenclora Dr. PA2: Pais 4C **98**
Glencloy St. G20: Glas 2A **62**
Glen Clunie G74: E Kil 1D **150**
Glen Clunie Dr. G53: Glas 3C **116**
Glen Clunie Pl. G53: Glas 3C **116**
Glencoats Dr. PA3: Pais 6E **77**
Glencoe Dr. ML1: Holy 2A **128**
Glencoe Pl. G13: Glas 2F **61**
ML3: Ham 3F **153**
Glencoe Rd. G73: Ruth 4F **121**
ML8: Carl 5G **165**
Glencoe St. G13: Glas 2F **61**
Glen Cona Dr. G53: Glas 2C **116**
Glenconner Way G66: Kirk 4G **31**
Glencorse Rd. PA2: Pais 3G **97**
Glencorse St. G32: Glas 4G **85**
Glen Ct. ML1: Moth 5B **144**
ML5: Coat 6H **89**
Glen Cova G74: E Kil 1B **150**
Glen Cova Dr. G68: Cumb 1E **35**
Glencraig St. ML6: Air 4G **91**
Glen Creran Cres. G78: Neil 3C **130**
Glen Cres. G13: Glas 2G **59**
Glencroft Av. G71: Tann 5C **108**
Glencroft Rd. G44: Glas 2H **119**
Glencryan Rd. G67: Cumb 5A **36**
Glendale Av. ML6: Air 5D **92**
Glendale Cres. G64: B'rig 1E **65**
Glendale Dr. G64: B'rig 1E **65**
Glendale Gro. ML5: Coat 2A **110**
Glendale Pl. G31: Glas 5D **84**
G64: B'rig 2E **65**
Glendale St. G31: Glas 5D **84**
Glendaruel Av. G61: Bear 3H **45**
Glendaruel Rd. G73: Ruth 5G **121**
Glendarvel Gdns. G22: Glas 5H **63**
Glendee Gdns. PA4: Renf 1F **79**
Glendee Rd. PA4: Renf 1F **79**
Glen Dene Way G53: Glas 3C **116**
Glendentan Rd. PA11: Bri W 4E **73**
Glendermott Ct. ML8: Carl 2F **165**
Glen Derry G74: E Kil 6D **138**
Glen Dessary G74: E Kil 3B **150**
Glendeveron Way ML1: Carf 5A **128**
Glen Devon G74: E Kil 2D **150**
Glendevon Cotts. G81: Clyd 4B **42**
Glendevon Pl. G81: Clyd 4B **42**
ML3: Ham 3F **153**
Glendevon Sq. G33: Glas 1B **86**
Glen Dewar Pl. G53: Glas 3C **116**
Glendinning Rd. G13: Glas 6E **45**
Glendoick Pl. G77: Newt M 4A **132**
Glen Doll G74: E Kil 1B **150**
Glen Doll Rd. G78: Neil 4B **130**
Glendorch Av. ML2: Wis 2A **146**
Glendore St. G14: Glas 1E **81**
Glen Douglas Dr. G68: Cumb 1E **35**
Glendoune Rd. G76: Clar 4C **134**
Glendower Way PA2: Pais 5C **96**
Glen Dr. ML1: Holy 2B **128**
Glenduffhill Rd. G69: Bail 6F **87**
Glen Dye G74: E Kil 1B **150**
Glen Eagles G74: E Kil 2C **150**
Gleneagles Av. G68: Cumb 6A **14**
Gleneagles Ct. *G64: B'rig 4C* ***48***
(off Hilton Rd.)
Gleneagles Dr. G64: B'rig 4C **48**
G77: Newt M 5H **133**
Gleneagles Gdns. G64: B'rig 4B **48**
Gleneagles Ga. G77: Newt M 5H **133**
Gleneagles La. Nth. G14: Glas 5C **60**
Gleneagles La. Sth. G14: Glas 6C **60**
Gleneagles Pk. G71: Both 5D **124**
Glenelg Cres. G66: Kirk 4G **31**
Glenelg Path ML5: Glenb 3G **69**
Glenelg Quad. G34: Glas 2B **88**
Glenelm Pl. ML4: Bell 1C **126**
Glen Esk G74: E Kil 1C **150**
Glen Esk Cres. G53: Glas 3C **116**
Glen Esk Dr. G53: Glas 3C **116**
Glen Esk Pl. G53: Glas 3C **116**
Glen Etive Pl. G73: Ruth 5G **121**
Glen Falloch G74: E Kil 2C **150**
Glen Falloch Cres. G78: Neil 4D **130**
Glen Farg G74: E Kil 2D **150**
Glenfarg Ct. ML3: Ham 3F **153**
Glenfarg Cres. G61: Bear 3H **45**
Glenfarg Rd. G73: Ruth 3D **120**
Glenfarg St. G20: Glas 1E **83**
Glenfarm Rd. ML1: N'hill 3E **129**
Glen Farrar G74: E Kil 2B **150**
Glen Feshie G74: E Kil 3B **150**
Glenfield Av. PA2: Pais 6H **97**
Glenfield Cres. PA2: Pais 6H **97**
Glenfield Gdns. PA2: Pais 6H **97**
Glenfield Grange PA2: Pais 1A **114**
Glenfield Gro. PA2: Pais 6H **97**
Glenfield Rd. G75: E Kil 5A **150**
PA2: Pais 6G **97**
Glen Finlet Cres. G78: Neil 4C **130**
Glenfinnan Dr. G20: Glas 3B **62**
G61: Bear 4H **45**
Glenfinnan Gro. ML4: Bell 3F **127**
Glenfinnan Pl. *G20: Glas 3B* ***62***
(off Glenfinnan Rd.)
Glenfinnan Rd. G20: Glas 3B **62**
Glenfruin Cres. PA2: Pais 4D **98**
Glen Fruin Dr. ML9: Lark 4G **161**
Glen Fruin Pl. *ML6: Chap 3D* ***112***
(off Glen Rannoch Dr.)
Glenfruin Rd. G72: Blan 1A **140**
Glen Fyne Rd. G68: Cumb 1D **34**
Glen Gairn G74: E Kil 1D **150**
Glen Gairn Cres. G78: Neil 3C **130**
Glen Gdns. PA5: Eld 2A **96**
Glen Garrell Pl. G65: Kils 2F **11**
Glengarriff Rd. ML4: Bell 5D **110**
Glen Garry G74: E Kil 3B **150**
Glengarry Dr. G52: Glas 6C **80**
Glengavel Cres. G33: Glas 3H **65**
Glengavel Gdns. ML2: Wis 2A **146**
Glengonnar St. ML9: Lark 5E **161**
GLENGOWAN 2C **160**
Glengowan Rd. PA11: Bri W 3E **73**
Glen Gro. G65: Kils 1H **11**
G75: E Kil 4F **149**
Glengyre St. G34: Glas 2A **88**
Glenhead Cres. G22: Glas 3G **63**
G81: Dun, Hard 6C **22**
Glenhead Dr. ML1: Moth 5F **143**
Glenhead Rd. G66: Lenz 3D **50**
G81: Clyd 2B **42**
Glenhead St. G22: Glas 3G **63**
Glenholme Av. PA2: Pais 4F **97**
Glenhove Rd. G67: Cumb 3A **36**
Gleniffer Av. G13: Glas 3A **60**
Gleniffer Braes Country Pk. 1A **114**

Gleniffer Ct. PA2: Pais 6F **97**
Gleniffer Cres. PA5: Eld 4A **96**
Gleniffer Dr. G78: Barr 2C **114**
Gleniffer Rd. PA2: Pais 6D **96**
  PA4: Renf 3D **78**
Gleniffer Vw. G78: Neil 1D **130**
  G81: Clyd 4F **43**
Glen Isla G74: E Kil 1C **150**
Glenisla Av. G69: Mood 3E **53**
Glen Isla Av. G78: Neil. 4C **130**
Glenisla St. G31: Glas 2F **105**
Glenkirk Dr. G15: Glas 5B **44**
Glen Kyle Dr. G53: Glas. 3C **116**
Glen La. PA3: Pais. 6A **78**
Glen Lednock Dr. G68: Cumb . . . 1D **34**
Glenlee St. ML3: Ham 4D **140**
Glen Lethnot G74: E Kil 1C **150**
Glen Livet Pl. G53: Glas 3C **116**
Glenlivet Rd. G78: Neil 3C **130**
Glen Lochay Gdns. G68: Cumb . . 1D **34**
Glenlora Dr. G53: Glas 6A **100**
Glenlora Ter. G53: Glas 6B **100**
Glen Loy Pl. G53: Glas. 3C **116**
Glenluce Dr. G32: Glas 2D **106**
Glenluce Gdns. G69: Mood 4E **53**
Glenluce Ter. G74: E Kil 1E **149**
Glenluggie Rd. G66: Kirk 6G **31**
Glenlui Av. G73: Ruth 2D **120**
Glen Luss Gdns. G68: Cumb 1D **34**
Glen Luss Pl. G53: Glas 3C **116**
  ML5: Coat 6F **91**
Glen Lyon G74: E Kil 2C **150**
Glen Lyon Ct. G68: Cumb 1D **34**
Glenlyon Ct. ML3: Ham 3F **153**
Glenlyon Pl. G73: Ruth 4E **121**
Glen Lyon Rd. G78: Neil 3C **130**
Glen Mallie G74: E Kil 2C **150**
Glenmalloch Pl. PA5: Eld 2A **96**
Glenmanor Av. G69: Mood 5C **52**
Glenmanor Rd. G69: Mood 5C **52**
Glenmare Av. G66: Kirk 6G **31**
Glen Mark G74: E Kil 1C **150**
Glen Mark Rd. G78: Neil 3C **130**
GLENMAVIS 5G **71**
Glenmavis Ct. ML8: Carl 4G **165**
Glenmavis Cres. ML8: Carl 4G **165**
Glenmavis Rd. ML6: Glenm 6G **71**
Glenmavis St. G4: Glas. . . 2F **83** (1D **4**)
Glen More G74: E Kil 2A **150**
Glenmore Av. G42: Glas. 5A **104**
  ML4: Bell 4D **126**
Glenmore Rd. ML1: N'hill 4C **128**
Glen Moriston G74: E Kil 2C **150**
Glen Moriston Rd.
  G53: Glas 4C **116**
  G68: Cumb 1D **34**
Glenmoss Av. PA8: Ersk 6D **40**
Glen Moy G74: E Kil 2B **150**
Glenmuir Dr. G53: Glas 2B **116**
Glen Muir Rd. G78: Neil. 3C **130**
Glen Nevis G74: E Kil 3B **150**
Glen Nevis Pl. G73: Ruth. 5E **121**
Glen Noble ML1: Cle 1G **145**
Glen Ochil Rd. ML6: Chap. 4D **112**
Glen Ogilvie G74: E Kil 1C **150**
Glenogle St. G32: Glas 1D **106**
Glenoran La. ML9: Lark. 1F **161**
Glenorchard Rd. G64: Balm. 3H **27**
Glen Orchy Ct. G68: Cumb 6D **12**
Glen Orchy Dr. G53: Glas. 3C **116**
  G68: Cumb 1D **34**
Glen Orchy Gro. G53: Glas 3D **116**
Glen Orchy Pl. G53: Glas 4D **116**
  G68: Cumb 1D **34**
  *ML6: Chap 4D **112***
    (off Glen Rannoch Dr.)
Glen Orchy Way G53: Glas. 4C **116**
Glen Orrin Way G78: Neil. 3C **130**
Glenpark Av. G46: Air 5E **93**
Glenpark Av. G46: T'bnk. 5F **117**
Glenpark Gdns. G72: Camb 6G **105**
Glenpark Ind. Est. G31: Glas 5D **84**
Glenpark Rd. G31: Glas. 5D **84**

Glenpark St. G31: Glas 5D **84**
  ML2: Wis 5G **145**
Glenpark Ter. G72: Camb 6G **105**
Glenpath G82: Dumb 2C **18**
Glenpatrick Rd. PA5: Eld 5A **96**
Glen Pl. G76: Clar 2C **134**
Glen Prosen G74: E Kil 1C **150**
Glen Quoich G74: E Kil 6D **138**
Glenraith Path G33: Glas 6B **66**
Glenraith Rd. G33: Glas 6B **66**
Glenraith Sq. G33: Glas 6B **66**
Glenraith Wlk. G33: Glas 6C **66**
Glen Rannoch Dr. ML6: Chap 4D **112**
Glen Rinnes Dr. G78: Neil 4D **130**
Glen Rd. G32: Glas 4B **86**
  G60: Old K 1F **41**
  G66: Cam G, Len 1C **6**
  G68: Dull 4F **13**
  G74: E Kil 5B **136**
    (not continuous)
  ML1: N'hse 6D **112**
  ML2: Wis 5G **145**
  ML6: Air 5E **93**
  PA7: B'ton 3G **39**
Glen Rosa Gdns. G68: Cumb. . . . 1D **34**
Glen Roy Dr. G78: Neil. 3C **130**
Glen Sannox Vw. G68: Cumb . . . 1D **34**
Glen Sannox Way G68: Cumb . . . 1D **34**
Glen Sannox Wynd G68: Cumb . . 1E **35**
Glen Sax Dr. PA4: Renf 2G **79**
Glen Shee G74: E Kil 1C **150**
Glen Shee Av. G78: Neil. 3C **130**
Glen Shee Cres. ML6: Chap 4D **112**
Glenshee Gdns. G31: Glas 1G **105**
Glenshee St. G31: Glas 1F **105**
Glenshee Ter. ML3: Ham 3F **153**
Glenshiel Av. PA2: Pais 4C **98**
Glenshira Av. PA2: Pais. 4C **98**
Glen Shirva Rd. G65: Twe 1D **32**
Glenside Av. G53: Glas 3B **100**
Glenside Cotts. *PA11: Bri W 3F 73*
    (off Mill of Gryffe Rd.)
Glenside Dr. G73: Ruth 1F **121**
Glenside Rd. G82: Dumb. 1H **17**
Glen Spean Pl. ML5: Coat 6F **91**
Glenspean St. G43: Glas 1A **118**
Glen St. G72: Camb 3D **122**
  G78: Barr 5E **115**
  ML1: Moth 6G **127**
  ML1: N'hill 3D **128**
  PA3: Pais 6H **77**
Glentanar Ct. PA1: Pais 1C **98**
Glentanar Dr. G69: Mood. 5E **53**
Glentanar Pl. G22: Glas 2F **63**
Glentanar Rd. G22: Glas 2F **63**
Glen Tanner G74: E Kil. 1D **150**
Glentarbert Rd. G73: Ruth. 4F **121**
Glen Tarbet Dr. G78: Neil. 3C **130**
Glen Tennet G74: E Kil 1C **150**
Glentore Quad. ML6: Air 1A **92**
Glen Twr. *ML1: Moth 5B 144*
    (off Glen Cl.)
Glentrool Gdns. G22: Glas 5H **63**
  G69: Mood 4E **53**
Glen Turret G74: E Kil 1C **150**
Glenturret St. G32: Glas 1A **106**
Glentyan Av. PA10: Kilb 1A **94**
Glen Urquhart G74: E Kil 2B **150**
Glenview G66: Kirk 5D **30**
Glen Vw. G67: Cumb 2C **36**
  ML3: Ham 5H **153**
Glenview ML6: Air 5D **92**
  ML9: Lark 1D **160**
Glenview Av. FK4: Bank 1E **15**
Glenview Cres. G69: Mood 4D **52**
Glenview Pl. G72: Blan 6B **124**
Glenview St. ML6: Glenm 5G **71**
Glenville Av. G46: Giff 4H **117**
Glenville Ga. G76: Busby. 4E **135**
Glenville Ter. G76: Busby 4E **135**
Glenward Av. G66: Len 3G **7**
Glenwell St. ML6: Glenm 6G **71**

Glenwood Av. ML6: Air 1C **112**
Glenwood Bus. Cen. G45: Glas . . 4A **120**
Glenwood Ct. G66: Lenz 2A **50**
Glenwood Dr. G46: T'bnk 5F **117**
Glenwood Gdns. G66: Lenz 2A **50**
Glenwood Path G45: Glas 4A **120**
Glenwood Pl. G45: Glas 4A **120**
  G66: Lenz 2A **50**
Glenwood Rd. G66: Lenz 2A **50**
Glidden Ct. ML2: Over 4A **158**
Globe Ct. G74: E Kil 4D **138**
Glorat Av. G66: Len 3G **7**
Gloucester Av. G73: Ruth. 2F **121**
  G76: Clar 2B **134**
Gloucester St. G5: Glas 6E **83**
Goals (Five a Side Football Cen.)
  . . . . 4F **43**
Goals Football Cen. 4D **102**
GOCKSTON 3H **77**
Gockston Rd. PA3: Pais 4H **77**
Goddard Pl. ML2: Newm 4F **147**
Gogar Pl. G33: Glas 3G **85**
Gogar St. G33: Glas 3G **85**
Goil Av. ML4: Bell 1H **125**
Goil Way *ML1: Holy. 2A 128*
    (off Howden Pl.)
Goldberry Av. G14: Glas 4B **60**
Goldberry La. *G14: Glas 4B 60*
    (off Esslemont Av.)
Goldenhill Ct. G81: Hard 1D **42**
Goldenlee Vw. PA6: C'lee 3A **74**
Goldie Rd. G71: Udd 3E **125**
Golf Av. ML4: Bell 4C **126**
Golf Course Rd. G64: Balm 5A **28**
  PA11: Bri W 3D **72**
Golf Ct. G44: Neth 5C **118**
Golf Dr. G15: Glas 6H **43**
  PA1: Pais 1E **99**
Golf Gdns. ML9: Lark. 3G **161**
GOLFHILL 1H **91**
Golfhill Dr. G31: Glas 3C **84**
Golfhill Quad. ML6: Air 1A **92**
Golfhill Rd. ML2: Wis 5D **144**
Golf Pl. ML4: Bell 4D **126**
Golf Rd. G73: Ruth 3D **120**
  G76: Clar 2B **134**
Golfview G61: Bear 2B **44**
Golf Vw. G81: Clyd 3B **42**
Golfview Dr. ML5: Coat 4G **89**
Golfview Pl. ML5: Coat 5G **89**
Golspie Av. ML6: Air 1G **111**
Golspie St. G51: Glas 3G **81**
Goodview Gdns.
  ML9: Lark. 3G **161**
Goosedubs *G1: Glas. 5G 83*
    (off Bridgegate)
Gooseholm Cres. G82: Dumb . . . 2G **17**
Gooseholm Rd. G82: Dumb. 2G **17**
Gopher Av. G71: View. 5F **109**
GORBALS 1G **103**
Gorbals Cross G5: Glas 6G **83**
  ML9: Lark 2E **161**
Gorbals Leisure Cen. 6G **83**
Gorbals St. G5: Glas 6F **83**
Gordon Av. G44: Neth 5C **118**
  G52: Hill 4G **79**
  G69: Bail 6F **87**
  PA7: B'ton 3G **39**
Gordon Ct. ML6: Air 3E **93**
Gordon Cres. G77: Newt M 3E **133**
Gordon Dr. G44: Neth 5C **118**
  G74: E Kil 6B **138**
Gordon La. G1: Glas 4F **83** (5D **4**)
Gordon Pl. ML4: Bell 4B **126**
Gordon Rd. G44: Neth 5C **118**
  ML3: Ham 5D **140**
Gordon Sq. PA5: John 3F **95**
Gordon St. G1: Glas 4F **83** (5D **4**)
  PA1: Pais 1A **98**
Gordon Ter. G72: Blan 5A **124**
  ML3: Ham 6D **140**
Gorebridge St. G32: Glas. 4G **85**
Goremire Rd. ML8: Carl 6G **165**
Gorget Av. G13: Glas 6C **44**

Gorget Pl. G13: Glas 6C 44
Gorget Quad. G13: Glas 6B 44
Gorse Cres. PA11: Bri W 4G 73
Gorse Dr. G78: Barr 3D 114
Gorsehall St. ML1: Cle 5H 129
Gorse Pl. G71: View 5F 109
Gorsewood G64: B'rig 6A 48
Gorstan Path G23: Glas 1B 62
Gorstan Pl. G20: Glas 4A 62
Gorstan St. G23: Glas 1B 62
Gosford La. G14: Glas 5A 60
Gotter Bank PA11: Q'riers 1A 72
Goudie St. PA3: Pais 4H 77
Gough La. G33: Glas 3F 85
(off Gough St.)
Gough St. G33: Glas 3F 85
Gourlay G74: E Kil 4D 138
Gourlay Dr. ML2: Over 5A 158
Gourlay St. G21: Glas 6H 63
(not continuous)
Gourock St. G41: Glas 1E 103
GOVAN 3G 81
GOVANHILL 3F 103
Govanhill St. G42: Glas 3F 103
(not continuous)
Govanhill Swimming Pool 3E 103
Govan Rd. G51: Glas 2D 80
Govan Station (Und.) 3G 81
Gowanbank Gdns. PA5: John. 3E 95
Gowanbrae G66: Lenz 1C 50
Gowanlea Av. G15: Glas 6A 44
Gowanlea Dr. G46: Giff 3B 118
Gowanlea Ter. G71: View 6F 109
Gowanside Pl. ML8: Carl. 3D 164
Gower St. G41: Glas 1A 102
Gower Ter. G41: Glas 6A 82
Gowkhall Av. ML1: N'hill 4F 129
GOWKTHRAPPLE 3G 157
Goyle Av. G15: Glas 4C 44
Grace Av. G69: Barg 6D 88
Grace St. G3: Glas 4D 82
Graeme Ct. ML1: Moth. 5F 127
Graffham Av. G46: Giff 4B 118
Grafton Pl. G1: Glas 3G 83 (3F 5)
Graham Av. G72: Camb 2D 122
G74: E Kil 1G 149
G81: Clyd 4D 42
ML3: Ham 3H 153
(not continuous)
Graham Dr. G62: Miln 3E 25
Graham Ho. G67: Cumb 3G 35
Graham Pl. G65: Kils 1G 11
ML9: Ashg 4B 162
Graham Rd. G82: Dumb 3D 16
Grahamsdyke Rd. G66: Kirk. 4E 31
Grahamshill Av. ML6: Air 3D 92
Grahamshill St. ML6: Air 3C 92
Grahamston Ct. PA2: Pais 5E 99
Grahamston Cres. PA2: Pais 5E 99
Grahamston Pk. G78: Barr. 2D 114
Grahamston Pl. PA2: Pais 5E 99
Graham St. G78: Barr 4D 114
ML1: Holy. 2A 128
ML2: Wis 1H 157
ML3: Ham 6A 142
ML6: Air. 4A 92
(not continuous)
PA5: John. 3E 95
Graham Ter. G64: B'rig 2D 64
Graignestock Pl. G40: Glas 6A 84
Graignestock St. G40: Glas 6A 84
Grainger Rd. G64: B'rig 6F 49
Grammar School Sq. ML3: Ham . . . 5A 142
Grampian Av. PA2: Pais. 5H 97
Grampian Ct. G61: Bear. 5C 24
Grampian Cres. G32: Glas 1B 106
ML6: Chap 4F 113
Grampian Pl. G32: Glas. 1B 106
Grampian Rd. ML2: Wis. 5F 145
Grampian St. G32: Glas 1B 106
Grampian Way G61: Bear 6B 24
G68: Cumb 3C 34
G78: Barr 6E 115

Granby La. G12: Glas 6B 62
Grandtully Dr. G12: Glas. 3A 62
Grange Av. G62: Miln. 3H 25
ML2: Wis 2E 157
Grange Gdns. G71: Both 6F 125
Grangeneuk Gdns. G68: Cumb 4E 35
Grange Rd. G42: Glas 5E 103
G61: Bear 2F 45
Grange St. ML1: Moth 5A 144
Grange Twr. ML1: Moth 1B 156
Gran St. G81: Clyd 1G 59
Grant Ct. ML3: Ham 5G 153
ML6: Air 3E 93
Grantholm Av. ML1: Holy. 1B 128
Grantlea Gro. G32: Glas 1D 106
Grantlea Ter. G32: Glas 1D 106
Grantley Gdns. G41: Glas 5B 102
Grantley St. G41: Glas 5B 102
Grantoften Path G75: E Kil 5F 149
Granton St. G5: Glas 3A 104
Grantown Av. ML6: Air. 5E 93
Grantown Gdns. ML6: Glenm 4H 71
Grants Cres. PA2: Pais 5H 97
Grant St. G3: Glas 2D 82 (1A 4)
Granville St. G3: Glas 3D 82
G81: C'csh 4D 42
Grasmere G75: E Kil. 6B 148
Grasmere Ct. ML3: Ham 5H 153
Grathellen Ct. ML1: Moth 1A 144
Gray Dr. G61: Bear 4F 45
Grayshill Rd. G68: Cumb. 6H 33
Gray's Rd. G71: Udd. 2F 125
Gray St. G3: Glas 2B 82
G66: Kirk 6H 31
ML1: Cle. 6H 129
ML9: Lark 1E 161
Great Av. ML3: Fern 2C 154
Great Dovehill G1: Glas. 5H 83
Gt. George La. G12: Glas. 6B 62
Gt. George St. G12: Glas 6B 62
Gt. Hamilton St. PA2: Pais 3A 98
Gt. Kelvin La. G12: Glas 1C 82
(off Glasgow St.)
Gt. Western Retail Pk. G15: Glas . . . 5G 43
Gt. Western Rd. G12: Glas 4G 61
G13: Glas 6H 43
G15: Glas 6H 43
G4: Glas 4G 61
G60: Bowl, Old K 5H 19
G81: Clyd, Dun, Hard 1H 41
Gt. Western Ter. G12: Glas 5A 62
Gt. Western Ter. La. G12: Glas 5A 62
Greenacres ML1: Moth 4E 143
Greenacres Ct. G53: Glas 3C 116
Greenacres Vw. ML1: Moth 4E 143
Greenacres Way G53: Glas 3C 116
Greenan Av. G42: Glas 6A 104
Greenbank G72: Blan 2A 140
Greenbank Av. G46: Giff 2G 133
Greenbank Dr. PA2: Pais 6H 97
Greenbank Gardens 4A 134
Green Bank Rd. G68: Cumb. 3E 35
Greenbank Rd. ML2: Wis. 6A 146
Greenbank St. G73: Ruth. 5C 104
Greenbank Ter. ML8: Carl 3F 165
Green Dale ML2: Wis. 4B 146
Greendyke St. G1: Glas 5H 83
GREENEND 1F 111
Greenend Av. PA5: John 5D 94
Greenend Pl. G32: Glas 4C 86
Greenend Vw. ML4: Bell 3B 126
Greenfarm Rd. G77: Newt M 4B 132
Green Farm Rd. PA3: Lin 5H 75
GREENFAULDS 6G 35
Greenfaulds Cres. G67: Cumb. 5A 36
Greenfaulds Rd. G67: Cumb 5A 36
(Greenfaulds Cres.)
G67: Cumb 6G 35
(Waverley Cres.)
Greenfaulds Station (Rail) 6H 35
GREENFIELD 5B 86
Greenfield Av. G32: Glas 4B 86
Greenfield Cres. ML2: Wis 5B 146
Greenfield Dr. ML2: Wis 5B 146

Greenfield Pl. G32: Glas 5B 86
Greenfield Quad. ML1: N'hill 3F 129
Greenfield Rd. G32: Glas. 4C 86
G76: Clar 3C 134
ML3: Ham. 3E 141
ML8: Carl 2F 165
Greenfield St. G51: Glas 4F 81
ML2: Wis 5B 146
GREENFOOT 2C 70
Greengairs Av. G51: Glas 3D 80
Green Gdns. ML1: Cle 5H 129
Greenhall Pl. G72: Blan 3A 140
GREENHEAD 1B 158
Greenhead Av. G82: Dumb 4H 17
Greenhead Gdns. G82: Dumb 4H 17
(not continuous)
Greenhead Rd. G61: Bear 3F 45
G66: Len 3G 7
G82: Dumb. 4H 17
ML2: Wis 1A 158
PA4: Inch 2G 57
Greenhead St. G40: Glas. 6A 84
GREENHILL 2D 90
Greenhill G64: B'rig 1E 65
Greenhill Av. G46: Giff. 6H 117
G69: G'csh 2C 68
Greenhill Bus. Pk. PA3: Pais. 5G 77
Greenhill Ct. G73: Ruth 5C 104
Greenhill Cres. PA3: Lin 5H 75
PA5: Eld 3B 96
Greenhill Dr. PA3: Lin 5A 76
Greenhill Ind. Est. ML5: Coat 2D 90
Greenhill Rd. G73: Ruth 5C 104
PA3: Pais 5G 77
GREENHILLS 6D 148
Greenhills Cres. G75: E Kil 6D 148
Greenhills Rd. G75: E Kil. 3A 148
Greenhills Sports Cen. 5E 149
Greenhills Sq. G75: E Kil 5C 148
Greenhill St. G73: Ruth. 6C 104
Greenhills Way G75: E Kil 5F 149
Greenholm Av. G71: Udd. 6C 108
G76: Clar 2C 134
Greenholme Ct. G44: Glas 1F 119
Greenholme St. G44: Glas 1F 119
Greenknowe Dr. ML8: Law 5D 158
Greenknowe Rd. G43: Glas 1H 117
Greenknowe St. ML2: Over 5H 157
Greenlaw Av. ML2: Wis 4A 146
PA1: Pais 6C 78
Greenlaw Ct. ML2: Wis 1H 157
Greenlaw Cres. PA1: Pais 5C 78
Greenlaw Dr. G77: Newt M 4C 132
PA1: Pais 6C 78
Greenlaw Ho. PA1: Pais. 6C 78
Greenlaw Ind. Est. PA3: Pais. 5B 78
Greenlaw Rd. G14: Glas. 3F 59
G77: Newt M 4C 132
Greenlea Rd. G69: Chry 1H 67
Greenlea St. G13: Glas 3E 61
GREENLEES 4B 122
Greenlees Gdns. G72: Camb. 4H 121
Greenlees Gro. ML5: Coat 6F 91
Greenlees Pk. G72: Camb. 4A 122
Greenlees Rd. G72: Camb. 5H 121
Green Loan ML1: New S 4A 128
Greenloan Av. G51: Glas 3D 80
Greenloan Vw. ML9: Lark 4F 161
(off Keir Hardie Rd.)
Greenlodge Ter. G40: Glas. 1B 104
Greenmoss Pl. ML4: Bell. 2D 126
Greenmount G22: Glas. 2E 63
Greenock Av. G44: Glas 2F 119
Greenock Rd. PA3: Pais. 3G 77
(not continuous)
PA7: B'ton 1A 38
Green Pl. G71: Both 5F 125
ML6: C'bnk. 3B 112
Greenrig G71: Udd. 1D 124
Greenrig Rd. G67: Cumb. 4A 36
Greenrig St. G33: Glas 6F 65
G71: Udd 1D 124
Green Rd. G73: Ruth 5C 104
PA2: Pais 2D 96

Greens Av. G66: Kirk 6C 30
Greens Cres. G66: Kirk 6C 30
Greens Health & Fitness. 3C 118
Greenshields Rd. G69: Bail. 6H 87
Greenside G76: Crmck. 1A 136
Greenside Cres. G33: Glas 6G 65
Greenside Pl. G61: Bear 5C 24
Greenside Rd. G81: Hard 6D 22
   ML1: N'hse. 6C 112
   ML2: Wis 1A 158
Greenside St. G33: Glas 6G 65
   ML1: N'hill 3F 129
   ML5: Coat 2D 90
Greens Rd. G67: Cumb 1H 55
GREENS, THE 6C 30
Green St. G40: Glas 6A 84
   G71: Both 5F 125
   G81: Clyd 4C 42
Green, The G40: Glas 1A 104
Greentree Dr. G69: Bail 2F 107
Greenview St. G43: Glas 5A 102
Greenway La. G72: Blan 3H 139
Greenways Av. PA2: Pais 3E 97
Greenways Ct. PA2: Pais 3E 97
Greenwood Av. G69: Mood 5D 52
   G72: Camb 1E 123
Greenwood Ct. G76: Clar 2C 134
Greenwood Cres. ML5: Coat 6E 91
Greenwood Dr. G61: Bear 3G 45
   PA5: John. 5D 94
Greenwood Quad. G81: Clyd 6F 43
Greenwood Rd. G76: Clar 2B 134
GREENYARDS INTERCHANGE 4B 36
Greer Quad. G81: Clyd 3D 42
Grenada Pl. G75: E Kil 2C 148
Grenadier Gdns. ML1: Moth 6F 143
Grenville Dr. G72: Camb 3H 121
Gresham Vw. ML1: Moth 1B 156
Greta Meek La. G66: Milt C. 5C 8
Gretna St. G40: Glas 1D 104
Greyfriars Rd. G71: Udd 5A 108
Greyfriars St. G32: Glas 4H 85
Greystone Av. G73: Ruth 1E 121
Greywood St. G13: Glas 2E 61
Grier Path G31: Glas 6F 85
Grier Pl. ML9: Lark 3D 160
Grierson La. *G33: Glas.* *3F 85*
                    (off Lomax St.)
Grierson St. G33: Glas 3F 85
Grieve Cft. G71: Both. 6D 124
Grieve Rd. G67: Cumb. 2A 36
Griffen Av. PA1: Pais 6B 76
Griffin Pl. ML4: Bell 5C 110
Griffiths Way ML8: Law 1H 163
Griqua Ter. G71: Both. 5F 125
Grogarry Rd. G15: Glas 3A 44
Grosvenor Cinema. *6B 62*
                    (off Ashton La.)
Grosvenor Cres. G12: Glas 6B 62
Grosvenor Cres. La. G12: Glas 6B 62
Grosvenor La. G12: Glas 6B 62
Grosvenor Ter. G12: Glas 6B 62
Groveburn Av. G46: T'bnk 3G 117
Grove Cres. ML9: Lark 3G 161
Grove Pk. G20: Glas. 6E 63
   G66: Lenz. 3D 50
Grovepark Ct. G20: Glas. 1E 83
Gro. Park Gdns. G20: Glas. 1E 83
Grovepark St. G20: Glas. 6E 63
Groves, The G64: B'rig. 1E 65
Grove, The G46: Giff 1H 133
   G78: Neil 3C 130
   PA10: Kilb. 1A 94
   PA11: Bri W 5G 73
   PA7: B'ton 4G 39
Grove Way ML4: Bell 2B 126
Grove Wood G71: View 4H 109
Grovewood Bus. Cen. ML4: Bell . . . 5A 110
Grove Wynd ML1: New S 4A 128
Grudie St. G34: Glas 3G 87
Gryfebank Av. PA6: C'lee 2E 75
Gryfebank Cl. PA6: C'lee 2E 75
Gryfebank Cres. PA6: C'lee 2E 75
Gryfebank Way PA6: C'lee 2E 75

Gryfewood Cres. PA6: C'lee 2E 75
Gryfewood Way PA6: C'lee 2E 75
Gryffe Av. PA11: Bri W 2E 73
   PA4: Renf 4D 58
Gryffe Cres. PA2: Pais 4D 96
Gryffe Gro. PA11: Bri W 3F 73
Gryffe Pl. *PA11: Bri W* *3F 73*
                    (off Main St.)
Gryffe Rd. PA11: Bri W. 4F 73
Gryffe St. G44: Glas 6E 103
Guildford St. G33: Glas 2C 86
Gullane Ct. ML3: Ham 3F 153
Gullane Cres. G68: Cumb 5H 13
Gullane St. G11: Glas 2H 81
Gunn Quad. ML4: Bell 4A 126
Guthrie Ct. ML1: Moth 3E 143
Guthrie Dr. G71: Tann 4E 109
Guthrie Pl. G64: Torr 5E 29
   G74: E Kil 1H 149
Guthrie St. G20: Glas. 3B 62
   ML3: Ham 5H 141
Gyle Pl. ML2: Wis 6C 146

H

Haberlea Av. G53: Glas 4C 116
Haberlea Gdns. G53: Glas 5C 116
                    (not continuous)
Haddington Way ML5: Coat 2A 110
Haddow Gro. G71: Tann 5E 109
Haddow St. ML3: Ham 6A 142
Hadrian Ter. ML1: Moth 1E 143
Hagart Rd. PA6: Hous 1B 74
Hagen Dr. ML1: Cle 6E 129
Hagg Cres. PA5: John 2E 95
Hagg Pl. PA5: John 2E 95
Hagg Rd. PA5: John 3E 95
HAGGS 1G 15
HAGGS CASTLE 3A 102
Haggs La. G41: Glas 3A 102
Haggs Rd. G41: Glas 4A 102
Haggswood Av. G41: Glas 3A 102
HAGHILL 4E 85
Haghill Rd. G31: Glas 5E 85
Hagmill Cres. ML5: Coat 3E 111
Hagmill Rd. ML5: Coat 3C 110
Haig Dr. G69: Bail. 1F 107
Haig St. G21: Glas 5B 64
Hailes Av. G32: Glas 6D 86
Haining Rd. PA4: Renf 6F 59
Haining, The PA4: Renf 1F 79
HAIRMYRES 3B 148
Hairmyres Dr. G75: E Kil 3B 148
Hairmyres Pk. G75: E Kil 3B 148
Hairmyres Station (Rail) 2B 148
HAIRMYRES RDBT. 2B 148
Hairmyres St. G42: Glas 3G 103
Hairst St. PA4: Renf 5F 59
Halbeath Av. G15: Glas 4H 43
Halbert St. G41: Glas 4C 102
Haldane La. *G14: Glas.* *6D 60*
                    (off Haldane St.)
Haldane Pl. G75: E Kil 4H 149
Haldane St. G14: Glas. 6D 60
Halfmerk Nth. G74: E Kil 1A 150
Halfmerk St. G74: E Kil 1A 150
HALFWAY 3D 122
Halgreen Av. G15: Glas 4G 43
Haliburton Cres. G34: Glas 4F 87
Halifax Way *PA4: Renf.* *2E 79*
                    (off Tiree Av.)
Hallbrae St. G33: Glas 1G 85
Hallburton Ter. G34: Glas 4G 87
Hallcraig Pl. ML8: Carl 3D 164
Hallcraig St. ML6: Air 3A 92
Halley Dr. G13: Glas 2G 59
Halley Pl. G13: Glas 2G 59
Halley Sq. G13: Glas 2H 59
Halley St. G13: Glas 2G 59
Hallforest St. G33: Glas 1B 86
Hallhill Cres. G33: Glas 5E 87
Hallhill Rd. G32: Glas 6B 86
   G33: Glas 5D 86

Hallhill Rd. G69: Bail. 5G 87
   PA5: John 6C 94
Halldale Cres. PA4: Renf 1H 79
Hallinan Gdns. ML2: Wis. 2F 157
Hall Pl. G33: Step. 4F 67
Hallrule Dr. G52: Glas 6C 80
HALLSIDE 3F 123
Hallside Av. G72: Camb 2E 123
Hallside Blvd. G72: Flem 4F 123
Hallside Cres. G72: Camb 2E 123
Hallside Dr. G72: Camb 2E 123
Hallside Gdns. ML2: Wis. 5C 146
Hallside Pl. G5: Glas 1G 103
Hallside Rd. G72: Flem 3F 123
                    (Hallside Blvd.)
   G72: Flem 3E 123
                    (Newton Sta. Rd.)
Hall St. G81: Clyd 6C 42
   ML1: New S 3A 128
   ML3: Ham 2H 153
Hallydown Dr. G13: Glas 4C 60
Halpin Cl. ML4: Bell. 2H 125
Halton Gdns. G69: Bail. 1F 107
Hamersley Pl. G75: E Kil 4D 148
Hamilcomb Rd. ML4: Bell 4C 126
Hamill Dr. G65: Kils 3B 12
HAMILTON 6A 142
Hamilton Academical F.C. 5E 91
Hamilton Av. G41: Glas 1H 101
Hamilton Bus. Pk. ML3: Ham 4H 141
Hamilton Central Station (Rail) 6A 142
Hamilton Ct. PA2: Pais 3A 98
Hamilton Cres. G61: Bear 6E 25
   G72: Camb 3C 122
   ML5: Coat. 6C 90
   PA4: Renf 4F 59
   PA7: B'ton. 4F 39
Hamilton Dr. G12: Glas 6C 62
   G46: Giff 5B 118
   G71: Both 6F 125
   G72: Blan 4H 139
   G72: Camb 2A 122
   ML1: Moth 5H 143
   ML6: Air 2B 92
   PA8: Ersk 4D 40
Hamilton Farm G73: Ruth 5G 105
HAMILTONHILL 5F 63
Hamiltonhill Cres. G22: Glas. 5F 63
Hamiltonhill Rd. G22: Glas 6F 63
HAMILTON INTERCHANGE. 5C 142
Hamilton Intl. Tech. Pk. (Technology Av.)
   G72: Blan 4A 140
Hamilton Intl. Tech. Pk. (Watt Pl.)
   G72: Blan 5A 140
Hamilton Mausoleum. 4B 142
Hamilton Pk. Av. G12: Glas 6C 62
Hamilton Pk. Nth. ML3: Ham 3H 141
Hamilton Pk. Racecourse 3H 141
Hamilton Pk. Sth. ML3: Ham 3H 141
Hamilton Pl. G75: E Kil 4G 149
   G78: Neil 2F 131
   ML1: N'hill 3C 128
   ML1: New S 3B 128
   ML3: Ham 5H 153
Hamilton Retail Pk. ML3: Ham 4G 141
Hamilton Rd. G32: Glas 2B 106
   G71: Both 6F 125
   G71: Udd 3F 107
   G72: Blan 4F 139
   G72: Camb, Flem 1A 122
   G73: Ruth. 5D 104
   G74: E Kil 4C 138
   ML1: Moth 4D 142
   ML4: Bell 3C 126
   ML9: Lark. 6H 155
Hamilton St. G42: Glas 4G 103
   G81: Clyd 2F 59
   G82: Dumb 3G 17
   ML8: Carl 4F 165
   ML9: Lark. 1E 161
   PA3: Pais 6B 78
Hamilton Ter. G81: Clyd 2F 59
Hamilton Twr. G71: Both 3B 124
Hamilton Vw. G71: Tann 6E 109

Hamilton Water Palace 5H 141
Hamilton West Station (Rail) 5G 141
Hamlet G74: E Kil. 4C 138
Hampden Dr. G42: Glas 6F 103
Hampden La. G42: Glas 5F 103
Hampden Pk. 6F 103
Hampden Ter. G42: Glas 5F 103
Hampden Way PA4: Renf 2F 79
Handel Pl. G5: Glas 1G 103
HANGINGSHAW 5G 103
Hangingshaw Pl. G42: Glas. 5G 103
Hannay St. PA1: Pais 6G 77
(off Well St.)
Hanover Cl. G42: Glas 5E 103
Hanover Ct. G1: Glas. 3G 83 (4F 5)
G11: Glas 1G 81
PA1: Pais 6C 78
PA5: John 2F 95
Hanover Gdns. G64: B'rig 6C 48
PA1: Pais 1G 97
(off Wilson St.)
Hanover Pl. G11: Glas 1G 81
Hanover St. G1: Glas 4G 83 (5E 5)
Hanson Pk. G31: Glas 3B 84
Hanson St. G31: Glas 4B 84
Hapland Av. G53: Glas 3C 100
Hapland Rd. G53: Glas 3C 100
Harbour La. PA3: Pais 6A 78
Harbour Pl. G11: Kils 2G 11
Harbour Rd. PA3: Pais 4A 78
Harburn Pl. G23: Glas 6C 46
Harbury Pl. G14: Glas 3H 59
Harcourt Dr. G31: Glas 3D 84
HARDGATE 1E 43
Hardgate Dr. G51: Glas 3C 80
Hardgate Gdns. G51: Glas 3C 80
Hardgate Path G51: Glas 3C 80
Hardgate Pl. G51: Glas 3C 80
Hardgate Rd. G51: Glas 3C 80
Hardie Av. G73: Ruth 5E 105
Hardie St. G72: Blan 2B 140
ML1: Moth 1G 143
ML3: Ham 1F 153
Hardmoor Gdns. G66: Kirk. 4E 31
Hardmoor Rd. G66: Kirk. 4E 31
Hardridge Av. G52: Glas. 3E 101
Hardridge Pl. G52: Glas. 3E 101
Hardridge Rd. G52: Glas 3D 100
Harefield Dr. G14: Glas 4B 60
Harelaw Av. G44: Glas 3C 118
G78: Barr 6F 115
G78: Neil 3D 130
Harelaw Cres. PA2: Pais 6G 97
HARELEESHILL 3F 161
Hareleeshill Rd. ML9: Lark 3F 161
Hareleeshill Sports Barn 4G 161
HARESTANES 4H 31
Harestanes Gdns. G66: Kirk 4G 31
Harestone Cres. ML2: Wis 1A 158
Harestone Rd. ML2: Wis 1A 158
Harhill St. G51: Glas 4F 81
Harkins Av. G72: Blan 2A 140
Harkness Av. G66: Milt C 6B 8
Harland Cotts. G14: Glas 6C 60
Harland St. G14: Glas 6C 60
Harlaw Gdns. G64: B'rig. 5F 49
Harley St. G51: Glas 5A 82
Harmetray St. G22: Glas 3H 63
Harmony Pl. G51: Glas 4G 81
Harmony Row G51: Glas 4G 81
(not continuous)
Harmony Sq. G51: Glas 4G 81
Harmsworth St. G11: Glas 1E 81
Harper Cres. ML2: Wis 5C 146
Harport St. G46: T'bnk 2E 117
Harriet Pl. G43: Glas 1H 117
Harriet St. G73: Ruth 6C 104
Harrington Rd. G74: E Kil 2G 149
Harris Cl. G77: Newt M 3B 132
Harris Cres. G60: Old K 2F 41
Harris Dr. G60: Old K 2F 41
Harris Gdns. G60: Old K 2G 41
Harrison Dr. G51: Glas. 5H 81
Harrison Quad. ML2: Wis 4C 146

Harris Rd. G23: Glas 6C 46
G60: Old K 2F 41
Harrow Ct. G15: Glas 4H 43
Harrow Pl. G15: Glas 4H 43
Hartfield Ct. G82: Dumb 3G 17
Hartfield Cres. G78: Neil 2E 131
Hartfield Gdns. G82: Dumb. 3G 17
Hartfield Ter. PA2: Pais 3B 98
Hartlaw Cres. G52: Glas 5A 80
Hartree Av. G13: Glas 1G 59
Hartstone Pl. G53: Glas 6B 100
Hartstone Rd. G53: Glas 6B 100
Hartstone Ter. G53: Glas 6B 100
Hart St. G31: Glas 6G 85
G81: Faif 6F 23
PA3: Lin 6H 75
Harvest Dr. ML1: Moth. 5F 143
Harvey St. G4: Glas 1G 83
Harvey Way ML4: Bell 6E 111
Harvie Av. G77: Newt M. 4C 132
Harvie St. G51: Glas 5B 82
Harwood Gdns. G69: Mood 4E 53
Harwood St. G32: Glas 4G 85
Hastie St. G3: Glas. 2B 82
Hastings G75: E Kil 4D 148
Hatfield Dr. G12: Glas 4F 61
Hathaway Dr. G46: Giff 5H 117
Hathaway La. G20: Glas 4C 62
Hathaway St. G20: Glas. 4C 62
Hathersage Av. G69: Bail. 6H 87
Hathersage Dr. G69: Bail. 6H 87
Hathersage Gdns. G69: Bail 6H 87
Hatton Gdns. G52: Glas 1A 100
Hattonhill ML1: Carf 5C 128
Hatton Path G52: Glas 1A 100
(off Hatton Gdns.)
Hatton Pl. ML1: Carf 5C 128
Hattonrigg ML4: Bell 1D 126
Hatton Rd. ML4: Bell 1D 126
Hatton Ter. ML1: Carf. 5C 128
Haughburn Pl. G53: Glas. 6B 100
Haughburn Rd. G53: Glas 6B 100
Haughburn Ter. G53: Glas 6C 100
HAUGHHEAD 1C 6
Haughhead Bri. G71: Udd 5A 108
Haugh Pl. ML3: Ham 2A 154
Haugh Rd. G3: Glas 3B 82
G65: Kils 3G 11
Haughton Av. G65: Kils 3A 12
Haughview Rd. ML1: Moth 3D 142
Havelock La. G11: Glas 1A 82
Havelock Pk. G75: E Kil 2C 148
Havelock St. G11: Glas 1A 82
Haven Pl. G75: E Kil. 5B 148
Havoc Rd. G82: Dumb 4B 16
Hawbank Rd. G74: E Kil. 6C 136
HAWBANK RDBT. 1D 148
Hawick Av. PA2: Pais 4F 97
Hawick Cres. ML9: Lark 3E 161
Hawick Dr. ML5: Coat. 2F 111
Hawick St. G13: Glas. 3G 59
ML2: Wis 4A 146
HAWKHEAD 3E 99
Hawkhead Av. PA2: Pais 3D 98
Hawkhead Rd. PA1: Pais 1D 98
Hawkhead Station (Rail) 1D 98
Hawksland Wlk. ML3: Ham 2A 154
Hawkwood G75: E Kil 6F 149
Hawkwood Rd. ML6: Glenm 5H 71
Hawthornden Gdns. G23: Glas. 5C 46
Hawthorn Dr. FK4: Bank. 1E 15
G78: Barr 6F 115
ML1: New S 4B 128
ML2: Wis 1A 158

Hawthorn Dr. ML5: Coat. 6F 91
ML6: Air 4D 92
Hawthorn Gdns. G72: Flem 3E 123
G76: Busby. 3C 134
ML4: Bell 3E 127
ML9: Lark. 3G 161
Hawthorn Gro. ML8: Law. 5D 158
Hawthorn Hill ML3: Ham 2A 154
Hawthornhill Rd. G82: Dumb 2B 16
Hawthorn Pl. G72: Blan 2C 140
Hawthorn Quad. G22: Glas 4G 63
Hawthorn Rd. G67: Cumb 1F 37
G76: Busby. 3C 134
PA8: Ersk 1A 58
Hawthorn St. G22: Glas 4G 63
G64: Torr 4E 29
G81: Clyd 3C 42
Hawthorn Ter. G71: View 6F 109
G75: E Kil 5D 148
Hawthorn Wlk. G72: Camb. 2F 121
Hawthorn Way G66: Milt C 6C 8
G82: Dumb 3B 16
PA8: Ersk 1A 58
Hay Av. PA7: B'ton 4A 40
Hayburn Cres. G11: Glas 6G 61
Hayburn Ga. G11: Glas 1H 81
Hayburn La. G12: Glas. 6G 61
Hayburn St. G11: Glas. 2G 81
Hay Dr. PA5: John 2H 95
Hayfield Ct. G5: Glas 1H 103
Hayfield St. G5: Glas 1H 103
Hayle Gdns. G69: Mood 4D 52
Haylynn St. G14: Glas 1E 81
Haymarket St. G32: Glas 4G 85
Haystack Pl. G66: Lenz 3D 50
HAYSTON 5A 30
Hayston Cres. G22: Glas 4F 63
Hayston Rd. G66: Kirk 5A 30
G68: Cumb 1G 35
Hayston St. G22: Glas 4F 63
Haywood St. G22: Glas. 3F 63
Hazel Av. G44: Glas 3D 118
G61: Bear 6G 25
G66: Lenz. 1D 50
G82: Dumb 2B 16
Hazel Av. PA5: John. 4G 95
Hazel Bank G66: Milt C 1B 30
Hazelbank ML1: Holy. 2B 128
Hazelbank Wlk. ML6: Air 3F 91
Hazeldean Cres. ML2: Wis 4A 146
Hazel Dene G64: B'rig 6D 48
Hazeldene La. ML9: Lark 4G 161
(off Keir Hardie Rd.)
Hazelden Gdns. G44: Glas 3C 118
Hazelden Pk. G44: Glas 3C 118
Hazelfield Gro. ML6: Chap. 4E 113
Hazel Gdns. ML1: Moth. 6G 143
Hazel Gro. G66: Lenz. 1D 50
ML8: Law 5D 158
Hazelhead G74: E Kil 1B 150
Hazellea Dr. G46: Giff 3C 118
Hazel Pk. ML3: Ham 1A 154
Hazel Path ML1: Cle 6H 129
Hazel Rd. FK4: Bank. 1E 15
G67: Cumb 2D 36
Hazel Ter. G71: View 6F 109
Hazelton ML1: Moth 4F 143
Hazel Wood ML2: Wis 4B 146
Hazelwood Av. G77: Newt M 5E 133
PA11: Bri W 4F 73
PA2: Pais 6C 96
Hazelwood Dr. G72: Blan 1A 140
Hazelwood Gdns. G73: Ruth 3E 121
Hazelwood La. PA11: Bri W 4F 73
Hazelwood Rd. G41: Glas 1A 102
PA11: Bri W 4F 73
Hazlitt Gdns. G20: Glas 3E 63
Hazlitt Pl. G20: Glas. 3E 63
Hazlitt St. G20: Glas. 3F 63
Headhouse Ct. G75: E Kil 3F 149
Headhouse Grn. G75: E Kil 3G 149
Headsmuir Av. ML8: Carl. 3D 164
Heath Av. G64: B'rig 1D 64
G66: Lenz. 3C 50

Heathcliffe Av. G72: Blan 6A 124
Heathcot Av. G15: Glas 5G 43
Heathcot Pl. G15: Glas 5F 43
Heather Av. G61: Bear 5D 24
   G78: Barr 2C 114
   G81: Hard 6C 22
   ML1: Holy 2A 128
Heatherbank Mus. of Social Work
   . . . . 1C 82
Heatherbank Wlk. ML6: Air 3F 91
HEATHERBELL 6H 69
Heatherbrae G64: B'rig 6A 48
Heather Dr. G66: Lenz 3A 50
Heather Gdns. G66: Lenz. 3A 50
Heather Gro. G75: E Kil. 4G 149
   (off Heathery Knowe)
Heatherlea Pl. ML5: Coat. 2F 111
Heather Pl. G66: Lenz 2A 50
   PA5: John. 3G 95
Heather Row ML8: Carl 1E 165
Heather Vw. G66: Len 2G 7
Heather Way ML1: New S 3A 128
Heathery Knowe G75: E Kil 4G 149
Heatheryknowe Rd.
   G69: Barg 4C 88
   (not continuous)
Heathery Rd. ML2: Wis 6F 145
Heathfield ML2: Wis 4G 157
Heathfield Av. G69: Mood 5D 52
Heathfield Dr. G62: Miln 2H 25
Heathfield St. G33: Glas 3C 86
Heath Rd. ML9: Lark 2F 161
Heathside Rd. G46: Giff 4B 118
Heathwood Dr. G46: T'bnk 4G 117
Hecla Av. G15: Glas 4H 43
Hecla Pl. G15: Glas 4H 43
Hecla Sq. G15: Glas 5H 43
Hector Rd. G41: Glas 5B 102
Helena Pl. G76: Clar 1C 134
Helena Ter. G81: Dun 1C 42
Helensburgh Dr. G13: Glas 3D 60
Helenslea G72: Camb 3D 122
Helenslea Pl. ML4: Bell 3B 126
Helenslee Ct. G82: Dumb 4D 16
Helenslee Cres. G82: Dumb 4E 17
Helenslee Rd. G82: Dumb. 4D 16
Helen St. G51: Glas 6F 81
   G52: Glas 6F 81
HELEN ST. INTERCHANGE 6F 81
Helenvale Ct. G31: Glas 6F 85
Helenvale St. G31: Glas. 1E 105
Helen Wynd ML9: Lark 3E 161
Helmsdale Av. G72: Blan 4A 124
Helmsdale Ct. G72: Camb 2D 122
Helmsdale Dr. PA2: Pais 3D 96
Hemlock St. G13: Glas 2F 61
Henderland Dr. G61: Bear 5E 45
Henderland Rd. G61: Bear 5E 45
Henderson Av. G72: Camb 1D 122
Henderson St. G20: Glas 6D 62
   G81: Clyd 1G 59
   ML5: Coat. 5B 90
   ML6: Air 3B 92
   PA1: Pais 6H 77
Henrietta St. G14: Glas 6C 60
Henry Bell Grn. G75: E Kil. 3H 149
   (off Muirhouse La.)
Henry St. G78: Barr 4D 114
Henry Wood Hall, The 3C 82
Hepburn Hill ML3: Ham 3F 153
Hepburn Rd. G52: Hill 4B 80
Herald Av. G13: Glas 6D 44
Herald Gro. ML1: Moth 5F 143
Herald Way PA4: Renf 2E 79
Herbertson Gro. G72: Blan. 6A 124
Herbertson St. G5: Glas 6F 83
   G72: Blan 2C 140
Herbert St. G20: Glas. 6D 62
Herbison Ct. ML9: Lark 1F 161
Hercules Way PA4: Renf 2F 79
Heriot Av. PA2: Pais 5C 96
Heriot Ct. PA2: Pais 5D 96
Heriot Cres. G64: B'rig 4C 48
Heriot Rd. G66: Lenz 4C 50

Heritage Ct. G77: Newt M 4E 133
Heritage Vw. ML5: Coat 3B 90
Heritage Way ML5: Coat 4B 90
Herma St. G23: Glas 1C 62
Hermes Way ML4: Moss 2H 127
Hermiston Av. G32: Glas 5C 86
Hermiston Pl. G32: Glas 5C 86
   ML1: Holy. 2A 128
   (off Windsor Rd.)
Hermiston Rd. G32: Glas 4B 86
Hermitage Av. G13: Glas 2C 60
Hermitage Cres. ML5: Coat. 2D 110
Herndon Ct. G77: Newt M 3G 133
Heron Ct. G81: Hard 2D 42
Heron Pl. PA5: John 6D 94
Heron St. G40: Glas 1B 104
Heron Way PA4: Renf 2E 79
Herries Rd. G41: Glas 4A 102
Herriet St. G41: Glas 2D 102
Herriot St. ML5: Coat 3A 90
Herschell St. G13: Glas 3F 61
Hertford Av. G12: Glas 3H 61
Hewett Cres. PA6: C'lee 2C 74
Hexham Gdns. G41: Glas. 4B 102
Heys St. G78: Barr 5E 115
Hickman St. G42: Glas 4F 103
Hickman Ter. G42: Glas 3G 103
Hickory Cres. G71: View 4G 109
Hickory St. G22: Glas. 4A 64
High Avon St. ML9: Lark 1D 160
HIGH BALMALLOCH 2G 11
High Barholm PA10: Kilb 2A 94
High Barrwood Rd. G65: Kils. 3A 12
High Beeches G76: Crmck 1A 136
HIGH BLANTYRE 4A 140
High Blantyre Rd. ML3: Ham 4D 140
Highburgh Dr. G73: Ruth 2D 120
Highburgh Rd. G12: Glas 6A 62
HIGH BURNSIDE 3E 121
High Burnside Av. ML5: Coat. 6A 90
High Calside PA2: Pais 2H 97
High Coats ML5: Coat 4D 90
High Comn. Rd. G75: E Kil 4B 150
Highcraig Av. PA5: John 4D 94
High Craigends G65: Kils. 3H 11
High Craighall Rd. G4: Glas. 1F 83
Highcroft Av. G44: Glas 2H 119
Highcross Av. ML5: Coat 1H 109
HIGH CROSSHILL 2D 120
Higherness Way ML5: Coat 2A 110
Highfield Av. G66: Kirk. 4E 31
   PA2: Pais 6H 97
Highfield Ct. G66: Kirk 5F 31
Highfield Cres. ML1: Moth 1A 144
   PA2: Pais 6H 97
Highfield Dr. G12: Glas 3H 61
   G73: Ruth 4E 121
   G76: Clar 2B 134
Highfield Gro. G66: Kirk. 4E 31
Highfield Pl. G12: Glas 3H 61
   G74: E Kil 6H 137
Highfield Rd. G66: Kirk 4E 31
   ML9: Lark 2F 161
High Flender Rd. G76: Clar 3A 134
HIGH GALLOWHILL 2B 50
Highgrove Ct. PA4: Renf 6G 59
Highgrove Rd. PA4: Renf 6G 59
High Kirk Vw. PA5: John 3F 95
HIGH KNIGHTSWOOD 1D 60
Highland Av. G72: Blan 1A 140
Highland La. G51: Glas 3A 82
HIGHLAND PARK 1G 11
Highland Pk. G65: Kils. 2G 11
Highland Pl. G65: Kils 1G 11
Highland Rd. G62: Miln 3G 25
High Mains Av. G82: Dumb 2C 18
High Mair PA4: Renf 1E 79
High Mdw. ML8: Carl. 5H 165
   (not continuous)
High Mill Rd. ML8: Carl. 3G 165
High Murray St. G72: Camb 2C 122
High Parksail PA8: Ersk. 1G 57
High Parks Cres. ML3: Ham 5H 153
High Patrick St. ML3: Ham 1A 154

High Pleasance ML9: Lark. 2E 161
High Rd. ML1: Moth. 2F 143
   PA2: Pais 2G 97
High Row Cotts. G64: B'rig 2D 48
Highstonehall Rd.
   ML3: Ham 4C 152
High St. G1: Glas 5H 83 (6G 5)
   G66: Kirk 4C 30
   G73: Ruth 5C 104
   G78: Neil 2D 130
   G82: Dumb 4E 17
   ML1: N'hill 3E 129
   ML6: Air 3H 91
   ML8: Carl 3F 165
   PA1: Pais 1H 97
   PA4: Renf 5F 59
   PA5: John 2E 95
High Street Station (Rail) . . . 4H 83 (6H 5)
High Whitehills Rd. G75: E Kil. . . 6F 149
Hilary Dr. G69: Bail 6F 87
Hilda Cres. G33: Glas 5G 65
Hillary Av. G73: Ruth 1F 121
Hill Av. G77: Newt M 5C 132
Hillbrae St. G51: Glas 5D 80
Hill Cres. G76: Busby 3C 134
Hillcrest G69: Chry 1B 68
   G76: Crmck 1H 135
Hillcrest Av. G32: Carm 5B 106
   G44: Glas 3C 118
   G67: Cumb 5G 35
   G81: Dun 6C 22
   ML2: Wis 6E 145
   ML5: Coat. 5E 91
   PA2: Pais 6G 97
Hillcrest Ct. G67: Cumb. 4H 35
Hillcrest Dr. G77: Newt M 4G 133
Hillcrest Rd. G32: Carm. 4C 106
   G61: Bear 3F 45
   G65: Queen 3C 10
   G71: Tann 6E 109
Hillcrest St. G62: Miln 3G 25
Hillcrest Ter. G71: Both 4F 125
Hillcrest Vw. ML9: Lark 3F 161
Hillcroft Ter. G64: B'rig 1B 64
Hillend Cotts. G66: Lenz 1C 50
Hillend Cres. G76: Clar 3A 134
   G81: Dun 1B 42
Hillend Rd. G22: Glas 2E 63
   G73: Ruth. 2D 120
   G76: Clar 3A 134
Hillfoot PA6: C'lee 3D 74
Hillfoot Av. G61: Bear 2F 45
   G73: Ruth 6C 104
   G82: Dumb 1C 18
   ML2: Wis 2B 146
Hillfoot Cres. ML2: Wis 2B 146
Hillfoot Dr. G61: Bear 2F 45
   ML2: Wis 2B 146
   ML5: Coat 5H 89
Hillfoot Gdns. G71: Tann 5C 108
   ML2: Wis 2B 146
Hillfoot Rd. ML6: Air 5A 92
Hillfoot Station (Rail) 2G 45
Hillfoot St. G31: Glas 4C 84
Hillfoot Ter. ML8: Carl 4G 165
HILLHEAD
   Glasgow 6B 62
   Kirkintilloch 4D 30
Hillhead Av. FK4: Bank. 1E 15
   G69: Mood 5D 52
   G73: Ruth. 3D 120
   ML1: Carf 5A 128
   ML8: Carl 3G 165
Hillhead Cres. ML1: Carf. 5A 128
   ML3: Ham 6C 140
Hillhead Dr. ML1: Carf. 6A 128
   ML6: Air 5A 92
Hillhead Pl. G73: Ruth 3D 120
Hillhead Rd. G21: Glas. 2F 65
   G66: Kirk 4D 30
Hillhead Station (Und.) 6B 62
Hillhead St. G12: Glas 1B 82
   G62: Miln 3G 25
Hillhead Ter. ML3: Ham. 6C 140

Hillhouse—Hornbeam Rd.

HILLHOUSE **6D 140**
Hillhouse Cres. ML3: Ham 6D **140**
Hillhouse Ga. ML8: Carl 5H **165**
Hillhouse Pk. Ind. Est.
ML3: Ham. 5E **141**
Hillhouse Rd. G72: Blan 4H **139**
ML3: Ham 5C **140**
Hillhouse St. G21: Glas 5C **64**
Hillhouse Ter. ML3: Ham. 6D **140**
HILLINGTON **6A 80**
Hillington East Station (Rail) **5B 80**
Hillington Gdns. G52: Glas 1C **100**
HILLINGTON INDUSTRIAL ESTATE
. . . . **3H 79**
HILLINGTON INTERCHANGE **2H 79**
Hillington Pk. Cir. G52: Glas 6C **80**
Hillington Quad. G52: Glas 6A **80**
Hillington Rd. G52: Hill 2H **79**
(not continuous)
Hillington Rd. Sth. G52: Glas 5A **80**
Hillington Shop. Cen. G52: Hill. 3H **79**
Hillington Ter. G52: Glas 6A **80**
Hillington West Station (Rail) **4H 79**
Hillkirk Pl. G21: Glas 5B **64**
Hillkirk St. G21: Glas 5B **64**
Hillkirk St. La. *G21: Glas. 5B* ***64***
(off Hillkirk St.)
Hillneuk Av. G61: Bear 2F **45**
Hillneuk Dr. G61: Bear 2G **45**
Hillpark Av. PA2: Pais 4H **97**
Hillpark Dr. G43: Glas 1H **117**
Hill Pl. ML1: Carf. 5C **128**
ML4: Bell 4B **126**
Hillrigg Av. ML6: Air 3C **92**
Hill Rd. G65: Kils. 1H **11**
G67: Cumb. 3G **35**
Hillsborough Rd. G69: Bail. 6F **87**
HILLSIDE **5B 114**
Hillside G65: Croy 6B **12**
PA6: C'lee. 3D **74**
Hillside Av. G61: Bear 2F **45**
G76: Clar 2B **134**
Hillside Cotts. ML5: Glenb. 3A **70**
Hillside Ct. G46: T'bnk. 4F **117**
Hillside Cres. G78: Neil. 2D **130**
ML1: N'hill 3D **128**
ML3: Ham 1H **153**
ML5: Coat. 1B **110**
Hillside Dr. G61: Bear 2G **45**
G64: B'rig. 5C **48**
G78: Barr 4C **114**
Hillside Gdns. La. *G11: Glas. 6H* ***61***
(off Nth. Gardner St.)
Hillside Gro. G78: Barr 5C **114**
Hillside La. ML3: Ham 1G **153**
Hillside Pk. G81: Hard. 1D **42**
Hillside Pl. ML1: N'hill 4D **128**
Hillside Quad. G43: Glas. 2H **117**
Hillside Rd. G43: Glas. 2H **117**
G78: Barr 5B **114**
G78: Neil 2D **130**
PA2: Pais 3C **98**
Hillside Ter. G60: Old K 1F **41**
G66: Milt C. 6B **8**
ML3: Ham 1G **153**
Hill St. G3: Glas 2E **83** (2A **4**)
G82: Dumb. 4D **16**
ML2: Wis 1G **157**
ML3: Ham 6D **140**
ML6: Chap 3D **112**
ML9: Lark 3E **161**
Hillsview G69: Chry. 1H **67**
Hillswick Cres. G22: Glas. 1F **63**
Hill Ter. ML1: Carf 5C **128**
Hilltop Av. ML4: Bell 6C **110**
Hilltop Ter. G69: Mood 5D **52**
Hill Vw. G75: E Kil 3G **149**
G82: Milt. 4F **19**
Hillview Av. G65: Kils 4H **11**
G66: Len 3G **7**
Hillview Cotts. G65: Twe 1D **32**
Hillview Cres. G71: Tann 5C **108**
ML4: Bell 5C **110**
ML9: Lark 3F **161**
Hillview Dr. G72: Blan 5A **124**
G76: Clar 2B **134**
Hill Vw. Gdns.
G64: B'rig 1E **65**
Hillview Pl. G76: Clar 2C **134**
G77: Newt M 5D **132**
Hillview Rd. PA11: Bri W 4G **73**
PA5: Eld 3H **95**
Hillview St. G32: Glas 6H **85**
Hillview Ter. G60: Old K. 2F **41**
Hiltonbank St. ML3: Ham. 5F **141**
Hilton Ct. G64: B'rig. 4C **48**
Hilton Gdns. G13: Glas. 2F **61**
Hilton Gdns. La. G13: Glas 2F **61**
Hilton Pk. G64: B'rig 3B **48**
Hilton Rd. G62: Miln 3E **25**
G64: B'rig 4B **48**
Hilton Ter. G13: Glas 2E **61**
G64: B'rig 3B **48**
G72: Camb 4G **121**
Hindsland Rd. ML9: Lark 4F **161**
Hinshaw St. G20: Glas 6E **63**
Hinshelwood Dr. G51: Glas 5G **81**
Hinshelwood Pl. G51: Glas 6H **81**
Hirsel Pl. G71: Both 5F **125**
Hobart Cres. G81: Clyd 2H **41**
Hobart Quad. ML2: Wis 6C **146**
Hobart Rd. G75: E Kil. 4E **149**
Hobart St. G22: Glas. 5F **63**
Hobden St. G21: Glas. 6C **64**
Hoddam Av. G45: Glas 4B **120**
Hoddam Ter. G45: Glas 4C **120**
Hodge Ct. G22: Glas. 3F **63**
Hoey Dr. ML2: Over 4A **158**
Hogan Ct. G81: Dun. 1B **42**
Hogan Way ML1: Cle 6E **129**
Hogarth Av. G32: Glas 4F **85**
Hogarth Cres. G32: Glas. 4F **85**
Hogarth Dr. G32: Glas 4F **85**
Hogarth Gdns. G32: Glas 4F **85**
HOGGANFIELD **1A 86**
Hogganfield St. G33: Glas 1F **85**
Hogg Av. PA5: John 4E **95**
Hogg Rd. ML6: Chap 1D **112**
Hogg St. ML6: Air 4A **92**
Holeburn La. G43: Glas 1A **118**
Holeburn Rd. G43: Glas. 1A **118**
HOLEHILLS. **2B 92**
Holehills Dr. ML6: Air 1B **92**
Holehills Pl. ML6: Air 1B **92**
HOLEHOUSE **2C 130**
Holehouse Brae G78: Neil 2C **130**
Holehouse Dr. G13: Glas 3A **60**
Holehouse Ter. G78: Neil. 2C **130**
Hollandbush Av. FK4: Bank 1E **15**
Hollandbush Cres. FK4: Bank. 1F **15**
Hollandbush Gro. ML3: Ham. 3H **153**
Hollandhurst Rd. ML5: Coat 2B **90**
Holland St. G2: Glas 3E **83** (4A **4**)
Hollinwell Rd. G23: Glas. 1B **62**
Hollowglen Rd. G32: Glas 5B **86**
Hollows Av. PA2: Pais 6D **96**
Hollows Cres. PA2: Pais 6D **96**
Hollows, The *G46: Giff 6H* ***117***
(off Ayr Rd.)
Holly Av. G66: Milt C 6B **8**
Hollybank Pl. G72: Camb. 3B **122**
Hollybank St. G21: Glas. 2C **84**
Hollybrook Pl. *G42: Glas 3F* ***103***
(off Jamieson St.)
Hollybrook St. G42: Glas 3F **103**
(not continuous)
Hollybush Av. PA2: Pais. 6F **97**
Hollybush Rd. G52: Glas 6H **79**
Holly Dr. G21: Glas 6C **64**
G82: Dumb. 2B **16**
Holly Gro. FK4: Bank 1F **15**
ML4: Moss. 2H **127**
Hollymount G61: Bear 5F **45**
Holly Pl. PA5: John 5G **95**
Holly St. G81: Clyd. 3C **42**
ML6: Air 4C **92**
Hollytree Gdns. G66: Len. 3E **7**
Hollywood Bowl. **1F 109**
Holm Av. G71: Udd 6C **108**
PA2: Pais 3B **98**
Holmbank Av. G41: Glas 6B **102**
Holmbrae Av. G71: Tann 6D **108**
Holmbrae Rd. G71: Tann. 6D **108**
Holmbyre Ct. G45: Glas 6F **119**
Holmbyre Rd. G45: Glas. 6F **119**
Holmbyre Ter. G45: Glas 5G **119**
Holmes Av. PA4: Renf 2E **79**
Holmes Quad. ML4: Bell 4C **126**
Holmfauldhead Pl. G51: Glas 3E **81**
Holmfauld Rd. G51: Glas. 3E **81**
Holmfield G66: Kirk 6E **31**
Holm Gdns. ML4: Bell 3E **127**
Holmhead Cres. G44: Glas. 1E **119**
Holmhead Pl. G44: Glas. 1E **119**
Holmhead Rd. G44: Glas 2E **119**
Holmhill Av. G72: Camb 3A **122**
Holmhills Dr. G72: Camb. 4H **121**
Holmhills Gdns. G72: Camb 3H **121**
Holmhills Gro. G72: Camb 3H **121**
Holmhills Pl. G72: Camb. 3H **121**
Holmhills Rd. G72: Camb 3H **121**
Holmhills Ter. G72: Camb 3H **121**
Holm La. G74: E Kil 2G **149**
Holmlea Rd. G42: Glas 6E **103**
G44: Glas 1E **119**
HOLMPARK **4H 39**
Holmpark PA7: B'ton 4G **39**
Holm Pl. ML9: Lark 3C **160**
PA3: Lin 4H **75**
Holms Cres. PA8: Ersk 5D **40**
Holms Pl. G69: G'csh. 2C **68**
Holm St. G2: Glas 4E **83** (6B **4**)
ML1: New S 4A **128**
ML8: Carl 3E **165**
Holmswood Av. G72: Blan 1B **140**
Holmwood Av. G71: Udd 6D **108**
Holmwood Gdns. G71: Udd. 6D **108**
Holyknowe Cres. G66: Len 3G **7**
Holyknowe Rd. G66: Len. 4G **7**
Holyrood Cres. G4: Glas 1D **82**
Holyrood Quad. *G20: Glas. 1D* ***82***
(off Holyrood Cres.)
Holyrood Sports Cen. **4G 103**
Holyrood St. ML3: Ham 4E **141**
HOLYTOWN. **2A 128**
Holytown Rd. ML4: Moss 2G **127**
Holytown Station (Rail) **4A 128**
Holywell St. G31: Glas. 6D **84**
Homeblair Ho. G46: Giff 2A **118**
Homefield Pl. G51: Glas 3E **81**
Homer Pl. ML4: Moss 2G **127**
Homeston Av. G71: Both 4E **125**
Honeybank Cres. ML8: Carl 2F **165**
Honeybog Rd. G52: Glas 5G **79**
Honeywell Cres. ML6: Chap 4E **113**
Hood St. G81: Clyd. 5E **43**
Hope Av. PA11: Q'riers. 1A **72**
Hope Cres. ML9: Lark 2F **161**
Hopefield Av. G12: Glas. 4A **62**
Hopehill Gdns. G20: Glas. 6E **63**
Hopehill Rd. G20: Glas 6E **63**
(not continuous)
Hopeman PA8: Ersk 4E **41**
Hopeman Av. G46: T'bnk. 3E **117**
Hopeman Dr. G46: T'bnk. 3E **117**
Hopeman Path G46: T'bnk. 2E **117**
Hopeman Rd. G46: T'bnk. 3E **117**
Hopeman St. G46: T'bnk 3E **117**
Hope St. G2: Glas 4F **83** (6C **4**)
ML1: Moth 2G **143**
ML2: Newm 5E **147**
ML3: Ham 6A **142**
ML4: Moss 2E **127**
ML8: Carl 3G **165**
Hopetoun Pl. G23: Glas 6C **46**
Hopetoun Ter. G21: Glas 6C **64**
Hopkins Brae G66: Kirk 4D **30**
Horatius St. ML1: Moth. 6D **126**
Hornal Rd. G71: Udd. 3D **124**
Hornbeam Dr. G81: Clyd 3C **42**
Hornbeam Rd. G67: Cumb. 6E **15**
G71: View 5F **109**

Horndean Ct. G64: B'rig 3C 48
Horne St. G22: Glas 4A 64
Hornock Rd. ML5: Coat 2B 90
Hornshill Dr. ML1: Cle 5H 129
Hornshill Farm Rd. G33: Step 3E 67
HORNSHILL INTERCHANGE 1E 67
Hornshill St. G21: Glas 5C 64
Horsbrugh Av. G65: Kils 2H 11
Horsburgh St. G33: Glas 1D 86
Horse Shoe Rd. G61: Bear 2E 45
Horsewood Rd. PA11: Bri W 4E 73
Horslethill Rd. G12: Glas 5A 62
Horslet St. ML5: Coat 1G 109
Horsley Brae ML2: Over 2C 162
Hospital Rd. ML2: Wis 3H 157
Hospital St. ML5: Coat 1C 110
Hotspur St. G20: Glas 4C 62
Houldsworth Ct. ML2: Wis 1A 158
Houldsworth La. G3: Glas 3C 82
                                (off Elliot St.)
Houldsworth St. G3: Glas 3C 82
House for an Art Lover 1G 101
Househillmuir Cres.
    G53: Glas 1C 116
Househillmuir La. G53: Glas 6C 100
                         (off Househillmuir Rd.)
Househillmuir Pl. G53: Glas 6C 100
Househillmuir Rd. G53: Glas 2A 116
HOUSEHILLWOOD 6B 100
Househillwood Cres.
    G53: Glas 6B 100
Househillwood Rd. G53: Glas 1A 116
Housel Av. G13: Glas 2B 60
HOUSTON. 1A 74
Houston St. PA5: John 2F 95
                              (off Houston Sq.)
Houstonfield Quad. PA6: Hous 1A 74
Houstonfield Rd. PA6: Hous 1A 74
Houston Pl. G5: Glas 5D 82
    PA5: Eld 3A 96
Houston Rd. PA11: Bri W 3F 73
    PA4: Inch 5D 56
    PA6: Hous 1A 74
                             (not continuous)
    PA7: B'ton 5C 38
Houston St. G5: Glas 6D 82
    ML2: Wis 2B 158
    ML3: Ham 2H 153
    PA4: Renf 5F 59
Houston Ter. G74: E Kil 1F 149
Houstoun Sq. PA5: John 2F 95
Howard Av. G74: E Kil 4A 138
Howard Ct. G74: E Kil 4A 138
Howard St. G1: Glas 5F 83 (6D 4)
    ML9: Lark 4G 161
    PA1: Pais 6C 78
Howatshaws Rd. G82: Dumb 1H 17
Howat St. G51: Glas. 3G 81
Howcraigs Ct. G81: Clyd 2F 59
                             (off Clydeholm Ter.)
Howden Av. ML1: N'hse. 5D 112
Howden Dr. PA3: Lin 6G 75
Howden Pl. ML1: Holy 2A 128
Howe Gdns. G71: Tann 6E 109
Howe Rd. G65: Kils 4H 11
Howes St. ML5: Coat 1D 110
Howe St. PA3: Pais 1D 96
Howford Rd. G52: Glas 1B 100
Howgate Av. G15: Glas 4H 43
Howgate Rd. ML3: Ham 3F 153
Howie Bldgs. G76: Clar 1C 134
Howieshill Av. G72: Camb 2B 122
Howieshill Rd. G72: Camb 3B 122
Howie St. ML9: Lark. 4F 161
Howletnest Rd. ML6: Air 5C 92
Howlet Pl. ML3: Ham. 2A 154
Howson Lea ML1: Moth. 5B 144
Howson Vw. ML1: Moth 2D 142
Howth Dr. G13: Glas 1F 61
Howth Ter. G13: Glas 1F 61
HOWWOOD ROAD 4E 95
Hoylake Pk. G71: Both. 5D 124
Hoylake Pl. G23: Glas 6C 46
Hozier Cres. G71: Tann 5D 108

Hozier Loan ML9: Lark 1F 161
                         (off Duncan Graham St.)
Hozier Pl. G71: Both. 4F 125
Hozier St. ML5: Coat 6C 90
    ML8: Carl 3F 165
Hub Leisure Cen 4D 42
                            (off Kilbowie Rd.)
Hudson Ter. G75: E Kil 3D 148
Hudson Way G75: E Kil 3E 149
Hughenden Dr. G12: Glas 5H 61
Hughenden Gdns. G12: Glas 5G 61
Hughenden La. G12: Glas 5H 61
Hughenden Rd. G12: Glas 5H 61
Hughenden Ter. G12: Glas 5H 61
Hugh Fraser Ct. G77: Newt M 4D 132
Hugo St. G20: Glas 4D 62
Humbie Ct. G77: Newt M 6E 133
Humbie Ga. G77: Newt M 6E 133
Humbie Gro. G77: Newt M 6E 133
Humbie Rd. G77: Newt M 6E 133
Hume Dr. G71: Both 4E 125
    G71: Udd 6C 108
Hume Pl. G75: E Kil 3F 149
Hume Rd. G67: Cumb 2A 36
Hume St. G81: Clyd 6D 42
Hunterfield Dr. G72: Camb 2G 121
HUNTERHILL 3C 98
Hunterhill Av. PA2: Pais. 2B 98
Hunterhill Rd. PA2: Pais 2B 98
Hunter Ho. Mus. 5C 138
Hunterian Gallery 1B 82
Hunterian Mus. 1B 82
Hunter Pl. G62: Miln 4E 25
    PA10: Kilb. 3A 94
Hunter Rd. G62: Miln 3E 25
    G73: Ruth 4E 105
    ML3: Ham 3F 141
Hunter's Av. G82: Dumb 2D 18
Hunters Dr. G77: Newt M 6B 132
Huntersfield Rd. PA5: John 4C 94
Hunters Hill Ct. G21: Glas 3B 64
Huntershill Ho. G64: B'rig 1B 64
Huntershill Rd. G64: B'rig 1B 64
Huntershill Village G64: B'rig. 1B 64
Huntershill Way G64: B'rig 2B 64
Hunter St. G4: Glas 5A 84
    G74: E Kil 1H 149
    ML4: Bell 2C 126
    ML6: Air 2H 91
    PA1: Pais 6A 78
Hunt Hill G68: Cumb 4G 33
Hunthill La. G72: Blan 3H 139
Hunthill Pl. G76: Busby 4E 135
Hunthill Rd. G72: Blan. 2H 139
HUNT HILL RDBT. 4G 33
Huntingdon Rd. G21: Glas 1A 84
Huntingdon Sq. G21: Glas 1A 84
Hunting Lodge Gdns. ML3: Ham. . . 1C 154
Huntingtower Rd. G69: Bail 1F 107
Huntly Av. G46: Giff 5B 118
    ML4: Bell 1C 126
Huntly Ct. G64: B'rig 1C 64
Huntly Dr. G61: Bear 6E 25
    G72: Camb 3B 122
    ML5: Coat 1H 109
Huntly Gdns. G12: Glas 6B 62
Huntly Ga. G46: Giff 4B 118
Huntly Path G69: Mood 5E 53
Huntly Quad. ML2: Wis 4H 145
Huntly Rd. G12: Glas 6A 62
    G52: Hill 3H 79
Huntly Ter. PA2: Pais 4C 98
Huntshill St. G21: Glas 3A 64
Hurlawcrook Rd. G75: E Kil 6A 150
HURLET. 6H 99
Hurlet Rd. PA2: Pais 4E 99
Hurlford Av. G13: Glas 2H 59
Hurly Hawkin G64: B'rig 1F 65
Hutcheson Rd. G46: Giff, T'bnk . . . 5G 117
Hutchesons' Hall 5F 5
Hutcheson St. G1: Glas 4G 83 (6F 5)
HUTCHESONTOWN 1H 103
Hutcheson Town Ct. G5: Glas 1G 103
Hutchinson Pl. G72: Flem 4E 123

Hutchison Ct. G46: Giff 6A 118
Hutchison Dr. G61: Bear 5G 45
Hutchison Pl. ML5: Coat 5B 90
Hutchison St. ML2: Over 4B 158
    ML3: Ham 3H 153
Hutton G12: Glas 3G 61
Hutton Av. PA6: C'lee 3C 74
Hutton Dr. G51: Glas 3E 81
    G74: E Kil 5H 137
Huxley St. G20: Glas 3D 62
Hyacinth Way ML8: Carl 5F 165
Hydepark St. G3: Glas 4D 82
Hyndal Av. G53: Glas 4C 100
HYNDLAND 6H 61
Hyndland Av. G11: Glas 1H 81
Hyndland Rd. G12: Glas 6H 61
Hyndland Station (Rail) 5G 61
Hyndland St. G11: Glas 1A 82
    G12: Glas 1A 82
Hyndlee Dr. G52: Glas 6C 80
Hyndshaw Rd. ML8: Carl 2F 165
Hyndshaw Vw. ML8: Law. 1A 164
Hyslop Pl. G81: Clyd 4C 42
Hyslop St. ML6: Air 3G 91

I

Iain Dr. G61: Bear 1C 44
Iain Nicholson Recreation Cen. 1C 68
Iain Rd. G61: Bear 2C 44
Ian Smith Ct. G81: Clyd 1F 59
IBROX 6H 81
Ibroxholm Av. G51: Glas 6H 81
Ibroxholm Oval G51: Glas 5H 81
Ibroxholm Pl. G51: Glas 6H 81
Ibrox Ind. Est. G51: Glas 5H 81
Ibrox Stadium 5G 81
Ibrox St. G51: Glas 5A 82
Ibrox Ter. G51: Glas 5H 81
Ibrox Ter. La. G51: Glas 5H 81
Ibrox Station (Und.) 5H 81
Ida Quad. ML4: Bell 2B 126
Iddesleigh Av. G62: Miln 3G 25
Ilay Av. G61: Bear. 1F 61
Ilay Ct. G61: Bear. 1G 61
Ilay Rd. G61: Bear. 1G 61
Imlach Pl. ML1: Moth 4F 143
Imperial Dr. ML6: Air. 4H 91
Inchbrae Rd. G52: Glas 1C 100
Inchcolm Gdns. G69: Mood 4E 53
Inchcolm Pl. G74: E Kil 1E 149
Inchcruin Pl. G15: Glas 3G 43
Inchfad Dr. G15: Glas. 4G 43
Inchfad Pl. G15: Glas. 4G 43
Inch Garvie G74: E Kil 2D 150
INCHINNAN 2H 57
Inchinnan Dr. PA4: Inch 6F 57
Inchinnan Ind. Est. PA4: Inch 5G 57
Inchinnan Rd. ML4: Bell 6B 110
    PA3: Pais 4A 78
    PA4: Renf 5D 58
Inch Keith G74: E Kil 2D 150
Inchkeith Pl. G32: Glas 4B 86
Inchlaggan Pl. G15: Glas 3G 43
Inchlee St. G14: Glas 1E 81
Inch Marnock G74: E Kil. 3C 150
Inchmoan Pl. G15: Glas. 3G 43
Inch Murrin G74: E Kil 2D 150
Inchmurrin Av. G66: Kirk 5H 31
Inchmurrin Dr. G73: Ruth 5F 121
Inchmurrin Gdns. G73: Ruth 5F 121
Inchmurrin Pl. G73: Ruth. 5F 121
Inchneuk Path ML5: Glenb. 3H 69
Inchneuk Rd. ML5: Glenb 3A 70
Inchnock Av. G69: G'csh 3D 68
Inchoch St. G33: Glas. 1E 87
Incholm La. G11: Glas 1E 81
                              (off Incholm St.)
Incholm St. G11: Glas 1E 81
Inchrory Pl. G15: Glas 3G 43
Inchwood Ct. G68: Cumb 6B 34
Inchwood Pl. G68: Cumb. 6B 34
Inchwood Rd. G68: Cumb 6B 34

Incle St. PA1: Pais 6B 78
India Dr. PA4: Inch. 3G 57
India St. G2: Glas 3E 83 (3A 4)
Industry St. G66: Kirk 6D 30
(not continuous)
Inga St. G20: Glas 2C 62
Ingerbreck Av. G73: Ruth. 3F 121
Ingleby Dr. G31: Glas. 4D 84
(Cumbernauld Rd.)
G31: Glas 4C 84
(Whitehill St.)
Ingleby Pl. G78: Neil 2E 131
Inglefield Ct. ML6: Air. 4A 92
Inglefield St. G42: Glas 3F 103
Ingleneuk Av. G33: Mille 4B 66
Ingleside G66: Lenz. 1C 50
Inglestone Av. G46: T'bnk 5G 117
Inglewood Cres. G75: E Kil 3C 148
PA2: Pais 3D 96
Inglis Pl. G75: E Kil 4H 149
Inglis St. G31: Glas 5C 84
ML2: Wis 1D 156
Ingliston Dr. PA7: B'ton 4F 39
Ingram St. G1: Glas 4G 83 (5E 5)
Inishail Rd. G33: Glas 2C 86
Inkerman Rd. G52: Glas 6H 79
Inner City Trad. Est.
G4: Glas 2G 5
Innerleithen Dr. ML2: Wis 3A 146
Innermanse Quad. ML1: N'hill 2F 129
Innerwick Dr. G52: Glas. 6B 80
Innes Ct. G74: E Kil 5G 137
ML6: Air 3E 93
Innspark G65: Kils 2H 11
International Av. G72: Blan 5B 140
Inveraray Dr. G64: B'rig. 3D 48
Inveraray Gdns. ML1: Carf 5C 128
Inverarish PA8: Ersk 2G 57
Inveravon Dr. ML1: Moth. 4D 142
Inverbervie PA8: Ersk. 5E 41
Invercanny Dr. G15: Glas 3H 43
Invercanny Pl. G15: Glas 3A 44
Invercargill G75: E Kil 4C 148
Inverclyde Gdns. G73: Ruth. 4F 121
Invercree Wlk. ML5: Glenb 3G 69
(off Dinyra Pl.)
Inveresk Pl. ML5: Coat 3C 90
Inveresk Quad. G32: Glas 5A 86
Inveresk St. G32: Glas 5H 85
Inverewe Av. G46: T'bnk 5D 116
Inverewe Dr. G46: T'bnk 5D 116
Inverewe Gdns. G46: T'bnk 5D 116
Inverewe Pl. G46: T'bnk 4D 116
Inverewe Way G77: Newt M 4A 132
Invergarry Av. G46: T'bnk 6D 116
Invergarry Ct. G46: T'bnk. 5E 117
Invergarry Dr. G46: T'bnk 5D 116
Invergarry Gdns. G46: T'bnk 6D 116
Invergarry Gro. G46: T'bnk 5D 116
Invergarry Pl. G46: T'bnk. 5E 117
Invergarry Quad. G46: T'bnk 5E 117
Invergarry Vw. G46: T'bnk 5E 117
Inverglas Av. PA4: Renf 2H 79
Invergordon Av. G43: Glas. 6D 102
Invergordon Pl. ML6: Air 5A 92
Invergyle Dr. G52: Glas 6B 80
Inverkar Dr. PA2: Pais 3E 97
Inverlair Av. G43: Glas. 1D 118
G44: Glas 1D 118
Inverleith St. G32: Glas 5F 85
Inverlochy St. G33: Glas 2D 86
Inverness St. G51: Glas 5D 80
Invernia Sq. G81: Clyd. 5D 42
Inveroran Dr. G61: Bear. 3H 45
Inver Rd. G33: Glas 4E 87
Invershiel Rd. G23: Glas 6B 46
Invershin Dr. G20: Glas 4B 62
Inverurie St. G21: Glas 6H 63
Invervale Av. ML6: Air 5F 93
Inzievar Ter. G32: Carm 4B 106
Iona ML6: Air 6D 92
Iona Av. G74: E Kil 5A 138
Iona Ct. G51: Glas 4H 81
Iona Cres. G60: Old K 2G 41

Iona Dr. PA2: Pais 6H 97
Iona Gdns. G60: Old K 2G 41
Iona La. G69: Mood 5E 53
Iona Path G72: Blan 2A 140
Iona Pl. G60: Old K 2G 41
ML5: Coat 2H 89
Iona Quad. ML2: Wis. 4C 146
Iona Ridge ML3: Ham 2C 152
Iona Rd. G73: Ruth 4G 121
ML2: Newm 3D 146
PA4: Renf 2E 79
Iona St. G51: Glas 4H 81
ML1: Moth 6F 127
Iona Wlk. ML5: Coat 1A 110
Iona Way G33: Step 5E 67
Iris Av. G45: Glas 4C 120
Irongray St. G31: Glas 4E 85
Irvine Cres. ML5: Coat. 4E 91
Irvine Dr. PA3: Lin 4F 75
Irvine Gdns. G66: Milt C 6B 8
Irvine Pl. G65: Kils 2F 11
Irvine St. G40: Glas 2D 104
ML6: Glenm 5H 71
Irvine Ter. ML3: Ham 3H 153
Irving Av. G81: Hard 1D 42
Irving Ct. G81: Hard. 1D 42
Irving Quad. G81: Hard 1D 42
Isabella Gdns. ML3: Fern 2D 154
Iser La. G41: Glas 5C 102
Isla Av. ML2: Newm. 3D 146
Island Rd. G67: Cumb 5F 35
Islay Av. G73: Ruth 4G 121
Islay Ct. ML3: Ham 1D 152
Islay Cres. G60: Old K 2G 41
PA2: Pais 6H 97
Islay Dr. G60: Old K 2G 41
G77: Newt M 4B 132
Islay Gdns. ML8: Carl. 5F 165
ML9: Lark 2F 161
Islay Quad. ML2: Wis. 2E 157
Islay Rd. G66: Kirk. 5G 31
Islay Way ML5: Coat 1H 109
Ivanhoe G74: E Kil 5D 138
Ivanhoe Ct. ML8: Carl 4D 164
Ivanhoe Cres. ML2: Wis 6H 145
Ivanhoe Dr. G66: Kirk. 5E 31
Ivanhoe Pl. ML1: Holy 2B 128
Ivanhoe Rd. G13: Glas. 1D 60
G67: Cumb 5G 35
PA2: Pais 4D 96
Ivanhoe Way PA2: Pais 6G 97
Ivybank Av. G72: Camb 3C 122
Ivy Gro. ML5: Coat. 5D 90
Ivy Pl. G72: Blan 1A 140
ML1: New S 4A 128
Ivy Rd. G71: View 5G 109
Ivy Ter. ML1: Holy 2A 128
Ivy Way ML6: Chap 2E 113

J

Jackson Ct. ML5: Coat. 5D 90
Jackson Dr. G33: Step 4F 67
Jackson Pl. ML8: Carl 2E 165
Jackson St. ML5: Coat. 4D 90
Jack's Rd. G71: Udd. 2E 125
Jack St. ML1: Moth 5B 144
ML3: Ham 3H 153
Jackton Rd. G75: E Kil 6A 148
Jacob's Ladder ML2: Over 5B 158
Jacob's Ladder Way ML2: Over. . . . 4A 158
Jade Ter. ML4: Bell 3C 126
Jagger Gdns. G69: Bail. 1F 107
Jamaica Dr. G75: E Kil 2C 148
Jamaica St. G1: Glas 5F 83 (6D 4)
James Dempsey Ct. ML5: Coat . . . 5B 90
James Dempsey Gdns.
ML5: Coat. 5B 90
James Dunlop Gdns. G64: B'rig . . . 2D 64
James Gray St. G41: Glas 5C 102
James Hamilton Dr. ML4: Bell 2D 126

James Hamilton Heritage Cen., The
. . . . 5F 137
James Hamilton Heritage Pk. . . . 5F 137
James Healy Dr. ML3: Ham 4G 153
James Hemphill Ct. G66: Len 3G 7
James Leeson Ct. G66: Milt C 5C 8
James Morrison St. G1: Glas 5H 83
James Nisbet St. G21: Glas 2B 84
James St. FK4: Hag 1G 15
G40: Glas 1A 104
ML1: Moth 2F 143
ML4: Bell 1A 126
ML8: Carl 4F 165
James Vw. ML1: New S. 4H 127
James Watt Av. G75: E Kil 3H 149
James Watt La. G2: Glas 6B 4
James Watt Pl. G74: E Kil 6D 136
James Watt Rd. G62: Miln 2F 25
James Watt St. G2: Glas 4E 83 (6B 4)
Jamieson Ct. G42: Glas 3F 103
G81: Hard. 6D 22
Jamieson Dr. G74: E Kil 1A 150
Jamieson St. G42: Glas 3F 103
(Batson St.)
G42: Glas 3F 103
(Cathcart Rd.)
Janebank Av. G72: Camb 3C 122
Jane Ct. ML9: Lark. 3E 161
Janefield Av. PA5: John. 3E 95
Janefield Pl. G66: Len 2F 7
G72: Blan 3A 140
Janefield St. G31: Glas. 6D 84
Jane Pl. G5: Glas. 1G 103
Jane Rae Gdns. G81: Clyd 1F 59
Jane's Brae G67: Cumb. 5H 35
JANE'S BRAE INTERCHANGE . . . 5H 35
Janesmith St. ML2: Wis 5C 144
Janetta St. G81: Clyd. 4C 42
Jardine St. G20: Glas. 6D 62
Jardine Ter. G69: G'csh 4D 68
Jarvie Av. ML6: Plain. 1G 93
Jarvie Cres. G65: Kils 4H 11
Jarvie Way PA2: Pais 5C 96
Jasmine Pl. G67: Cumb. 6D 34
Jasmine Way ML8: Carl 5E 165
Java St. ML1: Moth 6E 127
Jean Armour Dr. G81: Clyd 4E 43
Jeanette Av. ML3: Ham 4H 153
Jean Maclean Pl. G64: B'rig 3D 48
Jedburgh Av. G73: Ruth. 6D 104
Jedburgh Dr. PA2: Pais 4E 97
Jedburgh Gdns. G20: Glas. 6D 62
Jedburgh Pl. G74: E Kil 1H 149
ML5: Coat. 2B 110
Jedburgh St. G72: Blan 2B 140
ML2: Wis 4A 146
Jedworth Av. G15: Glas 4B 44
Jedworth Ct. G61: Bear 2E 45
(off Manse Rd.)
Jedworth Pl. G15: Glas 4C 44
Jedworth Rd. G15: Glas 4B 44
Jeffrey Pl. G65: Kils. 2G 11
Jellicoe St. G81: Clyd 4A 42
JELLYHILL 3C 48
Jennie Lee Dr. ML2: Over 4H 157
JENNY LIND 5D 116
Jenny Lind Ct. G46: T'bnk 5E 117
Jennys Well Ct. PA2: Pais 3E 99
Jennys Well Rd. PA2: Pais 3D 98
Jervis Ter. G75: E Kil 4D 148
Jerviston Ct. ML1: Carf 6A 128
Jerviston Rd. G33: Glas. 1C 86
ML1: Carf 5A 128
Jerviston St. ML1: Moth 1H 143
ML1: New S 4A 128
(not continuous)
Jerviswood ML1: Carf 6A 128
Jessie St. G42: Glas 3H 103
Jessiman Sq. PA4: Renf 2D 78
Jimmy Sneddon Way
ML1: Moth 5F 127
Joanna Ter. G72: Blan 1B 140
Jocelyn Sq. G1: Glas 5G 83
Jock Stein Sports Barn 5C 140

John Bassy Dr. FK4: Bank 1D **14**
John Bowman Gdns. ML4: Bell . . . 1D **126**
John Brannan Way ML4: Bell 1H **125**
John Brown Pl. G69: Chry 1A **68**
John Burnside Dr. G81: Faif. 6E **23**
John Ewing Gdns. ML9: Lark. 1E **161**
John Hendry Rd. G71: Udd 3E **125**
John Jarvie Sq. G65: Kils 2H **11**
John Knox La. ML3: Ham 5B **140**
John Knox St. G4: Glas 4A **84**
   G81: Clyd 1E **59**
John Lang St. PA5: John. 2G **95**
John Marshall Dr. G64: B'rig 1A **64**
John McEwan Way G64: Torr 5D **28**
John Murray Ct. ML1: Moth 6G **143**
John Pl. ML9: Lark. 6F **161**
Johnsburn Dr. G53: Glas 1B **116**
Johnsburn Rd. G53: Glas 1B **116**
Johnshaven PA8: Ersk 5E **41**
Johnshaven St. G43: Glas 6A **102**
John Smith Ct. ML3: Ham 3H **153**
   (off Hollandbush Gro.)
   ML6: Air 3H **91**
John Smith Gdns. ML5: Coat 6F **91**
John Smith Ga. G78: Barr 3E **115**
John Smith Swimming Pool 4H **91**
Johnson Dr. G72: Camb 2A **122**
Johnston Av. G65: Kils. 4H **11**
   G81: Clyd 1F **59**
JOHNSTONE 2F **95**
Johnstone Av. G52: Hill 3B **80**
Johnstone By-Pass PA5: John. . . . 3D **94**
   PA9: How 6A **94**
JOHNSTONE CASTLE 4G **95**
Johnstone Dr. G73: Ruth 6C **104**
Johnstone La. ML8: Carl 4H **165**
   (off Ramage Rd.)
Johnstone Rd. ML3: Ham 1A **154**
Johnstone Station (Rail) 3G **95**
Johnstone St. ML4: Moss 2E **127**
Johnstone Swimming Pool 2F **95**
Johnstone Ter. G65: Twe 2D **32**
Johnston Rd. G69: G'csh 3D **68**
Johnston St. ML6: Air 3B **92**
   PA1: Pais 1A **98**
John St. G1: Glas 4G **83** (5F **5**)
   G66: Kirk 4D **30**
   G72: Blan 2C **140**
   G78: Barr 4D **114**
   ML2: Wis 5C **144**
   ML3: Ham 6A **142**
   ML4: Bell 2C **126**
   ML8: Carl 4F **165**
   ML9: Lark. 3E **161**
John Wilson Dr. G65: Kils 2F **11**
John Wright Sports Cen. 1A **150**
Jones Wynd ML1: Cle. 6E **129**
Jonquil Way ML8: Carl. 5F **165**
Joppa St. G33: Glas 4G **85**
JORDANHILL. 4E **61**
Jordanhill Cres. G13: Glas 4D **60**
Jordanhill Dr. G13: Glas 4C **60**
Jordanhill La. G13: Glas 4E **61**
   (off Munro Rd.)
Jordanhill Station (Rail) 5F **61**
Jordan St. G14: Glas 1D **80**
Jordanvale Av. G14: Glas 1D **80**
Jowitt Av. G81: Clyd 6F **43**
Jubilee Bank G66: Lenz 4C **50**
Jubilee Ct. G52: Hill. 4H **79**
Jubilee Gdns. G61: Bear 3E **45**
Jubilee Ter. PA5: John. 3D **94**
Julian Av. G12: Glas. 5A **62**
Julian Ct. G12: Glas 5A **62**
   (off Julian Av.)
Julian La. G12: Glas 5A **62**
Juniper Av. G75: E Kil 5F **149**
Juniper Ct. G66: Lenz 2B **50**
Juniper Dr. G66: Milt C 1B **30**
Juniper Gro. ML3: Ham 1B **154**
Juniper Pl. G32: Glas. 1E **107**
   G71: View. 5H **109**
   PA5: John. 5G **95**
Juniper Rd. G71: View. 6H **109**

Juniper Ter. G32: Glas 1E **107**
Juniper Wynd ML1: Holy 2B **128**
   (off Dornoch Rd.)
Juno St. ML1: Moth 6F **127**
Jupiter St. ML1: Moth 6F **127**
Jura G74: E Kil 4B **150**
Jura Av. PA4: Renf 2F **79**
Jura Ct. G52: Glas 6E **81**
Jura Dr. G60: Old K 2G **41**
   G66: Kirk 5G **31**
   G72: Blan 4A **124**
   G77: Newt M 3B **132**
Jura Gdns. G60: Old K 2G **41**
   ML3: Ham. 1E **153**
   ML8: Carl 5G **165**
   ML9: Lark. 2G **161**
Jura Pl. G60: Old K 2G **41**
Jura Quad. ML2: Wis 2E **157**
Jura Rd. G60: Old K. 2G **41**
   PA2: Pais 6H **97**
Jura St. G52: Glas 6F **81**
Jura Wynd ML5: Glenb 3G **69**
Justice Cres. ML1: N'hill 3C **128**

K

Kaim Dr. G53: Glas 1C **116**
Karadale Gdns. ML9: Lark 3E **161**
Karol Path G4: Glas 1E **83**
Katewell Av. G15: Glas 3G **43**
Katewell Pl. G15: Glas. 3G **43**
Katherine St. ML6: Air 3E **93**
Kathkin Dr. G76: Clar 1A **134**
Katrine Av. G64: B'rig 6D **48**
   ML4: Bell 1H **125**
Katrine Ct. G20: Glas 1E **83**
   (off Cedar St.)
Katrine Cres. ML6: Air. 2H **91**
Katrine Dr. G77: Newt M 5H **133**
   PA2: Pais 3D **96**
Katrine Pl. G72: Camb 1A **122**
   ML5: Coat 1H **89**
Katrine Way G71: Both. 4E **125**
Katrine Wynd ML1: Holy 2A **128**
   (off Glencoe Dr.)
Katriona Path ML9: Lark 4G **161**
   (off Trinity Way)
Kay Gdns. ML1: Moth 3D **142**
Kaystone Rd. G15: Glas. 6A **44**
Kay St. G21: Glas. 5B **64**
Keal Av. G15: Glas 1A **60**
Keal Cres. G15: Glas. 1A **60**
Keal Dr. G15: Glas 1A **60**
Keal Pl. G15: Glas 1A **60**
Kearn Av. G15: Glas 6B **44**
Kearn Pl. G15: Glas. 6B **44**
Keats Pk. G71: Both 4F **125**
Keil Cres. G82: Dumb 4D **16**
Keir Cres. ML2: Wis 5H **145**
Keir Dr. G64: B'rig 5B **48**
Keir Hardie Av. ML1: Holy 2B **128**
Keir Hardie Ct. G64: B'rig 6C **48**
Keir Hardie Dr. G65: Kils 4H **11**
   ML4: Bell 3B **126**
Keir Hardie Pl. ML4: Bell 3B **126**
Keir Hardie Rd. ML9: Lark. 4F **161**
Keir Hardie Sports Cen. 1A **128**
Keir St. G41: Glas 2D **102**
Keir's Wlk. G72: Camb. 1A **122**
Keith Av. G46: Giff 4B **118**
Keith Ct. G11: Glas. 2A **82**
Keith Quad. ML2: Wis 4H **145**
Keith St. G11: Glas 1A **82**
   ML3: Ham 5B **142**
   ML4: Bell 1C **126**
Kelbourne Cres. ML4: Bell. 2B **126**
Kelbourne St. G20: Glas 5C **62**
Kelburne Ct. PA1: Pais. 6C **78**
Kelburne Dr. PA1: Pais 6D **78**
Kelburne Gdns. G69: Bail 2G **107**
   PA1: Pais 6C **78**
Kelburne Oval PA1: Pais 6C **78**
Kelburn St. G78: Barr. 6C **114**

Kelhead Av. G52: Glas. 6H **79**
   (not continuous)
Kelhead Dr. G52: Glas 6H **79**
Kelhead Path G52: Glas 6H **79**
Kelhead Pl. G52: Glas. 6H **79**
Kellas St. G51: Glas. 4G **81**
Kellie Gro. G74: E Kil 6F **137**
Kells Pl. G15: Glas. 3G **43**
Kelly's La. ML8: Carl 4H **165**
   (off Kelso Dr.)
Kelso Av. G73: Ruth. 6D **104**
   PA11: Bri W 4F **73**
   PA2: Pais 4E **97**
Kelso Cres. ML2: Wis 3H **145**
Kelso Dr. G74: E Kil 6A **138**
   ML8: Carl 4H **165**
Kelso Gdns. G69: Mood. 4D **52**
Kelso Pl. G14: Glas 3G **59**
Kelso Quad. ML5: Coat 3B **90**
Kelso St. G13: Glas 2H **59**
   G14: Glas 3G **59**
Kelton St. G32: Glas. 1B **106**
KELVIN 6A **150**
Kelvin Av. G52: Hill 2H **79**
KELVINBRIDGE RDBT. 5D **28**
Kelvinbridge Station (Rail) 1C **82**
Kelvin Ct. G12: Glas. 4G **61**
   G66: Kirk 4C **30**
Kelvin Cres. G61: Bear 5F **45**
KELVINDALE 3H **61**
Kelvindale G64: Torr 4E **29**
Kelvindale Bldgs. G12: Glas 4A **62**
Kelvindale Gdns. G20: Glas. 3A **62**
Kelvindale Pl. G20: Glas 3B **62**
Kelvindale Rd. G12: Glas 4H **61**
   G20: Glas 4H **61**
Kelvin Dr. G20: Glas. 5B **62**
   G64: B'rig 5C **48**
   G66: Kirk 5A **30**
   G69: Mood 5C **52**
   G75: E Kil 4H **149**
   G78: Barr 6F **115**
   ML6: Air 2B **92**
Kelvin Gdns. G65: Kils. 4H **11**
   ML3: Ham 5C **140**
KELVINGROVE 2C **82**
Kelvingrove Art Gallery & Mus.
   . . . . 2B **82**
Kelvingrove St. G3: Glas 3C **82**
Kelvin Hall International Sports Arena
   . . . . 2B **82**
Kelvin Hall Transport Mus. 2A **82**
Kelvinhall Station (Und.) 1A **82**
KELVINHAUGH 3B **82**
Kelvinhaugh Ga. G3: Glas 3B **82**
Kelvinhaugh Pl. G3: Glas 3B **82**
Kelvinhaugh St. G3: Glas 3A **82**
KELVINHEAD 1H **13**
Kelvinhead Rd. G65: Bant 1G **13**
Kelvin Pk. Sth. G75: E Kil 6A **150**
Kelvin Pl. G75: E Kil. 4A **150**
Kelvin Rd. G62: Miln 2E **25**
   G67: Cumb 5A **36**
   G71: Tann. 6C **108**
   G75: E Kil 4H **149**
   ML4: Bell 6D **110**
Kelvin Rd. Nth. G67: Cumb 5A **36**
KELVINSIDE 4H **61**
Kelvinside Av. G20: Glas 5C **62**
Kelvinside Dr. G20: Glas. 5D **62**
Kelvinside Gdns. G20: Glas 5C **62**
Kelvinside Gdns. E. G20: Glas . . . 6D **62**
Kelvinside Gdns. La. G20: Glas. . . 6C **62**
Kelvinside Ter. Sth. G20: Glas. . . . 6C **62**
Kelvinside Ter. W. G20: Glas. 6C **62**
Kelvin Sth. Bus. Pk. G75: E Kil . . . 6A **150**
Kelvin St. ML5: Coat 6E **91**
Kelvin Ter. G65: Twe 3D **32**
Kelvinvale G66: Kirk 4D **30**
Kelvin Vw. G64: Torr 5E **29**
   G65: Twe 3D **32**
Kelvinview Av. FK4: Bank. 1E **15**
Kelvin Way G12: Glas 2B **82**
   G3: Glas 2B **82**

Kelvin Way—Kilmartin La.

Kelvin Way G65: Kils 2G **11**
G66: Kirk 5A **30**
G71: Both 4E **125**
Kemp Av. PA3: Pais 2C **78**
Kemp Ct. ML3: Ham 6A **142**
Kempock St. G40: Glas 1E **105**
Kempsthorn Cres. G53: Glas 4B **100**
Kempsthorn Path *G53: Glas 4B* ***100***
(off Kempsthorn Cres.)
Kempsthorn Rd. G53: Glas 4A **100**
Kemp St. G21: Glas 5A **64**
ML3: Ham 6H **141**
Kenbank Cres. PA11: Bri W 3F **73**
Kenbank Rd. PA11: Bri W 3F **73**
Kendal Av. G12: Glas 3G **61**
G46: Giff 4A **118**
Kendal Dr. G12: Glas 3G **61**
Kendal Rd. G75: E Kil 5B **148**
Kendoon Av. G15: Glas 4G **43**
Kenhill Quad. ML6: Air 2A **92**
Kenilburn Av. ML6: Air 1B **92**
Kenilburn Cres. ML6: Air 1B **92**
Kenilworth G74: E Kil 5D **138**
Kenilworth Av. G41: Glas 5B **102**
ML2: Wis 6H **145**
PA2: Pais 5D **96**
Kenilworth Ct. G67: Cumb 5G **35**
ML1: Holy 2B ***128***
(off Rowantree Ter.)
ML8: Carl 4E **165**
Kenilworth Cres. G61: Bear 1C **44**
ML3: Ham 5D **140**
ML4: Bell 1C **126**
Kenilworth Dr. ML6: Air 3C **92**
Kenilworth Rd. G66: Kirk 5E **31**
Kenilworth Way PA2: Pais 4D **96**
Kenmar Gdns. G71: Tann 5C **108**
Kenmar Rd. ML3: Ham 4F **141**
Kenmar Ter. ML3: Ham 4F **141**
Kenmore Gdns. G61: Bear 2H **45**
Kenmore Rd. G67: Cumb 3B **36**
Kenmore St. G32: Glas 6A **86**
Kenmore Way ML5: Coat 2E **111**
ML8: Carl 2F **165**
Kenmuiraid Pl. ML4: Bell 4B **126**
Kenmuir Av. G32: Glas 2E **107**
Kenmuirhill Gdns. G32: Glas 3D **106**
Kenmuirhill Ga. G32: Glas 3D **106**
Kenmuirhill Rd. G32: Glas 3D **106**
Kenmuir Rd. G32: Carm, Glas 5C **106**
(not continuous)
G71: Udd 3E **107**
Kenmuir St. ML5: Coat 1F **109**
Kenmure Av. G64: B'rig 6A **48**
Kenmure Cres. G64: B'rig 6B **48**
Kenmure Dr. G64: B'rig 6B **48**
Kenmure Gdns. G64: B'rig 6A **48**
Kenmure La. G64: B'rig 6B **48**
Kenmure Rd. G46: Giff 3H **133**
Kenmure St. G41: Glas 2D **102**
Kenmure Way G73: Ruth 4D **120**
Kennedar Dr. G51: Glas 3E **81**
Kennedy Av. G65: Twe 2E **33**
Kennedy Ct. G46: Giff 3A **118**
Kennedy Dr. ML6: Air 4G **91**
Kennedy Gdns. ML2: Over 4H **157**
Kennedy Path G4: Glas 3H **83** (3G **5**)
Kennedy St. G4: Glas 3G **83** (3F **5**)
ML2: Wis 6A **146**
Kennelburn Rd. ML6: Chap 4D **112**
Kenneth Rd. ML1: Moth 4E **143**
Kennihill ML6: Air 1A **92**
KENNISHEAD 2E 117
Kennishead Av. G46: T'bnk 2E **117**
Kennishead Path *G46: T'bnk 2E* ***117***
(off Kennisholme Av.)
Kennishead Pl. G46: T'bnk 3E **117**
Kennishead Rd. G43: Glas 2E **117**
G46: T'bnk 3F **117**
G53: Glas 3B **116**
Kennishead Station (Rail) 2E 117
Kennisholm Av. G46: T'bnk 2E **117**
Kennisholm Path *G46: T'bnk 2E* ***117***
(off Kennisholme Av.)
Kennisholm Pl. G46: T'bnk 2E **117**
Kennoway Dr. G11: Glas 1F **81**
Kennoway La. *G11: Glas 1F* ***81***
(off Thornwood Av.)
Kennyhill Sq. G31: Glas 3D **84**
Kenshaw Av. ML9: Lark 5E **161**
Kenshaw Pl. ML9: Lark 5E **161**
Kensington Ct. *G12: Glas 5A* ***62***
(off Kingsborough Gdns.)
Kensington Dr. G46: Giff 6B **118**
Kensington Ga. G12: Glas 5A **62**
Kensington Ga. La. G12: Glas 5A **62**
Kensington Rd. G12: Glas 5A **62**
Kentallen Rd. G33: Glas 5E **87**
Kent Dr. G73: Ruth 2F **121**
Kentigern Ter. G64: B'rig 1D **64**
Kentmere Cl. G75: E Kil 5C **148**
Kentmere Dr. G75: E Kil 5C **148**
Kentmere Pl. G75: E Kil 5C **148**
Kent Pl. G75: E Kil 5B **148**
Kent Rd. G3: Glas 3C **82** (3A **4**)
Kent St. G40: Glas 5A **84**
Keppel Dr. G44: Glas 6A **104**
Keppochhill Dr. G21: Glas 6H **63**
Keppochhill Pl. G21: Glas 1H **83**
Keppochhill Rd. G21: Glas 6G **63**
Keppochhill Way G21: Glas 1H **83**
Keppoch St. G21: Glas 6H **63**
Kerfield La. *G15: Glas 3G* ***43***
(off Kerfield Pl.)
Kerfield Pl. G15: Glas 3G **43**
Kerr Cres. ML3: Ham 2G **153**
Kerr Dr. G40: Glas 6B **84**
ML1: Moth 3E **143**
Kerrera Pl. G33: Glas 5D **86**
Kerrera Rd. G33: Glas 5D **86**
Kerr Gdns. G71: Tann 5E **109**
Ker Rd. G62: Miln 2E **25**
Kerr Pl. G40: Glas 6B **84**
Kerr St. G40: Glas 6B **84**
G66: Kirk 5C **30**
G72: Blan 1C **140**
G78: Barr 5C **114**
PA3: Pais 6H **77**
Kerrycroy Av. G42: Glas 6H **103**
Kerrycroy Pl. G42: Glas 5H **103**
Kerrycroy St. G42: Glas 5H **103**
Kerrydale St. G40: Glas 1D **104**
Kerrylamont Av. G42: Glas 6A **104**
Kerry Pl. G15: Glas 4G **43**
Kershaw St. ML2: Over 4A **158**
Kersland Dr. G62: Miln 3H **25**
Kersland La. *G12: Glas 6B* ***62***
(off Kersland St.)
G62: Miln 3H **25**
Kersland St. G12: Glas 6B **62**
Kessington Dr. G61: Bear 3G **45**
Kessington Rd. G61: Bear 4G **45**
Kessington Sq. G61: Bear 4H **45**
Kessock Dr. G22: Glas 6F **63**
Kessock Pl. G22: Glas 6F **63**
Kestrel Ct. G81: Hard 2C **42**
Kestrel Pl. PA5: John 6D **94**
Kestrel Rd. G13: Glas 3C **60**
Kestrel Vw. ML4: Bell 4A **110**
Keswick Dr. ML3: Ham 5G **153**
Keswick Rd. G75: E Kil 5B **148**
Kethers La. ML1: Moth 2E **143**
Kethers St. ML1: Moth 2E **143**
Kew Gdns. G71: Tann 6F **109**
Kew La. G12: Glas 6B **62**
Kew Ter. G12: Glas 6B **62**
Keynes Sq. ML4: Bell 3F **127**
Keystone Av. G62: Miln 5G **25**
Keystone Quad. G62: Miln 5F **25**
Keystone Rd. G62: Miln 5G **25**
Kibbleston Rd. PA10: Kilb 2A **94**
Kidston Pl. G5: Glas 1G **103**
Kidston Ter. G5: Glas 1G **103**
Kierhill G68: Cumb 3E **35**
Kilallan Av. PA11: Bri W 2F **73**
KILBARCHAN 2A 94
Kilbarchan Rd. PA10: John 3C **94**
PA10: Kilb 3C **94**
Kilbarchan Rd. PA11: Bri W 4G **73**
PA5: John 4D **94**
Kilbarchan St. G5: Glas 6F **83**
Kilbeg Ter. G46: T'bnk 4D **116**
Kilberry St. G21: Glas 2C **84**
Kilbirnie Pl. G5: Glas 1E **103**
Kilbirnie St. G5: Glas 1E **103**
KILBOWIE 4D 42
Kilbowie Ct. G81: Clyd 4D **42**
Kilbowie Pl. ML6: Air 5D **92**
Kilbowie Rd. G67: Cumb 4A **36**
G81: Hard 2D **42**
Kilbreck Gdns. G61: Bear 5C **24**
Kilbreck La. ML1: N'hill 3C **128**
Kilbrennan Dr. ML1: Moth 2D **142**
Kilbrennan Rd. PA3: Lin 5H **75**
Kilbride St. G5: Glas 3H **103**
Kilbride Vw. G71: Tann 6E **109**
Kilburn Gro. G72: Blan 6B **124**
Kilburn Pl. G13: Glas 3B **60**
Kilcadzow Rd. ML8: Carl 4H **165**
Kilchattan Dr. G44: Glas 6G **103**
Kilchoan Rd. G33: Glas 1C **86**
Kilcloy Av. G15: Glas 3A **44**
Kildale Way G73: Ruth 5B **104**
Kildary Av. G44: Glas 2E **119**
Kildary Rd. G44: Glas 2E **119**
Kildermorie Path G34: Glas 3G **87**
Kildermorie Rd. G34: Glas 3F **87**
Kildonan Ct. ML2: Newm 2D **146**
Kildonan Dr. G11: Glas 1G **81**
Kildonan Pl. ML1: Moth 2E **143**
Kildonan St. ML5: Coat 4D **90**
Kildrostan St. G41: Glas 3D **102**
KILDRUM 2B 36
Kildrummy Pl. G74: E Kil 6F **137**
Kildrum Rd. G67: Cumb 2B **36**
KILDRUM SOUTH RDBT. **4B 36**
Kilearn Rd. PA3: Pais 4D **78**
Kilearn Sq. PA3: Pais 4D **78**
Kilearn Way PA3: Pais 4D **78**
(not continuous)
Kilfinan St. G22: Glas 2F **63**
Kilgarth St. ML5: Coat 1F **109**
Kilgraston Rd. PA11: Bri W 5E **73**
Kilkerran Ct. G77: Newt M 5B **132**
Kilkerran Dr. G33: Glas 3H **65**
Kilkerran Pk. G77: Newt M 5B **132**
Kilkerran Way G77: Newt M 5B **132**
Killearn Dr. PA1: Pais 1H **99**
Killearn St. G22: Glas 5F **63**
Killermont Av. G61: Bear 5G **45**
Killermont Ct. G61: Bear 4H **45**
Killermont Mdws. G71: Both 5C **124**
Killermont Rd. G61: Bear 4F **45**
Killermont St. G2: Glas 3G **83** (3E **5**)
Killermont Vw. G20: Glas 5G **45**
Killiegrew Rd. G41: Glas 3B **102**
Killin Ct. ML5: Coat 2D **110**
Killin Dr. PA3: Lin 6F **75**
Killin St. G32: Glas 2B **106**
Killoch Av. PA3: Pais 6E **77**
Killoch Dr. G13: Glas 2A **60**
G78: Barr 6F **115**
Killoch La. PA3: Pais 6E **77**
Killoch Rd. PA3: Pais 6E **77**
Killoch Way PA3: Pais 6E **77**
Kilmacolm Rd. PA11: Bri W 1C **72**
PA6: Hous 1B **74**
Kilmailing Rd. G44: Glas 2F **119**
Kilmair Pl. G20: Glas 4B **62**
Kilmaluag Ter. G46: T'bnk 4D **116**
Kilmannan Gdns. G62: Miln 2D **24**
Kilmany Dr. G32: Glas 6H **85**
Kilmany Gdns. G32: Glas 6H **85**
Kilmardinny Art Cen. 1G 45
Kilmardinny Av. G61: Bear 2F **45**
Kilmardinny Cres. G61: Bear 1F **45**
Kilmardinny Dr. G61: Bear 1F **45**
Kilmardinny Ga. G61: Bear 2F **45**
Kilmardinny Gro. G61: Bear 1F **45**
Kilmari Gdns. G15: Glas 3G **43**
Kilmarnock Rd. G43: Glas 2B **118**
Kilmartin La. ML8: Carl 2F **165**

Kilmartin Pl. G46: T'bnk 3E 117
  G71: Tann 4E 109
  ML6: Air 5D 92
Kilmaurs Dr. G46: Giff 4C 118
Kilmaurs St. G51: Glas 5F 81
Kilmeny Cres. ML2: Wis 4A 146
Kilmichael Av. ML2: Newm 3E 147
Kilmore Cres. G15: Glas 3G 43
Kilmorie Dr. G73: Ruth 6A 104
Kilmory Av. G71: Tann 6E 109
Kilmory Dr. G77: Newt M 3E 133
Kilmory Gdns. ML8: Carl 2F 165
Kilmory Rd. ML8: Carl 5H 165
Kilmuir Cres. G46: T'bnk 3D 116
Kilmuir Dr. G46: T'bnk 3E 117
        (not continuous)
Kilmuir Rd. G46: T'bnk 4D 116
  G71: Tann 4D 108
Kilmun St. G20: Glas 2A 62
Kilnburn Rd. ML1: Moth 2E 143
Kilncroft La. PA2: Pais 4A 98
Kilnside Rd. PA1: Pais 6B 78
Kilnwell Quad. ML1: Moth 2F 143
Kiloran Gro. G77: Newt M 5A 132
Kiloran Pl. G77: Newt M 4A 132
Kiloran St. G46: T'bnk 3F 117
Kilpatrick Av. PA2: Pais 3F 97
Kilpatrick Ct. G60: Old K 1E 41
Kilpatrick Cres. PA2: Pais 4H 97
Kilpatrick Dr. G61: Bear 5C 24
  PA4: Renf 3D 78
  PA8: Ersk 4F 41
Kilpatrick Gdns. G76: Clar 1H 133
Kilpatrick Station (Rail) 1F 41
Kilpatrick Vw. G82: Dumb 3H 17
Kilpatrick Way G71: Tann 5E 109
KILSYTH .3H 11
Kilsyth Heritage Mus. 3A 12
Kilsyth Rd. FK4: Bank 1C 14
  G65: Queen 5B 10
  G66: Kirk 4D 30
Kilsyth Swimming Pool 2G 11
Kiltarie Cres. ML6: Air 4F 93
Kiltearn Rd. G33: Glas 4F 87
Kiltongue Cotts. *ML6: Air.* *3F 91*
      (off Monkscourt Av.)
Kilvaxter Dr. G46: T'bnk 3E 117
Kilwinning Cres. ML3: Ham 2C 152
Kilwynet Way PA3: Pais 4C 78
Kimberley Gdns. G75: E Kil 3E 149
  ML2: Wis 5C 144
Kinalty Rd. G44: Glas 2E 119
Kinarvie Cres. G53: Glas 6H 99
Kinarvie Gdns. G53: Glas 6H 99
Kinarvie Pl. G53: Glas 6H 99
Kinarvie Rd. G53: Glas 6H 99
Kinarvie Ter. G53: Glas 6H 99
Kinbuck Pas. G22: Glas 5G 63
Kinbuck St. G22: Glas 5H 63
Kincaid Dr. G66: Len 2E 7
Kincaid Fld. G66: Milt C 6C 8
Kincaid Gdns. G72: Camb 1A 122
Kincaid Way G66: Milt C 6B 8
Kincardine Dr. G64: B'rig. 1D 64
Kincardine Pl. G64: B'rig 2E 65
  G74: E Kil 6C 138
Kincardine Sq. G33: Glas 2D 86
Kincath Av. G73: Ruth 4F 121
Kinclaven Av. G15: Glas. 4A 44
Kinclaven Gdns. G15: Glas 4B 44
Kinclaven Pl. G15: Glas. 4B 44
Kincraig St. G51: Glas 5D 80
Kinellan Rd. G61: Bear. 6F 45
Kinellar Dr. G14: Glas 3A 60
Kinfauns Dr. G15: Glas 3H 43
  G77: Newt M 4F 133
Kingarth St. G42: Glas 3E 103
  ML3: Ham 3H 153
King Edward La. *G13: Glas* *4E 61*
      (off Woodend Dr.)
King Edward Rd. G13: Glas 4F 61
Kingfisher Dr. G13: Glas 2H 59
Kingfisher Gdns. G13: Glas 2A 60

King George Ct. PA4: Renf 2G 79
King George Gdns. PA4: Renf 1G 79
King George Pk. Av. PA4: Renf 2G 79
King George Pl. PA4: Renf 2G 79
King George Way PA4: Renf 2G 79
Kinghorn Dr. G44: Glas 1G 119
Kinghorn La. G44: Glas 6G 103
Kinglas Ho. G82: Dumb. 1H 17
Kinglas Rd. G61: Bear 5C 44
King Pl. G69: Barg 6E 89
Kingsacre Rd. G44: Glas. 6G 103
  G73: Ruth 1A 120
Kingsbarns Dr. G44: Glas 6F 103
Kingsborough Gdns. G12: Glas 6H 61
Kingsborough Ga. G12: Glas 6H 61
Kingsborough La. G12: Glas 6H 61
Kingsborough La. E. G12: Glas 6H 61
Kingsbrae Av. G44: Glas 6G 103
King's Bri. G5: Glas 1H 103
Kingsbridge Cres. G44: Glas. 1H 119
Kingsbridge Dr. G44: Glas 1H 119
  G73: Ruth. 1A 120
Kingsbridge Pk. Gdns.
  G44: Glas 1H 119
Kingsburgh Dr. PA1: Pais. 6D 78
Kingsburn Dr. G73: Ruth 1C 120
Kingsburn Gro. G73: Ruth 1B 120
Kingscliffe Av. G44: Glas. 1G 119
Kings Ct. *ML3: Ham.* *5B 142*
      (off Castle St.)
Kingscourt Av. G44: Glas 6H 103
Kings Cres. G72: Camb 2B 122
King's Cres. ML8: Carl. 3G 165
Kings Cres. PA5: Eld 2A 96
Kingsdale Av. G44: Glas 6G 103
King's Dr. G40: Glas. 1A 104
  G68: Cumb 5H 13
Kings Dr. G77: Newt M. 6F 133
  ML1: New S 4H 127
Kingsdyke Av. G44: Glas. 6G 103
Kingsford Av. G44: Glas 3C 118
Kingsford Ct. G77: Newt M 3B 132
King's Gdns. G77: Newt M. 6G 133
Kingsgate Retail Pk. G74: Ners. . . .3H 137
Kingsheath Av. G73: Ruth 1A 120
Kingshill Av. G68: Cumb 4A 34
Kingshill Dr. G44: Glas 1G 119
Kingshill Vw. ML8: Law 1A 164
Kingshouse Av. G44: Glas 6G 103
Kingshurst Av. G44: Glas. 6G 103
Kings Inch Dr. G51: Glas 1A 80
King's Inch Rd. PA4: Renf 4F 59
Kingsknowe Dr. G73: Ruth. 1A 120
Kingsland Cres. G52: Glas 5B 80
Kingsland Dr. G52: Glas. 5B 80
Kingsland La. G52: Glas. 5C 80
Kingslea Rd. PA6: Hous 1B 74
Kingsley Av. G42: Glas 4F 103
Kingsley Ct. G71: Tann. 6E 109
Kingslynn Dr. G44: Glas. 1H 119
Kingslynn La. G44: Glas 1H 119
Kingsmuir Dr. G73: Ruth 1A 120
KING'S PARK 1A 120
King's Pk. G64: Torr. 4E 29
King's Pk. Av. G44: Glas. 1F 119
King's Pk. La. G44: Glas 1F 119
King's Park Station (Rail) 1G 119
King's Pk. Rd. G44: Glas 6F 103
King's Pl. G22: Glas 3F 63
King's Rd. PA5: Eld 3H 95
King's Theatre 3A 4
KINGSTON
  Bishopton 4A 40
  Glasgow 6E 83
Kingston Av. G71: Tann 5E 109
  G78: Neil 3D 130
  ML6: Air 4C 92
Kingston Bri. G5: Glas 5D 82
Kingston Flats G65: Kils 2H 11
Kingston Gro. PA7: B'ton. 4H 39
Kingston Ind. Est. G5: Glas. 6D 82
Kingston Pl. G81: Clyd 3H 41
Kingston Rd. G65: Kils 2H 11
  G78: Neil 5C 130

Kingston Rd. PA7: B'ton 5H 39
      (not continuous)
Kingston St. G5: Glas 5E 83
King St. G1: Glas 5G 83
  G65: Kils 3H 11
  G73: Ruth. 5C 104
  G81: Clyd 1H 109
  ML2: Newm 4D 146
  ML2: Wis 1H 157
  ML3: Ham 4D 140
  ML5: Coat. 5A 90
  ML9: Lark 2E 161
  PA3: Pais 6G 77
King's St. La. G65: Kils 3H 11
  G73: Ruth. 5C 104
King's Vw. G68: Cumb. 5H 13
Kings Vw. G73: Ruth 6B 104
Kingsway G14: Glas 4A 60
  G65: Kils 2H 11
  G66: Kirk 3H 31
  G74: E Kil 4A 138
King's Way G82: Dumb 2C 16
Kingsway Ct. G14: Glas 4A 60
Kingswood Dr. G44: Glas 1G 119
Kingswood Rd. PA7: B'ton 3F 39
Kingussie Dr. G44: Glas. 1G 119
Kiniver Dr. G15: Glas 6A 44
Kinkell Gdns. G66: Kirk 4H 31
Kinloch Av. G72: Camb 3B 122
  PA3: Lin 6G 75
Kinloch Dr. ML1: Moth 5F 127
Kinloch Rd. G77: Newt M 3C 132
  PA4: Renf 3D 78
Kinloch St. G40: Glas 1E 105
Kinloss Pl. G74: E Kil 1H 149
Kinmount Av. G44: Glas 6F 103
Kinmount La. G44: Glas. 6G 103
Kinnaird Av. G77: Newt M 4G 133
Kinnaird Cres. G61: Bear. 3H 45
Kinnaird Dr. PA3: Lin 5H 75
Kinnaird Pl. G64: B'rig. 2D 64
Kinnear Rd. G40: Glas 2C 104
Kinneil Ho. ML3: Ham 4A 142
Kinneil Pl. ML3: Ham 1D 152
Kinnell Av. G52: Glas. 2C 100
Kinnell Cres. G52: Glas. 2C 100
Kinnell Path G52: Glas. 2C 100
Kinnell Pl. G52: Glas 2D 100
Kinnell Sq. G52: Glas. 2C 100
KINNING PARK 1C 102
Kinning Pk. Ind. Est. G5: Glas. 6D 82
Kinning Park Station (Und.) 6B 82
Kinning St. G5: Glas 6E 83
Kinnoul Gdns. G61: Bear 6D 24
Kinnoul La. G12: Glas 6A 62
Kinnoull Pl. G72: Blan 2B 140
Kinpurnie Rd. PA1: Pais 6F 79
Kinross Av. G52: Glas 1B 100
Kinross Pk. G74: E Kil 6D 138
Kinsail Dr. G52: Glas 5H 79
Kinstone Av. G14: Glas 4A 60
Kintail Gdns. G66: Kirk 4H 31
Kintessack Pl. G64: B'rig 5F 49
Kintillo Dr. G13: Glas 3B 60
Kintore Pk. ML3: Ham 4F 153
Kintore Rd. G43: Glas 1D 118
Kintore Twr. G72: Camb. 4G 121
Kintra St. G51: Glas 5H 81
      (not continuous)
Kintyre Av. PA3: Lin 1G 95
Kintyre Cres. G77: Newt M 3C 132
  ML6: Plain 1F 93
Kintyre Gdns. G66: Kirk. 4H 31
Kintyre Rd. G72: Blan 1A 140
Kintyre St. G21: Glas 2C 84
Kintyre Wynd ML8: Carl 2F 165
Kipland Wlk. ML5: Coat 6F 91
Kippen Dr. G76: Busby. 4E 135
Kippen St. G22: Glas 3H 63
  ML6: Air 5F 91
Kipperoch Rd. G82: Dumb 1B 16
Kippford Pl. ML6: Chap 4F 113
Kippford St. G32: Glas 1C 106
Kipps Av. ML6: Air 3G 91

Kippsbyre Ct. ML6: Air. 4F **91**
(off Monkscourt Av.)
Kirkaig Av. PA4: Renf. 1H **79**
Kirk Bean Av. G73: Ruth 3C **120**
Kirkburn Av. G72: Camb. 3A **122**
Kirkcaldy Rd. G41: Glas. 3B **102**
Kirkconnel Av. G13: Glas 3H **59**
G68: Cumb. 4A **34**
Kirkconnel Dr. G73: Ruth. 2B **120**
Kirk Cres. G60: Old K 6E **21**
Kirkcudbright Pl. G74: E Kil . . . 6D **138**
Kirkdale Dr. G52: Glas 1E **101**
Kirkdene Av. G77: Newt M 4H **133**
Kirkdene Bank G77: Newt M . . . 4H **133**
Kirkdene Cres. G77: Newt M . . . 4H **133**
Kirkdene Gro. G77: Newt M. . . . 5H **133**
Kirkdene Pl. G77: Newt M 4H **133**
Kirkfieldbank Way ML3: Ham . . 6E **141**
Kirkfield Rd. G71: Both 4E **125**
Kirkford Rd. G69: Mood. 5C **52**
Kirkgate ML2: Newm 5D **146**
Kirk Glebe G78: Neil. 2E **131**
Kirkhall Rd. ML1: N'hill 3D **128**
KIRKHILL
Cambuslang 2B **122**
Newton Mearns 4G **133**
Kirkhill Av. G72: Camb. 4A **122**
Kirkhill Bowling Club 3H **121**
Kirkhill Cres. G78: Neil 1E **131**
Kirkhill Dr. G20: Glas 4B **62**
Kirkhill Gdns. G72: Camb 4A **122**
Kirkhill Ga. G77: Newt M. 5H **133**
Kirkhill Gro. G72: Camb. 4A **122**
Kirkhill Pl. G20: Glas. 4B **62**
ML2: Wis 1C **156**
Kirkhill Rd. G69: G'csh 4D **68**
G71: Tann. 5C **108**
G77: Newt M 4G **133**
ML2: Wis 2B **156**
Kirkhill Station (Rail) 2A **122**
Kirkhill St. ML2: Wis 2D **156**
Kirkhill Ter. G72: Camb 4A **122**
Kirkhope Dr. G15: Glas 6B **44**
Kirkinner Pl. PA11: Bri W 3F **73**
(off Main Rd.)
Kirkinner Rd. G32: Glas 2D **106**
KIRKINTILLOCH. 4C **30**
Kirkintilloch Ind. Est.
G66: Kirk 3C **30**
Kirkintilloch Rd. G64: B'rig . . . 2B **64**
G64: B'rig, Kirk. 1F **49**
G66: Kirk 2H **29**
(Campsie Rd.)
G66: Kirk 1G **49**
(Torrence Rd.)
G66: Lenz 2C **50**
Kirkland Gro. PA5: John. 2F **95**
KIRKLANDNEUK. 5D **58**
Kirklandneuk Cres. PA4: Renf . . 5C **58**
Kirklandneuk Rd. PA4: Renf . . . 5C **58**
Kirklands Cres. G65: Kils. 4H **11**
G71: Both 4E **125**
Kirklands Dr. G77: Newt M 6D **132**
Kirklands Pl. G77: Newt M 6D **132**
Kirkland St. G20: Glas 6D **62**
ML1: Moth 2F **143**
Kirk La. G43: Glas 6A **102**
G61: Bear 2E **45**
Kirklea Gdns. PA3: Pais 6E **77**
Kirkle Dr. G77: Newt M 4H **133**
Kirklee Cir. G12: Glas 5A **62**
Kirklee Gdns. G12: Glas. 4B **62**
Kirklee Gdns. La. G12: Glas . . . 4B **62**
Kirklee Ga. G12: Glas 4B **62**
Kirklee Pl. G12: Glas 5B **62**
Kirklee Quad. G12: Glas 5B **62**
Kirklee Quad. La. G12: Glas . . . 5B **62**
Kirklee Rd. G12: Glas 5A **62**
ML1: New S 6G **127**
ML4: Bell 3F **127**
Kirklee Ter. G12: Glas 5A **62**
Kirklee Ter. La. G12: Glas 5B **62**
Kirklee Ter. Rd. G12: Glas 5A **62**
Kirkliston St. G32: Glas 5H **85**

Kirk M. G72: Camb. 2A **122**
(off Greenlees Rd.)
Kirkmichael Av. G11: Glas. 6G **61**
Kirkmichael Gdns.
G11: Glas 6G **61**
Kirkmuir Dr. G73: Ruth 4D **120**
Kirkness St. ML6: Air. 3A **92**
Kirknethan ML2: Wis 2C **156**
Kirkoswald G74: E Kil 6D **138**
Kirkoswald Dr. G81: Clyd 4E **43**
Kirkoswald Rd. G43: Glas 1B **118**
ML1: N'hill 3E **129**
Kirkpatrick Dr. G33: Step 4E **67**
Kirkpatrick St. G40: Glas 6C **84**
Kirk Pl. G61: Bear. 2E **45**
G67: Cumb 6C **34**
G71: Udd 2C **124**
Kirkriggs Av. G73: Ruth 2D **120**
Kirkriggs Gdns. G73: Ruth. . . . 2D **120**
Kirkriggs Vw. G73: Ruth 2D **120**
Kirkriggs Way G73: Ruth. 2D **120**
(off Kirkriggs Gdns.)
Kirk Rd. G61: Bear 2E **45**
G76: Crmck 2H **135**
ML1: N'hse. 6D **112**
ML2: Wis 6H **145**
ML8: Carl 3E **165**
ML9: Dals. 3D **162**
PA6: Hous 1B **74**
Kirkshaw Ct. PA5: John 2F **95**
(off Walkinshaw St.)
KIRKSHAWS. 2A **110**
Kirkshaws Av. ML5: Coat. 2A **110**
Kirkshaws Pl. ML5: Coat 2B **110**
Kirkshaws Rd. ML5: Coat 2H **109**
Kirkstall Gdns. G64: B'rig 3D **48**
Kirkstone G77: Newt M 4H **133**
Kirkstone Cl. G75: E Kil 5B **148**
Kirk St. G62: Miln. 3E **25**
ML1: Moth 2G **143**
ML5: Coat. 5B **90**
(not continuous)
ML8: Carl 3E **165**
Kirkstyle Av. ML8: Carl. 4E **165**
Kirkstyle Cres. G78: Neil 2D **130**
ML6: Air. 1H **91**
Kirkstyle La. G78: Neil 2E **131**
Kirkstyle Pl. ML6: Glenm 5F **71**
Kirkstyle Av. G66: Kirk 6D **30**
KIRKTON 3E **131**
Kirkton G60: Old K 6E **21**
PA8: Ersk 4E **41**
Kirkton Av. G13: Glas 3A **60**
G72: Blan 4A **140**
G78: Barr 5D **114**
ML8: Carl 3E **165**
Kirkton Ct. ML8: Carl 4E **165**
Kirkton Cres. G13: Glas 3A **60**
G66: Milt C 6C **8**
ML5: Coat 2F **111**
Kirktonfield Dr. G78: Neil. 2F **131**
Kirktonfield Rd. G78: Neil 2E **131**
Kirkton Ga. G74: E Kil 1G **149**
KIRKTONHILL 4D **16**
Kirktonholme Cres. G74: E Kil . . 1F **149**
Kirktonholme Rd. G74: E Kil . . . 1D **148**
Kirkton Ho. G72: Blan 3B **140**
Kirkton Pk. G74: E Kil 1H **149**
Kirkton Pl. G72: Blan 3B **140**
G74: E Kil 1H **149**
(not continuous)
ML5: Coat. 1F **111**
Kirkton Rd. G72: Camb 2B **122**
G78: Neil 3D **130**
G82: Dumb 4D **16**
Kirkton Side G78: Barr. 6D **114**
Kirkton St. ML8: Carl 4F **165**
Kirkton Ter. G66: Cam G 1B **6**
Kirkvale Ct. G77: Newt M 4H **133**
Kirkvale Cres. G77: Newt M . . . 4H **133**
Kirkvale Dr. G77: Newt M 4H **133**
Kirkview G67: Cumb 1C **54**
Kirkview Ct. G67: Cumb. 1C **54**

Kirkview Cres. G77: Newt M . . . 6E **133**
Kirkview Gdns. G71: Tann 5D **108**
Kirkville Pl. G15: Glas 6B **44**
Kirkwall ML6: Cumb. 6A **14**
Kirkwall Av. G72: Blan 5A **124**
Kirkwell Rd. G44: Glas. 2F **119**
KIRKWOOD 1G **109**
Kirkwood Av. G33: Step 4G **67**
G81: Clyd 6F **43**
Kirkwood Pl. ML5: Coat. 6A **90**
Kirkwood Quad. G81: Clyd 6F **43**
Kirkwood Rd. G71: Tann 5D **108**
Kirkwood Sports Barn 1F **109**
Kirkwood St. G51: Glas 6A **82**
G73: Ruth 5C **104**
ML5: Coat. 5A **90**
Kirn St. G20: Glas 1A **62**
Kirriemuir G74: E Kil 4D **138**
Kirriemuir Av. G52: Glas 2C **100**
Kirriemuir Gdns. G64: B'rig . . . 5E **49**
Kirriemuir Pl. G52: Glas 1C **100**
(off Bucklaw Gdns.)
Kirriemuir Rd. G64: B'rig. 6E **49**
Kirtle Dr. PA4: Renf 1G **79**
Kirtle Pl. G75: E Kil 4A **148**
Kishorn Pl. G33: Glas. 2C **86**
Kitchener St. ML2: Wis 6G **145**
Kittoch Pl. G74: E Kil 1H **149**
KITTOCHSIDE 5C **136**
Kittochside Rd. G76: Crmck . . . 2A **136**
Kittoch St. G74: E Kil 1G **149**
Klondike Ct. ML1: New S 4B **128**
Knapdale St. G22: Glas 2E **63**
Knightsbridge St. G13: Glas . . . 2D **60**
Knightscliffe Av. G13: Glas . . . 1D **60**
Knights Ga. G71: Both 2C **124**
KNIGHTSWOOD 2D **60**
Knightswood Ct. G13: Glas . . . 3D **60**
Knightswood Cross G13: Glas . . 2D **60**
Knightswood Rd. G13: Glas. . . . 6C **44**
Knightswood Swimming Pool . . 3B **60**
Knightswood Ter. G72: Blan. . . . 6C **124**
Knivysbridge Pl. ML4: Bell 4B **126**
Knockburnie Rd. G71: Both . . . 3E **125**
Knockhall St. G33: Glas 1D **86**
Knockhill Dr. G44: Glas 6F **103**
Knockhill La. G44: Glas 6F **103**
Knockhill Rd. PA4: Renf 2D **78**
Knockside Av. PA2: Pais 6H **97**
Knock Way PA3: Pais. 4C **78**
Knollpark Dr. G76: Clar 2B **134**
Knowe Cres. ML1: N'hill 3D **128**
Knowehead Dr. G71: Udd 1C **124**
Knowehead Gdns. G41: Glas . . . 2C **102**
G71: Udd 1C **124**
Knowehead Rd. ML2: Wis 1A **158**
Knowehead Ter. G41: Glas 2C **102**
Knowenoble St. ML1: Cle 5H **129**
Knowe Rd. G69: Chry 1A **68**
PA3: Pais 4D **78**
Knowes Av. G77: Newt M 4E **133**
Knowes Rd. G77: Newt M 4F **133**
Knowe St. G62: Miln. 3F **25**
Knowetap St. G20: Glas 2C **62**
KNOWETOP 5H **143**
Knowetop Av. ML1: Moth 4H **143**
Knowetop Cres. G82: Dumb . . . 2C **16**
KNOWNOBLE 5H **129**
Knox Av. PA11: Bri W 4E **73**
Knoxland Sq. G82: Dumb 5G **17**
Knoxland St. G82: Dumb. 5G **17**
Knox Pl. G77: Newt M 5B **132**
Knox St. ML6: Air. 3B **92**
PA1: Pais 1F **97**
Koko's 4C **90**
Kronberg Way G75: E Kil 6F **149**
Kyleakin Dr. G72: Blan. 5H **123**
Kyleakin Rd. G46: T'bnk 4D **116**
Kyleakin Ter. G46: T'bnk 4D **116**
Kyle Ct. G72: Camb 1A **122**
Kyle Dr. G46: Giff 4C **118**
Kyle Gro. ML1: New S 4A **128**
Kylemore Cres. ML1: Moth 5F **127**

KYLEPARK 6B 108
Kylepark Av. G71: Udd. 1B 124
Kylepark Cres. G71: Udd. 6B 108
Kylepark Dr. G71: Udd. 6B 108
Kyle Quad. ML1: N'hill. 3C 128
    ML2: Wis 2E 157
Kylerhea Rd. G46: T'bnk 4D 116
Kyle Rd: Cumb 2B 36
Kyle Sq. G73: Ruth 2B 120
Kyle St. G4: Glas 2G 83 (2F 5)
    ML1: Moth 2D 142
Kyle Ter. G82: Dumb 2B 16

L

La Belle Allee G3: Glas 2C 82
    (off Claremont St.)
La Belle Pl. G3: Glas 2C 82
Laberge Gdns. ML1: New S. 4B 128
Laburnum Av. G75: E Kil. 5E 149
Laburnum Cl. G75: E Kil. 5E 149
Laburnum Cres. ML2: Wis. 4H 145
Laburnum Dr. G66: Milt C 6B 8
Laburnum Gdns. G66: Lenz. 2B 50
Laburnum Gro. G66: Lenz 2B 50
    ML5: Coat 6D 90
Laburnum Lea ML3: Ham 2A 154
Laburnum Pl. PA5: John 5G 95
Laburnum Rd. FK4: Bank 1E 15
    G41: Glas 1A 102
    G67: Cumb. 3D 36
    G71: View. 4G 109
Lachlan Cres. PA8: Ersk 6C 40
La Crusse Ter. G12: Glas 6C 62
Lacy St. PA1: Pais 6C 78
Ladeside Cl. G77: Newt M. 3C 132
Ladeside Dr. G65: Kils 2B 12
    PA5: John. 3D 94
Lade Ter. G52: Glas 1A 100
Ladhope Pl. G13: Glas. 1G 59
Ladyacres PA4: Inch 3H 57
Ladyacres Way PA4: Inch 3H 57
Lady Ann Cres. ML6: Air 5C 92
Lady Anne St. G14: Glas 4H 59
Ladybank G68: Cumb. 5H 13
Ladybank Ct. G74: E Kil 1G 149
Ladybank Dr. G52: Glas 1E 101
Ladybank Gdns. G74: E Kil 1G 149
Ladybank Pl. G74: E Kil 1G 149
Ladyburn St. PA1: Pais 1C 98
Ladyhill Dr. G69: Bail. 1G 107
Lady Isle Cres. G71: Udd. 1C 124
Lady Jane Ga. G71: Both 3B 124
Ladykirk Cres. G52: Glas 5B 80
    PA2: Pais 2B 98
Ladykirk Dr. G52: Glas 5B 80
Lady La. PA1: Pais. 1H 97
Ladyloan Av. G15: Glas 3G 43
Ladyloan Ct. G15: Glas 3H 43
Ladyloan Gdns. G15: Glas. 3H 43
Ladyloan Gro. G15: Glas 3H 43
Ladyloan Pl. G15: Glas 3G 43
Lady Mary Wlk. ML3: Ham 2A 154
Ladymuir Circ. PA8: Ersk 6D 40
Ladymuir Cres. G53: Glas 3C 100
Ladysmith Av. PA10: Kilb. 3B 94
Ladysmith St. ML2: Wis 5C 144
Lady Watson Gdns. ML3: Ham . . . 1E 153
Ladywell Rd. ML1: Moth. 3D 142
Ladywell St. G4: Glas 4A 84
Lady Wilson St. ML6: Air. 5B 92
Ladywood G62: Miln 3H 25
Lagan Rd. ML8: Carl 4F 165
Laggan Quad. ML6: Air 2G 91
Laggan Rd. G43: Glas 2C 118
    G64: B'rig 6D 48
    G77: Newt M 2D 132
    ML6: Air. 2H 91
Laggan Ter. PA4: Renf. 5D 58
Laggan Way ML2: Newm. 2D 146
Lagholm Dr. PA3: Lin. 6A 76
Lagoon Leisure Cen. 1B 98
Laidlaw Av. ML1: New S 4H 127

Laidlaw Gdns. G71: Tann 4D 108
Laidlaw St. G5: Glas 6E 83
    (not continuous)
Laidon Rd. ML6: Air 2H 91
Laidon Wlk. ML2: Newm. 3D 146
    (off Murdostoun Vw.)
Laighcartside St. PA5: John 2G 95
Laighlands Rd. G71: Both 5F 125
Laighmuir St. G71: Udd. 2D 124
LAIGH PARK 5A 78
Laighpark Av. PA7: B'ton 4H 39
Laighpark Vw. PA3: Pais 4A 78
Laigh Rd. G77: Newt M 4H 133
LAIGHSTONEHALL 1F 153
Laighstonehall Rd. ML3: Ham . . . 1F 153
Laightoun Ct. G67: Cumb 1C 54
Laightoun Dr. G67: Cumb 1C 54
Laightoun Gdns. G67: Cumb 1C 54
Lainshaw Dr. G45: Glas 5E 119
Laird Gro. G71: Tann 5E 109
Laird Pl. G40: Glas. 1B 104
Lairds Ga. G71: Both 2B 124
Lairds Hill G67: Cumb. 3G 35
Laird's Hill Ct. G65: Kils 3E 11
Laird's Hill Pl. G65: Kils 3E 11
Lairdsland Rd. G66: Kirk. 5D 30
Laird St. ML5: Coat 4D 90
Lairg Dr. G72: Blan 5A 124
Lairhills Rd. G75: E Kil 4G 149
Lamberton Dr. G52: Glas. 5B 80
LAMBHILL 2E 63
Lambhill Quad. G41: Glas. 6C 82
Lambhill St. G41: Glas. 6B 82
Lambie Cres. G77: Newt M 4C 132
Lamb St. G22: Glas 3F 63
    ML3: Ham 6A 142
Lamerton Rd. G67: Cumb 3C 36
Lamington Rd. G52: Glas. 1B 100
Lamlash Cres. G33: Glas. 3B 86
Lamlash Pl. G33: Glas 3B 86
    ML1: Moth 2E 143
Lamlash Sq. G33: Glas 3C 86
Lammermoor G74: E Kil. 5E 139
Lammermoor Av. G52: Glas. 1C 100
Lammermoor Cres. G66: Kirk 5F 31
Lammermoor Dr. G67: Cumb 6G 35
Lammermoor Gdns.
    G66: Kirk. 5F 31
Lammermoor Rd. G66: Kirk. 5F 31
Lammermoor Ter. ML2: Wis 6H 145
Lammermuir Ct. PA2: Pais 5A 98
Lammermuir Dr. PA2: Pais 5H 97
Lammermuir Gdns. G61: Bear. . . . 6C 24
Lammermuir Pl. ML1: Holy. 3B 128
    (off Cherry Pl.)
Lammermuir Way ML6: Chap 4F 113
Lammermuir Wynd ML9: Lark. . . . 6H 155
Lammer Wynd ML9: Lark 4G 161
    (off Pitlochry Dr.)
Lamont Av. PA7: B'ton 4A 40
Lamont Rd. G21: Glas. 3D 64
Lanark Av. ML6: Air 1H 111
Lanark Rd. ML8: Carl 4F 165
    ML8: Crsfd, Rose 4E 163
    ML9: Dals, Lark 4G 155
Lanark Rd. End ML9: Lark. 4G 155
Lanarkshire Ice Rink 4A 142
Lanark St. G1: Glas 5H 83
Lancaster Av. ML6: Chap. 4D 112
Lancaster Cres. G12: Glas. 5A 62
Lancaster Cres. La. G12: Glas. . . . 5A 62
Lancaster Rd. G64: B'rig 3D 48
Lancaster Ter. G12: Glas. 5A 62
Lancaster Ter. La. G12: Glas. 5A 62
Lancaster Way PA4: Renf. 2E 79
Lancefield Quay G3: Glas 4C 82
Lancefield St. G3: Glas 4D 82
Landemer Ct. G73: Ruth 1C 120
Landemer Dr. G73: Ruth 1B 120
Landressy Pl. G40: Glas 1B 104
Landressy St. G40: Glas 6B 84
Landsdowne Gdns. ML3: Ham. . . . 6B 142
Landsdowne Rd. ML9: Lark. 3G 161
Lane, The G68: Dull 5F 13

Lanfine Rd. PA1: Pais 1D 98
Langa Gro. G20: Glas. 2C 62
    (off Lochburn Gro.)
Langa St. G20: Glas 2C 62
Lang Av. PA4: Renf. 1E 79
    PA7: B'ton 4A 40
Langbank St. G5: Glas 6F 83
Langbar Cres. G33: Glas 4E 87
Langbar Gdns. G33: Glas 4F 87
Langbar Path G33: Glas 4D 86
    (off Langbar Cres.)
Langcraigs G82: Dumb 2G 17
Langcraigs Ct. PA2: Pais 5G 97
Langcraigs Dr. PA2: Pais 6G 97
Langcraigs Ter. PA2: Pais 6G 97
Langcroft Dr. G72: Camb 3C 122
Langcroft Pl. G51: Glas. 4C 80
Langcroft Rd. G51: Glas. 4C 80
Langcroft Ter. G51: Glas. 4D 80
Langdale G74: E Kil 6E 137
    G77: Newt M 4H 133
Langdale Av. G33: Glas 6G 65
Langdale Rd. G69: Mood 5D 52
Langdales Av. G68: Cumb 3F 35
Langdale St. G33: Glas 6G 65
Langfaulds Cres. G81: Faif. 6F 23
Langford Dr. G53: Glas 4A 116
Langford Pl. G53: Glas. 4B 116
Langhaul Av. G53: Glas 4H 99
Langhaul Ct. G53: Glas 4H 99
Langhaul Pl. G53: Glas 4H 99
Langhaul Rd. G53: Glas 4H 99
Langhill Dr. G68: Cumb 2F 35
Langholm G75: E Kil 5B 148
Langholm Ct. G69: Mood 5D 52
Langholm Cres. ML2: Wis. 3H 145
Langholm Path G72: Blan 2A 140
Langlands Av. G51: Glas. 4D 80
    G75: E Kil 6H 149
Langlands Ct. G51: Glas. 3F 81
Langlands Dr. G51: Glas 3C 80
    G75: E Kil 6H 149
Langlands Path G51: Glas 4E 81
    (off Langlands Rd.)
LANGLANDS-SEAFAR INTERCHANGE
    . . . . 5G 35
Langlands Ter. G82: Dumb 1H 17
Langlea Av. G72: Camb 3F 121
Langlea Ct. G72: Camb 3G 121
Langlea Dr. G72: Camb 2G 121
Langlea Gdns. G72: Camb 3G 121
Langlea Rd. G72: Camb 3G 121
Langlea Way G72: Camb 2G 121
Langlees Av. G77: Newt M 4H 133
Langley Av. G13: Glas 1B 60
Langley Gro. G72: Camb 3G 121
LANGLOAN 6A 90
Langloan Cres. ML5: Coat. 6A 90
Langloan Pl. ML5: Coat 5A 90
Langloan St. ML5: Coat 6A 90
Langlook Cres. G53: Glas 5H 99
Langlook Pl. G53: Glas 5H 99
Langlook Rd. G53: Glas. 5H 99
LANGMUIR 4H 31
Langmuir Av. G66: Kirk 4E 31
Langmuirhead Rd. G66: Auch. . . . 1H 65
Langmuir Rd. G66: Kirk. 4G 31
    G69: Barg 6E 89
Langmuir Way G69: Barg. 6E 89
Langness Rd. G33: Glas 3B 86
Langoreth Av. ML3: Ham 1D 152
Lang Pl. PA5: John. 2F 95
Langrig Rd. G21: Glas 4C 64
    G77: Newt M 6C 132
Langshaw Cres. ML8: Carl 3F 165
Langshot St. G51: Glas. 6B 82
LANGSIDE 5D 102
Langside Av. G41: Glas 4C 102
    G71: View. 1G 125
Langside Ct. G71: Both 6F 125
Langside Dr. G43: Glas 3C 118
    PA10: Kilb. 3A 94
Langside Gdns. G42: Glas 6E 103

Langside La. G42: Glas 4E **103**
Langside Pk. PA10: Kilb 3A **94**
Langside Pl. G41: Glas 5D **102**
Langside Rd. G42: Glas 5D **102**
  G71: Both 6F **125**
Langside Station (Rail) 1C **118**
Langside St. G81: Faif 1G **43**
Langstile Pl. G52: Glas 6H **79**
Langstile Rd. G52: Glas 6H **79**
Lang St. PA1: Pais 1C **98**
Langton Cres. G53: Glas 4C **100**
  G78: Barr 6F **115**
Langton Gdns. G69: Bail. 1F **107**
Langton Ga. G77: Newt M. 4C **132**
Langton Pl. G77: Newt M. 4C **132**
Langton Rd. G53: Glas 4C **100**
Langtree Av. G46: Giff 6G **117**
LANRIGG 6A **52**
Lanrig Pl. G69: Chry 1A **68**
Lanrig Rd. G69: Chry 6A **52**
Lansbury Gdns. PA3: Pais 4H **77**
Lansbury Ter. ML9: Lark 4G **161**
Lansdowne Cres. G20: Glas 1D **82**
Lansdowne Cres. La.
  G20: Glas 1D **82**
  (off Holyrood Cres.)
Lansdowne Dr. G68: Cumb 6H **13**
Lantana Gro. ML1: Moth 1F **143**
Lanton Dr. G52: Glas 6B **80**
Lanton Rd. G43: Glas. 2C **118**
Lappin St. G81: Clyd 1F **59**
Larbert St. G4: Glas 2F **83** (2D **4**)
Larch Av. G64: B'rig. 1D **64**
  G66: Lenz 1C **50**
Larch Ct. G67: Cumb 1D **36**
  G72: Blan 1A **140**
  G75: E Kil 6D **148**
Larch Cres. G66: Lenz 1C **50**
Larch Dr. FK4: Bank 1E **15**
  G75: E Kil 6D **148**
Larches, The G69: Mood 3E **53**
Larchfield Av. G14: Glas 5B **60**
  G77: Newt M 5E **133**
Larchfield Ct. G77: Newt M 5D **132**
Larchfield Cres. ML2: Wis. 3A **146**
Larchfield Dr. G73: Ruth 3D **120**
Larchfield Gdns. ML2: Wis 3B **146**
Larchfield Gro. ML2: Wis 2B **146**
Larchfield Pl. G14: Glas. 5B **60**
  ML2: Wis 3B **146**
Larchfield Rd. G61: Bear 6F **45**
Larch Gro. G66: Milt C 6B **8**
  G67: Cumb 1D **36**
  ML1: Holy 2B **128**
  ML3: Ham 1A **154**
Larchgrove Av. G32: Glas 5C **86**
Larchgrove Pl. G32: Glas. 4C **86**
Larchgrove Rd. G32: Glas 4C **86**
Larch Pl. G71: View 5H **109**
  G75: E Kil 6D **148**
  PA5: John. 5G **95**
Larch Rd. G41: Glas 1H **101**
  G67: Cumb 1D **36**
Larchwood Ter. G78: Barr 6F **115**
Largie Rd. G43: Glas 2D **118**
Largo Pl. G51: Glas 4E **81**
Larkfield Ct. G72: Blan. 3A **140**
Larkfield Dr. G72: Blan 3B **140**
Larkfield Rd. G66: Lenz 1E **51**
Larkfield St. G42: Glas. 2F **103**
LARKHALL 2E **161**
Larkhall Ind. Est. ML9: Lark 5G **161**
LARKHALL INTERCHANGE. 5A **156**
  Larkhall Leisure Cen. 3E **161**
Larkin Gdns. PA3: Pais 4H **77**
Larkin Way ML4: Bell. 6B **110**
Larksfield Dr. ML8: Carl 5G **165**
Larkspur Dr. G74: E Kil. 5E **137**
Larkspur Way ML8: Carl. 5F **165**
Lark Way ML4: Bell 5B **110**
Lashley Gro. ML2: Over. 4A **158**
Lasswade St. G14: Glas. 3G **59**
Latherton Dr. G20: Glas. 4B **62**
Latimer Gdns. G52: Glas 1A **100**

Latimer Path G52: Glas 1A **100**
  (off Hatton Gdns.)
Latta St. G82: Dumb 3G **17**
Lauchlin Pl. G66: Kirk 6H **31**
Lauchope Rd. ML1: N'hse. 6D **112**
Lauchope St. ML6: Chap 3E **113**
Lauder Cres. ML2: Wis 3H **145**
Lauderdale Dr. G77: Newt M 6C **132**
Lauderdale Gdns.
  G12: Glas 6H **61**
Lauderdale La. G12: Glas 6H **61**
Lauder Dr. G73: Ruth 1F **121**
  PA3: Lin 6H **75**
Lauder Gdns. G72: Blan. 5A **124**
  ML5: Coat 2F **111**
Lauder Grn. G74: E Kil 5B **138**
Lauder La. ML3: Ham 6C **140**
Lauder St. G5: Glas 1E **103**
Laughland Dr. ML1: N'hill 4D **128**
Laundry La. G33: Step. 4C **66**
Lauranne Pl. ML4: Bell 2A **126**
Laurel Av. G66: Lenz 1D **50**
  G81: Clyd 3H **41**
Laurel Bank ML3: Ham 3G **153**
Laurelbank ML5: Coat 3C **90**
Laurelbank Rd. G32: Carm 5C **106**
  G69: Chry. 2H **67**
Laurel Cl. G75: E Kil 6F **149**
Laurel Dr. G75: E Kil 6E **149**
  ML2: Wis 5D **144**
  ML9: Lark 3G **161**
Laurel Gdns. G71: Tann. 5D **108**
  ML6: Chap 3E **113**
Laurel La. *ML9: Lark*. 4G **161**
  (off Donaldson Rd.)
Laurel Pk. Gdns. G13: Glas 3C **60**
Laurel Pk. Sports Club. 3D **60**
Laurel Pl. G11: Glas 1G **81**
  G75: E Kil 6F **149**
Laurel Sq. FK4: Bank 1E **15**
Laurels, The G77: Newt M. 4D **132**
  ML1: Carf 5B **128**
Laurel St. G11: Glas 1G **81**
Laurel Wlk. G73: Ruth 4E **121**
Laurel Way G78: Barr 4D **114**
Laurence Dr. G15: Glas 4G **43**
Laurence Dr. G15: Glas 4G **43**
  G61: Bear 1D **44**
Laurence Gdns. G15: Glas. 4G **43**
Laurenstone Ter. *G74: E Kil*. 1B **150**
  (off Capelrig Rd.)
Lauren Vw. ML6: Air 4H **91**
Lauren Way PA2: Pais 4D **96**
Laurie Ct. G71: Tann 6E **109**
LAURIESTON 6F **83**
Laurieston Rd. G5: Glas 1F **103**
Laurieston Way G73: Ruth 3D **120**
Lavelle Dr. ML5: Coat 4E **91**
Lavender Dr. G75: E Kil 6F **149**
Lavender La. ML8: Carl 5E **165**
Laverock Av. ML3: Ham. 1C **154**
Laverockhall St. G21: Glas 6B **64**
Laverock Rd. ML6: Air. 1B **92**
Laverock Ter. G69: Mood 6D **52**
LAW 6D **158**
Law Dr. ML1: N'hill 3C **128**
Lawers Dr. G61: Bear. 1C **44**
Lawers La. ML1: N'hill 3C **128**
Lawers Rd. G43: Glas 2H **117**
  PA4: Renf 2E **79**
Lawfield Av. G77: Newt M 4H **133**
LAW HILL 1A **164**
Lawhill Av. G45: Glas 3H **119**
Lawhill Rd. ML8: Carl, Law. 6D **158**
Lawhope Mill Rd. ML6: Chap 2F **113**
Lawmarnock Cres.
  PA11: Bri W 4E **73**
Lawmarnock Rd. PA11: Bri W 5E **73**
Lawmoor Av. G5: Glas 3G **103**
Lawmoor Pl. G5: Glas 3G **103**
Lawmoor Rd. G5: Glas 2G **103**
Lawmoor St. G5: Glas 2G **103**
Lawmuir Cres. G81: Faif 6G **23**

Lawmuir Pl. ML4: Bell 5C **126**
Lawmuir Rd. ML4: Bell 4C **126**
  ML8: Law 6D **158**
LAWN PARK 4A **26**
Lawn Pk. G62: Miln 4A **26**
Lawn St. PA1: Pais. 6B **78**
LAW OF MAULDSLIE 1H **163**
Law Pl. G74: E Kil 5G **137**
Lawrence Av. G46: Giff 6A **118**
Lawrence St. G11: Glas 1A **82**
Lawrie St. G11: Glas 1H **81**
  ML2: Newm 4D **146**
Lawrie Way ML9: Lark. 4G **161**
LAW RDBT. 5G **137**
Lawson Av. ML1: Moth 6G **143**
Law St. G40: Glas 6C **84**
Law Vw. ML2: Over 5A **158**
Laxford Av. G44: Glas. 3E **119**
Laxford Pl. ML5: Coat 6F **91**
Laxford Rd. PA8: Ersk 6C **40**
Laxford Way ML1: N'hill. 3C **128**
Laxton Dr. G66: Lenz 3E **51**
Lea Av. G78: Neil 2D **130**
Leabank Av. PA2: Pais 5A **98**
Leadburn Rd. G21: Glas. 5E **65**
Leadburn St. G32: Glas 4G **85**
Leader St. G33: Glas 2F **85**
Leaend Rd. ML6: Air 2G **91**
Leander Cres. ML4: Moss. 2G **127**
  PA4: Renf 1G **79**
Learigg Rd. ML6: Plain 1H **93**
Learmonth Pl. G62: Miln 3F **25**
Leathem Pl. ML2: Wis 2C **156**
Leathen Pl. PA8: Ersk 6C **40**
Leckethill Av. G68: Cumb 6B **34**
Leckethill Ct. G68: Cumb. 6B **34**
Leckethill Pl. G68: Cumb. 6A **34**
Leckethill Vw. G68: Cumb 6B **34**
Leckie Ct. *ML3: Ham* 5G **141**
  (off Leckie Dr.)
Leckie Dr. ML3: Ham 5G **141**
Leckie St. G43: Glas 5A **102**
Ledaig Pl. G31: Glas 4E **85**
Ledaig St. G31: Glas 4E **85**
Ledard Rd. G42: Glas 5D **102**
Ledcameroch Cres. G61: Bear. 3D **44**
Ledcameroch Pk. G61: Bear 3D **44**
Ledcameroch Rd. G61: Bear 3D **44**
Ledgate G66: Kirk 4D **30**
Ledgowan Pl. G20: Glas 1B **62**
Ledi Dr. G61: Bear 6B **24**
Ledi Path ML1: N'hill 4C **128**
Ledi Rd. G43: Glas 2A **118**
Ledmore Dr. G15: Glas 3H **43**
Lednock Rd. G33: Step 4C **66**
  G52: Glas 6A **80**
Lee Av. G33: Glas 2G **85**
Leebank Dr. G44: Neth 6D **118**
Leeburn Av. PA6: Hous 2C **74**
Leeburn Gdns. PA6: Hous 2C **74**
Leechlee Rd. ML3: Ham 6A **142**
Lee Cres. G64: B'rig. 1C **64**
Leefield Dr. G44: Neth. 5D **118**
Leehill Rd. G21: Glas. 2A **64**
Lee Pl. ML4: Bell 3F **127**
Leesburn Pl. G74: E Kil 5H **137**
Lee's Ct. ML5: Coat 6C **90**
Leeside Rd. G21: Glas. 2A **64**
Leesland G71: Tann 5E **109**
Leeward Circ. G75: E Kil 2C **148**
Leewood Dr. G44: Neth 5E **119**
Le Froy Gdns. G75: E Kil 3E **149**
Le Froy La. G75: E Kil 3E **149**
Lefroy St. ML5: Coat 4A **90**
Legbrannock Av. ML1: N'hse. 6D **112**
Legbrannock Cres. ML1: N'hill 3D **128**
Legbrannock Rd. ML1: N'hse. 1E **129**
Leggatson Rd. G53: Glas. 4C **116**
Leglen Wood Cres. G21: Glas 3F **65**
Leglen Wood Dr. G21: Glas 3F **65**
Leglen Wood Gdns. G21: Glas 3F **65**
Leglen Wood Pl. G21: Glas 3G **65**
Leglen Wood Rd. G21: Glas 3F **65**
Leicester Av. G12: Glas 4H **61**

Leighton St. G20: Glas. 3C 62
   ML2: Wis 1H 157
Leisuredome Bishopbriggs Sports Cen.
   . . . . 3A 48
Leitchland Rd. PA2: Pais 5B 96
   PA5: Eld 5B 96
Leithington Rd. G46: Giff. 2G 133
Leithland Av. G53: Glas 4B 100
Leithland Rd. G53: Glas 4B 100
Leith St. G33: Glas 3F 85
Leman Dr. PA6: C'lee. 3D 74
Leman Gro. PA6: C'lee. 3D 74
Lembert Dr. G73: Clar 1B 134
Lendale La. G64: B'rig 3C 48
Lendalfoot Gdns. ML3: Ham 1B 152
Lendel Pl. G51: Glas 5B 82
Lenihall Dr. G45: Glas 5A 120
Lenihall Ter. G45: Glas 5A 120
Lennox Av. G14: Glas 6C 60
   G62: Miln 4G 25
   ML5: Coat. 4A 90
   PA7: B'ton 4H 39
Lennox Ct. G66: Kirk 5E 31
                (off Highfield Rd.)
Lennox Cres. G64: B'rig 1B 64
Lennox Dr. G61: Bear 1F 45
   G81: Faif. 6E 23
Lennox Gdns. G14: Glas 5D 60
Lennox Ho. G67: Cumb 3H 35
Lennox La. E. G14: Glas 6D 60
Lennox La. W. G14: Glas 6C 60
                (off Earlbank Av.)
   G14: Glas 5D 60
              (off Norse La. Nth.)
Lennox Pl. G66: Len. 3F 7
   G81: Clyd 4A 42
Lennox Rd. G66: Len 2E 7
   G67: Cumb 3H 35
   G82: Dumb. 4H 17
   G82: Milt. 4E 19
Lennox Sq. G66: Len 3F 7
                (off Service St.)
Lennox St. G20: Glas 2A 62
   G82: Dumb. 4G 17
   ML2: Wis 5C 146
Lennox Ter. PA3: Pais 3C 78
LENNOXTOWN 3F 7
Lennox Vw. G81: Clyd 4D 42
Lentran St. G34: Glas. 4A 88
Leny St. G20: Glas. 5D 62
LENZIE. 2C 50
Lenziemill Rd. G67: Cumb 6H 35
LENZIEMILL 5A 36
Lenzie Pl. G21: Glas 3B 64
Lenzie Rd. G33: Step. 2D 66
   G66: Kirk 6D 30
Lenzie Station (Rail) 3C 50
Lenzie St. G21: Glas 4B 64
Lenzie Ter. G21: Glas 3A 64
Lenzie Way G21: Glas 3A 64
Lesley Quad. ML4: Bell 5B 126
Leslie Av. G77: Newt M 2E 133
   PA7: B'ton 4H 39
Leslie Rd. G41: Glas 3C 102
Leslie St. G41: Glas 2D 102
   ML1: Moth 2H 143
Lesmuir Dr. G14: Glas 4H 59
Lesmuir Pl. G14: Glas 4H 59
Letham Ct. G43: Glas 2C 118
Letham Dr. G43: Glas 2C 118
   G64: B'rig 1E 65
Letham Grange G68: Cumb 1H 35
Lethamhill Cres. G33: Glas 2H 85
Lethamhill Pl. G33: Glas 2G 85
Lethamhill Rd. G33: Glas 2G 85
Letham Oval G64: B'rig 1F 65
Lethbridge Pl. G75: E Kil 3E 149
Letherby Dr. G44: Glas 6F 103
Letheron Dr. ML2: Wis 4H 145
Lethington Av. G41: Glas 5C 102
Lethington Pl. G41: Glas 5D 102
Letterfearn Dr. G23: Glas 6C 46
Letterickhills Cres. G72: Flem 4E 123

Lettoch St. G51: Glas. 4G 81
Leven Av. G64: B'rig 6D 48
Leven Ct. G78: Barr 2D 114
   G82: Dumb 3E 17
Leven Dr. G61: Bear 3F 45
   ML3: Ham 3F 153
Levenford Ter. G82: Dumb 4E 17
Levengrove Ct. G82: Dumb 4E 17
Levengrove Ter. G82: Dumb 4E 17
Leven Path ML1: Holy 2A 128
                (off Graham St.)
Leven Pl. PA8: Ersk 6C 40
Leven Quad. ML6: Air 1H 91
Leven Rd. ML5: Coat. 2G 89
Leven Sq. PA4: Renf 5D 58
Leven St. G41: Glas 2D 102
   G82: Dumb. 4G 17
   ML1: Moth 4G 143
Leven Ter. ML1: Carf 5C 128
Leven Valley Ent. Cen.
   G82: Dumb. 3D 16
Leven Vw. G81: Clyd 4D 42
Leven Way G67: Cumb 4H 35
      (in Cumbernauld Shop. Cen.)
   G75: E Kil 5B 148
   PA2: Pais 4C 96
Levernbridge Ct. G53: Glas 6H 99
Levernbridge Gro. G53: Glas 6H 99
Levernbridge Pl. G53: Glas 1H 115
Levernbridge Rd. G53: Glas 1H 115
Levernbridge Way G53: Glas 1H 115
Levern Cres. G78: Barr 5D 114
Leverndale Ct. G53: Glas 4H 99
Levern Gdns. G78: Barr 4D 114
Leverngrove Ct. G53: Glas 1H 115
Levern Rd. G53: Glas. 1G 115
Levernside Av. G53: Glas 5C 100
   G78: Barr 5C 114
Levernside Cres. G53: Glas 4B 100
Levernside Rd. G53: Glas 4C 100
Lewis Av. ML2: Wis 4C 146
   PA4: Renf 2F 79
Lewis Cres. G60: Old K 2G 41
   PA10: Kilb. 3C 94
Lewis Dr. G60: Old K 2F 41
Lewis Gdns. G60: Old K 2G 41
   G61: Bear 1B 44
Lewis Gro. G60: Old K 2G 41
Lewis Pl. G60: Old K 2G 41
   G77: Newt M 3B 132
   ML6: Air 5D 92
Lewiston Dr. G23: Glas 6B 46
              (off Lewiston Rd.)
Lewiston Pl. G23: Glas 6B 46
              (off Lewiston Rd.)
Lewiston Rd. G23: Glas 6B 46
Lexwell Av. PA5: Eld 2B 96
Leyden Ct. G20: Glas 4C 62
Leyden Gdns. G20: Glas 4D 62
Leyden St. G20: Glas. 4C 62
Leys Pk. ML3: Ham 5E 141
Leys, The G64: B'rig 6C 48
Libberton Way ML3: Ham 6E 141
Liberty Av. G69: Barg 6E 89
Liberty Path G72: Blan 2B 140
Liberty Rd. ML4: Bell 3C 126
Libo Av. G53: Glas. 4D 100
Libo Pl. PA8: Ersk 5C 40
Library Gdns. G72: Camb 1H 121
Library La. G46: T'bnk 4F 117
Library Rd. ML2: Wis 6H 145
Lickprivick Rd. G75: E Kil 6D 148
Liddell Gro. G75: E Kil 4F 149
Liddells Ct. G64: B'rig 2C 64
Liddell St. G32: Carm 4C 106
Liddel Rd. G67: Cumb 4G 35
                 (Seafar Rd.)
   G67: Cumb 4A 36
                 (Torbrex Rd.)
Liddesdale Pl. G22: Glas 2A 64
Liddesdale Rd. G22: Glas 2F 63
Liddesdale Sq. G22: Glas 2H 63
Liddesdale Ter. G22: Glas 2A 64

Liddesdale Pas. G22: Glas 2G 63
Liddoch Way G73: Ruth 5B 104
Liff Gdns. G64: B'rig. 1F 65
Liff Pl. G34: Glas 2A 88
LIGHTBURN
   Cambuslang. 4E 123
   Glasgow 4A 86
Lightburn Pl. G32: Glas 4B 86
Lightburn Rd. G31: Glas. 5E 85
   G72: Camb, Flem 3D 122
Lighthouse, The 6D 4
Lilac Av. G67: Cumb 6E 15
   G81: Clyd 2H 41
Lilac Ct. G67: Cumb 6E 15
Lilac Cres. G71: View. 5F 109
Lilac Gdns. G64: B'rig 1D 64
Lilac Hill G67: Cumb 6F 15
   ML3: Ham 1B 154
Lilac Pl. G67: Cumb 6F 15
Lilac Way ML1: Holy 2B 128
Lilac Wynd G72: Flem 3E 123
Lillie Art Gallery 3H 25
Lillyburn Pl. G15: Glas 3G 43
Lilybank Av. G69: Muirh 2A 68
   G72: Camb 3B 122
   ML6: Air 1B 92
Lilybank Gdns. G12: Glas 1B 82
Lilybank Gdns. La.
   G12: Glas 1B 82
           (off Lilybank Gdns.)
Lilybank La. G12: Glas. 1B 82
           (off Lilybank Gdns.)
Lilybank St. ML3: Ham 5G 141
Lilybank Ter. G12: Glas 1B 82
Lilybank Ter. La. G12: Glas 1B 82
          (off Gt. George St.)
Lily St. G40: Glas 2D 104
Lime Cres. G67: Cumb. 2E 37
   ML6: Air 4C 92
Lime Gro. G66: Lenz 2D 50
   G72: Blan 6A 124
   ML1: Moth 5G 143
Limegrove St. ML4: Bell 6C 110
Limekilns Rd. G67: Cumb 1H 55
Limekilns St. G81: Faif. 6F 23
Lime La. G14: Glas 6D 60
Lime Loan ML1: Holy. 3B 128
Lime Rd. G82: Dumb 3F 17
Limeside Av. G73: Ruth. 6D 104
Limeside Gdns. G73: Ruth. 6E 105
Limes, The G44: Glas 3F 119
Lime St. G14: Glas. 6D 60
Limetree Av. G71: View. 5F 109
Limetree Ct. ML3: Ham 4E 141
Limetree Cres. G77: Newt M 5D 132
Limetree Dr. G81: Clyd 3C 42
Limetree Quad. G71: View 5G 109
Limetree Wlk. G66: Milt C 1B 30
Limeview Av. PA2: Pais 6F 97
Limeview Cres. PA2: Pais 6F 97
Limeview Rd. PA2: Pais. 6F 97
Limeview Way PA2: Pais 6F 97
Linacre Dr. G32: Glas. 6C 86
Linacre Gdns. G32: Glas 6D 86
LINBURN 6D 40
Linburn Pl. G52: Glas. 5A 80
Linburn Rd. G52: Glas. 4G 79
   PA8: Ersk 6C 40
LINCLIVE INTERCHANGE 6B 76
Linclive Spur PA3: Lin. 6B 76
Linclive Ter. PA3: Lin. 6B 76
Lincluden Path G41: Glas 1D 102
Lincoln Av. G13: Glas. 2C 60
   G71: Tann. 4D 108
Lincuan Av. G46: Giff 6A 118
Lindams G71: Udd 2D 124
Lindcres Av. G73: Ruth 6D 104
Linden Av. ML2: Wis 3A 146
Linden Ct. G81: Hard 1C 42
Linden Dr. FK4: Bank 1E 15
   G81: Hard. 1C 42

Linden Lea G66: Milt C 6B **8**
  ML3: Ham. 5F **141**
Linden Pl. G13: Glas 2F **61**
Linden St. G13: Glas 2F **61**
Linden Way G13: Glas 2F **61**
Lindores Dr. G74: E Kil. 2E **149**
Lindores Pl. G74: E Kil. 2E **149**
Lindores St. G42: Glas 5F **103**
Lindrick Dr. G23: Glas 6C **46**
Lindsaybeg Ct. G69: Chry 1A **68**
Lindsaybeg Rd. G66: Lenz. 3D **50**
  G69: Chry. 5H **51**
  G69: Lenz. 4G **51**
Lindsay Dr. G12: Glas 3H **61**
Lindsayfield Av. G75: E Kil 6D **148**
Lindsayfield Rd. G75: E Kil 6D **148**
Lindsay Gro. G74: E Kil 1H **149**
Lindsay Pl. G12: Glas 3H **61**
  G66: Lenz. 4D **50**
  G74: E Kil 2A **150**
  PA5: John. *2G 95*
           (off John Lang St.)
Lindsay Rd. G74: E Kil 2H **149**
Lindsay Ter. G66: Len 3G **7**
Lindum Cres. ML1: Moth. 1D **142**
Lindum St. ML1: Moth. 1D **142**
Linfern Rd. G12: Glas 6A **62**
Linghope Pl. ML2: Wis. 3F **157**
Lingley Av. ML6: Air 5A **92**
Linhope Pl. G75: E Kil 4A **148**
Links Rd. G32: Glas 2D **106**
  G44: Glas 3G **119**
Links, The G68: Cumb 5B **14**
Links Vw. ML9: Lark 3G **161**
Linksview Rd. ML1: Carf 6B **128**
Linkwood Av. G15: Glas 4H **43**
Linkwood Cres. G15: Glas 4H **43**
Linkwood Dr. G15: Glas 4H **43**
Linkwood Gdns. G15: Glas. 4B **44**
Linkwood Pl. G15: Glas 4H **43**
Linlithgow Gdns. G32: Glas. 6D **86**
Linn Crematorium G45: Glas 5E **119**
Linn Cres. PA2: Pais 6G **97**
Linndale Dr. G45: Glas 6G **119**
Linndale Gdns. G45: Glas 6G **119**
Linndale Gro. G45: Glas 6G **119**
Linndale Rd. G45: Glas 6G **119**
Linn Dr. G44: Neth 4D **118**
Linnet Av. PA5: John 6C **94**
Linnet Pl. G13: Glas. 2H **59**
Linnet Rd. ML4: Bell 3D **126**
Linnet Way ML4: Bell 5B **110**
Linn Gdns. G68: Cumb. 3B **34**
Linn Glen G66: Len 3H **7**
Linnhead Dr. G53: Glas 1B **116**
Linnhead Pl. G14: Glas 5B **60**
Linnhe Av. G44: Glas 3E **119**
  G64: B'rig. 6D **48**
  ML3: Ham. 2E **153**
Linnhe Ct. ML9: Lark 6H **155**
Linnhe Cres. ML2: Wis 2H **157**
Linnhe Dr. G78: Barr 2D **114**
Linnhe Pl. G72: Blan 5A **124**
  PA8: Ersk 6C **40**
Linnpark Av. G44: Neth 5D **118**
Linnpark Ct. G44: Neth 4D **118**
Linn Pk. Gdns. PA5: John 3G **95**
Linnpark Ind. Est. G45: Glas 4G **119**
Linnvale Way G68: Dull 5E **13**
Linn Valley Dr. G45: Glas 4H **119**
Linside Av. PA1: Pais 1C **98**
Lint Butts G72: Blan 2A **140**
Lintfield Loan *G71: Udd*. *2E 125*
           (off Bellshill Rd.)
Linthaugh Rd. G53: Glas 3A **100**
Linthaugh Ter. G53: Glas 4D **100**
LINTHOUSE 3E **81**
Linthouse Bldgs. G51: Glas 3E **81**
Linthouse Rd. G51: Glas 2E **81**
Lintie Rd. ML1: N'hill 3C **128**
Lintlaw G72: Blan. 5B **124**
Lintlaw Dr. G52: Glas. 5B **80**
Lintmill Ter. G78: Neil 3C **130**
Linton Pl. ML5: Coat 2A **110**

Linton St. G33: Glas. 3G **85**
Lintwhite Ct. *PA11: Bri W* *4G 73*
          (off Lintwhite Cres.)
Lintwhite Cres. PA11: Bri W 3G **73**
LINVALE 6G **43**
Linwell Cres. PA2: Pais 6H **97**
LINWOOD .6A **76**
Linwood Av. G74: E Kil. 1B **148**
  G76: Busby 2D **134**
Linwood Ct. G44: Glas 2E **119**
Linwood Ind. Est. PA3: Lin 1H **95**
Linwood Rd. PA1: Pais 6B **76**
  PA3: Pais 6B **76**
Linwood Sports Complex 4G **75**
Linwood Ter. ML3: Ham. 5F **141**
Lion Bank G66: Kirk. 4D **30**
Lismore G74: E Kil. 3C **150**
Lismore Av. ML1: Moth. 1D **142**
  PA4: Renf 2F **79**
Lismore Dr. ML5: Coat 1H **109**
  PA2: Pais 6H **97**
  PA3: Lin 6F **75**
Lismore Gdns. PA10: Kilb 3C **94**
Lismore Hill ML3: Ham 6B **140**
Lismore Pl. G69: Mood 4E **53**
  G77: Newt M 4B **132**
Lismore Rd. G12: Glas 4H **61**
Lister Gdns. G76: Busby 4E **135**
Lister Hgts. *G4: Glas* *4A 84*
             (off Drygate)
Lister Pl. G52: Hill 4A **80**
Lister Rd. G52: Hill 4H **79**
          (not continuous)
Lister St. G4: Glas 2H **83** (2H **5**)
Lister Twr. *G75: E Kil* *3H 149*
           (off Sinclair Pl.)
Lister Wlk. ML4: Bell 6E **111**
Lithgow Av. G66: Kirk. 6E **31**
Lithgow Cres. PA2: Pais 3C **98**
Lithgow Dr. ML1: Cle. 6H **129**
Lithgow Pl. G74: E Kil 1D **148**
Lit. Drum Rd. G68: Cumb 5F **33**
LITTLE EARNOCK 2E **153**
Littlehill St. G21: Glas. 5C **64**
Littleholm Pl. G81: Clyd 3A **42**
Lit. John Gdns. ML2: Newm 5D **146**
Littlemill Av. G68: Cumb. 4A **34**
Littlemill Cres. G53: Glas 5A **100**
Littlemill Dr. G53: Glas 5A **100**
Littlemill Gdns. G53: Glas 5A **100**
Littlemill La. G60: Bowl. 5A **20**
Lit. Mill Way ML1: Carf 6B **128**
Littlesdale Av. PA2: Pais 6B **96**
Littleston Gdns. PA8: Ersk. 6D **40**
Little St. G3: Glas 4D **82**
Littleton Dr. *G23: Glas* *6B 46*
           (off Littleton St.)
Littleton St. G23: Glas 6B **46**
Lively Pl. *G72: Blan* *2A 140*
           (off Burnbrae Rd.)
Livery Wlk. *PA11: Bri W*. *3F 73*
           (off Main St.)
Livingston Dr. ML6: Plain 1G **93**
Livingstone Av. G52: Hill 3A **80**
Livingstone Blvd. G72: Blan 4A **140**
Livingstone Cl. G75: E Kil 4F **149**
Livingstone Cres. G72: Blan 6B **124**
Livingstone Dr. G75: E Kil 3F **149**
Livingstone Gdns. ML9: Lark 2F **161**
Livingstone La. G71: Both. 4E **125**
Livingstone Pk. G65: Kils. 1F **11**
Livingstone Pl. ML6: Air 4B **92**
Livingstone St. G81: Clyd 6E **43**
  ML3: Ham 5D **140**
Lloyd Av. G32: Glas 3A **106**
Lloyd Dr. ML1: Carf 6A **128**
Lloyds St. ML5: Coat 6C **90**
Lloyd St. G31: Glas 3C **84**
  G73: Ruth. 4D **104**
  ML1: Carf 6A **128**
Loanbank Pl. G51: Glas. 4G **81**
Loanbank Quad. G51: Glas. 4F **81**
Loancroft Av. G69: Bail 2A **108**

Loancroft Gdns. G71: Udd 2C **124**
Loancroft Ga. G71: Udd. 2C **124**
Loancroft Ho. G69: Bail 2H **107**
Loancroft Pl. G69: Bail. 2H **107**
Loanend Cotts. G72: Flem 6F **123**
Loanfoot Av. G13: Glas 2A **60**
  G78: Neil 3D **130**
Loanfoot Rd. G72: Blan 4B **140**
LOANHEAD 1E **79**
Loanhead Av. ML1: N'hill. 4D **128**
  PA3: Lin 5G **75**
  PA4: Renf 6F **59**
Loanhead Cres. ML1: N'hill. 4D **128**
Loanhead La. PA3: Lin 5G **75**
Loanhead Rd. ML1: N'hill 4C **128**
  PA3: Lin 5G **75**
Loanhead St. G32: Glas 4H **85**
  ML5: Coat. 2A **110**
Loaning *ML9: Lark*. *3G 161*
         (off Hareleeshill Rd.)
Loaninghead Dr.
  G82: Dumb. 1H **17**
Loaning, The G46: Giff 1G **133**
  G61: Bear 2E **45**
  G66: Kirk 6C **30**
  ML1: Moth 2E **143**
Loan Lea Cres. ML9: Lark 4F **161**
Loan, The G62: Miln 1C **24**
Lobnitz Av. PA4: Renf. 6F **59**
Lochaber Dr. G73: Ruth 3F **121**
Lochaber Path G72: Blan 2B **140**
Lochaber Pl. G74: E Kil 6H **137**
Lochaber Rd. G61: Bear 5G **45**
Lochaber Wlk. G66: Milt C. 4C **8**
Lochachray Gdns. G32: Glas 1C **106**
Lochachray St. G32: Glas 1C **106**
Lochalne Av. PA2: Pais 3E **97**
Lochaline Dr. G44: Glas 3E **119**
Lochalsh Cres. G66: Milt C 5C **8**
Lochalsh Dr. PA2: Pais. 3E **97**
Lochalsh Pl. G72: Blan 5H **123**
Lochar Cres. G53: Glas 3D **100**
Lochard Dr. PA2: Pais 4E **97**
Lochar Pl. G75: E Kil 4A **148**
Loch Assynt G74: E Kil. 3B **150**
Loch Awe G74: E Kil. 3A **150**
Loch Awe Pl. ML5: Coat 5B **90**
Lochay St. G32: Glas 1C **106**
Lochbrae Dr. G73: Ruth 3E **121**
Lochbridge Rd. G34: Glas 4G **87**
Lochbroom Dr. G77: Newt M 3F **133**
  PA2: Pais 3E **97**
Loch Brora Cres. ML5: Coat 5A **90**
Lochbrown Ct. G77: Newt M 3F **133**
Lochbuie La. ML6: Glenm. 5G **71**
Lochburn Cres. G20: Glas 2C **62**
Lochburn Gro. *G20: Glas* *2C 62*
         (off Lochburn Cres.)
Lochburn Pas. G20: Glas 2C **62**
Lochburn Rd. G20: Glas. 3B **62**
Lochdochart Rd. *G34: Glas* *4B 88*
           (off Lentran St.)
Lochdochart Rd. G34: Glas 3A **88**
Lochearn Cres. ML6: Air 1H **91**
  PA2: Pais 3E **97**
Lochearnhead Rd. G33: Step. 4B **66**
Lochend Av. G69: G'csh. 2C **68**
Lochend Cres. G61: Bear. 4D **44**
Lochend Dr. G61: Bear. 4D **44**
Lochend Path G34: Glas 2H **87**
Lochend Rd. G34: Glas 2H **87**
  G61: Bear 4E **45**
  G69: G'csh 2B **88**
            (Easterhouse)
  G69: G'csh 2D **68**
           (Mount Ellen)
Lochend St. ML1: Moth 3H **143**
Locher Av. PA6: C'lee 2E **75**
Locherburn Av. PA6: C'lee 3D **74**
Locherburn Gro. PA6: C'lee 3D **74**
Locherburn Pl. PA6: C'lee 3D **74**
Locher Cres. PA6: C'lee 3E **75**
Locher Gait PA6: C'lee 3E **75**
Locher Gdns. PA6: C'lee. 3E **75**

Locher Pl. ML5: Coat 2F 111
Locher Rd. PA11: Bri W 6H 73
Locher Way PA6: C'lee 3E 75
Lochfauld Rd. G23: Glas 5E 47
LOCHFIELD 4B 98
Lochfield Cres. PA2: Pais 4B 98
Lochfield Dr. PA2: Pais 4C 98
Lochfield Gdns. G34: Glas 2B 88
Lochfield Rd. PA2: Pais 4A 98
Lochgarry Way ML5: Coat 1H 109
Lochgilp St. G20: Glas 2A 62
Loch Goil G74: E Kil 2A 150
Lochgoin Gdns. G15: Glas 3G 43
Lochgreen Pl. ML3: Ham 3F 153
　　ML5: Coat 1G 89
Lochgreen St. G33: Glas 6F 65
Lochhead Av. PA3: Lin 6H 75
Lochiel Ct. ML6: Air 4F 91
　　　　　　　　　(off Monkscourt Av.)
Lochiel Dr. G66: Milt C 5C 8
Lochiel La. G73: Ruth 3F 121
Lochiel Rd. G46: T'bnk 3F 117
Lochinch Pl. G77: Newt M 4A 132
Lochinvar Rd. G67: Cumb 6F 35
Lochinver Cres. PA2: Pais 3E 97
Lochinver Dr. G44: Glas 3E 119
Lochinver Gro. G72: Camb 2B 122
Loch Laidon Ct. G32: Glas 1C 106
Loch Laidon St. G32: Glas 1D 106
Loch Laxford G74: E Kil 3B 150
Loch Lea G66: Kirk 3F 31
Lochlea G74: E Kil 5D 138
Lochlea Av. G81: Clyd 4E 43
Lochlea Loan ML9: Lark 3G 161
　　　　　　　　　　　(off Catrine St.)
Lochlea Rd. G43: Glas 1B 118
　　G67: Cumb 2B 36
　　G73: Ruth 2G 121
　　　　　　　　　　　　(Burnside)
　　G73: Ruth 2B 120
　　　　　　　　　　　　　(Spittal)
　　G76: Busby 4C 134
Lochlea Way ML1: N'hill 3E 129
Lochleven La. G42: Glas 6E 103
Lochleven Rd. G42: Glas 6E 103
LOCHLIBO 6C 114
Lochlibo Av. G13: Glas 3H 59
Lochlibo Cres. G78: Barr 6C 114
Lochlibo Rd. G78: Neil 3A 130
Lochlibo Ter. G78: Barr 6C 114
Loch Long G74: E Kil 3A 150
Loch Loyal G74: E Kil 3B 150
Lochmaben Rd. G52: Glas 1H 99
Loch Maree G74: E Kil 3B 150
Loch Meadie G74: E Kil 3B 150
Lochnagar Dr. G61: Bear 6B 24
Lochnagar Way ML9: Lark 3G 161
　　　　　　　　　(off Keir Hardie Way)
Loch Naver G74: E Kil 3B 150
Lochore Av. PA3: Pais 4B 78
Loch Pk. ML2: Wis 6A 146
Loch Pk. Av. ML8: Carl 5E 165
Loch Pk. Pl. ML9: Lark 4E 161
Lochpark Stadium 5F 165
Loch Pl. PA11: Bri W 3F 73
Lochranza Ct. ML1: Carf 5B 128
Lochranza Dr. G75: E Kil 6D 148
Lochranza La. G75: E Kil 6E 149
Loch Rd. G33: Step 4D 66
　　G62: Miln 2H 25
　　G66: Kirk 6D 30
　　ML6: Chap 3D 112
　　PA11: Bri W 3F 73
Loch Shin G74: E Kil 3B 150
Lochside G61: Bear 4F 45
　　G69: G'csh 3D 68
Lochside St. G41: Glas 4C 102
Lochsloy Ct. G22: Glas 5H 63
Loch St. ML6: C'bnk 3B 112
Loch Striven G74: E Kil 2A 150
Loch Torridon G74: E Kil 3B 150
Loch Vw. ML6: C'bnk 3B 112

Lochview Cres. G33: Glas 6H 65
Lochview Dr. G33: Glas 6H 65
Lochview Gdns. G33: Glas. 6H 65
Lochview Pl. G33: Glas 6H 65
Lochview Quad. ML4: Bell 4B 126
Lochview Rd. G61: Bear. 4E 45
　　ML5: Coat 2G 89
Lochview Ter. G69: G'csh 4D 68
Loch Voil St. G32: Glas 1D 106
Lochwood Loan G69: Mood 4E 53
Lochwood St. G33: Glas 1G 85
Lochy Av. PA4: Renf 2H 79
Lochy Gdns. G64: B'rig 6D 48
Lochy Pl. PA8: Ersk 6C 40
Lochy St. ML2: Wis 2G 157
Locke Rd. ML1: Cle. 6F 129
Lockerbie Av. G43: Glas 1D 118
Locket Yett Vw. ML4: Bell 2A 126
Lockhart Av. G72: Camb 1D 122
Lockhart Dr. G72: Camb 1D 122
　　G77: Newt M 6D 132
Lockhart Pl. ML2: Wis 5C 146
Lockhart St. G21: Glas. 1D 84
　　ML3: Ham 5G 153
　　ML8: Carl 3F 165
Lockhart Ter. G74: E Kil 1B 150
Locksley Av. G13: Glas 1C 60
　　G67: Cumb. 1G 55
Locksley Ct. G67: Cumb 1G 55
Locksley Cres. G67: Cumb 1G 55
Locksley Pl. G67: Cumb 1G 55
Locksley Rd. G67: Cumb. 1G 55
　　PA2: Pais 4D 96
Locksley Way PA2: Pais. 4D 96
Locks St. ML5: Coat. 5F 91
Lodge Twr. ML1: Moth 5A 144
　　　　　　　　　(off Glassford St.)
Logan Av. G77: Newt M 3C 132
Logandale Av. ML2: Newm 3D 146
Logan Dr. G68: Cumb 2F 35
　　PA3: Pais 5G 77
Logan Gdns. ML1: Cle 1H 145
Loganlea Dr. ML1: Carf 6A 128
Logans Rd. ML1: Moth 2D 142
Logan St. G5: Glas 3H 103
　　G72: Blan 2C 140
Loganswell Dr. G46: T'bnk 5E 117
Loganswell Gdns.
　　G46: T'bnk 5E 117
Loganswell Pl. G46: T'bnk 5E 117
Loganswell Rd. G46: T'bnk 5E 117
Logan Twr. G72: Camb 3E 123
Logie Pk. G74: E Kil 6A 138
Logie Sq. G74: E Kil 6A 138
Lomax St. G33: Glas. 3F 85
Lomond G75: E Kil 6G 149
Lomond Av. PA4: Renf 2D 78
Lomond Ct. G67: Cumb 6E 35
　　G78: Barr 5E 115
　　G82: Dumb 3E 17
Lomond Cres. G67: Cumb 6E 35
　　PA11: Bri W 3E 73
　　PA2: Pais 5H 97
Lomond Dr. G64: B'rig 4B 48
　　G67: Cumb 6D 34
　　G71: Both 4F 125
　　G77: Newt M 2D 132
　　G78: Barr 3D 114
　　G82: Dumb 1H 17
　　ML2: Wis 1G 157
　　ML6: Air 2G 91
Lomond Gdns. PA5: Eld 3A 96
Lomond Gro. G67: Cumb 6E 35
Lomond Pl. G33: Step 5D 66
　　G67: Cumb 6D 34
　　ML5: Coat. 2A 90
　　PA8: Ersk 6C 40
　　　　　　　　　　(not continuous)
Lomond Rd. G61: Bear. 5E 45
　　G66: Lenz. 2D 50
　　G71: Tann 4D 108
　　ML5: Coat 1G 89
Lomondside Av. G76: Clar 1A 134
Lomond St. G22: Glas 4F 63

Lomondveiw Ind. Est.
　　PA5: John 2F 95
　　　　　　　　　　　(off High St.)
Lomond Vw. G67: Cumb 6E 35
　　G81: Clyd 4D 42
　　　　　　　　　　(off Church St.)
　　ML3: Ham 1D 152
Lomond Wlk. ML1: N'hill 3C 128
Lomond Wlk. ML9: Lark. 1F 161
　　　　　　　　　(off Ashburn Loan)
Lomond Way ML1: Holy. 2A 128
　　　　　　　　　　(off Graham St.)
London Dr. G32: Glas 3E 107
London La. G1: Glas 5H 83
　　　　　　　　　(off St Andrews St.)
London Rd. G1: Glas 5H 83
　　G32: Glas 4A 106
　　G40: Glas 1D 104
London St. ML9: Lark. 1E 161
　　PA4: Renf 4F 59
London Way G1: Glas 5H 83
Lonend PA1: Pais 1B 98
Longay Pl. G22: Glas 1G 63
Longay St. G22: Glas 1G 63
Long Calderwood Cotts.
　　G74: E Kil 5C 138
　　　　　　　(off Maxwellton Rd.)
Long Crags Vw. G82: Dumb 1H 17
LONGCROFT 1G 15
Longcroft Dr. PA4: Renf 5E 59
Longden St. G81: Clyd 1F 59
Long Dr. G75: E Kil. 4A 150
Longford St. G33: Glas 3F 85
Longlee G69: Bail. 1H 107
Longmeadow PA5: John 4D 94
Longmorn Pl. ML1: Carf 6B 128
Long Row G66: Kirk. 6H 31
　　G69: Bail. 5A 88
Longstone Pl. G33: Glas 3B 86
Longstone Rd. G33: Glas 3B 86
Longwill Ter. G67: Cumb 1B 36
Lonsdale Av. G46: Giff 4A 118
Loom Wlk. PA10: Kilb 2A 94
　　　　　　　　　　(not continuous)
Lora Dr. G52: Glas 1E 101
Lord Way G69: Barg 6D 88
Loretto Pl. G33: Glas 3H 85
Loretto St. G33: Glas 3H 85
Lorimer Cres. G75: E Kil 4F 149
Lorn Av. G69: Chry 1B 68
Lorne Ct. G20: Glas 1E 83
　　　　　　　　　　　(off Cedar St.)
Lorne Cres. G64: B'rig 5F 49
Lorne Dr. ML1: Moth 5F 127
　　PA3: Lin 6G 75
Lorne Pl. ML5: Coat 6F 91
Lorne Rd. G52: Hill 3H 79
Lorne St. G51: Glas 5B 82
　　ML3: Ham 5G 141
Lorne Ter. G72: Camb 4H 121
Lorn Pl. G66: Kirk 4A 32
Lorraine Gdns. G12: Glas 5A 62
Lorraine Gdns. La. G12: Glas 5A 62
　　　　　　　　　(off Lorraine Gdns.)
Lorraine Rd. G12: Glas 5A 62
Loskin Dr. G22: Glas. 2F 63
Lossie Cres. PA4: Renf 1H 79
Lossie St. G33: Glas 2F 85
Lothian Cres. PA2: Pais 4H 97
Lothian Dr. G76: Clar 1B 134
Lothian Gdns. G20: Glas 6C 62
Lothian St. G52: Hill 3G 79
　　　　　　　　　　(not continuous)
Lothian Way G74: E Kil 6C 138
Louden Hill Dr. G33: Glas 3G 65
Louden Hill Gdns. G33: Glas 3G 65
Louden Hill Pl. G33: Glas 3G 65
Louden Hill Rd. G33: Glas. 3G 65
Louden Hill Way G33: Glas 3G 65
Louden St. ML6: Air. 4A 92
Loudon G75: E Kil 6G 149
Loudon Gdns. PA5: John 2G 95
Loudonhill Av. ML3: Ham 3A 154
Loudon Rd. G33: Mille 5B 66

Loudon St. ML2: Wis 3H 145
Loudon Ter. G61: Bear 6D 24
(off Grampian Way)
Louise Gdns. ML1: Holy 2H 127
Louisville Av. ML2: Wis 4B 146
LOUNSDALE 3E 97
Lounsdale Av. PA2: Pais 2F 97
Lounsdale Cres. PA2: Pais 3E 97
Lounsdale Dr. PA2: Pais 3F 97
Lounsdale Gro. PA2: Pais 2F 97
Lounsdale Ho. PA2: Pais 4D 96
Lounsdale Pl. G14: Glas 5B 60
Lounsdale Rd. PA2: Pais 3F 97
Lounsdale Way PA2: Pais 2F 97
Lourdes Av. G52: Glas 1D 100
Lourdes Ct. G52: Glas 1D 100
Lovat Av. G61: Bear 6E 25
Lovat Dr. G66: Kirk 5B 30
Lovat Path ML9: Lark 3G 161
(off Shawrigg Rd.)
Lovat Pl. G52: Hill 4G 79
G73: Ruth 3F 121
Love Av. PA11: Q'riers 1A 72
Love St. PA3: Pais 5A 78
Low Barholm PA10: Kilb 3B 94
LOW BLANTYRE 6C 124
Low Broadlie Rd. G78: Neil 1D 130
Low Craigends G65: Kils 3A 12
Low Cres. G81: Clyd 1G 59
Lwr. Admiralty Rd. G60: Old K 2F 41
Lwr. Auchingramont Rd.
    ML3: Ham 5A 142
Lwr. Bourtree Dr. G73: Ruth 3E 121
Lower Millgate G71: Udd 1D 124
Lwr. Mill Rd. G76: Busby 3D 134
Low Flender Rd. G76: Clar 4B 134
Low Moss Ind. Est. G64: B'rig 3E 49
Lowndes St. G78: Barr 5E 115
Low Parksail PA8: Ersk 1G 57
Low Parks Mus. 5A 142
Low Patrick St. ML3: Ham 6B 142
Low Pleasance ML9: Lark 2F 161
Low Quarry Gdns. ML3: Ham 1H 153
Low Rd. PA2: Pais 2G 97
Lowther Av. G61: Bear 6C 24
Lowther Ter. G12: Glas 5A 62
LOW WATERS 2A 154
Low Waters Rd. ML3: Ham 3H 153
Loyal Av. PA8: Ersk 6D 40
Loyal Gdns. G61: Bear 6B 24
Loyal Pl. PA8: Ersk 6D 40
Loyne Dr. PA4: Renf 1H 79
Luath St. G51: Glas 3G 81
Lubas Av. G42: Glas 6H 103
Lubas Pl. G42: Glas 6H 103
Lubnaig Dr. PA8: Ersk 6D 40
Lubnaig Gdns. G61: Bear 6C 24
Lubnaig Pl. ML6: Air 1G 91
Lubnaig Rd. G43: Glas 2C 118
Lubnaig Wlk. ML1: Holy 2A 128
Luckiesfauld G78: Neil 3D 130
Luckingsford Av. PA4: Inch 2H 57
Luckingsford Dr. PA4: Inch 2G 57
Luckingsford Rd. PA4: Inch 2G 57
Lucy Brae G71: Tann 5C 108
Ludovic Sq. PA5: John 2F 95
Luffness Gdns. G32: Glas 3B 106
Lugar Dr. G52: Glas 1E 101
Lugar Pl. G44: Glas 2B 120
Lugar St. ML5: Coat 3D 90
Luggiebank Pl. G69: Barg 1E 109
Luggiebank Rd. G66: Kirk 5D 30
(not continuous)
Luggie Gro. G66: Kirk 6G 31
Luggie Rd. ML8: Carl 3D 164
Luggie Vw. G67: Cumb 6C 34
Luing ML6: Air 5E 93
Luing Rd. G52: Glas 6E 81
Luma Gdns. G51: Glas 4C 80
LUMLOCH 1G 65
Lumloch St. G21: Glas 5C 64
Lumsden La. G3: Glas 2B 82
(off Lumsden St.)
Lumsden St. G3: Glas 3B 82

Lunan Dr. G64: B'rig 1E 65
Lunan Pl. G51: Glas 4E 81
Lunar Path ML6: Chap 4D 112
Luncarty Pl. G32: Glas 2A 106
Luncarty St. G32: Glas 2A 106
Lunderston Cl. G53: Glas 1B 116
Lunderston Dr. G53: Glas 6A 100
Lunderston Gdns. G53: Glas 1B 116
Lundie Gdns. G64: B'rig 1F 65
Lundie St. G32: Glas 2G 105
Luss Brae ML3: Ham 1C 152
Lusset Glen G60: Old K 1F 41
Lusset Rd. G60: Old K 1F 41
Lusset Vw. G81: Clyd 4D 42
Lusshill Ter. G71: Udd 3H 107
Luss Rd. G51: Glas 4F 81
Lybster Cres. G73: Ruth 4F 121
Lyell Gro. G74: E Kil 6G 137
Lyell Pl. G74: E Kil 6G 137
Lyle Cres. PA7: B'ton 3F 39
Lyle Pl. PA2: Pais 3B 98
Lyle Rd. ML6: Air 4F 93
Lyle's Land PA6: Hous 1B 74
Lylesland Ct. PA2: Pais 3A 98
Lyle Sq. G62: Miln 3E 25
(Hilton Rd.)
G62: Miln 3E 25
(Kelvin Rd.)
Lyman Dr. ML2: Wis 2A 146
Lymburn St. G3: Glas 3B 82
Lymekilns Rd. G74: E Kil 1F 149
Lyndale Pl. G20: Glas 1B 62
Lyndale Rd. G20: Glas 1B 62
Lyndhurst Gdns. G20: Glas 6D 62
Lyndhurst Gdns. La. G20: Glas . . . 6C 62
(off Lothian Gdns.)
Lyne Cft. G64: B'rig 3C 48
Lynedoch Cres. G3: Glas 2D 82
Lynedoch Cres. La. G3: Glas 2D 82
(off Woodlands Rd.)
Lynedoch Pl. G3: Glas 2D 82
Lynedoch St. G3: Glas 2D 82
Lynedoch Ter. G3: Glas 2D 82
Lyne St. ML2: Wis 4G 145
Lynnburn Av. ML4: Bell 1C 126
Lynn Ct. ML9: Lark 3E 161
Lynn Dr. G62: Miln 3A 26
Lynne Dr. G23: Glas 6C 46
Lynnhurst G71: Tann 6D 108
Lynn Wlk. G71: Udd 2E 125
(off Bellshill Rd.)
Lynton Av. G46: Giff 6G 117
Lynwood Rd. ML2: Newm 3G 147
Lyoncross Av. G78: Barr 5F 115
Lyoncross Cres. G78: Barr 4F 115
Lyoncross Rd. G53: Glas 2B 100
Lyon Rd. PA2: Pais 4D 96
PA3: Lin 1H 95
PA8: Ersk 6C 40
Lyons Quad. ML2: Wis 5D 144
Lysander Way PA4: Renf 2F 79
Lysa Va. Pl. ML4: Bell 2A 126
Lytham Dr. G23: Glas 6C 46
Lytham Mdws. G71: Both 5C 124
Lyttelton G75: E Kil 5D 148

M

Mabel St. ML1: Moth 4G 143
Macadam Gdns. ML4: Bell 1C 126
Macadam Pl. G75: E Kil 3G 14
Maleny Gro. G77: Newt M 6B 132
McAlister Av. ML6: Air 3D 92
McAlpine St. G2: Glas 4E 83 (6A 4)
ML2: Wis 1H 157
McArdle Av. ML1: Moth 2D 142
McArron Way G67: Cumb 4H 35
(in Cumbernauld Shop. Cen.)
Macarthur Av. ML6: Glenm 6F 71
Macarthur Ct. G74: E Kil 6E 137
Macarthur Cres. G74: E Kil 5E 137
(not continuous)

Macarthur Dr. G74: E Kil 6E 137
Macarthur Gdns. G74: E Kil 6E 137
McArthur Pk. G66: Kirk 6C 30
McArthur St. G43: Glas 6A 102
Macarthur Wynd G72: Camb 2C 122
McAslin Ct. G4: Glas 3H 83 (3H 5)
McAslin St. G4: Glas 3A 84 (3H 5)
Macbeth G74: E Kil 4B 138
Macbeth Pl. G31: Glas 1F 105
Macbeth St. G31: Glas 1F 105
McBride Av. G66: Kirk 6C 30
MacCabe Gdns. G66: Len 4H 7
McCallum Av. G73: Ruth 6D 104
McCallum Ct. G74: E Kil 5D 136
McCallum Gdns. ML4: Bell 5B 126
McCallum Pl. G74: E Kil 5D 136
McCallum Rd. ML9: Lark 4F 161
McCarrison Rd. ML2: Newm 3E 147
McCash Pl. G66: Kirk 6C 30
McCloy Gdns. G53: Glas 2H 115
McClue Av. PA4: Renf 6D 58
McClue Rd. PA4: Renf 5E 59
McClurg Ct. ML1: Moth 4G 143
McCormack Gdns. ML1: N'hill 3E 129
McCourt Gdns. ML4: Moss 2E 127
(off Main St.)
McCracken Av. PA4: Renf 1D 78
McCracken Dr. G71: View 5G 109
McCreery St. G81: Clyd 1F 59
Maccrimmon Pk. G74: E Kil 5D 136
McCrorie Pl. PA10: Kilb 2A 94
McCulloch Av. G71: View 1G 125
McCulloch St. G41: Glas 1D 102
McCulloch Way G78: Neil 2D 130
McCullochs Wlk. G66: Len 3F 7
Macdairmid Dr. ML3: Ham 4F 153
Macdonald Av. G74: E Kil 5C 136
Macdonald Cres. G65: Twe 2D 32
McDonald Av. PA5: John 4E 95
Macdonald Cres. G65: Twe 2D 32
McDonald Cres. G81: Clyd 1F 59
MacDonald Gro. ML4: Bell 5B 126
McDonald Pl. G78: Neil 2E 131
ML1: Holy 2A 128
Macdonald St. G73: Ruth 6C 104
ML1: Moth 4H 143
Macdougal Dr. G72: Camb 2C 122
Macdougall St. G43: Glas 6A 102
Macdougal Quad. ML4: Bell 5B 126
Macdowall St. PA3: Pais 5H 77
PA5: John 2F 95
Macduff PA8: Ersk 5E 41
Macduff Pl. G31: Glas 1F 105
Macduff St. G31: Glas 1F 105
Macedonian Gro. ML1: N'hill 3C 128
Mace Rd. G13: Glas 6C 44
McEwan Gdns. G74: E Kil 5C 136
Macfarlane Cres. G72: Camb 2C 122
Macfarlane Rd. G61: Bear 4G 45
McFarlane St. G40: Glas 5A 84
PA3: Pais 4G 77
Macfie Pl. G74: E Kil 5D 136
McGhee St. G81: Clyd 3D 42
McGowan Pl. ML3: Ham 4E 141
McGown St. PA3: Pais 5H 77
McGregor Av. ML6: Air 3D 92
PA4: Renf 1D 78
Macgregor Ct. G72: Camb 2C 122
McGregor Dr. G82: Dumb 1C 18
McGregor Path ML5: Glenb 3G 69
McGregor Rd. G67: Cumb 4G 35
McGregor St. G51: Glas 5F 81
G81: Clyd 1F 59
ML2: Wis 5D 144
McGrigor Rd. G62: Miln 2F 25
MACHAN 4F 161
Machan Av. ML9: Lark 2E 161
Machanhill ML9: Lark 2F 161
Machanhill Vw. ML9: Lark 3F 161
Machan Rd. ML9: Lark 3E 161
Machrie Dr. G45: Glas 3B 120
G77: Newt M 3A 132
Machrie Rd. G45: Glas 3A 120

Machrie St. G45: Glas 4A 120
 ML1: Moth 2D 142
McInnes Ct. ML2: Wis 1H 157
McInnes Pl. ML2: Over 4H 157
McIntosh Ct. G31: Glas 4B 84
 (off McIntosh St.)
McIntosh Pl. G31: Glas 4B 84
Macintosh Pl. G75: E Kil 4E 149
McIntosh Quad. ML4: Bell 5B 126
McIntosh St. G31: Glas 4B 84
McIntosh Way ML1: Moth 4E 143
McIntyre Pl. PA2: Pais 3A 98
Macintyre St. G3: Glas 4D 82
McIntyre Ter. G72: Camb 1A 122
McIver St. G72: Camb 1D 122
Macivor Cres. G74: E Kil 5C 136
McKay Ct. G77: Newt M 5C 132
McKay Cres. PA5: John 3G 95
McKay Gro. ML4: Bell 2B 126
McKay Pl. G74: E Kil 5C 136
 G77: Newt M 5C 132
MacKean St. PA3: Pais 5G 77
McKechnie St. G51: Glas 3G 81
MacKeith St. G40: Glas 1B 104
McKenna Dr. ML6: Air 4G 91
McKenzie Av. G81: Clyd 3D 42
Mackenzie Dr. PA10: Kilb 4B 94
Mackenzie Gdns. G74: E Kil 5C 136
McKenzie St. PA3: Pais 6G 77
Mackenzie Ter. ML4: Bell 6C 110
McKeown Gdns. ML4: Bell 3F 127
McKerrell St. PA1: Pais 6C 78
Mackie's Mill Rd. PA5: Eld 5B 96
MacKinlay Pl. G77: Newt M 5D 132
Mackinlay St. G5: Glas 1F 103
MacKinnon Mills ML5: Coat 2C 110
Mack St. ML6: Air 3A 92
McLaren Ct. G46: Giff 6H 117
McLaren Cres. G20: Glas 2C 62
McLaren Dr. ML4: Bell 3F 127
McLaren Gro. G74: E Kil 5C 136
McLaren Pl. G44: Neth 5D 118
McLaurin Cres. PA5: John 4D 94
Maclay Av. PA10: Kilb 3A 94
McLean Av. PA4: Renf 2E 79
Maclean Ct. G74: E Kil 5D 136
McLean Dr. ML4: Bell 5B 126
Maclean Gro. G74: E Kil 5D 136
Maclean Pl. G67: Cumb 6C 34
 (off Airdrie Rd.)
McLean Pl. PA3: Pais 4H 77
Maclean Rd. G74: E Kil 5D 136
 G78: Neil 3E 131
Maclean Sq. G51: Glas 5B 82
Maclean St. G51: Glas 5B 82
Mclean St. G81: Clyd 1G 59
 (off Wood Quad.)
McLees La. ML1: Moth 2D 142
Maclehose Rd. G67: Cumb 2C 36
McLelland Dr. ML6: Plain 1H 93
Maclellan St. G41: Glas 6B 82
Mclennan Galleries 3F 83 (3C 4)
McLennan St. G42: Glas 5F 103
Macleod Pl. G74: E Kil 6B 138
McLeod Rd. G82: Dumb 1C 18
Macleod St. G4: Glas 4A 84 (5H 5)
Macleod Way G72: Camb 2C 122
McMahon Dr. ML2: Newm 3E 147
McMahon Gro. ML4: Bell 1D 126
Macmillan Gdns. G71: Tann 5E 109
McMillan Rd. ML2: Wis 1D 156
Macmillan St. ML9: Lark 3D 160
McMillan Way ML8: Law 6D 158
McNair St. G32: Glas 6A 86
McNeil Av. G81: Clyd 6G 43
McNeil Dr. ML1: Holy 6G 111
McNeil Gdns. G5: Glas 1H 103
Macneill Dr. G74: E Kil 5D 136
Macneill Gdns. G74: E Kil 5D 136
Macneill St. ML9: Lark 2D 160
McNeil Pl. ML2: Over 4A 158
McNeil St. G5: Glas 1H 103
Macneish Way G74: E Kil 5D 136
Macnicol Ct. G74: E Kil 5C 136

Macnicol Pk. G74: E Kil 5C 136
Macnicol Pl. G74: E Kil 5C 136
McPhail St. G40: Glas 1A 104
McPhater St. G4: Glas 2F 83 (2D 4)
McPherson Cres. ML6: Chap 4E 113
McPherson Dr. G71: Both 4F 125
Macpherson Pk. G74: E Kil 6E 137
McPherson St. G1: Glas . . . 5H 83 (6G 5)
 ML4: Moss 2F 127
Macphie Rd. G82: Dumb 1C 18
Macquisten Bri. G41: Glas 6B 102
Macrae Ct. PA5: John 4E 95
 (off Tannahill Cres.)
Macrae Gdns. G74: E Kil 6E 137
Macrimmon Pl. G75: E Kil 3G 149
McShannon Gro. ML4: Bell 4C 126
McSparran Rd. G65: Croy 1B 34
MacTaggart Rd. G67: Cumb 5G 35
Madison Av. G44: Glas 2F 119
Madison La. G44: Glas 2F 119
Madison Pl. G72: Blan 2B 140
Madras Pl. G40: Glas 2B 104
 G78: Neil 2E 131
Madras St. G40: Glas 2B 104
Mafeking St. G51: Glas 5H 81
 ML2: Wis 5D 144
Mafeking Ter. G78: Neil 2C 130
Magdalen Way PA2: Pais 6B 96
Magna St. ML1: Moth 1D 142
Magnolia Dr. G72: Flem 4F 123
Magnolia Gdns. ML1: N'hill 4C 128
Magnolia Pl. G71: View 5G 109
Magnolia St. ML2: Wis 4H 145
Magnus Cres. G44: Glas 3F 119
Magnus Rd. PA6: C'lee 3C 74
Mahon Ct. G69: Mood 6D 52
Maidens G74: E Kil 6F 137
Maidens Av. G77: Newt M 4G 133
Maidland Rd. G53: Glas 5C 100
Mailerberg Gdns. G69: Mood 4D 52
Mailie Wlk. ML1: N'hill 4C 128
Mailing Av. G64: B'rig 5D 48
Mainhead Ter. G67: Cumb 6B 14
Mainhill Av. G69: Bail 6B 88
Mainhill Dr. G69: Bail 6A 88
Mainhill Pl. G69: Bail 5B 88
Mainhill Rd. G69: Barg 6C 88
Main Rd. G67: Cumb 2B 54
 PA2: Pais 1H 97
 PA5: Eld 3H 95
Mains Av. G46: Giff 6H 117
Mains Castle 4F 137
Mainscroft PA8: Ersk 6G 41
Mains Dr. PA8: Ersk 6G 41
Mains Hill PA8: Ersk 6F 41
Mainshill Av. PA8: Ersk 6F 41
Mainshill Gdns. PA8: Ersk 6F 41
Mains Pl. ML4: Bell 4C 126
Mains River PA8: Ersk 6G 41
Mains Rd. G74: E Kil 6G 137
 G74: E Kil, Ners 4G 137
Main St. G40: Glas 2B 104
 G46: T'bnk 4F 117
 G62: Miln 4G 25
 (not continuous)
 G64: Torr 5D 28
 G65: Kils 2H 11
 G65: Twe 1D 32
 G66: Len 3F 7
 G67: Cumb 6B 14
 G69: Bail 1H 107
 G69: Chry 1A 68
 G71: Both 5E 125
 G71: Udd 1D 124
 G72: Blan 3H 139
 G72: Camb 1A 122
 G73: Ruth 5C 104
 G74: E Kil 1H 149
 G76: Busby 3D 134
 G78: Barr 5D 114
 G78: Neil 2D 130
 ML1: Cle 1H 145
 ML1: Holy 2A 128
 ML2: Newm 6E 147

Main St. ML2: Over 5A 158
 ML2: Wis 5F 145
 ML4: Bell 2B 126
 ML5: Coat 4C 90
 (not continuous)
 ML5: Glenb 3H 69
 ML6: C'bnk 2C 112
 ML6: Chap 2E 113
 ML6: Plain 1G 93
 PA11: Bri W 3F 73
 PA6: Hous 1A 74
Mains Wood PA8: Ersk 6H 41
Mair St. G51: Glas 5C 82
Maitland Bank ML9: Lark 2G 161
Maitland Dr. G64: Torr 4D 28
Maitland Pl. PA4: Renf 1D 78
Maitland St. G4: Glas 2F 83 (1D 4)
Malcolm Gdns. G74: E Kil 1E 149
Malcolm St. ML1: Moth 3E 143
Maleny Gro. G77: Newt M 6B 132
Mal Fleming's Brae G65: Kils 4B 12
Malin Pl. G33: Glas 3H 85
Mallaig Path G51: Glas 4D 80
 (off Mallaig Rd.)
Mallaig Pl. G51: Glas 4D 80
Mallaig Rd. G51: Glas 4D 80
Mallard Cres. G75: E Kil 6C 148
Mallard La. G71: Both 4E 125
Mallard Pl. G75: E Kil 6C 148
Mallard Rd. G81: Hard 2D 42
Mallard Ter. G75: E Kil 6C 148
Mallard Way ML4: Bell 4B 110
Malleable Gdns. ML1: Moth 5E 127
MALLETSHEUGH 5B 132
Malletsheugh Rd. G77: Newt M 6A 132
 (not continuous)
Malloch Cres. PA5: Eld 3H 95
Malloch Pl. G74: E Kil 1B 150
Malloch St. G20: Glas 4C 62
Mallotts Vw. G77: Newt M 6B 132
Malov Ct. G75: E Kil 6G 149
Malplaquet Ct. ML8: Carl 4H 165
Malta Ter. G5: Glas 1F 103
Maltbarns St. G20: Glas 6E 63
Malvaig La. G72: Blan 3A 140
Malvern Ct. G31: Glas 5C 84
Malvern Way PA3: Pais 3H 77
Mambeg Dr. G51: Glas 3E 81
Mamore Pl. G43: Glas 1A 118
Mamore St. G43: Glas 1A 118
Manchester Dr. G12: Glas 3G 61
M & D's Theme Pk. 6A 126
Mandora Ct. ML8: Carl 4H 165
Manitoba Cres. G75: E Kil 2D 148
Mannering G74: E Kil 5D 138
Mannering Ct. G41: Glas 5A 102
Mannering Rd. G41: Glas 5A 102
 PA2: Pais 6C 96
Mannering Way PA2: Pais 5C 96
Mannoch Pl. ML5: Coat 2F 111
Mannofield G61: Bear 3D 44
Manor Dr. ML6: Air 3G 91
Manor Ga. G77: Newt M 6F 133
Manor Pk. ML3: Ham 1H 153
Manor Pk. Av. PA2: Pais 4F 97
Manor Rd. G14: Glas 5E 61
 G15: Glas 6H 43
 G69: G'csh 4D 68
 PA2: Pais 4D 96
Manor Vw. ML6: C'bnk 3B 112
 ML9: Lark 3G 161
Manor Way G73: Ruth 3E 121
Manresa Pl. G4: Glas 1F 83
Manse Av. G61: Bear 2F 45
 G71: Both 5E 125
 ML5: Coat 1H 109
Manse Brae G44: Glas 1F 119
 G72: Flem 5F 123
 ML9: Ashg, Dals 6D 162
Manse Bri. ML8: Carl 4G 165
Manse Ct. G65: Kils 4H 11
 G78: Barr 4F 115
 ML8: Law 1A 164
Manse Cres. PA6: Hous 1B 74

Mansefield Av.—Maxwell Cres.

Mansefield Av. G72: Camb 3A **122**
Mansefield Cres. G60: Old K 6E **21**
G76: Clar 3B **134**
Mansefield Dr. G71: Udd. 1D **124**
Mansefield Rd. G76: Clar 3C **134**
ML3: Ham 5H **153**
Manse Gdns. G32: Glas. 1D **106**
Manse La. G74: E Kil. 6H **137**
Mansel St. G21: Glas. 4B **64**
Manse Pl. ML6: Air 4A **92**
Manse Rd. G32: Glas. 1D **106**
G60: Bowl. 5B **20**
G61: Bear 2E **45**
G65: Kils 4H **11**
G69: Barg 5C **88**
G76: Crmck 2H **135**
G78: Neil 2D **130**
ML1: Moth 1G **155**
ML2: Newm 5D **146**
Manse Rd. Gdns. G61: Bear. 2F **45**
Manse St. ML5: Coat. 5B **90**
PA4: Renf 5F **59**
Manse Vw. ML1: N'hill 3F **129**
ML9: Lark 3F **161**
MANSEWOOD **2A 118**
Mansewood Dr. G82: Dumb 2H **17**
Mansewood Rd. G43: Glas 1H **117**
Mansfield Rd. G52: Hill. 4H **79**
ML4: Bell 3B **126**
Mansfield St. G11: Glas. 1A **82**
Mansion Ct. G72: Camb. 1A **122**
Mansionhouse Av. G32: Carm 5C **106**
Mansionhouse Dr. G32: Glas 5C **86**
Mansionhouse Gdns.
G41: Glas 6C **102**
Mansionhouse Gro. G32: Glas. 2E **107**
Mansionhouse Rd. G32: Glas 1E **107**
G41: Glas 6C **102**
PA1: Pais 6C **78**
Mansion St. G22: Glas. 4G **63**
G72: Camb 1A **122**
Manson Pl. G75: E Kil 6B **150**
Manus Duddy Ct. G72: Blan. 1B **140**
Maple Av. G66: Milt C 6B **8**
G77: Newt M 5D **132**
G82: Dumb. 2B **16**
Maple Bank ML3: Ham 1B **154**
Maple Ct. G67: Cumb. 6F **15**
ML5: Coat. 1B ***110***
(off Ailsa Rd.)
Maple Cres. G72: Flem. 4F **123**
Maple Dr. G66: Lenz 2A **50**
G78: Barr 6F **115**
G81: Clyd 2B **42**
ML9: Lark. 6A **156**
PA5: John. 5F **95**
Maple Gro. G75: E Kil 6D **148**
Maple Pl. FK4: Bank. 1E **15**
G71: View. 5H **109**
G75: E Kil. 5D **148**
PA5: John. 5G **95**
Maple Quad. ML6: Air. 5D **92**
Maple Rd. G41: Glas 1H **101**
G67: Cumb 6F **15**
ML1: Holy. 2B **128**
Maple Ter. G75: E Kil. 5D **148**
Maple Wlk. G66: Milt C 6B **8**
Maple Way G72: Blan 2A **140**
Maplewood ML2: Wis 2D **156**
Mar Av. PA7: B'ton. 4H **39**
Marchbank Gdns. PA1: Pais. 1F **99**
Marchfield G64: B'rig. 4A **48**
Marchfield Av. PA3: Pais. 3H **77**
Marchglen Pl. G51: Glas 4D **80**
Marchmont Gdns. G64: B'rig 4B **48**
Marchmont Ter. *G12: Glas. 6A* ***62***
(off Observatory Rd.)
March St. G41: Glas. 3D **102**
Mardale G74: E Kil 6E **137**
Mar Dr. G61: Bear. 6F **25**
Maree Dr. G52: Glas. 1E **101**
G67: Cumb. 6D **34**
Maree Gdns. G64: B'rig. 6D **48**
Maree Rd. PA2: Pais 3E **97**
Maree Wlk. *ML2: Newm 3D* ***146***
(off Banavie Rd.)
Maree Way G72: Blan 1B **140**
Marfield St. G32: Glas. 4G **85**
Mar Gdns. G73: Ruth 3F **121**
Margaret Av. FK4: Hag. 1G **15**
Margaret Pl. ML4: Bell. 2A **126**
Margaret Rd. ML3: Ham 3F **141**
Margaret's Pl. ML9: Lark. 2E **161**
Margaret St. ML5: Coat. 1C **110**
Margaretta Bldgs. G44: Glas 1E **119**
Margaretvale Dr. ML9: Lark. 3E **161**
Marguerite Av. G66: Lenz 1C **50**
Marguerite Dr. G66: Lenz 1C **50**
Marguerite Gdns. G66: Lenz 1C **50**
G71: Both 5F **125**
Marguerite Gro. G66: Lenz 1C **50**
Marguerite Pl. G66: Milt C. 5B **8**
Marian Dr. ML1: Carf. 5C **128**
Maric La. ML6: Plain 1G **93**
Marigold Av. ML1: Moth 1G **143**
Marigold Way ML8: Carl 5F **165**
Marina Ct. ML4: Bell 4B **126**
Marine Cres. G51: Glas 5C **82**
Marine Gdns. G51: Glas. 5C **82**
Mariner Ct. G81: Clyd 5C **42**
Marion St. ML4: Moss 2F **127**
Mariscat Rd. G41: Glas 3C **102**
Marjory Dr. PA3: Pais 4C **78**
Marjory Rd. PA4: Renf. 2C **78**
Markdow Av. G53: Glas 4A **100**
Market Cl. G65: Kils. 3H **11**
Market Ct. *G65: Kils. 3H* ***11***
(off Market St.)
Markethill Rd. G74: E Kil, Roger . . . 3F **137**
(not continuous)
MARKETHILL RDBT. **6G 137**
Market Pl. G65: Kils. 3H **11**
G71: View. 6G **109**
ML8: Carl 3F **165**
Market Rd. G66: Kirk. 6G **31**
G71: View. 6G **109**
ML8: Carl 3F **165**
Market Sq. G65: Kils 3H **11**
Market St. G65: Kils. 3H **11**
G71: View. 6G **109**
ML6: Air 4A **92**
Marlach Pl. G53: Glas 5A **100**
Marlborough Av. G11: Glas 6F **61**
Marlborough La. Nth. G11: Glas 6F **61**
Marlborough La. Sth. *G11: Glas 6F* ***61***
(off Broomhill Dr.)
G52: Hill 4B ***80***
(off Nasmyth Rd. Nth.)
Marlborough Pk. G75: E Kil 4C **148**
Marldon La. G11: Glas 6F **61**
Marley Way G66: Milt C. 5B **8**
Marlfield Gdns. ML4: Bell 6C **110**
Marlow St. G41: Glas. 1C **102**
Marlow Ter. G41: Glas 1C **102**
Marmion Ct. PA2: Pais 5D **96**
Marmion Cres. ML1: Moth. 5F **127**
Marmion Dr. G66: Kirk. 5F **31**
Marmion Pl. G67: Cumb 6G **35**
Marmion Rd. G67: Cumb. 6G **35**
PA2: Pais 5C **96**
Marne St. G31: Glas 4D **84**
Marnoch Dr. ML5: Glenb 2H **69**
Marnoch Way G69: Mood 5D **52**
MARNOCK **3G 69**
Marnock Ter. PA2: Pais 2C **98**
Marquis Ga. G71: Both 2C **124**
Marrswood Grn. ML3: Ham 5E **141**
Marshall Gro. ML3: Ham 6F **141**
Marshall La. ML2: Wis 6G **145**
Marshall's La. PA1: Pais 1A **98**
Marshall St. ML2: Wis 1F **157**
ML9: Lark 2E **161**
Martha Pl. ML9: Lark. 3F **161**
Martha St. G1: Glas. 3G **83** (4F **5**)
Martin Ct. ML3: Ham 6G **141**
Martin Cres. G69: Bail 6A **88**
Martin Pl. ML1: N'hill. 4C **128**
Martinside G75: E Kil. 6G **149**
Martin St. G40: Glas 2B **104**
ML5: Coat. 4F **91**
Martlet Dr. PA5: John 6C **94**
Mart St. G1: Glas. 5G **83**
(not continuous)
Martyn St. ML6: Air. 4G **91**
Martyrs Pl. G64: B'rig 1C **64**
Marwick St. G31: Glas. 4D **84**
Mary Dr. ML4: Bell 4A **126**
Mary Fisher Cres. G82: Dumb. 3C **18**
Mary Glen ML2: Wis 4B **146**
MARYHILL **1A 62**
Maryhill Rd. G20: Glas 3B **62** (1A **4**)
G61: Bear 5F **45**
Maryhill Shop. Cen. G20: Glas 4C **62**
Maryhill Station (Rail) **1A 62**
Maryknowe Rd. ML1: Carf. 5C **128**
Maryland Dr. G52: Glas 6E **81**
Maryland Gdns. G52: Glas. 6E **81**
Maryland Rd. G82: Dumb 1H **17**
Mary Rae Rd. ML4: Bell 4A **126**
Mary Sq. G69: Barg. 6D **88**
Maryston St. G33: Glas 1F **85**
Mary St. ML3: Ham 1G **153**
PA2: Pais 3A **98**
PA5: John. 2G **95**
Maryville Av. G46: Giff. 5A **118**
Maryville Gdns. G46: Giff 5A **118**
MARYVILLE INTERCHANGE **5A 108**
Maryville La. G71: Tann 5B **108**
Maryville Vw. G71: Tann 4B **108**
Marywood Sq. G41: Glas. 3D **102**
Mary Young Pl. G76: Busby 3D **134**
Masonfield Av. G68: Cumb 3F **35**
Mason La. ML1: Moth. 3G **143**
(not continuous)
Mason St. ML1: Moth 3G **143**
ML9: Lark. 4G **161**
Masterton Pl. G21: Glas 6G **63**
Masterton Way G71: Tann 4F **109**
Matherton Av. G77: Newt M 4H **133**
Mathieson Rd. G73: Ruth 4E **105**
Mathieson St. PA1: Pais 6D **78**
Matilda Rd. G41: Glas 2C **102**
Matthew McWhirter Pl.
ML9: Lark. 1F **161**
Mauchline G74: E Kil. 6D **138**
Mauchline Av. G66: Kirk 3G **31**
Mauchline Ct. G66: Kirk 3G **31**
ML3: Ham 1B **152**
Mauchline St. G5: Glas 1E **103**
Maukinfauld Ct. G32: Glas. 2F **105**
Maukinfauld Gdns. G31: Glas 1G **105**
Maukinfauld Rd. G32: Glas 2G **105**
Mauldslie Dr. ML8: Law 5D **158**
Mauldslie Pl. ML9: Ashg. 5B **162**
Mauldslie Rd. ML8: Carl 2F **163**
Mauldslie St. G40: Glas. 1D **104**
ML4: Bell 3C **126**
ML5: Coat. 6C **90**
Maule Dr. G11: Glas 1G **81**
Mausoleum Dr. ML3: Ham. 4A **142**
Mavis Bank G64: B'rig 1B **64**
G72: Blan 2A **140**
Mavisbank Gdns. G51: Glas. 5C **82**
ML4: Bell 1C **126**
Mavisbank Rd. G51: Glas 4B **82**
Mavisbank St. ML2: Newm 4G **147**
ML6: Air. 3G **91**
Mavisbank Ter. PA1: Pais 2B **98**
PA5: John 3F **95**
Mavis Valley Rd.
G64: B'rig 3A **48**
Mavor Av. G74: E Kil 5H **137**
MAVOR RDBT. **5H 137**
Maxton Av. G78: Barr. 4C **114**
Maxton Cres. ML2: Wis 3A **146**
Maxton Gro. G78: Barr. 5C **114**
Maxton Ter. G72: Camb 4H **121**
Maxwell Av. G41: Glas. 1C **102**
G61: Bear 4E **45**
G69: Bail 1G **107**
Maxwell Ct. G41: Glas 1C **102**
Maxwell Cres. G72: Blan. 3B **140**

Maxwell Dr. G41: Glas 1A **102**
  G69: Bail 6F **87**
  G74: E Kil 1H **149**
  PA8: Ersk 4D **40**
Maxwell Gdns. G41: Glas 1B **102**
Maxwell Gro. G41: Glas 1B **102**
Maxwell La. G41: Glas 1C **102**
Maxwell Oval G41: Glas 1D **102**
Maxwell Park Station (Rail)
  . . . . 3B **102**
Maxwell Path ML9: Lark 3G **161**
  (off Keir Hardie Rd.)
Maxwell Pl. G41: Glas 2E **103**
  G65: Kils 2H **11**
  G71: Udd 1E **125**
  ML5: Coat. 6B **90**
  PA11: Bri W 3F **73**
Maxwell Rd. G41: Glas 1D **102**
  PA7: B'ton 4H **39**
Maxwell St. G1: Glas 4G **83** (6E **5**)
  (Argyle St.)
  G1: Glas 5G **83**
  (Broomielaw)
  G69: Bail 1H **107**
  G81: Clyd 3B **42**
  PA3: Pais 6A **78**
Maxwell Ter. G41: Glas 1C **102**
Maxwellton Av. G74: E Kil 1A **150**
Maxwellton Ct. PA1: Pais 1G **97**
Maxwellton Pl. G74: E Kil 6B **138**
Maxwellton Rd. G74: E Kil 6B **138**
  PA1: Pais 1F **97**
Maxwellton St. PA1: Pais 1G **97**
Maxwelton Rd. G33: Glas 1F **85**
Maybank La. G42: Glas 4E **103**
Maybank St. G42: Glas 4E **103**
Mayberry Cres. G32: Glas 6D **86**
Mayberry Gdns. G32: Glas 6D **86**
Mayberry Gro. G32: Glas 6D **86**
Mayberry Pl. G72: Blan 1B **140**
Maybole Cres. G77: E Kil 5G **133**
Maybole Gdns. ML3: Ham 1B **152**
Maybole Gro. G77: Newt M 5G **133**
Maybole Pl. ML5: Coat. 2F **111**
Maybole St. G53: Glas 1H **115**
Mayfield Av. G76: Clar 2C **134**
Mayfield Gdns. ML8: Carl 6G **165**
Mayfield Pl. ML5: Coat 2C **110**
  ML8: Carl 6G **165**
Mayfield Rd. ML3: Ham 5D **140**
Mayfield St. G20: Glas 4D **62**
May Gdns. ML3: Ham 4G **141**
May Rd. PA2: Pais 6A **98**
May St. ML3: Ham 4H **141**
May Ter. G42: Glas 5F **103**
  G46: Giff 4A **118**
McCloy Gdns. G53: Glas 2H **115**
McCulloch Way G78: Neil 2D **130**
Meadow Av. G72: Blan 3B **140**
Meadowbank La. G71: Udd 1C **124**
Meadowbank Pl. G77: Newt M 4D **132**
Meadowbank St. G82: Dumb 3E **17**
  (not continuous)
Meadowburn G64: B'rig 3C **48**
Meadowburn Av. G66: Lenz 2E **51**
  G77: Newt M 4D **132**
Meadowburn Rd. ML2: Wis 6A **146**
Meadow Ct. G82: Dumb 2F **17**
Meadowfield Pl. ML2: Newm 3G **147**
Meadowhead Av. G69: Mood 5D **52**
Meadowhead Rd. ML2: Wis 5C **144**
  (not continuous)
Meadowhead Rd. ML6: Plain 1F **93**
MEADOWHILL 2F **161**
Meadowhill G77: Newt M 4D **132**
Meadowhill St. ML9: Lark 2F **161**
Meadow La. G71: Both. 5F **125**
  PA4: Renf 4F **59**
Meadowpark St. G31: Glas 4D **84**
  (not continuous)
Meadow Path ML6: Chap. 4D **112**
Meadow Rd. G11: Glas 1G **81**
  G82: Dumb 3F **17**
  ML1: Moth 4H **143**

Meadows Av. ML9: Lark 2F **161**
  PA8: Ersk 6G **41**
Meadows Dr. PA8: Ersk 6G **41**
Meadow Side ML3: Ham 5H **153**
Meadowside Av. PA5: Eld 3B **96**
Meadowside Gdns. ML6: Air 4D **92**
Meadowside Ind. Est. PA4: Renf . . . 3F **59**
Meadowside Pl. ML6: Air 4D **92**
Meadowside Quay Sq. G11: Kils . . . 2G **81**
Meadowside Quay Wlk.
  G11: Glas 2F **81**
Meadowside Rd. G65: Queen 3C **10**
Meadowside St. G11: Glas 2G **81**
  PA4: Renf 4F **59**
Meadow Sports Cen. 3F **17**
Meadows., The PA6: Hous 2D **74**
Meadow St. ML5: Coat 1D **110**
Meadow Vw. G67: Cumb 1C **36**
  ML6: Plain 1G **93**
Meadow Wlk. ML5: Coat 5D **90**
Meadow Way G77: Newt M 4D **132**
Meadowwell St. G32: Glas 6B **86**
Meadside Av. PA10: Kilb 1A **94**
Meadside Rd. PA10: Kilb. 1A **94**
Mealkirk St. G81: Faif 6E **23**
MEARNS 6E **133**
MEARNS CASTLE 6G **133**
Mearns Castle. 6G **133**
Mearns Ct. ML3: Ham 4A **154**
Mearnscroft Gdns. G77: Newt M . . . 6F **133**
Mearnscroft Rd. G77: Newt M 6F **133**
Mearnskirk Rd. G77: Newt M 6D **132**
Mearns Rd. G76: Clar 3H **133**
Mearns Rd. G77: Newt M. 6E **133**
  ML1: Moth 1E **143**
Mearns Way G64: B'rig 5F **49**
Medlar Ct. G72: Flem 4F **123**
Medlar Rd. G67: Cumb 3D **36**
Medrox Gdns. G67: Cumb 2B **54**
Medwin Ct. G75: E Kil 4A **148**
Medwin Gdns. G75: E Kil 4A **148**
Medwin St. G72: Camb 2D **122**
Medwyn St. G14: Glas 6D **60**
  (not continuous)
Meek Pl. G72: Camb 2B **122**
Meetinghouse La. PA1: Pais 6A **78**
Megan Ga. G40: Glas. 1B **104**
Megan St. G40: Glas 1B **104**
Meigle Rd. ML6: Air 1H **111**
Meikle Av. PA4: Renf 1E **79**
Meikle Cres. ML3: Ham. 4G **153**
MEIKLE EARNOCK 4G **153**
Meikle Earnock Rd. ML3: Ham 5D **152**
Meiklehill Ct. G66: Kirk 4E **31**
  (not continuous)
Meiklehill Rd. G66: Kirk 4E **31**
Meiklem St. ML4: Moss. 2E **127**
Meiklerig Cres. G53: Glas 3C **100**
MEIKLERIGGS 3F **97**
Meiklerigg Ct. PA2: Pais 3F **97**
Meikleriggs Dr. PA2: Pais 4E **97**
Meikle Rd. G53: Glas 5C **100**
Meiklewood Rd. G51: Glas 5D **80**
  (not continuous)
Melbourne Av. G75: E Kil 4E **149**
  G81: Clyd 2H **41**
Melbourne Ct. G46: Giff. 4B **118**
Melbourne Grn. G75: E Kil 3E **149**
Melbourne St. G31: Glas 5B **84**
Meldon Pl. G51: Glas 4D **80**
Meldrum Gdns. G41: Glas 3B **102**
Meldrum Mains ML6: Glenm. 5G **71**
Meldrum St. G81: Clyd. 1F **59**
Melford Av. G46: Giff 5B **118**
  G66: Kirk 5B **30**
Melford Ct. G81: Clyd. 5E **43**
Melford Rd. ML4: Bell 1H **125**
Melford Way PA3: Pais 3D **78**
Melfort Av. G41: Glas. 1H **101**
  G81: Clyd 4D **42**
Melfort Gdns. PA10: John 4C **94**
Melfort Path ML2: Newm 2D **146**
  (off Kildonan Ct.)

Melfort Quad. ML1: N'hill 4D **128**
  (off Glenmore Rd.)
Melfort Rd. ML3: Ham 6C **140**
Mellerstain Dr. G14: Glas 3G **59**
Mellerstain Gro. G14: Glas 3H **59**
Melness Pl. G51: Glas. 4D **80**
Melrose Av. G69: Barg. 6D **88**
  G73: Ruth. 6D **104**
  ML1: Holy. 1B **128**
  ML6: Chap. 3D **112**
  PA2: Pais 4E **97**
  PA3: Lin 6H **75**
Melrose Ct. G73: Ruth. 6D **104**
  (off Dunard Rd.)
Melrose Cres. ML2: Wis 4G **145**
Melrose Gdns. G20: Glas 6D **62**
  G65: Twe 1C **32**
  (off Glen Shirva Rd.)
  G71: Tann. 4D **108**
Melrose Pl. G72: Blan 6A **124**
  ML5: Coat. 4B **90**
  ML9: Lark. 4E **161**
Melrose Rd. G67: Cumb 6G **35**
Melrose St. G4: Glas 1A **4**
  ML3: Ham 4F **141**
Melrose Ter. G74: E Kil 6H **137**
  ML3: Ham 3F **141**
Melvaig Pl. G20: Glas 4B **62**
Melvick Pl. G51: Glas 4D **80**
Melville Ct. G1: Glas 6F **5**
Melville Cres. ML1: Moth 3H **143**
Melville Dr. ML1: Moth 3G **143**
Melville Gdns. G64: B'rig 5C **48**
Melville Pk. G74: E Kil. 6B **138**
Melville Pl. ML8: Carl 3E **165**
Melville St. G41: Glas 2D **102**
Memel St. G21: Glas 4A **64**
Memus Av. G52: Glas 1C **100**
Mennock Ct. ML3: Ham 1C **152**
Mennock Dr. G64: B'rig 3C **48**
Mennock St. ML1: Cle 5H **129**
Menock Rd. G44: Glas 1F **119**
Menteith Av. G64: B'rig 6D **48**
Menteith Dr. G73: Ruth 5F **121**
Menteith Gdns. G61: Bear 5C **24**
Menteith Loan ML1: Holy 2A **128**
Menteith Pl. G73: Ruth 5F **121**
Menteith Rd. ML1: Moth 2G **143**
Menzies Dr. G21: Glas. 4C **64**
Menzies Pl. G21: Glas 4C **64**
Menzies Rd. G21: Glas 3D **64**
Merchant La. G1: Glas. 5G **83**
Merchants Cl. PA10: Kilb 2A **94**
Merchants Ho. 5E **5**
Merchiston Av. PA3: Lin. 6F **75**
Merchiston Dr. PA5: Brkfld 6D **74**
Merchiston St. G32: Glas. 4G **85**
Merkins Av. G82: Dumb. 1H **17**
MERKLAND 4G **31**
Merkland Ct. G11: Glas 2H **81**
  G66: Kirk. 4F **31**
Merkland Dr. G66: Kirk 4G **31**
Merkland Pl. G66: Kirk 4F **31**
Merkland Rd. ML5: Coat 1G **89**
Merkland St. G11: Glas 1H **81**
Merksworth Way PA3: Pais 4A **78**
  (off Mosslands Rd.)
Merlewood Av. G71: Both 3F **125**
Merlin Av. ML4: Bell 6C **110**
Merlinford Av. PA4: Renf. 6G **59**
Merlinford Cres.
  PA4: Renf 6G **59**
Merlinford Dr. PA4: Renf 6G **59**
Merlinford Way PA4: Renf 6G **59**
Merlin Way PA3: Pais 4D **78**
Merrick Ct. ML6: Air 1B **92**
Merrick Gdns. G51: Glas 6H **81**
  G61: Bear 6C **24**
Merrick Path G51: Glas 6H **81**
  (off Merrick Gdns.)
Merrick Ter. G71: View. 6F **109**
Merrick Way G73: Ruth 4D **120**
Merryburn Av. G46: Giff 2B **118**
Merrycrest Av. G46: Giff 3A **118**

Merrycroft Av. G46: Giff 3B 118
Merryflats G65: Twe 1D 32
Merryland Pl. G51: Glas 4H 81
Merryland St. G51: Glas 4H 81
(not continuous)
MERRYLEE 3B 118
Merrylee Cres. G46: Giff 2A 118
Merrylee Pk. Av. G46: Giff 3A 118
Merrylee Pk. M. G46: Giff 2A 118
Merrylee Rd. G43: Glas 2D 118
G44: Glas 2D 118
Merrylees Rd. G72: Blan 2A 140
Merryston Ct. ML5: Coat 5A 90
Merrystone St. ML5: Coat 4B 90
Merry St. ML1: Carf 6B 128
ML1: Moth 2G 143
(not continuous)
Merryton Av. G15: Glas 4B 44
G46: Giff 3A 118
Merryton Gdns. G15: Glas 4B 44
Merryton Rd. ML1: Moth 1B 156
ML9: Lark 5H 155
Merryton St. ML9: Lark 6H 155
Merryton Twr. ML1: Moth 1B 156
Merryvale Av. G46: Giff 2B 118
Merryvale Pl. G46: Giff 2A 118
Merton Dr. G52: Glas 6A 80
Meryon Gdns. G32: Glas 2D 106
Meryon Rd. G32: Glas 2D 106
Methil St. G14: Glas 6C 60
Methlan Pk. G82: Dumb 5E 17
Methlick Av. ML6: Air 1G 111
Methuen Rd. PA3: Pais 2B 78
Methven Av. G61: Bear 2H 45
Methven Pl. G74: E Kil 1E 149
Methven Rd. G46: Giff 3G 133
Methven St. G31: Glas 2F 105
G81: Clyd 3B 42
Methven Ter. ML5: Coat 2D 90
Metropole La. G1: Glas 5G 83
Mews La. PA3: Pais 4B 78
Mey Ct. G77: Newt M. 5A 132
Mey Pl. G77: Newt M. 5A 132
M8 Food Pk. G21: Glas 1H 83
Michael McParland Dr.
G64: Torr 5D 28
Michael Ter. ML6: Chap 4D 112
Micklehouse Oval G69: Bail 5H 87
Micklehouse Pl. G69: Bail 5H 87
Micklehouse Rd. G69: Bail 5H 87
Micklehouse Wynd G69: Bail 5H 87
Midas Pl. ML4: Moss 2G 127
Mid Barrwood Rd. G65: Kils 4A 12
Mid Carbarns ML2: Wis. 2D 156
Midcroft G64: B'rig 4A 48
Midcroft Av. G44: Glas 2H 119
Middlefield G75: E Kil 6G 149
Middlehouse Ct. ML8: Carl 3D 164
Middlemuir Av. G66: Lenz 2D 50
Middlemuir Rd. G66: Lenz 1D 50
Middlerigg Rd. G68: Cumb 3F 35
Middlesex Gdns G41: Glas 5C 82
Middlesex St. G41: Glas 6C 82
Middleton Av. ML9: Lark 5F 161
Middleton Dr. G62: Miln 3H 25
Middleton Rd. PA3: Lin 5A 76
PA3: Pais 5F 77
Middleton St. G51: Glas 5A 82
Middleward St. G81: Faif 6F 23
Midfaulds Av. PA4: Renf 1G 79
Midland St. G1: Glas 4F 83 (6C 4)
Midlem Dr. G52: Glas 6C 80
Midlem Oval G52: Glas 6C 80
Midlock St. G51: Glas 6A 82
Midlothian Dr. G41: Glas 4B 102
Mid Park G75: E Kil 3G 149
Mid Rd. G67: Cumb 1H 55
Midton Rd. PA9: How 6B 94
Midton St. G21: Glas 6B 64
Mid Wharf St. G4: Glas 1G 83 (1F 5)
Migvie Pl. G20: Glas 4B 62
Milford G75: E Kil 4D 148
Milford St. G33: Glas 3A 86
Millands Av. G72: Blan 6A 124

Millarbank St. G21: Glas 5A 64
Millar Gro. ML3: Ham 5E 141
Millar Pk. ML3: Ham 5F 141
Millars Pl. G66: Lenz 3D 50
MILLARSTON 1E 97
Millarston Av. PA1: Pais 1E 97
Millarston Ct. PA1: Pais. 1F 97
Millarston Dr. PA1: Pais 1E 97
Millarston Ind. Est. PA1: Pais . . . 2E 97
Millar St. PA1: Pais 6B 78
Millar Ter. G73: Ruth 4D 104
Millbank Av. ML4: Bell. 4D 126
Millbank Rd. ML2: Wis 1F 157
Millbeg Cres. G33: Glas 5E 87
Millbeg Pl. G33: Glas 6E 87
Mill Brae PA11: Bri W 3F 73
Millbrae Av. G69: Chry 1B 68
Millbrae Ct. G42: Glas 6D 102
ML5: Coat 6H 89
Millbrae Cres. G42: Glas 6C 102
G81: Clyd 2F 59
Millbrae Gdns. G42: Glas 6D 102
Millbrae Rd. G43: Glas 6C 102
Millbrix Av. G14: Glas 4A 60
Millbrook G74: E Kil. 1D 148
Millburn Av. G73: Ruth 1C 120
G81: Clyd 1G 59
PA4: Renf 6F 59
Millburn Ct. G75: E Kil 4A 148
Millburn Cres. G82: Dumb 4H 17
Millburn Dr. PA4: Renf. 6G 59
Millburn Gdns. G75: E Kil 4A 148
Millburn La. ML9: Lark 3G 161
Millburn Pl. ML9: Lark 5F 161
Millburn Rd. G82: Dumb 4H 17
ML9: Ashg 4B 162
PA4: Renf 6F 59
Millburn St. G21: Glas 2C 84
G66: Len 3F 7
ML1: Moth 2G 143
Millburn Way G75: E Kil 4A 148
PA4: Renf 6G 59
Mill Ct. G73: Ruth 5C 104
ML3: Ham 1G 153
Mill Cres. G40: Glas 2B 104
G64: Torr 4E 29
Millcroft Rd. G67: Cumb 4B 36
(Sth. Carbrain Rd.)
G67: Cumb 3G 55
(Summerhill & Garngibbock Rd)
G73: Ruth 3B 104
Milldam Rd. G81: Faif 6E 23
Millennium Ct. G34: Glas 3A 88
Millennium Gdns. G34: Glas 3A 88
Millennium Pk. 2D 82
(off Ashley St.)
Miller Cl. G64: B'rig 1F 65
Miller Ct. G82: Dumb 3H 17
Miller Dr. G64: B'rig 1F 65
Millerfield Pl. G40: Glas 2D 104
ML3: Ham 6B 142
Millerfield Rd. G40: Glas. 2D 104
Miller Gdns. G64: B'rig 1F 65
Miller Pl. G64: B'rig 1F 65
Millerslea G82: Milt 4F 19
(off Colquhoun Rd.)
MILLERSNEUK 3E 51
Millersneuk Av. G66: Lenz 3D 50
Millersneuk Ct. G66: Lenz 3D 50
Millersneuk Cres. G33: Mille. . . . 4A 66
Millersneuk Dr. G66: Lenz 3D 50
Millersneuk Rd. G66: Lenz 3D 50
(not continuous)
Miller's Pl. ML6: Air 4B 92
MILLERSTON 5C 134
Millerston St. G40: Glas 5C 84
Miller St. G1: Glas 4G 83 (6E 5)
G69: Bail 1H 107
G81: Clyd 6D 42
G82: Dumb. 3H 17
ML2: Wis 6G 145
ML3: Ham 6B 142
ML5: Coat 6D 90
ML8: Carl 3F 165

Miller St. ML9: Lark 2E 161
PA5: John 2H 95
Miller Wlk. G64: B'rig 1F 65
Millfield Av. ML1: Moth. 1H 143
PA8: Ersk 6D 40
Millfield Cres. PA8: Ersk 6E 41
Millfield Dr. PA8: Ersk 1E 57
Millfield Gdns. PA8: Ersk. 6E 41
Millfield Hill PA8: Ersk 6D 40
Millfield La. PA8: Ersk 6D 40
Millfield Mdw. PA8: Ersk 6D 40
Millfield Pl. PA8: Ersk 6D 40
Millfield Vw. PA8: Ersk 6D 40
Millfield Wlk. PA8: Ersk. 1E 57
Millfield Wynd PA8: Ersk. 6D 40
Millford Dr. PA3: Lin 6H 75
Millgate G71: Tann 5D 108
Millgate Av. G71: Tann 5D 108
Millgate Ct. G71: Udd 6D 108
Millgate Rd. ML3: Ham. 2G 153
Mill Gro. ML3: Ham. 1G 153
MILLHEUGH 3C 160
Millheugh Brae ML9: Lark 3C 160
Millheugh Pl. G72: Blan. 3A 140
Millheugh Rd. ML3: Ham 6C 160
ML9: Lark 3C 160
Millholm Rd. G44: Glas 3F 119
Millhouse Cres. G20: Glas. 2A 62
Millhouse Dr. G20: Glas 2H 61
Millichen Rd. G23: Glas 3B 46
Milliken Dr. PA10: Kilb. 3C 94
MILLIKENPARK 4C 94
Millikenpark Station (Rail) 5C 94
Milliken Pk. Rd. PA10: Kilb. 4C 94
Milliken Pl. PA10: Kilb. 3C 94
(off Easwald Bank)
Milliken Rd. PA10: Kilb 3C 94
Mill Loan ML6: Air 3A 92
Mill of Gryffe Rd.
PA11: Bri W 3F 73
Mill Pk. ML3: Ham. 1G 153
Mill Pl. PA3: Lin 5G 75
Millport Av. G44: Glas 6G 103
Millrig G75: E Kil 6F 149
Millri. G66: Lenz 3D 50
Mill Rd. G65: Queen 4C 10
G71: Both 6E 125
G72: Camb 3D 122
(Hamilton Rd.)
G72: Camb 1C 122
(Westburn Rd.)
G78: Barr 4D 114
G81: Clyd 2F 59
ML1: Moth 2H 143
ML2: Newm 6G 147
ML6: Air 2A 92
ML8: Carl 4E 165
Millroad Dr. G40: Glas 5A 84
Millroad Gdns. G40: Glas 5B 84
(off Millroad Dr.)
Millroad St. G40: Glas 5A 84
(not continuous)
Millstream Ct. PA1: Pais 1B 98
Mill St. G40: Glas. 2B 104
G73: Ruth. 6C 104
(not continuous)
PA1: Pais 1B 98
Mill St. Ind. Est. ML6: Air 3A 92
Mill Vennel PA4: Renf 6F 59
Millview G78: Barr 4F 115
Millview Mdws. G78: Neil 2C 130
Millview Pl. G53: Glas 3B 116
Millview Ter. G78: Neil 2C 130
Mill Way G66: Kirk. 6G 31
Millwood St. G41: Glas 5C 102
MILNBANK 3C 84
Milnbank St. G31: Glas 3C 84
Milncroft Pl. G33: Glas 2A 86
Milncroft Rd. G33: Glas 2A 86
Milner La. G13: Glas 4E 61
Milner Rd. G13: Glas 4E 61
MILNGAVIE 3H 25
Milngavie Station (Rail) 4H 25
Milngavie Rd. G61: Bear 4F 45

Milnpark Gdns. G41: Glas 6B **82**
Milnpark St. G41: Glas. 6C **82**
MILNWOOD. 3E **127**
Milnwood Dr. ML1: Moth. 5E **127**
  ML4: Bell 3E **127**
Milovaig Av. G23: Glas 6B **46**
Milovaig St. G23: Glas. 6B **46**
Milrig Rd. G73: Ruth 6B **104**
Milroy Gdns. ML4: Bell 5C **110**
MILTON
  Dumbarton 4F **19**
  Glasgow 1G **63**
Milton Av. G72: Camb 2G **121**
Milton Brae G82: Milt. 1F **19**
Milton Ct. *G66: Kirk* *5E **31***
  (off Highfield Rd.)
  G82: Milt. 3F **19**
  ML6: Air. 3A **92**
Milton Cres. ML8: Carl 4F **165**
Milton Douglas Rd.
  G81: Dun, Hard 2C **42**
Milton Dr. G64: B'rig 2B **64**
Milton Gdns. G71: Tann 5C **108**
Milton Hill G82: Milt. 4F **19**
Milton Mains Rd. G81: Clyd 2C **42**
MILTON OF CAMPSIE. 5C **8**
Milton Rd. G66: Kirk 3C **30**
  G66: Len 4G **7**
  G74: E Kil 1C **148**
  ML8: Carl 5B **164**
Milton St. G4: Glas 2F **83** (2D **4**)
  ML1: Moth 1G **143**
  ML3: Ham 5E **141**
  ML6: Air 3A **92**
  ML8: Carl 3E **165**
Milton Ter. ML3: Ham 4E **141**
Milverton Av. G61: Bear. 1C **44**
Milverton Rd. G46: Giff 6G **117**
Mimosa Rd. PA11: Bri W 3F **73**
Mimosas, The *PA11: Bri W* *3F **73***
  (off Mimosa Rd.)
Minard Rd. G41: Glas 4C **102**
Minard Way G71: Tann 6E **109**
Mincher Cres. ML1: Moth 5G **143**
Minch Way ML6: Air 6C **92**
Minella Gdns. ML4: Bell 5C **110**
Minerva Ct. *G3: Glas* *3C **82***
  (off Houldsworth St.)
Minerva St. G3: Glas 3C **82**
Minerva Way G3: Glas. 3B **82**
Mingarry La. G20: Glas 5C **62**
Mingarry St. G20: Glas. 5C **62**
Mingulay Cres. G22: Glas 1H **63**
Mingulay Pl. G22: Glas 1A **64**
Mingulay St. G22: Glas. 1H **63**
Minister's Pk. G74: E Kil 5B **136**
Minmoir Rd. G53: Glas 6H **99**
Minster Wlk. G69: Barg 6D **88**
Minstrel Rd. G13: Glas 6D **44**
Minto Av. G73: Ruth. 3F **121**
Minto Cres. G52: Glas 6F **81**
Minto Pk. ML2: Wis 3A **146**
Minto St. G52: Glas 6F **81**
Mireton St. G22: Glas. 4F **63**
Mirren Ct. PA3: Pais 4B **78**
Mirren Dr. G81: Dun 6B **22**
Mirrlees Dr. G12: Glas. 5A **62**
Mirrlees La. G12: Glas 5A **62**
Mitchell Arc. G73: Ruth. 5D **104**
Mitchell Av. G72: Camb 1E **123**
  PA4: Renf. 1D **78**
Mitchell Ct. G74: E Kil 1E **149**
Mitchell Dr. G62: Miln 4A **26**
  G73: Ruth. 1D **120**
Mitchell Gro. G74: E Kil 1E **149**
Mitchell Hill Rd. G45: Glas 5B **120**
Mitchell La. G1: Glas 4F **83** (5D **4**)
Mitchell Rd. G67: Cumb 3A **36**
Mitchell St. G1: Glas. 4F **83** (6D **4**)
  ML5: Coat 1F **109**
  ML6: Air 3H **91**
Mitchell Theatre, The 3D **82**
Mitchison Rd. G67: Cumb 2A **36**
Mitre Ct. G11: Glas. 5F **61**

Mitre Ga. G11: Glas 6F **61**
Mitre La. G14: Glas 5E **61**
Mitre La. W. G14: Glas 5D **60**
Mitre Rd. G11: Glas 5F **61**
  G14: Glas 5D **60**
Moat Av. G13: Glas 2C **60**
Mochrum Rd. G43: Glas. 1C **118**
Moffat Ct. G75: E Kil 4A **148**
Moffat Gdns. G75: E Kil 4A **148**
Moffathill ML6: Gart. 6E **93**
Moffat Pl. G72: Blan. 6B **124**
  G75: E Kil 4A **148**
  ML5: Coat 1F **111**
  ML6: Air 3F **93**
Moffat Rd. ML6: Air 4F **93**
Moffat St. G5: Glas 1H **103**
Moffat Vw. ML6: Plain 1G **93**
Mogarth Av. PA2: Pais 5D **96**
Moidart Av. PA4: Renf 5D **58**
Moidart Ct. G78: Barr 3D **114**
Moidart Cres. G52: Glas 6F **81**
Moidart Gdns. G66: Kirk 4H **31**
  G77: Newt M 3E **133**
Moidart Pl. G52: Glas 6F **81**
Moidart Rd. G52: Glas 6E **81**
Moir St. G1: Glas. 5H **83**
Molendinar St. G1: Glas. 5H **83**
Molendinar Ter. G78: Neil 3C **130**
MOLLINSBURN 3H **53**
MOLLINSBURN JUNC. 4G **53**
Mollinsburn Rd. G67: Cumb 3A **54**
  ML5: Anna 6B **54**
Mollinsburn St. G21: Glas. 6A **64**
Mollins Ct. G68: Cumb 2H **53**
Mollins Rd. G68: Cumb. 1G **53**
MOLLINS RDBT. 3H **53**
Monach Rd. G33: Glas. 3C **86**
Monar Dr. G22: Glas. 6F **63**
Monar Pl. G22: Glas. 6F **63**
Monart Pl. G20: Glas 4D **62**
Monar Way *ML2: Newm* *3D **146***
  (off Murdostoun Vw.)
Moncrieff Av. G66: Lenz. 2C **50**
Moncrieffe Rd. ML6: Chap 1D **112**
Moncrieff Gdns. G66: Lenz 2D **50**
Moncrieff St. PA3: Pais 6A **78**
Moncur St. G40: Glas. 5A **84**
  (not continuous)
Moness Dr. G52: Glas 1E **101**
Money Gro. ML1: Moth 5B **144**
Monieburgh Cres. G65: Kils. 2A **12**
Monieburgh Rd. G65: Kils 2A **12**
Monifieth Av. G52: Glas. 2D **100**
Monikie Gdns. G64: B'rig. 6F **49**
Monkcastle Dr. G72: Camb 1A **122**
Monkdyke Ho. PA4: Renf 6F **59**
Monkland Av. G66: Kirk, Lenz. 6D **30**
Monkland La. ML5: Coat. 1A **110**
Monklands Ind. Est. ML5: Coat 3B **110**
Monkland St. ML6: Air 4B **92**
Monkland Ter. ML5: Glenb 3H **69**
Monkland Vw. G71: Tann 4E **109**
  ML6: C'bnk. 3B **112**
Monkland Vw. Cres. G69: Barg 1D **108**
Monksbridge Av. G13: Glas. 6C **44**
Monkscourt Av. ML6: Air 3G **91**
Monkscroft Av. G11: Glas. 6G **61**
Monkscroft Ct. G11: Glas 1G **81**
Monkscroft Gdns. G11: Glas. 6G **61**
Monks Rd. ML6: Air. 6C **92**
Monkton Dr. G15: Glas. 5B **44**
Monkton Gdns. G77: Newt M. 5G **133**
Monmouth Av. G12: Glas. 3G **61**
Monreith Av. G61: Bear. 5D **44**
Monreith Rd. G43: Glas. 1B **118**
Monreith Rd. E. G44: Glas 2E **119**
Monroe Dr. G71: Tann 4D **108**
Monroe Pl. G71: Tann 4D **108**
Montague La. G12: Glas 5H **61**
Montague St. G4: Glas. 1D **82**
Montalto Av. ML1: Carf 6A **128**
Montclair Pl. PA3: Lin 5H **75**

Montego Grn. G75: E Kil 2C **148**
Monteith Dr. G76: Clar. 1D **134**
Monteith Gdns. G76: Clar 1D **134**
Monteith Pl. G40: Glas. 6A **84**
  G72: Blan 1C **140**
Monteith Row G40: Glas 5H **83**
Montford Av. G44: Glas. 6H **103**
  G73: Ruth. 6A **104**
Montgarrie St. G51: Glas. 5D **80**
Montgomery Av. ML5: Coat 4B **90**
  PA3: Pais 4D **78**
Montgomery Ct. PA3: Pais. 4D **78**
Montgomery Cres. ML2: Wis. 2E **157**
Montgomery Dr. G46: Giff 6A **118**
  PA10: Kilb. 1A **94**
Montgomery Pl. G74: E Kil 1H **149**
  ML9: Lark 3F **161**
Montgomery Rd. PA3: Pais 3C **78**
Montgomery St. G72: Camb 2D **122**
  G74: E Kil 1H **149**
  ML9: Lark. 1E **161**
Montgomery Ter. G40: Glas 1C **104**
  G66: Milt C 6B **8**
Montgomery Wynd *G74: E Kil* . . . *1H **149***
  (off Montgomery St.)
Montraive St. G73: Ruth 4E **105**
Montrave Path G52: Glas. 1D **100**
Montrave St. G52: Glas 1D **100**
Montreal Ho. G81: Clyd 1H **41**
Montreal Pk. G75: E Kil 2E **149**
Montrose Av. G32: Carm 4B **106**
  G52: Hill 3G **79**
Montrose Ct. PA2: Pais 5D **96**
Montrose Cres. ML3: Ham 5H **141**
Montrose Dr. G61: Bear 6E **25**
Montrose Gdns. G62: Miln. 2H **25**
  G65: Kils 2G **11**
  G72: Blan 5A **124**
Montrose La. ML3: Ham 5G **141**
Montrose Pl. PA3: Lin 5G **75**
Montrose Rd. PA2: Pais. 5D **96**
Montrose St. G1: Glas 4H **83** (5G **5**)
  G81: Clyd 5D **42**
  ML1: Moth 6F **127**
Montrose Ter. G64: B'rig 2E **65**
  PA11: Bri W 4F **73**
Montrose Way PA2: Pais 5D **96**
Monument Dr. G33: Glas 4G **65**
Monymusk Gdns. G64: B'rig. 5F **49**
Monymusk Pl. G15: Glas. 2G **43**
MOODIESBURN. 5D **52**
Moodiesburn St. G33: Glas 1F **85**
Moorburn Av. G46: Giff 4H **117**
Moorburn Pl. PA3: Lin 5E **75**
Moorcroft Dr. ML6: Air. 4E **93**
Moorcroft Rd. G77: Newt M. 6C **132**
Moore Dr. G61: Bear. 4F **45**
Moore Gdns. ML3: Ham. 4A **154**
Moore St. G31: Glas. 5B **84**
  ML1: New S 4A **128**
Moorfield Cres. ML6: Air 4F **93**
Moorfield Rd. G72: Blan 3A **140**
Moorfoot G64: B'rig 5E **49**
Moorfoot Av. G46: T'bnk 4G **117**
  PA2: Pais 4H **97**
Moorfoot Dr. ML2: Wis. 6F **145**
Moorfoot Path PA2: Pais. 5H **97**
Moorfoot St. G32: Glas. 5G **85**
Moorfoot Way G61: Bear. 5B **24**
Moorhill Cres. G77: Newt M 6C **132**
Moorhill Rd. G77: Newt M. 5C **132**
Moorhouse Av. G13: Glas 3H **59**
  PA2: Pais 3F **97**
Moorhouse St. G78: Barr 5E **115**
Moorings, The PA2: Pais 2F **97**
Moorland Dr. ML6: Air 4F **93**
MOORPARK 1D **78**
Moorpark Av. G52: Glas. 5H **79**
  G69: Muirh 2A **68**
  ML6: Air 4E **93**
Moorpark Ct. PA4: Renf. 1D **78**
Moorpark Pl. G52: Glas. 5H **79**
Moorpark Sq. PA4: Renf 1D **78**
Moor Rd. G62: Miln 3H **25**

Moorside St. ML8: Carl 3G 165
Morag Av. G72: Blan 6A 124
Moraine Av. G15: Glas 6A 44
Moraine Cir. G15: Glas 6A 44
Moraine Dr. G15: Glas 6A 44
   G76: Clar 1B 134
Moraine Pl. G15: Glas 6B 44
Morar Av. G81: Clyd 3D 42
Morar Ct. G67: Cumb 5D 34
   G81: Clyd 3D 42
   ML3: Ham 2E 153
   ML5: Coat 2H 89
   ML6: Air 1G 91
   PA7: B'ton 5A 40
Morar Dr. G61: Bear 4H 45
   G67: Cumb 6D 34
   G73: Ruth 4D 120
   G81: Clyd 3D 42
   PA2: Pais 3D 96
   PA3: Lin 6G 75
Morar Pl. G74: E Kil 6H 137
   G77: Newt M 2D 132
   G81: Clyd 3D 42
   PA4: Renf 5D 58
Morar Rd. G52: Glas 6E 81
   G81: Clyd 3D 42
Morar St. ML2: Wis 2G 157
Morar Ter. G71: View 6F 109
   G73: Ruth 4F 121
Morar Way ML1: N'hill 4C 128
Moravia Av. G71: Both 4E 125
Moray Av. ML6: Air 6A 92
Moray Ct. G73: Ruth 5C 104
Moray Dr. G64: Torr 4D 28
   G76: Clar 2D 134
Moray Gdns. G68: Cumb 6H 13
   G71: Tann 5D 108
   G76: Clar 1D 134
Moray Ga. G71: Both 3C 124
Moray Pl. G41: Glas 3C 102
   G64: B'rig 6E 49
   G66: Kirk 4G 31
   G69: Chry 1B 68
   G72: Blan 3A 140
   PA3: Lin 5G 75
Moray Quad. ML4: Bell 2C 126
Moray Way ML1: Holy 2A 128
Mordaunt St. G40: Glas 2C 104
Moredun Cres. G32: Glas 4C 86
Moredun Dr. PA2: Pais 4F 97
Moredun Rd. PA2: Pais 4F 97
Moredun St. G32: Glas 4C 86
Morefield Rd. G51: Glas 4D 80
Morgan M. G42: Glas 2F 103
Morgan St. ML3: Ham 1H 153
   ML9: Lark 2D 160
Morina Gdns. G53: Glas 4C 116
Morion Rd. G13: Glas 1D 60
Morison Ho. G67: Cumb 3A 36
             (off Burns Rd.)
Moriston Ct. G72: Newm 3D 146
Morland G74: E Kil 4D 138
Morley St. G42: Glas 6E 103
Morna La. G14: Glas 1E 81
           (off Glendore St.)
MORNINGSIDE 6G 147
Morningside Rd.
   ML2: Newm 4E 147
Morningside St. G33: Glas 3F 85
Morrin Path G21: Glas 6A 64
Morrin St. G21: Glas 5A 64
Morris Cres. G72: Blan 2B 140
   ML1: Cle 6E 129
Morrishall Rd. G74: E Kil 5C 138
Morrison Dr. G66: Len 4G 7
Morrison Gdns. G64: Torr 5E 29
Morrison Pl. PA11: Bri W 3F 73
           (off Main St.)
Morrison Quad. G81: Clyd 6G 43
Morrison St. G5: Glas 5E 83
   G81: Dun 1B 42

Morris St. ML3: Ham 2H 153
   ML9: Lark 4G 161
Morriston Cres. PA4: Renf 2H 79
Morriston Pk. Dr. G72: Camb 1A 122
Morriston St. G72: Camb 1A 122
Morton Gdns. G41: Glas 4A 102
Morton St. ML1: Moth 1G 143
Morton Ter. PA11: Bri W 3E 73
      (off Horsewood Rd.)
Morvan St. G52: Glas 6E 81
Morven Av. G64: B'rig 6E 49
   G72: Blan 6A 124
   PA2: Pais 5H 97
Morven Dr. G76: Clar 1B 134
   PA3: Lin 6G 75
Morven Gait PA8: Ersk 1A 58
Morven Gdns. G71: Tann 5D 108
Morven La. G72: Blan 6A 124
Morven Rd. G61: Bear 1E 45
   G72: Camb 4H 121
Morven St. ML5: Coat 3C 90
Morven Way G66: Kirk 5H 31
   PA3: Both 4F 125
Mosesfield St. G21: Glas 4B 64
Mosque Av. G5: Glas 6G 83
Mossacre Rd. ML2: Wis 5A 146
Moss Av. PA3: Lin 5H 75
Mossbank G72: Blan 3B 140
   G75: E Kil 3B 148
Mossbank Av. G33: Glas 5H 65
Mossbank Cres. ML1: N'hill 3F 129
Mossbank Dr. G33: Glas 5H 65
Mossbank Rd. ML2: Wis 5A 146
Mossbell Rd. ML4: Bell 1A 126
Mossblown St. ML9: Lark 2D 160
Mossburn Rd. ML2: Wis 6B 146
Mossburn St. ML2: Wis 2B 158
Mosscastle Rd. G33: Glas 1C 86
Mossdale G74: E Kil 6E 137
Mossdale Ct. ML4: Bell 2F 127
Mossdale Gdns. ML3: Ham 1C 152
Moss Dr. G78: Barr 2C 114
   PA8: Ersk 2F 57
Mossedge Ind. Est. PA3: Lin 5A 76
MOSSEND 2E 127
Mossend La. G33: Glas 3D 86
Mossend St. G33: Glas 3D 86
Mossgiel G75: E Kil 4D 148
Mossgiel Av. G73: Ruth 2C 120
Mossgiel Cres. G76: Busby 4D 134
Mossgiel Dr. G81: Clyd 4E 43
Mossgiel Gdns. G66: Kirk 4F 31
   G71: Tann 5C 108
Mossgiel La. ML9: Lark 4G 161
      (off Keir Hardie La.)
Mossgiel Pl. G73: Ruth 2C 120
Mossgiel Rd. G43: Glas 1B 118
     (Doonfoot Rd., not continuous)
   G43: Glas 6B 102
           (Newlands Rd.)
   G67: Cumb 2B 36
         (not continuous)
Mossgiel Ter. G72: Blan 5A 124
Mosshall Av. ML1: N'hill 3C 128
Mosshall Gro. ML1: N'hill 3F 129
Mosshall Rd. ML1: N'hse 6D 112
Mosshall St. ML1: N'hill 3F 129
Mosshead Rd. G61: Bear 6F 25
Moss Hgts. Av. G52: Glas 6D 80
Mosshill Rd. ML4: Bell 5D 110
Moss Knowe G67: Cumb 3C 36
Mossland Dr. ML2: Wis 5A 146
Mossland Rd. G52: Hill 3F 79
   PA4: Renf 2H 79
Mosslands Rd. PA3: Pais 3H 77
Mosslingal G75: E Kil 6G 149
Mossmulloch G75: E Kil 6G 149
MOSSNEUK 4B 148
Mossneuk Av. G75: E Kil 3A 148
Mossneuk Cres. ML2: Wis 5B 146
Mossneuk Dr. G75: E Kil 4B 148
   ML2: Wis 5A 146
   PA2: Pais 5G 97
Mossneuk Pk. ML2: Wis 5A 146

Mossneuk Rd. G75: E Kil 3B 148
Mossneuk St. ML5: Coat 2B 110
MOSSPARK 2E 101
Mosspark Av. G52: Glas 2F 101
   G62: Miln 2G 25
Mosspark Blvd. G52: Glas 1E 101
Mosspark Dr. G52: Glas 1C 100
Mosspark La. G52: Glas 2E 101
Mosspark Oval G52: Glas 2E 101
Mosspark Rd. G62: Miln 2G 25
   ML5: Coat 3H 89
Mosspark Sq. G52: Glas 2E 101
Mosspark Station (Rail) 2C 100
Moss Path G69: Bail 2F 107
Moss Rd. G51: Glas 3D 80
   G66: Kirk 6H 31
   G66: Lenz 1B 50
   G67: Cumb 2E 37
   G69: Muirh 2A 68
   ML2: Wis 6C 146
   ML6: Air 5A 92
   PA11: Bri W 3G 73
   PA6: Hous 1H 75
Moss Side Av. ML6: Air 3G 91
Mossside Dr. G41: Glas 3D 164
   ML8: Carl 5A 92
Mossside Rd. G41: Glas 4B 102
Moss St. PA1: Pais 6A 78
Mossvale Cres. G33: Glas 1C 86
Mossvale La. PA3: Pais 5H 77
Mossvale Path G33: Glas 6C 66
Mossvale Rd. G33: Glas 6B 66
Mossvale Sq. G33: Glas 1B 86
   PA3: Pais 5H 77
Mossvale St. PA3: Pais 4H 77
Mossvale Ter. G69: Mood 4E 53
Mossvale Wlk. G33: Glas 1C 86
Mossvale Way G33: Glas 1C 86
Mossview Cres. ML6: Air 5A 92
Mossview La. G52: Glas 6C 80
Mossview Quad. G52: Glas 6D 80
Mossview Rd. G33: Step 4E 67
Mosswell Rd. G62: Miln 2H 25
Mossywood Ct. G68: Cumb 6B 34
Mossywood Pl. G68: Cumb 6B 34
Mossywood Rd. G68: Cumb 6B 34
Mote Hill ML3: Ham 5A 142
Motehill Rd. PA3: Pais 5C 78
MOTHERWELL 3G 143
Motherwell Bus. Cen.
   ML1: Moth 2H 143
Motherwell Concert Hall &
   Theatre Complex 4H 143
Motherwell F.C. 5H 143
Motherwell Heritage Cen. 3F 143
           (off High Rd.)
Motherwell Rd. ML1: Carf 6C 128
   ML1: N'hse 2G 129
   ML3: Ham 5C 142
   ML4: Bell 2C 126
Motherwell Station (Rail) 2G 143
Motherwell St. ML6: Air 2C 92
Moulin Cir. G52: Glas 1A 100
Moulin Pl. G52: Glas 1A 100
Moulin Rd. G52: Glas 1A 100
Moulin Ter. G52: Glas 1A 100
Mountainblue St. G31: Glas 6C 84
Mt. Annan Dr. G44: Glas 6F 103
MOUNTBLOW 2G 41
Mountblow Rd. G81: Clyd, Dun 1H 41
Mt. Cameron Dr. Nth. G74: E Kil . . . 3A 150
Mt. Cameron Dr. Sth. G74: E Kil . . . 3A 150
MOUNT ELLEN 2C 68
MOUNT FLORIDA 5F 103
Mount Florida Station (Rail) 5E 103
Mountgarrie Path G51: Glas 4D 80
Mountgarrie Rd. G51: Glas 4D 80
Mt. Harriet Av. G33: Step 3E 67
Mt. Harriet Dr. G33: Step 3D 66
Mountherrick G75: E Kil 6G 149
Mt. Lockhart G71: Udd 3H 107
Mt. Lockhart Gdns. G71: Udd 3H 107
Mt. Lockhart Pl. G71: Udd 3H 107
Mt. Pleasant Cres. G66: Milt C 5B 8
Mt. Pleasant Ho. G60: Old K 1E 41

Mt. Pleasant Pl.—Napier Pl.

Mt. Pleasant Pl. *G60: Old K* 1F **41**
(off Station Rd.)
G60: Old K 1F **41**
(off Mt. Pleasant Rd.)
Mt. Pleasant Rd. G60: Old K 6F **21**
Mt. Stewart St. ML8: Carl 3E **165**
Mount St. G20: Glas 6D **62**
Mt. Stuart St. G41: Glas 5C **102**
Mount, The ML1: Moth 3F **143**
MOUNT VERNON 3D **106**
Mt. Vernon Av. G32: Glas 3E **107**
ML5: Coat 4A **90**
Mount Vernon Station (Rail) 3F **107**
Mournian Way ML3: Ham 2H **153**
Mowbray G74: E Kil 5C **138**
Mowbray Av. G69: G'csh 4D **68**
Moyne Rd. G53: Glas 3A **100**
Moy Path *ML2: Newm* 3D **146**
(off Murdostoun Vw.)
Muckcroft Rd. G66: Kirk, Lenz 3H **51**
G69: Chry, Lenz 3H **51**
Mugdock Rd. G62: Miln 3G **25**
Mugdock Rd. S. G62: Miln 3G **25**
Muirbank Av. G73: Ruth 6B **104**
Muirbank Gdns. G73: Ruth 6B **104**
Muirbrae Rd. G73: Ruth 3D **120**
Muirbrae Way G73: Ruth 3D **120**
Muirburn Av. G44: Glas 3C **118**
Muir Ct. G44: Neth 5C **118**
(not continuous)
Muircroft Dr. ML1: Cle 5H **129**
Muirdrum Av. G52: Glas 2D **100**
Muirdyke Rd. ML5: Coat 3H **89**
ML5: Glenb 5B **70**
Muirdykes Av. G52: Glas 6A **80**
Muirdykes Rd. G52: Glas 6A **80**
PA3: Pais 4F **77**
Muiredge Ct. G71: Udd 1D **124**
Muiredge Ter. G69: Bail 1H **107**
MUIREND 3D **118**
Muirend Av. G44: Glas 3D **118**
Muirend Rd. G44: Glas 3C **118**
Muirend Station (Rail) 3D **118**
Muirfield Ct. G44: Glas 3D **118**
Muirfield Cres. G23: Glas 6C **46**
Muirfield Mdws. G71: Both 5C **124**
Muirfield Rd. G68: Cumb 6A **14**
MUIRHEAD
Glasgow 1H **107**
North Lanarkshire 2A **68**
MUIRHEAD-BRAEHEAD INTERCHANGE 3A **36**
Muirhead Cotts. G66: Kirk 6H **31**
Muirhead Ct. G69: Bail 1A **108**
Muirhead Dr. ML1: N'hill 3F **129**
ML8: Law 5E **159**
PA3: Lin 6G **75**
Muirhead Gdns. G69: Bail 1A **108**
Muirhead Ga. G71: Tann 5F **109**
Muirhead Gro. G69: Bail 1A **108**
Muirhead Rd. G69: Bail 2H **107**
G78: Neil 4A **130**
MUIRHEAD RDBT. 2B **36**
Muirhead St. G66: Kirk 6C **30**
Muirhead Ter. ML1: Moth 5G **143**
Muirhead Way G64: B'rig 6F **49**
Muirhill Av. G44: Glas 3C **118**
Muirhill Cres. G13: Glas 2A **60**
MUIRHOUSE 1B **156**
Muirhouse Av. ML1: Moth 6B **144**
ML2: Newm 3F **147**
Muirhouse Dr. ML1: Moth 1B **156**
Muirhouse La. G75: E Kil 3H **149**
Muirhouse Pk. G61: Bear 5D **24**
Muirhouse Rd. ML1: Moth 1B **156**
Muirhouse St. G41: Glas 2E **103**
Muirhouse Twr. ML1: Moth 6B **144**
Muirhouse Works G41: Glas 2E **103**
Muirkirk Dr. G13: Glas 2F **61**
ML3: Ham 1B **152**
Muirlee Rd. ML8: Carl 4H **165**
Muirlees Cres. G62: Miln 3E **25**
Muirmadkin Rd. ML4: Bell 2D **126**
Muirpark Av. PA4: Renf 1E **79**
Muirpark Dr. G52: Glas 5A **80**
G64: B'rig 1C **64**
Muirpark St. G11: Glas 1H **81**
Muirpark Ter. G64: B'rig 1B **64**
Muir Rd. G82: Dumb 1H **17**
Muirshiel Av. G53: Glas 1C **116**
Muirshiel Ct. G53: Glas 2C **116**
Muirshiel Cres. G53: Glas 1C **116**
Muirshot Rd. ML9: Lark 1F **161**
Muirside Av. G32: Glas 2E **107**
G66: Kirk 5G **31**
Muirside Pl. ML2: Newm 3D **146**
Muirside Rd. G69: Bail 1H **107**
PA3: Pais 4F **77**
Muirside St. G69: Bail 1H **107**
Muirskeith Cres. G43: Glas 1D **118**
Muirskeith Pl. G43: Glas 1D **118**
Muirskeith Rd. G43: Glas 1D **118**
Muir St. G64: B'rig 6C **48**
G72: Blan 3B **140**
ML1: Moth 1F **143**
ML3: Ham 5H **141**
ML5: Coat 4A **90**
ML8: Law 5D **158**
ML9: Lark 2E **161**
PA4: Renf 5F **59**
Muir Ter. PA3: Pais 4C **78**
Muirton Dr. G64: B'rig 4B **48**
Muiryfauld Dr. G31: Glas 1G **105**
Muiryhall St. ML5: Coat 4C **90**
Muiryhall St. E. ML5: Coat 4D **90**
Mulben Cres. G53: Glas 6H **99**
Mulben Pl. G53: Glas 6H **99**
Mulben Ter. G53: Glas 5H **99**
Mulberry Cres. ML6: Chap 2E **113**
Mulberry Dr. G75: E Kil 6E **149**
Mulberry Rd. G43: Glas 2B **118**
G71: View 4G **109**
Mulberry Way G75: E Kil 6E **149**
Mulberry Wynd G72: Flem 4F **123**
Mull G74: E Kil 3C **150**
ML6: Air 6D **92**
Mullardoch St. *G23: Glas* 6B **46**
(off Rothes Dr.)
Mull Av. PA2: Pais 6A **98**
PA4: Renf 2E **79**
Mull Ct. ML3: Ham 2D **152**
Mullen Ct. G33: Step 4F **67**
Mull Quad. ML2: Wis 4C **146**
Mull St. G21: Glas 1D **84**
Mulvey Cres. ML6: Air 4G **91**
Mungo Pk. G75: E Kil 3F **149**
Mungo Pl. G71: Tann 4E **109**
Munlochy Rd. G51: Glas 4D **80**
Munro Ct. G81: Dun 1B **42**
Munro Dr. G66: Milt C 6B **8**
Munro La. G13: Glas 4E **61**
Munro La. E. G13: Glas 4E **61**
Munro Pl. G13: Glas 2E **61**
G74: E Kil 6B **138**
Munro Rd. G13: Glas 4E **61**
Murano St. G20: Glas 4D **62**
Murchison G12: Glas 3G **61**
Murchison Dr. G75: E Kil 4D **148**
Murchison Rd. PA6: C'lee 2C **74**
Murdoch Ct. *PA5: John* 4E **95**
(off Tannahill Cres.)
Murdoch Dr. G62: Miln 5B **26**
Murdoch Pl. ML1: New S 4H **127**
Murdoch Sq. ML4: Bell 6E **111**
Murdock Rd. G75: E Kil 3G **149**
Murdostoun Gdns. ML2: Wis 4H **145**
Murdostoun Rd. ML2: Newm 1G **147**
Murdostoun Vw. ML2: Newm 3D **146**
Muriel La. G78: Barr 4E **115**
Muriel St. G78: Barr 4E **115**
Murray Av. G65: Kils 4H **11**
Murray Business Area PA3: Pais 5G **77**
Murray Bus. Area PA3: Pais 5H **77**
Murray Cres. ML2: Newm 2E **147**
Murrayfield G64: B'rig 4C **48**
Murrayfield Dr. G61: Bear 6E **45**
Murrayfield St. G32: Glas 4G **85**
Murray Gdns. G66: Milt C 5C **8**
Murray Gro. G61: Bear 5B **24**
Murrayhill G75: E Kil 3F **149**
Murray Path G71: Udd 1C **124**
Murray Pl. G78: Barr 3F **115**
G82: Dumb 1C **18**
ML4: Bell 6A **110**
Murray Rd. G71: Both 4E **125**
ML8: Law 1H **163**
Murray Rd., The G75: E Kil 3E **149**
MURRAY RDBT., THE 3H **149**
Murray Sq., The G75: E Kil 4G **149**
Murray St. PA3: Pais 5G **77**
PA4: Renf 6E **59**
Murray Ter. ML1: Moth 2D **142**
MURRAY, THE 4G **149**
Murrin Av. G64: B'rig 6F **49**
Murroch Av. G82: Dumb 1H **17**
Murroes Rd. G51: Glas 4D **80**
Mus. of 602 (City of Glasgow) Squadron 4G **79**
Mus. of Piping 2D **4**
Mus. of Scottish Country Life 5B **136**
Musgrove Pl. G75: E Kil 3E **149**
Muslin St. G40: Glas 1B **104**
Muttonhole Rd. ML3: Ham 3H **151**
M.V. Gipsy Princess 5H **11**
Mybole Dr. ML6: Air 1A **112**
Mybster Pl. G51: Glas 4D **80**
Myers Cres. G71: Udd 2E **125**
Myreside Pl. G32: Glas 5F **85**
Myreside St. G32: Glas 5F **85**
Myres Rd. G53: Glas 5D **100**
Myrie Gdns. G64: B'rig 5D **48**
Myroch Pl. G34: Glas 2A **88**
Myrtle Av. G66: Lenz 2C **50**
Myrtle Dr. ML1: Holy 2B **128**
ML2: Wis 5D **144**
Myrtle Hill La. G42: Glas 5G **103**
Myrtle La. ML9: Lark 4F **161**
Myrtle Pk. G42: Glas 4F **103**
Myrtle Pl. G42: Glas 4G **103**
Myrtle Rd. G71: View 5F **109**
G81: Clyd 3H **41**
Myrtle Sq. G64: B'rig 1C **64**
Myrtle St. G72: Blan 6B **124**
Myrtle Vw. Rd. G42: Glas 5G **103**
Myrtle Wlk. G72: Camb 1H **121**
Myvot Av. G67: Cumb 1D **54**
Myvot Rd. G67: Cumb 1D **54**
(Condorrat)
G67: Cumb 3A **54**
(Mollinsburn)

N

Naburn Ga. G5: Glas 1G **103**
Nagle Gdns. ML1: Cle 1F **145**
Nairn Av. G72: Blan 5A **124**
ML4: Bell 1C **126**
Nairn Cres. ML6: Air 6A **92**
Nairn Pl. G74: E Kil 6C **138**
G81: Clyd 4B **42**
Nairn Quad. ML2: Wis 4H **145**
Nairnside Rd. G21: Glas 2E **65**
Nairn St. G3: Glas 2B **82**
G72: Blan 3A **140**
G81: Clyd 4B **42**
ML9: Lark 3D **160**
Nairn Way G68: Cumb 6A **14**
Naismith St. G32: Carm 5C **106**
Naismith Wlk. ML4: Bell 6E **111**
Nansen St. G20: Glas 6E **63**
Napier Ct. G60: Old K 2G **41**
G68: Cumb 3D **14**
Napier Cres. G82: Dumb 4C **16**
Napier Dr. G51: Glas 3H **81**
Napier Gdns. PA3: Lin 5A **76**
Napier Hill G75: E Kil 3G **149**
Napier La. G75: E Kil 3G **149**
Napier Pk. G68: Cumb 4C **14**
Napier Pl. G51: Glas 3H **81**
G60: Old K 2G **41**
G68: Cumb 3C **14**

228 A-Z Glasgow

Napier Rd.—Newlands Dr.

Napier Rd. G51: Glas . . . 3H **81**
G52: Hill . . . 2H **79**
G68: Cumb . . . 4C **14**
Napiershall La. *G20: Glas* . . . *1D 82*
(off Napiershall St.)
Napiershall Pl. G20: Glas . . . 1D **82**
Napiershall St. G20: Glas . . . 1D **82**
Napier Sq. ML4: Bell . . . 6D **110**
Napier St. G51: Glas . . . 3H **81**
G81: Clyd . . . 2E **59**
PA3: Lin . . . 5A **76**
PA5: John . . . 2E **95**
Napier Ter. G51: Glas . . . 3H **81**
Napier Way G68: Cumb . . . 4C **14**
Naproch Pl. G77: Newt M . . . 4A **134**
Naseby Av. G11: Glas . . . 6F **61**
Naseby La. G11: Glas . . . 6F **61**
Nasmyth Av. G61: Bear . . . 5B **24**
G75: E Kil . . . 4H **149**
Nasmyth Bank G75: E Kil . . . 4H **149**
Nasmyth Rd. G52: Hill . . . 4A **80**
Nasmyth Rd. Nth. G52: Hill . . . 4A **80**
(not continuous)
Nasmyth Rd. Sth. G52: Hill . . . 4A **80**
Nassau Pl. G75: E Kil . . . 2C **148**
National Bank La.
G1: Glas . . . 4F **83** (5D **4**)
Navar Pl. PA2: Pais . . . 3C **98**
Naver St. G33: Glas . . . 2G **85**
Naylor La. ML6: Air . . . 3B **92**
Needle Grn. ML8: Carl . . . 3F **165**
Neidpath G69: Bail . . . 1G **107**
Neidpath Av. ML5: Coat . . . 2D **110**
Neidpath E. G74: E Kil . . . 1F **149**
Neidpath Pl. ML5: Coat . . . 2C **110**
Neidpath Rd. ML8: Carl . . . 2E **165**
Neidpath Rd. E. G46: Giff . . . 3G **133**
Neidpath Rd. W. G46: Giff . . . 2G **133**
Neidpath W. G74: E Kil . . . 1F **149**
Neilsland Dr. ML1: Moth . . . 3D **142**
ML3: Ham . . . 4G **153**
Neilsland Oval G53: Glas . . . 5D **100**
Neilsland Rd. ML3: Ham . . . 2F **153**
Neilsland Sq. G53: Glas . . . 4D **100**
ML3: Ham . . . 2G **153**
Neilsland St. ML3: Ham . . . 2G **153**
Neilson Ct. ML3: Ham . . . 1A **154**
Neilson St. ML4: Bell . . . 2C **126**
NEILSTON . . . **2E 131**
Neilston Av. G53: Glas . . . 2C **116**
Neilston Ct. G53: Glas . . . 2C **116**
Neilston Leisure Cen. . . . 2E **131**
Neilston Pl. G65: Kils . . . 2F **11**
Neilston Rd. G78: Neil . . . 1E **131**
PA2: Pais . . . 2A **98**
Neilston Station (Rail) . . . **2D 130**
Neilston Wlk G65: Kils . . . 2F **11**
(not continuous)
Neil St. PA4: Renf . . . 4F **59**
Neilvaig Dr. G73: Ruth . . . 4D **120**
Neistpoint Dr. G33: Glas . . . 3A **86**
Nelson Av. ML5: Coat . . . 1A **110**
Nelson Cres. ML1: Moth . . . 5B **144**
Nelson Mandela Pl.
G2: Glas . . . 3G **83** (4E **5**)
Nelson Pl. G69: Bail . . . 1H **107**
Nelson St. G5: Glas . . . 5E **83**
G69: Bail . . . 1H **107**
Nelson Ter. G74: E Kil . . . 3A **150**
Neptune St. G51: Glas . . . 4H **81**
Neptune Way ML4: Moss . . . 2G **127**
NERSTON . . . **3A 138**
Nerston Rd. G74: Ners, Roger . . . 3G **137**
Ness Av. PA5: John . . . 5C **94**
Ness Dr. G72: Blan . . . 6C **124**
G74: E Kil . . . 2B **150**
Ness Gdns. G64: B'rig . . . 6D **48**
ML9: Lark . . . 5E **161**
Ness Rd. PA4: Renf . . . 5D **58**
Ness St. G33: Glas . . . 2G **85**
ML2: Wis . . . 3H **157**
Ness Ter. ML3: Ham . . . 2E **153**
Ness Way ML1: Holy . . . 2A **128**
Nethan Av. ML2: Wis . . . 1C **156**
Nethan Ga. ML3: Ham . . . 6G **141**
Nethan Path ML9: Lark . . . 5E **161**
Nethan Pl. ML3: Ham . . . 5H **153**
Nethan St. G51: Glas . . . 3G **81**
ML1: Moth . . . 5E **127**
Nether Auldhouse Rd. G43: Glas . . . 1H **117**
Netherbank Rd. ML2: Wis . . . 1D **156**
Netherbog Av. G82: Dumb . . . 3H **17**
Netherbog Rd. G82: Dumb . . . 3H **17**
Netherburn Av. G44: Neth . . . 5D **118**
PA6: C'lee . . . 3E **75**
Netherburn Gdns. PA6: C'lee . . . 3E **75**
Netherburn Rd. ML9: Ashg . . . 5C **162**
Netherby Dr. G41: Glas . . . 1B **102**
Nethercairn Pl. G77: Newt M . . . 4A **134**
Nethercairn Rd. G43: Glas . . . 3A **118**
Nethercliffe Av. G44: Neth . . . 5D **118**
Nethercommon Ind. Est.
PA3: Pais . . . 3A **78**
(not continuous)
Nethercraigs Ct. PA2: Pais . . . 6F **97**
Nethercraigs Dr. PA2: Pais . . . 5G **97**
Nethercraigs Rd. PA2: Pais . . . 6F **97**
Nethercroy Rd. G65: Croy . . . 6A **12**
Netherdale G77: Newt M . . . 4H **133**
Netherdale Cres. ML2: Wis . . . 1C **156**
Netherdale Dr. PA1: Pais . . . 1H **99**
Netherdale Rd. ML2: Wis . . . 1E **157**
Nethergreen Cres. PA4: Renf . . . 6D **58**
Nethergreen Wynd PA4: Renf . . . 6D **58**
Netherhall Rd. ML2: Wis . . . 1D **156**
Netherhill Av. G44: Neth . . . 6D **118**
Netherhill Cotts. *PA3: Pais* . . . *4C 78*
(off Netherhill Rd.)
Netherhill Cres. PA3: Pais . . . 5C **78**
Netherhill Rd. G69: Mood . . . 6D **52**
PA3: Pais . . . 5B **78**
Netherhill Way PA3: Pais . . . 4D **78**
Netherhouse Av. G66: Lenz . . . 3E **51**
ML5: Coat . . . 2B **110**
Netherhouse Pl. G34: Glas . . . 3C **88**
Netherhouse Rd. G34: Glas . . . 4B **88**
G69: Barg . . . 4B **88**
NETHER KIRKTON . . . **1F 131**
NETHERLEE . . . **5D 118**
Netherlee Pl. G44: Glas . . . 3E **119**
Netherlee Rd. G44: Glas . . . 2E **119**
Nethermains Rd. G62: Miln . . . 5G **25**
Netherpark Av. G44: Neth . . . 6D **118**
Netherplace . . . 5A **132**
Netherplace Cres. G77: Newt M . . . 5C **132**
Netherplace Rd. G53: Glas . . . 5B **100**
G77: Newt M . . . 5A **132**
Netherpool Cres. G53: Glas . . . 5B **100**
NETHERTON
Glasgow . . . **1E 61**
Wishaw . . . **2E 157**
Netherton Av. G13: Glas . . . 2E **61**
Netherton Ct. G45: Glas . . . 5B **120**
G77: Newt M . . . 3F **133**
Netherton Dr. G78: Barr . . . 5F **115**
Netherton Farm La. G61: Glas . . . 1F **61**
Netherton Hill G66: Len . . . 3C **6**
Netherton Ind. Est. ML2: Wis . . . 1E **157**
Netherton Oval G66: Len . . . 3D **6**
Netherton Rd. G13: Glas . . . 1E **61**
G75: E Kil . . . 6C **148**
(Mallard Cres.)
G75: E Kil . . . 5E **149**
(Owen Av.)
G77: Newt M . . . 3F **133**
ML2: Wis . . . 1C **156**
Netherton St. ML2: Wis . . . 1F **157**
Nethervale Av. G44: Neth . . . 6D **118**
Netherview Rd. G44: Neth . . . 6E **119**
Netherway G44: Neth . . . 6D **118**
Netherwood Av. G68: Cumb . . . 5C **34**
Netherwood Ct. G68: Cumb . . . 5C **34**
ML1: Moth . . . *1B 156*
(off Muirhouse Rd.)
Netherwood Gro. G68: Cumb . . . 5C **34**
Netherwood Pl. G68: Cumb . . . 5B **34**
Netherwood Rd. G68: Cumb . . . 5B **34**
ML1: Moth . . . 6B **144**
Netherwood Twr. ML1: Moth . . . 1B **156**
Netherwood Way G68: Cumb . . . 5C **34**
Nethy Way PA4: Renf . . . 2H **79**
Neuk Av. G69: Muirh . . . 2A **68**
PA6: Hous . . . 2C **74**
Neuk Cres. PA6: Hous . . . 1C **74**
Neuk, The ML2: Wis . . . 6E **145**
Neuk Way G32: Carm . . . 5C **106**
PA6: Hous . . . 2C **74**
Neva Pl. *PA11: Bri W* . . . *3F 73*
(off Main St.)
Neville G74: E Kil . . . 4C **138**
Nevis Av. ML3: Ham . . . 1E **153**
Nevis Ct. G78: Barr . . . 6E **115**
ML1: Moth . . . 5G **143**
ML5: Coat . . . 2E **111**
Nevis Dr. G64: Torr . . . 4D **28**
Nevison St. ML9: Lark . . . 3F **161**
Nevis Rd. G43: Glas . . . 2H **117**
G61: Bear . . . 6B **24**
PA4: Renf . . . 2D **78**
Nevis Way PA3: Glas A . . . 2A **78**
Newark Dr. G41: Glas . . . 2B **102**
ML2: Wis . . . 3A **146**
PA2: Pais . . . 5G **97**
Newark Pl. ML2: Wis . . . 3B **146**
NEWARTHILL . . . **3F 129**
Newarthill Rd. ML1: Carf . . . 5C **128**
New Ashtree St. ML2: Wis . . . 6E **145**
Newbank Ct. G31: Glas . . . 1G **105**
Newbank Gdns. G31: Glas . . . 1F **105**
Newbank Rd. G31: Glas . . . 1G **105**
Newbarns St. ML8: Carl . . . 2F **165**
Newbattle Av. ML6: C'bnk . . . 3B **112**
Newbattle Ct. G32: Glas . . . 3B **106**
Newbattle Gdns. G32: Glas . . . 3B **106**
Newbattle Pl. G32: Glas . . . 3B **106**
Newbattle Rd. G32: Glas . . . 3A **106**
Newbold Av. G21: Glas . . . 2A **64**
NEWBRIDGE END . . . **5F 165**
New Broomfield Stadium . . . 5C **92**
Newburgh PA8: Ersk . . . 4E **41**
Newburgh St. G43: Glas . . . 6B **102**
Newcastleton Dr. G23: Glas . . . 6C **46**
New City Rd. G4: Glas . . . 1E **83** (1B **4**)
(not continuous)
Newcraigs Dr. G76: Crmck . . . 2H **135**
Newcroft Dr. G44: Glas . . . 2H **119**
New Cross *ML6: Air* . . . *4A 92*
(off Stirling St.)
New Cross Cen. ML3: Ham . . . 6A **142**
Newdyke Av. G66: Kirk . . . 5E **31**
Newdyke Rd. G66: Kirk . . . 5E **31**
New Edinburgh Rd.
G71: Tann, View . . . 6C **108**
ML4: Bell . . . 2A **126**
Newfield Cres. ML3: Ham . . . 5F **141**
Newfield La. G71: Both . . . 4F **125**
Newfield Pl. G46: T'bnk . . . 5F **117**
G73: Ruth . . . 6A **104**
Newfield Sq. G53: Glas . . . 1A **116**
Newford Gro. G76: Busby . . . 4D **134**
Newgrove Gdns. G72: Camb . . . 1A **122**
Newhall St. G40: Glas . . . 2B **104**
Newhaven Rd. G33: Glas . . . 3B **86**
Newhaven St. G32: Glas . . . 4A **86**
Newhills Rd. G33: Glas . . . 4E **87**
NEWHOUSE . . . **5H 113**
Newhouse Ind. Est. ML1: N'hse . . . 6C **112**
(Greenside Rd.)
ML1: N'hse . . . 5D **112**
(York Rd.)
NEWHOUSE INTERCHANGE . . . **5G 113**
Newhousemill Rd.
G72: Blan . . . 4F **151**
Newhousemill Rd. G74: E Kil . . . 4C **150**
ML3: Ham . . . 3H **151**
Newhut Rd. ML1: Moth . . . 1F **143**
New Inchinnan Rd. PA3: Pais . . . 4A **78**
Newington St. G32: Glas . . . 5H **85**
New Kirk Rd. G61: Bear . . . 2E **45**
New Lairdsland Rd. G66: Kirk . . . 4C **30**
NEWLANDS . . . **2C 118**
Newlands Dr. ML3: Ham . . . 3H **153**

A-Z Glasgow 229

Newlandsfield Rd. G43: Glas 6B **102**
Newlands Gdns. PA5: Eld 4A **96**
NEWLANDSMUIR 6B **148**
Newlandsmuir Rd. G75: E Kil 5B **148**
Newlands Pl. G74: E Kil. 2G **149**
Newlands Rd. G43: Glas 6B **102**
   G71: Tann 5D **108**
   G75: E Kil 6A **148**
                          (Newlandsmuir)
   G75: E Kil 4C **148**
                             (Westwood)
Newlands Squash & Tennis Club
   . . . . 1D **118**
Newlands Ter. G66: Milt C 5C **8**
   ML8: Carl 3F **165**
New La. ML6: C'bnk. 3B **112**
New Line Pend G74: E Kil 1H **149**
                         (off Kittoch Pl.)
New Luce Dr. G32: Glas. 2D **106**
NEWMAINS
   Renfrew 2E **79**
   Wishaw 5E **147**
Newmains Av. PA4: Inch 4F **57**
Newmains Rd. PA4: Renf 1D **78**
Newmill Rd. G21: Glas. 4E **65**
Newmilns St. G53: Glas. 1H **115**
NEW MONKLAND 5G **71**
Newnham Rd. PA1: Pais 1G **99**
Newpark Cres. G72: Camb. 6A **106**
New Pk. St. ML3: Ham 4G **141**
New Plymouth G75: E Kil 4C **148**
New Rd. G72: Camb. 3E **123**
Newrose Av. ML4: Bell. 6D **110**
Newshot Ct. G81: Clyd 2F **59**
                        (off Clydeholm Ter.)
Newshot Dr. PA8: Ersk 5F **41**
New Sneddon St. PA3: Pais 5A **78**
                           (not continuous)
Newstead Gdns. G23: Glas 6C **46**
NEW STEVENSTON 3A **128**
New Stevenston Rd. ML1: Carf 5B **128**
                           (not continuous)
New St. G72: Blan 2A **140**
   G81: Dun 1C **42**
   PA1: Pais 1A **98**
   PA10: Kilb. 2A **94**
NEWTON 1G **123**
Newton Av. G72: Camb 1D **122**
   G78: Barr 6F **115**
   PA3: Pais 4D **78**
   PA5: Eld 2C **96**
Newton Brae G72: Newt 1F **123**
Newton Ct. G77: Newt M 6D **132**
Newton Dr. G71: Tann 6E **109**
   ML2: Newm 4E **147**
   PA5: Eld 2C **96**
Newton Farm Rd. G72: Newt 6F **107**
Newtongrange Av. G32: Glas 2B **106**
Newtongrange Gdns.
   G32: Glas 3B **106**
Newton Gro. G77: Newt M 6D **132**
Newtonlea Av. G77: Newt M 5E **133**
NEWTON MEARNS 5D **132**
Newton Pl. G3: Glas 2D **82**
   G77: Newt M 6E **133**
Newton Rd. G66: Lenz 3E **51**
   PA7: B'ton 4F **39**
Newton Station (Rail) 2E **123**
Newton Sta. Rd.
   G72: Flem, Newt 3E **123**
Newton St. G3: Glas 3E **83** (3A **4**)
   ML5: Coat. 1A **110**
   PA1: Pais 1G **97**
Newton Ter. G3: Glas 3D **82**
                        (off Sauchiehall St.)
   PA1: Pais 2D **96**
Newton Ter. La. G3: Glas 3D **82**
                          (off Elderslie St.)
Newton Way PA3: Pais 4D **78**
Newtown St. G65: Kils 3H **11**
Newtyle Dr. G53: Glas 4H **99**
Newtyle Pl. G53: Glas 4H **99**
   G64: B'rig 6F **49**

Newtyle Rd. PA1: Pais. 1D **98**
New Vw. Cres. ML4: Bell 4C **126**
New Vw. Dr. ML4: Bell. 4C **126**
New Vw. Pl. ML4: Bell. 4C **126**
New Wynd G1: Glas. 5G **83** (6F **5**)
Next Generation Health Club 1F **61**
Niamh Ct. PA4: Inch 2G **57**
Nicholas St. G1: Glas 4H **83** (5H **5**)
Nicholson St. G5: Glas 6F **83**
Nicklaus Way ML1: N'hse 6E **113**
Nicolson Ct. G33: Step 4D **66**
Nicol St. ML6: Air 2C **92**
Niddrie Rd. G42: Glas 3D **102**
Niddrie Sq. G42: Glas 3D **102**
Niddry St. PA3: Pais. 6B **78**
Nigel Gdns. G41: Glas 4B **102**
Nigel St. ML1: Moth. 3F **143**
Nigg Pl. G34: Glas 3G **87**
Nightingale Pl. PA5: John 6D **94**
Nikitas Av. ML9: Lark 6F **161**
Nimmo Dr. G51: Glas 4E **81**
Nimmo Pl. ML2: Wis 6A **146**
Ninian Av. PA6: C'lee 3C **74**
Ninian Rd. ML6: Air 6B **92**
Ninian's Ri. G66: Kirk. 6E **31**
Nisbet St. G31: Glas 6F **85**
Nisbett Pl. ML6: Chap 2E **113**
Nisbett St. ML6: Chap 3E **113**
Nisbet St. G53: Glas 4H **99**
Nith Dr. ML3: Ham 3E **153**
   PA4: Renf 1G **79**
Nith La. ML2: Newm 3D **146**
                             (off King St.)
Nith Path ML1: Cle. 5H **129**
Nith Pl. PA5: John 5C **94**
Nith Quad. ML1: N'hill 4C **128**
Nithsdale G74: E Kil 6D **138**
Nithsdale Cres. G61: Bear 1C **44**
Nithsdale Dr. G41: Glas 3D **102**
Nithsdale Pl. G41: Glas 2D **102**
Nithsdale Rd. G41: Glas 1H **101**
                          (Dumbreck Rd.)
   G41: Glas 3D **102**
                         (Pollokshaws Rd.)
Nithsdale St. G41: Glas 3D **102**
Nith St. G33: Glas. 2F **85**
Nith Way PA4: Renf 1G **79**
NITSHILL 2A **116**
Nitshill Rd. G53: Glas, T'bnk 1H **115**
Nitshill Station (Rail) 2A **116**
Niven St. G20: Glas 3A **62**
Noble Rd. ML4: Bell. 2C **126**
Nobles Pl. ML4: Bell 3B **126**
Nobles Vw. ML4: Bell. 3B **126**
Noldrum Av. G32: Carm 5C **106**
Noldrum Gdns. G32: Carm. 5C **106**
Norbreck Dr. G46: Giff 3A **118**
Norby Rd. G11: Glas. 6F **61**
Noremac Way ML4: Bell 6B **110**
Norfield Dr. G44: Glas 6F **103**
Norfolk Ct. G5: Glas 6F **83**
Norfolk Cres. G64: B'rig. 4A **48**
Norfolk St. G5: Glas 6F **83**
Norham St. G41: Glas 4C **102**
Norman St. G40: Glas 2B **104**
Norse La. Nth. G14: Glas. 5C **60**
Norse La. Sth. G14: Glas 5C **60**
Norse Pl. G14: Glas. 5C **60**
Norse Rd. G14: Glas 5C **60**
Northall Quad. ML1: Carf 6A **128**
Northampton Dr. G12: Glas 3H **61**
Northampton La. G12: Glas 3H **61**
                    (off Northampton Dr.)
North & South Rd. ML1: Cle 1C **146**
North Av. G72: Camb 1H **121**
   G81: Clyd 4C **42**
   ML1: New S 5A **128**
   ML8: Carl 3D **164**
North Bank PA6: Hous 1B **74**
                            (off North St.)
Northbank Av. G66: Kirk 5C **30**
   G72: Camb. 1D **122**
Nth. Bank Pl. G81: Clyd 1E **59**

Northbank Rd. G66: Kirk 5C **30**
Northbank St. G72: Camb 1D **122**
Nth. Bank St. G81: Clyd 1E **59**
NORTH BARR 4E **41**
Nth. Barr Av. PA8: Ersk 4E **41**
NORTH BARRWOOD 3A **12**
Nth. Berwick Av. G68: Cumb 6H **13**
Nth. Berwick Cres. G75: E Kil 5C **148**
Nth. Berwick Gdns. G68: Cumb . . . 6H **13**
Nth. Biggar Rd. ML6: Air. 3B **92**
Nth. Birbiston Rd. G66: Len 3F **7**
Northbrae Pl. G13: Glas. 3B **60**
North Bri. St. ML6: Air. 3H **91**
Nth. British Rd. G71: Udd 1D **124**
Northburn Av. ML6: Air 2B **92**
Northburn Pl. ML6: Air 1B **92**
Northburn Rd. ML5: Coat 2E **91**
Northburn St. ML6: Plain 1H **93**
Nth. Bute St. ML5: Coat 1D **110**
Nth. Caldeen Rd. ML5: Coat 6E **91**
Nth. Calder Dr. ML6: Air 5D **92**
Nth. Calder Gro. G71: Udd 3H **107**
Nth. Calder Pl. G71: Udd. 3G **107**
Nth. Calder Rd. G71: View 4G **109**
Nth. Campbell Av. G62: Miln 4F **25**
Nth. Canal Bank G4: Glas 1G **83**
Nth. Canal Bank St.
   G4: Glas. 1G **83** (1E **5**)
Nth. Carbrain Rd. G67: Cumb 5G **35**
NORTH CARDONALD 4B **80**
Nth. Claremont La. G62: Miln 3G **25**
Nth. Claremont St. G3: Glas 2C **82**
Nth. Corsebar Rd. PA2: Pais 3G **97**
North Ct. G1: Glas 4G **83** (5E **5**)
North Ct. La. G1: Glas. 4G **83** (5E **5**)
Northcroft Rd. G69: Mood 5C **52**
Nth. Croft St. PA3: Pais 6B **78**
Nth. Dean Pk. Av. G71: Both 4E **125**
Nth. Douglas St. G81: Clyd 1E **59**
North Dr. G1: Glas. 4F **83** (6D **4**)
   PA3: Lin 5H **75**
Nth. Dryburgh Rd. ML2: Wis. 4G **145**
Nth. Dumgoyne Av. G62: Miln 2F **25**
Nth. Elgin Pl. G81: Clyd. 2E **59**
Nth. Elgin St. G81: Clyd 2E **59**
Nth. Erskine Pk. G61: Bear 2D **44**
NORTHFIELD 2F **11**
Northfield G75: E Kil 4B **148**
Northfield Rd. G65: Kils 2F **11**
Northfield St. ML1: Moth. 1G **143**
Nth. Frederick St. G1: Glas. . . 4G **83** (5F **5**)
Nth. Gardinar St. G11: Glas. 1H **81**
Nth. Gate Quad. G21: Glas 2E **65**
Northgate Rd. G21: Glas. 2E **65**
Nth. Gower St. G51: Glas. 6A **82**
Nth. Grange Rd. G61: Bear 1E **45**
Nth. Hanover St. G1: Glas . . . 3G **83** (5F **5**)
Northinch Ct. G14: Glas. 1D **80**
Northinch St. G14: Glas. 1D **80**
Nth. Iverton Pk. Rd. PA5: John . . . 2G **95**
NORTH KELVIN 6C **62**
Nth. Kilmeny Cres. ML2: Wis 3A **146**
Northland Av. G14: Glas. 4C **60**
Northland Dr. G14: Glas 4C **60**
Northland Gdns. G14: Glas 4C **60**
Northland La. G14: Glas. 5C **60**
North La. PA3: Lin 5A **76**
NORTH LODGE 5F **143**
Nth. Lodge Av. ML1: Moth 5G **143**
Nth. Lodge Rd. PA4: Renf 5E **59**
Nth. Moraine La. G15: Glas. 5C **44**
NORTH MOTHERWELL 2D **142**
Northmuir Dr. ML2: Wis. 5B **146**
Northmuir Rd. G15: Glas. 3B **44**
Nth. Orchard St. ML1: Moth. 2F **143**
Nth. Park Av. G46: T'bnk 3F **117**
   G78: Barr 4D **114**
Northpark St. G20: Glas. 5D **62**
Nth. Pk. Vs. G46: T'bnk 4F **117**
Nth. Portland St. G1: Glas . . . 4H **83** (5G **5**)
North Rd. G68: Cumb. 5C **34**
   ML4: Bell 2C **126**
   PA5: John 3E **95**
North Sq. ML5: Coat 3A **90**

North St. G3: Glas 2D **82** (2A **4**)
  ML1: Moth 1H **143**
  ML9: Lark 1E **161**
  PA3: Pais 5A **78**
  PA6: Hous 1A **74**
Northumberland St. G20: Glas . . 5C **62**
North Vw. G61: Bear 5D **44**
North Vw. Rd. PA11: Bri W 5H **73**
Nth. Wallace St. G4: Glas . . 2H **83** (2G **5**)
Northway G72: Blan 6A **124**
Northwood Dr. ML2: Newm 3E **147**
Nth. Woodside Leisure Cen. . . . 1E **83**
Nth. Woodside Rd. G20: Glas . . . 6D **62**
  (not continuous)
Norval St. G11: Glas 1G **81**
Norwich Dr. G12: Glas 4H **61**
Norwood Av. G66: Kirk 5B **30**
Norwood Dr. G46: Giff 6G **117**
Norwood Pk. G61: Bear 4F **45**
Norwood Ter. G71: Tann 6E **109**
Nottingham Av. G12: Glas 3H **61**
Nottingham La. G12: Glas 3H **61**
  (off Northampton Dr.)
Novar Dr. G12: Glas 5G **61**
Novar Gdns. G64: B'rig 5A **48**
Novar St. ML3: Ham 1H **153**
Nuneaton St. G40: Glas 2C **104**
Nuneaton St. Ind. Est.
  G40: Glas 2C **104**
Nurseries Rd. G69: Bail 5F **87**
Nursery Av. PA7: B'ton 3C **40**
Nursery Ct. ML8: Carl 2E **165**
Nursery Dr. ML9: Ashg 5C **162**
Nursery La. G41: Glas 3D **102**
Nursery Pk. ML8: Carl 3E **165**
Nursery Pl. G72: Blan 3B **140**
Nursery St. G41: Glas 2E **103**
Nutberry Ct. G42: Glas 4F **103**

O

Oak Av. G61: Bear 6F **25**
  G75: E Kil 5D **148**
Oakbank Av. ML2: Wis 2E **157**
Oakbank Dr. G78: Barr 6F **115**
Oakbank Ind. Est. G20: Glas . . . 6F **63**
Oakbank St. ML6: Air. 4D **92**
Oakburn Av. G62: Miln 4F **25**
Oakburn Cres. G62: Miln 3F **25**
Oak Cres. G69: Bail 1G **107**
Oakdene Av. G71: Tann 6F **109**
  ML4: Bell 6C **110**
Oakdene Cres. ML1: N'hill 4C **128**
Oak Dr. G66: Lenz 2B **50**
  G72: Camb 3C **122**
Oak Fern Dr. G74: E Kil 5F **137**
Oak Fern Gro. G74: E Kil 5F **137**
Oakfield Av. G12: Glas 1C **82**
Oakfield Dr. ML1: Moth 3G **143**
Oakfield La. G12: Glas 1C **82**
  (off Gibson St.)
Oakfield Rd. ML1: Moth 3G **143**
Oakfield Twr. ML1: Moth 4G **143**
Oak Gro. ML6: Chap 2E **113**
Oakhill Av. G69: Bail. 2F **107**
Oak Lea ML3: Ham 1B **154**
Oaklea Cres. G72: Blan 1A **140**
Oakley Dr. G44: Neth 4D **118**
Oakley Ter. G31: Glas 4B **84**
Oak Pk. G64: B'rig 6D **48**
  ML1: Moth 5F **143**
Oak Pl. G71: View 6G **109**
  G75: E Kil 5D **148**
  ML5: Coat. 6E **91**
Oakridge Cres. PA3: Pais 6F **77**
Oak Rd. G67: Cumb 1E **37**
  G81: Clyd 2B **42**
  PA2: Pais 4C **98**
Oakshaw Brae PA1: Pais 6H **77**
Oakshawhead PA1: Pais 6H **77**
Oakshaw St. E. PA1: Pais 6H **77**
Oakshaw St. W. PA1: Pais 6H **77**
Oakside Pl. ML3: Ham 4H **153**

Oaks, The G44: Glas 3F **119**
  PA5: John 3E **95**
Oak St. G2: Glas 4E **83** (5A **4**)
Oaktree Gdns. G45: Glas 3B **120**
  G82: Dumb 3C **18**
Oakwood Av. PA2: Pais 4F **97**
Oakwood Cres. G34: Glas 2B **88**
Oakwood Dr. G34: Glas 2B **88**
  G77: Newt M 5F **133**
  ML5: Coat 6H **89**
Oakwood Vw. ML1: Holy 2B **128**
Oak Wynd G72: Flem 4F **123**
Oates Gdns. ML1: Moth 5B **144**
Oatfield St. G21: Glas 5D **64**
OATLANDS 3H **103**
Oban Ct. G20: Glas 5C **62**
Oban Dr. G20: Glas 5C **62**
Oban La. G20: Glas 5C **62**
Oban Pass G20: Glas 5C **62**
Observatory La. G12: Glas 6B **62**
Observatory Rd. G12: Glas 6A **62**
Ochel Path ML6: Chap 4F **113**
Ochil Dr. G78: Barr 6D **114**
  PA2: Pais 5H **97**
Ochil Pl. G32: Glas 1A **106**
Ochil Rd. G61: Bear 6B **24**
  G64: B'rig 6E **49**
  PA4: Renf 2D **78**
Ochil St. G32: Glas 1A **106**
  ML2: Wis 5F **145**
Ochiltree Av. G13: Glas 2F **61**
Ochiltree Dr. ML3: Ham 2C **152**
Ochil Vw. G71: Tann 5E **109**
Odense Ct. G75: E Kil 5G **149**
Odeon Cinema 5D **82**
Ogilvie Athletic Ground 5A **66**
Ogilvie Ct. ML6: Air 3E **93**
  (off Katherine St.)
Ogilvie Pl. G31: Glas 1F **105**
Ogilvie St. G31: Glas 1F **105**
Old Aisle Rd. G66: Kirk 6F **31**
Old Albert St. ML5: Coat 4C **90**
Old Avon Rd. ML3: Ham 1C **154**
OLD BALORNOCK 4D **64**
Old Bore Rd. ML6: Air. 3E **93**
Old Bothwell Rd. G71: Both . . . 6F **125**
Old Bridgend ML8: Carl 4F **165**
Old Bridge of Weir Rd.
  PA6: Hous 1A **74**
Old Castle Gdns. G44: Glas . . . 1F **119**
Old Castle Rd. G44: Glas 1E **119**
Old Chu. Gdns. G69: Barg 6E **89**
Old Coach Rd. G74: E Kil 6H **137**
Old Cross ML6: Air. 3A **92**
Old Dalmarnock Rd.
  G40: Glas 1B **104**
Old Dalnottar Rd. G60: Old K. . . 2F **41**
Old Dullatur Rd. G68: Dull 5F **13**
Old Dumbarton Rd. G3: Glas . . 2A **82**
Old Edinburgh Rd. G71: Tann . . 4B **108**
  ML4: Bell 1A **126**
Old Farm La. G61: Glas 1F **61**
Old Farm Rd. PA2: Pais 4F **99**
Old Ferry Rd. PA8: Ersk. 3D **40**
Old Gartloch Rd. G69: G'csh . . . 3H **69**
Old Glasgow Rd. G67: Cumb. . . 1H **35**
  G71: Udd 6B **108**
  (not continuous)
Old Govan Rd. PA4: Renf 6H **59**
Old Greenock Rd. PA4: Inch . . . 6C **40**
  (East Craigend)
  PA4: Inch 2G **57**
  (Inchinnan)
  PA7: B'ton 2A **38**
  PA8: Ersk 6C **40**
Oldhall Rd. PA1: Pais 6E **79**
OLDHILL 6G **79**
Old Howwood Rd. PA9: How . . . 6C **94**
Old Humbie Rd. G77: Newt M . . 6E **133**
OLD INNS INTERCHANGE 5B **14**
OLD INNS RDBT. 5B **14**
OLD KILPATRICK 1E **41**
Old Lanark Rd. ML8: Carl. 4F **165**
  (not continuous)

Old Manse Rd. G32: Glas 1D **106**
  ML2: Wis 3E **157**
Old Mill Ga. G73: Ruth 1C **120**
  (off Mill St.)
Old Mill Pk. Ind. Est. G66: Kirk. . 4C **30**
Old Mill Rd. G71: Both. 6E **125**
  G71: Udd 2D **124**
  (Bellshill Rd.)
  G71: Udd 1D **124**
  (Lwr. Millgate)
  G72: Camb 2D **122**
  G74: E Kil 1H **149**
  G81: Dun, Hard 1C **42**
  PA2: Pais 2F **97**
Old Mill Vw. G65: Croy 1B **34**
OLD MONKLAND 1A **110**
Old Monkland Rd. ML5: Coat . . 2H **109**
Old Playfield Rd. G76: Crmck . . 1H **135**
Old Quarry Rd. G68: Cumb . . . 2H **53**
Old Rd. PA5: Eld 2H **95**
Old Rutherglen Rd. G5: Glas . . . 6G **83**
Old School Ct. ML5: Coat 1C **110**
Old Schoolhouse La. PA6: Hous . . 1B **74**
Old Shettleston Rd. G32: Glas. . 6H **85**
Old Sneddon St. PA3: Pais 6A **78**
Old Stable Row ML5: Coat 4D **90**
Old St. G81: Dun 1B **42**
Old Union St. ML6: Air. 4B **92**
Old Vic Ct. G74: E Kil 5B **138**
  (off Bosworth Rd.)
Old Wishaw Rd. ML8: Carl. 2E **165**
  ML8: Law. 6G **159**
Old Wood Rd. G69: Bail. 2G **107**
Old Wynd G1: Glas 5G **83** (6F **5**)
Olifard Av. G71: Both 4F **125**
Oliphant Ct. PA2: Pais 5D **96**
Oliphant Cres. G76: Busby 4C **134**
  PA2: Pais 5C **96**
Oliphant Oval PA2: Pais 5C **96**
Olive Bank G71: View 4G **109**
Olive Ct. ML1: Holy 2B **128**
  (off Elm Rd.)
Olive St. G33: Glas 5F **65**
Ollach PA8: Ersk 2G **57**
Olympia G74: E Kil 2H **149**
Olympia Arc. G74: E Kil. 3H **149**
  (off Olympia Ct.)
Olympia Ct. G74: E Kil 2H **149**
Olympia St. G40: Glas 6B **84**
Olympia, The G74: E Kil 3H **149**
  (off Olympia Ct.)
Olympia Way G74: E Kil. 2H **149**
Omoa Rd. ML1: Cle 6G **129**
O'Neill Av. G64: B'rig 1D **64**
Onslow G75: E Kil 4E **149**
Onslow Dr. G31: Glas 4C **84**
Onslow Rd. G81: Clyd 5E **43**
Onslow Sq. G31: Glas 4C **84**
Ontario Pk. G75: E Kil 2D **148**
Ontario Pl. G75: E Kil 2D **148**
Onyx St. ML4: Bell 3C **126**
Oran Gdns. G20: Glas 4C **62**
Oran Ga. G20: Glas 4C **62**
Oran Pl. G20: Glas 5C **62**
Oran St. G20: Glas 4C **62**
ORBISTON 3C **126**
Orbiston Ct. ML1: Moth 4A **144**
Orbiston Dr. G81: Faif. 6F **23**
  ML4: Bell 4D **126**
Orbiston Gdns. G32: Glas 6A **86**
Orbiston Pl. G81: Faif 6F **23**
Orbiston Rd. ML4: Bell 5D **126**
  (Community Rd.)
  ML4: Bell 3B **126**
  (Crofthead Cres.)
Orbiston Sq. ML4: Bell 4B **126**
Orbiston St. ML1: Moth 3H **143**
Orcades Dr. G44: Glas 3F **119**
Orchard Av. G71: Both 6F **125**
Orchard Brae G66: Lenz 3E **51**
Orchard Ct. G32: Carm. 5B **106**
  G46: T'bnk 4G **117**
Orchard Dr. G46: Giff. 4H **117**
  (not continuous)

Orchard Dr. G72: Blan 1A 140
  G73: Ruth. 5B 104
Orchard Fld. G66: Lenz 3E 51
Orchard Ga. ML9: Lark. 3E 161
Orchard Grn. G74: E Kil 5B 138
Orchard Gro. G46: Giff. 3H 117
  ML5: Coat. 5D 90
ORCHARD PARK
  Lenzie. 4E 51
  Thornliebank 4H 117
Orchard Pk. G46: Giff. 4A 118
Orchard Pk. Av. G46: T'bnk 3G 117
Orchard Pl. G66: Kirk 6G 31
  ML3: Ham 6H 141
  ML4: Bell 4B 126
Orchard St. G69: Bail 2F 107
  ML1: Moth 2F 143
  ML2: Over 5H 157
  ML3: Ham 6H 141
  ML8: Carl 4F 165
  PA1: Pais 1A 98
  PA4: Renf 5F 59
Orchardton Rd. G68: Cumb 1G 53
  (Mollins Rd.)
  G68: Cumb. 2H 53
  (Old Quarry Rd.)
Orchardton Woods Ind. Pk.
  G68: Cumb. 5G 33
Orchid Pl. G66: Len 3E 7
Orchy Av. G76: Clar 6D 118
Orchy Cres. G61: Bear 5D 44
  ML6: Air 6C 92
  PA2: Pais 4D 96
Orchy Dr. G76: Clar 6D 118
Orchy Gdns. G76: Clar 6D 118
Orchy St. G44: Glas 1E 119
Orchy Ter. G74: E Kil 2B 150
Orefield Pl. G74: E Kil 6G 137
Oregon Pl. G5: Glas 1G 103
Orion Pl. ML4: Moss 2G 127
Orion Way G72: Camb 1A 122
  ML8: Carl 3D 164
Orkney Pl. G51: Glas 4H 81
Orkney Quad. ML2: Wis 5B 146
Orkney St. G51: Glas 4H 81
Orlando G74: E Kil 4C 138
Orleans Av. G14: Glas 6E 61
Orleans La. G14: Glas 6E 61
  (off Victoria Pk. Dr. Nth.)
Orlington Ct. ML5: Coat. 3B 90
Ormiston Av. G14: Glas 5C 60
Ormiston Dr. ML3: Ham. 3G 153
Ormiston La. G14: Glas 5C 60
  (off Norse La. Sth.)
Ormiston La. Nth. G14: Glas 5C 60
  (off Norse La. Nth.)
Ormonde Av. G44: Neth 4D 118
Ormonde Ct. G44: Neth 4C 118
Ormonde Cres. G44: Neth 4D 118
Ormonde Dr. G44: Neth 4D 118
Ornsay St. G22: Glas 2H 63
Oronsay Ct. G60: Old K 1G 41
Oronsay Cres. G60: Old K 1G 41
  G61: Bear 4H 45
Oronsay Gdns. G60: Old K. 1G 41
Oronsay Pl. G60: Old K 1G 41
Oronsay Sq. G60: Old K 1G 41
Orr Church Sq. PA1: Pais. 6H 77
Orr Sq. PA1: Pais 6A 78
Orr St. G40: Glas 6B 84
  (not continuous)
  PA1: Pais 6A 78
  PA2: Pais 2A 98
Orr Ter. G78: Neil 3C 130
Orton Pl. G51: Glas 5G 81
Osborne Cres. G74: T'hall 6F 135
Osborne St. G1: Glas 5G 83 (6E 5)
  G81: Clyd 4C 42
Oskaig Path G51: Glas 2G 57
Osprey Cres. ML2: Wis 5G 145
Osprey Dr. G71: Tann 6E 109
Osprey Ho. PA3: Tann 3A 78
Ossian Av. PA1: Pais 6H 79

Ossian Rd. G43: Glas. 1C 118
Oswald St. G1: Glas 5F 83 (6C 4)
Oswald Wlk. G62: Miln 5A 26
Otago La. G12: Glas. 1C 82
Otago La. Nth. G12: Glas. 1C 82
  (off Otago St.)
Otago Pk. G75: E Kil 2C 148
Otago St. G12: Glas. 1C 82
Othello G74: E Kil. 5B 138
Ottawa Cres. G81: Clyd 3H 41
Otterburn Dr. G46: Giff. 6A 118
Otterswick Pl. G33: Glas 1C 86
Oudenarde Ct. ML8: Carl. 4H 165
Our Lady of Good Aid R.C. Cathedral
  . . . . 2G 143
Oval Path G52: Glas 2E 101
Oval, The G76: Clar 6D 118
  ML5: Glenb 3G 69
Overbrae Pl. G15: Glas. 2H 43
Overburn Av. G82: Dumb 3F 17
Overburn Cres. G82: Dumb 2F 17
Overburn Ter. G82: Dumb 2G 17
Overcroy Rd. G65: Croy. 1B 34
Overdale Av. G42: Glas 5D 102
Overdale Gdns. G42: Glas 5D 102
Overdale Pl. ML2: Over 5A 158
Overdale St. G42: Glas 5D 102
Overjohnstone Dr. ML2: Wis 5D 102
Overlea Av. G73: Ruth 1F 121
Overlee Rd. G76: Busby 2D 134
Overnewton Pl. G3: Glas 3B 82
Overnewton Sq. G3: Glas 2B 82
Overnewton St. G3: Glas 2B 82
Overton Cres. PA5: John 2H 95
Overton Rd.
  G72: Camb, Flem 3D 122
  PA5: John. 3G 95
Overton St. G72: Camb 3D 122
Overtoun Av. G82: Dumb 4H 17
Overtoun Dr. G73: Ruth 6C 104
  G81: Clyd 3B 42
Overtoun Rd. G81: Clyd 3A 42
OVERTOWN 5A 158
Overtown Av. G53: Glas 1A 116
Overtown Ct. G81: Clyd 4A 42
Overtown Rd. ML2: Wis 4B 158
Overtown St. G40: Glas 6C 84
Overwood Dr. G44: Glas 1G 119
  G82: Dumb 3H 17
Overwood Gro. G82: Dumb 3H 17
Owen Av. G75: E Kil 4E 149
Owendale Av. ML4: Bell. 6D 110
Owen Pk. G75: E Kil. 4F 149
Owen St. ML1: Moth 1G 143
O'Wood Av. ML1: Holy. 1B 128
Oxford Dr. PA3: Lin 5H 75
Oxford La. G5: Glas. 6F 83
  PA4: Renf 6E 59
Oxford Rd. PA4: Renf 6E 59
Oxford St. G5: Glas. 5F 83
  G66: Kirk 5C 30
  ML5: Coat. 5B 90
OXGANG 6F 31
Oxgang Pl. G66: Kirk 6E 31
Oxhill Pl. G82: Dumb. 4D 16
Oxhill Rd. G82: Dumb 3D 16
Oxton Dr. G52: Glas 6B 80

P

Pacific Dr. G51: Glas 5A 82
Paddock St. ML5: Coat 1F 111
Paddock, The G76: Busby 4E 135
Paidmyre Cres. G77: Newt M 6D 132
Paidmyre Gdns. G77: Newt M 6D 132
Paidmyre Rd. G77: Newt M 6C 132
PAISLEY. 1H 97
Paisley Arts Cen. 1A 98
Paisley Canal Station (Rail) 2A 98
Paisley Cen., The PA1: Pais 1A 98
Paisley Gilmour Street Station (Rail)
  . . . . 6A 78
Paisley Mus. & Art Gallery 6H 77

Paisley Rd. G5: Glas 5D 82
  G78: Barr 2D 114
  PA4: Renf 3C 78
Paisley Rd. W. G51: Glas 6A 82
  (not continuous)
  G52: Glas 1H 99
Paisley St James Station (Rail) . . . 5G 77
Palacecraig St. ML5: Coat. 2C 110
Palace Gdns. Retail Pk.
  ML3: Ham 5B 142
Palace Grounds Rd. ML3: Ham. 5B 142
Palace of Art 6G 81
Palace of Paisley, The 1B 98
Palacerigg Country Pk. 6E 37
Paladin Av. G13: Glas 1B 60
Palermo St. G21: Glas 5A 64
Palladium Pl. G14: Glas 6D 60
Palmer Av. G13: Glas. 6D 44
Palmerston G75: E Kil 4C 148
Palmerston Pl. G3: Glas 3B 82
  PA5: John. 5C 94
Palm Pl. G71: View 4F 109
Pandora Way G71: Tann. 6E 109
Pankhurst Pl. G74: E Kil 1H 149
Panmure Cl. G22: Glas 5E 63
Panmure Pl. G22: Glas 4E 63
Panmure St. G20: Glas 5E 63
Parkandarroch Cres. ML8: Carl 4G 165
Park Av. G3: Glas 1D 82
  G62: Miln 4G 25
  G64: B'rig 4C 48
  G65: Twe 1D 32
  G66: Kirk 5C 30
  G78: Barr 6D 114
  G82: Dumb. 4H 17
  ML1: Holy. 2A 128
  ML8: Carl 2F 165
  PA2: Pais 4G 97
  PA5: Eld 3A 96
Park Bank PA8: Ersk. 6F 41
Park Brae PA8: Ersk. 1G 57
Parkbrae Av. G20: Glas 3E 63
Parkbrae Dr. G20: Glas 3E 63
Parkbrae Gdns. G20: Glas 3E 63
Parkbrae Ga. G20: Glas 3E 63
Parkbrae La. G20: Glas 3E 63
Parkburn Av. G66: Kirk. 1C 50
Park Burn Ct. ML3: Ham 3D 140
Park Burn Ind. Est.
  ML3: Ham 3E 141
Parkburn Rd. G65: Kils 2H 11
Park Cir. G3: Glas 2C 82
  ML8: Carl 2F 165
Park Cir. La. G3: Glas 2C 82
Park Cir. Pl. G3: Glas 2D 82
Park Ct. G46: Giff. 4H 117
  G64: B'rig. 4D 48
  G81: Clyd 3A 42
Park Cres. G61: Bear 2B 44
  G64: B'rig 5C 48
  G64: Torr 4E 29
  G72: Blan 3A 140
  G82: Dumb 2F 17
  ML6: Air 3G 91
  PA4: Inch 2G 57
Park Dr. G3: Glas 1C 82
  G73: Ruth. 6C 104
  G74: T'hall 6G 135
  ML1: Newm 4E 147
  ML3: Fern 2E 155
  PA8: Ersk 1F 57
Park Gdns. G3: Glas 2C 82
  PA10: Kilb. 1B 94
Park Gdns. La. G3: Glas 2C 82
  (off Clifton St.)
Park Ga. G3: Glas. 1F 57
  PA8: Ersk 1F 57
Park Ga. Pl. ML4: Bell 2B 126
Park Glade PA8: Ersk 1F 57
Park Grn. PA8: Ersk 1F 57

Park Gro. PA8: Ersk 1G **57**
Parkgrove Av. G46: Giff 3B **118**
Parkgrove Ter. G3: Glas 2C **82**
Parkgrove Ter. La. *G3: Glas* *2C 82*
(off Derby St.)
PARKHALL **2B 42**
Parkhall Rd. G81: Clyd 3B **42**
Parkhall St. G74: E Kil 1H **149**
Parkhall Ter. G81: Clyd 2B **42**
PARKHEAD **6F 85**
Parkhead Cross G31: Glas 6F **85**
Parkhead La. ML6: Air. 3A **92**
Parkhead St. ML1: Moth 4H **143**
ML6: Air 3A **92**
Park Hill PA8: Ersk 6F **41**
Parkhill Dr. G73: Ruth 6C **104**
Parkhill Rd. G43: Glas 5B **102**
Parkholm La. G5: Glas 5D **82**
PARKHOUSE **3H 115**
Park Ho. ML3: Ham 4H **141**
Parkhouse Path G53: Glas 3B **116**
Parkhouse Rd. G53: Glas 3H **115**
G78: Barr 3H **115**
Parkinch PA8: Ersk 1G **57**
Parklands Oval G53: Glas 3H **99**
Parklands Rd. G44: Neth 4D **118**
Parklands Vw. G53: Glas 4H **99**
Park La. G40: Glas 6B **84**
G65: Kils 3H **11**
G72: Blan 1B **140**
ML8: Carl 4E **165**
Parklea G64: B'rig 4A **48**
Parklee Dr. G76: Crmck 2A **136**
PARK MAINS **2G 57**
Park Moor PA8: Ersk 1F **57**
PARKNEUK **1G 151**
Parkneuk Rd. G43: Glas 3H **117**
G72: Blan 1G **151**
Parkneuk St. ML1: Moth 1F **143**
Parknook Way *ML9: Lark* *2F 161*
(off Muirshot Rd.)
Park Pl. G74: T'hall 6G **135**
ML4: Bell 4A **126**
ML5: Coat 1F **111**
PA3: Lin 5A **76**
PA5: John 3F **95**
Park Quad. G3: Glas 2C **82**
ML2: Wis 2E **157**
Park Rd G4: Glas 1C **82**
Park Ridge PA8: Ersk 1F **57**
Park Rd. G32: Carm 5C **106**
G46: Giff 5A **118**
G62: Miln 4G **25**
G64: B'rig 5C **48**
G69: Barg 6D **88**
G69: Chry 1A **68**
G81: Clyd 4B **42**
ML1: New S 4A **128**
ML3: Ham 6H **141**
ML4: Bell 3C **126**
ML6: C'bnk 3B **112**
PA11: Bri W 2F **73**
PA2: Pais 5H **97**
PA4: Inch 2H **57**
PA5: John 3F **95**
Parksail PA8: Ersk 2G **57**
Parksail Dr. PA8: Ersk 1G **57**
Parkside Gdns. G20: Glas 3E **63**
Parkside Pl. G20: Glas 3E **63**
Parkside Rd. ML1: Moth 3D **142**
Park St. G66: Kirk 6H **31**
G82: Dumb 4G **17**
ML1: Cle. 4H **129**
ML1: Moth 2G **143**
ML1: New S 4A **128**
ML5: Coat 3D **90**
ML6: Air 3G **91**
ML8: Carl 4F **165**
Park St. Sth. G3: Glas 2C **82**
Parks Vw. ML3: Ham 5H **153**
Park Ter. G3: Glas 2C **82**
G46: Giff 5A **118**
G74: E Kil 2G **149**
Park Ter. E. La. G3: Glas 2D **82**

Park Ter. La. G3: Glas 2C **82**
Park Top PA8: Ersk. 6G **41**
Parkvale Cres. PA8: Ersk. 1H **57**
Parkvale Dr. PA8: Ersk. 1H **57**
Parkvale Gdns. PA8: Ersk 1H **57**
Parkvale Pl. PA8: Ersk. 1H **57**
Parkvale Way PA8: Ersk 1H **57**
Parkview G82: Miln 3F **19**
Parkview Av. G66: Kirk 6D **30**
Parkview Ct. G66: Kirk. 6D **30**
Parkview Cres. ML2: Newm. 5E **147**
Parkview Dr. G33: Step 3E **67**
ML5: Coat 4A **90**
Parkville Dr. G72: Blan 3C **140**
(not continuous)
Parkville Rd. ML4: Bell 6E **111**
Parkway G32: Carm 5C **106**
Park Way G67: Cumb 1B **36**
Parkway PA8: Ersk 1F **57**
Parkway Ct. G69: Bail 4H **87**
ML5: Coat 5A **90**
Parkway Pl. ML5: Coat 6A **90**
Park Winding PA8: Ersk. 1G **57**
Park Wood PA8: Ersk. 6G **41**
Parlbrae Pl. G22: Glas 6E **91**
Parnell St. ML6: Air. 6H **91**
Parnie St. G1: Glas 5G **83**
Parry Ter. G75: E Kil 2D **148**
Parsonage Row G1: Glas . . . 4H **83** (6H **5**)
Parsonage Sq. G1: Glas 4H **83** (6H **5**)
(not continuous)
Parson St. G4: Glas 3A **84** (3H **5**)
PARTICK **1H 81**
Partick Bri. St. G11: Glas 2A **82**
PARTICKHILL **1H 81**
Partickhill Av. G11: Glas 6H **61**
Partickhill Ct. G11: Glas 6H **61**
Partickhill Rd. G11: Glas. 6H **61**
Partick Station (Rail, Und.) 1H **81**
Partick St. ML5: Coat 1B **110**
Partick Thistle F.C. 5E **63**
Patchy Pk. ML9: Lark 5E **161**
Paterson Pl. G61: Bear 5C **24**
Paterson's Laun G64: Balm 6A **28**
Paterson St. G5: Glas 6E **83**
(not continuous)
ML1: Moth 2G **143**
Paterson Ter. G75: E Kil 4F **149**
Pathead Gdns. G33: Glas. 3H **65**
Pather St. ML2: Wis 1H **157**
Pathhead Rd. G76: Crmck 2H **135**
Patna Ct. ML3: Ham 2C **152**
Patna St. G40: Glas 2D **104**
PATNER **2H 157**
Paton St. G31: Glas 4D **84**
Patrick St. PA2: Pais 2B **98**
Patterson Dr. ML8: Law 5E **159**
PATTERTON **1D 132**
Patterton Dr. G78: Barr. 6F **115**
Patterton Station (Rail) 1D **132**
Pattison St. G81: Clyd 4A **42**
Pavilion Theatre 3D **4**
Paxton Ct. *G74: E Kil* *5H 137*
(off Paxton Cres.)
Paxton Cres. G74: E Kil 5H **137**
Payne St. G4: Glas 1G **83** (1E **5**)
Peace Av. PA11: Q'riers 1B **72**
Peacock Av. PA2: Pais. 3D **96**
Peacock Cross ML3: Ham 5G **141**
Peacock Cross Ind. Est.
ML3: Ham 5G **141**
Peacock Dr. ML3: Ham 5G **141**
PA2: Pais 3D **96**
Peacock Loan *ML8: Carl.* *2F 165*
(off Carranbute Rd.)
Pearce La. G51: Glas. 3G **81**
Pearce St. G51: Glas. 3G **81**
Pearl St. ML4: Bell. 4D **126**
Pearson Dr. PA4: Renf 1F **79**
Pearson Pl. PA3: Lin 6H **75**
Peathill Av. G69: Chry 6H **51**

Peathill St. G21: Glas 6G **63**
Peat Pl. G53: Glas 2A **116**
Peat Rd. G53: Glas 2A **116**
PA11: Bri W 4G **73**
Pedmyre La. G76: Crmck 2G **135**
Peebles Dr. G73: Ruth 6F **105**
Peebles Path ML5: Coat. 2F **111**
Peel Av. ML1: Moth. 5G **143**
Peel Brae G66: Kirk 4C **30**
Peel Ct. G72: Camb 1A **122**
Peel Glen Gdns. G15: Glas 2A **44**
Peel Glen Rd. G15: Glas 3A **44**
Peel La. G11: Glas 1H **81**
PEEL PARK **1A 148**
Peel Pk. Ind. Est. G74: E Kil 1A **148**
Peel Pk. Pl. G74: E Kil 2B **148**
Peel Pl. G71: Both 4E **125**
ML5: Coat 6H **89**
Peel Rd. G74: T'hall 6F **135**
Peel St. G11: Glas 1H **81**
Peel Vw. G81: Clyd. 4F **43**
Pegasus Av. ML8: Carl. 3E **165**
PA1: Pais 6B **76**
Pegasus Rd. ML4: Moss 2G **127**
Peinchorran PA8: Ersk. 2G **57**
Peiter Pl. *G72: Blan* *2A 140*
(off Burnbrae Rd.)
Pembroke G74: E Kil 5D **138**
Pembroke St. G3: Glas 3D **82**
Pencaitland Dr. G32: Glas 2A **106**
Pencaitland Gro. G32: Glas 3A **106**
Pencaitland Pl. G23: Glas 6C **46**
Pendale Ri. G45: Glas 4H **119**
Pend Cl. PA5: John 4F **95**
Pendeen Cres. G33: Glas 6E **87**
Pendeen Pl. G33: Glas 5F **87**
Pendeen Rd. G33: Glas 6E **87**
Pendicle Cres. G61: Bear 4D **44**
Pendicle Rd. G61: Bear 4D **44**
Pendle Ct. G69: G'csh 3D **68**
Penfold Cres. G75: E Kil. 3F **149**
Penicuik St. G32: Glas 5F **85**
PENILEE **5G 79**
Penilee Rd. G52: Hill 3F **79**
Penilee Ter. G52: Glas. 4G **79**
Peninver Dr. G51: Glas 3E **81**
Penman Av. G73: Ruth. 5B **104**
Pennan PA8: Ersk. 5E **41**
Pennan Pl. G14: Glas. 4A **60**
Penneld Rd. G52: Glas 6H **79**
Penniecroft Av. G82: Dumb 2H **17**
Pennine Gro. ML6: Chap 4F **113**
Pennyroyal Ct. G74: E Kil 5F **137**
Penrith Av. G46: Giff 4A **118**
Penrith Dr. G12: Glas. 3G **61**
Penrith Pl. G75: E Kil. 5B **148**
Penryn Gdns. G32: Glas 2D **106**
Penston Rd. G33: Glas 3D **86**
Pentland Av. PA3: Lin 6G **75**
Pentland Ct. G78: Barr. 6D **114**
ML5: Coat 2E **111**
ML6: Air. 1B **92**
Pentland Cres. ML9: Lark 6G **155**
PA2: Pais 5H **97**
Pentland Dr. G64: B'rig 5F **49**
G78: Barr 6D **114**
PA4: Renf 3D **78**
Pentland Pl. G61: Bear 6B **24**
Pentland Rd. G43: Glas 2A **118**
G69: Chry 1B **68**
ML2: Wis 5E **145**
Penzance Way G69: Mood 4C **52**
Peockland Gdns. PA5: John 2G **95**
Peockland Pl. PA5: John 6A **84**
People's Palace (Museum) 6A **84**
Peploe Dr. G74: E Kil 4D **138**
Perchy Vw. ML2: Wis. 2A **158**
Percy Dr. G46: Giff. 6A **118**
Percy Rd. PA4: Renf 3C **78**
Percy St. G51: Glas 6B **82**
ML9: Lark 1E **161**
Perran Gdns. G69: Mood 5C **52**
Perray Av. G82: Dumb 2B **16**
Perrays Cres. G82: Dumb 2A **16**

Perrays Dr. G82: Dumb 3A 16
Perrays Way G82: Dumb 2A 16
Perth Av. ML6: Air 1A 112
Perth Cres. G81: Clyd 2H 41
Perth St. G3: Glas 4D 82
                              (not continuous)
Peter Coats Bldg. PA2: Pais 2A 98
Peter Dr. G66: Kirk 4D 30
PETERSBURN 5E 93
Petersburn Pl. ML6: Air 5D 92
Petersburn Rd. ML6: Air 6C 92
PETERSHILL 6D 64
Petershill Ct. G21: Glas 6D 64
Petershill Dr. G21: Glas 5D 64
Petershill Pl. G21: Glas 5D 64
Petershill Rd. G21: Glas 6B 64
Peterson Dr. G13: Glas 1G 59
Peterson Gdns. G13: Glas 1G 59
Petition Pl. G71: Udd 2E 125
Pettigrew St. G32: Glas 6A 86
Peveril Av. G41: Glas 4B 102
    G73: Ruth 2E 121
Peveril Ct. G73: Ruth 3E 121
Pharonhill St. G31: Glas 6G 85
Philip Murray Rd. ML4: Bell 1H 125
PHILIPSHILL 5A 136
Philipshill Ga. G74: E Kil 5A 136
Philipshill Rd. G76: Crmck 6A 136
Phoenix Bus. Pk., The PA1: Pais . . . 6C 76
Phoenix Ct. G74: E Kil 4D 138
                              (off Bosworth Rd.)
Phoenix Cres. ML4: Bell 5A 110
Phoenix Ind. Est. PA3: Glas A 3A 78
Phoenix Pl. ML1: New S 4A 128
    PA5: Eld 2B 96
Phoenix Retail Pk., The
    PA1: Pais 1D 96
Phoenix Rd. G4: Glas 1E 83 (1A 4)
    ML4: Moss 2G 127
Phyliss Jane Ct. ML2: Wis 2H 157
Piazza Shop. Cen. PA1: Pais 6A 78
Picadilly St. G3: Glas 4D 82 (6A 4)
PICKERSTONHILL 2F 129
Pickerstonhill ML1: N'hill 3E 129
Picketlaw Dr. G76: Crmck 2H 135
Picketlaw Farm Rd. G76: Crmck . . . 2G 135
Piershill St. G32: Glas 4H 85
Pikeman Rd. G13: Glas 3C 60
Pillans Ct. ML3: Ham 3E 141
Pilmuir Av. G44: Glas 3D 118
Pilrig St. G32: Glas 4G 85
Pilton Rd. G15: Glas 3A 44
Pine Av. G72: Flem 4F 123
Pine Cl. G67: Cumb 1E 37
Pine Ct. G67: Cumb 1E 37
    G75: E Kil 6D 148
    ML5: Coat. 1A 110
                              (off Ailsa Rd.)
Pine Cres. G67: Cumb 1E 37
    G75: E Kil 6D 148
    PA5: John. 4G 95
Pine Gro. G67: Cumb 1E 37
    G71: View 5F 109
    ML1: Holy. 2B 128
    ML6: C'bnk. 3B 112
Pinelands G64: B'rig 3C 48
Pine Lawn ML2: Wis 4B 146
Pine Pk. ML3: Ham 2A 154
Pine Pl. G5: Glas 1G 103
    G67: Cumb 1E 37
Pine Quad. ML6: Chap 2E 113
Pine Rd. G67: Cumb 6E 15
    G81: Clyd 3H 41
    G82: Dumb 3F 17
Pines, The G44: Glas 3F 119
Pine St. G66: Len 3G 7
    ML6: Air. 4D 92
    PA2: Pais 3C 98
Pinewood Av. G66: Lenz. 2A 50
Pinewood Ct. G66: Lenz. 2A 50
    G82: Dumb. 2H 17
Pinewood Pl. G66: Lenz. 2A 50
Pinewood Sq. G15: Glas 4B 44
Pinkerton Av. G73: Ruth 5A 104

Pinkston Dr. G21: Glas 1H 83 (1H 5)
Pinkston Rd. G21: Glas 6H 63 (1H 5)
    G4: Glas 1H 83
Pinmore Pl. G53: Glas 2H 115
Pinmore St. G53: Glas 2H 115
Pinwherry Dr. G33: Glas 3H 65
Pinwherry Pl. G71: Both 4E 125
Piper Av. PA6: C'lee 3C 74
Piper Rd. ML6: Air 6C 92
    PA6: C'lee. 3C 74
Pirnie Pl. G65: Kils 3H 11
Pirnmill Av. ML1: Moth 2D 142
Pitcairn Cres. G75: E Kil 3B 148
Pitcairn Gro. G75: E Kil 3C 148
Pitcairn Pl. G75: E Kil 3B 148
Pitcairn St. G31: Glas 1G 105
Pitcairn Ter. ML3: Ham 5E 141
Pitcaple Dr. G43: Glas 1H 117
Pitlochry Dr. G52: Glas 1B 100
    ML9: Lark. 4G 161
Pitmedden Rd. G64: B'rig 5F 49
Pitmilly Rd. G15: Glas 3C 44
Pitreavie Ct. ML3: Ham 3F 153
Pitreavie Pl. G33: Glas 2C 86
Pit Rd. G66: Kirk 6A 32
    ML4: Bell 1B 126
Pitt St. G2: Glas. 4E 83 (5B 4)
Pladda Rd. PA4: Renf. 2F 79
Pladda St. ML1: Moth 2D 142
PLAINS 1G 93
Plaintrees Ct. PA2: Pais. 4A 98
Plane Pl. G71: View. 4G 109
Planetree Pl. PA5: John 4G 95
Planetree Rd. G81: Clyd 2C 42
PLANTATION 5B 82
Plantation Av. ML1: Holy. 1B 128
Plantation Pk. Gdns. G51: Glas. . . . 6B 82
                              (not continuous)
Plantation Sq. G51: Glas. 5C 82
Plant St. G31: Glas. 5E 85
Platthorn Dr. G74: E Kil 2H 149
Platthorn Rd. G74: E Kil. 2H 149
Play Drome, The. 6D 42
Playfair St. G40: Glas 2C 104
Plaza, The G74: E Kil 2G 149
Pleaknowe Cres. G69: Mood. 5C 52
Pleamuir Pl. G68: Cumb 4E 35
Plean St. G14: Glas 4A 60
Pleasance St. G43: Glas 5A 102
Pleasance Way G43: Glas 6B 102
Plotcock Castle (Remains of) 4A 160
Plotcock Rd. ML3: Ham 4A 160
Plover Dr. G75: E Kil 6C 148
Plover Pl. PA5: John 6C 94
Plusgarten Loan ML2: Newm 2D 146
Pochard Way ML4: Bell 5B 110
Poet's Vw. G66: Kirk. 6F 31
Poindfauld Ter. G82: Dumb 3G 17
Pointhouse Rd. G3: Glas 3A 82
Pollock Av. ML3: Ham 6D 140
Pollock Rd. G61: Bear 4G 45
    G77: Newt M 5C 132
Pollock St. ML1: Moth. 2G 143
    ML4: Bell 2E 127
POLLOK 6C 100
Pollok Av. G43: Glas 5H 101
Pollok Country Pk. 4G 101
Pollok Dr. G64: B'rig 5A 48
Pollok Ho. 5F 101
Pollok La. G74: E Kil 6B 138
Pollok Leisure Pool 6C 100
Pollok Pl. G74: E Kil 6B 138
POLLOKSHAWS 6A 102
Pollokshaws East Station (Rail) 6B 102
Pollokshaws Rd. G41: Glas 4C 102
    G43: Glas 6H 101
Pollokshaws Sports Cen. 5A 102
                              (off Ashtree Rd.)
Pollokshaws West Station (Rail)

. . . . 6H 101
POLLOKSHIELDS 2C 102
Pollokshields East Station (Rail)

. . . . 2E 103

Pollokshields Sq. G41: Glas 3C 102
Pollokshields West Station (Rail)

. . . . 3D 102
Pollok Township Cen. G53: Glas . . . 6C 100
POLMADIE 3H 103
Polmadie Av. G5: Glas. 3H 103
Polmadie Ind. Est. G5: Glas 3A 104
Polmadie Rd. G42: Glas 4G 103
Polmadie St. G42: Glas 4G 103
Polnoon Av. G13: Glas 3A 60
Polquhap Cl. G53: Glas 5A 100
Polquhap Gdns. G53: Glas 5A 100
Polquhap Pl. G53: Glas 5A 100
Polquhap Rd. G53: Glas 5A 100
Polson Dr. PA5: John 3E 95
Polsons Cres. PA2: Pais 3H 97
Polwarth La. G12: Glas 6H 61
Polwarth St. G12: Glas 6H 61
Pomona Pl. ML3: Ham 1D 152
Poplar Av. G11: Glas 6H 61
    G77: Newt M 6D 132
    PA5: John. 4G 95
    PA7: B'ton 5H 39
Poplar Ct. ML5: Coat 1A 110
Poplar Cres. PA7: B'ton. 5H 39
Poplar Dr. G66: Lenz 2A 50
    G66: Milt C 6C 8
    G81: Clyd 2B 42
Poplar Gdns. G75: E Kil 6E 149
Poplar Pl. G71: View 5H 109
    G72: Blan 6A 124
    ML1: Holy. 3B 128
Poplar Rd. G82: Dumb. 3F 17
Poplars, The G61: Bear 5D 24
Poplar St. ML6: Air 4D 92
Poplar Way G72: Flem 4F 123
Poplin St. G40: Glas. 2B 104
Porchester St. G33: Glas 1D 86
Portal Rd. G13: Glas 1C 60
PORT DUNDAS 1G 83
Port Dundas Ind. Est. G4: Glas 1G 83
Port Dundas Pl. G2: Glas . . 3G 83 (3E 5)
Port Dundas Rd. G4: Glas . . 2F 83 (1D 4)
PORT EGLINTON 1E 103
PORTERFIELD 1D 78
Porterfield Rd. PA4: Renf 6D 58
Porters La. ML6: Chap. 3D 112
Porter St. G51: Glas. 6A 82
Porters Well G71: Udd 2C 124
Portessie PA8: Ersk 5E 41
Portland Pk. ML3: Ham 1A 154
Portland Pl. ML3: Ham 1A 154
Portland Rd. G68: Cumb 6H 13
    PA2: Pais 2D 98
Portland Sq. ML3: Ham 1A 154
Portland St. ML5: Coat 3D 90
Portland Wynd ML9: Lark. 1F 161
                              (off Muirshot Rd.)
Portlethen PA8: Ersk 5E 41
Portman St. G41: Glas 6C 82
Portmarnock Dr. G23: Glas 1C 62
Porton Pl. PA7: B'ton 4G 39
Portpatrick Rd. G60: Old K 6D 20
Portreath Rd. G69: Mood 4D 52
Portree Av. ML5: Coat 1A 110
Portree Pl. G15: Glas. 3G 43
Portsoy PA8: Ersk. 5E 41
Portsoy Av. G13: Glas 1H 59
Portsoy Pl. G13: Glas 1G 59
Port St. G3: Glas 4D 82
Portugal St. G5: Glas 6F 83
Portwell ML3: Ham 5A 142
POSSIL PARK 4G 63
Possilpark & Parkhouse Station (Rail)

. . . . 3F 63
Possil Pk. Millennium Cen. 5F 63
Possil Pk. Trad. Cen. G22: Glas . . . 4G 63
Possil Rd. G4: Glas 1F 83
Postgate ML3: Ham 5A 142
Potassels Rd. G69: Muirh 2A 68
Potrail Pl. ML3: Ham 6E 141
Potter Cl. G32: Glas. 2G 105
Potter Gro. G32: Glas. 2G 105
POTTERHILL 4H 97

Potterhill Av. PA2: Pais 5A 98
Potterhill Rd. G53: Glas 3A 100
Potter Path G32: Glas 2G 105
Potter Pl. G32: Glas 2G 105
Potter St. G32: Glas 2G 105
Potts Way ML1: Moth 6E 127
Powbrone G75: E Kil 6G 149
POWBURN 5C 108
Powburn Cres. G71: Udd 6B 108
Powderdrome Bowl 5E 91
Powerleague Soccer Cen.
    Glasgow 3A 84 (2H 5)
    Hamilton 3G 141
    Paisley 2C 98
Powfoot St. G31: Glas 6F 85
Powforth Cl. ML9: Lark 2C 160
Powrie St. G33: Glas 6C 66
Prentice La. G71: Tann 5E 109
Prentice Rd. ML1: Moth 4D 142
Prestonfield G62: Miln 4E 25
Preston Pl. G42: Glas 3F 103
Preston St. G42: Glas 3F 103
Prestwick Ct. G68: Cumb 1H 35
Prestwick Pl. G77: Newt M 5G 133
Prestwick St. G53: Glas 1A 116
Priestfield Ind. Est. G72: Blan 4B 140
Priestfield St. G72: Blan 3A 140
PRIESTHILL 1A 116
Priesthill & Darnley Station (Rail)
    . . . . 2C 116
Priesthill Av. G53: Glas 1C 116
Priesthill Cres. G53: Glas 1C 116
Priesthill Gdns. G53: Glas 2C 116
Priesthill Rd. G53: Glas 1B 116
PRIESTKNOWE RDBT. 2H 149
Prieston Rd. PA11: Bri W 4E 73
Primrose Av. ML4: Bell 6C 110
    ML9: Lark 5E 161
Primrose Ct. G14: Glas 6D 60
Primrose Cres. ML1: Moth 4G 143
Primrose Pl. G67: Cumb 6D 34
    G71: View 5G 109
Primrose St. G14: Glas 6C 60
Primrose Way G66: Len 4G 7
    ML8: Carl 5E 165
Prince Albert Rd. G12: Glas 6H 61
Prince Edward St. G42: Glas 3E 103
Prince of Wales Gdns. G20: Glas . . 1A 62
Prince Pl. ML2: Newm 3E 147
Prince's Gdns. G12: Glas 6H 61
Prince's Gdns. La. G12: Glas 6H 61
Princes Ga. G71: Both 3C 124
    G73: Ruth 5C 104
Princes Mall G74: E Kil 2G 149
    (off Olympia)
Princes Pk. PA7: B'ton 3C 40
Prince's Pl. G12: Glas 6A 62
Princess Anne Quad. ML1: Holy . . . 2H 127
    (off Sherry Av.)
Princess Cres. PA1: Pais 6D 78
Princess Dr. G69: Barg 6E 89
Princess Sq. G74: E Kil 2G 149
Princess Sq. Shop. Cen.
    G1: Glas 6E 5
Princess Rd. ML1: New S 3H 127
Princess Sq. G78: Barr 4F 115
    ML2: Newm 4D 146
Princes St. G73: Ruth 5C 104
    ML1: Moth 1G 143
Prince's Ter. G12: Glas 6A 62
Prince's Ter. La. G12: Glas 6A 62
Printers Land G76: Busby 3E 135
Printers Lea G66: Len 3E 7
Priorscroft Bowling Club 1B 98
    (off Cochran St.)
Priorwood Ct. G13: Glas 3D 60
Priorwood Gdns. G13: Glas 3D 60
Priorwood Ga. G77: Newt M 5A 132
Priorwood Pl. G13: Glas 3D 60
Priorwood Rd. G77: Newt M 5A 132
Priorwood Way G77: Newt M 5A 132
Priory Av. PA3: Pais 4C 78
Priory Dr. G71: Udd 6B 108
Priory Ga. ML2: Over 4H 157

Priory Pl. G13: Glas 2D 60
    G68: Cumb 4A 34
Priory Rd. G13: Glas 2D 60
Priory St. G72: Blan 1B 140
Priory Ter. ML2: Wis 1C 156
Pro Bowl 4D 30
Procession Rd. PA2: Pais 1A 114
Professors Sq. G12: Glas 1B 82
Pro Lane Bowl 5A 150
Pro Life Fitness Cen. 5A 78
Prosen St. G32: Glas 2G 105
Prospect Av. G71: Udd 1C 124
    G72: Camb 1H 121
Prospect Ct. G72: Blan 4B 140
Prospect Dr. ML9: Ashg 5B 162
Prospecthill Cir. G42: Glas 4H 103
Prospecthill Cres. G42: Glas 5A 104
Prospecthill Gro. G42: Glas 5E 103
Prospecthill Pl. G42: Glas 5A 104
Prospecthill Rd. G42: Glas 5E 103
Prospecthill Sq. G42: Glas 4H 103
Prospecthill Way G42: Glas 6E 103
    (off Prospecthill Gro.)
Prospect Rd. G43: Glas 5B 102
    G68: Dull 5E 13
Provandhall Cres. G69: Bail 2H 107
Provand's Lordship 4H 5
Provan Hall 2F 87
Provanhill St. G21: Glas 2B 84
PROVAN INTERCHANGE 2E 85
PROVANMILL 6G 65
Provanmill Pl. G33: Glas 6F 65
    (off Provanmill Rd.)
Provanmill Rd. G33: Glas 6F 65
Provan Rd. G33: Glas 2E 85
Provan Wlk. G34: Glas 2E 87
Provost Cl. PA5: John 2F 95
Provost Dr. Ct. PA4: Renf 1F 79
Provost Ga. ML9: Lark 2E 161
P.S. Waverley 5D 82
Purdie G74: E Kil 4D 138
Purdie St. ML3: Ham 4E 141
Purdon St. G11: Glas 1H 81
Pyatshaw Rd. ML9: Lark 4F 161

Q

Quadrant Rd. G43: Glas 1C 118
Quadrant Shop. Cen. ML5: Coat . . . 4C 90
Quadrant, The G76: Clar 1C 134
QUARRELTON 3E 95
Quarrelton Gro. PA5: John 4F 95
Quarrelton Rd. PA5: John 3E 95
QUARRIER'S VILLAGE 1A 72
Quarry Av. G72: Camb 4D 122
Quarrybank PA10: Kilb 3C 94
Quarrybrae Av. G76: Clar 2B 134
Quarrybrae Gdns. G71: View 1G 125
Quarrybrae St. G31: Glas 6F 85
Quarry Dr. G66: Kirk 5F 31
Quarryknowe G73: Ruth 6B 104
Quarry Knowe PA11: B'ton 2D 16
Quarry Knowe Pl. ML4: Bell 4B 126
Quarryknowe St. G31: Glas 6G 85
    G81: Faif 6F 23
Quarry La. G66: Len 2F 7
    G82: Dumb 4E 17
Quarry Pk. G75: E Kil 3G 149
Quarry Pl. G72: Camb 1G 121
    G82: Dumb 2D 16
    ML3: Ham 6A 142
Quarry Rd. G75: E Kil 6F 149
    G78: Barr 3D 114
    ML6: Air 2H 91
    ML8: Carl 3H 163
    ML9: Lark 3E 161
    PA2: Pais 4B 98
Quarryside St. ML6: Glenm 5G 71
Quarry St. ML1: New S 3A 128
    ML2: Wis 6G 145
    ML3: Ham 6A 142
    ML5: Coat 5F 91

Quarry St. ML9: Lark 4F 161
    PA5: John 2F 95
Quarrywood Av. G21: Glas 5E 65
Quarrywood Rd. G21: Glas 5E 65
Quay Pend G82: Dumb 4E 17
Quay Rd. G73: Ruth 4C 104
Quay Rd. Nth. G73: Ruth 4C 104
Quay St. G82: Dumb 4F 17
Quay, The G5: Glas 5D 82
Quebec Dr. G75: E Kil 3E 149
Quebec Grn. G75: E Kil 2E 149
Quebec Ho. G81: Clyd 1H 41
Quebec Wynd G32: Carm 5C 106
Queen Elizabeth Av. G52: Hill 4G 79
Queen Elizabeth Ct. G81: Clyd . . . 4C 42
    ML1: Moth 2F 143
Queen Elizabeth Gdns. G5: Glas . . 1G 103
Queen Margaret Ct. G20: Glas 5C 62
    (off Fergus Dr.)
Queen Margaret Dr. G12: Glas 6B 62
Queen Margaret Rd. G20: Glas . . . 5C 62
Queen Mary Av. G42: Glas 4E 103
    G81: Clyd 5F 43
Queen Mary Gdns. G81: Clyd 4C 42
Queen Mary St. G40: Glas 1C 104
Queen's Av. G72: Camb 1B 122
Queensbank Av. G69: G'csh 2C 68
Queensberry Av. G61: Bear 6E 25
    G76: Clar 2C 134
Queensborough Gdns. G12: Glas . . 5G 61
Queensby Av. G69: Bail 6H 87
Queensby Dr. G69: Bail 5H 87
Queensby Pl. G69: Bail 5A 88
Queensby Rd. G69: Bail 5H 87
Queen's Ct. G62: Miln 5G 25
Queen's Cres. G4: Glas 1D 82 (1A 4)
    G69: Barg 6D 88
Queens Cres. ML1: New S 4H 127
Queen's Cres. ML4: Bell 3B 126
    ML6: Chap 2D 112
    ML8: Carl 3G 165
Queensdale Av. ML9: Lark 5F 161
Queensdale Rd. ML9: Lark 5F 161
Queen's Dr. G42: Glas 3D 102
    G68: Cumb 5H 13
Queens Dr. ML3: Ham 5H 153
    PA7: B'ton 4H 39
Queen's Dr. La. G42: Glas 4E 103
Queensferry St. G5: Glas 3A 104
Queen's Gdns. G12: Glas 6A 62
Queen's Ga. G76: Clar 1C 134
Queen's Ga. La. G12: Glas 6A 62
Queens Gro. G66: Lenz 3C 50
Queenside Cres. PA8: Ersk 6D 40
Queensland Ct. G52: Glas 5C 80
Queensland Dr. G52: Glas 5C 80
Queensland Gdns. G52: Glas 5C 80
Queensland La. E. G52: Glas 5C 80
Queensland La. W. G52: Glas 5C 80
Queenslie Ind. Est. G33: Glas 3D 86
Queenslie St. G33: Glas 1F 85
Queen's Pk. Av. G42: Glas 4F 103
Queen's Pk. F.C. 6F 103
Queen's Park Station (Rail) 3E 103
Queens Pl. G12: Glas 6A 62
Queen's Rd. PA5: Eld 3A 96
Queen's St. ML1: Cle 5H 129
Queen St. G1: Glas 4G 83 (6E 5)
    G66: Kirk 5C 30
    G73: Ruth 5C 104
    ML1: Moth 2G 143
    ML2: Newm 3D 146
    ML3: Ham 4E 141
    PA1: Pais 1G 97
    PA4: Renf 6F 59
Queen Street Station (Rail)
    . . . . 3G 83 (4E 5)
Queens Way G64: Torr 5D 28
Queensway G74: E Kil 6B 136
Queen Victoria Ct. G14: Glas 5C 60
Queen Victoria Dr. G13: Glas 5C 60
    G14: Glas 5C 60
Queen Victoria Ga. G13: Glas 4C 60

Queen Victoria St. ML6: Air 4H 91
QUEENZIEBURN 3C 10
Queenzieburn Ind. Est.
G65: Queen 4D 10
Quendale Dr. G32: Glas 2H 105
Quentin St. G41: Glas 4C 102
Quinton Gdns. G69: Bail 6G 87

R

Raasay Cres. ML6: Air 5E 93
Raasay Dr. PA2: Pais 6H 97
Raasay Gdns. G77: Newt M 4B 132
Raasay Pl. G22: Glas 1G 63
Raasay St. G22: Glas 1G 63
Racecourse Vw. ML3: Ham 4A 142
RADNOR PARK 3C 42
Radnor St. G3: Glas 2B 82
G81: Clyd 4C 42
(not continuous)
Raeberry St. G20: Glas 6D 62
Raebog Cres. ML6: Air 1H 91
Raebog Rd. ML6: Glenm 5G 71
Raeburn Av. G74: E Kil 5B 138
PA1: Pais 1B 98
Raeburn Cres. ML3: Ham 6C 140
Raeburn Pl. G74: E Kil 5B 138
Raeburn Wlk. ML4: Bell 6D 110
Raeside Av. G77: Newt M 6D 132
Raes Rd. ML8: Carl 5B 164
Raeswood Dr. G53: Glas 5H 99
Raeswood Gdns. G53: Glas 5H 99
Raeswood Pl. G53: Glas 5H 99
Raeswood Rd. G53: Glas 5H 99
Raewell Cres. ML4: Bell 4B 126
Rafford St. G51: Glas 4G 81
Raglan St. G4: Glas 1E 83
Railway Rd. ML6: Air 4F 91
Raith Av. G45: Glas 3H 119
Raithburn Av. G45: Glas 3G 119
Raithburn Rd. G45: Glas 4G 119
Raith Cottage Vis. Cen. 6H 125
Raith Dr. G68: Cumb 4H 33
ML4: Bell 3D 126
RAITH INTERCHANGE. 5G 125
RALSTON 1F 99
Ralston Av. PA1: Pais 2H 99
Ralston Cotts. PA1: Pais 1F 99
Ralston Ct. G52: Glas 1H 99
Ralston Dr. G52: Glas 1H 99
Ralston Path G52: Glas 1H 99
Ralston Pl. G52: Glas 1H 99
Ralston Rd. G61: Bear 2E 45
G78: Barr 5E 115
Ralston St. ML6: Air 4G 91
PA1: Pais 1C 98
Ramage Rd. ML8: Carl 5H 165
Ramillies Ct. G81: Clyd 5E 43
ML8: Carl 4G 165
Rampart Av. G13: Glas 1A 60
Ramsay Av. PA5: John 4E 95
Ramsay Ct. G77: Newt M 6E 133
Ramsay Cres. PA10: Kilb 3B 94
Ramsay Hill G74: E Kil 6A 138
Ramsay Ind. Est. G66: Kirk 4B 30
Ramsay Pl. ML5: Coat 6G 89
PA5: John 4E 95
Ramsay St. G81: Clyd 4B 42
Ramsey Wynd ML4: Bell 6D 110
Ram St. G32: Glas 6H 85
Ranaldard Gdns. G73: Ruth 4F 121
Randolph Av. G76: Clar 6E 119
Randolph Dr. G76: Clar 6D 118
Randolph Gdns. G76: Clar 6D 118
Randolph Ga. G11: Glas 5F 61
Randolph La. G11: Glas 6F 61
Randolph Rd. G11: Glas 5F 61
RANFURLY 5G 73
Ranfurly Ct. PA11: Bri W 4F 73
Ranfurly Dr. G68: Cumb 1G 35
Ranfurly Pl. PA11: Bri W 4F 73
Ranfurly Rd. G52: Glas 6H 79
PA11: Bri W 5F 73

Range Av. ML1: Moth 5C 144
Range Pl. ML3: Ham 2A 154
Rangers F.C. 5G 81
Rangers F.C. Training Cen. &
Youth Academy 5A 26
Rangerhouse Rd. G75: E Kil 6H 149
Range Rd. ML1: Moth 5B 144
Range Rd. Ind. Est. ML1: Moth. . . 6C 144
(Range Av.)
ML1: Moth 5B 144
(Range Rd.)
Range St. ML1: Moth. 5B 144
Rankin Dr. G77: Newt M 3C 132
Rankine Av. G75: E Kil 4A 150
Rankine Pl. G75: E Kil 4A 150
PA5: John 2F 95
Rankine St. PA5: John 2F 95
Rankin Gait Cen. ML8: Carl 3F 165
(off High St.)
Rankin St. ML8: Carl 3F 165
Rankin Way G78: Barr 4G 115
Rannoch Av. G64: B'rig 6D 48
G77: Newt M 2D 132
ML3: Ham 2E 153
ML5: Coat 2H 89
Rannoch Ct. G67: Cumb 1D 54
G72: Blan 4D 140
Rannoch Dr. G61: Bear 2H 45
G66: Kirk 4H 31
G67: Cumb. 1D 54
ML2: Wis 2H 157
PA4: Renf 5E 59
Rannoch Gdns. G64: B'rig 6E 49
Rannoch Grn. G74: E Kil 6H 137
Rannoch La. G69: Mood 5E 53
Rannoch Pl. PA2: Pais 2C 98
Rannoch Rd. G71: Tann 4C 108
ML6: Air 2H 91
PA5: John 4E 95
Rannoch St. G44: Glas 1E 119
Rannoch Ter. ML9: Lark 4G 161
Rannoch Way G71: Both 4E 125
RAPLOCH 2D 160
Raploch Av. G14: Glas 5B 60
Raploch Cres. G81: Faif 6F 23
Raploch La. G14: Glas 5B 60
Raploch Rd. ML9: Lark 2D 160
Raploch St. ML9: Lark 2D 160
RASHIEBURN 5E 41
Rashieburn PA8: Ersk 5E 41
Rashieglen PA8: Ersk. 5E 41
Rashiehill PA8: Ersk 5E 41
Rashielee Rd. PA8: Ersk 5E 41
Rashiewood PA8: Ersk 5F 41
Rashilee Av. PA8: Ersk. 5F 41
Rathlin St. G51: Glas 3G 81
Rathlin Ter. G82: Dumb 2C 16
Ratho Dr. G21: Glas 5A 64
G68: Cumb 6F 13
Ratho Pk. ML3: Ham 4F 153
Rattray PA8: Ersk 4E 41
Rattray St. G32: Glas 2G 105
Ravel Row G31: Glas 6F 85
Ravelston Rd. G61: Bear 5E 45
(not continuous)
Ravelston St. G32: Glas 5F 85
Ravel Wynd G71: Tann 5F 109
Ravenscliffe Dr. G46: Giff 4H 117
Ravens Ct. G64: B'rig 1B 64
Ravenscourt G74: T'hall 6G 135
Ravenscraig Av. PA2: Pais 4G 97
Ravenscraig Ct. ML4: Bell 2D 126
Ravenscraig Dr. G53: Glas 1B 116
Ravenscraig Ter. G53: Glas 2C 116
Ravenshall ML1: Cle 1H 145
Ravenshall Rd. G41: Glas 5A 102
Ravenshill Dr. ML1: Cle. 6H 129
Ravenstone Dr. G46: Giff 2A 118
Ravenswood Av. PA2: Pais 6C 96
Ravenswood Dr. G41: Glas 4B 102
Ravenswood Rd. G69: Bail 6A 88
Raven Wynd ML2: Wis 5H 145
RAWYARDS 2C 92

Rawyards Av. ML6: Air 1B 92
Raymond Pl. G75: E Kil 2E 149
Rayne Pl. G15: Glas. 3B 44
Ream Av. ML6: Air 5F 93
Reay Av. G74: E Kil 1D 148
Reay Gdns. G74: E Kil 1D 148
Rebrae Pl. G66: Kirk 4E 31
Redan St. G40: Glas. 6B 84
Redbrae Rd. G66: Kirk. 4D 30
Red Bri. Ct. ML5: Coat. 3C 90
Redburn Av. G46: Giff 1H 133
Redburn Ct. G67: Cumb 5F 15
Redburn Pl. G67: Cumb 6F 15
Redburn Rd. G67: Cumb 5F 15
Redcastle Sq. G33: Glas 2E 87
Redcliffe Dr. G75: E Kil 3D 148
Red Deer Rd. G75: E Kil 3E 149
Rederech Cres. ML3: Ham 1D 152
Redford St. G33: Glas. 3F 85
Redgate Pl. G14: Glas 5B 60
Redgrave G74: E Kil 4C 138
Redhill Rd. G68: Cumb 2F 35
Redhills Vw. G66: Len 4G 7
Redholme ML9: Lark 4F 161
(off Keir Hardie Rd.)
Redhouse La. ML8: Carl. 2F 165
Redhurst Cres. PA2: Pais 6F 97
Redhurst La. PA2: Pais. 6G 97
Redhurst Way PA2: Pais. 6F 97
Redlands La. G12: Glas 5A 62
Redlands Rd. G12: Glas 5A 62
Redlands Ter. G12: Glas 5A 62
Redlands Ter. La. G12: Glas 5A 62
Redlawood Pl. G72: Newt 1G 123
Redlawood Rd. G72: Newt 1G 123
Redmoss Rd. G66: Milt C 6B 8
G81: Dun 1B 42
Redmoss St. G22: Glas 4F 63
Rednock St. G22: Glas. 5G 63
Redpath Dr. G52: Glas. 5B 80
Red Rd. G21: Glas 5D 64
Red Rd. Ct. G21: Glas 6D 64
Red Road Recreation Cen. 6E 65
Redwing Gdns. ML2: Wis. 2F 157
Redwood Av. G74: E Kil 2A 148
Redwood Ct. G74: E Kil 2A 148
Redwood Cres. G71: View 5G 109
G72: Flem 3F 123
G74: E Kil 6A 136
PA7: B'ton 4A 40
Redwood Dr. G21: Glas 6C 64
G74: E Kil 3A 148
Redwood Gro. ML5: Coat 5D 90
Redwood Pl. G66: Lenz 2B 50
G71: View. 5G 109
G74: E Kil 1A 148
Redwood Rd. G67: Cumb 3D 36
ML1: Holy. 2C 128
Redwood Way G72: Flem 4F 123
Reelick Av. G13: Glas 1G 59
Reelick Quad. G13: Glas 1G 59
Reema Rd. ML4: Bell. 1D 126
Reen Pl. G71: Both. 3F 125
Regency Ct. ML3: Ham 1C 154
Regency M. G69: Bail 1A 108
Regency Way G71: New S 3H 127
Regent Dr. G73: Ruth. 5C 104
Regent Moray St. G3: Glas 2B 82
Regent Pk. Sq. G41: Glas 3D 102
Regent Pl. G81: Clyd 3A 42
Regents Ga. G71: Both 3B 124
Regent Shop. Cen. G66: Kirk. 5C 30
Regent Sq. G66: Lenz 3C 50
Regent St. G66: Kirk 5C 30
G81: Clyd 3A 42
PA1: Pais 6D 78
Regent Way ML3: Ham 6A 142
Register Av. ML4: Bell 4C 126
Register Rd. G65: Kils 3A 12
Regwood St. G41: Glas 5B 102
Reid Av. G61: Bear. 1G 45
PA3: Lin 6H 75
Reid Gro. ML1: Moth 5B 144
Reid Pl. G40: Glas 1B 104

Reid St. G40: Glas 2B **104**
  G73: Ruth 5D **104**
  ML3: Ham 4D **140**
  ML5: Coat 3C **90**
  PA6: Air 2B **92**
Reidvale St. G31: Glas 5B **84**
Reilly Rd. PA6: Hous 6B **38**
Reith Dr. G75: E Kil 4F **149**
Remus Pl. ML4: Moss 2G **127**
Renfield La. G2: Glas 4F **83** (5D **4**)
Renfield St. G2: Glas 4F **83** (5D **4**)
  PA4: Renf 5F **59**
RENFREW 5F **59**
Renfrew Community Mus. 5F **59**
Renfrew Ct. *G1: Glas* *3G 5*
                        (off St Mungo Av.)
  G2: Glas. 3G **83** (3E **5**)
Renfrew La. G2: Glas 3F **83** (3D **4**)
Renfrew Pl. ML5: Coat 1G **109**
Renfrew Rd. G51: Glas 3B **80**
  PA3: Pais 5B **78**
  PA4: Renf 1A **80**
Renfrew St. G3: Glas 2E **83** (2A **4**)
  ML5: Coat 1G **109**
Rennie Ct. G74: E Kil 6C **136**
Rennie Rd. G65: Kils 2F **11**
Renshaw Dr. G52: Glas 5B **80**
Renshaw Rd. PA5: Eld 4A **96**
  PA7: B'ton 4H **39**
Renton Rd. G82: Dumb 1D **16**
Renton St. G4: Glas 2G **83** (1E **5**)
Resipol Rd. G33: Step 4E **67**
Reston Dr. G52: Glas 5B **80**
Reuther Av. G73: Ruth. 6D **104**
Revoch Dr. G13: Glas 2A **60**
Reynolds Av. G75: E Kil 4A **150**
Reynolds Dr. G33: Step 4F **67**
Reynolds Path ML2: Wis 2B **158**
Rhannan Rd. G44: Glas 2E **119**
Rhannan Ter. G44: Glas 2E **119**
Rhindhouse Pl. G69: Bail 6B **88**
Rhindhouse Rd. G69: Bail 6C **88**
Rhindmuir Av. G69: Bail 6A **88**
Rhindmuir Ct. G69: Bail 5A **88**
Rhindmuir Cres. G69: Bail 5B **88**
Rhindmuir Dr. G69: Bail 5A **88**
Rhindmuir Gdns. G69: Bail 5A **88**
Rhindmuir Gro. G69: Bail 5B **88**
Rhindmuir Path G69: Bail 5B **88**
Rhindmuir Pl. G69: Bail 5A **88**
Rhindmuir Rd. G69: Bail 5B **88**
Rhindmuir Vw. G69: Bail 5B **88**
Rhindmuir Wynd G69: Bail 5B **88**
Rhinds St. ML5: Coat 1F **109**
Rhinsdale Cres. G69: Bail 6A **88**
Rhumhor Gdns. PA10: Kilb 3C **94**
Rhu Quad. ML2: Over 5A **158**
Rhymer St. G21: Glas 2A **84**
Rhymie Rd. G32: Glas 2D **106**
Rhynie Dr. G51: Glas 6H **81**
Riach Gdns. ML1: Moth 6E **127**
Ribblesdale G74: E Kil 6E **137**
Riccardon G75: E Kil 4D **148**
Riccarton St. G42: Glas 2G **97**
Riccartsbar Av. PA2: Pais 2G **97**
Rice Way ML1: Moth 5B **144**
Richmond Av. G76: Clar 2C **134**
Richmond Ct. G73: Ruth 5E **105**
Richmond Dr. G64: B'rig 3D **48**
  G72: Camb 2G **121**
  G73: Ruth 6E **105**
  PA3: Lin 4G **75**
Richmond Gdns. G69: Chry 1H **67**
Richmond Gro. G73: Ruth 6E **105**
Richmond Pl. G73: Ruth 5E **105**
Richmond Rd. G73: Ruth 6F **105**
Richmond St. G1: Glas 4H **83** (5G **5**)
  G81: Clyd 6E **43**
Riddell St. G81: Clyd 4D **42**
  ML5: Coat 4E **91**
Riddon Av. G13: Glas 1G **59**
Riddon Pl. G13: Glas 1G **59**
RIDDRIE 2F **85**
Riddrie Cres. G33: Glas 3G **85**

RIDDRIE KNOWES 3G **85**
Riddrie Knowes G33: Glas 3G **85**
Riddrievale Ct. G33: Glas 2G **85**
Riddrievale St. G33: Glas 2G **85**
Rigby St. G31: Glas 6G **85**
Rigg Pl. G33: Glas 4E **87**
Riggside Rd. G33: Glas 1C **86**
Riggs, The G62: Miln 2G **25**
Riggead Ga. *G74: E Kil* *2G 149*
                             (off Princess Sq.)
Righead Ind. Est. ML4: Bell 6A **110**
RIGHEAD RDBT. 2F **149**
Riglands Way PA4: Renf 6E **59**
Riglaw Pl. G13: Glas 2A **60**
Rigmuir Rd. G51: Glas 4C **80**
Rimsdale St. G40: Glas 6C **84**
Ringford St. G21: Glas 6B **64**
Ripon Dr. G12: Glas 3G **61**
Risk St. G81: Clyd 3B **42**
  G82: Dumb 4E **17**
Ristol Rd. G13: Glas 4B **60**
Ritchie Cres. PA5: Eld 2A **96**
Ritchie Pk. PA5: John 2H **95**
Ritchie Pl. G77: Newt M 5C **132**
Ritchie St. G5: Glas 1E **103**
  ML2: Wis 6D **144**
Riverbank Dr. ML4: Bell 4E **127**
Riverbank St. G43: Glas 6A **102**
River Ct. G76: Busby 3D **134**
Riverdale Gdns. ML3: Ham 2A **154**
Riverford Rd. G43: Glas 6A **102**
  G73: Ruth 4E **105**
River Rd. G32: Carm 6B **106**
Riversdale La. G14: Glas 4A **60**
Riverside G62: Miln 3G **25**
  G66: Len 1C **6**
  PA6: Hous 2D **74**
Riverside Ct. G44: Neth 4D **118**
Riverside Gdns. G76: Busby 4D **134**
Riverside La. G82: Dumb 4E **17**
Riverside Pk. G44: Neth 5E **119**
Riverside Pl. G72: Camb 1E **123**
Riverside Rd. G43: Glas 6C **102**
  ML9: Lark 5E **161**
Riverside Ter. G76: Busby 4D **134**
Riverside Wlk. ML1: Moth 1H **143**
Riverton Dr. G75: E Kil 3D **148**
Riverview Dr. G5: Glas 5E **83**
Riverview Gdns. G5: Glas 5E **83**
Riverview Pl. G5: Glas 5E **83**
R.N.I.B. Springfield Cen.
  G64: B'rig 6D **48**
Roaden Av. PA2: Pais 6D **96**
Roaden Rd. PA2: Pais 6D **96**
Roadside G67: Cumb 6A **14**
Robb Ter. G66: Kirk 1G **51**
Robert Burns Av. G81: Clyd 4E **43**
  ML1: N'hill 3E **129**
Robert Burns Quad. ML4: Bell . . . 2B **126**
Robert Dr. G51: Glas 4G **81**
Roberton St. ML6: Chap 2E **113**
Robert Smillie Cres. ML9: Lark . . . 4E **161**
Robertson Av. G41: Glas 3A **102**
  PA4: Renf 6D **58**
Robertson Cl. PA4: Renf 6E **59**
Robertson Cres. G78: Neil 2D **130**
Robertson Dr. G74: E Kil 1B **150**
  ML4: Bell 3C **126**
Robertson La. G2: Glas 6B **4**
Robertson St. G1: Glas 5F **83** (6C **4**)
  G78: Barr 5D **114**
  ML3: Ham 4D **140**
  ML6: Air 4G **91**
Robertson Ter. G69: Bail 6A **88**
Roberts Quad. ML4: Bell 4D **126**
Roberts St. G81: Clyd 4A **42**
  ML2: Wis 6G **145**
Robert St. G51: Glas 4G **81**
Robert Templeton Dr.
  G72: Camb 2B **122**
Robert Wynd ML2: Newm 3E **147**
Robet Gilson Gdns. ML5: Coat . . . 6D **90**
Robin Pl. ML2: Wis 6H **145**

Robin Way G32: Carm 5C **106**
ROBROYSTON 3G **65**
Robroyston Av. G33: Glas 6G **65**
ROBROYSTON INTERCHANGE 4H **65**
Robroyston Rd. G33: Glas 4F **65**
  G64: B'rig 6H **49**
  G66: Auch 6H **49**
Robshill Ct. G77: Newt M 5D **132**
Roblsee Dr. G46: Giff 4H **117**
Roblsee Rd. G46: Giff, T'bnk. 5G **117**
Robson Gro. G42: Glas. 2F **103**
Rochdale Pl. G66: Kirk 5C **30**
Rochsoles Cres. ML6: Air 1A **92**
Rochsoles Dr. ML6: Air 1H **91**
Rochsolloch Farm Cotts.
  ML6: Air 4G **91**
Rochsolloch Rd. ML6: Air 5F **91**
Rockall Dr. G44: Glas. 3F **119**
Rockbank Pl. G40: Glas 6C **84**
  G81: Hard 1E **43**
Rockbank St. G40: Glas 6C **84**
Rockburn Cres. ML4: Bell 6C **110**
Rockburn Dr. G76: Clar 1A **134**
Rockcliffe St. G40: Glas 2B **104**
Rock Dr. PA10: Kilb 3B **94**
Rockfield Pl. G21: Glas 4E **65**
Rockfield Rd. G21: Glas 4E **65**
Rockhampton Av. G75: E Kil 4D **148**
Rockmount Av. G46: T'bnk 3G **117**
  G78: Barr 6F **115**
Rock St. G4: Glas 6F **63**
Rockwell Av. PA2: Pais 5G **97**
Roddinghead Rd. G46: Giff 3G **133**
Rodger Av. G77: Newt M 4C **132**
Rodger Dr. G73: Ruth 1C **120**
Rodger Pl. G73: Ruth 1C **120**
Rodil Av. G44: Glas 3G **119**
Rodney St. G4: Glas 1F **83**
Roebank Dr. G78: Barr 6E **115**
Roebank St. G31: Glas. 3D **84**
                              (not continuous)
Roffey Pk. Rd. PA1: Pais 6F **79**
Rogart St. G40: Glas 6B **84**
                              (not continuous)
Rogerfield Rd. G69: Barg 4A **88**
ROGERTON 3F **137**
Roland Cres. G77: Newt M. 6F **133**
Roman Av. G15: Glas 6A **44**
  G61: Bear 2F **45**
Roman Bath House 2F **45**
Roman Ct. G61: Bear 2F **45**
Roman Cres. G60: Old K 6D **20**
Roman Dr. G61: Bear 2F **45**
  ML4: Bell 3D **126**
Roman Gdns. G61: Bear. 2F **45**
Roman Hill Rd. G81: Hard 6D **22**
Roman Pl. ML4: Bell 4A **126**
Roman Rd. G61: Bear 2E **45**
  G66: Kirk 5B **30**
  G81: Hard 1C **42**
  ML1: Moth 1F **143**
                              (not continuous)
Roman Way G71: View 1G **125**
Romney Av. G44: Glas. 2G **119**
Romulus Ct. ML1: Moth. 6E **127**
Ronaldsay Dr. G64: B'rig 5F **49**
Ronaldsay Pas. G22: Glas 2H **63**
Ronaldsay Pl. G67: Cumb 5F **35**
Ronaldsay St. G22: Glas 2G **63**
Ronald St. ML5: Coat. 3C **90**
Rona St. G21: Glas 1D **84**
Rona Ter. G72: Camb 4H **121**
Ronay St. G22: Glas. 2H **63**
  ML2: Wis 4C **146**
Rooksdell Av. PA2: Pais 4G **97**
Ropework La. G1: Glas. 5G **83**
Rorison Pl. ML9: Ashg. 4B **162**
Rosa Burn Av. G75: E Kil 6D **148**
ROSEBANK
  Carlwe 5E **163**
  Glasgow 5G **31**
Rosebank PA5: John 3F **95**
Rosebank Av. G66: Kirk 4E **31**
  G72: Blan 6C **124**

Rosebank Dr. G71: View 6G 109
  G72: Camb 3C 122
Rosebank Gdns. G71: Udd 3H 107
Rosebank La. G71: Both 4F 125
Rosebank Pl. G68: Dull 5E 13
  G71: Udd 3H 107
  ML3: Ham 6E 141
Rosebank Rd. ML2: Over. 5A 158
  ML4: Bell 5D 110
Rosebank St. ML6: Air. 3E 93
Rosebank Ter. G69: Barg 1D 108
Rosebank Twr. G72: Camb 1A 122
                     (off Main St.)
Roseberry La. ML6: Chap 2E 113
Roseberry Pl. ML3: Ham 5E 141
Roseberry Rd. ML6: Chap 1D 112
Roseberry St. G5: Glas 2A 104
Roseburn Ct. G67: Cumb 5F 15
Rose Cres. ML3: Ham 5D 140
Rose Dale G64: B'rig 1D 64
Rosedale G74: E Kil 6E 137
Rosedale Av. PA2: Pais 6B 96
Rosedale Dr. G69: Baul 1G 107
Rosedale Gdns. G20: Glas 1A 62
Rosedene Ter. ML4: Bell 1C 126
Rosefield Gdns. G71: Udd 6C 108
Rosegreen Cres. ML4: Bell 5C 110
ROSEHALL 2D 110
Rosehall Av. ML5: Coat 1D 110
Rosehall Ind. Est. ML5: Coat. 2C 110
Rosehall Rd. ML4: Bell 1B 126
Rosehall Ter. ML2: Wis 2E 157
Rosehill Dr. G67: Cumb 1C 54
Rosehill Pl. G67: Cumb 1C 54
Rosehill Rd. G64: Torr. 5D 28
Rose Knowe Rd. G42: Glas 5H 103
Roselea Dr. G62: Miln 2H 25
Roselea Gdns. G13: Glas 2F 61
Roselea Pl. G72: Blan 6A 124
Roselea Rd. G71: Tann 5C 108
Roselea St. ML9: Lark 1F 161
Rosemary Cres. G74: E Kil. 5F 137
Rosemary Pl. G74: E Kil. 5F 137
Rosemount G68: Cumb 6H 13
Rose Mt. Ct. ML6: Air 3C 92
Rosemount Gdns. ML6: Air 4A 92
Rosemount La. ML9: Lark 4G 161
               (off Dickson St.)
  PA11: Bri W 5D 72
Rosemount Mdws. G71: Both 5D 124
Rosemount St. G21: Glas 2B 84
Rosendale Way G72: Blan 2C 140
Roseneath Ga. G74: E Kil 1E 149
Roseness Pl. G33: Glas 3A 86
Rosepark Av. G71: View 1G 125
Rosepark Cotts. ML5: Coat 2B 110
Rose St. G3: Glas 3F 83 (3C 4)
  G66: Kirk 5D 30
  G67: Cumb 6D 34
  ML1: Moth 4A 144
Rosevale Cres. ML4: Bell 3E 127
Rosevale Gdns. ML3: Ham 1F 153
Rosevale Rd. G61: Bear 3E 45
Rosevale St. G11: Glas 1G 81
Rosewood Av. ML4: Bell 6D 110
  PA2: Pais 4F 97
Rosewood Path ML4: Bell 2A 126
Rosewood St. G13: Glas 2E 61
Roslea Dr. G31: Glas 4C 84
Roslin Twr. G72: Camb 4G 121
Roslyn Dr. G69: Barg 6D 88
Rosneath St. G51: Glas 3G 81
Ross Av. G66: Kirk 5F 31
  PA4: Renf 2C 78
Ross Cres. ML1: Moth 4E 143
Ross Dr. G71: View 4G 109
  ML1: Moth 4E 143
  ML6: Air. 1G 111
Rossendale Ct. G43: Glas 5A 102
Rossendale Rd. G43: Glas 5A 102
Ross Gdns. ML1: Moth 4E 143
ROSSHALL 2A 100
Rosshall Av. PA1: Pais 1E 99
Ross Hall Pl. PA4: Renf 6F 59

Rosshill Av. G52: Glas 6H 79
Rosshill Rd. G52: Glas 6H 79
Rossie Cres. G64: B'rig 1E 65
Rossie Gro. G77: Newt M 4B 132
ROSSLAND 5H 39
Rossland Cres. PA7: B'ton 4G 39
Rossland Gdns. PA7: B'ton 4G 39
Rossland Pl. PA7: B'ton 5H 39
Rossland Vw. PA7: B'ton 4G 39
Rosslea Dr. G46: Giff 5A 118
Rosslea Cres. G46: Giff 4G 117
Rosslyn Av. G73: Ruth 6D 104
  G74: E Kil 6H 137
Rosslyn Ct. ML3: Ham 5E 141
Rosslyn Rd. G61: Bear 1B 44
  ML9: Ashg 5B 162
Rosslyn Ter. G12: Glas 5A 62
Ross Pl. G73: Ruth 3F 121
  G74: E Kil 6C 138
Ross St. G40: Glas 5H 83
  ML5: Coat. 4C 90
  PA1: Pais 2C 98
Ross Ter. ML3: Ham 2E 155
Rostan Rd. G43: Glas 2A 118
Rosyth Rd. G5: Glas 3A 104
Rosyth St. G5: Glas 3A 104
Rotherwick Dr. PA1: Pais 1G 99
Rotherwood Av. G13: Glas 6C 44
  PA2: Pais 5D 96
Rotherwood Pl. G13: Glas 1D 60
Rotherwood Way PA2: Pais 5D 96
Rothesay Cres. ML5: Coat. 1D 110
Rothesay Pl. G74: E Kil 2G 149
  ML5: Coat 1D 110
Rothesay St. G74: E Kil 2G 149
Rothes Dr. G23: Glas 6A 46
Rothes Pl. G23: Glas 6A 46
Rottenrow G1: Glas. 3H 83 (4G 5)
  G4: Glas 4A 84 (5H 5)
Rottenrow E. G4: Glas 4H 83 (5H 5)
Roughcraig St. ML6: Air. 1A 92
Roughrigg Rd. ML6: Air. 5F 93
Roukenburn St. G46: T'bnk 3E 117
Rouken Glen Pk. 6F 117
Rouken Glen Rd. G46: T'bnk 5F 117
Roundel, The ML2: Wis 1A 158
Roundhill Dr. PA5: Eld 2C 96
Roundknowe Rd. G71: Udd 4A 108
Round Riding Rd. G82: Dumb 3G 17
Rowallan Gdns. G11: Glas 6G 61
Rowallan La. G11: Glas 6F 61
  G76: Clar 2C 134
Rowallan Rd. G46: T'bnk 5F 117
Rowallan Ter. G33: Mille 5B 66
Rowallen La. E. G11: Glas 6G 61
Rowan Av. ML6: Milt C 6B 8
  PA4: Renf 5E 59
Rowanbank Pl. ML3: Air 3E 91
Rowan Ct. G72: Flem 3F 123
  ML2: Wis 1D 156
  PA2: Pais 3A 98
Rowan Cres. G66: Lenz 2C 50
  ML6: Chap 2E 113
Rowandale Av. G69: Bail 1G 107
Rowand Av. G46: Giff 5A 118
Rowanden Av. ML4: Bell 1C 126
Rowan Dr. FK4: Bank 1E 15
  G61: Bear 6F 25
  G81: Clyd 3B 42
  G82: Dumb 3A 16
Rowan Gdns. G41: Glas 1H 101
Rowan Ga. PA2: Pais 3B 98
Rowan La. ML1: New S 4A 128
Rowanlea PA5: John 5F 95
Rowanlea Av. PA2: Pais 6B 96
Rowanlea Dr. G46: Giff 3B 118
Rowanpark Dr. G78: Barr 2C 114
Rowan Pl. G72: Blan 1B 140
  G72: Camb 1C 122
  ML5: Coat. 1A 110
Rowan Ri. ML3: Ham. 1A 154
Rowan Rd. G41: Glas. 1H 101
  G67: Cumb. 2D 36
  PA3: Lin 4F 75

Rowans Gdns. G71: Both 3F 125
Rowans, The G64: B'rig 5B 48
Rowan St. ML2: Wis 4H 145
  PA2: Pais 3A 98
Rowantree Av. G71: View 6G 109
  G73: Ruth. 2D 120
  ML1: N'hse 6C 112
Rowantree Gdns.
  G73: Ruth. 2D 120
Rowantree Pl. G66: Len 4G 7
Rowan Tree Pl. ML9: Lark 3H 161
Rowantree Pl. PA5: John 4F 95
             (off Rowantree Rd.)
Rowantree Rd. PA5: John 4F 95
Rowantree Ter. G66: Len 4G 7
  ML1: Holy. 2B 128
Rowanwood Cres. ML5: Coat 6H 89
Rowena Av. G13: Glas 6D 44
Rownlea ML6: Plain 1F 93
             (off Craigiea Ter.)
Roxburgh Dr. G61: Bear 6E 25
  ML5: Coat. 1F 111
Roxburgh Pk. G74: E Kil 2H 149
Roxburgh Pl. G72: Blan 2B 140
             (off Jedburgh St.)
Roxburgh Rd. PA2: Pais. 6B 96
Roxburgh St. G12: Glas 6B 62
Royal Bank Pl. G1: Glas. 5E 5
Royal Cres. G3: Glas 3C 82
Royal Dr. ML3: Ham 1C 154
Royal Exchange Ct. G1: Glas 6E 5
Royal Exchange Sq.
  G1: Glas. 4G 83 (5E 5)
Royal Highland Fusiliers Mus.
  . . . . 2E 83 (2A 4)
Royal Inch Cres. PA4: Renf 4F 59
Royal Scottish Academy of
  Music & Drama 3F 83 (3D 4)
Royal Ter. G3: Glas 2C 82
  ML2: Wis 2A 146
Royal Ter. La. G3: Glas 2C 82
Royellen Av. ML3: Ham. 1D 152
ROYSTON 2B 84
Roystonhill G21: Glas 2B 84
Roystonhill Pl. G21: Glas. 2B 84
Royston Rd. G21: Glas. 2A 84
  G33: Glas 6G 65
Royston Sq. G21: Glas. 2A 84
Roy St. G21: Glas. 6H 63
Rozelle Av. G15: Glas 4B 44
  G77: Newt M 5B 132
Rozelle Dr. G77: Newt M 5B 132
Rozelle Pl. G77: Newt M 5B 132
Rubislaw Dr. G61: Bear 4E 45
Ruby St. G40: Glas. 1C 104
Ruby Ter. ML4: Bell 3C 126
RUCHAZIE 2B 86
Ruchazie Pl. G33: Glas 3H 85
Ruchazie Rd. G33: Glas 3H 85
RUCHILL 4D 62
Ruchill Pl. G20: Glas. 4D 62
Ruchill Sports Cen. 3D 62
Ruchill St. G20: Glas. 4C 62
Ruel St. G44: Glas 6E 103
Rufflees Av. G78: Barr 3F 115
Rugby Av. G13: Glas 1B 60
Rullion Pl. G33: Glas 3H 85
Rumford St. G40: Glas 2B 104
Runciman Pl. G74: E Kil 5B 138
Rundell Dr. G66: Milt C 6C 8
Rupert St. G4: Glas 1D 82
Rushyhill St. G21: Glas 5C 64
Ruskin La. G12: Glas 6C 62
Ruskin Pl. G12: Glas 6C 62
  G65: Kils 3H 11
Ruskin Sq. G64: B'rig 6C 48
Ruskin Ter. G12: Glas 6C 62
  G73: Ruth. 4D 104
Russell Colt St.
  ML5: Coat. 3C 90
Russell Dr. G61: Bear. 1E 45
Russell Gdns. G71: Tann 5E 109
  G77: Newt M 5C 132
Russell La. ML2: Wis 1G 157

Russell Pl. G75: E Kil. 4E **149**
   G76: Busby. 4E **135**
   PA3: Lin 5F **75**
Russell Rd. G81: Dun 6A **22**
Russell St. ML2: Wis. 1G **157**
   ML3: Ham 4D **140**
   ML4: Moss 2F **127**
   ML6: Chap 3E **113**
   PA3: Pais 4H **77**
   PA5: John. 2G **95**
Rutherford Av. G61: Bear 5B **24**
   G66: Kirk 1H **51**
Rutherford Ct. G81: Clyd 5C **42**
Rutherford Grange G66: Lenz . . . 1C **50**
Rutherford La. G75: E Kil. 3H **149**
Rutherford Sq. G75: E Kil 3G **149**
RUTHERGLEN. 5C **104**
Rutherglen Ind. Est. G73: Ruth 4B **104**
                (Glasgow Rd.)
   G73: Ruth. 4C **104**
                 (Quay Rd.)
Rutherglen Mus. 5D **104**
Rutherglen Rd. G5: Glas 2H **103**
   G73: Ruth. 3A **104**
Rutherglen Station (Rail) 5D **104**
Rutherglen Swimming Pool 6C **104**
Ruthven Av. G46: Giff. 6B **118**
Ruthven La. G12: Glas. 6A **62**
   ML5: Glenb 3G **69**
Ruthven Pl. G64: B'rig 1E **65**
Ruthven St. G12: Glas 6B **62**
Rutland Ct. *G51: Glas* *5C **82***
             (off Rutland Cres.)
Rutland Cres. G51: Glas 5C **82**
Rutland Pl. G51: Glas 5C **82**
Ryan Rd. G64: B'rig 6D **48**
Ryan Way G73: Ruth 4E **121**
Ryat Dr. G77: Newt M 3C **132**
Ryat Grn. G77: Newt M 3C **132**
              (not continuous)
Ryatt Linn PA8: Ersk 6D **40**
Rydal Gro. G75: E Kil 5B **148**
Rydal Pl. G75: E Kil. 5B **148**
Ryden Mains Rd. ML6: Glenm 5F **71**
Ryde Rd. ML2: Wis 6A **146**
Ryebank Rd. G21: Glas 4E **65**
Rye Cres. G21: Glas. 4D **64**
Ryecroft Dr. G69: Bail 6H **87**
Ryedale Pl. G15: Glas 3A **44**
Ryefield Av. ML5: Coat 4H **89**
   PA5: John. 4D **94**
Ryefield Pl. PA5: John 4D **94**
Ryefield Rd. G21: Glas. 4D **64**
Ryehill Pl. G21: Glas 4E **65**
Ryehill Rd. G21: Glas. 4E **65**
Ryemount Rd. G21: Glas 4E **65**
Rye Rd. G21: Glas 4D **64**
Ryeside Rd. G21: Glas 4D **64**
Rye Way PA2: Pais. 4C **96**
Rylands Dr. G32: Glas 1D **106**
Rylands Gdns. G32: Glas 1E **107**
Rylees Cres. G52: Glas 5G **79**
Rylees Pl. G52: Glas. 5G **79**
Rylees Rd. G52: Glas 5G **79**
Rysland Av. G77: Newt M 4E **133**
Rysland Cres. G77: Newt M 4E **133**
Ryvra Rd. G13: Glas 3D **60**

S

Sachelcourt Av. PA7: B'ton 5H **39**
Sackville Av. G13: Glas 4F **61**
Sackville La. G13: Glas 4F **61**
Saddell Rd. G15: Glas 3B **44**
Sadlers Wells Ct. *G74: E Kil* *5B **138***
            (off Bosworth Rd.)
Saffron Cres. ML2: Wis. 2D **156**
Saffronhall Cres. ML3: Ham 5H **141**
Saffronhall La. ML3: Ham 5H **141**
St Abb's Dr. PA2: Pais 4E **97**
St Aidan's Path ML2: Wis 3A **146**
St Andrew's Av. G64: B'rig. 5A **48**
St Andrews Av. G71: Both 6E **125**

St Andrew's Brae G82: Dumb 1H **17**
St Andrew's Ct. G75: E Kil 5E **149**
St Andrews Ct. ML1: Holy 1A **128**
   ML4: Bell *2D **126***
           (off Anderson Ct.)
   ML8: Carl 3E **165**
St Andrew's Cres. G41: Glas 1C **102**
   G82: Dumb. 2H **17**
   PA3: Glas A 2G **77**
St Andrew's Dr. G41: Glas 3A **102**
St Andrews Dr. G61: Bear 6D **24**
St Andrew's Dr. G68: Cumb 5B **140**
   ML3: Ham 5B **140**
St Andrews Dr. ML5: Coat 5A **90**
St Andrew's Dr. PA11: Bri W 4E **73**
   PA3: Glas A 3H **77**
St Andrew's Dr. W. PA3: Glas A . . . 2G **77**
St Andrew's Gdns. ML6: Air. 3B **92**
St Andrew's Ga. ML4: Bell. 2B **126**
St Andrew's La. *G1: Glas.* *5H **83***
             (off Gallowgate)
St Andrew's Path *ML9: Lark* *4G **161***
           (off Glen Fruin Dr.)
St Andrews Pl. G65: Kils 2G **11**
St Andrew's Rd. G41: Glas 1D **102**
   PA4: Renf 6E **59**
St Andrew's Sports Cen. 5G **149**
St Andrew's Sq. G1: Glas. 5H **83**
St Andrew's St. G1: Glas. 5H **83**
St Andrews St. ML1: Holy 2A **128**
St Andrew's Wlk. ML2: Wis 3A **146**
St Andrew's Way *ML1: Moth* *4A **144***
            (off Glassford St.)
St Anne's Av. PA8: Ersk 1H **57**
St Anne's Wynd PA8: Ersk 1H **57**
St Ann's Dr. G46: Giff 5A **118**
St Blanes Dr. G73: Ruth. 1A **120**
St Boswell's Cres. PA2: Pais 4E **97**
St Boswells Dr. ML5: Coat 1F **111**
St Bride's Av. G71: View 6G **109**
St Bride's Rd. G43: Glas 6B **102**
St Brides Way G71: Both 3E **125**
St Bryde St. G74: E Kil. 1H **149**
St Catherine's Rd. G46: Giff 5A **118**
St Clair Av. G46: Giff 4A **118**
St Clair St. G20: Glas. 1D **82**
St Columba Dr. G66: Kirk. 6E **31**
St Cyrus Gdns. G64: B'rig 6E **49**
St Cyrus Rd. G64: B'rig 6E **49**
St Davids Dr. ML6: Air. 1C **112**
St David's Pl. ML9: Lark 2E **161**
St Denis Way ML5: Coat 3B **90**
St Edmunds Gro. G62: Miln. 2G **25**
St Edmunds La. G62: Miln. 2G **25**
St Enoch Av. G71: View 5G **109**
St Enoch Pl. G1: Glas . . . . . . *4F **83** (6D 4)*
St Enoch Shop. Cen.
   G1: Glas. 5G **83** (6E 5)
St Enoch Sq. G1: Glas 5F **83** (6D 4)
St Enoch Station (Und.) 5F **83** (6D 4)
St Fillans Dr. PA6: Hous 1A **74**
St Fillans Rd. G33: Step 4C **66**
St Flanan Rd. G66: Kirk. 4B **32**
St Francis Rigg G5: Glas 1G **103**
ST GEORGE'S CROSS INTERCHANGE
   . . . . 1A **4**
St Georges Cross Station (Und.)
   . . . . 1E **83** (1A 4)
St George's Pl. G4: Glas 1A **4**
St George's Rd. G3: Glas 2D **82** (2A 4)
   G4: Glas. 1E **83** (1A 4)
St George's Ter. *PA11: Bri W* *3E **73***
           (off Horsewood Rd.)
St Germains G61: Bear. 3E **45**
St Giles Pk. ML3: Ham 1F **153**
St Giles Way ML3: Ham 1F **153**
St Helena Cres. G81: Hard. 1E **43**
St Ives Rd. G69: Mood 4D **52**
St James Av. PA3: Pais 4F **77**
St James Bus. Cen. PA1: Pais. 1B **96**
St James Ct. ML5: Coat. 1A **110**
ST JAMES E. INTERCHANGE 3G **77**
St James' St. PA3: Pais 6A **78**

St James Way ML5: Coat. 2A **110**
ST JAMES W. INTERCHANGE. 3F **77**
St John's Ct. G41: Glas 1C **102**
St John's Quad. G41: Glas 1C **102**
St John's Rd. G41: Glas. 2C **102**
St John St. ML5: Coat 4C **90**
St Joseph's Ct. G21: Glas 2B **84**
St Joseph's Pl. G21: Glas 2B **84**
St Joseph's Vw. G21: Glas. 2B **84**
St Kenneth Dr. G51: Glas. 3D **80**
St Kilda Dr. G14: Glas 5E **61**
St Kilda Way ML2: Wis 4C **146**
St Lawrence Pk. G75: E Kil 2E **149**
ST LEONARDS. 2C **150**
St Leonard's Dr. G46: Giff 4A **118**
St Leonards Rd. G74: E Kil 1B **150**
St Leonards Sq. G74: E Kil 2C **150**
St Leonards Wlk. ML5: Coat 2E **111**
St Lukes Bus. Cen. *G5: Glas* *6G **83***
           (off St Lukes Pl.)
St Lukes Pl. G5: Glas. 6G **83**
St Lukes's Av. ML8: Carl 5E **165**
St Lukes Ter. G5: Glas. 6G **83**
St Machan's Way G66: Len 2F **7**
St Machars Rd. PA11: Bri W 4G **73**
St Margarets Av. G65: Bant 1G **13**
   PA3: Pais 4B **78**
St Margarets Ct. *ML4: Bell* *2D **126***
             (off Dean St.)
   PA3: Pais *4B **78***
           (off Renfrew Rd.)
St Margarets Dr. ML2: Wis 2E **157**
St Margaret's Pl. *G1: Glas.* *5G **83***
            (off Bridgegate)
St Mark Gdns. G32: Glas. 6H **85**
St Mark's Ct. ML2: Wis 3A **146**
St Mark St. G32: Glas. 6G **85**
            (not continuous)
St Marnock St. G40: Glas. 6C **84**
St Martins Ga. ML5: Coat 1C **110**
St Mary's Ct. G2: Glas. 5D **4**
   ML2: Wis 1H **157**
St Mary's Cres. G78: Barr 5E **115**
St Mary's Gdns. G78: Barr 5F **115**
St Mary's La. G2: Glas. 5D **4**
St Mary's Rd. G64: B'rig 5A **48**
   ML4: Bell 2A **126**
St Mary's Way G82: Dumb. 4F **17**
ST MAURICE'S RDBT. 4C **34**
St Michael Rd. ML2: Wis. 2C **156**
St Michaels Ct. G31: Glas 6E **85**
St Michaels La. G31: Glas. 6E **85**
St Mirren F.C. 5A **78**
St Mirren Pk. 6B **78**
St Mirren R.C. Cathedral 6B **78**
St Mirren Sports & Leisure Complex
   . . . . 5A **78**
St Mirren's Rd. G65: Kils 3A **12**
St Mirren St. PA1: Pais 1A **98**
St Monance St. G21: Glas. 4B **64**
St Monicas Way ML5: Coat 1H **109**
St Mungo Av. G4: Glas 3G **83** (3F 5)
St Mungo Ct. PA11: Bri W 3G **73**
St Mungo Mus. of Religious Life & Art
   . . . . 3A **84**
St Mungo Pl. G4: Glas. 3H **83** (3H 5)
   ML3: Ham 5B **140**
St Mungo's Cathedral. 3A **84**
St Mungo's Cres. ML1: Carf 5B **128**
St Mungo's Rd. G67: Cumb. 4H **35**
St Mungo St. G64: B'rig 1B **64**
St Mungo's Wlk. *G67: Cumb.* *3H **35***
       (in Cumbernauld Shop. Cen.)
St Ninian's Cres. PA2: Pais 3B **98**
St Ninians Gro. ML2: Wis 3B **146**
St Ninian's Pl. ML3: Ham 6D **140**
St Ninian's Rd. ML3: Ham. 6D **140**
   PA2: Pais 3B **98**
St Ninian Ter. G5: Glas 6G **83**
St Peters La. G2: Glas 4E **83** (5B 4)
St Peter's Path *G4: Glas.* *1E **83***
           (off St Peter's St.)
St Peter's St. G4: Glas 1E **83** (1B 4)
St Roberts Gdns. G53: Glas. 2C **116**

St Rollox Brae. G21: Glas 1A 84
St Rollox Bus. & Retail Pk.
  G21: Glas 1B 84
St Ronan's Dr. G41: Glas 4B 102
St Ronans Dr. G73: Ruth 1E 121
St Ronan's Dr. ML3: Ham 3G 153
St Stephen's Av. G73: Ruth 4F 121
St Stephen's Cres. G73: Ruth 4G 121
St Valentine Ter. G5: Glas 1H 103
St Vigean's Av. G77: Newt M 6B 132
St Vigeans Pl. G77: Newt M 6C 132
St Vincent Cres. G3: Glas 3B 82
St Vincent Cres. La. G3: Glas 3B 82
St Vincent La. G2: Glas 3E 83 (4B 4)
St Vincent Pl. G1: Glas 4G 83 (5E 5)
  G75: E Kil 3C 148
  ML1: Moth 2G 143
St Vincent St. G2: Glas 3E 83 (4A 4)
  G3: Glas 3D 82 (4A 4)
St Vincent Ter. G3: Glas 3D 82 (4A 4)
St Winifred's Way ML2: Wis 5G 145
Salamanca St. G31: Glas 6F 85
  (not continuous)
Salasaig Ct. G33: Glas 4A 86
Salen St. G52: Glas 6F 81
Salford Pl. G66: Kirk 4C 30
  (off Glasgow Rd.)
Saline St. ML6: Air 5F 91
Salisbury G74: E Kil 5D 138
Salisbury Cres. ML1: Moth 1D 142
Salisbury Pl. G81: Clyd 2H 41
Salisbury St. G5: Glas 1F 103
Salkeld St. G5: Glas 1E 103
Salmona St. G22: Glas 5F 63
Salterland Rd. G53: Glas 2G 115
Saltire Cres. ML9: Lark 3G 161
Saltmarket G1: Glas 5G 83
Saltmarket Pl. G1: Glas 5G 83
Saltoun La. G12: Glas 6B 62
Saltoun St. G12: Glas 6A 62
Salvia St. G72: Camb 1H 121
Samson Cres. ML8: Carl 5H 165
Sandaig Rd. G33: Glas 6E 87
Sandale Path G72: Blan 3A 140
Sandalwood Av. G74: E Kil 5F 137
Sandalwood Ct. G74: E Kil 5F 137
Sanda St. G20: Glas 5C 62
Sandbank Av. G20: Glas 2B 62
Sandbank Cres. G20: Glas 3B 62
Sandbank Dr. G20: Glas 2B 62
Sandbank St. G20: Glas 1B 62
Sandbank Ter. G20: Glas 2B 62
Sandend PA8: Ersk 4E 41
Sandend Rd. G53: Glas 6A 100
Sanderling Pl. G75: E Kil 6C 148
  PA5: John 6D 94
Sanderling Rd. PA3: Glas A 3H 77
Sanderson Av. G71: View 1H 125
Sandfield Av. G62: Miln 2G 25
Sandfield St. G20: Glas 4C 62
Sandford Gdns. G69: Bail 6H 87
Sandgate Av. G32: Glas 2D 106
Sandhaven Pl. G53: Glas 6A 100
Sandhaven Rd. G53: Glas 6A 100
Sandhead Cres. ML6: Chap 4E 113
Sandholes Rd. PA5: Brkfld 6C 74
Sandholes St. PA1: Pais 1G 97
Sandholm Pl. G14: Glas 4H 59
Sandholm Ter. G14: Glas 4H 59
Sandiefield Rd. G5: Glas 1G 103
Sandielands Av. PA8: Ersk 2H 57
Sandilands Cres. ML1: Moth 4D 142
Sandilands St. G32: Glas 6B 86
Sandmill St. G21: Glas 2C 84
Sandpiper Dr. G75: E Kil 6C 148
Sandpiper Pl. G75: E Kil 6C 148
Sandpiper Way ML4: Bell 5A 110
Sandra Rd. G64: B'rig 5E 49
Sandra Way PA2: Pais 6H 97
Sandringham Av. G77: Newt M . . 3G 133
Sandringham Ct. G77: Newt M . . 4G 133
Sandringham Dr. PA5: Eld 4H 95
Sandwood G52: Glas 6A 80

Sandwood Cres. G52: Glas 6A 80
Sandwood Path G52: Glas 6A 80
Sandwood Rd. G52: Glas 1A 100
Sandyfaulds Sq. G5: Glas 1G 103
Sandyfaulds St. G5: Glas 1H 103
Sandyford Av. ML1: N'hse 5D 112
Sandyford Pl. G3: Glas 3C 82
  (off Claremont St.)
  ML1: N'hse 6D 112
Sandyford Pl. La. G3: Glas 3C 82
Sandyford Rd. G3: Glas 3A 82
  ML1: N'hse 6D 112
  PA3: Pais 3C 78
SANDYHILLS 1D 106
Sandyhills Cres. G32: Glas 2B 106
Sandyhills Dr. G32: Glas 2B 106
Sandyhills Gro. G32: Glas 3B 106
Sandyhills Pl. G32: Glas 2B 106
Sandyhills Rd. G32: Glas 2B 106
Sandyknowes Rd. G67: Cumb . . . 5A 36
Sandy La. G11: Glas 1G 81
  ML8: Carl 3F 165
  PA4: Renf 2E 79
Sannox Dr. ML1: Moth 2D 142
Sannox Gdns. G31: Glas 3D 84
Sanquhar Dr. G53: Glas 5A 100
Sanquhar Gdns. G53: Glas 5A 100
  G72: Blan 5H 123
Sanquhar Pl. G53: Glas 5A 100
Sanquhar Rd. G53: Glas 5A 100
Sanson La. ML8: Carl 5H 165
Sapphire Rd. ML4: Bell 4C 126
Saracen Head La. G1: Glas 5A 84
Saracen St. G22: Glas 6G 63
Sarazen Ct. ML1: Cle 1E 145
Sardinia La. G12: Glas 6B 62
Saskatoon Pl. G75: E Kil 2D 148
Saucel Hill Ter. PA2: Pais 2A 98
Saucel St. PA1: Pais 1A 98
Sauchiehall Cen. G2: Glas 3C 4
Sauchiehall La. G2: Glas . . . 3E 83 (3A 4)
  (not continuous)
Sauchiehall St. G3: Glas 2B 82 (2A 4)
Sauchiesmoor Rd. ML8: Carl . . . 5G 165
Saughs Av. G33: Glas 3H 65
Saughs Dr. G33: Glas 3H 65
Saughs Ga. G33: Glas 3H 65
Saughs Pl. G33: Glas 3H 65
Saughs Rd. G33: Glas 3H 65
  G33: Mille. 3A 66
Saughton St. G32: Glas 4G 85
Saunders Ct. G78: Barr 4D 114
Savoy Cen. G2: Glas 3F 83 (3C 4)
Savoy St. G40: Glas 1B 104
Sawmillfield St. G4: Glas 1F 83
Sawmill Rd. G11: Glas 1F 81
Saxon Rd. G13: Glas 2D 60
Scadlock Rd. PA3: Pais 5F 77
Scalpay G74: E Kil 2C 150
Scalpay Pas. G22: Glas 2H 63
Scalpay Pl. G22: Glas 2H 63
Scalpay St. G22: Glas 2G 63
Scapa St. G23: Glas 1C 62
Scapesland Ter. G82: Dumb 3G 17
Scaraway Dr. G22: Glas 1H 63
Scaraway Pl. G22: Glas 1H 63
Scaraway St. G22: Glas 1G 63
Scaraway Ter. G22: Glas 1H 63
Scarba Dr. G43: Glas 2H 117
Scarba Quad. ML2: Wis 2E 157
Scarffe Av. PA3: Lin 6F 75
Scarhill Av. ML6: Air 6H 91
Scarhill La. ML6: Air 6A 92
Scarhill St. ML1: Cle 5H 129
  ML5: Coat. 2B 110
Scarrel Dr. G45: Glas 3C 120
Scarrel Gdns. G45: Glas 3C 120
Scarrel Rd. G45: Glas 3C 120
Scarrel Ter. G45: Glas 3C 120
Scavaig Cres. G15: Glas 3G 43
Schaw Ct. G61: Bear 1E 45
Schaw Dr. G61: Bear 1D 44
  G81: Faif. 6G 23

Schaw Rd. PA3: Pais 5C 78
Scholar's Ga. G75: E Kil 5F 149
School Av. G72: Camb 2B 122
Schoolhouse La. G72: Blan 3A 140
School La. G66: Len 3F 7
  G66: Milt C 5C 8
  G82: Dumb. 3D 16
  ML8: Carl 4E 165
School Quad. ML6: Air 1H 91
School Rd. G33: Step. 3E 67
  G64: Torr 4E 29
  G77: Newt M 5D 132
  ML2: Newm 5F 147
    (Morningside)
  ML2: Newm 5E 147
    (Newmains)
  PA1: Pais 6G 79
School St. ML3: Ham. 2H 153
  ML5: Coat. 1C 110
  ML6: Chap 3D 112
School Wynd PA1: Pais 6A 78
Scioncroft Av. G73: Ruth 6E 105
Scone Pl. G74: E Kil 6F 137
  G77: Newt M 5H 133
Scone St. G21: Glas. 6G 63
Scone Wlk. G69: Bail 2G 107
Sconser St. G23: Glas 6C 46
Scorton Gdns. G69: Bail 1F 107
Scotcart Indoor Kart Racing
  . . . . 1C 122
Scotia Cres. ML9: Lark 4E 161
Scotia Gdns. ML3: Ham. 4G 153
Scotia St. ML1: Moth 2E 143
Scotland St. G5: Glas. 6D 82
Scotland Street School Mus. 6D 82
Scotland St. W. G41: Glas 6B 82
Scotsblair Av. G66: Kirk. 1C 50
Scotsburn Rd. G21: Glas 5E 65
SCOTSTOUN 5B 60
Scotstoun Athletic Track 5C 60
SCOTSTOUNHILL 3B 60
Scotstounhill Station (Rail). 4B 60
Scotstoun Leisure Cen. 5D 60
Scotstoun St. G14: Glas 6C 60
Scott Av. G60: Bowl 5B 20
  G66: Milt C 5C 8
  PA5: John. 5E 95
Scott Cres. G67: Cumb. 6F 35
Scott Dr. G61: Bear 1C 44
  G67: Cumb 6F 35
Scott Gro. ML3: Ham 1H 153
Scott Hill G74: E Kil 6A 138
Scott Ho. G67: Cumb 2A 36
Scottish Enterprise Technology Pk.
  G75: E Kil 4A 150
Scottish Exhibition & Conference Cen.
  . . . . 4B 82
Scottish Maritime Mus.
  Dumbarton 4F 17
  Renfrew 6A 60
Scottish National Football Mus. . 6F 103
Scott Pl. ML4: Bell 6D 110
  PA5: John 5E 95
Scott Rd. G52: Hill 3H 79
Scott's Pl. ML6: Air 3B 92
Scott's Rd. PA2: Pais 2D 98
Scott St. G3: Glas 3E 83 (3B 4)
  G69: Bail 1H 107
  G81: Clyd 3A 42
  ML1: Moth 2G 143
  ML3: Ham 2H 153
  ML9: Lark 3F 161
SEAFAR 3G 35
Seafar Rd. G67: Cumb. 5G 35
SEAFAR RDBT. 5G 35
Seafield Av. G61: Bear 6F 25
Seafield Cres. G68: Cumb 4A 34
Seafield Dr. G73: Ruth 4F 121
Seaforth Cres. G78: Barr 2D 114
Seaforth La. G69: Mood. 5E 53
Seaforth Rd. ML4: Bell 4B 126
Seaforth Rd. G52: Hill 4A 80
  G81: Clyd 6D 42

Seaforth Rd. Nth. G52: Hill 4A **80**
Seaforth Rd. Sth. G52: Hill 4A **80**
Seagrove St. G32: Glas 5F **85**
Seamill Gdns. G74: E Kil 1F **149**
Seamill Path G53: Glas 2H **115**
Seamill St. G53: Glas 2H **115**
Seamore St. G20: Glas 1D **82**
Seath Av. ML6: Air 4G **91**
Seath Rd. G73: Ruth 4C **104**
Seath St. G42: Glas 3G **103**
Seaton Ter. ML3: Ham 5E **141**
Seaward Pl. G41: Glas 6D **82**
Seaward St. G41: Glas 6C **82**
(not continuous)
SEAWARD ST. INTERCHANGE . . 6C 82
Second Av. G33: Mille 4B **66**
    G44: Glas 1F **119**
    G61: Bear 4F **45**
    G66: Auch 6C **50**
    G71: Tann 4C **108**
    G81: Clyd 4B **42**
    G82: Dumb 3C **18**
    PA4: Renf 2E **79**
Second Av. La. G44: Glas 6F **103**
Second Gdns. G41: Glas 1G **101**
Second Rd. G72: Blan 4C **140**
Second St. G71: Tann 5D **108**
SEEDHILL 1C **98**
Seedhill PA1: Pais 1B **98**
Seedhill Rd. PA1: Pais 1B **98**
Seggielea La. G13: Glas 3D **60**
(off Helensburgh Dr.)
Seggielea Rd. G13: Glas 3D **60**
Seil Dr. G44: Glas 3F **119**
Selborne Pl. G13: Glas 4E **61**
Selborne Pl. La. G13: Glas 4E **61**
Selborne Rd. G13: Glas 4E **61**
Selby Gdns. G32: Glas 6D **86**
Selby Pl. ML5: Coat 1H **89**
Selby St. ML5: Coat 1H **89**
Selkirk Av. G52: Glas 1C **100**
    PA2: Pais 4E **97**
Selkirk Dr. G73: Ruth 6E **105**
Selkirk Pl. G74: E Kil 6D **138**
    ML3: Ham 1A **154**
Selkirk St. G72: Blan 2B **140**
    ML2: Wis 4A **146**
    ML3: Ham 1A **154**
Selkirk Way ML4: Bell 6D **110**
    ML5: Coat 2G **111**
Sella Rd. G64: B'rig 5F **49**
Selvieland Rd. G52: Glas 6H **79**
Semphill Gdns. G74: E Kil 1B **150**
Sempie St. ML3: Ham 5D **140**
Sempill Av. PA8: Ersk 5D **40**
Semple Av. PA7: B'ton 4H **39**
Semple Pl. PA3: Lin 4H **75**
Senga Cres. ML4: Bell 6C **110**
Seres Rd. G76: Clar 1B **134**
Sergeantlaw Rd. PA2: Pais 6E **97**
Service St. G66: Len 2E **7**
Seton Ter. G31: Glas 4B **84**
Settle Gdns. G69: Bail 1F **107**
Seven Sisters G66: Lenz 2E **51**
Seventh Av. G71: Tann 5D **108**
Seventh Rd. G72: Blan 4C **140**
Severn Rd. G75: E Kil 4B **148**
Seymour Grn. G75: E Kil 3D **148**
Seyton Av. G46: Giff 6A **118**
Seyton Ct. G46: Giff 6A **118**
Seyton La. G74: E Kil 6G **137**
Shaftesbury Av. G81: Clyd 5B **42**
Shaftesbury Ct. G74: E Kil 4C **138**
Shaftesbury Cres. ML1: N'hill 4D **128**
Shafton Pl. G13: Glas 1E **61**
Shafton Rd. G13: Glas 1E **61**
Shaftesbury St. G3: Glas . . 3D **82** (4A **4**)
(not continuous)
Shakespeare Av. G81: Clyd 3B **42**
Shakespeare St. G20: Glas 4C **62**
Shamrock St. G4: Glas 2E **83** (1B **4**)
    G66: Kirk 5D **30**
Shandon Cres. ML4: Bell 6C **110**
Shandon Ter. ML3: Ham 6D **140**

Shand Pl. ML8: Carl 2F **165**
Shand St. ML2: Wis 6H **145**
Shandwick Sq. G34: Glas 3G **87**
Shandwick St. G34: Glas 3G **87**
Shanks Av. G78: Barr 5E **115**
Shanks Cres. PA5: John 3E **95**
Shanks Pk. Ind. Est. G78: Barr . . . 3E **115**
Shanks St. G20: Glas 4C **62**
    ML6: Air 2A **92**
Shanks Way G78: Barr 2E **115**
Shannon St. G20: Glas 4D **62**
Shapinsay St. G22: Glas 1H **63**
Sharmanka Kinetic Gallery & Theatre
    . . . . 5G **83**
(off Trongate)
Sharp Av. ML5: Coat 1G **109**
Sharp St. ML1: Moth 2D **142**
Shaw Av. PA7: B'ton 4A **40**
Shawbridge Arc. G43: Glas 5A **102**
Shawbridge Ind. Est.
    G43: Glas 6A **102**
Shawbridge St. G43: Glas 6H **101**
Shawburn Cres. ML3: Ham 5F **141**
Shawburn St. ML3: Ham 5F **141**
Shaw Ct. G77: Newt M 5F **133**
    PA8: Ersk 4D **40**
Shaw Cres. ML2: Wis 2D **156**
SHAWFIELD 3B **104**
Shawfield Cres. ML8: Law 6D **158**
Shawfield Dr. G5: Glas 3A **104**
Shawfield Ind. Est. G73: Ruth 3B **104**
Shawfield Rd. G73: Ruth 3B **104**
Shawfield Stadium 3B **104**
Shawgill Ct. ML8: Law 1H **163**
SHAWHEAD 2B **110**
Shawhead Av. ML5: Coat 1D **110**
Shawhead Cotts. ML5: Coat 3D **110**
Shawhead Ind. Est. ML5: Coat . . . 2E **111**
Shawhill Cres. G77: Newt M 6E **133**
Shawhill Rd. G41: Glas 5A **102**
    G43: Glas 5A **102**
Shawholm Cres. G43: Glas 6H **101**
(not continuous)
SHAWLANDS 5C **102**
Shawlands Arc. G41: Glas 5B **102**
Shawlands Station (Rail) 5B **102**
Shawmoss Rd. G41: Glas 4A **102**
Shawpark St. G20: Glas 3C **62**
Shawrigg Rd. ML9: Lark 3G **161**
Shaw Rd. G62: Miln 5G **25**
    G77: Newt M 5E **133**
SHAWSBURN 3A **162**
Shaws Rd. ML9: Lark 6F **161**
Shaw St. G51: Glas 3G **81**
    ML9: Lark 5F **161**
Shawwood Cres. G77: Newt M . . . 6E **133**
Shearer Dr. ML3: Ham 4G **153**
Shears La. PA4: Renf 6F **59**
Sheddens Pl. G32: Glas 6G **85**
Sheepburn Rd. G71: Udd 6C **108**
Sheila St. G33: Glas 5G **65**
Sheiling Hill ML3: Ham 5A **142**
Sheldaig Rd. G22: Glas 1F **63**
Sheldrake Pl. PA5: John 6D **94**
Shelley Ct. G12: Glas 4F **125**
Shelley Dr. G71: Both 4F **125**
    G81: Clyd 3C **42**
Shelley Rd. G12: Glas 4F **61**
Shells Rd. G66: Kirk 4E **31**
Sherbrooke Av. G41: Glas 2A **102**
Sherbrooke Dr. G41: Glas 1A **102**
Sherbrooke Gdns. G41: Glas 2A **102**
Sherbrooke Pl. G75: E Kil 2E **149**
Sherburn Gdns. G69: Bail 2F **107**
Sherdale Av. ML6: Chap 3D **112**
Sheriff Pk. Av. G73: Ruth 6C **104**
Sherry Av. ML1: Holy 2H **127**
Sherry Dr. ML3: Ham 2E **153**
Sherry Hgts. G72: Camb 1A **122**
Sherwood Av. G71: Udd 2E **125**
    PA1: Pais 5C **78**
Sherwood Dr. G46: T'bnk 4G **117**
Sherwood Pl. G15: Glas 4B **44**

Shetland Dr. G44: Glas 3F **119**
SHETTLESTON 6B **86**
Shettleston Rd. G31: Glas 5E **85**
Shettleston Station (Rail) 6B **86**
Shiel Av. G74: E Kil 6H **137**
Shielbridge Gdns. G23: Glas 6C **46**
Shiel Ct. G78: Barr 2D **114**
Shieldaig Dr. G73: Ruth 3D **120**
Shieldburn Rd. G51: Glas 4C **80**
SHIELDHALL 3C **80**
Shieldhall Gdns. G51: Glas 4C **80**
Shieldhall Rd. G51: Glas 3B **80**
Shieldhill G75: E Kil 4H **149**
Shieldhill Rd. ML8: Carl 5E **165**
Shieldmuir Station (Rail) 5C **144**
Shieldmuir St. ML2: Wis 5C **144**
Shiel Dr. ML9: Lark 6H **155**
Shilford Av. G13: Glas 2A **60**
Shillay St. G22: Glas 1A **64**
Shillingworth Pl. PA11: Bri W 5F **73**
Shilton Dr. G53: Glas 2C **116**
Shilton La. PA7: B'ton 3C **40**
Shinwell Av. G81: Clyd 6F **43**
Shipbank La. G1: Glas 5G **83**
(off Clyde St.)
Shira Ter. G74: E Kil 2B **150**
Shirley Quad. ML1: Moth 6F **143**
SHIRREL 6C **110**
Shirrel Av. ML4: Bell 6C **110**
Shirrel Rd. ML1: Holy 3A **128**
Shirva Lea G65: Twe 1D **32**
Shiskine Pl. G20: Glas 1A **62**
Shiskine St. G20: Glas 1A **62**
Sholto Cres. ML4: Bell 6H **109**
Shore St. G40: Glas 3B **104**
Shortridge St. G20: Glas 4C **62**
SHORTROODS 4A **78**
Shortroods Av. PA3: Pais 4H **77**
Shortroods Cres. PA3: Pais 4H **77**
Shortroods Rd. PA3: Pais 4H **77**
Shotts St. G33: Glas 3D **86**
Showcase Cinema (Kirkwood) . . . 1F **109**
Showcase Cinema (Paisley) 6C **76**
Shuna Gdns. G20: Glas 4C **62**
Shuna Pl. G20: Glas 4C **62**
    G77: Newt M 3B **132**
Shuna St. G20: Glas 3C **62**
Shuttle St. G1: Glas 4H **83** (6G **5**)
    G65: Kils 3H **11**
    PA1: Pais 1A **98**
    PA10: Kilb 1A **94**
Sidland Rd. G21: Glas 4E **65**
Sidlaw Av. G78: Barr 6E **115**
    ML3: Ham 1D **152**
Sidlaw Ct. ML5: Coat 2E **111**
Sidlaw Dr. ML2: Wis 6F **145**
Sidlaw Rd. G61: Bear 1B **44**
Sidlaw Way ML6: Chap 4F **113**
    ML9: Lark 6H **155**
Sielga Pl. G34: Glas 3G **87**
Siemens Pl. G21: Glas 1D **84**
Siemens St. G21: Glas 1D **84**
Sievewright St. G73: Ruth 4E **105**
SIGHTHILL 1A **84**
Sighthill Loan ML9: Lark 1F **161**
(off Muirshot Rd.)
SIKESIDE 6F **91**
Sikeside Pl. ML5: Coat 6F **91**
Sikeside St. ML5: Coat 6F **91**
Silkin Av. G81: Clyd 6F **43**
Silk St. PA1: Pais 6B **78**
Silvan Pl. G76: Busby 4E **135**
SILVERBANK 1G **121**

Silverburn Cres. ML1: N'hill 4D **128**
Silverburn St. G33: Glas 3G **85**
Silverdale G74: E Kil 6E **137**
Silverdale St. G40: Glas. 1E **105**
Silverfir Ct. G5: Glas 1H **103**
Silver Firs ML1: N'hill 4C **128**
Silverfir St. G5: Glas 2H **103**
Silver Glade G52: Glas. 1B **100**
Silvergrove St. G40: Glas 1A **104**
SILVERTON 4H **17**
Silverton Av. G82: Dumb 4H **17**
SILVERTONHILL 1B **154**
Silvertonhill Av. ML3: Ham 3A **154**
Silvertonhill La. G82: Dumb 4H **17**
Silvertonhill Pl. ML3: Ham 4H **153**
SILVERWELLS 6E **125**
Silverwells G71: Both 6E **125**
Silverwells Ct. G71: Both 6E **125**
Silverwells Cres. G71: Both 6F **125**
Silverwood Ct. G71: Both. 6F **125**
Simons Cres. PA4: Renf 4F **59**
Simpson Ct. G71: Udd 1D **124**
   G81: Clyd 5C **42**
Simpson Dr. G75: E Kil 4F **149**
Simpson Gdns. G78: Barr 5D **114**
Simpson Hgts. *G4: Glas.* *4A 84*
   (off John Knox St.)
Simpson Pl. G75: E Kil 4F **149**
Simpson St. G20: Glas 6D **62**
Simpson Way ML4: Bell 6E **111**
Simshill Rd. G44: Glas 4F **119**
Sinclair Av. G61: Bear 1E **45**
Sinclair Dr. G42: Glas 6D **102**
   ML5: Coat 4H **89**
Sinclair Gdns. G64: B'rig 1D **64**
Sinclair Gro. ML4: Bell 5B **126**
Sinclair Pk. G75: E Kil 3H **149**
Sinclair Pl. G75: E Kil 3H **149**
Sinclair St. G62: Miln 3G **25**
   G81: Clyd 1F **59**
Singer Rd. G75: E Kil 5H **149**
   G81: Clyd 4B **42**
Singer Station (Rail) 5D **42**
Singer St. G81: Clyd 4D **42**
Sir Matt Busby Sports Complex . . . 2B **126**
Sir Michael Pl. PA1: Pais 1H **97**
Sixth Av. PA4: Renf 2E **79**
Sixth St. G71: Tann 4C **108**
Skaethorn Rd. G20: Glas 2H **61**
Skara Wlk. *ML2: Newm.* *2D 146*
   (off Kildonan Ct.)
Skaterigg Dr. G13: Glas 4F **61**
Skaterigg Gdns. G13: Glas 4F **61**
Skaterigg La. *G13: Glas.* *4E 61*
   (off Chamberlain Rd.)
Skelbo Path G34: Glas 2B **88**
Skelbo Pl. G34: Glas 2B **88**
Skellyton Cres. ML9: Lark 3F **161**
Skene Rd. G51: Glas 6H **81**
Skerne Gro. G75: E Kil 5B **148**
Skerray Quad. G22: Glas 1G **63**
Skerray St. G22: Glas 1G **63**
Skerryvore Pl. G33: Glas 3B **86**
Skerryvore Rd. G33: Glas 3B **86**
Skibo La. G46: T'bnk 4E **117**
Skimmers Hill G66: Milt C. 1B **30**
Skipness Av. ML8: Carl 5G **165**
Skipness Dr. G51: Glas 4D **80**
Skirsa Ct. G23: Glas 1E **63**
Skirsa Pl. G23: Glas 2D **62**
Skirsa Sq. G23: Glas 2E **63**
Skirsa St. G23: Glas 1D **62**
Skirving St. G41: Glas 5C **102**
Skovlunde Way G75: E Kil 5G **149**
Skye G74: E Kil 2C **150**
Skye Av. PA4: Renf 2E **79**
Skye Ct. G67: Cumb 5F **35**
Skye Cres. G60: Old K 2G **41**
   PA2: Pais 6H **97**
Skye Dr. G60: Old K 2G **41**
   G67: Cumb 5F **35**
Skye Gdns. G61: Bear 1B **44**
Skye Pl. G67: Cumb 5F **35**
Skye Quad. ML2: Wis 4C **146**

Skye Rd. G67: Cumb 5F **35**
   G73: Ruth 4F **121**
Skye Wynd ML3: Ham 2D **152**
Slakiewood Av. G69: G'csh 2C **68**
Slatefield G66: Len. 3F **7**
Slatefield Ct. *G31: Glas* *5C 84*
   (off Slatefield St.)
Slatefield St. G31: Glas 5C **84**
Sleaford Av. ML1: Moth 5F **143**
Slenavon Av. G73: Ruth 4F **121**
Slessor Dr. G75: E Kil 4G **149**
Slioch Sq. ML1: N'hill 3C **128**
Sloy St. G22: Glas 5H **63**
   ML2: Wis 2G **157**
Small Cres. G72: Blan 2B **140**
Sma'Shot Cottages 1A **98**
Smeaton Av. G64: Torr 5D **28**
Smeaton Dr. G64: B'rig 3C **48**
Smeaton St. G20: Glas 3D **62**
Smith Av. ML2: Wis 4G **157**
Smith Cl. G64: B'rig 1F **65**
Smith Cres. G81: Hard 2D **42**
Smith Gdns. G64: B'rig. 1F **65**
Smith Gro. G64: B'rig 1F **65**
Smithhills St. PA1: Pais. 6A **78**
Smith Pk. Pl. G76: Busby 4D **134**
Smith Quad. ML5: Coat 4E **91**
Smith's La. PA3: Pais 5A **78**
SMITHSTONE 2B **34**
Smithstone Cres. G65: Croy 6A **12**
Smithstone Rd. G68: Cumb. 3B **34**
Smith St. G14: Glas 1E **81**
   (not continuous)
Smith Ter. G73: Ruth 4D **104**
Smithview ML2: Over. 4A **158**
Smith Way G64: B'rig 1F **65**
Smithycroft ML3: Ham 1C **154**
Smithycroft Rd. G33: Glas 3F **85**
Smithyends G67: Cumb. 6B **14**
Smollett Rd. G82: Dumb 4H **17**
Snaefell Av. G73: Ruth. 3E **121**
Snaefell Cres. G73: Ruth. 2E **121**
Snead Vw. ML1: Cle. 6E **129**
Sneddon Av. ML2: Wis. 2A **158**
Sneddon St. ML3: Ham 3D **140**
Sneddon Ter. ML3: Ham 3D **140**
Snowdon Pl. G5: Glas 1H **103**
Snowdon St. G5: Glas 1H **103**
Snuff Mill Rd. G44: Glas 2E **119**
Solar Ct. ML9: Lark 5F **161**
Sollas Pl. G13: Glas. 1G **59**
Solsgirth Gdns. G66: Kirk 4H **31**
Solway Ct. ML3: Ham. 3F **153**
Solway Pl. G69: Chry. 6B **52**
Solway St. G40: Glas. 3B **104**
Somerford Rd. G61: Bear. 6F **45**
Somervell St. G72: Camb 1H **121**
Somerville Dr. G42: Glas 5F **103**
   G75: E Kil 4G **149**
Somerville La. G75: E Kil 4H **149**
Somerville Ter. G75: E Kil 4H **149**
Sorby St. G31: Glas 6F **85**
Sorley St. G11: Glas. 1F **81**
Sorn St. G40: Glas 2D **104**
Souterhouse Path ML5: Coat 6B **90**
Souterhouse Rd. ML5: Coat. 6B **90**
Southampton Dr. G12: Glas 3H **61**
Southampton La. *G12: Glas.* *3H 61*
   (off Burlington Av.)
Sth. Annandale St. G42: Glas 3F **103**
South Av. G72: Blan 4B **140**
   G81: Clyd 5C **42**
   ML8: Carl 4E **165**
   PA2: Pais 5B **98**
   PA4: Renf 6F **59**
Southbank Bus. Pk. G66: Kirk 6C **30**
Southbank Dr. G66: Kirk 6C **30**

Southbank Rd. G66: Kirk 6B **30**
Sth. Bank St. G31: Glas 6F **85**
Sth. Bank St. G81: Clyd 2E **59**
SOUTHBAR 1E **57**
Southbar Av. G13: Glas 2A **60**
Southbar Rd. PA4: Inch 3E **57**
SOUTH BARRWOOD 4A **12**
Sth. Barrwood Rd. G65: Kils 4A **12**
Sth. Biggar Rd. ML6: Air 4B **92**
South Brae G66: Len 5E **7**
Southbrae Av. PA11: Bri W 4D **72**
Southbrae Dr. G13: Glas 4C **60**
Southbrae La. *G13: Glas* *4E 61*
   (off Selborne Rd.)
Sth. Bridge St. ML6: Air 3A **92**
Sth. Caldeen Rd. ML5: Coat 6D **90**
Sth. Calder ML1: Moth 1H **143**
Sth. Campbell St. PA2: Pais 2A **98**
Sth. Carbrain Rd. G67: Cumb. 5H **35**
SOUTH CARDONALD 1C **100**
Sth. Chester St. G32: Glas. 6A **86**
Sth. Circular Rd. ML5: Coat 4C **90**
Sth. Claremont La. G62: Miln 4G **25**
Sth. Commonhead Av. ML6: Air . . . 2H **91**
Southcroft Rd. G73: Ruth. 4A **104**
Southcroft St. G51: Glas 4H **81**
Sth. Crosshill Rd. G64: B'rig 6C **48**
Sth. Dean Pk. Av. G71: Both 5E **125**
Southdeen Av. G15: Glas. 4A **44**
Southdeen Rd. G15: Glas 4A **44**
Sth. Douglas St. G81: Clyd 1E **59**
South Dr. PA3: Lin 5H **75**
Sth. Dumbreck Rd. G65: Kils 3F **11**
Sth. Elgin Pl. G81: Clyd 2E **59**
Sth. Elgin St. G81: Clyd 2E **59**
Southend Pl. ML4: Bell 3B **126**
Southend Rd. G81: Hard 2D **42**
Southern Av. G73: Ruth. 2D **120**
Southerness Dr. G68: Cumb 6A **14**
Sth. Erskine Pk. G61: Bear 2D **44**
Southesk Av. G64: B'rig 4B **48**
Southesk Gdns. G64: B'rig 4B **48**
Sth. Exchange Ct. G1: Glas 6E **5**
Southfield Av. PA2: Pais 5A **98**
Southfield Cres. G53: Glas 5C **100**
   ML5: Coat. 6E **91**
Southfield Rd. G68: Cumb 4E **35**
Sth. Frederick St. G1: Glas . . . 4G **83** (5F **5**)
Southgate G62: Miln 4G **25**
   G74: E Kil *2G 149*
   (off Olympia Ct.)
Sth. Glassford St. G62: Miln 4H **25**
Sth. Halfhill Rd. G32: Glas 6B **86**
Southhill Av. G73: Ruth 1E **121**
Southinch Av. G14: Glas 3G **59**
Southlea Av. G46: T'bnk 4G **117**
South Loan G69: Chry 1B **68**
Southloch Gdns. G21: Glas 6B **64**
Southloch St. G21: Glas. 6B **64**
Sth. Mains Rd. G62: Miln. 4F **25**
Sth. Medrox St. ML5: Glenb 2G **69**
Sth. Moraine La. G15: Glas. 5C **44**
South Mound PA6: Hous 1A **74**
Sth. Muirhead Rd. G67: Cumb 3A **36**
Southmuir Pl. G20: Glas 4B **62**
Sth. Nimmo St. ML6: Air 4B **92**
SOUTH NITSHILL 3A **116**
South Pk. ML3: Ham 1H **153**
Southpark Av. G12: Glas 1B **82**
Sth. Park Av. G78: Barr 4D **114**
Sth. Park Dr. PA2: Pais 3A **98**
Sth. Park Gro. ML3: Ham 6H **141**
Sth. Park La. G12: Glas. 1C **82**
Sth. Park Ter. G12: Glas. 1C **82**
South Pl. ML4: Bell 3B **126**
South Portland St. G5: Glas 5F **83**
Sth. Portland St. G5: Glas 6F **83**
   (not continuous)
South Rd. G76: Busby 4E **135**
Sth. Robertson Pl. ML6: Air 4G **91**
Sth. Scott St. G69: Bail 1H **107**
Southside Cres. G5: Glas. 1G **103**
Sth. Spiers Wharf G4: Glas. . . 1F **83** (1D **4**)

South St. G14: Glas 5A 60
  PA4: Inch 5F 57
  PA6: Hous 1A 74
Sth. Vesalius St. G32: Glas 6A 86
South Vw. G72: Blan 6A 124
  G81: Clyd 4B 42
  ML4: Bell 3A 126
Southview Av. G76: Busby 4D 134
Southview Ct. G64: B'rig 2B 64
Southview Cres. PA11: Bri W. . . . 2F 73
Southview Dr. G61: Bear 2C 44
Southview Gro. G61: Bear 2C 44
Southview Pl. G69: G'csh 3C 68
Southview Ter. G64: B'rig 2B 64
Sth. William St. PA5: John 3F 95
Southwell Rd. PA1: Pais 6G 79
Southwood Dr. G44: Glas 2G 119
  G4: Glas 1C 82
Sth. Woodside Rd. G20: Glas . . . 6D 62
Soutra Pl. G33: Glas 3B 86
Sovereigns Ga. G71: Both 5C 124
Spalehall Dr. ML1: N'hill 4F 129
SPATESTON 6C 94
Spateston Rd. PA5: John 6C 94
Spean Av. G74: E Kil 2B 150
Spean St. G44: Glas 6E 103
Spectrum Ho. G81: Clyd 5D 42
Speirsfield Ct. PA1: Pais 2H 97
Speirsfield Gdns. PA2: Pais. 2A 98
Speirshall Cl. G14: Glas 4H 59
Speirshall Ter. G14: Glas 3G 59
Speirs Rd. G61: Bear 4G 45
  PA5: John. 2H 95
Spencer Dr. PA2: Pais 5B 96
Spencerfield Gdns. ML3: Ham . . 6B 142
Spencer St. G13: Glas 2F 61
  G81: Clyd 4C 42
Spence St. G20: Glas 1A 62
Spey Av. PA2: Pais 5C 96
Spey Ct. ML2: Newm 3D 146
  ML6: Air 6C 92
Spey Dr. ML5: Coat 1A 110
  PA4: Renf 1G 79
Spey Gdns. ML3: Ham 3F 153
Spey Gro. G75: E Kil 4A 148
Spey Pl. PA5: John 5C 94
Spey Rd. G61: Bear 5C 44
Spey St. G33: Glas 3H 85
Spey Ter. G75: E Kil 4B 148
Spey Wlk. G67: Cumb 4H 35
  (in Cumbernauld Shop. Cen.)
  ML1: Holy. 1C 128
Spey Wynd ML9: Lark 5E 161
Spiersbridge Av. G46: T'bnk . . . 5E 117
               (Nitshill Rd.)
  G46: T'bnk 4F 117
        (Spiersbridge Rd.)
Spiersbridge Bus. Pk.
  G46: T'bnk 4E 117
Spiersbridge La. G46: T'bnk . . . 4E 117
Spiersbridge Rd. G46: T'bnk . . . 5F 117
Spiersbridge Ter. G46: T'bnk . . . 4E 117
Spiers Gro. G46: T'bnk 4F 117
Spiers Pl. PA3: Lin. 4A 76
Spiers Rd. G61: Bear 4H 45
  PA6: Hous 1B 74
Spiers Wharf G4: Glas 1F 83 (1D 4)
Spindlehowe Rd. G71: Tann . . . 1E 125
  G71: Udd 2D 124
Spinners Gdns. PA2: Pais 2F 97
Spinners La. G81: Hard 6D 22
SPITTAL 2B 120
Spittal Rd. G73: Ruth 3B 120
Spittal Ter. G72: Flem 5H 123
Spoolers Rd. PA1: Pais 2F 97
Spoutmouth G1: Glas 5H 83
Springbank Rd. PA3: Pais 4H 77
Springbank St. G20: Glas 5D 62
Springbank Ter. PA3: Pais 4H 77
SPRINGBOIG 5C 86
Springboig Av. G32: Glas 5C 86
Springboig Rd. G32: Glas 4C 86
SPRINGBURN 5B 64
Springburn Leisure Cen. 5B 64

Springburn Mus. 5B 64
             (off Ayr St.)
Springburn Pl. G74: E Kil 6C 136
Springburn Rd. G21: Glas 2A 84
Springburn Shop. Cen. G21: Glas . . 5B 64
Springburn Station (Rail) 5B 64
Springburn Way G21: Glas 5A 64
Springcroft Av. G69: Bail 5H 87
Springcroft Cres. G69: Bail 5H 87
Springcroft Dr. G69: Bail 5G 87
Springcroft Gdns. G69: Bail 5A 88
Springcroft Gro. G69: Bail 5H 87
Springcroft Wynd G69: Bail 5H 87
Springfield Av. G'rig 1C 64
  G71: Udd 2D 124
  PA1: Pais 1D 98
Springfield Ct. G1: Glas 4G 83 (6E 5)
  G64: B'rig. 6D 48
Springfield Cres. G64: B'rig. 1C 64
  G71: Udd 2D 124
  G72: Blan 2A 140
  ML8: Carl 5F 165
Springfield Dr. G78: Barr 6G 115
Springfield Gro. G78: Barr 6F 115
Springfield Pk. PA5: John 3G 95
Springfield Pk. Rd. G73: Ruth . . 1E 121
Springfield Quay G5: Glas 5D 82
Springfield Rd. G31: Glas 1E 105
  G40: Glas 2C 104
  G64: B'rig. 6C 48
  G67: Cumb 1A 36
  G78: Barr, Neil 2F 131
  ML6: Air 3E 93
Springfield Sq. G64: B'rig 1C 64
Springfield Woods PA5: John . . . 3G 95
SPRINGHALL. 3F 121
Springhall Ct. G73: Ruth 4F 121
      (off Slenavon Av.)
SPRINGHILL. 1G 131
Springhill Av. ML5: Coat 1G 109
  ML6: Air 3B 92
Springhill Dr. Sth. G69: Bail 5G 87
Springhill Farm Gro. G69: Bail . . 5G 87
Springhill Farm Pl. G69: Bail . . . 5G 87
Springhill Farm Rd. G69: Bail . . . 5G 87
Springhill Farm Way G69: Bail . . 5G 87
Springhill Gdns. G41: Glas 4C 102
Springhill Parkway G69: Bail . . . 5G 87
Springhill Pl. ML5: Coat 1G 109
Springhill Rd. G69: Bail 6F 87
  G76: Busby 2D 134
  G78: Barr 5D 114
  G78: Neil 4G 131
Springholm Dr. ML6: Air 1H 91
Springkell Av. G41: Glas 2H 101
Springkell Dr. G41: Glas 3H 101
Springkell Gdns. G41: Glas 3B 102
Springkell Ga. G41: Glas 3B 102
Springside Gdns. G15: Glas. 3A 44
Springside Pl. G15: Glas. 3A 44
Springvale Dr. PA2: Pais 3D 96
Springvale Ter. G21: Glas 5A 64
SPRINGWELL 4D 122
Springwell Cres. G72: Blan 2D 140
SPRINGWELLS 3D 140
Springwells Av. ML6: Air 3C 92
Springwells Cres. ML6: Air 3C 92
Spruce Av. G72: Blan 1A 140
  ML3: Ham 1A 154
  PA5: John. 4G 95
Spruce Ct. ML3: Ham. 2A 154
  ML5: Coat. 1B 110
Spruce Dr. G66: Lenz 2A 50
  G72: Flem 3F 123
Spruce Rd. G67: Cumb 1D 36
  G71: View. 4G 109
Spruce St. G22: Glas 4H 63
Spruce Way G72: Flem 3F 123
  ML1: Holy 3B 128
Spynie Pl. G64: B'rig 5F 49
Spynie Way ML2: Newm 3D 146
          (off Iona Rd.)
Squire St. G14: Glas 1D 80
Sraehouse Wynd ML8: Carl. . . . 4H 165

Stabcross Bus. Pk. G3: Glas 3C 82
      (off St Vincent Cres.)
Stable Gro. PA1: Pais. 2F 97
Stable Pl. G62: Miln. 2F 25
Stable Rd. G62: Miln 2F 25
Staffa G74: E Kil 3C 150
Staffa Av. PA4: Renf 2E 79
Staffa Dr. G66: Kirk 5H 31
  ML6: Air 4F 93
  PA2: Pais 6A 98
Staffa Rd. G72: Camb 4H 121
Staffa St. G31: Glas 3D 84
Staffin Dr. G23: Glas 6B 46
Staffin Path G23: Glas 6C 46
      (off Staffin St.)
Staffin St. G23: Glas 6C 46
Stafford St. G4: Glas. 2G 83 (2G 5)
  ML4: Bell 3B 126
Stag Ct. G71: View. 1G 125
Stag St. G51: Glas 4H 81
Staig Wynd ML1: Moth 5A 144
Staineybraes Pl. ML6: Air 1H 91
Stalker St. ML2: Wis 5C 144
Stamford Pl. G31: Glas 6D 84
Stamford Rd. G31: Glas. 6D 84
Stamford St. G31: Glas 6D 84
  G40: Glas 6D 84
STAMPERLAND 6D 118
Stamperland Av. G76: Clar 2D 134
Stamperland Cres. G76: Clar . . . 1C 134
Stamperland Dr. G76: Clar 2D 134
Stamperland Gdns. G76: Clar . . . 6D 118
Stamperland Hill G76: Clar 1C 134
Stanalane St. G46: T'bnk 3F 117
Standburn Rd. G21: Glas 2F 65
Stand Comedy Club, The 1C 82
Standford Hall G72: Camb. 1A 122
      (off Main St.)
Staneacre Pk. ML3: Ham. 6B 142
Stanecraigs Pl. ML2: Newm 3D 146
Stanefield Dr. ML1: N'hill. 3E 129
Stanely Av. PA2: Pais 5F 97
Stanely Cres. PA2: Pais 5F 97
Stanely Dr. PA2: Pais. 4G 97
Stanely Rd. PA2: Pais 4G 97
Stanford St. G81: Clyd 6E 43
Stanhope Dr. G73: Ruth 2F 121
Stanhope Pl. ML2: Wis 4G 157
Stanistone Rd. ML8: Carl 3G 165
Stanka Av. PA2: Pais 2G 97
STANLEY 4G 97
Stanley Blvd. G72: Blan 5B 140
Stanley Dr. G64: B'rig 5D 48
  ML4: Bell 1C 126
  PA5: Brkfld 6C 74
Stanley Gro. PA2: Pais 5F 97
Stanley La. PA5: Brkfld 6C 74
Stanley Pk. ML6: Air 3B 92
Stanley Pl. G72: Blan. 6B 124
Stanley Rd. PA2: Pais 3H 97
Stanley St. G41: Glas 6C 82
  ML3: Ham 5D 140
Stanley St. La. G41: Glas 6C 82
Stanmore Rd. G42: Glas. 5F 103
Stanrigg St. ML6: Plain 1G 93
Stark Av. G81: Dun. 1A 42
Starling Way ML4: Bell 5A 110
Startpoint St. G33: Glas 3A 86
Station Brae G78: Neil 1C 130
Station Bldgs. G67: Cumb 5A 36
Station Cres. PA4: Renf. 5G 59
Station Pk. G69: Bail 1A 108
Station Pl. ML8: Law 5E 159
Station Rd. G20: Glas 1A 62
  G33: Mille. 4A 66
  G33: Step 4D 66
  G46: Giff 4A 118
  G60: Old K 1F 41
  G61: Bear 3C 44
  G62: Bard 6E 27
  G62: Miln 3G 25
  G65: Kils 2H 11
  G66: Len 3F 7
  G66: Lenz 3C 50

Station Rd. G69: Bail 1A 108
G69: Muirh 2A 68
G71: Both 5E 125
G71: Udd 1C 124
G72: Blan 1C 140
G76: Busby 4E 135
G78: Neil 2D 130
G82: Dumb 3E 17
ML1: Cle 6H 129
ML1: New S 4B 128
ML2: Wis 1G 157
ML6: Air 3E 93
ML6: Plain 1H 93
ML8: Carl 4E 165
ML8: Law 6D 158
ML9: Lark 1F 161
PA1: Pais 2E 97
PA10: Kilb 3A 94
PA11: Bri W 4G 73
PA4: Renf 5F 59
PA7: B'ton 5H 39
Station Row ML8: Carl 5E 159
Station Way G71: Udd 1D 124
Station Wynd PA10: Kilb 3B 94
Staybrae Dr. G53: Glas 4H 99
Staybrae Gro. G53: Glas 4H 99
Steading, The ML2: Wis 4H 145
Steel St. G1: Glas 5H 83
ML2: Wis 1H 157
Steeple Sq. PA10: Kilb 2A 94
Steeple St. PA10: Kilb 2A 94
Stemac La. ML6: Plain 1G 93
Stenhouse Av. G69: Muirh 2A 68
Stenton Cres. ML2: Wis. 2D 156
Stenton Pl. ML2: Wis. 2D 156
Stenton St. G32: Glas 4G 85
Stepends Rd. ML6: Air 5H 93
Stepford Path G33: Glas 4G 87
Stepford Pl. G33: Glas 4F 87
Stepford Rd. G33: Glas. 4F 87
Stepford Sports Pk. 5G 87
Stephen Cres. G69: Bail 6F 87
Stephenson Pl. G75: E Kil 3F 149
Stephenson Sq. G75: E Kil 3F 149
Stephenson St. G52: Hill 3G 79
Stephenson Ter. G75: E Kil 3F 149
STEPPS 4C 66
Steppshill Ter. G33: Step. 4C 66
Stepps Rd. G33: Glas. 2C 86
G66: Auch. 5E 51
STEPPS RD. INTERCHANGE 2C 86
Stepps Station (Rail) 4E 67
Stevens La. ML1: New S 4A 128
Stevenson Pl. ML4: Bell 6D 110
Stevenson St. G40: Glas 5A 84
(not continuous)
G81: Clyd 3B 42
ML8: Carl 3E 165
PA2: Pais 2A 98
Stevenston Ct. ML1: New S 3A 128
Stevenston St. ML1: New S 3A 128
Stewart Av. G72: Blan 2A 140
G77: Newt M 3E 133
PA4: Renf 2D 78
Stewart Ct. G73: Ruth 6E 105
G78: Barr 3E 115
ML5: Coat. 5E 91
(off Clifton Pl.)
Stewart Cres. G78: Barr 3F 115
ML2: Newm 3E 147
Stewart Dr. G69: Barg 5F 89
G76: Clar 1B 134
G81: Hard 1D 42
STEWARTFIELD 5E 137
Stewartfield Dr. G74: E Kil 5F 137
Stewartfield Rd. G74: E Kil 6E 137
Stewartfield Way G74: E Kil 6A 136
Stewart Gdns ML5: Coat 4E 91
Stewart Gill Pl. ML3: Ashg 4B 162
Stewarton Dr. G72: Camb 2G 121
Stewarton Ho. ML2: Wis 1H 157
(off Stewarton St.)
Stewarton Rd. G46: T'bnk 6D 116
G77: Newt M 4A 132

Stewarton St. ML2: Wis. 1H 157
Stewarton Ter. ML2: Wis 1H 157
Stewart Pl. G78: Barr 3F 115
ML8: Carl 3F 165
Stewart Quad. ML1: Holy. 1B 128
Stewart Rd. PA2: Pais 5B 98
Stewarts La. ML2: Wis 6A 146
Stewart St. G4: Glas 2F 83 (1D 4)
G62: Miln 4G 25
G78: Barr 3F 115
G81: Clyd 4A 42
ML3: Ham. 4E 141
(not continuous)
ML4: Moss 2E 127
ML5: Coat. 3C 90
ML8: Carl 2E 165
Stewartville St. G11: Glas 1H 81
Stirling Av. G61: Bear. 5E 45
Stirling Dr. G61: Bear 1D 44
G64: B'rig 4A 48
G73: Ruth. 2D 120
G74: E Kil 6A 138
ML3: Ham 5C 140
PA3: Lin 6F 75
PA5: John. 3D 94
Stirlingfauld Pl. G5: Glas. 6F 83
Stirling Gdns. G64: B'rig 4A 48
Stirling Ho. G81: Clyd 5D 42
(off Clyde St.)
Stirling Pl. G66: Len 3G 7
Stirling Rd. G4: Glas 3H 83 (4H 5)
G65: Kils. 2A 12
G66: Kirk 4D 30
G82: Dumb, Milt. 1G 17
ML6: Air, Rigg 1B 92
ML6: Chap 1D 112
ML6: Carl 1E 165
Stirling Rd. Ind. Est.
ML6: Air 1B 92
Stirling St. G67: Cumb. 1B 36
ML1: Moth 5B 144
ML5: Coat 1H 109
ML6: Air. 4H 91
Stirling Way G69: Bail 1G 107
PA4: Renf 2F 79
Stirrat St. G20: Glas. 3A 62
PA3: Pais. 4F 77
Stobcross Rd. G3: Glas 3A 82
Stobcross St. G3: Glas 4C 82 (5A 4)
ML5: Coat. 5C 90
Stobcross Wynd G3: Glas. 4B 82
Stobhill Cotts. G21: Glas. 2C 64
Stobhill Rd. G21: Glas. 2B 64
Stobo G74: E Kil 5C 138
Stobo Ct. G74: E Kil 5C 138
Stobo St. ML2: Wis 4A 146
Stobs Dr. G78: Barr 2D 114
Stobs Pl. G34: Glas 2A 88
Stock Av. PA2: Pais 2A 98
Stock Exchange G2: Glas 5E 5
Stockholm Cres. PA2: Pais 2A 98
Stockiemuir Av. G61: Bear. 6D 24
Stockiemuir Ct. G61: Bear 6E 25
Stockiemuir Rd. G61: Bear 1D 44
G62: Miln 3C 24
Stocks Rd. ML1: Cle 1D 146
Stock St. PA2: Pais 3A 98
Stockwell Pl. G1: Glas. 5G 83
Stockwell St. G1: Glas 5G 83 (6F 5)
Stoddard Sq. PA5: Eld 2B 96
Stonebyres Ct. ML3: Ham 6E 141
Stonecraig Rd. ML2: Wis 1H 157
Stonedyke Cres. ML8: Carl 2G 165
Stonedyke Gro. G15: Glas 5B 44
Stonedyke Rd. ML8: Carl 2G 165
STONEFIELD 1C 140
Stonefield Av. G12: Glas 3A 62
PA2: Pais 4B 98
Stonefield Cres. G72: Blan 3A 140
G76: Clar 1A 134
PA2: Pais 4B 98
Stonefield Dr. PA2: Pais. 4B 98
Stonefield Gdns. ML8: Carl 2F 165
PA2: Pais 4B 98
Stonefield Grn. PA2: Pais 4A 98

Stonefield Gro. PA2: Pais 4A 98
Stonefield Pk. PA2: Pais 5A 98
Stonefield Pk. Gdns.
G72: Blan 1C 140
Stonefield Pl. G72: Blan 3H 139
Stonefield Rd. G72: Blan 2A 140
Stonefield St. ML6: Air 2A 92
Stonehall Av. ML3: Ham 1F 153
Stonehaven Cres. ML6: Air 6G 91
Stonelaw Dr. G73: Ruth. 6D 104
Stonelaw Rd. G73: Ruth 6D 104
Stonelaw Towers G73: Ruth. 1E 121
Stoneside Dr. G43: Glas 1G 117
Stoneside Sq. G43: Glas 1G 117
Stoney Brae PA2: Pais 5A 98
(not continuous)
Stoneyetts Rd. G69: Mood 4D 52
Stoneymeadow Rd. G72: Blan 3E 139
G74: E Kil 5B 138
Stony Brae PA1: Pais 6A 78
PA3: Pais 6A 78
Stonyflatt Av. G82: Dumb 2H 17
Stonyflatt Rd. G82: Dumb 2H 17
Stonyhurst St. G22: Glas 5F 63
(not continuous)
Stonylee Rd. G67: Cumb 4A 36
Storie St. PA1: Pais 1A 98
(not continuous)
Stormyland Way G78: Barr 5E 115
Stornoway Cres. ML2: Wis 4C 146
Stornoway St. G22: Glas 1G 63
Stow Brae PA1: Pais 1A 98
Stow St. PA1: Pais 1A 98
Strachan St. ML4: Bell 3C 126
Strachur St. G22: Glas 2E 63
Strain Cres. ML6: Air. 5B 92
Straiton Dr. ML3: Ham 1B 152
Straiton Pl. G72: Blan 1B 140
Straiton St. G32: Glas 4G 85
Stranraer Dr. G15: Glas 5C 44
Stratford G74: E Kil 4D 138
Stratford St. G20: Glas. 4B 62
Strathallan Gdns. G66: Kirk. 5D 30
(off Willowbank Gdns.)
Strathallon Pl. G73: Ruth. 4F 121
(off St Stephen's Av.)
Strathaven Rd. G75: E Kil 3A 150
ML3: Ham 6G 153
Strathavon Cres. ML6: Air 1A 92
Strathblane Cres. ML6: Air 6H 71
Strathblane Dr. G75: E Kil 3A 148
Strathblane Gdns. G13: Glas 1E 61
Strathblane Rd. G62: Miln 3H 25
G66: Cam G 1A 6
Strathbran St. G31: Glas 1F 105
STRATHBUNGO 3D 102
Strathcairn Cres. ML6: Air. 6H 71
Strath Carron ML8: Law 6E 159
Strathcarron Cres. PA2: Pais 5D 98
Strathcarron Dr. PA2: Pais. 4D 98
Strathcarron Pl. G20: Glas. 3B 62
PA2: Pais 5D 98
Strathcarron Rd. PA2: Pais 5D 98
Strathcarron Way PA2: Pais. 4D 98
Strathclyde Arts Cen. 6A 4
Strathclyde Bus. Cen.
G72: Flem 4E 123
Strathclyde Bus. Pk. ML4: Bell 3A 110
Strathclyde Country Pk. 1A 142
Strathclyde Dr. G73: Ruth 6C 104
Strathclyde Homes Stadium 5G 17
Strathclyde Path G71: Udd 1C 124
Strathclyde Rd. G82: Dumb. 2G 17
ML1: Moth 3D 142
Strathclyde St. G40: Glas. 3C 104
Strathclyde Vw. G71: Both 6F 125
Strathcona Dr. G13: Glas 2F 61
Strathcona Gdns. G13: Glas 2G 61
Strathcona La. G75: E Kil 4G 149
Strathcona Pl. G73: Ruth 3F 121
G75: E Kil 4G 149
Strathcona St. G13: Glas 3F 61
Strathconon Gdns. G75: E Kil 2A 148
(off Strathnairn Dr.)

Strath Dearn ML8: Law	6E 159
Strathdearn Gro. G75: E Kil	3A 148
Strathdee Av. G81: Hard	2D 42
Strathdee Rd. G44: Neth	5C 118
Strathdon Av. G44: Neth	5C 118
PA2: Pais	3G 97
Strathdon Dr. G44: Neth	5D 118
Strathdon Pl. G75: E Kil	3A 148
(off Strathnairn Dr.)	
Strathearn Gro. G66: Kirk	4H 31
Strathearn Rd. G76: Clar	3C 134
Strath Elgin ML8: Law	6D 158
Strathendrick Dr. G44: Glas	1F 149
Strathfillan Rd. G74: E Kil	6E 159
Strath Halladale ML8: Law	6E 159
Strathhalladale Ct. G75: E Kil	3A 148
(off Strathmore Gro.)	
Strathkelvin Av. G64: B'rig	2B 64
Strathkelvin La. G75: E Kil	3A 148
Strathkelvin Retail Pk. G64: B'rig	3E 49
Strathlachan Av. ML8: Carl	4G 165
Strathleven Pl. G82: Dumb	4F 17
Strathmore Av. G72: Blan	6A 124
PA1: Pais	1F 99
Strathmore Cres. ML6: Air	1A 92
Strathmore Gdns. G73: Ruth	3F 121
Strathmore Gro. G75: E Kil	3A 148
Strathmore Ho. G74: E Kil	2G 149
(off Princess Sq.)	
Strathmore Pl. ML5: Coat	6F 91
Strathmore Rd. G22: Glas	2F 63
ML3: Ham	6A 142
Strathmore Wlk. ML5: Coat	6F 91
Strathmungo Cres. ML6: Air	1H 91
Strath Nairn ML8: Law	6E 159
Strathnairn Av. G75: E Kil	3A 148
Strathnairn Ct. G75: E Kil	3A 148
Strathnairn Dr. G75: E Kil	3A 148
Strathnairn Way G75: E Kil	3A 148
Strath Naver ML8: Law	6E 159
Strathnaver Gdns. G75: E Kil	3A 148
Strathord Pl. G69: Mood	3E 53
Strathord St. G32: Glas	2A 106
Strath Peffer ML8: Law	6D 158
Strathpeffer Av. ML6: Air	1A 92
Strathpeffer Dr. G75: E Kil	3A 148
(off Strathnairn Dr.)	
Strathspey Av. G75: E Kil	3A 148
Strathspey Cres. ML6: Air	6H 71
Strathtay Av. G44: Neth	5C 118
G75: E Kil	3A 148
Strathtummel Cres. ML6: Air	6H 71
Strathview Gro. G44: Neth	5C 118
Strathview Pk. G44: Neth	5C 118
Strathview Rd. ML4: Bell	4A 126
Strathy Pl. G20: Glas	3B 62
Strathyre Gdns. G61: Bear	2H 45
G69: Mood	4E 53
G75: E Kil	3A 148
ML6: Glenm	4H 71
Strathyre Rd. G72: Blan	3D 140
Strathyre St. G41: Glas	5C 102
Stratton Dr. G46: Giff	5H 117
Strauss Av. G81: Clyd	6G 43
Stravaig Path PA2: Pais	6E 97
Stravaig Wlk. PA2: Pais	6E 97
Stravanan Ct. G45: Glas	5A 120
Stravanan Gdns. G45: Glas	5H 119
Stravanan Pl. G45: Glas	5H 119
Stravanan Rd. G45: Glas	6H 119
Stravanan St. G45: Glas	5H 119
Stravanan Ter. G45: Glas	5H 119
Stravenhouse Rd. ML8: Law	1G 163
Strawberry Fld. Rd. PA6: C'lee	2B 74
Strawhill Ct. G76: Busby	2D 134
Strawhill Rd. G76: Clar	2C 134
Strayhgryffe Cres. PA11: Bri W	2E 73
Streamfield Gdns. G33: Glas	2G 65
Streamfield Ga. G33: Glas	2F 65
Streamfield Lea G33: Glas	1G 65
(off Brookfield Dr.)	
Streamfield Pl. G33: Glas	2G 65
Strenabey Av. G73: Ruth	3F 121
Striven Ct. ML5: Coat	2D 110

Striven Cres. ML2: Wis	2G 157
Striven Gdns. G20: Glas	6D 62
Striven Ter. ML3: Ham	2E 153
Stroma St. G21: Glas	1D 84
Stromness St. G5: Glas	1E 103
Strone Gdns. G65: Kils	3F 11
Stronend St. G22: Glas	4F 63
Strone Path ML5: Glenb	3G 69
Strone Pl. ML6: Air	6C 92
Strone Rd. G33: Glas	4B 86
Stronsay Pl. G64: B'rig	5F 49
Stronsay St. G21: Glas	1D 84
Stronvar Dr. G14: Glas	5B 60
Stronvar La. G14: Glas	5B 60
Stroud Rd. G75: E Kil	6E 149
Strowan Cres. G32: Glas	1B 106
Strowan's Rd. G82: Dumb	2C 18
Strowan St. G32: Glas	1B 106
Strowan's Well Rd. G82: Dumb	2C 18
Struan Av. G46: Giff	4A 118
Struan Gdns. G44: Glas	2E 119
Struan Rd. G44: Glas	2E 119
Struie St. G34: Glas	3G 87
Struma Dr. G76: Clar	1A 134
Struther & Swinhill Rd.	
ML9: Lark	6G 161
STRUTHERHILL	5F 161
Strutherhill ML9: Lark	4F 161
Strutherhill Ind. Est. ML9: Lark	5G 161
Struthers Cres. G74: E Kil	5B 138
Struther St. ML9: Lark	5F 161
Stuart Av. G60: Old K	2F 41
G73: Ruth	2D 120
Stuart Dr. G64: B'rig	1A 64
ML9: Lark	4G 161
Stuart Ho. G67: Cumb	2B 36
Stuarton Pk. G74: E Kil	1G 149
Stuart Quad. ML2: Wis	2E 157
Stuart Rd. G76: Crmck	1H 135
G82: Dumb	1C 18
PA7: B'ton	3H 39
Stuart St. G60: Old K	2F 41
G74: E Kil	1H 149
Stuartville ML5: Coat	4D 90
Succoth St. G13: Glas	1F 61
Sudbury Cres. G75: E Kil	2D 148
Suffolk St. G40: Glas	5H 83
Sugworth Av. G69: Bail	6H 87
Suisnish PA8: Ersk	2G 57
Sumburgh St. G33: Glas	4H 85
Summerfield Cotts. G14: Glas	1E 81
Summerfield Rd. G67: Cumb	1C 54
Summerfield St. G40: Glas	2D 104
Summerhill & Garngibbock Rd.	
G67: Cumb	5E 55
Summerhill Av. ML9: Lark	3E 161
Summerhill Dr. G15: Glas	3B 44
Summerhill Gdns. G15: Glas	3B 44
Summerhill Pl. G15: Glas	3B 44
Summerhill Rd. G15: Glas	3A 44
G76: Busby	2D 134
Summerhill Way ML4: Bell	3B 126
Summerlea Rd. G46: T'bnk	3F 117
SUMMERLEE	3B 90
Summerlee Cotts. ML5: Coat	4B 90
Summerlee Heritage Trust	3B 90
Summerlee Rd. ML2: Wis	5C 144
ML9: Lark	6H 155
Summerlee St. G33: Glas	3C 86
ML5: Coat	4B 90
SUMMERSTON	6B 46
Summerston Station (Rail)	1B 62
Summer St. G40: Glas	6B 84
Summertown Path G51: Glas	4H 81
Summertown Rd. G51: Glas	4H 81
Summyside Oval PA2: Pais	4A 98
Sunart Av. PA4: Renf	5D 58
Sunart Ct. ML3: Ham	2E 153
Sunart Gdns. G64: B'rig	6E 49
Sunart Rd. G52: Glas	6E 81
G64: B'rig	6E 49
Sunart St. ML2: Wis	2G 157
Sunbury Av. G76: Clar	2A 134
Sundale Av. G76: Clar	3B 134

Sunderland Av. G82: Dumb	3C 16
Sunflower Gdns. ML1: Moth	1F 143
Sunningdale Av. G77: Newt M	4F 133
Sunningdale Dr. PA11: Bri W	5E 73
Sunningdale Rd. G23: Glas	1B 62
Sunningdale Wynd G71: Both	4C 124
Sunnybank Dr. G76: Clar	3B 134
Sunnybank Gro. G76: Clar	3B 134
Sunnybank St. G40: Glas	2D 104
Sunnyhill G65: Twe	2D 32
Sunnylaw Dr. PA2: Pais	3F 97
Sunnylaw St. G22: Glas	5F 63
SUNNYSIDE	3C 90
Sunnyside Av. G71: Udd	2D 124
ML1: Holy	2B 128
Sunnyside Cres. ML1: Holy	2A 128
Sunnyside Dr. G15: Glas	6A 44
G69: Barg	6D 88
G76: Clar	1B 134
Sunnyside Pl. G15: Glas	6A 44
G78: Barr	5D 114
ML1: Holy	2A 128
Sunnyside Rd. ML1: Cle	1H 145
ML3: Ham, Quar	3A 160
ML5: Coat	4C 90
ML9: Lark	2B 160
PA2: Pais	4H 97
Sunnyside St. ML9: Lark	1D 160
Sunnyside Ter. ML1: Holy	2A 128
Surrey La. G5: Glas	1F 103
Surrey St. G5: Glas	1F 103
Sussex St. G41: Glas	6C 82
Sutcliffe Ct. G13: Glas	2E 61
Sutcliffe Rd. G13: Glas	2E 61
Sutherland Av. G41: Glas	2H 101
G61: Bear	6E 25
Sutherland Ct. G41: Glas	1C 102
Sutherland Cres. ML3: Ham	5E 141
Sutherland Dr. G46: Giff	6B 118
G82: Dumb	2C 18
ML6: Air	6G 91
Sutherland La. G12: Glas	1B 82
Sutherland Pl. ML4: Bell	5B 126
Sutherland Rd. G81: Clyd	5D 42
Sutherland St. G72: Blan	4A 140
PA1: Pais	6H 77
Sutherland Way G74: E Kil	6C 138
Sutherness Dr. G33: Glas	4A 86
Swaledale G74: E Kil	6E 137
Swallow Dr. PA5: John	6C 94
Swallow Gdns. G13: Glas	2H 59
Swallow Rd. G81: Faif	6F 23
ML2: Wis	5H 145
Swan Pl. PA5: John	6C 94
Swanston St. G40: Glas	3C 104
Swan St. G4: Glas	2G 83 (1F 5)
G81: Clyd	4B 42
Swan Way ML8: Law	1H 163
Sweeney Dr. ML2: Wis	3E 157
Sween Av. G44: Glas	3E 119
Sween Dr. ML3: Ham	2E 153
Sween Path ML4: Bell	4E 127
(off Millbank Av.)	
Sweethill Ter. ML5: Coat	2F 111
Sweethill Wlk. ML4: Bell	6E 111
Sweethope Gdns. G71: Both	5F 125
Sweethope Pl. G71: Both	4E 125
Swift Bank ML3: Ham	2C 152
Swift Cl. ML2: Wis	6H 145
Swift Cres. G13: Glas	1H 59
Swift Pl. G75: E Kil	5A 148
PA5: John	6D 94
Swindon St. G81: Clyd	4A 42
SWINHILL	6G 161
Swinstie Rd. ML1: Cle	1A 146
SWINTON	5G 87
Swinton Av. G69: Bail	6A 88
Swinton Cres. G69: Bail	6A 88
ML5: Coat	1F 109
Swinton Dr. G52: Glas	6B 80
Swinton Gdns. G69: Bail	6B 88
Swinton Path G69: Bail	6B 88
Swinton Pl. G52: Glas	6B 80
ML5: Coat	1F 109
(off Swinton Cres.)	

Swinton Rd. G69: Bail	6A 88
Swinton Vw. G69: Bail	6B 88
Swisscot Av. ML3: Ham	3F 153
Swisscot Wlk. ML3: Ham	3F 153
Switchback Rd. G61: Bear	5F 45
Swordale Path G34: Glas	3G 87
(off Kildermorie Rd.)	
Swordale Pl. G34: Glas	3G 87
Sword St. G31: Glas	5B 84
ML6: Air	4H 91
Sycamore Av. G66: Lenz	2D 50
G71: View	6G 109
PA5: John	4G 95
Sycamore Ct. G75: E Kil	5F 149
ML5: Coat	1B 110
(off Ailsa Rd.)	
Sycamore Cres. G75: E Kil	5E 149
ML6: Air	5D 92
Sycamore Dr. G81: Clyd	3C 42
ML3: Ham	1B 154
ML6: Air	5D 92
Sycamore Gro. G72: Blan	1A 140
Sycamore Pl. G75: E Kil	5F 149
ML1: N'hill	4C 128
Sycamore Way G66: Milt C	6C 8
G72: Flem	3F 123
G76: Crmck	2H 135
Sydenham Ct. G12: Glas	5H 61
(off Westbourne Gdns. La.)	
Sydenham La. G12: Glas	6A 62
Sydenham Rd. G12: Glas	6A 62
Sydes Brae G72: Blan	5H 139
Sydney Dr. G75: E Kil	4E 149
Sydney Pl. G75: E Kil	3E 149
Sydney St. G31: Glas	5A 84
G81: Clyd	3H 41
Sykehead Av. ML4: Bell	2D 126
Sykeside Rd. ML6: Air	1G 111
Sykes Ter. G78: Neil	2F 131
Sylvania Way G81: Clyd	5D 42
Sylvania Way Sth. G81: Clyd	6D 42
Symington Dr. G81: Clyd	5C 42
Symington Sq. G75: E Kil	3H 149
Syriam Pl. G21: Glas	5B 64
Syriam St. G21: Glas	4B 64

T

Tabard Pl. G13: Glas	1C 60
Tabard Rd. G13: Glas	1C 60
Tabernacle La. G72: Camb	2A 122
Tabernacle St. G72: Camb	2A 122
Taggart Rd. G65: Croy	2B 34
Taig Rd. G66: Kirk	6H 31
Tait Av. G78: Barr	3F 115
Takmadoon Rd. G65: Kils	2A 12
Talbot G74: E Kil	5C 138
Talbot Ct. G13: Glas	4B 60
Talbot Dr. G13: Glas	4B 60
Talbot Pl. G13: Glas	4B 60
Talbot Ter. G13: Glas	4B 60
G71: Tann	5C 108
Talisman Av. G82: Dumb	3C 16
Talisman Cres. ML1: Moth	5F 127
Talisman Rd. G13: Glas	3C 60
PA2: Pais	6C 96
Tallant Rd. G15: Glas	4B 44
Tallant Ter. G15: Glas	4C 44
Talla Rd. G52: Glas	5A 80
Tall Ship at Glasgow Harbour, The	
	3A 82
Tamarack Cres. G71: View	4G 109
Tamar Dr. G75: E Kil	5B 148
Tambowie Av. G62: Miln	3F 25
Tambowie Cres. G62: Miln	3F 25
Tambowie St. G13: Glas	1E 61
Tamshill St. G20: Glas	3D 62
Tanar Av. PA4: Renf	2G 79
Tanar Way PA4: Renf	1G 79
TANDLEHILL	3B 94
Tandlehill Rd. PA10: Kilb	4A 94
Tanera Av. G44: Glas	2G 119
Tanfield Pl. G32: Glas	4C 86

Tanfield St. G32: Glas	4C 86
Tankerland Rd. G44: Glas	1E 119
Tannadice Av. G52: Glas	2C 100
Tannadice Path G52: Glas	1C 100
(off Tannadice Av.)	
Tanna Dr. G52: Glas	2F 101
Tannahill Cen. PA3: Pais	5E 77
Tannahill Cres. PA5: John	4E 95
(not continuous)	
Tannahill Dr. G74: E Kil	6C 138
Tannahill Rd. G43: Glas	1D 118
PA3: Pais	5F 77
Tannahill's Cottage	1G 97
Tannahill Ter. PA3: Pais	5F 77
Tannoch Dr. G62: Miln	2G 25
G67: Cumb	6H 35
Tannoch Pl. G67: Cumb	6H 35
TANNOCHSIDE	4F 109
Tannochside Dr. G71: Tann	4E 109
Tannochside Pk. G71: Tann	4F 109
Tannock St. G22: Glas	5F 63
Tantallon Ct. ML8: Carl	2E 165
Tantallon Dr. ML5: Coat	2G 89
PA2: Pais	4E 97
Tantallon Pk. G74: E Kil	1F 149
Tantallon Rd. G41: Glas	5C 102
G69: Bail	2G 107
G71: Both	4F 125
Tanzieknowe Av. G72: Camb	4B 122
Tanzieknowe Dr. G72: Camb	4B 122
Tanzieknowe Pl. G72: Camb	4A 122
Tanzieknowe Rd. G72: Camb	4A 122
Taransay St. G51: Glas	3G 81
Tarbert Av. G72: Blan	5A 124
ML2: Wis	2G 157
Tarbert Ct. ML3: Ham	2E 153
Tarbert Pl. ML8: Carl	4G 165
Tarbert Way ML5: Coat	1A 110
Tarbolton Cres. ML6: Chap	5D 112
Tarbolton Dr. G81: Clyd	4E 43
Tarbolton Path ML9: Lark	2D 160
Tarbolton Rd. G43: Glas	1B 118
G67: Cumb	3B 36
Tarbolton Sq. G81: Clyd	4F 43
Tarbrax Way ML3: Ham	6E 141
Tarfside Av. G52: Glas	1C 100
Tarfside Gdns. G52: Glas	1D 100
Tarfside Oval G52: Glas	1D 100
Target Rd. ML6: Air	5B 92
Tarland St. G51: Glas	5F 81
Tarn Gro. G33: Glas	1G 65
Tarras Dr. PA4: Renf	2G 79
Tarras Pl. G72: Camb	2D 122
Tasman Dr. G75: E Kil	4D 148
Tasmania Quad. ML2: Wis	6C 146
Tassie Pl. G74: E Kil	1A 150
Tassie St. G41: Glas	5B 102
Tattershall Dr. G33: Glas	1C 86
Tavistock Dr. G43: Glas	2B 118
Tay Av. PA4: Renf	6G 59
Tay Ct. G75: E Kil	4A 148
Tay Cres. G33: Glas	2G 85
G64: B'rig	6D 48
Tay Gdns. ML3: Ham	3F 153
Tay Gro. G75: E Kil	4A 148
Tayinloan Dr. ML8: Carl	5H 165
Tay La. ML2: Newm	4E 147
Tay Loan ML1: Holy	2A 128
(off Windsor Rd.)	
Taylor Av. ML1: Carf	5D 128
PA10: Kilb	2A 94
Taylor Pl. G4: Glas	3H 83 (3H 5)
Taylor St. G4: Glas	3H 83 (4H 5)
(not continuous)	
G81: Clyd	1E 59
Taymouth St. G32: Glas	2B 106
Taynish Dr. G44: Glas	3F 119
Tay Pl. G75: E Kil	4A 148
G82: Dumb	1H 17
ML9: Lark	5E 161
PA5: John	5C 94
Tay Rd. G61: Bear	5D 44
G64: B'rig	6D 48

Tayside ML6: Air	2H 91
Tay St. ML5: Coat	2G 89
Tay Ter. G75: E Kil	3A 148
Tay Wlk. G67: Cumb	4H 35
(in Cumbernauld Shop. Cen.)	
Teak Pl. G71: View	4H 109
Teal Ct. ML4: Bell	5A 110
Teal Cres. G75: E Kil	6B 148
Teal Dr. G13: Glas	2A 60
Tealing Av. G52: Glas	1C 100
Tealing Cres. G52: Glas	1C 100
Teasel Av. G53: Glas	4B 116
Teawell Rd. G77: Newt M	4D 132
Technology Av. G72: Blan	5A 140
Teesdale G74: E Kil	6E 137
Teign Gro. G75: E Kil	6C 148
Teith Av. PA4: Renf	1H 79
Teith Dr. G61: Bear	4D 44
Teith Pl. G72: Camb	2D 122
Teith St. G33: Glas	2G 85
Telephone La. G12: Glas	1A 82
(off Highburgh Rd.)	
Telford Av. ML9: Lark	5G 161
Telford Ct. G81: Clyd	5C 42
Telford Pl. G67: Cumb	5A 36
Telford Rd. G67: Cumb	5A 36
G75: E Kil	3F 149
Telford St. ML4: Bell	1C 126
Telford Ter. G75: E Kil	3H 149
(off Telford Rd.)	
Teme Pl. G75: E Kil	4B 148
Templar Av. G13: Glas	6D 44
TEMPLE	2F 61
Temple Gdns. G13: Glas	2F 61
Templeland G53: Glas	3C 100
Templeland Rd. G53: Glas	3C 100
Temple Locks Ct. G13: Glas	2F 61
Temple Locks Pl. G13: Glas	2F 61
Temple Rd. G13: Glas	2G 61
Templeton Bus. Cen.	
G40: Glas	6A 84
Templeton St. G40: Glas	6A 84
Tenement Ho. G3: Glas	2E 83 (2A 4)
Tennant Av. G74: E Kil	1C 148
Tennant Complex, The	
G74: E Kil	1C 148
Tennant St. PA4: Renf	5F 59
Tennent St. ML5: Coat	6D 90
Tennyson Dr. G31: Glas	1G 105
Tenters Way PA2: Pais	2F 97
Tern Pl. PA5: John	6D 94
Terregles Av. G41: Glas	3H 101
Terregles Cres. G41: Glas	3A 102
Terregles Dr. G41: Glas	3A 102
Teviot Av. G64: B'rig	4C 48
PA2: Pais	5C 96
Teviot Cres. G61: Bear	5D 44
Teviotdale G74: E Kil	1F 149
(off Strathfillan Rd.)	
G77: Newt M	4H 133
Teviot Dr. PA7: B'ton	5A 40
Teviot Path G72: Blan	2A 140
Teviot Pl. G72: Camb	2E 123
Teviot Sq. G67: Cumb	4H 35
(in Cumbernauld Shop. Cen.)	
Teviot St. G3: Glas	3A 82
ML5: Coat	1H 89
Teviot Ter. PA5: John	5C 94
Teviot Wlk. G67: Cumb	4H 35
(in Cumbernauld Shop. Cen.)	
Teviot Way G67: Cumb	4H 35
(in Cumbernauld Shop. Cen.)	
Tewkesbury Rd. G74: E Kil	4D 138
Thane Rd. G13: Glas	3C 60
Thanes Ga. G71: Both	2C 124
Thankerton Av. ML1: Holy	2H 127
Thankerton Rd. ML9: Lark	4F 161
Tharsis St. G21: Glas	2B 84
Theatre Royal	3F 83 (3A 4)
Third Av. G33: Mille	4B 66
G44: Glas	6F 103
G66: Auch	5D 50
G82: Dumb	3C 18
PA4: Renf	1E 79

Third Av. La. G44: Glas 6F 103
Third Gdns. G41: Glas 1G 101
Thirdpart Cres. G13: Glas 2G 59
Third Rd. G72: Blan 4C 140
Third St. G71: Tann 5D 108
Thirlmere G75: E Kil. 6B 148
Thistle Bank G66: Lenz 3D 50
Thistlebank PA11: Bri W 2E 73
Thistlebank Gdns.
  ML5: Coat. 2A 110
Thistle Cres. ML9: Lark 3F 161
Thistledown Gro.
  ML5: Coat. 5E 91
Thistle Gdns. ML1: Holy 2A 128
Thistleneuk G60: Old K 6E 21
Thistle Pl. G74: E Kil 6G 137
Thistle Quad. ML6: Air. 2B 92
Thistle Rd. ML1: New S. 4A 128
Thistle St. G5: Glas 6G 83
  G66: Kirk 5D 30
  ML1: Cle. 6H 129
  ML6: Air 2B 92
  PA2: Pais 3G 97
Thistle Ter. G5: Glas 1G 103
Thomas Muir Av. G64: B'rig. 1C 64
Thomas Muir Mus. 6C 48
Thomas St. PA1: Pais 1F 97
Thompson Av. G66: Kirk. 5E 31
Thompson Brae PA1: Pais 2A 98
Thompson Pl. G81: Hard 1E 43
Thompson St. PA4: Renf 1E 79
Thomson Av. ML2: Wis 2D 156
  PA5: John 2E 95
Thomson Dr. G61: Bear 1F 45
  ML1: Moth 4F 143
  ML4: Bell 2H 125
  ML6: Air 5H 91
Thomson Gro. G72: Camb 6A 106
Thomson St. G31: Glas 5C 84
  ML8: Carl 3F 165
  PA5: John 3E 95
Thorn Av. G74: T'hall 6G 135
Thornbank St. G3: Glas 3A 82
Thornbridge Av. G12: Glas 4A 62
  G69: Bail 6H 87
Thornbridge Gdns. G69: Bail 6G 87
Thornbridge Rd. G69: Bail 6G 87
Thorncliffe Gdns. G41: Glas. 3C 102
Thorncroft Dr. G44: Glas 3H 119
Thorndale Gdns. FK4: Alla 1H 15
Thorndean Av. ML4: Bell 3D 126
Thorndean Cres. ML4: Bell 3D 126
Thorndene PA5: Eld 2H 95
Thorndene Av. ML1: Carf 5C 128
Thornden La. G14: Glas 5A 60
Thorn Dr. G61: Bear 1D 44
  G73: Ruth 3E 121
Thorndyke G74: E Kil 4C 138
Thorne Brae PA5: John 2G 95
Thornhill PA5: John 3H 95
Thornhill Av. G72: Blan 1B 140
  PA5: Eld 3H 95
Thornhill Dr. PA5: Eld 3H 95
Thornhill Gdns. G77: Newt M 6D 132
  PA5: John 2G 95
Thornhill La. G71: Both 4F 125
Thornhill Path G31: Glas 6F 85
Thornhill Rd. ML3: Ham 5C 140
Thornhill Way ML5: Coat 2F 111
Thorniecroft Dr. G67: Cumb 1E 55
Thorniecroft Pl. G67: Cumb 1E 55
Thorniebank G46: T'bnk 1B 150
Thorniewood Gdns. G71: Tann. 6E 109
Thorniewood Rd. G71: Tann 5D 108
Thornkip Pl. ML5: Coat 6F 91
Thornlea Dr. G46: Giff 3B 118
Thornlea St. ML8: Carl 5G 165
Thornley Av. G13: Glas 3B 60
THORNLIEBANK. 4F 117
Thornliebank Ind. Est.
  G46: T'bnk 4E 117
Thornliebank Rd. G43: Glas 1H 117
Thornliebank Station (Rail). 3G 117
Thornlie Gill ML2: Wis 1H 157

THORNLY PARK. 5B 98
Thornly Pk. Av. PA2: Pais 5B 98
Thornly Pk. Dr. PA2: Pais. 5B 98
Thornly Pk. Gdns. PA2: Pais 4B 98
Thornly Pk. Rd. PA2: Pais 4A 98
Thorn Rd. G61: Bear 2C 44
  ML4: Bell 2D 126
Thornside Rd. PA5: John. 2G 95
THORNTONHALL. 6G 135
Thorntonhall Station (Rail) 6F 135
Thornton La. G20: Glas 2C 62
Thornton Pl. ML3: Ham 5H 153
Thornton Rd. G74: T'hall 6G 135
Thornton St. G20: Glas. 2B 62
  ML5: Coat 1H 89
Thorntree Av. ML3: Ham 4D 140
Thorntree Way G71: Both. 4F 125
Thornwood Av. G11: Glas 1G 81
  G66: Lenz 2A 50
Thornwood Cres. G11: Glas 6F 61
Thornwood Dr. G11: Glas 1F 81
  (not continuous)
  PA11: Bri W 4D 72
  PA2: Pais 3F 97
Thornwood Gdns. G11: Glas 1F 81
Thornwood Pl. G11: Glas 6F 61
Thornwood Quad. G11: Glas 6F 61
Thornwood Rd. G11: Glas 1F 81
Thornwood Ter. G11: Glas 1F 81
  (not continuous)
Thornyburn Dr. G69: Bail 1B 108
Thornyburn Pl. G69: Bail 1A 108
Thorny Pk. Ct. PA2: Pais 5A 98
Thorp Ct. PA5: John. 3G 95
Three Queens Sq. G81: Clyd 6D 42
Three Rivers Wlk. G75: E Kil 3D 148
Threestonehill Av. G32: Glas 5B 86
Threshold Pk. G74: E Kil 1A 150
Threshold Rd. G74: E Kil 1A 150
Thriplee Rd. PA11: Bri W 3E 73
Thrnyland Way PA8: Ersk 2F 57
Thrums G74: E Kil 4D 138
Thrums Av. G64: B'rig 6E 49
Thrums Gdns. G64: B'rig 6E 49
Thrushbush La. ML6: Air 1B 92
Thrushbush Quad. ML6: Air. 1A 92
Thrushbush Rd. ML6: Air. 1A 92
Thrushcraig Cres. PA2: Pais 3B 98
Thrush Pl. PA5: John. 6D 94
Thurso St. G11: Glas 2A 82
Thurston Rd. G52: Glas 6A 80
Thyme Sq. ML1: Moth 1G 143
Tianavaig PA8: Ersk. 2G 57
Tibbermore Rd. G11: Glas 6G 61
Tiber Av. ML1: Moth 6E 127
Tighnasheen Way G72: Blan 1B 140
Tillanburn Rd. ML1: N'hill 4F 129
Tillet Oval PA3: Pais 4H 77
Tillie St. G20: Glas 6D 62
Till St. ML2: Wis 3H 145
Tillycairn Av. G33: Glas 1D 86
Tillycairn Dr. G33: Glas 1D 86
Tillycairn Pl. G33: Glas 1E 87
Tillycairn Rd. G33: Glas 1E 87
Tillycairn St. G33: Glas 1E 87
Tilt Rd. ML2: Newm. 3D 146
Tilt St. G33: Glas 1G 85
Time Capsule, The 5B 90
Timmons Gro. ML4: Moss 2F 127
Timmons Ter. ML6: Chap. 4D 112
Tinker's La. ML1: Moth 3E 143
Tintagel Gdns. G69: Mood 4D 52
TINTOCK. 3A 32
Tintock Dr. G66: Kirk 4F 31
Tintock Pl. G68: Dull 5F 13
Tintock Rd. G66: Kirk. 3H 31
Tinto Ct. ML5: Coat 2E 111
Tinto Cres. ML2: Wis 1A 158

Tinto Dr. G78: Barr. 6D 114
Tinto Rd. G43: Glas 2A 118
  G61: Bear 1B 44
  G64: B'rig 6F 49
  ML6: Air 5B 92
Tinto Sq. PA4: Renf 2D 78
Tinto St. ML2: Wis 1A 158
Tinto Vw. ML3: Ham 3A 154
Tinto Vw. Rd. ML9: Shaw 6H 161
Tinto Way G75: E Kil 6D 148
  ML1: Cle. 5H 129
Tinwald Path G52: Glas 6C 80
Tiree G74: E Kil 4C 150
Tiree Av. PA2: Pais 6H 97
  PA4: Renf 3E 79
Tiree Ct. G67: Cumb 5F 35
Tiree Cres. ML2: Newm. 2D 146
Tiree Dr. G67: Cumb 5F 35
Tiree Gdns. G60: Old K 1G 41
  G61: Bear 1B 44
  ML6: Glenm 4H 71
Tiree Grange ML3: Ham 2D 152
Tiree Pl. G60: Old K. 1G 41
  G77: Newt M 4B 132
  ML5: Coat 1H 109
Tiree Rd. G67: Cumb 5F 35
Tiree St. G21: Glas 1E 85
Tirry Av. PA4: Renf. 1H 79
Tirry Way PA4: Renf. 1H 79
Titwood Rd. G41: Glas 3A 102
  (not continuous)
Tiverton Av. G32: Glas 2D 106
Tivoli Ct. G75: E Kil 5G 149
Tobago Pl. G40: Glas 6B 84
  G75: E Kil 2C 148
Tobago St. G40: Glas 6A 84
Tobermory Rd. G73: Ruth 4F 121
Todburn Dr. PA2: Pais 6B 98
Todd Pl. G31: Glas 4E 85
Todd St. G31: Glas 4E 85
Todhills G75: E Kil 3H 149
  (off Todhills Nth.)
Todhills Nth. G75: E Kil 3H 149
Todhills Sth. G75: E Kil 3H 149
Todholm Cres. PA2: Pais 3D 98
Todholm Rd. PA2: Pais 3D 98
Todholm Ter. PA2: Pais 3D 98
Tofthill Av. G64: B'rig 5B 48
Tofthill Gdns. G64: B'rig 5B 48
Tolbooth Steeple 5H 83
  (off Saltmarket)
Tollbrae Av. ML6: Air 4B 92
TOLLCROSS. 2A 106
Tollcross Pk. Gdns. G32: Glas 2G 105
Tollcross Pk. Gro. G32: Glas 2H 105
Tollcross Pk. Leisure Cen. 2H 105
Tollcross Pk. Vw. G32: Glas 2G 105
Tollcross Rd. G31: Glas 6F 85
Tollhouse Gdns. ML4: Bell 4E 127
Toll La. G51: Glas 5C 82
Tollpark Cres. ML2: Newm 4E 147
Tollpark Pl. G68: Cumb 3E 15
Tollpark Rd. G68: Cumb 3D 14
TOLL PLAZA INTERCHANGE 4D 40
Toll St. ML1: Moth. 4H 143
Toll, The G76: Clar. 1C 134
Toll Wynd ML3: Ham 4G 153
Tolsta St. G23: Glas 6C 46
Tomtain Brae G68: Cumb. 6B 34
Tomtain Ct. G68: Cumb 6B 34
Toner Gdns. ML2: Over 4H 157
Tontine La. G1: Glas. 5H 83 (6G 5)
Tontine Pl. G73: Ruth 3G 121
Topaz Ter. ML4: Bell 4C 126
Toppersfield PA10: Kilb 3C 94
Torbreck St. G52: Glas 6F 81
Torbrex Rd. G67: Cumb 4A 36
Torburn Av. G46: Giff 3H 117
TORBUSH. 5F 147
Tordene Path G68: Cumb 2F 35
Torgyle St. G23: Glas 6B 46
Tormeadow Rd. G77: Newt M 4D 132
Tormore St. G51: Glas 5D 80
Tormusk Dr. G45: Glas 3C 120

Tormusk Gdns. G45: Glas 3C 120
Tormusk Gro. G45: Glas 3C 120
Tormusk Rd. G45: Glas 3B 120
Torness St. G11: Glas 1A 82
Torogay Pl. G22: Glas 1A 64
Torogay St. G22: Glas 2G 63
Torogay Ter. G22: Glas. 1G 63
Toronto Wlk. G32: Carm 5C 106
Torphin Cres. G32: Glas 5A 86
Torphin Wlk. G32: Glas 5B 86
TORRANCE 5D 28
Torrance Av. ML6: Air 4D 92
Torrance Rd. G74: E Kil 1G 149
TORRANCE RDBT. 6B 150
Torran Dr. PA8: Ersk 2A 58
Torran Rd. G33: Glas 4F 87
Torranyard Ter. ML3: Ham 2C 152
Torr Av. PA11: Q'riers. 1A 72
Torrence Rd. G64: B'rig, Torr. . . 5D 28
Torr Gdns. G22: Glas 5H 63
Torriden Pl. ML5: Coat. 6A 90
Torriden St. ML5: Coat. 6A 90
Torridon Av. G41: Glas 2G 101
    ML1: N'hill 4D 128
Torridon Ct. G20: Glas 1E 83
                        (off Cedar St.)
Torridon Gdns. G77: Newt M . . . 5H 133
Torridon Path G41: Glas. 2G 101
                    (off Dumbreck Pl.)
Torrington Gdns. G61: Bear 6D 24
Torrington Av. G46: Giff 1G 133
Torrington Cres. G32: Glas 2D 106
Torrin Rd. G23: Glas 6B 46
Torrisdale Pl. ML5: Coat 4A 90
Torrisdale St. G42: Glas 3D 102
    ML5: Coat. 4A 90
Torr La. PA11: Q'riers. 1A 72
Torr Pl. G22: Glas 5H 63
Torr Rd. G64: B'rig 6F 49
    PA11: Bri W 2C 72
Torr St. G22: Glas 5H 63
Torryburn Rd. G21: Glas. 5E 65
Torwood Brae ML3: Ham 1D 152
Torwood La. G69: Mood. 5E 53
TORYGLEN 5A 104
Toryglen Rd. G73: Ruth 5B 104
Toryglen St. G5: Glas 3H 103
Tourmaline Ter. ML4: Bell 4D 126
Tournai Path G72: Blan 2B 140
Toward Ct. G72: Blan 6C 124
Toward Rd. G33: Glas 4C 86
Toward Way PA2: Pais 6H 97
Tower Av. G78: Barr 3F 115
Tower Castle 4G 95
                        (off Tower Pl.)
Towerhill Rd. G13: Glas. 6C 44
Tower Pl. G20: Glas 5H 63
    G62: Miln 3H 25
    PA5: John. 4G 95
Tower Rd. G64: Balm, Torr 2G 27
    G67: Cumb 1H 55
    PA5: John 4F 95
Towerside Cres. G53: Glas 3A 100
Towerside Rd. G53: Glas 3A 100
Towers Pl. ML6: Air 4F 93
Towers Rd. ML6: Air 3E 93
Tower St. G41: Glas 6C 82
Tower Ter. PA1: Pais 1H 97
Towerview Dr. G69: G'csh 6A 68
Towie Pl. G71: Udd 1D 124
TOWNEND 2F 17
Townend Rd. G82: Dumb 3F 17
TOWNHEAD
    Coatbridge 2H 89
    Glasgow 4G 83 (6F 5)
    Kirkintilloch 5D 30
Townhead G66: Kirk. 5D 30
Townhead Av. ML1: Holy. 5G 111
Townhead Dr. ML1: N'hill 4F 129
TOWNHEAD INTERCHANGE . . . 3A 84
                    (M8, JUNCTION 15)
Townhead Pl. G71: Tann 5E 109
Townhead Rd. G77: Newt M 5C 132
    ML5: Coat. 1E 89

Townhead St. G65: Kils 3H 11
    ML3: Ham 6B 142
Townhead Ter. PA1: Pais 1H 97
Townhill Rd. ML3: Ham 6B 140
Townhill Ter. ML3: Ham 6C 140
Townmill Rd. G31: Glas. 3B 84
Townsend St. G4: Glas 1G 83 (1E 5)
Traction Bus. Pk. ML1: Moth 4E 143
TRADESTON 6E 83
Tradeston Ind. Est.
    G5: Glas 1D 102
Tradeston St. G5: Glas 6E 83
Trafalgar Ct. G68: Dull 5F 13
Trafalgar St. G40: Glas 2B 104
    G81: Clyd 4B 42
Trainard Av. G32: Glas 1H 105
Tramway. 2E 103
Tranent Path ML1: Cle 5H 129
Tranent Pl. G33: Glas. 3G 85
    ML1: Cle. 5H 129
Traquair Av. ML2: Wis 4A 146
    PA2: Pais 5C 96
Traquair Dr. G52: Glas 1B 100
Traquair Wynd G72: Blan 2A 140
                        (off Winton Cres.)
Treeburn Av. G46: Giff 4H 117
Treemain Rd. G46: Giff 1G 133
Trees Pk. Av. G78: Barr 3D 114
Trefoil Av. G41: Glas 5B 102
Trefoil Pl. PA6: Hous 1B 74
                        (off North St.)
Trent Pl. G75: E Kil. 5A 148
Trent St. ML5: Coat 1H 89
Tresta Rd. G23: Glas 1C 62
Triangle, The G64: B'rig. 6C 48
Tribboch St. ML9: Lark 2D 160
Trident Way PA4: Renf 2E 79
Trigg St. PA2: Pais 2E 97
Trinidad Grn. G75: E Kil 2C 148
Trinidad Way G75: E Kil 2C 148
Trinity Av. G52: Glas 1C 100
Trinity Dr. G72: Camb 4C 122
Trinity Way ML9: Lark 4G 161
Trinley Rd. G13: Glas. 6D 44
Triton Pl. ML4: Moss 2H 127
Tronda Path G34: Glas 3F 87
Trondra Pl. G34: Glas 3F 87
Trongate G1: Glas 5G 83 (6F 5)
Tron Theatre 5H 83
                        (off Trongate)
Troon Av. G75: E Kil 5C 148
Troon Ct. G75: E Kil 5D 148
Troon Dr. PA11: Bri W 4E 73
Troon Gdns. G68: Cumb 5H 13
Troon Pl. G77: Newt M 5G 133
Troon St. G40: Glas 2D 104
Trossachs Av. ML1: Holy 2A 128
Trossachs Ct. G20: Glas 6E 63
Trossachs Rd. G73: Ruth 5F 121
Trossachs St. G20: Glas 6E 63
Troubridge Av. PA10: Kilb 4B 94
Troubridge Cres. PA10: Kilb . . . 3B 94
Trovaig PA8: Ersk 2G 57
Trows Rd. ML2: Over 5H 157
Truce Rd. G13: Glas 1B 60
Truro Av. G69: Mood 4D 52
Tryst Rd. G67: Cumb 4H 35
                        (not continuous)
Tryst Sports Cen. 3A 36
Tryst Wlk. G67: Cumb 3A 36
Tudor La. Sth. G14: Glas 6E 61
Tudor St. G69: Bail 2F 107
Tulley Wynd ML1: Moth 5F 127
Tulliallan Pl. G74: E Kil 3A 150
Tullis Ct. G40: Glas 1A 104
Tullis St. G40: Glas 1A 104
Tulloch-Ard Pl. G73: Ruth 4F 121
Tulloch Gdns. ML1: Moth 5B 144
Tulloch St. G44: Glas 1E 119
Tullymet Rd. ML3: Ham 3H 153
Tummel Dr. ML6: Air 1H 91
Tummel Grn. G74: E Kil 6G 137
Tummel Way PA2: Pais. 4D 96
Tummel St. G33: Glas 1G 85

Tummel Wlk. G67: Cumb 4H 35
                (in Cumbernauld Shop. Cen.)
Tummel Way G67: Cumb. 3H 35
                (in Cumbernauld Shop. Cen.)
Tunnel St. G3: Glas 4C 82
Tuphall Rd. ML3: Ham. 1H 153
Tureen St. G40: Glas 5A 84
                        (off Millroad Dr.)
Turnberry Av. G11: Glas. 6H 61
Turnberry Cres. ML5: Coat. 1A 110
    ML6: Chap 4E 113
Turnberry Dr. G73: Ruth. 2B 120
    G77: Newt M 5G 133
    ML3: Ham 1B 152
    PA11: Bri W 5E 73
Turnberry Gdns. G68: Cumb 6H 13
Turnberry Pl. G75: E Kil. 5D 148
    G82: Dumb 3C 16
Turnberry Rd. G11: Glas. 6G 61
Turnberry Wynd G71: Both. 4C 124
Turnbull St. G1: Glas 5H 83
Turner Rd. G21: Glas 1B 84
    PA3: Pais 3B 78
Turners Av. PA1: Pais 2F 97
Turner St. ML5: Coat 5B 90
Turnhill Av. PA8: Ersk 2F 57
Turnhill Cres. PA8: Ersk 2F 57
Turnhill Dr. PA8: Ersk. 1F 57
Turnhill Gdns. PA8: Ersk 2F 57
Turnlaw G75: E Kil 6F 149
Turnlaw Rd. G72: Camb 6A 122
Turnlaw St. G5: Glas 1H 103
Turnyland Mdws. PA8: Ersk 2F 57
Turquoise Ter. ML4: Bell 4D 126
Turret Cres. G13: Glas 1C 60
Turret Rd. G13: Glas 6C 44
Turriff St. G5: Glas 1F 103
Twechar Recreation Cen. 2D 32
Tweed Av. PA2: Pais 3D 96
Tweed Ct. ML6: Air 6C 92
Tweed Cres. G33: Glas 2F 85
    ML2: Wis 4A 146
    PA4: Renf. 6G 59
Tweed Dr. G61: Bear 4D 44
Tweed La. ML1: Holy 2B 128
Tweedmuir Pl. ML5: Coat. 2F 111
Tweed Pl. PA5: John 5C 94
Tweedsmuir Rd. G52: Glas 6E 49
Tweedsmuir Cres. G61: Bear . . . 6E 25
Tweedsmuir Pk. ML3: Ham 3G 153
Tweedsmuir Rd. G52: Glas 1B 100
Tweed St. G75: E Kil 4B 148
    ML5: Coat 2D 110
    ML9: Lark 4E 161
Tweedvale Av. G14: Glas 3G 59
Tweedvale Pl. G14: Glas 3G 59
Tweed Wlk. G67: Cumb 4H 35
                (in Cumbernauld Shop. Cen.)
Twinlaw St. G34: Glas 2B 88
Tylney Rd. PA1: Pais 6F 79
Tyndrum Rd. G61: Bear 2H 45
Tyndrum St. G4: Glas 2G 83 (1E 5)
Tynecastle Cres. G32: Glas 4B 86
Tynecastle Path G32: Glas 4B 86
Tynecastle Pl. G32: Glas 4B 86
Tynecastle St. G32: Glas 4B 86
Tyne Pl. G75: E Kil 5A 148
Tynron Ct. ML3: Ham 2C 152
Tynwald Av. G73: Ruth 3F 121

U

UCI Cinema
    Clydebank 6D 42
    East Kilbride 3H 149
UDDINGSTON 2D 124
Uddingston Rd. G71: Both. 4D 124
Uddingston Station (Rail) 1C 124
UDSTON 5E 141
Udston Rd. ML3: Ham 5C 140
Udston Ter. ML3: Ham 4D 140
UGC Cinema 6E 85
Uig Pl. G33: Glas 6E 87

Uist Cres. G33: Step. 5E 67
Uist Dr. G66: Kirk. 5G 31
Uist Pl. ML6: Air 5D 92
Uist St. G51: Glas. 4F 81
Uist Way ML2: Wis 4C 146
Ullswater G75: E Kil. 6B 148
Ulundi Rd. PA5: John 3D 94
Ulva St. G52: Glas 6F 81
Ulverston Ter. ML3: Ham. 5H 153
Umachan Rd. PA8: Ersk 2G 57
Underwood Dr. ML2: Newm. 2E 147
Underwood La. PA1: Pais 6H 77
Underwood Rd. G73: Ruth. 1E 121
PA3: Pais 6G 77
Underwood St. G41: Glas 5C 102
Union Ct. PA2: Pais 3A 98
Union Pl. G1: Glas. 4F 83 (5D 4)
Union St. G1: Glas. 4F 83 (5D 4)
G66: Kirk 5C 30
ML1: New S 3A 128
ML3: Ham 5G 141
ML8: Carl 4F 165
ML9: Lark 2E 161
PA2: Pais 3A 98
Unitas Cres. ML8: Carl. 4E 165
Unitas Rd. ML4: Moss 2E 127
Unity Pl. G4: Glas. 1E 83
University Av. G12: Glas 1B 82
University Gdns. G12: Glas 1B 82
University of Glasgow Vis. Cen. . . . 1B 82
University Pl. G12: Glas. 1A 82
Unsted Pl. PA1: Pais 1C 98
Unthank Rd. ML4: Moss 2E 127
Uphall Pl. G33: Glas 4G 85
Upland La. G14: Glas. 5C 60
(off Danes La. Nth.)
Upland Rd. G14: Glas 5C 60
U.P. La. G65: Kils 3H 11
Uplawmoor Rd. G78: Neil 4A 130
Up. Bourtree Ct. G73: Ruth 3E 121
Up. Bourtree Dr. G73: Ruth 3D 120
Up. Glenburn Rd. G61: Bear 2C 44
Up. Mill St. ML6: Air 3A 92
U.P. Rd. G65: Kils 3H 11
Urquhart Cres. PA4: Renf 1E 79
Urquhart Dr. G74: E Kil 6A 138
Urrdale Rd. G41: Glas 6H 81
Usmore Pl. G33: Glas. 6E 87

V

Vaila Pl. G23: Glas. 2E 63
Vaila St. G23: Glas 1D 62
Valence Twr. G71: Both 3B 124
Valerio Ct. G72: Blan 1B 140
Valetta Pl. G81: Clyd 4H 41
Valeview Ter. G42: Glas 5E 103
G82: Dumb. 1G 17
Vale Wlk. G64: B'rig. 1E 65
Vallantine Cres. G71: Tann 5E 109
Vallay St. G22: Glas. 1H 63
Valleybank G65: Bant. 1F 13
Valley Ct. ML3: Ham 1G 153
Valleyfield G66: Milt C 5A 8
G75: E Kil 2F 149
Valleyfield Dr. G68: Cumb. 4A 34
Valleyfield St. G21: Glas 6A 64
Valley Vw. G72: Camb 1C 122
ML1: Moth 6B 144
Vancouver Ct. G75: E Kil 2D 148
Vancouver Dr. G75: E Kil 2D 148
Vancouver La. G14: Glas. 5D 60
(off Norse La. Nth., not continuous)
Vancouver Pl. G81: Clyd 4H 41
Vancouver Rd. G14: Glas 5C 60
Vanguard St. G81: Clyd 5E 43
Vanguard Way PA4: Renf 2E 79
Vardar Av. G76: Clar 1A 134
Vardon Lea ML1: Cle 6E 129
Varna La. G14: Glas. 6E 61
Varna Rd. G14: Glas. 5E 61
Varnsdorf Way ML6: Air 5D 92
Vasart Pl. G20: Glas 5D 62

Veir Ter. G82: Dumb. 4E 17
Veitches Ct. G81: Dun 1C 42
Veitch Pl. G66: Len 3F 7
Vennacher Rd. PA4: Renf 5C 58
Vennard Gdns. G41: Glas. 3C 102
Vermont Av. G73: Ruth 6C 104
Vermont St. G41: Glas 6B 82
Vernon Bank G74: E Kil 6G 137
Vernon Dr. PA3: Lin 5G 75
Verona Av. G14: Glas. 5C 60
Verona Gdns. G14: Glas. 5C 60
Verona La. G14: Glas. 5C 60
Vesalius St. G32: Glas. 6A 86
Viaduct Rd. G76: Busby. 2D 134
Vicarfield St. G51: Glas 4H 81
VICARLAND .2A 122
Vicarland Pl. G72: Camb 3A 122
Vicarland Rd. G72: Camb 2A 122
Vicars Wlk. G72: Camb 2B 122
Vickers St. ML1: Moth. 1D 142
Victoria Av. G78: Barr 3D 114
ML8: Carl 4E 165
Victoria Baths .5F 59
Victoria Bri. G5: Glas 5G 83
Victoria Cir. G12: Glas. 6A 62
Victoria Ct. ML9: Lark 1E 161
Victoria Cres. G65: Kils 3F 11
G76: Busby 2D 134
G78: Barr 3D 114
ML2: Wis 5D 144
ML6: Air. 5G 91
Victoria Cres. La. G12: Glas 6A 62
Victoria Cres. Pl. G12: Glas. 6A 62
Victoria Cres. Rd. G12: Glas 6A 62
Victoria Cross G42: Glas 3E 103
Victoria Dr. G78: Barr 3D 114
Victoria Dr. E. PA4: Renf 1E 79
Victoria Dr. W. PA4: Renf 6D 58
Victoria Gdns. G78: Barr 3D 114
ML6: Air. 4H 91
PA2: Pais. 3G 97
Victoria Glade G68: Dull. 5F 13
Victoria Gro. G78: Barr 3D 114
Victoria Pk. G65: Kils 3F 11
Victoria Pk. Cnr. G14: Glas 6D 60
Victoria Pk. Dr. Nth. G14: Glas 5D 60
Victoria Pk. Dr. Sth. G14: Glas 6D 60
(not continuous)
Victoria Pk. Gdns. Nth. G11: Glas 6F 61
Victoria Pk. Gdns. Sth. G11: Glas 6F 61
Victoria Pk. La. Nth. G14: Glas 6D 60
Victoria Pk. La. Sth. G14: Glas 6D 60
(off Westland Dr.)
Victoria Pk. St. G14: Glas 6D 60
Victoria Pl. G62: Miln 4H 25
G65: Kils 3G 11
G73: Ruth. 5C 104
(off King St.)
G78: Barr 3E 115
G81: Hard. 1D 42
ML4: Bell 3B 126
ML6: Air. 5G 91
Victoria Quad. ML1: Holy 2H 127
Victoria Rd. G33: Step. 4C 66
G42: Glas 4E 103
G66: Lenz. 3C 50
G68: Dull. 5F 13
G73: Ruth. 1D 120
G78: Barr 3D 114
PA2: Pais 3G 97
PA5: Brkfld. 6D 74
Victoria St. G66: Kirk. 5C 30
G72: Blan 3B 140
G73: Ruth. 5C 104
G82: Dumb. 5G 17
ML2: Newm 5E 147
ML3: Ham. 3F 141
ML9: Lark 2E 161
Victoria Ter. G68: Dull 5F 13
Victor St. ML6: Plain 1G 93
Victory Dr. PA10: Kilb 1A 94
VICTORY GARDENS 1E 79
Victory Way G69: Bail 1H 107
Viewbank G46: T'bnk. 4G 117

Viewbank Av. ML6: C'bnk 3B 112
Viewbank St. ML5: Glenb 4B 70
VIEWFIELD 4B 126
Viewfield G69: Mood. 3C 52
ML6: Air .5G 91
Viewfield Av. G64: B'rig. 1A 64
G66: Lenz. 2C 50
G66: Milt C 6B 8
G69: Bail 6F 87
G72: Blan 6C 124
Viewfield Dr. G64: B'rig 1A 64
G69: Bail 6F 87
Viewfield La. G12: Glas. 1C 82
Viewfield Rd. FK4: Bank 1D 14
G64: B'rig. 1A 64
ML4: Bell 4B 126
ML5: Coat 1F 109
Viewglen Ct. G45: Glas. 6H 119
Viewmount Dr. G20: Glas. 2B 62
VIEWPARK 6G 109
Viewpark G62: Miln 4H 25
Viewpark Av. G31: Glas 3D 84
Viewpark Ct. G73: Ruth 1E 121
Viewpark Dr. G73: Ruth. 1D 120
Viewpark Gardens 1F 125
Viewpark Gdns. PA4: Renf 1D 78
Viewpark Pl. ML1: Moth 3E 143
Viewpark Rd. ML1: Moth. 3E 143
Viewpark Shop. Cen.
G71: View. 1H 125
Viewpoint Pl. G21: Glas. 3B 64
Viewpoint Rd. G21: Glas. 3B 64
Vigilant Ho. PA3: Pais 4A 78
Viking Cres. PA6: C'lee 3D 74
Viking Rd. ML6: Air 6B 92
Viking Ter. G75: E Kil 5G 149
Viking Way G46: T'bnk 2F 117
PA4: Renf 2E 79
Villafield Av. G64: B'rig 4C 48
Villafield Dr. G64: B'rig. 4C 48
Villafield Loan G64: B'rig 4C 48
Village Gdns. G72: Blan. 6C 124
Village Rd. G72: Flem 2E 123
Vincent Ct. ML4: Bell 3C 126
(off Gardenside)
Vine St. G11: Glas 1H 81
Vinicombe La. G12: Glas 6B 62
(off Vinicombe St.)
Vinicombe St. G12: Glas 6B 62
Vintner St. G4: Glas 1G 83
Viola Pl. G64: Torr 5E 29
Violet Gdns. ML8: Carl. 5E 165
Violet Pl. ML1: Holy. 1B 128
Violet St. PA1: Pais 1C 98
Virginia Ct. G1: Glas 4G 83 (6E 5)
Virginia Gdns. G62: Miln 5A 26
Virginia Pl. G1: Glas 4G 83 (6E 5)
Virginia St. G1: Glas 4G 83 (6E 5)
Viscount Av. PA4: Renf. 2E 79
Viscount Ga. G71: Both 2C 124
Vivian Av. G62: Miln. 4F 25
Voil Dr. G44: Glas. 3E 119
Vorlich Ct. G78: Barr 6E 115
Vorlich Gdns. G61: Bear 6C 24
Vorlich Wynd ML1: N'hill 3C 128
Vulcan St. G21: Glas 5A 64
(not continuous)
ML1: Moth 1G 143

W

Waddell Av. ML6: Glenm 5F 71
Waddell Ct. G5: Glas 6H 83
Waddell St. G5: Glas 1H 103
ML6: Air. 2A 92
Waid Av. G77: Newt M. 3C 132
Waldemar Rd. G13: Glas. 2C 60
Waldo St. G13: Glas 2F 61
Walkerburn Dr. ML2: Wis 3A 146
Walkerburn Rd. G52: Glas. 1B 100
Walker Ct. G11: Glas 2H 81
Walker Dr. PA5: Eld 3H 95
Walker Path G71: Tann 5E 109

Walker St. G11: Glas 2H 81	Wardrop St. G51: Glas 3G 81	Watson St. ML1: Moth 4G 143
PA1: Pais 1H 97	PA1: Pais 1A 98	ML9: Lark 2D 160
Walkinshaw Rd. PA4: Inch 6F 57	Wards Cres. ML5: Coat 6A 90	Watsonville Pk. ML1: Moth 3G 143
Walkinshaw St. G40: Glas 1C 104	Ware Rd. G34: Glas 4F 87	Watt Cres. ML4: Bell 6D 110
PA5: John 2F 95	Warilda Av. G81: Clyd 5E 43	Watt La. PA11: Bri W 4G 73
(Collier St.)	Warlock Dr. PA11: Bri W 2F 73	Watt Low Av. G73: Ruth 1B 120
PA5: John 2F 95	Warlock Rd. PA11: Bri W 2F 73	Watt Pl. G62: Miln 2F 25
(High St.)	Warnock Cres. ML4: Bell 3D 126	G72: Blan 5A 140
Wallace Av. PA5: Eld 2A 96	Warnock Rd. G77: Newt M 3C 132	Watt Rd. G52: Hill 4H 79
PA7: B'ton 4H 39	Warnock St. G31: Glas 3A 84	PA11: Bri W 4F 73
Wallace Dr. G33: B'rig 1F 65	Warren Rd. ML3: Ham 3H 153	Watt St. G5: Glas 5D 82
ML9: Lark 3G 161	Warren St. G42: Glas 4F 103	ML6: Air 2C 92
Wallacegait PA4: Renf 6D 58	Warren Wlk. G66: Len 4G 7	Waukglen Av. G53: Glas 5B 116
Wallace Gdns. G64: Torr 4D 28	Warrington Ct. G33: Glas 3H 85	Waukglen Cres. G53: Glas 4C 116
Wallace Ga. G33: B'rig 1F 65	Warriston Cres. G33: Glas 3F 85	Waukglen Dr. G53: Glas 4B 116
Wallace Ho. G67: Cumb 3G 35	Warriston Pl. G32: Glas 4B 86	Waukglen Gdns. G53: Glas 5B 116
Wallace Pl. G73: B'rig 1F 65	Warriston St. G33: Glas 3F 85	Waukglen Path G53: Glas 4B 116
G72: Blan 6C 124	Warriston Way G73: Ruth 3F 121	Waukglen Pl. G53: Glas 4B 116
ML3: Ham 1C 154	(off Kilbride Rd.)	Waukglen Rd. G53: Glas 4B 116
Wallace Rd. ML1: New S 5B 128	Warroch St. G3: Glas 4D 82	Waulking Mill Rd.
PA4: Renf 2C 78	Warwick G74: E Kil 5C 138	G81: Faif, Hard 6E 23
Wallace St. G5: Glas 5E 83	Warwick Gro. ML3: Ham 4C 140	Waulkmill Av. G78: Barr 3F 115
G33: B'rig 1F 65	Warwick Vs. G81: Clyd 2G 59	Waulkmill Dr. G46: T'bnk 3E 117
G73: Ruth 6C 104	(off Edward St.)	Waulkmill Way G78: Barr 3F 115
G81: Clyd 1D 58	Washington Rd. G66: Kirk 5B 30	Waverley G74: E Kil 5D 138
G82: Dumb 5G 17	PA3: Pais 3B 78	G81: Clyd 5E 43
ML1: Moth 2F 143	Washington St. G3: Glas . . . 4E 83 (6A 4)	Waverley Ct. G71: Both 5E 125
ML5: Coat 6C 90	Watchmeal Cres. G81: Faif 6E 23	PA2: Pais 5D 96
ML6: Plain 1G 93	Waterbank Rd. G76: Crmck 3H 135	Waverley Cres. G66: Kirk. 5E 31
PA3: Pais 5A 78	WATERFOOT 6B 134	G67: Cumb 6F 35
Wallacewell Cres. G21: Glas. 4D 64	Waterfoot Av. G53: Glas. 5C 100	ML3: Ham 5D 140
Wallacewell Pl. G21: Glas. 4D 64	Waterfoot Bank G74: T'hall 6C 134	Waverley Dr. G73: Ruth 6E 105
Wallacewell Quad. G21: Glas 3E 65	Waterfoot Rd. G74: T'hall 6C 134	ML2: Wis 5H 145
Wallacewell Rd. G21: Glas. 4C 64	Waterfoot Rd. G77: Newt M 6F 133	ML6: Air 2B 92
Wallace Wynd ML8: Law 5E 159	Waterfoot Row G76: Water 6B 134	Waverley Gdns. G41: Glas 4C 102
Wallbrae Rd. G67: Cumb. 5A 36	Waterfoot Ter. G53: Glas 5C 100	PA5: Eld 3B 96
Waller Gdns. G41: Glas 4B 102	(off Waterfoot Av.)	WAVERLEY PARK 4B 102
Wallneuk PA3: Pais 6B 78	Waterford Rd. G46: Giff. 4H 117	Waverley Pk. G66: Kirk 5D 30
Wallneuk Rd. PA3: Pais 6B 78	Waterhaughs Gdns. G33: Glas 2F 65	Waverley Rd. PA2: Pais 6D 96
Walls St. G1: Glas 4H 83 (6G 5)	Waterhaughs Gro. G33: Glas 2F 65	Waverley St. G41: Glas 4C 102
Walmer Cres. G51: Glas 5A 82	Waterhaughs Pl. G33: Glas 2F 65	ML3: Ham 5D 140
Walnut Ct. G66: Milt C 6B 8	Waterlands Gdns. ML8: Carl 2G 165	ML5: Coat 2D 90
Walnut Cres. G22: Glas 4H 63	Waterlands Pl. ML8: Law 1A 164	ML9: Lark 5E 161
PA5: John 4H 95	Waterlands Rd. ML8: Law 5F 159	Waverley Ter. G72: Blan 4A 140
Walnut Dr. G66: Lenz 1B 50	WATERLOO 2B 158	G82: Dumb 3B 16
Walnut Ga. G72: Flem 3F 123	Waterloo Cl. G66: Kirk. 4D 30	Waverley Way PA2: Pais 6D 96
Walnut Pl. G22: Glas 4G 63	Waterloo Gdns. G66: Kirk 4D 30	Weardale La. G33: Glas 3C 86
G71: View 4G 109	(off John St.)	Weardale St. G33: Glas 3C 86
Walnut Rd. G22: Glas 4G 63	Waterloo La. G2: Glas 4F 83 (5C 4)	Weaver Av. G77: Newt M 2C 132
Walpole Pl. PA5: John 6D 94	Waterloo St. G2: Glas 4E 83 (5B 4)	Weaver Cres. ML6: Air 6A 92
Walter St. G31: Glas 4D 84	G66: Kirk 4D 30	Weaver La. PA10: Kilb 1A 94
ML2: Wis 6B 146	Watermill Av. G66: Lenz 3D 50	Weaver Pl. G75: E Kil 4A 148
Walton Av. G77: Newt M 3C 132	Water Rd. G78: Barr 4E 115	Weavers Av. PA2: Pais 2F 97
Walton Ct. G46: Giff 5A 118	Water Row G51: Glas. 3G 81	Weaver's Cottage 2A 94
Walton St. G41: Glas 5C 102	Watershaugh Dr. ML1: Cle 5H 129	(off Weavers Ct.)
G78: Barr 4E 115	WATERSIDE	Weaver's Cottage Mus., The 3A 92
Wamba Av. G13: Glas 1E 61	Barrhead 2G 115	Weavers St. G74: E Kil 1H 149
Wamba Pl. G13: Glas. 1E 61	Kirkintilloch 6H 31	(off Parkhall St.)
Wamphray Pl. G75: E Kil 4A 148	Waterside Av. G77: Newt M 5C 132	PA10: Kilb. 2A 94
Wandilla Av. G81: Clyd 5F 43	Waterside Cotts. G66: Kirk 6H 31	Weavers Ga. PA1: Pais 2E 97
Wanlock St. G51: Glas 3G 81	Waterside Ct. G76: Crmck. 2H 135	Weavers Rd. PA2: Pais. 2F 97
Wardend Rd. G64: Torr 4D 28	Waterside Dr. G77: Newt M 5C 132	Weaver St. G4: Glas 4H 83 (5H 5)
Warden Rd. G13: Glas 2D 60	Waterside Gdns. G72: Flem 4E 123	Weaver Ter. PA2: Pais 2C 98
Wardhill Rd. G21: Glas 4D 64	G76: Crmck 2H 135	Webster Groves ML2: Wis 4B 146
Wardhouse Rd. PA2: Pais 6G 97	ML3: Ham 2A 154	Webster St. G40: Glas 2C 104
Wardie Path G33: Glas 4F 87	Waterside La. PA10: John 3C 94	G81: Clyd 1G 59
Wardie Pl. G33: Glas 4F 87	Waterside Rd. G66: Kirk 6E 31	Wedderlea Dr. G52: Glas 6A 80
Wardie Rd. G33: Glas. 4F 87	(not continuous)	Wedsley Ct. G41: Glas 1C 102
Wardlaw Av. G73: Ruth 6D 104	G76: Crmck 4H 135	Weensmoor Rd. G53: Glas 3H 115
Wardlaw Cres. G75: E Kil 4H 149	Waterside St. G5: Glas 1H 103	Weeple Dr. PA3: Lin 5G 75
Wardlaw Dr. G73: Ruth 5D 104	Waterside Ter. PA10: Kilb 3C 94	Weighhouse Cl. PA1: Pais 1A 98
Wardlaw Rd. G61: Bear 6F 45	(off Kilbarchan Rd.)	Weigh Ho. Rd. ML8: Carl. 2E 165
WARDPARK 4C 14	Waterside Way PA10: Kilb 3C 94	Weir Av. G78: Barr 5E 115
Wardpark Ct. G67: Cumb 5D 14	Water Sports Cen. 3C 142	Weir Pl. ML8: Law. 1H 163
Wardpark E. Ind. Est. G68: Cumb . . 3E 15	Watling Pl. G75: E Kil 2C 148	Weir's La. ML8: Carl 3F 165
Wardpark Nth. Ind. Est.	Watling St. G71: Tann 4C 108	Weir St. ML5: Coat 4C 90
G68: Cumb 4C 14	ML1: Moth 6D 126	PA3: Pais 6B 78
Wardpark Pl. G67: Cumb. 5D 14	Watson Av. G73: Ruth 6B 104	Weirwood Av. G69: Bail 1F 107
Wardpark Rd. G67: Cumb 5C 14	PA3: Lin 5H 75	Weirwood Gdns. G69: Bail 1F 107
WARDPARK RDBT. 4D 14	Watson Cres. G65: Kils 3A 12	Welbeck Rd. G53: Glas 2B 116
Wardpark Sth. Ind. Est.	Watson Pl. G72: Blan 2H 139	Weldon Pl. G65: Croy 2B 34
G67: Cumb 5D 14	Watson St. G1: Glas 5H 83 (6H 5)	Welfare Av. G72: Camb 3D 122
Wardrop Pl. G74: E Kil. 6H 137	G71: Udd 2D 124	Welland Pl. G75: E Kil 4A 148
	G72: Blan 2H 139	Wellbank Pl. G71: Udd 2D 124

Wellbeck Ho. *G74: E Kil* 1H **149**
(off Stuart St.)
Wellbrae Hill ML9: Lark. 3E **161**
Wellbrae Rd. ML3: Ham 2F **153**
Wellbrae Ter. G69: Mood 5D **52**
Wellcroft Pl. G5: Glas. 1F **103**
(not continuous)
Wellcroft Rd. ML3: Ham 6C **140**
Wellcroft Ter. ML3: Ham 6C **140**
Wellesley Cres. G68: Cumb 4A **34**
G75: E Kil 4B **148**
Wellesley Dr. G68: Cumb 4H **33**
G75: E Kil 3B **148**
Wellesley Pl. G68: Cumb 4H **33**
Wellfield Av. G46: Giff. 4H **117**
Wellfield St. G21: Glas 5B **64**
Wellgate Ct. ML9: Lark 1E **161**
Wellgate St. ML9: Lark 1E **161**
Well Grn. G43: Glas. 5A **102**
Well Grn. Ct. *G43: Glas* 5A **102**
(off Well Grn.)
Wellhall Ct. ML3: Ham. 5F **141**
Wellhall Rd. ML3: Ham. 1C **152**
Wellhouse Cres. G33: Glas 4E **87**
Wellhouse Gdns. G33: Glas 4F **87**
Wellhouse Gro. G33: Glas 4F **87**
Wellhouse Path G34: Glas 4F **87**
Wellhouse Rd. G33: Glas 3F **87**
Wellington G75: E Kil 4D **148**
Wellington La. G2: Glas 4E **83** (5B **4**)
(not continuous)
Wellington Path G69: Bail 1H **107**
Wellington Pl. G81: Clyd 4H **41**
ML2: Wis 3B **158**
ML5: Coat 6G **89**
Wellington Rd. G64: B'rig 3D **48**
Wellington St. G2: Glas. 4F **83** (6C **4**)
ML2: Wis 4C **144**
ML6: Air 2A **92**
PA3: Pais 5H **77**
Wellington Way PA4: Renf 2E **79**
Wellknowe Av. G74: T'hall 6G **135**
Wellknowe Pl. G74: T'hall 6F **135**
Wellknowe Rd. G74: T'hall 6G **135**
Well La. G66: Len 3F **7**
Wellmeadow Cl. G77: Newt M 4D **132**
Wellmeadow Grn.
G77: Newt M 3D **132**
Wellmeadow Rd. G43: Glas 1H **117**
Wellmeadow St. PA1: Pais 1H **97**
Wellmeadow Way
G77: Newt M 4D **132**
Wellpark La. G78: Neil 3D **130**
Wellpark Rd. FK4: Bank. 1D **14**
ML1: Moth 3E **143**
Wellpark St. G31: Glas 4A **84**
Wellpark Ter. G78: Neil 3D **130**
Well Rd. PA10: Kilb 2A **94**
Wellshot Cotts. G65: Kils. 4H **11**
Wellshot Dr. G72: Camb 2H **121**
Wellshot Rd. G32: Glas 2H **105**
WELLSIDE 3D **122**
Wellside Av. ML6: Air 2A **92**
Wellside Dr. G72: Camb 3C **122**
Wellside La. ML6: Air 2B **92**
Wellside Quad. ML6: Air 1A **92**
Wellsquarry Rd. G76: Crmck. 5E **137**
Wells St. G81: Clyd 4B **42**
Well St. PA1: Pais 6G **77**
PA3: Pais 6G **77**
Wellview Dr. ML1: Moth 3F **143**
Wellwynd ML6: Air 3H **91**
Wellwynd Gdns. ML6: Air 3H **91**
Welsh Dr. G72: Blan. 3B **140**
ML3: Ham 4G **153**
Welsh Row ML6: C'bnk 2C **112**
Wemyss Av. G77: Newt M 2C **132**
Wemyss Dr. G68: Cumb. 4A **34**
Wemyss Gdns. G69: Bail 2G **107**
Wendur Way PA3: Pais 3A **78**
Wenlock Rd. PA2: Pais 3B **98**
Wensleydale G74: E Kil 6E **137**
Wentworth Dr. G23: Glas 6C **46**
Wesley St. ML6: Air. 4H **91**

Westacres Rd. G77: Newt M 5A **132**
WEST ARTHURLIE 6C **114**
West Av. G33: Step 4D **66**
G71: View 1F **125**
G72: Blan 4C **140**
ML1: New S 5A **128**
ML6: Plain 1G **93**
ML8: Carl 4D **164**
PA1: Pais 1B **96**
PA4: Renf 6F **59**
WEST BALGROCHAN 3D **28**
W. Balgrochan Rd. G64: Torr 4D **28**
Westbank Ct. *G12: Glas* 1C **82**
(off Westbank Quad.)
Westbank La. *G12: Glas* 1C **82**
(off Gibson St.)
Westbank Quad. G12: Glas 1C **82**
Westbourne Cres. G61: Bear 2C **44**
Westbourne Dr. G61: Bear 2C **44**
Westbourne Gdns. La. G12: Glas . . 5A **62**
Westbourne Gdns. Nth. G12: Glas. . 5A **62**
Westbourne Gdns. Sth. G12: Glas. . 5A **62**
Westbourne Gdns. W. G12: Glas. . . 5H **61**
Westbourne Rd. G12: Glas 5H **61**
Westbourne Ter. La. Nth.
G12: Glas 5H **61**
Westbourne Ter. La. Sth.
G12: Glas 5H **61**
West Brae PA1: Pais 1H **97**
Westbrae Dr. G14: Glas 5E **61**
Westbrae Rd. G77: Newt M 3F **133**
West Bridgend G82: Dumb 3E **17**
WESTBURN 1E **123**
Westburn Av. G72: Camb. 1D **122**
PA3: Pais 6E **77**
Westburn Cres. G73: Ruth. 6B **104**
G81: Hard. 6D **22**
Westburn Dr. G72: Camb 6B **106**
Westburn Farm Rd. G72: Camb. . . . 1B **122**
Westburn Rd. G72: Camb, Newt . . 2B **122**
W. Burnside St. G65: Kils 3H **11**
W. Campbell St. G2: Glas . . . 4E **83** (6B **4**)
PA1: Pais 1F **97**
W. Canal St. ML5: Coat 5B **90**
Westcastle Ct. G45: Glas 4H **119**
Westcastle Cres. G45: Glas 4H **119**
Westcastle Gdns. G45: Glas 4H **119**
Westcastle Gro. G45: Glas 4H **119**
W. Chapelton Av. G61: Bear. 3F **45**
W. Chapelton Cres. G61: Bear 3F **45**
W. Chapelton Dr. G61: Bear. 3F **45**
W. Chapelton La. G61: Bear. 3F **45**
Westcliff G82: Dumb 3B **16**
W. Clyde St. ML9: Lark 3F **161**
Westclyffe St. G41: Glas 4C **102**
W. Coats Rd. G72: Camb. 3H **121**
West Ct. G81: Clyd 3A **42**
PA1: Pais 1E **97**
WEST CRAIGEND 6E **41**
WEST CRINDLEDYKE 3D **146**
West Cross ML2: Wis 6G **145**
West Dr. ML6: Air. 5E **93**
WEST DRUMOYNE 4D **80**
Westend G61: Bear 5G **45**
Westend Ct. ML8: Law 1H **163**
W. End Dr. ML4: Bell 3A **126**
Westend Pk. St. G3: Glas 2D **82**
W. End Pl. ML4: Bell 3B **126**
WESTER AUCHINLOCH 6D **50**
Westerburn St. G32: Glas 5H **85**
Wester Carriagehill PA2: Pais 3H **97**
Wester Cleddens Rd. G64: B'rig . . . 5C **48**
Wester Cochno Holdings
G81: Hard. 5D **22**
Wester Comn. Dr. G22: Glas 5E **63**
Wester Comn. Rd. G22: Glas 5E **63**
Westercraigs G31: Glas 4B **84**
Westercraigs Ct. G31: Glas 4B **84**
Westerdale G74: E Kil 6E **137**
Westerfield Rd. G76: Crmck 5H **135**
Westergate Shop. Cen. G2: Glas . . . 6C **4**
Wester Gill ML6: Air. 5E **93**
Westergreens Av. G66: Kirk. 1B **50**

Westerhill Rd. G64: B'rig 3D **48**
WESTER HOLYTOWN 2G **127**
Westerhouse Ct. ML8: Carl 3D **164**
Westerhouse Path *G34: Glas*. 3G **87**
(off Arnisdale Rd.)
Westerhouse Rd. G34: Glas. 3F **87**
WESTERHOUSE ROAD INTERCHANGE
. . . . 3F **87**
Westerkirk Dr. G23: Glas 6C **46**
Westerlands G12: Glas 3G **61**
Westerlands Dr. G77: Newt M 5B **132**
Westerlands Gdns. G77: Newt M . . . 5B **132**
Westerlands Gro. G77: Newt M. . . . 5B **132**
Westerlands Pl. G77: Newt M 4B **132**
Westermains Av. G66: Kirk 6B **30**
Wester Mavisbank Av. ML6: Air 3G **91**
Wester Moffat Av. ML6: Air 3E **93**
Wester Moffat Cres. ML6: Air 4E **93**
Wester Myvot Rd. G67: Cumb. 3C **54**
Western Av. G73: Ruth 5B **104**
Western Baths Club 6B **62**
Western Isles Rd. G60: Old K 1G **41**
Western Rd. G72: Camb 3G **121**
Wester Rd. G32: Glas 1D **106**
Westerton G66: Len 3H **7**
Westerton Av. G61: Bear 1F **61**
G76: Busby. 4E **135**
ML9: Lark 4E **161**
Westerton Ct. G76: Busby. 4E **135**
Westerton La. G76: Busby 4E **135**
Westerton Rd. G68: Dull 5F **13**
Westerton Station (Rail). 6E **45**
WESTERWOOD 6A **14**
W. Fairholm St. ML9: Lark 6H **155**
WEST FERRY INTERCHANGE 1A **38**
WESTFIELD
Cumbernauld 6B **34**
Kilsyth 2F **11**
Westfield G82: Dumb. 3C **16**
Westfield Av. G73: Ruth 6B **104**
Westfield Cres. G61: Bear 5E **45**
Westfield Dr. G52: Glas 6A **80**
G61: Bear 5E **45**
G68: Cumb 6A **34**
Westfield Ind. Area G68: Cumb 1H **53**
Westfield Ind. Est. G68: Cumb 2A **54**
Westfield Pl. G68: Cumb. 1H **53**
Westfield Rd. G46: T'bnk 5G **117**
G65: Kils. 2F **11**
G68: Cumb. 1H **53**
ML1: N'hse 6C **112**
Westfields G64: B'rig 4A **48**
Westgarth Pl. G74: E Kil 6C **136**
West Ga. ML2: Wis 6B **146**
Westgate Way ML4: Bell 3B **126**
W. George La. G2: Glas 3E **83** (4A **4**)
W. George St. G2: Glas 3E **83** (4A **4**)
(not continuous)
ML5: Coat. 3C **90**
W. Glebe Ter. ML3: Ham 1G **153**
W. Graham St. G4: Glas 2E **83** (1B **4**)
W. Greenhill Pl. G3: Glas 3C **82**
W. Hamilton St. ML1: Moth 3G **143**
W. High St. G66: Kirk. 4C **30**
Westhorn Dr. G32: Glas 4A **106**
Westhouse Av. G73: Ruth 6A **104**
Westhouse Gdns. G73: Ruth 6A **104**
W. Kirk St. ML6: Air. 4H **91**
Westknowe Gdns. G73: Ruth. 2D **120**
Westland Dr. G14: Glas 6D **60**
Westland Dr. La. *G14: Glas*. 6D **60**
(off Westland Dr.)
Westlands Gdns. PA2: Pais 3H **97**
West La. PA1: Pais 1F **97**
Westlea Pl. ML6: Air 5B **92**
W. Lodge Rd. PA4: Renf 5E **59**
WEST MAINS 1D **148**
W. Mains Rd. G74: E Kil 1D **148**
WEST MARYSTON 4B **88**
Westminster Ter. *G3: Glas*. 3C **82**
(off Royal Cres.)
Westmoreland St. G42: Glas 3E **103**
Westmuir Pl. G73: Ruth. 5B **104**
Westmuir St. G31: Glas 6F **85**

W. Nile St. G1: Glas 4F 83 (5D 4)
    G2: Glas. 3F 83 (4D 4)
West of Scotland Go-Kart Circuit
    . . . . 5A 156
West of Scotland Indoor Bowling Club
    . . . . 3A 104
West of Scotland R.U.F.C. 5H 25
Westpark Dr. PA3: Pais 6F 77
West Pl. ML2: Newm 4E 147
Westport G75: E Kil 2C 148
WEST PORTON 3G 39
W. Porton Pl. PA7: B'ton 3F 39
Westragh St. G65: Kils 3H 11
W. Prince's La. G4: Glas 1C 82
W. Prince's St. G4: Glas 1D 82 (1A 4)
Westray Av. G77: Newt M 2C 132
Westray Cir. G22: Glas 3G 63
Westray Ct. G67: Cumb 5G 35
Westray Pl. G22: Glas 2H 63
    G64: B'rig 5F 49
Westray Rd. G67: Cumb 5G 35
Westray Sq. G22: Glas 2G 63
Westray St. G22: Glas 2G 63
Westray Wynd ML2: Newm 3D 146
    (off Iona Rd.)
W. Regent La. G2: Glas 3F 83 (4C 4)
W. Regent St. G2: Glas 3E 83 (3B 4)
    (not continuous)
West Rd. G64: Torr 4D 28
    PA10: Kilb. 1A 94
W. Scott Ter. ML3: Ham. 2H 153
Westside Gdns. G11: Glas. 1H 81
W. Stewart St. ML3: Ham 5G 141
West St. G5: Glas 1E 103
    G81: Clyd 1G 59
    PA1: Pais 1G 97
WEST ST. INTERCHANGE 6D 82
West Street Station (Und.) 6E 83
W. Thomson St. G81: Clyd. 4C 42
W. Thornlie St. ML2: Wis 1G 157
W. Westbrae Cres. ML3: Ham 2F 153
W. Whitby St. G31: Glas 1E 105
WESTWOOD 3D 148
Westwood Av. G46: Giff. 4H 117
Westwood Cres. ML3: Ham 1F 153
Westwood Gdns. PA3: Pais 6F 77
Westwood Hill G75: E Kil. 3D 148
Westwood Quad. G81: Clyd 6F 43
Westwood Rd. G43: Glas. 1H 117
    G75: E Kil. 2D 148
    ML2: Newm 2D 146
Westwood Sq. G75: E Kil. 3D 148
Weymouth Dr. G12: Glas 3G 61
Weymouth La. G12: Glas. 4H 61
    (off Chelmsford Dr.)
Whamflet Av. G69: Bail 4A 88
Whamond Twr. ML1: Moth 4G 143
Wheatfield Rd. G61: Bear 4D 44
Wheatholm Cres. ML6: Air 2B 92
Wheatholm St. ML6: Air 2B 92
Wheatland Av. G72: Blan. 1A 140
Wheatlandhead Ct. G72: Blan 1A 140
WHEATLANDS 1A 140
Wheatlands Dr. PA10: Kilb. 1A 94
Wheatlands Farm Rd. PA10: Kilb . . 1A 94
Wheatley Ct. G32: Glas 6A 86
Wheatley Cres. G65: Kils. 4H 11
Wheatley Dr. G32: Glas 6A 86
Wheatley Loan G64: B'rig 1E 65
Wheatley Pl. G32: Glas 6A 86
WHIFFLET 6D 90
Whifflet Ct. ML5: Coat. 6D 90
    (off Whifflet St.)
Whifflet Station (Rail) 6D 90
Whifflet St. ML5: Coat. 2C 110
Whin Av. G78: Barr 3D 114
Whinfell Dr. G75: E Kil 5C 148
Whinfell Gdns. G75: E Kil 5C 148
Whinfield Av. G72: Camb 6G 105
Whinfield Rd. G53: Glas 3A 116
WHINHALL 2G 91
Whinhall Av. ML6: Air. 2G 91
Whinhall Rd. ML6: Air. 2G 91
Whin Hill G74: E Kil 5B 138

Whinhill Pl. G53: Glas 2A 100
Whinhill Rd. G53: Glas 2A 100
    PA2: Pais 3D 98
WHINKNOWE 5C 162
Whinknowe ML9: Ashg 5B 162
Whin Loan G65: Queen 2A 10
Whinney Gro. ML2: Wis. 5C 146
Whinnie Knowe ML9: Lark 4D 160
Whinpark Av. ML4: Bell 4B 126
Whin Pl. G74: E Kil 4B 138
Whins Rd. G41: Glas 4A 102
Whin St. G81: Clyd. 3C 42
Whirlie Ct. PA6: C'lee 2C 74
Whirlie Dr. PA6: C'lee 3B 74
Whirlie Rd. PA6: C'lee 2B 74
WHIRLIES RDBT., THE 5A 138
Whirlow Gdns. G69: Bail 6G 87
Whirlow Rd. G69: Bail 6G 87
Whistleberry Cres. ML3: Ham 2F 141
Whistleberry Dr. ML3: Ham 2E 141
Whistleberry Ind. Pk.
    ML3: Ham. 2E 141
Whistleberry Pk. ML3: Ham 2E 141
Whistleberry Retail Pk.
    G72: Blan 2D 140
Whistleberry Rd. G72: Blan. 2D 140
    ML3: Ham. 2E 141
Whistlefield Ct. G61: Bear 4E 45
Whitacres Path G53: Glas 3A 116
Whitacres Rd. G53: Glas 3H 115
Whitburn St. G32: Glas 4H 85
Whiteadder Pl. G75: E Kil 4A 148
White Av. G82: Dumb 4H 17
Whitebill Rd. ML3: Ham 1A 154
Whitebridge Av. PA3: Pais 1D 96
Whitebridge Cl. PA3: Pais 1D 96
White Cart Rd. PA3: Glas A 2A 78
White-Cart Twr. G74: E Kil 4B 150
    (off Easdale)
WHITECRAIGS 2G 133
Whitecraigs Ct. G46: Giff. 1G 133
Whitecraigs Pl. G23: Glas 1C 62
Whitecraigs Station (Rail) 1G 133
WHITECROOK 6E 43
Whitecrook St. G81: Clyd 1D 58
Whitefield G66: Len 2E 7
Whitefield Av. G72: Camb 3A 122
Whitefield Rd. G51: Glas 6A 82
Whitefield Ter. G66: Len 2E 7
    G72: Camb 2B 122
Whiteford Av. G82: Dumb 1H 17
Whiteford Ct. ML3: Ham 5G 153
Whiteford Cres. G82: Dumb 2H 17
Whiteford Pl. G82: Dumb 2H 17
Whiteford Rd. G33: Step 4F 67
    PA2: Pais 3C 98
Whitehall St. G3: Glas. 4D 82
WHITEHAUGH 6C 78
Whitehaugh Av. PA1: Pais 6D 78
Whitehaugh Cres. G53: Glas 3A 116
    (not continuous)
Whitehaugh Dr. PA1: Pais 6D 78
Whitehaugh Rd. G53: Glas 3A 116
    (not continuous)
WHITEHILL 3F 141
Whitehill Av. G33: Step 3D 66
    G66: Kirk. 4F 31
    G68: Cumb 3F 35
    ML6: Air. 2A 92
Whitehill Ct. G31: Glas 4C 84
    G66: Kirk. 4F 31
Whitehill Cres. G66: Kirk 4F 31
    G81: Faif. 6G 23
    ML8: Carl 2F 165
Whitehill Farm Rd. G33: Step 4D 66
Whitehill Gdns. G31: Glas. 4C 84
Whitehill Gro. G77: Newt M 6F 133
Whitehill La. G61: Bear 3D 44
Whitehill Pl. G31: Glas 4C 84
Whitehill Pool 4D 84
Whitehill Rd. G61: Bear. 2D 44
    ML3: Ham. 3F 141
WHITEHILLS 5G 149
Whitehills PA8: Ersk 5E 41

Whitehills Dr. G75: E Kil. 4G 149
Whitehills Pl. G75: E Kil 4G 149
Whitehill Sports Barn 3F 141
Whitehills Ter. G75: E Kil 5G 149
Whitehill St. G31: Glas 4C 84
    (not continuous)
Whitehill St. La. G31: Glas 4C 84
Whitehill Ter. G69: G'csh 5D 68
Whitehorse Wlk. G75: E Kil 3D 148
Whitehurst G61: Bear. 1C 44
Whitehurst Pk. G61: Bear 1C 44
WHITEINCH 6C 60
Whiteinch Bus. Pk. G14: Glas 1D 80
Whiteinch Homes G14: Glas 6D 60
    (off Westland Dr.)
Whitekirk Pl. G15: Glas. 5A 44
Whitelaw Av. ML5: Glenb 4B 70
Whitelaw Cres. ML4: Bell. 3F 127
Whitelaw Gdns. G64: B'rig 4C 48
Whitelaw St. G20: Glas 2A 62
Whitelaw Ter. G65: Twe 1D 32
Whitelee G75: E Kil 6F 149
Whitelee Cres. G77: Newt M 3B 132
Whitelee Ga. G77: Newt M 3B 132
Whitelees Rd. G67: Cumb 5E 15
WHITELEES RDBT. 6F 15
Whiteloans G71: Both 4F 125
Whitemoss Av. G44: Glas 3D 118
    G74: E Kil 2H 149
Whitemoss Gro. G74: E Kil 1A 150
Whitemoss Rd. G74: E Kil 2H 149
WHITEMOSS RDBT. 2A 150
Whitepond Av. ML4: Bell 4B 126
Whiterigg Ct. ML6: Air 3F 91
    (off Monkscourt Av.)
Whiteshaw Av. ML8: Carl 3D 164
Whiteshaw Dr. ML8: Carl. 3D 164
Whiteshaw Rd. ML8: Law 2B 164
Whitestone Av. G68: Cumb 3D 34
White St. G11: Glas 1H 81
    G81: Clyd 2F 59
WHITESTRIPE 3F 147
Whitevale St. G31: Glas. 5C 84
    G40: Glas 5C 84
Whithope Rd. G53: Glas 3H 115
Whithope Ter. G53: Glas 3H 115
Whithorn Cres. G69: Mood 4D 52
WHITLAWBURN 4H 121
Whitlawburn Av. G72: Camb 3G 121
Whitlawburn Rd. G72: Camb 3G 121
Whitlawburn Shop. Cen.
    G72: Camb 4G 121
    (off Western Rd.)
Whitlawburn Ter. G72: Camb 3G 121
Whitriggs Rd. G53: Glas 2H 115
Whitslade Pl. G34: Glas 2F 87
Whitslade St. G34: Glas 2G 87
Whitsun Dale G74: E Kil 6E 137
WHITTAGREEN 4D 128
Whittagreen Av. ML1: N'hill. 4D 128
Whittagreen Ct. ML1: N'hill 4D 128
Whittagreen Cres. ML1: N'hill 4D 128
Whittingehame Gdns. G12: Glas . . . 4G 61
Whittingehame Dr.
    G13, G12: Glas 4F 61
Whittinghame La. G13: Glas 4F 61
Whittington St. ML5: Coat 5C 90
Whittlemuir Av. G44: Glas 3D 118
Whitton Dr. G46: Giff 3B 118
Whitton St. G20: Glas 1A 62
Whitworth Dr. G81: Clyd 5C 42
Whitworth St. G20: Glas. 3E 63
Whyte Av. G72: Camb 1G 121
Whyte Cnr. G82: Milt 4F 19
Wick Av. ML6: Air 1G 111
Wickets, The PA1: Pais 2C 98
Wickham Av. G77: Newt M 3D 132
Wigton Av. G77: Newt M 2C 132
Wigtoun Pl. G67: Cumb. 1B 36
WILDMANBRIDGE 4F 159
Wildman Rd. ML8: Law 5F 159
Wilfred Av. G13: Glas 2D 60
Wilkie Cres. ML9: Lark 3F 161

Wilkie Loan ML4: Bell 1D 126
Wilkie Rd. G71: Udd 2E 125
William Dr. ML3: Ham. 4H 153
William Mann Dr. G77: Newt M . . 5B 132
WILLIAMSBURGH 1C 98
Williamsburgh Ct. PA1: Pais. 1C 98
Williamsburgh Ter. PA1: Pais 6C 78
Williamson Av. G82: Dumb 3G 17
Williamson Pl. PA5: John 3H 95
Williamson St. G40: Glas 1E 105
    G81: Clyd 3D 42
William Spiers Pl. ML9: Lark 4F 161
William St. G3: Glas. 3D 82 (4A 4)
    G65: Kils 3H 11
    G81: Dun, Hard 1C 42
    ML3: Ham 4F 141
    ML5: Coat 1D 110
    PA1: Pais 1G 97
    PA5: John 2F 95
William Ure Pl. G64: B'rig. 2D 48
WILLIAMWOOD 1B 134
Williamwood Dr. G44: Neth. 5C 118
Williamwood Rd. G44: Neth 5D 118
Williamwood Pk. G44: Neth. 5D 118
Williamwood Pk. W. G44: Neth. . . 5D 118
Williamwood Station (Rail). 6B 118
Willock Pl. G20: Glas. 2C 62
Willoughby Dr. G13: Glas 3F 61
Willoughby La. G13: Glas 3F 61
Willow Av. G64: B'rig. 1C 64
    G66: Lenz 2C 50
    ML1: New S 5A 128
    PA5: Eld 3A 96
Willowbank ML9: Lark 6A 156
Willowbank Cres. G3: Glas 1D 82
Willowbank Gdns. G66: Kirk 5D 30
Willowbank St. G3: Glas 1D 82
Willow Ct. G75: E Kil 5D 148
    G81: Clyd 3B 42
Willow Cres. ML5: Coat. 1C 110
Willowdale Cres. G69: Bail 1G 107
Willowdale Gdns. G69: Bail. 1G 107
Willow Dr. FK4: Bank 1E 15
    G66: Milt C 6C 8
    G72: Blan 1A 140
    ML6: Air 4C 92
    PA5: John 4F 95
Willowford Rd. G53: Glas 3H 115
Willow Gro. ML1: Holy 2B 128
Willow La. G32: Glas 3B 106
Willow Pl. G71: View 3G 95
    PA5: John 3G 95
Willows, The G76: Crmck 1H 135
Willow St. G13: Glas 2F 61
Willow Tea Rooms 3C 4
Willow Way ML3: Ham 2A 154
Willox Pk. G82: Dumb 2G 17
Willwood Rd. ML2: Wis. 2A 146
Wilmot Rd. G13: Glas 5D 60
Wilsgait St. ML1: Cle 5H 129
Wilson Av. PA3: Lin 5G 75
Wilson Ct. ML4: Bell 2B 126
Wilson Pl. G74: E Kil 5A 138
    G77: Newt M 5C 132
Wilson St. G1: Glas 4G 83 (6F 5)
    ML1: Moth 2H 143
    ML3: Ham 4E 141
    ML5: Coat 4E 91
    ML6: Air 2H 91
    ML9: Lark 4F 161
    PA1: Pais 1G 97
    PA4: Renf 5F 59
Wiltonburn Path G53: Glas 3A 116
Wiltonburn Rd. G53: Glas 3A 116
Wilton Ct. G20: Glas 6C 62
                 (off Wilton St.)
Wilton Cres. La. G20: Glas 6D 62
Wilton Dr. G20: Glas 6D 62
Wilton Rd. ML8: Carl 5G 165
Wilton St. G20: Glas 5C 62
    ML5: Coat 1H 89
Wilverton Rd. G13: Glas 1E 61
Winburne Cres. ML3: Ham. 5F 141
Winchester Dr. G12: Glas 3H 61
Windemere Gdns. ML3: Ham 5G 153

Windermere G75: E Kil 6B 148
Windermere St. ML4: Bell 3B 126
Windhill Cres. G43: Glas 2H 117
Windhill Pl. G43: Glas 2A 118
Windhill Rd. G43: Glas 2H 117
Windlaw Ct. G45: Glas. 5H 119
Windlaw Gdns. G44: Neth 3D 118
Windlaw Pk. Gdns. G44: Neth. . . 3D 118
Windlaw Rd. G76: Crmck 6H 119
Windmill Ct. ML1: Moth 4H 143
Windmillcroft Quay G5: Glas . . . 5E 83
               (off Riverview Pl.)
Windmillhill St. ML1: Moth. 3H 143
Windmill Rd. ML3: Ham 5H 141
Windrow Ter. ML2: Wis 2A 146
Windsor Ct. ML8: Carl 3F 165
Windsor Cres. G81: Clyd 4C 42
    PA1: Pais 5C 78
    PA5: Eld 4H 95
Windsor Dr. ML6: Glenm 5H 71
Windsor Gdns. ML3: Ham 3E 141
Windsor Path G69: Barg 5D 88
                  (off Park Rd.)
    ML9: Lark. 3G 161
                 (off Carrick St.)
Windsor Pl. PA11: Bri W 3F 73
                 (off Main Rd.)
Windsor Quad. ML8: Carl. 3F 165
Windsor Rd. ML1: Holy 2A 128
    PA4: Renf 1E 79
Windsor St. G20: Glas 1E 83
    G32: Glas 5C 86
    ML5: Coat 2A 110
Windsor Ter. G20: Glas 1E 83
Windsor Wlk. G71: View 6F 109
Windward Rd. G75: E Kil 2C 148
Windyedge & Hareshaw Rd.
    ML1: Cle. 4H 129
Windyedge Cres. G13: Glas. 4C 60
Windyedge Pl. G13: Glas. 4C 60
Windyridge ML3: Ham. 2A 154
Windyridge Pl. G72: Blan. 2A 140
Windy Yetts G65: Twe 2D 32
Wingate Cres. G74: E Kil 5C 138
Wingate Dr. G74: E Kil 5C 138
Wingate Pk. G74: E Kil. 5C 138
Wingate St. ML2: Wis 5D 144
Wingfield Gdns. G71: Both 6F 125
Winifred St. G33: Glas 5F 65
Winning Ct. G72: Blan 6C 124
Winning Quad. ML2: Wis 6D 144
Winning Row G31: Glas 6F 85
Winnipeg Dr. G75: E Kil 3D 148
Winston Cres. G66: Len 3F 7
Winter Gdns. 6B 62
Wintergreen Ct. G74: E Kil 5F 137
Wintergreen Dr. G74: E Kil 5F 137
Winton Av. G46: Giff 5A 118
Winton Cres. G72: Blan 2A 140
Winton Dr. G12: Glas 4A 62
Winton Gdns. G71: Tann 6D 108
Winton La. G12: Glas 4A 62
Winton Pk. G75: E Kil. 2C 148
Wirran Pl. G13: Glas 1G 59
Wishart Av. G81: Faif, Hard 6E 23
Wishart St. G31: Glas 4A 84
WISHAW 5H 145
Wishaw High Rd. ML1: Cle 1H 145
WISHAWHILL 5F 145
Wishawhill St. ML2: Wis 6F 145
Wishaw Low Rd. ML1: Cle 3G 145
Wishaw Rd. ML2: Wis 2B 158
Wishaw Sports Cen. 1F 157
Wishaw Station (Rail) 1G 157
Wisner Ct. G46: T'bnk 3F 117
Wisteria La. ML8: Carl 5F 165
Wiston St. G72: Camb 2E 123
Witchwood Ct. ML5: Coat 1H 89
Witcutt Way ML2: Wis 2E 157
Wolcott Dr. G72: Blan 1B 140
Wolfe Av. G77: Newt M 2C 132
Wolseley St. G5: Glas 2H 103
Women's Library 6F 5

Wood Aven Dr. G74: E Kil. 5F 137
Woodbank Cres. G76: Clar. 3C 134
    PA5: John 3F 95
Woodburn Av. G72: Blan 1C 140
    G76: Clar 3C 134
    ML6: Air 5H 91
Woodburn Ct. G73: Ruth 1D 120
Woodburn Pl. PA6: C'lee 4E 75
Woodburn Rd. G43: Glas 2B 118
    ML1: N'hse. 6D 112
Woodburn St. ML1: Moth 1G 143
Woodburn Ter. ML9: Lark 3G 161
Woodburn Way G62: Miln 4G 25
    G68: Cumb 3E 35
Wood Cres. ML1: Moth 1G 143
Woodcroft Av. G11: Glas 6F 61
Wooddale ML1: Moth. 5F 143
Woodend G72: Blan 3B 140
    ML9: Lark. 4G 161
            (off Keir Hardie Dr.)
Woodend Ct. G32: Glas 3E 107
Woodend Dr. G13: Glas 4E 61
    ML6: Air 2C 92
    PA1: Pais 1F 99
Woodend Gdns. G32: Glas. 3D 106
Woodend La. G13: Glas 4E 61
Woodend Pl. PA5: Eld 3H 95
Woodend Rd. G32: Glas 3D 106
    G73: Ruth 3C 120
    ML8: Carl 3G 165
Wood Farm Rd. G46: T'bnk 5G 117
Woodfield G71: View 1G 125
Woodfield Av. G64: B'rig 6D 48
Woodfoot Path G53: Glas. 3B 116
Woodfoot Pl. G53: Glas 3A 116
Woodfoot Quad. G53: Glas 3B 116
Woodfoot Rd. G53: Glas 3A 116
    ML3: Ham 1E 153
Woodford Pl. PA3: Lin 5G 75
Woodford St. G41: Glas 6C 102
Woodgreen Av. G44: Glas 1F 119
Woodgreen Ct. ML2: Wis 3G 157
Woodhall ML1: Holy 5A 112
Woodhall Av. ML1: Holy 2H 127
    ML3: Ham 5F 141
Woodhall Av. ML5: Coat 2A 110
    ML6: C'bnk 3B 112
Woodhall Cott. Rd.
    ML6: C'bnk 4C 112
Woodhall Mill Rd. ML6: Chap . . . 4B 112
Woodhall Pl. ML5: Coat 2B 110
Woodhall Rd. ML2: Wis 5D 146
    ML6: C'bnk 3B 112
Woodhall St. G40: Glas 3D 104
    ML6: Chap 4D 112
Woodhead Av. G66: Kirk 6D 30
    G68: Cumb 6B 34
    G71: Both 1F 141
Woodhead Ct. G68: Cumb 6B 34
Woodhead Cres. G71: Tann 6D 108
    ML3: Ham 3E 153
Woodhead Gdns. G71: Both 1F 141
Woodhead Ind. Est. G60: Chry . . . 3H 67
Woodhead La. ML3: Ham 3F 153
Woodhead Path G53: Glas 2A 116
Woodhead Pl. G68: Cumb 6B 34
Woodhead Rd. G53: Glas 2H 115
    G68: Cumb 6B 34
    G69: Chry 3H 67
Woodhead Ter. G69: Chry 2H 67
Woodhead Vw. G68: Cumb 6B 34
Woodhill Rd. G21: Glas 3D 64
    G64: B'rig 6E 49
Woodholm Av. G44: Glas 1G 119
Woodhouse Dr. G76: Busby 4E 135
Woodhouse St. G13: Glas 2E 61
Woodilee Cotts. G66: Lenz 1E 51
Woodilee Ind. Est. G66: Lenz . . . 1E 51
Woodilee Rd. G66: Kirk, Lenz . . . 6E 31
Woodilee Rd. ML1: N'hill 3E 129
Woodland Av. G66: Kirk. 5B 30
    ML6: Air 1C 112
    PA2: Pais 5A 98

Woodland Cres. G72: Camb 3B 122
Woodland Gdns. G76: Crmck 2H 135
  ML3: Ham 1B 154
Woodlands Av. G69: G'csh 2C 68
  G71: Both 4E 125
  ML8: Law 5D 158
Woodlands Ct. G46: T'bnk 5F 117
  G60: Old K 2F 41
Woodlands Cres. G46: T'bnk 4F 117
  G71: Both 4D 124
  PA5: John 4D 94
Woodlands Dr. G4: Glas 1D 82
  ML1: Holy 2H 127
  ML5: Coat 4H 89
Woodlands Gdns. G71: Both 3D 124
Woodlands Ga. G3: Glas 2D 82
  G46: T'bnk 4F 117
Woodlands Gro. G62: Miln 2G 25
Woodlands Pk. G46: T'bnk 5F 117
Woodlands Pl. ML5: Coat 4H 89
Woodlands Rd. G3: Glas . . . 1D 82 (2A 4)
  G46: T'bnk 5F 117
  ML1: Moth 6H 143
  ML1: N'hse 6D 112
Woodlands St. G62: Miln 3G 25
  ML1: Moth 5H 143
Woodlands Ter. G3: Glas 2C 82
  G71: Both 4E 125
Woodlands, The ML4: Bell 4F 127
Woodland Ter. ML9: Lark 4G 161
Woodland Way G67: Cumb 2B 36
Wood La. G64: B'rig 1E 65
Woodlea Av. ML6: Air 1C 112
Woodlea Dr. G46: Giff 3B 118
  ML3: Ham 3H 153
Woodlea Pl. ML6: Air 2C 92
Woodlinn Av. G44: Glas 2F 119
Woodmill Dr. G64: Torr 4E 29
Woodmill Gdns. G67: Cumb 1B 54
Woodneuk Av. G69: G'csh 3D 68
Woodneuk Ct. PA1: Pais 1E 97
Woodneuk La. G69: G'csh 4D 68
  G69: G'csh 4D 68
Woodneuk St. ML6: Coat 4D 112
Woodneuk Ter. G69: G'csh 4D 68
Wood Quad. G81: Clyd 1G 59
Woodrop St. G40: Glas 3D 104
Woodrow ML1: Holy 5G 111
Woodrow Av. ML1: Carf 5B 128
Woodrow Cir. G41: Glas 1B 102
Woodrow Pl. G41: Glas 1A 102
Woodrow Rd. G41: Glas 1B 102
Woodside ML1: Holy 5G 111
  PA6: Hous 2D 74
Woodside Av. G46: T'bnk 4G 117
  G65: Kils 3B 12
  G66: Lenz 1D 50
  G73: Ruth 6E 105
  ML3: Ham 1A 154
  PA11: Bri W 2F 73
Woodside Ct. ML3: Ham 1A 154
  ML5: Coat 6H 89
            (off Woodside St.)
Woodside Cres. G3: Glas 2D 82
  G78: Barr 5F 115
  ML2: Newm 3F 147
  PA1: Pais 1G 97
Woodside Dr. G76: Water 6B 134
  ML6: C'bnk 3A 112
Woodside Gdns. G76: Clar 2B 134
  G76: Crmck 2H 135
  ML5: Coat 1H 109
Woodside Gro. G73: Ruth 6E 105
Woodside La. PA5: Brkfld 5D 74

Woodside Pl. G3: Glas 2D 82
  G71: View 5G 109
Woodside Pl. La. G3: Glas 2D 82
Woodside Rd. G76: Crmck 2H 135
  PA5: Brkfld 5C 74
Woodside St. ML1: Moth 5B 144
  ML1: New S 4A 128
  ML5: Coat 2H 109
            (not continuous)
  ML6: Chap 3D 112
Woodside Ter. G3: Glas 2D 82
Woodside Ter. La. G3: Glas 2A 4
Woodside Twr. ML1: Moth 5B 144
Woodside Wlk. ML3: Ham 1A 154
Woodstock Av. G41: Glas 4B 102
  G66: Kirk 5F 31
  PA2: Pais 5C 96
Woodstock Dr. ML2: Wis 5A 146
Woodstock Way PA2: Pais 5C 96
Wood St. G31: Glas 3D 84
  ML1: Moth 1H 143
  ML5: Coat 4A 90
  ML6: Air 2B 92
  PA2: Pais 2D 98
Woodvale Av. G46: Giff 1H 133
  G61: Bear 5H 45
  ML6: Air 1D 112
Woodvale Dr. PA3: Pais 6E 77
Woodview G71: View 5H 109
Woodview Dr. ML4: Bell 6E 111
  ML6: Air 6A 92
Woodview La. ML6: Air 6A 92
Woodview Rd. ML9: Lark 5E 161
Woodview Ter. ML3: Ham 5F 141
Woodville Pk. G51: Glas 5H 81
Woodville Pk. Ind. Est. *G51: Glas . . . 5H 81*
            (off Woodville Pk.)
Woodville St. G51: Glas 5H 81
Woodyard Rd. G82: Dumb 4E 17
Woodyett Pk. G76: Busby 4D 134
Woodyett Rd. G76: Busby 4D 134
Wordsworth Way G71: Both 4F 125
Worsley Cres. G77: Newt M 3C 132
Wraes Av. G78: Barr 3F 115
Wraes Vw. G78: Barr 6B 114
Wraisland Cres. PA7: B'ton 3F 39
Wrangholm Cres. ML1: New S 4B 128
Wrangholm Dr. ML1: New S 4A 128
Wren Ct. ML4: Bell 5A 110
Wren Pl. ML2: Wis 6H 145
  PA5: John 6D 94
Wright Av. G78: Barr 5C 114
Wrightlands Cres.
  PA8: Ersk 1A 58
Wright St. PA4: Renf 1B 78
Wright Way ML1: New S 4A 128
Wye Cres. ML5: Coat 2H 89
Wykeham Pl. G13: Glas 3C 60
Wykeham Rd. G13: Glas 3C 60
Wyler Twr. ML3: Ham 6A 142
Wylie G74: E Kil 4D 138
Wylie Av. G77: Newt M 2D 132
Wylie St. ML3: Ham 1H 153
Wyndford Dr. G20: Glas 4B 62
Wyndford Pl. G20: Glas 4B 62
Wyndford Rd. G20: Glas 4A 62
  G68: Cumb 3D 14
Wyndford Ter. G71: View 6F 109
Wyndham Ct. *G12: Glas 5B 62*
            (off Wyndham St.)
Wyndham St. G12: Glas 5B 62
Wynd, The G67: Cumb 6B 14
Wyneford Rd. FK4: Bank 1D 14
Wynyard Grn. G75: E Kil 3D 148
Wyper Pl. G40: Glas 5C 84

Wyvil Av. G13: Glas 6E 45
Wyvis Av. G13: Glas 1H 59
  G61: Bear 6C 24
Wyvis Ct. G77: Newt M 6D 132
Wyvis Pl. G13: Glas 1H 59
  G77: Newt M 6C 132
Wyvis Quad. G13: Glas 1H 59

X

XS Superbowl 5B 78

Y

Yair Dr. G52: Glas 5A 80
Yarrow Ct. G72: Camb 2D 122
Yarrow Cres. ML2: Wis 5H 145
  PA7: B'ton 5A 40
Yarrow Gdns. G20: Glas 6D 62
Yarrow Gdns. La. *G20: Glas 6D 62*
            (off Yarrow Gdns.)
Yarrow Pk. G74: E Kil 2A 150
Yarrow Rd. G64: B'rig 3C 48
Yarrow Way G72: Blan 1B 140
Yate Gro. G31: Glas 6D 84
Yate St. G31: Glas 6D 84
  G40: Glas 6D 84
Yetholm Gdns. G74: E Kil 5H 137
Yetholm St. G14: Glas 3G 59
Yetholm Ter. ML3: Ham 6C 140
Yett Rd. ML1: N'hill 4D 128
Yetts Cres. G66: Kirk 5F 31
Yetts Hole Rd. ML6: Glenm 6D 54
Yew Dr. G21: Glas 6C 64
Yew Pl. PA5: John 4F 95
Yews Cres. ML3: Ham 4F 141
Yokerburn Pl. G13: Glas 2G 59
Yokerburn Ter. G81: Clyd 2F 59
Yoker Ferry Rd. G14: Glas 3G 59
Yoker Ind. Est. G14: Glas 3H 59
Yoker Mill Gdns. G13: Glas 2G 59
Yoker Mill Rd. G13: Glas 2G 59
Yoker Station (Rail) 2F 59
Yoker Sports Cen. 3H 59
York Dr. G73: Ruth 2F 121
Yorkhill Pde. G3: Glas 2A 82
Yorkhill St. G3: Glas 3B 82
York Rd. ML1: N'hse 5D 112
  ML6: Chap 5D 112
York St. G2: Glas 4E 83 (6B 4)
  G81: Clyd 5F 43
  ML2: Wis 1H 157
York Way PA4: Renf 2E 79
Younger Quad. G64: B'rig 6C 48
Young Pl. G71: Tann 5E 109
  G75: E Kil 6A 150
  ML2: Newm 4F 147
Young St. G81: Clyd 3D 42
  ML2: Wis 6H 145
Young Ter. G21: Glas 5C 64
Young Wynd ML4: Bell 5C 110
Yukon Ter. G75: E Kil 3D 148
Yvetot Ct. ML8: Carl 2E 165

Z

Zambesi Dr. G72: Blan 6A 124
Zena Cres. G33: Glas 5E 65
Zena Pl. G33: Glas 5F 65
Zena St. G33: Glas 5E 65
Zetland Rd. G52: Hill 3H 79

HOSPITALS and HOSPICES

covered by this atlas

with their map square reference

N.B. Where Hospitals and Hospices are not named on the map, the reference given is for the road in which they are situated.

ACCORD HOSPICE —3E **99**
Hawkhead Hospital Grounds
Hawkhead Rd.
PAISLEY
Renfrewshire
PA2 7BL
Tel: 0141 5812000

ACORN STREET DAY HOSPITAL —1B **104**
23 Acorn St.
GLASGOW
G40 4AN
Tel: 0141 5564789

AIRBLES ROAD CENTRE —4H **143**
59 Airbles Rd.
MOTHERWELL
ML1 2TJ
Tel: 01698 261331

ALEXANDER HOSPITAL —3A **90**
Blair Rd.
COATBRIDGE
Lanarkshire
ML5 2EW
Tel: 01236 422661

BLAWARTHILL HOSPITAL —3A **60**
129 Holehouse Dr.
GLASGOW
G13 3TG
Tel: 0141 211 9000

CANNIESBURN HOSPITAL —5E **45**
Switchback Rd.
Bearsden
GLASGOW
G61 1QL
Tel: 0141 2115600

CLELAND HOSPITAL —1A **146**
Bellside Rd.
Cleland
MOTHERWELL
Lanarkshire
ML1 5NR
Tel: 01698 245000

COATHILL HOSPITAL —1C **110**
Hospital St.
COATBRIDGE
Lanarkshire
ML5 4DN
Tel: 01698 245000

COWGLEN HOSPITAL —6D **100**
10 Boystone Rd.
GLASGOW
G53 6XJ
Tel: 0141 2119200

DRUMCHAPEL HOSPITAL —5B **44**
129 Drumchapel Rd.
GLASGOW
G15 6PX
Tel: 0141 2116000

DUMBARTON JOINT HOSPITAL —3C **16**
Cardross Rd.
DUMBARTON
G82 5JA
Tel: 01389 762317

DYKEBAR HOSPITAL —6D **98**
Grahamston Rd.
PAISLEY
Renfrewshire
PA2 7DE
Tel: 0141 8845122

ERSKINE HOSPITAL (PRINCESS LOUISE
SCOTTISH HOSPITAL) —2C **40**
Bishopton
BISHOPTON
Renfrewshire
PA7 5PU
Tel: 0141 8121100

GARTNAVEL GENERAL HOSPITAL —5G **61**
1053 Great Western Rd.
GLASGOW
G12 0YN
Tel: 0141 2113000

GARTNAVEL ROYAL HOSPITAL —4F **61**
1055 Great Western Rd.
GLASGOW
G12 0XH
Tel: 0141 2113600

GLASGOW DENTAL HOSPITAL
—3E **83** (3B **4**)
378 Sauchiehall St.
GLASGOW
G2 3JZ
Tel: 0141 2119600

GLASGOW HOMOEOPATHIC HOSPITAL
—5G **61**
1053 Great Western Rd.
GLASGOW
G12 0YN
Tel: 0141 2111600

GLASGOW NUFFIELD HOSPITAL, THE
—4H **61**
25 Beaconsfield Rd.
GLASGOW
G12 0PJ
Tel: 0141 3349441

GLASGOW ROYAL INFIRMARY —3A **84**
84 Castle St.
GLASGOW
G4 0SF
Tel: 0141 2114000

GOLDEN JUBILEE NATIONAL HOSPITAL
—5A **42**
Beardmore St.
CLYDEBANK
Dunbartonshire
G81 4HX
Tel: 01419 515000

HAIRMYRES HOSPITAL —2B **148**
Eaglesham Rd.
East Kilbride
GLASGOW
G75 8RG
Tel: 01355 220292

HAWKHEAD HOSPITAL —3E **99**
Hawkhead Rd.
PAISLEY
Renfrewshire
PA2 7BL
Tel: 0141 8898151

JOHNSTONE HOSPITAL —1G **95**
Bridge of Weir Rd.
JOHNSTONE
Renfrewshire
PA5 8YX
Tel: 01505 331471

KIRKLANDS HOSPITAL —3F **125**
Fallside Rd.
Bothwell
GLASGOW
G71 8BB
Tel: 01698 245000

LENNOX CASTLE HOSPITAL —2C **6**
Glen Rd.
Lennoxtown
GLASGOW
G66 7LB
Tel: 01360 329200

LEVERNDALE HOSPITAL —3H **99**
Crookston Rd.
GLASGOW
G53 7TU
Tel: 0141 2116400

LIGHTBURN HOSPITAL —4B **86**
966 Carntyne Rd.
GLASGOW
G32 6ND
Tel: 0141 2111500

MANSIONHOUSE UNIT, THE —5D **102**
100 Mansionhouse Rd.
GLASGOW
G41 3DX
Tel: 0141 2016161

MARIE CURIE CENTRE, HUNTERS HILL
—3B **64**
107 Belmont Rd.
GLASGOW
G21 3AY
Tel: 0141 5582555

MERCHISTON HOSPITAL —6E **75**
Bridge of Weir Rd.
Brookfield
JOHNSTONE
Renfrewshire
PA5 8TY
Tel: 01505 328261

Hospitals & Hospices

MONKLANDS DISTRICT GENERAL
HOSPITAL —4G **91**
Monkscourt Av.
AIRDRIE
Lanarkshire
ML6 0JS
Tel: 01236 748748

PARKHEAD HOSPITAL —6F **85**
81 Salamanca St.
GLASGOW
G31 5ES
Tel: 0141 211 8300

PRINCE & PRINCESS OF WALES HOSPICE
—5F **83**
71 Carlton Pl.
GLASGOW
G5 9TD
Tel: 0141 4295599

PRIORY HOSPITAL, GLASGOW, THE
—5D **102**
38 Mansionhouse Rd.
GLASGOW
G41 3DW
Tel: 0141 6366116

QUEEN MOTHER'S MATERNITY HOSPITAL
—2A **82**
Dalnair St.
Yorkhill
GLASGOW
G3 8SH
Tel: 0141 2010550

RED DEER DAY HOSPITAL —3E **149**
Alberta Av., East Kilbride
GLASGOW
G75 8NH
Tel: 01355 244254

ROADMEETINGS HOSPITAL —5H 165
Goremire Rd.
CARLUKE
Lanarkshire
NL8 4PS
Tel: 01555 77221

ROSS HALL HOSPITAL —2A **100**
221 Crookston Rd.
GLASGOW
G52 3NQ
Tel: 0141 8103151

ROYAL ALEXANDRA HOSPITAL —3H **97**
Corsebar Rd.
PAISLEY
Renfrewshire
PA2 9PN
Tel: 0141 887 9111

ROYAL HOSPITAL FOR SICK CHILDREN
—2A **82**
Dalnair St.
Yorkhill
GLASGOW
G3 8SJ
Tel: 0141 2010000

ST ANDREW'S HOSPICE —3A **92**
Henderson St.
AIRDRIE
Lanarkshire
ML6 6DJ
Tel: 01236 766951

ST MARGARET'S HOSPICE —2F **59**
East Barns St.
CLYDEBANK
Dunbartonshire
G81 1EG
Tel: 0141 9521141

ST VINCENT'S HOSPICE —6B **94**
Midton Rd.
Howwood
JOHNSTONE
Renfrewshire
PA9 1AF
Tel: 01505 705635

SHETTLESTON DAY HOSPITAL —1H **105**
152 Wellshot Rd.
GLASGOW
G32 7AX
Tel: 0141 3038800

SOUTHERN GENERAL HOSPITAL —3D **80**
Govan Rd.
GLASGOW
G51 4TF
Tel: 0141 2011100

STOBHILL GENERAL HOSPITAL —3C **64**
133 Balornock Rd.
GLASGOW
G21 3UW
Tel: 0141 2013000

STRATHCLYDE HOSPITAL —4F **143**
Airbles Rd.
MOTHERWELL
Lanarkshire
ML1 3BW
Tel: 01698 245000

UDSTON HOSPITAL —5D **140**
Farm Rd.
HAMILTON
Lanarkshire
ML3 9LA
Tel: 01698 245000

VICTORIA INFIRMARY —5E **103**
Langside Rd.
GLASGOW
G42 9TY
Tel: 0141 2016000

VICTORIA MEMORIAL COTTAGE HOSPITAL
—3F **11**
19 Glasgow Rd.
Kilsyth
GLASGOW
G65 9AG
Tel: 01236 822172

WESTER MOFFAT HOSPITAL —3F **93**
Towers Rd.
AIRDRIE
Lanarkshire
ML6 8LW
Tel: 01236 763377

WESTERN INFIRMARY —1A **82**
Dumbarton Rd.
GLASGOW
G11 6NT
Tel: 0141 2112000

WISHAW GENERAL HOSPITAL —6E **145**
Netherton St.
WISHAW
Lanarkshire
ML2 0DP
Tel: 01698 361100